Envisioning 2060

Opportunities and Risks for Emerging Markets

Envisioning 2060

Opportunities and Risks for Emerging Markets

Editors
Harinder S. Kohli
Rajat Nag
Ieva Vilkelyte

PENGUIN
ENTERPRISE

An imprint of Penguin Random House

PENGUIN ENTERPRISE

USA | Canada | UK | Ireland | Australia
New Zealand | India | South Africa | China

Penguin Enterprise is part of the Penguin Random House group of companies
whose addresses can be found at global.penguinrandomhouse.com

Published by Penguin Random House India Pvt. Ltd
4th Floor, Capital Tower 1, MG Road,
Gurugram 122 002, Haryana, India

First published in Penguin Enterprise by Penguin Random House India 2022

10 9 8 7 6 5 4 3 2 1

ISBN 9780670096916

Typeset in Helvetica Neue LT Std
Printed at Replika Press Pvt. Ltd, India

www.penguin.co.in

Dedicated to

MICHEL CAMDESSUS

Founding Co-Chair of the Emerging Markets Forum,
Governor Emeritus of Banque De France,
and
Former Managing Director of the International Monetary Fund

*For inspiring everyone he has touched,
in his nine decades so far*

Table of Contents

List of Boxes, Figures, and Tables

Boxes

Figures

Tables

Foreword

During my fifty-year professional career in economic development, I have had the privilege to witness, first hand, enormous progress across all continents of the world, politically, socially and economically. When I was born, most of today's emerging and developing countries (EMDEs) were either colonized by foreign powers, under their tutelage, or ruled by homegrown dictators or autocrats. The world was in the midst of the bloody Second World War. When I started my professional career, most countries in Asia and Africa were learning how to manage themselves as independent nations, hunger was rife in the EMDEs, absolute poverty averaged 50 per cent, and most people lived in rural areas. Since then, billions of people have been lifted out of poverty. Globally, the absolute poverty rate measure has by now fallen from around 50 per cent to below 10 per cent, and most of the global population is classified as middle- or upper-middle-class and lives in urban centres. Several erstwhile developing countries (e.g. Taiwan, Singapore, Korea, Chile, etc.) are now classified as advanced economies. Never in the history of mankind has so much economic and social progress been made over a single lifetime.

Yet, this progress has also brought to the fore new issues. The imminent threat to the health and well-being of our fragile planet casts a dark shadow over our ability to effectively tackle the critical issues of inequality and inequities, the uneven distribution of the benefits of globalization, the limits of unfettered global supply chains, and the fragility of the global monetary and financial system. We are also discovering that the post-pandemic world is likely to be very different from what it was in 2019. Finally, the solutions to all major issues require actions both at the national and global levels. Yet, the present global governance and multilateral system is ill-suited to effectively tackle such overarching issues just when it is most needed. This book explores these individual issues in depth, in an analytical and clear-eyed manner, to allow us all to assess the alternatives available to those guiding the long-term path of the EMDEs—in the context of the evolution of the entire global economy. Can we expect the EMDEs to replicate, in relative terms, their past record of progress through 2060?

I commend Harinder Kohli and his co-editors, Rajat Nag and Ieva Vilkelyte, for shouldering this huge undertaking and persuading such an illustrious group of authors to explore in depth as to where our world may be headed and lay out the major opportunities and key risks emerging market economies are likely to face between now and 2060. Their basic objective is not to offer definitive projections of what the future will be or to provide over-arching answers to the questions posed in various chapters, but only to inform and stimulate a debate on the major issues and, through that, hopefully contribute to more informed policy choices by countries individually and collectively. I believe that the editors have truly succeeded in their endeavour.

Even though the authors started off on the premise that their undertaking was largely to raise questions and provide an analytical framework for examining them, I am impressed by the concrete set of proposals and recommendations that practically every chapter makes. I guess they could not resist going that extra mile! I believe that that 'bonus' will be of enormous value to policymakers everywhere.

Finally, I wish to congratulate the editors for moulding the work of twenty-two different authors, from different professional backgrounds, cultures and writing styles into a cohesive and eminently readable book.

Gautam Kaji
Chairman, Centennial Group International and former Managing Director, World Bank

Acknowledgements

This book was inspired by Michel Camdessus, the founding and longest-serving Co-Chairman of the Emerging Markets Forum (EMF), who has also been the intellectual force behind the EMF since its inception in 2005. We were sustained by his active support and encouragement during a period of over a year and a half, when the book was conceived, shaped and reshaped, and finally realized. In addition to offering inspiration and invaluable advice throughout this process, and despite his very busy schedule, he offered to contribute written inputs for this book. Further, he painstakingly read draft chapters by others and made insightful comments. This made our job as the editors and co-authors much more feasible.

We are also much obliged to the following world-renowned experts who so generously accepted our invitation to contribute chapters included in the book: Montek Singh Ahluwalia, Manu Bhaskaran, Soumitra Dutta, Sir Suma Chakrabarti, Kevin Cleaver, Jose Fajgenbaum, Katie Ford, Enrique García, Werner Hermann, Claudio Loser, Harpaul Alberto Kohli, Ramesh A. Mashelkar, Celestin Monga, Utkarsh Patel, Jean Louis Sarbib, Laura Shelton, Bernard Snoy, V. K. Tulasidhar and Hasan Tuluy. We are most grateful to all the authors for adhering to tight deadlines and for responding so graciously to our comments that were necessary to mould their chapters into a cohesive book.

Such projects are ultimately the result of a team effort and it certainly was the case with this book. We owe special thanks to Harpaul Alberto Kohli for making numerous runs of his model of the global economy, often demanded at short notice, to facilitate as well as reflect the work of other authors.

The book also benefitted greatly from comments on draft chapters from numerous colleagues within the EMF and Centennial Group. Authors of individual chapters also sought comments from a wide range of other experts, as acknowledged by them.

We wish to offer special thanks to Ieva Vilkelyte and Laura Shelton for converting various data into easily digestible graphics and tables. Ms Parita Patel helped edit several chapters, under a very tight deadline, to bring a greater cohesion between material written by twenty-two authors from very different cultures and writing styles. Ieva Vilkelyte, Laura Shelton and Katie Ford worked tirelessly for checking the facts, doing final copy editing and formatting the chapters. They also deserve special credit for creating eye-catching illustrations. Ieva worked tirelessly to put together the final manuscript and did a fantastic job in putting together a flawless final manuscript in collaboration with our publisher. Sugata Ghosh played a key role in facilitating the publication of the book.

Finally, we are truly obligated to Ankit Juneja, his editorial colleagues, and other staff at Penguin Random House (India), our publisher, for their support and help in making the book a reality under an extremely tight deadline.

Harinder S. Kohli   Rajat Nag   Ieva Vilkelyte

Editors
February 2022

Chapter 1: Introduction

Introduction[1]

Chapter 1

Harinder S. Kohli

Primary Focus

This volume takes a long-term perspective—the next forty years (comprising two generations) through 2060—of the likely evolution of the economic and social landscape of emerging market economies. While the primary focus is on EMDEs and their main economic and social opportunities as well as the primary challenges and policy issues before them, it does so in the context of prospects and likely evolution of the global economy as a whole.

Why This Book?

In 2016, the EMF published *The World in 2050*. In addition to two editions in English, the book was also published in Spanish, Chinese and French (a shortened version). The world has undergone major, in many ways fundamental, changes since 2016. This has led EMF and the editors to prepare this sequel. While in some respects, this book is an updated version of the 2016 book, in many other respects, it either covers new ground or departs from the earlier thinking, given the major developments in the world during the intervening five years.

The COVID-19 pandemic is a global and cataclysmic event that has fundamentally affected the entire world: from Park Avenue penthouses to Syrian refugee camps and favelas in Rio. Arguably, WWII was the last event with such a global reach (although it was deadlier). Other pandemics were either mostly regionally bound (Ebola and SARS-1), or mostly affected specific social groups (AIDS). The economic, financial and social costs of the still-raging COVID-19 pandemic are already much greater and widespread than that of the 2007–8 global financial crisis.

Importantly, the current pandemic has brought into sharper relief several major, underlying global developments and emerging challenges to the existing international economic order:

- The growth of inequality between and within nations (UNU-WIDER 2021);
- Renewed debate about the prior unrelenting march towards globalization and the dependency on value chains—some regions and countries are now wanting to 'onshore production' of many goods and services, and to protect national technological capacity to enhance national security and domestic jobs (The Economist 2020);
- The potential reversal of the convergence between rich countries and emerging markets that had allowed a historic reduction in poverty globally over the past fifty plus years (Centennial 2021);

---

1. This book was finalized before the onset of hostilities in Ukraine in late February 2022. These hostilities are already leading to major changes in geopolitics and could have significant impacts on the global economy depending on when and how peace is restored.

- The transformation of work and the impact of digital technologies (positive and negative) (Laura LaBerge et al. 2021); and
- The strains on multilateralism and global governance (WHO, WTO, United Nations, multilateral development banks (MDBs), the European Union, etc.) (Humphrey et al. 2015).

The pandemic could create further significant and potentially lasting behavioural changes – location of work, use of distance education, e-commerce, accelerated digitization of societies, etc.—with a major impact on work patterns, automation, service delivery and cities.

Such profound changes are also accelerating at a time when the international order born out of WWII, already shaken by the collapse of the Soviet Union and the rise of China, is under additional pressure as the promise of globalization has fallen short in many of the countries that defined the post-WWII order:

- Rising concerns, worldwide, about climate change (IPCC 2021);
- The rise of nationalism and right-wing authoritarianism in the United States, Europe (e.g. Brexit and some new EU members), and several other parts of the world as well as left-wing populism in other regions (Latin America) (CFR 2021);
- Linked to this political shift, increased scorn for elites—seen as the winners of an inequitable globalization—that bleeds into a mistrust of expertise and even science (Hetherington and Ladd 2020);
- A declining trust of people in public institutions and established political parties (Hetherington and Ladd 2020);
- A fragmentation of multilateral institutions, as legacy organizations (UN, IMF, World Bank, WTO, WHO, UNEP, etc.) have not evolved fast enough to reflect the new distribution of economic power and new organizations (AIIB, NDB, GCF etc.) have emerged as a result (Humphrey et al. 2015); and
- China, as a key player, emphasizing the superiority of its development model at a time when liberal democracies are struggling (Centennial 2021).

In many ways, the consequences of this pandemic and associated health crises are more immediate and visible than the impact of climate change. But both these threats exhibit a similar dynamic: they represent a global phenomenon affecting almost everyone and demanding a global and coordinated response. To successfully address these twin challenges, as well as other issues highlighted above, will require much greater and much more effective international cooperation, greater trust between governments and citizens, and a renewed belief in science and evidence-based policies. The pandemic and related social issues also suggest the need to rethink the role of the government in ensuring provision of essential public services and safety nets to the public.

In short, the world economy and institutions after COVID-19 will look markedly different than where they were at the end of 2019. This is the primary motivation behind this book.

The COVID-19 Pandemic

During 2020–21, the pandemic unleashed by COVID-19 wreaked havoc in the lives and livelihoods of people in practically every country in the world. It is widely considered the worst global pandemic and health crises in over a century.

According to WHO, by December 2021, over 215 million had tested positive for COVID-19 and over 4.5 million had died. It is not clear when, if ever, this pandemic will end. While hardly any country has been spared, until early 2021, advanced economies in North America and Europe (with their sophisticated healthcare systems) were most affected, with Latin America, the next most affected region. Asia and Africa, the most populous regions of the world, had escaped the worst. But since the emergence of the Delta variant in early 2021, they too have suffered much (with China being a major exception due to its draconian measures to restrict movement of people internally). With the sudden emergence of the Omicron variant in late 2021, a new wave of the disease is spreading throughout the world.

Beyond the huge losses of lives and massive number of people who fell ill, the pandemic has had a fundamental impact on the lives of people around the world. To contain the spread of the pandemic, country after country shut down all economic activities and mandated their citizens to stay indoors. Curfews were imposed. As a result, many people had to remain confined to their homes for a year or more. Millions of businesses were closed (despite significant stimulus programs by many countries). 2021 witnessed the biggest drop in the global economic activity since the Great Depression in the 1930s. Countries closed their borders (even within the EU). As a result, unemployment and the rate of poverty rose in most countries. There is also some evidence that inequality—both between countries and within countries—increased (Centennial 2021). Early signs indicate that, because of the changing nature of the way work is being done now, not all the jobs lost due to the pandemic may return in the post-pandemic world (Taylor 2021). All in all, the pandemic has had and is having a devastating toll on human beings, mostly impacting the less well off in both advanced economies and EMDEs.

One bright spot during 2020 was the success of scientists to successfully discover and test vaccines against COVID-19 in record time. By December 2020, three vaccines (Pfizer, Moderna and AstraZeneca) had been approved in North America and/or Europe for emergency use. Soon thereafter, China, Russia and India deployed their own vaccines. While in abstract, it is an impressive performance, these numbers hide two realities. First, until mid-2021, almost 90 per cent of vaccine orders had been placed by advanced economies in North America and Europe, far exceeding their needs to fully vaccinate their entire populations (OXFAM 2021). Second, almost all major producers (United States, EU and India), other than China and Russia, prohibited exports of vaccines to other nations. This vaccine nationalism was in direct contradiction of the long-standing expressions of global solidarity and principles of free global trade by the countries concerned. Fortunately, during September 2021, at a global leaders meeting, convened by President Biden and the UN Secretary General, the United States announced a new global initiative to donate 1 billion dosages, the European Union too pledged large donations, India promised to resume exports from October 2021, and other countries agreed to pitch in (China had been the first country to promise significant donations to poor countries, followed by India), to vaccinate 70 per cent of global population by the end of 2022.

Following this high-profile global meeting, the pace of vaccinations worldwide picked up. By 31 January 2022, just over 4 billion persons or nearly 53 per cent of the global population had been fully vaccinated (63 per cent were partially vaccinated), according to Oxford University World Data Lab (2021). However, large disparities between countries and regions persisted. While by end-January 2022, vaccination rates were 180 per 100 adults in the higher income economies and 178 per 100 in upper middle-income countries, they had reached only 98 per 100 people in the lower middle-income countries but were still only at 14 per 100 persons in low-income countries. The global average was 129 per 100; the country vaccination rates varied from a high of 303 per 100 for Cuba to a low of 0.5 per 100 for Congo.

The Impact of the Pandemic on Emerging Economies

The current pandemic is having a devastating impact on economic performance in both advanced economies and in the emerging world (except for East Asia). The collapse in world-wide activity in 2020 did begin to reverse in 2021. But with the emergence of new variants of the virus in mid- and late-2021, it remains unclear whether the recovery in advanced economies achieved in 2021 will continue in 2022. In any case, globally, it will take time to fully reverse the disruptive impacts on the level and structure of production, and thus on absolute and relative incomes. This, in turn, has far-reaching social and political implications worldwide.

The impact of recent events on international trade and cooperation are, and will likely remain, significant. The pandemic hit when the major economies of the world had already begun distancing themselves from global cooperation and new, less global (i.e., more regional, or bilateral) trade arrangements were being developed, accelerating a breakdown in the previous multilateral and open trade and investment flow regimes. Underlying all this is the increasing tension between a rising China and the traditional economic powers in North America and Europe. In early 2022, tensions between them and Russia had also risen sharply.

In these circumstances, emerging economies will need to deal with several correlated but clearly identifiable effects:

1. The need to mitigate the impact on the economy and emerge without major dislocations.
2. The disruptive impact of the pandemic on international trade and technology flows.
3. The secular decline in terms of trade for commodity exporters and ensuing/concomitant exchange rate adjustments over the longer term.
4. Possible revisions in global value chains with greater emphasis on domestic or geo-graphically closer sources of inputs; and
5. Increasing debt burdens and loss of macro-financial sustainability in the least-developed countries (especially Sub-Saharan Africa) as well as many middle-income countries (in Africa and Latin America).

Advanced economies and some emerging economies (e.g. China, Vietnam) have been able to counteract the sharp decline in activity due to lockdowns and related business disturbances. The ability of most other emerging and developing economies to take equivalent actions has been limited by fiscal constraints, by their narrow domestic financial markets and by limited or no access to foreign capital. This has resulted in a reduced effectiveness of countercyclical actions, with possible inflationary and balance of payments consequences.

The increase in domestic public borrowing by advanced economies has absorbed signif-icant resources and will continue to do so into the future (IMF 2021b). This, along with higher risks among emerging economies, will likely limit capital flows to these countries. Furthermore, China's actions to revive economic activity at home may limit funds for investment abroad and hamper potential growth around the emerging world. These circumstances point to a problem-atic recovery in the medium term and increased poverty.

EMF has adapted its in-house Global Growth Model to reflect these developments, taking into account the fact that, during the last few decades, there has been a secular decline in the growth of the global productivity frontier. The latest scenarios generated by the model suggest that, as result of the pandemic, the world economy, as a whole, will lose at least one year of output and that, even with global growth resuming in 2021, global GDP will not be on track to return to the pre-pandemic trend line. Asia will remain the most dynamic region, while Latin America and Europe will suffer the most from the recent events. Independent of the effects of the pandemic, there is also a slight slowdown in the long-term global productivity growth, though there are some encouraging signs of a recent uptick. Finally, the book discusses the headwinds faced by the global economy due to climate change.

This book discusses the above developments and paints a picture of how the post-COVID-19 world economy and different emerging economies may evolve over time, as well as highlights the key issues the countries will have to confront. The initial chapters provide the broader context from within which the specific issues are discussed in the chapters that follow.

In addition, the book includes chapters devoted to two broader issues: (1) the reasons and implications of the secular trend in the slowdown in global productivity growth (which if left unchecked, will have a huge impact on the long-term well-being of people worldwide), and what can be done to reverse it ('build back better'); and (2) explore in some depth the reasons why Latin America and Africa are badly lagging behind Asia (as these trends will ultimately threaten global solidarity and even peace) and what can be done to reverse these trends. Contrasting the chapters on these two lagging regions is one on Emerging Asia (excluding China) making a case as to why its economies may be poised to accelerate growth.

The volume comprises of a total of twenty-one chapters and is structured as follows.

Section I sets the stage for the rest of book. After this introduction, the first section comprises three more chapters. The next chapter attempts to give an overview of the world we all live in today, but in doing so it also tries to give readers a sense of how much progress the world has made—economically, socially, and politically—since WWII ended in 1945 and country after country in Asia and Africa achieved independence. At the same time, the chapter describes the many challenges that the global community still needs to jointly confront.

With this as the background, Chapter 3 invites the readers to peek into the future by looking at ten global megatrends which are likely to fundamentally drive the long-term trajectory of most emerging as well as advanced economies: demographics; urbanization; rising incomes combined with increased inequality and inequities; rise of a massive middle class; climate change; accelerating technological development; changes in work and jobs; changing attitudes towards globalization and value chains; weakening of global cooperation and a seeming widespread retreat towards nationalism; and finally, transformation of the structure of the global economy, with the steady rise of emerging economies (particularly Asia).

The chapter on global megatrends is followed by, perhaps the most quantitative part of the book, Chapter 4, which presents alternative scenarios of the post-pandemic global economy through 2060, derived from an in-house econometric model of some 195 economies in the world. None of these scenarios—central, pessimistic, or optimistic—should be seen as the authors' projections of how the world would be some forty years from now, but rather as a policy tool to ask what-if questions and explore the sensitivities of the future development paths of individual countries, regions or even the world, depending on what policies are followed, what happens to the global megatrends discussed above, and what happens with the global productivity frontier. The broad messages of the various scenarios are that growth in the global productivity frontier and country policies are the two most critical determinants of the future economic path. Overall, emerging economies as a group would continue to increase their share of global GDP, that within the EMDEs, Asia would outperform the rest of the world; and the three commodity-exporting regions (Latin America, Africa and the Middle East) would underperform unless they make major structural reforms and transform their economies. The reforms will need to be designed and implemented at individual country levels, with support from the international community.

Section III discusses several conceptual issues and comprises of two chapters. Chapter 5 highlights the importance of improving domestic governance to achieve sustainable and just development. This is a difficult and politically sensitive subject. Global economic growth, fuelled in part by increased globalization, has increased incomes and reduced poverty dramatically around the world over the past several decades. It is no exaggeration to claim that never have so many people around the world been lifted out of poverty in so short a time. Yet, the incidence of the benefits and costs of economic growth has been asymmetric. Most countries have been less than fully successful in addressing such asymmetries and finding politically acceptable means of compensating the losers. Significant human deprivations and inequality within and between countries remain. Increasing social discontent and political polarization has been the result. Lack of good governance is a fundamental issue that plagues many emerging market economies: more and more people have been losing faith in the institutions and the political elites that rule them. Without restoring their credibility by improving domestic governance, long-term economic and social development cannot be achieved. Restoring trust in them and improving domestic governance in all its aspects is fundamental to the long-term well-being and growth of the countries. Recognizing the inherent, and often deep-rooted complexities of the process, this short chapter presents some insights as to what countries can do to reverse the recent trends.

Chapter 6 is a natural continuum from Chapter 5. It explores the important issue as to what sets apart countries and societies which have been able to achieve prosperity over a sustained period, compared to those that have been unable to do so (everything else being more or less the same). Based on extensive literature survey, the chapter presents a conceptual framework that can help explore measures to foster prosperity. Its main message is: one cannot engineer prosperity, but one can create better or worse conditions for prosperity to occur. Part I briefly touches on what renowned economists have said so far on the subject of 'safeguarding prosperity'; Part II presents the effects of the social rules of the game on prosperity, their determinants, and the possibility of controlling them. Part III discusses pragmatically selected approaches to adjusting the rules.

Section III covers eight cross-cutting issues that will have an important bearing on the long-term trajectory of emergence for emerging market economies, indeed of the entire global economy and societies. Satisfactory resolution of these issues is crucial for the realization of the optimistic scenario outlined in Chapter 4. On the other hand, if most of these problems are allowed to fester: the pessimistic scenario may be the unfortunate outcome.

This section starts with Chapter 7 that discusses a major topical issue of worldwide significance: two faces of development. In the midst of rising prosperity in the world, the world is also witnessing increasing inequities and vulnerabilities. While inequality had started rising in the US in the 1980s, it became a major issue in emerging economies more recently. But by now, it has become a global problem. The chapter discusses both inequality between countries (which had been steadily declining before the pandemic, though still large) and intra-country inequalities (which are rising). This analysis is followed by a persuasive summary of the reasons of why economic policy makers should be concerned about this phenomenon, in addition to political leaders and socialists. The chapter includes a menu of recommendations on how to tackle this major issue; each country would need to tailor its own action agenda based on its specific circumstances. The overall approach skirts the traditional ideological divides by proposing actions that emphasize policies that would permit the inequities to be bridged by creating new opportunities for the poor and giving them tools to gain from the opportunities without reducing incentives for others; in the literature, it is sometimes referred to as 'equalizing opportunities to equalize outcomes'.

Chapter 8 discusses another issue of global significance: reformation of the international monetary and financial system. This chapter argues that a fundamental reform of the system is urgent to prevent another, even costlier global financial crisis. The chapter makes a convincingly strong case about more fundamental bases too, for urgently agreeing on a new architecture for the global monetary and financial system to replace the one which was essentially conceived more than seventy-five years ago at Bretton Woods in 1945, in the aftermath of World War II. If the system is already outdated to meet the needs of the present world economy, surely it is even more certain that it will be unable to perform its proper role and functions as the world economy becomes much larger, even more globalized, and much more complex by 2060. This will require creation of a true lender of last resort—perhaps by transforming the International Monetary Fund—and creating an international reserve currency to replace the US dollar (a truly globally traded SDR) to resolve a host of problems that make the current international monetary and financial system both very fragile and unstable. Such a fundamental change will require close cooperation between the major economic powers in the world, particularly the US, China and European Union. The Emerging Markets Forum has advocated similar reforms at multiple times in the past, including by supporting the work of the high-level Palais Royal Initiative, which presented its recommendations at the G20 Summit in 2011. If the author of this chapter is correct—that the risks of another global financial crisis are very high—then inaction in this critical area would be very costly to the entire global community.

Climate change is obviously the third cross-cutting issue that touches every human being. Many global leaders have called it an existential threat to mankind. So much has been written about this problem, considering two recent events: release of the sixth report of the IPCC in mid-2021 and the COP 26 meeting in Glasgow in November 2021. Given this, Chapter 9 tries to add value to the debate on the subject by discussing as to why emerging market economies need to take urgent actions to fight climate change and what they can and should do in this regard. The chapter does so by presenting strong evidence as to how the emerging market economies as a group will suffer much more than the advanced economies in case global temperature rises by 2°C instead of 1.5°C, and therefore it is in their self-interest to aggressively fight climate change. It also presents an interesting proposal on how to distribute the limited global carbon emissions budget in the future, and discusses at length the vexing issue of how to cover the massive financing needs of emerging market economies to restructure the economies to mitigate and adapt to the rising global temperatures.

The discussion on climate is followed by the only other sectoral discussion in the book and that is on agriculture, in Chapter 10. The chapter discusses the basic drivers of global demand of agricultural production by major regions of the world, including changes in prices of agriculture products. An interesting section of the chapter offers the comparison between what IPCC-5's agriculture analysis said about the likely impact of climate change on global agriculture output—a dire outlook—and the actual outcome pre-COVID-19 pandemic (record global agricultural production in 2019). The author ascribes this to the unexpected success of the farmers worldwide to adapt to climate change, contrary to what the IPCC scientists had anticipated. However, even though this chapter does not express a definitive opinion about the future—because IPCC-6 has not yet released its detailed analysis on agriculture—it is not as pessimistic about the future as Chapter 9. It should be noted though that since this chapter was finalized agriculture prices have risen significantly, although it is not clear at this time whether that is due to temporary breakdown in supply chains (as in most other parts of the global economy) or due to climate change.

Chapter 11 is the first of two chapters to explore the accelerating technological revolution underway right now. This chapter gives an overview of a broad range of technological developments and breakthroughs that are expected to revolutionize all aspects of human life in the coming decades. They include biotechnology and medical science, superfast computers, 6G and satellite Internet, new materials, Internet of Things, artificial intelligence, green energy technologies including green hydrogen, quantum computing, and so on. The chapter will be fascinating to read for anyone interesting in knowing where the world is headed in the future. Overall, the chapter paints an optimistic view of the future and postulates that the world economy is ready for a burst in productivity growth (see Chapter 13).

The next chapter, Chapter 12, describes how some of these technological developments are already changing how people work and their impact on jobs (mainly in the services sector). In a nutshell, the basic messages of the chapter are that: a fundamental transformation of societies is underway; that the pandemic acted as a catalyst in accelerating this transformation; and that it is being led by Generation Z. The chapter acknowledges that while the changes described are currently predominantly in the advanced economies, it anticipates these trends to spread to EMDEs also. It ends by making some policy recommendations on how countries can prepare for and facilitate this process. Policy makers in emerging markets need to take proactive actions (build nationwide IT infrastructure and digitization, accelerate STEM literacy among the youth, emphasize innovation and entrepreneurship and promote openness) so as not to suffer from a new digital divide in this fast-changing global scene.

The above two chapters set the stage for Chapter 13 on total factor productivity growth in general. It explores a question that many economists have been debating for a while as to what is happening to the long-term trends in total factor productivity in the world, and between the major regions and countries. The answer to this question, in turn, has major implications for the long-term economic growth prospects, as Chapter 4 indicated. This chapter finds that there have actually been three recent distinct episodes in global productivity growth: it grew at a robust pace until the late 1980's, then it slowed significantly for about a decade; and more recently, until the pandemic, there were signs of green shoots, suggesting a major uptick in productivity. This uptick was particularly evident in East and South Asia, and appears to be driven by the penetration of newer technologies in the services sector. The chapter concludes with six policy recommendations for emerging market economies.

Chapter 14 analyses past productivity trends in three commodity exporting regions (Latin America and the Caribbean, Sub-Saharan Africa and the Middle East) vs. non-commodity-exporting regions by controlling the impact of the commodity cycles on their economic growth and terms of trade. Based on sophisticated regression analyses, the authors conclude that the nominal GDP/GNI growth rates during the past twenty-odd years overestimated their real performance; therefore, the past estimates of total factor productivity, too, are an overestimate. This explains the underperformance of these three regions compared to Asia, and the need for a major transformation of these economies if they are to improve their performance in the future and do not want to be left behind by the rest of the world. The chapter thus reinforces the findings of Chapter 14.

This brings us to Section V comprising three regional essays. The editors decided to commission a separate essay on the African continent (Chapter 15). There were three basic reasons for this. First, in terms of demographics, Africa is by far the fastest-growing region in the world, and before the end of this century, it would have doubled its share of world population. Its future is important not only for its own people but also for the world. Second, many development experts consider Africa as the final development frontier (Baier and Hamel 2018). Without this region doing much better, the world cannot get rid of absolute poverty and deprivations. And third, a poor and poorly governed Africa could be a threat to global peace and security. The authors of this chapter—intimately familiar with its challenges but also passionate about its future—present a hopeful but clear-eyed view and a fresh perspective on how to move forward. In addition to pinpointing four policy issues key to achieving the much-needed transformation of the continent, the chapter presents two fresh messages. First, Africa and African leaders must take the lead in conceiving and implementing its transformation; it cannot and must not be designed by outsiders (as in the past). And second, in the future, there must be a more symmetric cooperation between Africa and the rest of the world.

Chapter 16 is about how to transform the lagging economies in the Latin America and Caribbean region. While this region does not face the threat of a demographic time-bomb and still has relatively much higher per capita income levels than Africa, the chapter demonstrates that in relative terms, it too has been falling behind the more dynamic East and South Asian economies. In many fundamental respects, Latin America and Africa share similar structural issues: overdependence on primary commodities, inability to diversify their economies despite decades-long efforts, lack of international competitiveness, low domestic savings and investment rates, and so on. The average Latin citizen is not satisfied with the status quo, if not entirely disillusioned with her/his political leadership—whether from the Right or the Left. The chapter argues that a major reason for this lies in the economic and social policies followed by many regional economies in the past. Countries have lurched from policies ideologically driven either by the left or the right. It argues that the answer lies in pursuit of much more balanced development policies, by adding social equity and environmental sustainability considerations to the traditional economic growth and macroeconomic stability objectives; in addition, much greater attention needs to be paid to governance and institutional development.

Chapter 17 on Emerging Asia, is included for the opposite reasons. While the current population of Emerging Asia as defined here (India plus ASEAN, but minus China) is similar to Africa, its total GDP is much higher and growth prospects significantly brighter. This volume includes this chapter for two basic reasons. First, very often, discussion around Asia is dominated by China. References to ASEAN and India appear as an afterthought. This chapter explicitly excludes China in discussing Emerging Asia. And second, it presents an unusually optimistic view as to how this part of the world is poised to take off in the next few years to take advantage of technological breakthroughs described elsewhere in the book. If only Africa and Latin America (as well as the Middle East) can emulate what Emerging Asia is reportedly poised to accomplish, the optimistic scenario portrayed in Chapter 4 would be realized globally.

Chapter 18 discusses how to improve global governance in order to tackle more effectively the issues discussed in earlier chapters. Effective resolution of most of the issues outlined above requires close cooperation and collaboration at the global level, as they cannot be tackled at the national level alone. It is vital to get the multilateral agenda right—one that is more focussed on the issues of concern to emerging and developing economies, to reduce the transaction costs for emerging markets in the work of the multilateral system; and to establish a louder voice for emerging markets in this system. In the post-COVID-19 world, the re-shaped global governance and multilateral system does not imply going back to what has existed since the Bretton Woods Conference, but rather, reimagining the system. It will have to reflect new global economic and political realities. Future global governance and the multilateral system needs to consider the much greater weight of emerging economies (particularly in Asia) in global GDP, trade, and savings for them to remain relevant and effective. Existing development finance institutions also need to focus on issues of most concern to the EMDEs and become much more effective in what they do. The chapter calls for the convening of a Bretton Woods 2.0 Conference to bring about such fundamental changes.

Section VI comprises two chapters that bring everything together.

Chapter 19, appropriately titled 'The Missing Link' adds a special—noneconomic—dimension to the rest of the book, and thus enhances it significantly. Its main point is that in recent decades, the unfettered pursuit of profits and material wealth combined with increasing loyalties to peoples' own tribes or countries, have weakened not only the moral and ethical values of societies but also created suspicions about—if not hatred against—people with different backgrounds (e.g. faith, race, country of origin) as well as damaged the planet. It calls for the creation of a new global culture and restoration of a greater sense of ethics in societies, as well as care for the well-being of the planet.

Chapter 20 concludes with a short summary that brings together the basic messages of the book. It does so by presenting two contrasting—extreme—scenarios that can be derived from the various chapters of the book: one portraying a prosperous and more equitable world if most countries succeed in tackling the key issues outlined in the book, and the other a pessimistic outcome resulting in a much more divergent and unstable world by 2060 if most countries fail to act decisively. It highlights eight issues which will make the most difference as to which scenario the next generations will inherit. The chapter concludes on a positive note: human ingenuity combined with technological breakthroughs and driven by the enthusiasm and idealism of the youth makes the first scenario eminently achievable. But, this is by no means inevitable.

Finally, the book ends with a most inspirational epilogue by Michel Camdessus, to whom this volume is dedicated. Only a true global citizen, a statesman with his unique worldwide perspective, and a man of unmatched wisdom as well as impeccable moral values can convey such a profound and heartfelt message to all of humanity. It is a must-read for all.

Chapter 2: The World Today — Progress to Date and Major Challenges

The World Today—Progress to Date and Major Challenges

Chapter 2 | Harinder S. Kohli

The World Today

Before looking forward towards the next forty years, this chapter looks back at the developments in the recent past and where the world stands today. The basic message of this brief overview is that the past half century has been a period of unprecedented historic, economic and social progress worldwide, and that the world is poised for further historic transformation in its economies and societies, provided its some 200 countries successfully tackle the major challenges outlined later in this volume.

A More Interconnected and Interdependent world

Our world is more interconnected and interdependent than ever before. The lives of the 7.8 billion human beings that inhabit the world today are intertwined through trade, urbanization, rise of the middle classes, health, migration, conflicts, social media, etc. Yet, despite rising material well-being for most, we also increasingly share concerns about a variety of issues. Many of these concerns—rising inequality, unequal distribution of benefits of globalization, and climate change—cut across traditional boundaries between advanced and emerging economies.

There are still vast differences in per capita incomes of people living in advanced countries in North America, Europe and Oceania, and those of emerging economies. At the same time, as this chapter shows, the earlier sharp contrasts between advanced and developing countries have started to gradually come down as people in higher income countries and large numbers in the middle-income countries in East Asia and Latin America have come to share many common characteristics. Many of their common challenges arise from newly widespread affluence and globalization, which is why solutions to these challenges also require global and regional cooperation as well as better governance at the national level. At the same time, unfortunately, the situation in much of Sub-Saharan Africa and parts of South Asia remain starkly different. These two regions face deep-rooted problems; they represent the final frontiers of economic and social development.

A vivid example of how interconnected the world has become and how some major issues now affect people throughout the world is the COVID-19 pandemic. During 2020–21, the pandemic wreaked havoc in the lives and livelihoods of people in practically every country in the world. It is widely considered to be the worst global pandemic and health crisis in over a century.

According to the World Health Organization, until December 2021, over 272 million had tested positive for COVID-19 and over 5.3 million had died. It is not clear when, if ever, this pandemic will end. While hardly any country was spared, until early 2021, advanced countries in North America and Europe (despite their sophisticated healthcare systems) were affected the most, with Latin

America emerging as the next most affected region. Asia and Africa, the most populous regions of the world, had escaped the worst until early 2021. But since the emergence of the Delta variant, they, too, suffered much (with China being a major exception due to its draconian measures to restrict movement of people internally). At this rate, it was unclear as to how dangerous the newest variant—Omicron—would prove.

Beyond the huge losses of lives and the large number of people who fell ill, the pandemic has had a fundamental impact on the lives of people around the world. To contain the spread of the pandemic, country after country ordered widespread lockdowns. In many cases, curfews were imposed. As a result, many people had to remain confined to their homes for a year or more. Millions of businesses closed down despite the introduction of significant stimulus programmes by many countries.

As a result, 2020 witnessed the biggest drop in global economic activity since the Great Depression in the 1930s. Countries closed their borders (even within the European Union). As a result, unemployment and the rate of poverty rose in most countries. There is also some evidence that inequality—both between countries and within countries—also increased. Early signs indicate that, because of the changing nature of the way work is done now, not all the jobs lost due to the pandemic will return in the post-pandemic world (see Chapter 14, 'The Productivity Conundrum'). All in all, the pandemic has had and is having a devastating toll on human beings, mostly impacting the less well-off in both advanced and emerging markets and developing economies (EMDE).

Demographics: Population Trends and Ageing

Of the 7.8 billion people in the world in 2020, the largest number live in Asia (4.4 billion people, or around 56 per cent of total global population).

Within Asia, East Asia and the Pacific have by far the largest population of any sub-region in the world: 2.8 billion. These includes two of the world's most populous countries—China (1.35 billion) and Indonesia (251 million). The next three East Asian countries with the highest populations are Japan (120 million), the Philippines (99 million) and Vietnam (91 million). The second most populous sub-region in the world, also in Asia, is South Asia. It has 1.6 billion people as of 2020, with India having 1.26 billion. Another 200 million live in Pakistan, and 149 million in Bangladesh.

However, there is one major difference in recent demographic trends in the two Asian regions. While in East Asia, population growth has slowed significantly (it was 19 per cent for the past twenty years) and is well below the global average of 27 per cent, in South Asia, the population has been growing faster—at an average rate of 33 per cent—and above the global average (though still much slower than Sub-Saharan Africa at 52 per cent). In 2020, total global population grew by just 1 per cent over 2019.

The three advanced regions—Europe, North America and Oceania—have by now essentially stable absolute population sizes; as a result, their share in the total global population has been gradually declining. While Latin America is still growing, many of its countries are also exhibiting declining population growth rates (like Brazil and Chile).

Within these headline counts, various regions do have different demographic profiles. The larger regions are especially heterogeneous. For example, there are significant differences between countries within Africa and Asia. Given the scope and length of this chapter, it is not possible to delve into the details of all 200 countries that comprise the world. The discussion here is limited to the demographic profiles of the eight broader regions of the world, as defined in this book.

Advanced countries in North America, Europe and Oceania (and those in Asia), as a group, have entered a period of ageing societies because of two phenomena: (i) the declining population growth rates mentioned previously, and (ii) improved health outcomes that have led to people living significantly longer now, compared to previous generations. In many countries, total population appears to be peaking or even to have started declining. In much of Europe, the US, and advanced Asian economies (Japan and South Korea), national birth rates have fallen below replacement rate. Japan, Germany and many Eastern European countries are already showing declines in the absolute sizes of their populations. China, the world's most populated country and still a developing economy, has already joined the growing list of countries showing a decline in absolute population. It will be the first nation in history to become old before becoming rich.

Economic Output and Income Levels

In 2020, global economic output totalled US$81.9 trillion in market exchange rates, and US$127.6 trillion in Purchasing Power Parity (PPP) (2018) terms (Centennial Group 2021). Of this, US$56.7 trillion (PPP) was produced in the advanced economies (44.5 per cent), and US$70.9 trillion (55.5 per cent) in EMDEs. The per capita income of advanced economies averaged, in PPP terms, US$50,620 and that of EMDEs averaged US$10,770.

Five of the fifteen largest economies in the world (in PPP terms) are in Asia (China, India, Indonesia, Korea and Japan) and another six straddle across the North Atlantic (Canada, France, Germany, Italy, United Kingdom and the US); Australia is the tenth. Table 2.1 shows the size of these fifteen economies in GDP and GDP per capita in PPP terms.

The share of EMDEs in global economic output has been steadily rising in recent decades due to the higher economic growth of countries such as China, India, Indonesia and Vietnam. As a result, the two Asian sub-regions together account for almost half of global output in PPP terms (42.4 per cent in 2020).

East Asia (which includes China, Indonesia, Japan, Singapore and South Korea) alone accounts for more than a third (35 per cent) of global GDP. South Asia (which includes three large nations: Bangladesh, India and Pakistan) produces another 8 per cent of world output, thanks to its large population and despite its still much lower per capita income and productivity compared to the advanced countries and even East Asia. North America and Europe have the next two largest shares of global output because of their high per capita income (and productivity) but also, significant population base. Africa, Latin America, the Middle East and Oceania combined account only for 16 per cent of the global GDP, despite their large geographic sizes and natural resource bases.

In 2020, there were still vast differences in per capita incomes of people in advanced economies and those living in EMDEs, despite enormous progress made by the latter in reducing poverty during the past seventy-odd years. While due to superior economic growth of countries in East and South Asia (Bangladesh, China, India, Indonesia, South Korea, Thailand and Vietnam), inter-country inequalities had come down significantly before the pandemic (compared to, say, the 1950s), there is still a very large gap in the per capita income (and, therefore, overall quality of life) of people in the Organisation for Economic Co-operation and Development (OECD) countries and the rest of the world. The gap is even more striking between the

Table 2.1: Top fifteen economies, 2020 (in PPP terms)

Country	GDP (PPP)	Country	GDP per capita (PPP)
China	23,435	Luxembourg	114,550
United States	20,320	Singapore	92,945
India	8,646	Ireland	92,653
Japan	5,157	Qatar	88,266
Germany	4,365	Switzerland	70,339
Russia	3,976	United Arab Emirates	63,873
Indonesia	3,205	Brunei	63,717
Brazil	3,061	Norway	63,491
France	2,912	United States	61,390
United Kingdom	2,873	Iceland	57,971
Turkey	2,472	Hong Kong, China	57,606
Italy	2,389	Denmark	57,511
Mexico	2,373	Netherlands	56,736
Korea	2,243	Sweden	54,021
Canada	1,796	Taiwan (China)	53,631

Source: Centennial Group 2021

Table 2.2: GDP by regions, 2020

Region	GDP (MkFx)	GDP (PPP)
East Asia and the Pacific	26,037	44,155
South Asia	3,067	9,940
Oceania	1,523	1,499
Sub Saharan Africa	1,615	4,184
The Middle East & North Africa	2,665	6,007
Latin America & Caribbean	4,187	9,304
Europe	20,907	30,430
North America	21,914	22,116
World Total	81,915	127,634

Source: Centennial Group 2021

OCED countries (including in Asia) and those in much of Sub-Saharan Africa and South Asia, as illustrated in Table 2.3. Per capita incomes in Northern America are twelve times that of Sub-Saharan Africa.

Table 2.3: Average per capita income by regions, 2019 (GNI PPP)

Region	GNI per capita (PPP)
East Asia and the Pacific	18,349
South Asia	6,463
Oceania	47,245
Sub-Saharan Africa	3,824
The Middle East and North Africa	16,876
Latin America and the Caribbean	16,356
Europe	39,287
Northern America	64,417
World Average	17,535

Source: World Bank 2021b

Intra-country Inequalities

Globally, until recently, income inequality had been declining over the last fifty-plus years. As Figure 2.1 illustrates, this can be attributed to decreasing inter-country inequality due to faster growth of many large EMDEs. In the past twenty years, EMDEs have annually grown, on average, roughly 4 per cent faster than the advanced countries (see Chapter 4). However, 65 per cent of global inequality is still due to inter-country income gaps (IMF 2017).

While inter-country income inequalities have been coming down, the trend is unfortunately just the opposite for intra-country inequalities, both in terms of income and wealth. This is true

Figure 2.1: GDP PPP per capita, advanced and emerging economies

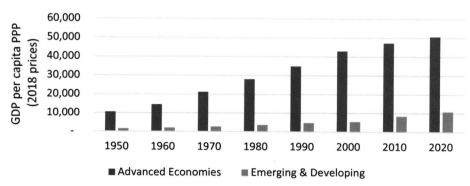

Source: Centennial Group 2021

for both advanced economies and EMDEs. As a result, inequality has now become a global phenomenon and a major political issue in an increasing number of countries. The global numbers in this area are heavily influenced by recent developments in several large countries, such as China, India and the US (since the mid-1980s). Further, the pandemic has hit the vulnerable sections of societies worldwide disproportionately, further aggravating the situation.

Finally, some recent studies suggest that the current pandemic had led to a decline in per capita incomes in both advanced and emerging market economies. However, low-income economies experienced larger declines compared to advanced economies and EMDEs as a whole.

The bottom line is that as a result of three factors—large inter-country inequalities (despite enormous progress over the past fifty years); major, and often rising, intra-country inequalities; and the recent drop in per capita incomes, particularly in most low-income countries—we today live in a world that suffers from major disparities in per capita income and living standards.

Rise of the Middle Classes

In 2021, for the first time in known history, almost half of the people on Earth had achieved middle-class[1] income levels.

In 2022, we are likely to witness an important social and economic milestone when more than half of the people in the world would be in either middle class or upper income groups. In most societies, middle classes have not only represented stability and continuity but have also put greater emphasis on better work ethic, education, savings, and demanded more accountability from public and political bodies. As these values spread widely through a society and take deeper hold in more countries around the world, they are likely to not only lead to better economic outcomes but also demands for better governance. Indeed, over the longer term, the

Table 2.4: Per cent of population classified as middle and upper class, 2020

Region	Per cent of Population
Asia and the Pacific	52
South Asia	20
Oceania	98
Sub-Saharan Africa	11
The Middle East & North Africa	51
Latin America & Caribbean	57
Europe	96
North America	99
Average (World)	47

Source: Centennial Group 2021

1. A commonly used definition of the middle class is the one designated by the World Bank—per capita income of US$11/ day or more (2018 dollars).

emergence of middle classes, together with parallel developments in some other areas—like social media and civic societies—discussed later in this chapter, could be a powerful force for change.

The percentage of people classified as middle class in each region is shown in the Table 2.4.

Urbanization

A majority of the world's population (4.36 billion or 56 per cent) today lives in urban areas. Greater economic development in EMDEs has been accompanied by an acceleration in rural–urban migration, particularly in Asia (both East and South). The ongoing rapid urbanization in EMDEs again will have far-reaching economic, social, political and governance ramifications.

Interestingly, in terms of urbanization, some EMDEs today exhibit characteristics that are similar (or closer) to those of the advanced economies than those of less dynamic emerging economies. For example, as Figure 2.2 shows, Latin America is now the most urbanized region of the world after Europe (and ahead of North America), followed by the Middle East and East Asia. South Asia and Sub-Saharan Africa are still mostly rural.

In EMDEs, these urbanization rates have already resulted in the formation of many megacities. Indeed, Asia and the Pacific already have the largest number of cities with more than 10 million people (11 out of 33 such cities in the world): Bangkok, Beijing, Chongqing, Guangzhou, Jakarta, Metro Manila, Osaka, Shanghai, Shenzhen, Tianjin, and Tokyo. South Asia accounts for eight more such cities: Bengaluru, Chennai, Delhi, Dhaka, Karachi, Kolkata, Lahore and Mumbai. Latin America has another six (Bogota, Buenos Aires, Lima, Mexico City, Rio de Janeiro and Sao Paulo), and Sub-Saharan Africa already has two (Kinshasa and Lagos). Compared to these EMDEs, North America and Europe together have only three cities with more than 10 million residents: Los Angeles, New York and Paris.

For the EMDEs, challenges involved in urban management are magnified by four other factors:
- Due to the inequalities and the large number of poor people (particularly in Sub-Saharan Africa and South Asia), cities in most EMDEs have large and crowded slum areas, with meagre, if any, public services; most are crime-ridden.

Figure 2.2: Urbanization levels by region

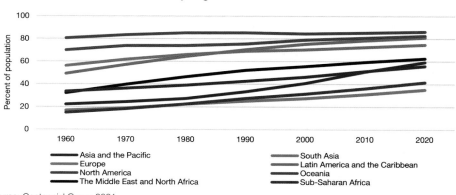

- The rapid pace of urbanization (especially in Africa and South Asia), as mentioned. Managing rapid expansion of already crowded and inadequately served cities constitutes a massive challenge.
- EMDEs have the most polluted large cities in the world with unhealthy air, inadequate supply of clean water and poor sewage systems. Climate change is likely to make living conditions even worse for people in these cities.
- And finally, limited financial and managerial resources to cope with the urgent urban management challenges (including public safety) even as the public's tolerance for inaction is wearing thin.

Human Development

Comparing the overall Human Development Index (HDI), produced by the United Nations Development Program (UNDP), of the advanced economies and EMDEs, reveals a clear relation between human development and income levels. However, looking deeper, this co-relationship does not always hold across all regions. Indeed, distinctions between advanced and developing countries are not as sharp when looking at HDI as they are for per capita income, except in the case of most countries in Sub-Saharan Africa and South Asia.

For example, as shown in Table 2.5, most HDIs for East Asia, Latin America and the Middle East are approaching those of North America and Europe, in a sharp contrast to those of Sub-Saharan Africa. Looking at individual indicators, several East Asian countries outperform even North America and Europe in critical education tests. At the same time, South Asia and Africa lag badly in crucial areas of maternal health, child mortality and nutrition. And even Latin America and the Caribbean, despite their otherwise high overall HDI, lags significantly in the education index.

As expected, even within regions, there are disparities. In South Asia, Bangladesh has a much better HDI than India, despite a similar per capita income. There are similar anomalies in Africa; for example, Ethiopia does better than Nigeria despite being much poorer.

While greater investment in human development is necessary in most EMDEs, more efficient use of the resources presently directed towards it is equally, if not more, critical. Many studies

Table 2.5: Human Development Index by region, 2019

Region	Human Development Index	Education Index
Asia and the Pacific	0.721	0.671
South Asia	0.676	0.570
Oceania	0.938	0.925
Sub-Saharan Africa	0.544	0.470
The Middle East and North Africa	0.749	0.648
Latin America and the Caribbean	0.748	0.681
Europe	0.878	0.838
Northern America	0.928	0.897

Source: UNDP 2021

have indicated, for example, that educational outcomes in Latin America fall well short of expectations despite the region spending fiscal resources (as per cent of GDP) similar to those spent by the OECD countries (Inter-American Development Bank 2017).

Access to Basic Infrastructure

There is clearly a major infrastructure gap between the advanced countries and EMDEs, except for China. Key indicators of infrastructure stock show that advanced countries in Asia, Europe, North America, and Oceania (Japan, Singapore and South Korea) deliver much better infrastructure services to their citizens—both due to the existing stock and because of much better management and operation of this stock—than the EMDEs. China is an exception as, in many respects, it has infrastructure similar or even better than in many OECD countries. However, it is also a fact that within the advanced countries, there are significant differences. And some countries, like the US, which were the world leaders at one time, have had difficulties in renewing their infrastructure stock and are now trying to catch up.

But the biggest global challenges relating to infrastructure lie in the EMDEs, most of all in Sub-Saharan Africa: supply of clean water, sanitation, rural roads, access to 24x7 power, ports, highways, telecommunications and wideband Internet.

In terms of sheer volume, the largest investments remain to be made in Asia because of its much larger population, its forecasted higher economic growth, and, of course, its larger existing stock, which requires renewal and maintenance.

To the extent infrastructure is the backbone of development, EMDEs cannot promote inclusive growth or improve their productivity and competitiveness (thus, the longer-term economic well-being of their people) without overcoming the current gaps in the provision of infrastructure services to both the public at large and businesses.

Climate Change

Climate change is an existential threat to mankind. The latest (sixth) Intergovernmental Panel on Climate Change (IPCC) report, put together by hundreds of top international scientists and released by the UN in August 2021, has issued a 'code red alert' to the entire global community, warning that our planet appears on a trajectory to warm by 1.5°C by 2040. Almost every human being is likely to be adversely affected by more frequent extreme weather events, including heavy floods, droughts, and melting of glaciers.

IPCC adds credible scientific data and arguments to the already mounting day-to-day evidence that climate change is already here and that it is starting to affect people everywhere. The latest IPCC report also suggests that, overall, EMDEs will be hurt much more by it than advanced countries. Yet, it is the advanced countries—driven by grassroots groups—who appear much more energized to contain global warming. Within the advanced economies, the European Union currently is in the lead in considering concrete actions to reduce carbon emissions. The new US administration also promises major actions.

Until a few years ago, climate change was regarded, by most, as a long-term threat and its exact impact debatable. It is now evident that climate change already has started to have negative—sometimes disastrous—impacts on all regions of the world. The major debate now is about what the global community can and will do to contain temperature rise within 2°C by

2100 (COP 21 had set a more ambitious target of limiting the rise to only 1.5°C, which now seems elusive).

One concrete piece of evidence of climate change is that during the past decade, the world has experienced six of the hottest ten years on record. July 2021 was the hottest month ever in history. This global warming is leading to a much greater frequency of extreme weather conditions, such as unprecedented floods, droughts and fires. For example, in July 2021, Central Europe saw unusually heavy rains in multiple countries that led to flooding, with many towns getting submerged and leading to large losses of life and property. Simultaneously, in North America while the East Coast saw heavy rains and floods, the West Coast suffered massive forest fires, mainly due to record heat and prolonged drought. Across the Pacific Ocean, China had massive floods. In the Middle East, prolonged droughts caused many hydro-electric plants to curtail production, leading to major power shortages in several countries also in the same month. And simultaneously there were massive fires in Russia (Siberia), Turkey and Greece. Sub-Saharan Africa has suffered more frequent droughts and parts of South America have seen numerous lakes shrink or even dry up altogether. Glaciers are melting worldwide—in the Himalayas, Alps, Andes, Alaska and Antarctica. Scientists have ascribed most of these events to ongoing climate change.

EMDEs face a diverse set of environmental issues, including extreme flooding due to rising seas, heavy rainfall, and storm surges from typhoons. Of the top ten countries ranked highest on the Global Climate Risk Index 2021 (Eckstein, Künzel, and Schäfer 2021), three are in Asia, another five in Sub-Saharan Africa, and the remaining two are in Latin America and the Caribbean. In addition to disrupting daily lives and causing widespread damage to public property and infrastructure, these changes in weather patterns have fundamental implications for billions of people as to where and how they will live and what they will eat. For example, a rise in global temperature of 2°C is projected to lead to a rise in sea levels of 50 to 100 centimetres, directly impacting between 190 and 480 million people currently living in affected areas. In Asia alone, many cities (such as Bangkok, Colombo, Dhaka, Jakarta, Kolkata, Manila and Mumbai), in which millions of people live, will be almost entirely submerged. Similarly, millions of people in Sub-Saharan Africa will have to abandon their current places of inhabitation as droughts choke off supply of water. Such developments would result in hundreds of millions of environmental refugees worldwide.

People in EMDEs are already suffering from other, more local and immediate environmental problems. Because of a variety of reasons—poor urban management and lack of environmental standards imposed on local industry—major rivers in many EMDEs are heavily polluted, and even dying, in many cases. Forests are receding (for example, the Amazon forest in Brazil). The most polluted cities in the world are in the EMDEs (almost all in Asia).

It is also clear that it is in the self-interest of everyone—in advanced countries as well as EMDEs—to work together to mitigate and adapt to climate change by taking actions at local, national, regional and global levels. Only such actions, both individual and collective, can meet this existential threat to mankind head-on. This, in turn, will help the most vulnerable people in the world.

People Living under Democracy

Today, the vast majority of people in the world—both in advanced economies and EMDEs—are ruled by democratically elected governments. Some 1.7 billion people live under 'hard autocracies' and over 6 billion people or 76 per cent live under some form of democracy. Comparatively, most Asians and Africans were under colonial rule as recently as 1945, and much of Latin America had either military dictatorships or was ruled by tyrants. Few citizens of today's EMDEs had a right to vote; in 2020, most do.

This is not to say that all democracies are equally developed or effective in reflecting the will and desires of the electorates. But at least 6 billion people of the 7.8 billion people of the world have a right to vote, and thus, some say in who governs them. Within this overall universe, experts have classified how effective various democracies are. One such classification and how countries fall in each category, by region, is shown in Table 2.6.

Emergence of Civic Society: A Potential Major Force for Change

A major positive development in the past few decades has been the emergence of civic society as a major voice of ordinary citizens and an important force in public affairs in more and more countries. The interconnectedness of the Internet and the ability to amplify one's voice outside of physically limited areas has allowed for the emergence of a new wave of activism and engagement around the world. This new global and interconnected civic society has taken many shapes in recent years, ranging from Western 'Slacktivism' to the revolutions of the Arab Spring and the emergence of Q-Anon. As technology progresses, the barrier of entry to engage with these forces—and civil society as a whole—continues to decrease.

This separation of location and interest, however, has resulted in a disconnect between those who care about certain issues, those who are most affected by those issues, and those who are most able to address them. For example, fighting against climate change has become a massive movement in the West, so much so that the poster child of the movement is a young Swedish woman. However, there is little movement in countries who rely on heavily polluting industries to support their economies.

Social Media: Another Promising Fast-emerging Global Phenomenon

A major global phenomenon of the past two decades is the spread of social media. It is rapidly becoming a major force both for peer-to-peer communications and for social activism (see Chapter 12, 'Future Technological Landscape').

The explosion in the rise of social media in the past decade or so has been driven by four factors. First, wide availability of (lower cost) mobile connectivity—including in rural areas—not just in advanced countries but also in most EMDEs. Second, almost universal use of mobile phones (India reportedly has 1.5 billion mobile phones for a total population of 1.28 billion). Third, the continually growing diaspora of populations in urban centres seeking to retain some connection with their communities. And fourth, availability of multiple, easy-to-use, newer platforms like WhatsApp, WeChat, Signal, TikTok, and so on, in addition to the more mature platforms like Facebook, Twitter and YouTube.

The result is billions of messages being exchanged daily amongst millions of chat groups. While most are for sharing personal information, many are being actively used to discuss (and

Table 2.6: Number of countries and population by government type and region

Category	# of Countries	Population (mil)
Working Democracy	**34**	**750.0**
Asia and the Pacific	3	201.6
Europe	24	447.2
Latin America and the Caribbean	3	24.5
The Middle East and North Africa	1	8.7
Northern America	1	37.7
Oceania	2	30.3
Deficient Democracy	**48**	**1,254.1**
Asia and the Pacific	7	286.1
Europe	10	89.3
Latin America and the Caribbean	11	329.0
The Middle East and North Africa	1	11.8
Northern America	1	331.0
South Asia	4	51.9
Sub-Saharan Africa	14	155.0
Hybrid Regime	**37**	**2,761.6**
Asia and the Pacific	9	447.0
Europe	3	47.6
Latin America and the Caribbean	6	226.7
The Middle East and North Africa	4	58.2
South Asia	1	1,380.0
Sub-Saharan Africa	14	602.1
Moderate Autocracy	**34**	**1,255.3**
Asia and the Pacific	7	359.0
Europe	4	248.5
Latin America and the Caribbean	4	39.3
The Middle East and North Africa	4	191.5
South Asia	1	164.7
Sub-Saharan Africa	14	252.3
Hard Autocracy	**20**	**1,716.1**
Asia and the Pacific	6	1,498.1
Latin America and the Caribbean	1	28.4
The Middle East and North Africa	7	101.8
Sub-Saharan Africa	6	87.8

Source: Lauth, Hans-Joachim and Oliver Schlenkrich 2021

advocate) social and political issues, and how to organize to influence policies at the national or even global levels.

Social media's influence is likely to increase dramatically in EMDEs over time. It could potentially become a powerful force in improving governance, both domestic and global, in the next few decades. At the same time, we have recently witnessed in some open societies that social media can also be used to spread false information and undercut the rule of law, even in advanced economies. Countries will need to remain vigilant regarding these risks that follow the misuse of social media, and adopt policies to minimize its risks, but in ways that neither overly restrict people's freedom of expression nor prevent innovation.

Chapter 3: Ten Global Megatrends

Ten Global Megatrends

Chapter
3

Harinder S. Kohli, Ieva Vilkelyte and Harpaul Alberto Kohli

Introduction

Almost all studies on long-term prospects identify the drivers that would, together, have a funda-mental influence on the future trajectory of an economy. Emerging Markets Forum's earlier studies of this nature have also followed a similar approach by identifying the key international and domestic drivers. With time, as the global economy has continued to evolve and major individual economies have become more fully integrated within the global economy, it has become clear that most countries and regions are increasingly influenced by similar, if not the same, long-term megatrends. These megatrends, when combined with certain key domestic factors (like the quality and effec-tiveness of domestic institutions, governance, infrastructure, business climate as well as political leadership), are expected to be the key determinants for economies worldwide.

This chapter highlights ten global megatrends that are critical to the long-term prospects of emerging market economies. These global megatrends are also relevant to the advanced econo-mies, as the fortunes of most countries worldwide have become increasingly intertwined and the earlier sharp distinctions between advanced and developing countries are becoming blurred. For example, in terms of demographics, as recently as only thirty years ago, while most developed countries were characterized by stable and mostly urbanized populations, most developing coun-tries still had fast-growing, young, and mostly rural populations. Well before 2060, these distinctions essentially will have disappeared between today's so called advanced economies and many emerg-ing and developing economies (EMDEs). Except for Sub-Saharan Africa and the Middle East (and some parts of South Asia), almost all countries in the world—whether developed or developing—will share the challenges related to ageing and stable (if not even shrinking) populations. A vast majority of the global population will live in urban areas and will have achieved either middle-class or upper income status, like what happened in North America and Western Europe soon after the end of the Second World War. Similarly, the new challenges posed by climate change and the opportunities offered by technological developments will be common to all countries. The same can be said for most other megatrends discussed in this chapter, though the degree and timing of their impact will vary by region, depending on each country's circumstances. The megatrends will act as a tailwind for some economies at times and as a headwind for others, depending on how countries anticipate and or respond to them.

While the megatrends are discussed individually below, it is important to remember that they interact with each other. Often, they reinforce each other. For example, higher economic growth combined with better urban management leads to faster urban growth and better absorption of new technology, both of which in turn boost overall productivity of an economy, leading to a larger and more prosperous middle class. But some megatrends can also potentially offset each other. For example, climate change and competition for finite natural resources due to the expected addition of 4 billion additional middle-class consumers between now and 2060 could significantly reduce sustainable rates of global economic growth (in absence of the technological changes that are being envisaged). Fortunately, major technological advances have the potential to overcome these challenges and allow raising of living standards. However, the same technological breakthroughs are also leading to significant changes in how we work, making many workers redundant even while creating new jobs for others. Without retraining, and concerted efforts by both the state and private sector to reintegrate them into the labour force, they may end up being the unintended losers. Instead of looking at each megatrend as a standalone phenomenon, these megatrends should thus be looked at together in assessing how they may impact a particular society, economy, region or the world.

3.1 Global Population Trends: Peaking of Global Population . . . Except for Africa

Many recent highly respected studies (Volsett et al. 2020), suggest a fast-changing outlook for the global population through 2100, compared to what many demographers had expected just a few years ago, and certainly compared to alarming reports of a global 'population explosion' by many in the 1960s. The latest studies point to a possible peaking of the global population before the end of this century. They anticipate dramatic declines in the absolute population of dozens of countries in Europe and Asia.[1]

In 1980, the world population was 4.4 billion. Asia had almost six out of ten people in the world (2.5 billion), with Africa having only about one-tenth of the world population (467 million). The population of emerging market economies had grown by 54 per cent between 1960 and 1980, while that of the advanced countries by only 24 per cent. Since then, there have been major changes in population size, growth rates and trends. By 2020, total global population had risen to 7.8 billion. Asia's share had fallen slightly to 56 per cent (4.4 billion) while Africa had significantly increased its share of global population to 17.1 per cent. Europe's share of the global population had declined to 10.8 per cent from 16.6 per cent in 1980. While global population growth rate had slowed down to only 1 per cent per annum, Africa was growing at a rate of 2.5 per cent, which explained its fast-rising share of global population.

The Lancet study forecasts global population to peak in 2064 at 9.63 billion. It will then gradually decline to 8.79 billion by year 2100 (the UN had projected in 2015 that the global population will be 9.7 billion by 2100). Lancet's reference (base case) projections further give the following figures for the five most populous countries: India (1.09 billion); Nigeria (791 million); China (732 million); the USA (336 million); and Pakistan (248 million).

The study also suggests major shifts in the age structure in many parts of the world. Overall, it forecasts 2.37 billion people (27 per cent of total) to be sixty-five years or older and 1.7 billion (19 per cent of total) to be younger than twenty years by year 2100. Perhaps, the most dramatic finding of this study is that by 2050, the total fertility rate in as many as 151 countries

---

1. The data for this megatrend comes from the Lancet October 2020 study, with references to historic statistics from the UN Population office.

will be below the replacement level (2.1); by year 2100, the number of such countries would rise to 183. As a result, many countries will see a dramatic decline in population. For example, Japan, Thailand, and Spain would see declines of more than 50 per cent between 2017 and 2100. China, the world's most populous country, is forecast to see a decline of about 48 per cent. Africa will be the only region still with a growing and young population. These trends are illustrated in the pie charts below.

These developments will have far-reaching health, social, economic, fiscal and political implications.

Figure 3.1: Share of world population

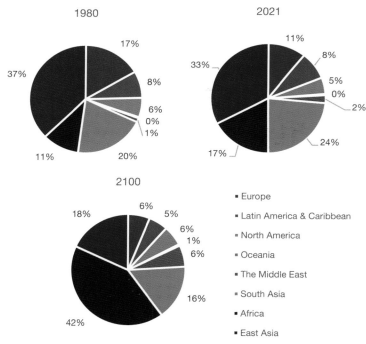

Source: Centennial Group2021

3.2 Urbanization: A Fast-urbanizing World; Asia and Africa Catch Up with Others

Most of the world's population (4.36 billion or 56 per cent) today lives in urban areas. Greater economic development in EMDEs has been accompanied by an acceleration in rural-urban migration, particularly in Asia.

In terms of urbanization, some EMDEs already exhibit characteristics similar to those of the advanced economies. For example, Latin America is now the most urbanized region of the world after Europe and North America, followed by the Middle East and East Asia. South

Asia and Sub-Saharan Africa are still mostly rural. Figure 3.2 traces the urbanization trends of eight global regions.

In EMDEs, these urbanization rates have already resulted in the formation of many megacities. Regionally, Asia and the Pacific has the largest number of cities with more than 10 million people (eleven out of thirty-three such cities in the world). Latin America has another six and Sub-Saharan Africa already has two. Compared to these EMDEs, Europe and North America together have only three cities with more than 10 million people.

Building on the work of the UN Statistical Office, Centennial Group's global model has projected possible future evolution of global urbanization trends as follows. By 2060, global urban population will likely rise to 7.25 billion (72 per cent of total). This means an increase of as many as 2.8 billion additional people in urban areas (an increase of 64 per cent). As much as 78.6 per cent of this increase in global urban population will occur in Sub-Saharan Africa, South Asia and East Asia, which are projected to experience a 234, 105 and 29 per cent increase in urban population, respectively. In terms of countries, four countries alone—China, India, Nigeria and Pakistan—are expected to add over 1 billion additional people to their urban population.

For all EMDEs, but particularly for countries in Sub-Saharan Africa and South Asia, challenges involved in urban management are magnified by five factors. First, due to the inequalities and large number of poor, cities in most EMDEs have large and crowded slum areas, with very poor, if any, public services; most are also crime-ridden. These pose huge governance challenges. Second, managing rapid expansion of already crowded and inadequately served cities further adds to those challenges. Third, EMDEs have the most polluted large cities in the world with unhealthy air, inadequate supply of clean water, and poor sewage systems. Fourth, climate change poses a major new challenge on top of the above. All urban areas will require far-reaching adaptation and mitigation measures to make them more resilient. In many cases, existing infrastructure may need to be totally rebuilt and coastal cities redesigned. And finally, EMDEs have limited financial and managerial resources to cope with the above urgent urban management challenges (including public safety) even as the public's tolerance is wearing thin.

Figure 3.2: Change in population 2021–60

Source: Centennial Group 2021

3.3 Rapid Rise of the Middle Class:[2] The Impending Dominance of Consumer Classes

One of the distinguishing features of the twenty-first century will be the emergence of large—and in many countries even a dominant—middle class worldwide. 2022 will mark a major historic milestone as a majority of the world population would be either middle-class or higher, as defined by the World Bank (annual per capita income above US$1,036). By 2060, the world will have been further transformed in terms of people's income levels and consumption, provided the world economy stays on its current course (a major if).

During the twentieth century, in many regions of the world, a majority of people reached middle-income status. By the 1960's, the vast majority of North Americas and Western Europeans had become middle-class, or higher, benefitting from the post-WWII economic recovery. This transatlantic transformation was followed by Japan and the so-called newly industrializing countries (NICs) in Asia—South Korea, Taiwan, Hong Kong and Singapore. In parallel, Latin America, historically the richest of the developing regions, also greatly increased the size of its population classified as middle-income. After the major economic reform in China in the 1980s and in India in the 1990s, these two world's most populous countries exhibited some of the highest economic growth rates in the world, their poverty rates fell sharply, and the size of middle classes started to grow rapidly. Finally, in Europe, the fall of the Berlin Wall led to the economic revival of most emerging economies in Eastern Europe (after a lag of a few years), boosting incomes and middle-income classes. All these developments combined together have brought the world to a stage today when it appears to be on the cusp of further major transformation.

By 2060, according to the Centennial's in house model of the global economy, 80 per cent of the world population will be either middle-class or upper-income. In the next forty years, 4 billion more people would join this group, almost exclusively in the EMDEs. In addition to the current three developed regions (North America, Europe and Oceania), East Asia too will have almost all its population in the ranks of middle-class and upper-income (when measured by current international standards). Latin America—which used to be the richest developing region in the 1960s—would still have a third of its population falling below this threshold, as defined today by the World Bank. But Africa will have less than half its population reaching this threshold, even in 2060.

Past experiences in many countries suggests that, over time, the middle classes can play a very positive role in building a society and becoming its backbone by putting much greater emphasis on education and work ethics; increasing savings while at the same time increasing demand for quality goods; having greater aspirations for their future generations; and demanding greater transparency and accountability from their governments. On the other hand, unless channelled appropriately, rising demand from 4 billion additional new middle-class consumers could also add huge pressures onto our planet's finite natural resources.[3]

---

2. Middle class defined by 2020 standards using World Bank definition of annual per capita income above US$1,036. Having per capita income levels that classify individuals (and their families) as middle-class at this thresh-hold means that they have escaped the worst of poverty and can have a reasonable level of living standards in terms of nutrition, shelter, education and health care.
3. See also Chapter 4 by Claudio Loser, Harpaul Alberto Kohli and Laura Shelton.

Figure 3.3: Share of middle- and upper-class population in 2060

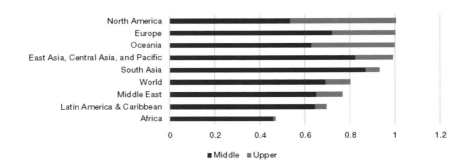

Source: Centennial Group 2021

3.4 Inequality and Inequities: Inter-country vs. Intra-country

In looking at inequality and inequities globally, three distinct aspects need to be considered: inter-country inequalities; intra-country inequalities; and non-income related disparities due to people's lack of access to basic services such as clean water supply, sanitation, health services, education, and shelter.

According to the most recent (2019) World Bank study on (income) inequality, inter-country inequalities have been gradually decreasing in recent decades due to higher per capita GDP growth of emerging and developing economies (EMDEs) relative to the advanced economies. A recent Centennial Group study suggests that between years 2000 and 2019 EMDEs' growth was about 4 percentage points higher than that of the advanced economies. Due to this superior performance of EMDEs, globally, inter-country inequities fell from accounting 80 per cent to 65 per cent. Such a significant fall in inter-country inequality had not occurred since the Industrial Revolution. However, it will still take a long time to close this remaining large gap (Figure 3.4a).

Centennial Group's in-house global model portrays how these inter-country inequalities may evolve between now and 2060 under its baseline scenario (Figure 3.4b). The model suggests that most EMDEs—particularly in the two Asian regions where more than 50 per cent of the world's population currently lives—will continue to converge with the advanced economies and combined with their slowing (or declining) population growth rates, their per capita incomes will continue to catch up with wealthier countries. However, while Latin America and Africa will also close their relative income gaps, they will catch up much slower than Asia.

It is much more difficult to anticipate the future direction of intra-country income inequalities. What is obvious is that as inter-country inequities become less pronounced, intra-country disparities in incomes (urban–rural, regional, by ethnic groups, by gender, etc.) will become more important. At the same time, eradicating them will require sustained policy and institutional actions at individual country level. It is not possible to anticipate how the recent worrisome trends in many countries of rising intra-country inequities can be reversed. Least of all it is not feasible to model such outcomes at the global level. What is clear, though, is that they are a major political issue which cannot be ignored anymore.

Beyond the issues of income inequity at the national level, is the much more vexing issue of broader social disparities in most EMDEs. There are very wide disparities faced by citizens within countries in getting access to basic public services such as education, health care, clean water, sanitation, transportation, public safety, and so on. As in the case of income inequities, these disparities in access to social services vary by region, ethnic groups, gender, etc. Again, they can be remedied only by actions at the national level. It is not possible to anticipate the feasibility and pace of such actions at individual country level, and therefore to project their outcomes.[4]

Figure 3.4: GDP per capita PPP (2018 US$)

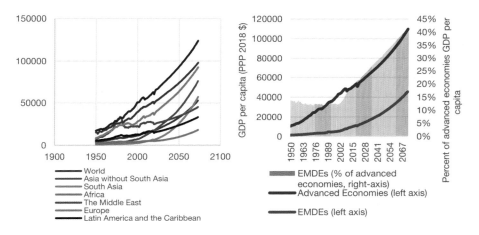

Source: Centennial Group 2021

3.5 Climate Change: The Time to Act Is Now . . . Locally, Nationally and Globally

While the pandemic poses a global threat in the immediate future, climate change is the most serious threat faced by the entire mankind over the medium- to long-term. The latest (sixth) Intergovernmental Panel on Climate Change (IPCC) report, released by the UN in August 2021, has warned that our planet is on a trajectory to warm by 1.5°C by 2040. Under that scenario, almost every human being is likely to be adversely affected by more frequent extreme weather events, including heavy floods, droughts and melting of glaciers. Overall, EMDEs and within them, the poorest segments of societies, will be hurt the most.

EMDEs face a diverse set of environmental issues, including extreme flooding due to rising seas, heavy rainfall, and storm surges from typhoons. Of the top ten countries ranked highest on the Global Climate Risk Index 2021, three are in Asia, another five in Sub-Saharan Africa, and the remaining two are in Latin America and the Caribbean. These changes in weather patterns have fundamental implications for billions of people as to where and how they will live.

---

4. For further discussion of these complex issues see Chapter 7 by Jose Fajgenbaum, Ieva Vilkelyte and Harpaul A. Kohli.

A rise in global temperature of 2°C (a question of when and not if) is projected to lead to a rise in sea levels of 50 to 100 centimetres, directly impacting between 190 and 480 million people currently living in affected areas. In Asia alone, many cities in which millions of people live, will be almost entirely submerged. Similarly, millions in Sub-Saharan Africa will have to abandon their current places of inhabitation as droughts choke off supply of water. Such developments will result in perhaps hundreds of millions of environmental refugees worldwide. Additionally, the ongoing changes in climate could have a major adverse impact on agriculture and food production as well as rural employment. Further, over the longer term, as glaciers melt (e.g., in the Himalayas), even agriculture production on irrigated lands would suffer as water flows in rivers begin to ebb.

A recent study published in the journal *Nature Climate Change* (October 2021) concluded that at least 85 per cent of the world's population and 80 per cent of world's land area has been affected by human-induced climate change. It is clearly in the self-interest of everyone— in advanced countries as well as EMDEs—to work together to mitigate and adapt to climate change by taking actions at local, national, regional and global levels. The coming decades will be the ultimate test of the ability and willingness of the global community—governments, businesses, local communities, civic societies as well as international institutions—to act together to preserve the planet for future generations.[5]

Figure 3.5: Number of disasters

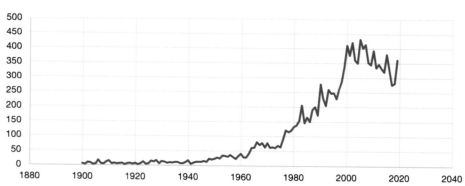

Source: EMDAT 2020

3.6 International Trade and Changes in Value Chains: A Less Globalized World?

The world may be at an important inflection point with respect to the future direction of globalization. There is now an increasing worldwide debate about the merits of unfettered globalization and the current (over-) dependency on global value chains, which was based on the principles of the free flow of goods, services and capital across international borders. Many regions and countries now want to give greater preference instead to 'onshore production' of at least some

---

5. For further discussion of climate change and role of emerging markets see Chapter 9 by Montek Singh Ahluwalia and Utkarsh Patel, and Chapter 10 on agriculture development, climate change and technological developments by Kevin Cleaver.

goods and services (for example, to protect critical technological capacities to enhance national security and domestic jobs).

The share of merchandise trade in the total world GDP rose from about 17 per cent in 1960 to 44 per cent in 2019; except for the short period around the global financial crisis of 2007–09, since after 1960 global trade had steadily risen faster than global GDP (Figure 3.6). As a result, major world economies became linked together as never before and consumers worldwide gained significantly. But many recent developments—not all of them linked with the pandemic—suggest that the past may not be a prelude to the future.

The Case for Globalization of Trade, Investments and Capital Flows

Economic theory—based on the concept of countries using their comparative advantage to produce specific goods and services—suggests that open trade between countries (though within agreed rules) normally leads to the best economic outcome for all concerned. The empirical evidence from the past fifty years supports economic theory (including the more recent 'new trade theory' explaining the explosion of trade between similar economies such as Europe and North America, within Europe and with Japan and Korea). Increased globalization of trade, investment, and capital flows, led to higher global economic growth rates, and bene- fitted most countries and consumers as well as led to major reductions in poverty worldwide. This in turn has led to continued strong support for international and regional trade in Asia (the world's fastest growing and most populous region) as well as in Europe. In the past fifty years, developing countries that have embraced globalization (such as East Asia) have exhibited superior economic performance; similar to the experience in North America and Europe. The regions and countries that have followed inward-looking policies (Latin America and the Middle East) have not done as well, despite their much richer resource endowments. Most international economists continue to believe that globalization, and an open and fair global trading system, benefits all countries and consumers everywhere.

Headwinds Against Globalization and Isolated Calls for Decoupling

In the past few years, there has been a backlash against globalization, particularly in many G7 countries, which used to be its most ardent supporters in the past. As it is, intellectuals in many emerging market economies and regions (e.g. Latin America, Africa and India) have been suspicious about unfettered free trade and capital flows. But questions about the downsides of globalization became more common with the hallowing of the rust belts in North America and Western Europe, and the realization amongst the broader societies that, without active public intervention, many people were being left behind due to no fault of their own. For a long time, most proponents of globalization—including the multilateral institutions—focussed primarily on the benefits of globalization and had not paid adequate attention to its potential negative impacts and what to do about them. This in turn led to the rise of populist leaders and weak- ening of support for free international trade in many key advanced countries; calls for bringing jobs back home and decoupling from global supply chains started becoming common. Four additional factors have accentuated the situation further. First, is the increasing ineffectiveness of the WTO. There are many reasons for this, but a primary one is that since the major expan- sion of its membership, under its system requiring unanimous agreement amongst all members for all major decisions, the institution seems unable to function effectively. A prime example of this is the decades-long stalemate in the Doha negotiations on further reforms in global trading rules. Second, are the increased concerns about national security related to high tech companies and products. This is leading some countries to either outrightly ban or limit trading with companies (or some of their products) from countries not deemed friendly (5G network technologies). Third, rising tensions between China—the world's largest trading nation—and many of its trading partners. This is leading the concerned countries as well as many private businesses to reconsider their reliance on the global supply chains, as in the past. And finally, in many cases technological breakthroughs are making onshoring of production possible, which allows companies to shorten the supply chains without any significant cost penalty.

Overall, most trade experts remain cautiously optimistic about prospects of continued trade expansion. In the absence of a global trade agreement under WTO, regional trade agreements are expected to flourish. Intra-European Union trade is likely to remain robust. The EU has already pencilled in a trade agreement with Japan. It is also discussing a deal with MERCOSUR (four countries in Latin America). In Asia, the fastest growing region of the world, there is continued strong interest in enhancing international trade; the coming in force on 1 January 2022, of the Regional Comprehensive Economic Partnership (RCEP) under the ASEAN+6 initiative and the more recent Chinese initiative to supplement as well as join the Trans-Pacific Partnership (TPP) trade agreement could be forerunners of a new generation of mega-FTAs until a global agreement is finally reached.

The current political backlash in some advanced countries against globalization may have a silver lining, in that it could curb the excesses of the past and lead to economic and social policies designed to help productively reintegrate people dislocated in mid-career by the changes brought about both by fast-paced globalization and technological changes into the labour markets,.

Figure 3.6: Merchandise trade (per cent of GDP)

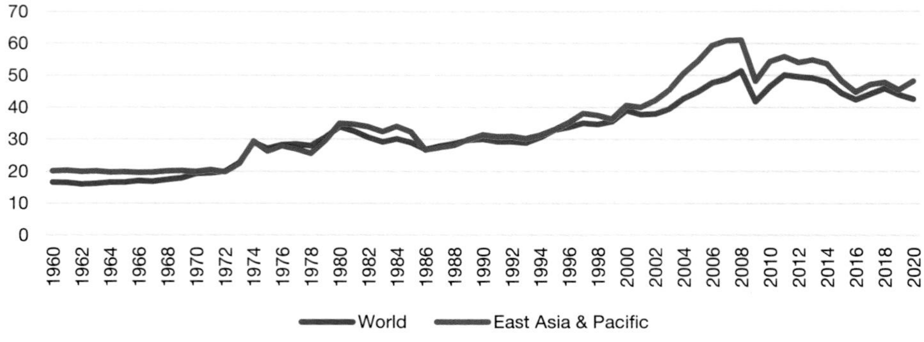

Source: World Bank 2021b

3.7 Technological Progress: Potential Solutions to the World's Evolving Challenges

There is mounting evidence that the pace of technological progress is accelerating. New scientific discoveries are leading to technological breakthroughs that have the potential to help the world tackle current and future global challenges such as climate change, pandemics, inequality and to promote inclusive growth. They—including the so-called breakthrough technologies—will be key to pushing the global productivity frontier further during the coming decades, and hopefully reverse the recent trend in sagging productivity growth in most economies.

Information Technology

During our lifetime, massive breakthroughs in information technologies—including computing power—has revolutionized the use of computers in the daily lives of people and in businesses. So far, every eighteen months, technical progress has doubled the speed of microprocessors. Simultaneously, costs have come down dramatically. The buzzwords in the computer world are smaller, faster, cheaper, pipelined, super-scalar and parallel. Laboratories around the world are busy exploring novel technologies that may one day herald the arrival of a new generation of computers and microelectronic devices. Quantum techniques, which capitalize on the non-classical behaviour of devices, seem around the corner. Other scientists are taking non-silicon routes by developing data storage systems that can potentially use photonically activated biomolecules. Yet others are exploring nano-mechanical logic gaps. Future developments in information technologies appear limitless, and their potential uses exciting.

Information Sharing

A parallel, equally important development involves information sharing. Satellites, television, mobile telephony and the Internet (also see below)—leveraged by new social media—have already revolutionized the way in which information is gathered, stored, searched and shared within and across national boundaries. Emergence of the World Wide Web and the rapid rise of new global business giants like Google, Apple, Facebook and Twitter, have further transformed information sharing. Amazon disrupted the traditional retail business model only a decade ago. The impending introduction of drones by Amazon, Walmart and others may, yet again, revolutionize the consumer delivery business. The latest examples of how the communication revolution can be harnessed to deliver superior, or even totally new, products and services to the consumers are Uber, YouTube, Netflix and TikTok. Many, many more will certainly emerge by 2060.

Mobile Internet

97 per cent of US consumers owned a mobile phone in 2021. But the phenomenon is not limited to the United States or other advanced countries. It is already present worldwide, providing instant access to information to anyone with a smartphone. The International Telecommunications Union estimated that in 2020 some 85 per cent of people in the world had access to mobile Internet. By 2060, practically all Internet connections will be through mobile devices; most new Internet users will be using mobile devices. The mobile world will be omnipresent by 2060, including to billions of consumers in today's emerging economies.

Communications Revolution: Fuelling and Satisfying Rising Aspirations

A few years ago, digital or electronic communications were primarily the preserve of advanced countries. In the past ten years, this revolution has spread to emerging economies. Just twenty years ago, three of 1,000 Indians had access to a telephone (mainly fixed lines). In 2021, India had over 1.1 billion cell phone connections, or eight out of ten Indians. This communications revolution is fast spreading throughout the developing world, including Africa. Similarly, Internet penetration is beginning to explode; introduction of low-cost Internet services via satellites to remote areas (including in Africa) could be a major game changer (both Amazon and Tesla are planning such services). The pace of change of this communication revolution will only accelerate.

. . . But Easier Communication Also Means Exploding Expectations and Social Upheaval

Instant and universal communications and access to information is a powerful social force, both good and not so good. Events that occured in Egypt and Tunisia about a decade ago as well as the dramatic rise of ISIS in the Middle East and Africa earlier this century, have demonstrated the power of the communications revolution in impacting even more traditional societies and politics. Social media can also lead to the spread of misinformation and conspiracy theories and undermine democracies and rule of law even in the most sophisticated societies. The immense power of the unfolding communications revolution can facilitate human progress, but it can also be misused to disrupt societies, or even disturb global peace and harmony.

Automation of Work and Artificial Intelligence

By 2050, computers will be able to perform tasks typically considered 'human' – such as complex analyses, subtle judgments and creative problem-solving. People will be able to interact with a machine in the way that one would with a co-worker. Humans will work side by side with machines and robots, instead of being totally replaced by them. Instant access to information and substantial enhancement in the quality and pace of decision-making, and consequently, performance, will be the result. Indeed, thinking machines with processing powers that far exceed those of the human brain will become a distinct possibility by 2060. Overall, this could lead to a yet another leap in productivity. Some have called it the Fourth Industrial Revolution, which is already beginning to trigger a jump in productivity.

Delivering Services to the Bottom of the Pyramid

Many emerging market economies are leapfrogging from a cash-based society to mobile payments—not very different from the communications industry, where during the past half century, many emerging economies went from post offices to mobile phones without pausing for the wire-line infrastructure to be laid out. Even ten years ago, M-Pesa in Kenya was one of the most successful mobile payment ecosystems in the world with clients representing 60 per cent of Kenya's population (Mbiti and Weil 2011). In 2021, India and China led the world in the number of electronic transactions. The ubiquity of mobile phones plus robust Internet services would help governments, businesses and individuals overcome a number of pressing and persistent issues (e.g. the lack of access to financial services, computers and Internet connectivity, even corruption), and deliver much-needed services to poor segments. In India, almost 1 billion citizens are already enrolled in the unique ID system that permits them to receive public payments and services faster and without interference from civil servants. It will also lead to universal access to financial services.

Green Technologies to Fight Climate Change

2020 was a record year for renewables. Globally, 260 gigawatts of renewable energy capacity was added in 2020, exceeding expansion in 2019 by close to 50 per cent—and breaking all previous records (Ingram 2021). More than 80 per cent of all new electricity capacity added that year was renewables, with solar and wind accounting for 91 per cent of new renewables. 2021 was even better. Cost of renewables has become competitive, if not lower, than electricity generated from fossil fuels, and costs are dropping further. New breakthroughs are expected in storage and transmission technologies. Green hydrogen is another promising technology to fight climate change. Electric cars are expected to replace combustion engine vehicles within the next ten to fifteen years. They, along with new battery and other green technologies, will help countries achieve their net zero emission pledges made in COP 26 to contain global warming between 1.5-2.0°C.[6]

Figure 3.7: Mobile cellular subscriptions and Internet users

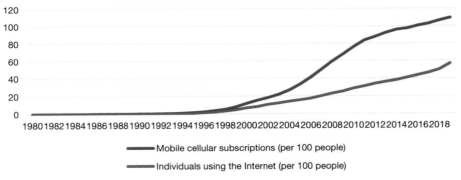

Mobile cellular subscriptions (per 100 people)

Individuals using the Internet (per 100 people)

Source: World Bank 2021b

3.8 Future of Work and Jobs: What about Those Being Left Behind?

The COVID-19 pandemic has caused major disruptions in the way people live and work throughout the world. Extended lockdowns and closures of offices and other businesses, restrictions on travel and more generally, the fear of contracting the virus by mingling with other people, has led to new ways of working and carrying out day-to-day functions (attending meetings by Zoom and remote work from home), learning (distant schooling through virtual classes), shopping (on Internet and delivery by package delivery companies like Amazon), and eating (carry out delivery by Uber).

As and when the pandemic gets over, or at least is brought under control, and countries resume a modicum of normal economic and social activities, many of the above disruptions would become a distant memory. But it is also likely that the pandemic could induce further

---

6. Find more information about this megatrend in Chapter 11 'Future Technological Landscape: Possible Solutions to Emerging Societal Challenges' by R.A. Mashelkar.

significant and potentially lasting behavioural changes—location of work, use of distance education, e-commerce, etc.—with permanent transformation of work patterns, service delivery, and cities. This is because many of the changes seen during the pandemic were already underway, though in a less pronounced manner, because of changing social patterns and ongoing technological advances.

By 2060, we should expect dramatic changes in the way people work and the structure of jobs in most parts of the world. Technology has always had a strong impact on both. Invention of the steam engines, printing presses, textile mills, railroads and steamer ships in the nineteenth century, of phones, airplanes and computers in the twentieth century and of robotics, mobile phones and worldwide Internet as well as various forms of social media in the twenty-first century have offered new services to consumers as well as created hundreds of millions of new jobs while also making redundant a large number of old industries and the workers in them.

As discussed in the previous section, the pace of technological change is accelerating, including in digital technologies (computing and communications), robotics, biotechnology, artificial intelligence, advances in material sciences and so on. They are creating new opportunities in terms of new products and services, which will also lead to creation of new jobs (including in data management). At the same time, many traditional jobs in agriculture, labour intensive manufacturing and even today's services sector (e.g. tedious office work, accounting, health care) will gradually disappear. While, as in the past, ongoing technological progress is expected to lead to a net gain of jobs, there will be people and regions who will be left behind. Countries in Sub-Saharan Africa would be at particular risk in this transformation of the jobs landscape unless they urgently take steps to remedy shortcomings in two crucial areas. First, to upgrade their human capital to take advantage of the coming opportunities. Second, to close the current large digital divide by providing access to fast Internet and computers to all students to train them for the future. In any case, all countries must work proactively to anticipate and formulate policies and programmes to support people who are likely to be made redundant by future changes in work patterns and jobs.[7]

3.9 Weakening of Global Cooperation and Solidarity: Retreat Towards Nationalism?

The global community's response to calls for equitable distribution of vaccines to contain COVID-19 is a prime example of the breakdown of international cooperation and solidarity in times of global crisis. This is despite repeated declarations by all major powers professing global solidarity (and principles of free global trade) and their support for multilateral institutions. Instead, during the initial days of the pandemic, each country looked after its own interests. Many took extreme steps like sealing off their borders (even within the European Union) and banning exports of vaccines within their jurisdictions; most of these restrictions had been lifted by end 2021. As a result, while by December 2021, between 60–80 per cent of North Americans and Europeans had been fully vaccinated, less than 10 per cent of the populations in the least developed countries had been vaccinated.

---

7. For a detailed discussion see Chapter 12 by Professor Soumitra Dutta.

While the above may, arguably, be an extreme case which hopefully is now being remedied, the strains on the multilateralism have been evident for some time. And the effectiveness of the global multilateral organizations (the UN system, the European Union, NATO, the IMF, World Bank and other international financial institutions, WHO, WTO, etc.), both individually and as a group, has slowly deteriorated in the past few decades. While the specific reasons vary for individual institutions, there are also some common reasons why multilateralism is increasingly being questioned and nationalism is being favoured even in countries which led the creation of the current multilateral system to begin with, and why many legacy multilateral institutions seem to be losing influence.

In many respects, the global role and influence of multilateralism and the legacy multilateral institutions appear to have peaked after the fall of the Berlin Wall and of the Soviet Union. Earlier, these institutions had a cohesive economic philosophy and governance mechanisms (dominated by the G7) and the system was generally seen as delivering expected results (peace, security, increasing global trade, financial stability, drop in global poverty, etc.). As a result, the system had enjoyed wide credibility.

But, after the fall of the Berlin Wall and the breakup of the Soviet Union, not only did the membership of international institutions expand very rapidly but they also had to tackle a different set of issues (systemic transformation of the former Soviet Union and communist countries in Eastern Europe, instead of focusing primarily on poverty alleviation and reconstruction as they had since the 1950s). Simultaneously, they had to continuously adjust to the changing needs, first of rapidly growing China and then India. In the meantime, the world was being increasingly confronted by new issues like inequality, climate change and now the pandemic. More recently, there has been a proliferation of multilateral institutions, in the view of some new shareholders, as the legacy organizations (IMF, World Bank, WTO, WHO, UNEP, etc.) did not evolve fast enough to reflect the new distribution of economic power in the world. As a result, many new organizations (AIIB, NDB, BRI, GCF, etc.) have emerged.

Finally, China, by now a major lender to other emerging economies, is emphasizing the superiority of its development model (that emphasizes a continued dominant role of the state) at a time when liberal democracies are struggling. This is a direct challenge to the economic approach long advocated by the legacy multilateral institutions as well as bilateral assistance agencies of most advanced countries.

The current situation is clearly untenable. The COVID-19 pandemic crisis and threats from climate change, both represent global phenomena that demand a global and coordinated response. To successfully address such challenges, the world requires much greater and much more effective international cooperation. All-out efforts are necessary to rebuild trust in multilateralism and make the legacy multilateral institutions more effective.

3.10 Transformation of the Global Economy: Rise of the Emerging Economies

During the next forty years, further major transformation of the global economy is anticipated. This transformation will lead to enormous shifts in the structure and size of the global economy, as the world economy triples in size. The major highlights of our analysis based on the Centennial global economic model's central scenario are as below:

HARINDER S. KOHLI, IEVA VILKELYTE AND HARPAUL ALBERTO KOHLI

3

- The absolute size of global economy would reach US$409 trillion (in 2018 prices) in PPP terms and US$276 trillion in market exchange terms, compared to US$128 trillion and US$82 trillion, respectively, in 2020.
- Average global per capita income could reach US$41,000 in PPP terms and US$28,700 in market exchange rates, compared to US$16,600 and US$12,200, respectively, today.
- As a result, the world would be much more prosperous than today. By 2060, 54 per cent of the global population in as many as eighty-five countries would have income levels equal to or higher than those enjoyed by an average citizen in southern Europe (Greece, Italy, Spain and Portugal) in 2020.
- Almost all people in four regions of the world—North America, Europe (including developing Europe), Oceania and East Asia— would be either middle-class, or upper-income by today's standards. Given the strong strides being made by East Asia, by 2060, the current distinction between that region and advanced countries is likely to fade.
- In terms of the recovery from the sharp recession suffered by the global economy in 2020 due to the COVID-19 pandemic, a two-track recovery is expected. Most advanced countries would have reached pre-pandemic-level economic activity by early 2022, but the EMDEs (except for China) will take much longer to recover, perhaps another two to three years.
- The structure of the global economy will see enormous shifts with the centre of gravity of the world economy gradually moving to the Indo-Pacific region (East and South Asia). In 1980, the G7 countries accounted for 51 per cent of global GDP (in PPP terms). In 2020, their share had fallen to 31 per cent. By 2060, East Asia alone will account for 34 per cent of global GDP, and South Asia for an additional 21 per cent. The two Asia's combined would have 55 per cent global output, while North America would have 12 per cent and Europe (including the UK), 15 per cent.
- The three commodity-exporting regions—Africa, Latin America and the Caribbean and the Middle East—are projected to exhibit sub-par economic performance, despite their rich natural (and in theory, human), resources. As a result, they are likely to be outperformed by the two Asian regions. Unless, these trends can be reversed, and soon, their continued sub-par performance would have adverse global consequences.
- In per capita income terms, there will still be major differences in the average per capita incomes of people in different regions. The regional averages are predicted to be as follows: North America ($106,000); Europe ($75,000); Oceania ($83,000); East Asia ($59,000); South Asia ($37,000); Middle East ($39,000); Latin America ($21,000) and Africa ($13,000).
- Climate change, that could cause downward pressures on economic growth, has not been factored into this scenario. Centennial's global model has also simulated other scenarios, including a 'pessimistic' scenario with lower outcomes.[8]

---

8. For a fuller discussion on the coming transformation of the global economy, see Chapter 4 by Claudio Loser, Harpaul Alberto Kohli and Laura Shelton.

Figure 3.8: Global share of GDP

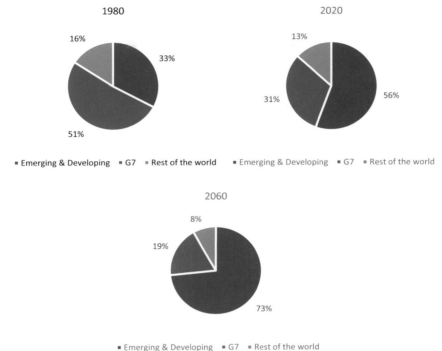

1980

16%
33%
51%

■ Emerging & Developing   ■ G7   ■ Rest of the world

2020

13%
31%   56%

■ Emerging & Developing   ■ G7   ■ Rest of the world

2060

8%
19%
73%

■ Emerging & Developing   ■ G7   ■ Rest of the world

Source: Centennial Group 2021

Concluding Remarks: Underscoring the Relationship between the Megatrends

The ten megatrends described above will have a major—in some cases even decisive—impact on the future evolution of individual economies as well as of the global economy. At the same time, as mentioned at the start of this chapter, it is important that these megatrends are not seen in isolation, but within a broader context of how they interact with each other. These megatrends do not operate in isolation—as if they were vertical cylinders—but operate within the context of other megatrends. In many cases, they would reinforce each other, but sometimes they may offset the impact each would have on an economy or society. How different megatrends interact with each other is not always universal; often the situation would vary by individual economies or region.

For example, urbanization and surging consumer demand due to the growing income levels of populations will require larger infrastructure investments, particularly in emerging market economies. Similarly, making cities more climate resilient will also require massive investments programmes. On the other hand, in countries—both advanced and emerging—with declining (or stagnant) and ageing populations some of the existing infrastructure will turn out to be over-sized, as will many social facilities for the young (schools and playgrounds). Similarly, while many of the megatrends (urbanization, rise of the middle classes, increased global trade and technological changes) should lead to higher economic growth, others could act as headwinds to slow it down: the potential risk of social dissatisfaction due to inequality; not tackling of climate change; drive for nationalism hampering international trade; inability of some of the low-income countries to bridge the digital divide and train their low skilled population. Many of these issues and how they may be tackled by the policy makers are discussed later in this volume.

Chapter 4: World Economy after the Pandemic—Alternative Long-term Scenarios

World Economy after the Pandemic—Alternative Long-term Scenarios

Chapter 4 | Claudio Loser, Harpaul Kohli and Laura Shelton

Introduction and General Trends

This chapter focuses on recent developments in the world and presents scenarios for the global economy emerging from the COVID-19 pandemic and through 2060, with a primary focus on Emerging and Developing Economies (EMDEs). For future scenarios, it uses the Centennial growth model as a basis.

In the period 2000–19, the average annual rate of growth for EMDEs at 5.6 per cent was almost four percentage points higher than that of Advanced Economies (AEs) at 1.9 per cent. However, in the period 2014–19, with a slowdown in the rate of growth to 1.2 per cent for AEs, and 3.5 per cent for EMDEs, the difference was only of about two percentage points. Furthermore, except for Emerging Asia and, to a lesser extent, Developing Europe, per capita income for Emerging economies grew by less than that of AEs. The world growth path was abruptly and traumatically interrupted by the emergence of COVID-19, and world GDP will reach the levels expected before the onslaught of the virus, only with a considerable lag. Currently, predicted behaviour of productivity, labour growth, and investment will likely not be as expected before the COVID-19 pandemic. Still, the long-term trend of the EMDEs gaining a greater share of the global GDP will continue.

Furthermore, beyond the current slowdown, as more residents of EMDEs join the middle class, they will have greater impact on the world economic structure and governance. Nonetheless, the path to the future will not be uniformly distributed. Emerging Eastern Asia, and more specifically China, is not expected to show a decline in growth with respect to earlier projections/scenarios. Other regions, and more markedly Latin America, the Middle East and Sub-Saharan Africa, will see a much lower rate of growth.

The current pandemic has had a major impact on economic performance in both AEs and EMDEs. Economic consequences equivalent to those born out of the pandemic have not been experienced since WWII. Even with the massive and growing vaccination effort, the economic crisis is taking time to revert, and the recovery is far from smooth. The adverse impact on both the level and structure of production, and thus on relative incomes, is having far-reaching social and political implications. The impact of recent events and policies on international trade and cooperation are, and will likely remain, significant. In this regard, it is important to note the following facts:

1. Output losses for the world for the period 2020–22 with respect to what was projected in late 2019, could amount to a total of US$18 trillion.
2. For EMDEs, losses could be 17 per cent of 2019 GDP.
3. These output losses are unlikely to ever be recovered.

4. The unemployment rate in advanced economies rose to 6.5 per cent in 2020, to the highest level in the last thirty years, but has come down, and may reach 5.8 per cent in 2022, with an expected continued subsequent decline.
5. EMDEs debt stands at 64 per cent of GDP, the highest in this century.
6. There is a potential to slow or even reverse the convergence between rich countries and emerging market economies that has contributed to the reduction of poverty.

Thus, despite the observed recovery and underlying trends, the path ahead cannot be taken for granted. The strong performance of earlier years was largely the result of a combination of factors, such as opening up to trade worldwide, greater mobilization of domestic and external resources, a steady improvement in education levels and infrastructure services, the effects of the demographic (population growth) dividend, the acquisition of new technologies, the increased role of global value chains, and for many, the commodity boom of the 2000s (reversed in 2012–13 and aggravated by the pandemic in its initial phase, although commodity prices are now experiencing an increase), and, importantly, stronger institutions. This shock has the potential to slow or even reverse some of these trends that have contributed to the reduction of poverty.

Even so, the short-term prospects indicate a solid recovery. As discussed in the most recent IMF World Economic Outlook of October 2021,[1] and by the Organisation for Economic Co-operation and Development (OECD) in a separate report, issued in September 2021,[2] a year and a half into the COVID-19 pandemic, growing vaccine coverage generates some optimism, although there are marked concerns about the unevenness of both the rate of vaccination and economic performance. The contraction of activity in 2020 was unprecedented in living memory in its speed and synchronized nature. Although difficult to pin down precisely, International Monetary Fund (IMF) estimates suggest that the contraction could have been three times as large without the enormous policy support.

After an estimated contraction of –3.1 per cent in 2020, the estimates are the global economy grew by 5.9 per cent in 2021, and will moderate to 4.9 per cent in 2022, indicating a slight downward revision from earlier estimates. The OECD came out with a slightly more conservative estimate of 5.7 per cent growth in 2021, with a slowdown to 4.5 per cent in 2022. These estimates indicate that world output has exceeded pre-pandemic levels, even though they clearly have not reached the projected levels expected prior to 2020. While remaining upbeat about the prospects for growth, risks remain of a considerable downside on account of the different rates of health recovery, the breakdown in net international value chain, a tightening in the labour markets and the consequent increase in the rate of inflation in most countries.

According to the IMF, global growth is expected to moderate to 3.3 per cent by 2026— reflecting projected damage to supply potential and pre-pandemic forces, including an ageing-related slowdown in labour force growth in AEs and some EMDEs. Thanks to the policy response, the COVID-19 recession has had limited impact on AEs, but EMDEs have been hit harder and are expected to suffer more significant medium-term losses. Output losses have been large for countries that rely on tourism and commodity exports and for those with

---

1. The estimates and projections are based on the IMF WEO of October 2021. Revisions to these numbers may have appeared after completion of this study in late 2021.
2. 'Interim Report', OECD Economic Outlook 2020, no. 2, September 2021.

limited policy space to respond. Many of these countries entered the crisis in precarious fiscal situations and with less capacity to mount major health care policy responses or to support livelihoods. The projected recovery follows a severe contraction that has had particularly adverse employment and earnings impacts on the young, women, workers with relatively lower educational attainment and the informal sector. Income inequality has increased significantly because of the pandemic. About 100 million more people are estimated to have fallen below the threshold of extreme poverty in 2020 compared to pre-pandemic projections, aggravated by serious disruptions in education, with only a moderate subsequent reversal. Evidence suggests that inequality between and within countries has increased due to the pandemic, a trend that is likely to continue in the near future (Fajgenbaum et al. 2021). Risks around the short-term projection are on the downside. Slower-than-anticipated vaccine rollout has allowed the virus to mutate further. Financial conditions are likely to tighten rapidly, as inflation expectations increase more rapidly than anticipated. A double hit to EMDEs from pandemic dynamics and tighter external financial conditions would set back their recovery and result in slower growth, offset only in part by the recovery of commodity prices, particularly metals and fuels. However, these increases may reverse as specific bottlenecks in AEs are corrected.

Price pressures for a significant part reflect unusual pandemic-related developments and transitory supply-demand mismatches, although the pressures in the labour markets in AEs are likely to persist. Inflation is expected to remain higher than in the pre-pandemic ranges in most countries through 2022, and it is considerably uncertain if prices will decelerate significantly in later years. Elevated inflation is also expected in some EMDEs, related in part to high food prices, but also considerable macroeconomic imbalances. Central banks are now expected to tighten monetary policy, even if slowly. Price pressures may become persistent and central banks may need to take pre-emptive action.

Future developments will depend on the path of the current health crisis, the effectiveness of policy actions to limit persistent economic damage while rebuilding macroeconomic sustainability and the evolution of international financial conditions and commodity prices. Policymakers may have to prioritize policies to strengthen social protection, ensuring adequate resources for health care and broad education support, in addition to resources to address climate change, among other challenges. Where elevated debt levels limit scope for action, effort should also be directed at creating fiscal space through improved revenue policies and management, reducing wasteful subsidies and tightening expenditure controls.

There is no single policy path for all countries, especially regarding progress toward normalization. Hence, countries need to tailor their policy responses to the stage of the recovery, and structural characteristics of the economy. While the transition remains a main policy goal, countries will need to remain focussed on longer-term challenges to strengthen total factor productivity. In addition to the required work by major central banks and multilateral institutions, hard work is required to navigate the external financial conditions in emerging markets and the impact diverse country policies have on capital flows. Strong international cooperation will remain vital for achieving these objectives and ensuring that emerging market economies and low-income developing countries continue to narrow the gap between their living standards and those of high-income countries. This coordination includes achieving adequate worldwide vaccine production and distribution, providing help for financially constrained economies to gain sufficient access to international liquidity to continue their process of growth and convergence and resolving issues underlying current trade and technology conflicts.

The strength of the recovery is projected to vary significantly across countries, depending on access to medical action, policy support, exposure to cross-country spillovers, movements in terms of trade and specific characteristics at the time of entering the crisis (Figure 4.1 and Table 4.1). Thus, by early 2022, China could effectively have approached the same path as before the pandemic surge, although affected by new supply and policy constraints. Meanwhile, most of the rest of the world will be at the same level of output as the pre-pandemic level, but below the previously estimated trajectory, and clearly with a lower per capita income in most countries.

Figure 4.1: GDP 2017–23

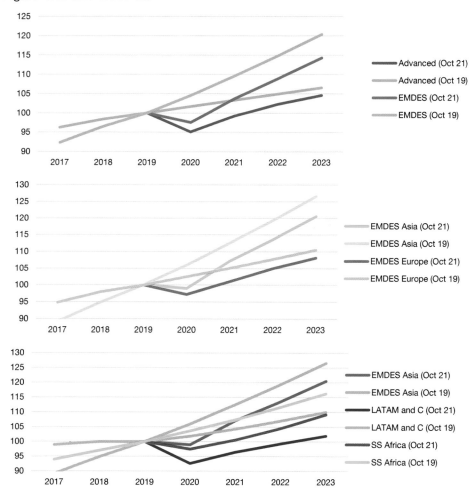

Source: Centennial Group 2021

Table 4.1: World Economic Outlook projections (per cent change)

	Estimates			Projections
	2019	2020	2021	2022
World Output	2.8	−3.1	5.9	4.9
Advanced Economies	1.6	−4.5	5.2	4.5
Emerging Market and Developing Economies	3.7	−2.1	6.4	5.1
Emerging and Developing East Asia	5.7	1.0	6.8	5.7
South Asia	4.4	−5.9	8.3	8.0
Emerging and Developing Europe	2.5	−2.0	6.0	3.6
Latin America and the Caribbean	0.1	−7.0	6.3	3.0
The Middle East and Central Asia	1.4	−2.8	4.1	4.1
Sub-Saharan Africa	3.2	−1.7	3.7	3.8

Source: IMF 2021b and Centennial Group 2021

Among major AEs, only the US will have recovered and increased output beyond the levels of 2019, as would be the case for the non-G7 AEs as a group. By contrast, the rest of the G7 countries would only recover over the course of 2022.

Among EMDEs, Emerging and Developing Asia shows strong although slower recovery. Emerging Europe has rebounded, although Russia will likely only reach 2019 levels of output in 2022. Sub-Saharan Africa also recovered in 2021, although its largest economies will take longer, particularly in the case of South Africa. The Middle East and Central Asia will have recovered by 2022. Finally, the region that had been lagging behind all others prior to the pandemic, Latin America and the Caribbean, is recovering faster than previously estimated, helped by improved growth prospects in Mexico, Brazil and, to a lesser extent, Argentina, offset by the stagnation of Venezuela. These growth patterns have major effects in the medium and long run as discussed below.

A quantification of the short-term losses resulting from the pandemic noted above illustrates the magnitude of the economic costs of COVID-19. In this regard, it is important to note the following facts:

1. Losses may be much higher for Emerging and Developing Asia with the exclusion of China (37 per cent of the relevant GDP), mainly on account of India (45 per cent) but also reflecting the impact on the ASEAN-5 group (31 per cent), both constituting the bulk of non-China Asia GDP.
2. Losses for China could be in the order of US$1.6 trillion, or 11 per cent of the GDP.
3. The losses for Latin America could be in the order of 20 per cent of the GDP, 17 per cent for Sub-Saharan Africa, and 15 per cent for the Middle East, while for all advanced countries, the losses could amount to some 9 per cent of the GDP.

Development in the Twenty-first Century

A review of the recent performance of the EMDEs points out a continuation of the process of reduction in poverty that prevailed for so many years, although interrupted by the pandemic crisis. The rate of growth of the EMDEs increased from 3.5 per cent during the period 1981–90 to 5.6 per cent a year during the last decade of the twentieth century. It then rose again during the period 2001–12 to 6.2 per cent. The rates of growth were not uniform, but the trend was observed in all regions (Figure 4.2). The rate of growth of the AEs declined over the last decade of the twentieth century and averaged 1.7 per cent a year during the period 2001–12, seriously affected by the Great Recession of 2008–09. Therefore, the share of EMDEs in total world GDP, in PPP terms rose from 33 per cent in 1980 to 39 per cent in 2000 and to 51 per cent in 2012, although smaller at market prices.

Figure 4.2: Comparative GDP growth by regions and periods

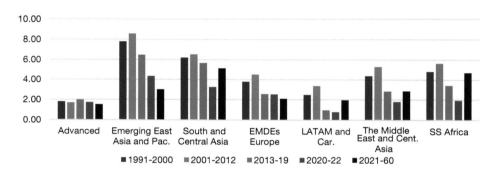

Source: Centennial Group 2021

By contrast, the AEs' rate of growth increased, even if slightly, in the period 2013–19, to about 2 per cent a year, while that of emerging economies declined markedly, from 6.2 per cent in the period 2001–12 to 4.5 per cent, largely as commodity exporters suffered declines in their terms of trade as prices fell. By that time, the share of EMDEs in total GDP in PPP terms had increased to 55 per cent compared to 51 per cent in 2012, showing a deceleration compared to previous periods, even though the share has and will continue to increase.

As noted, performance was not uniform throughout the period among regions, with primary producing regions like Sub-Saharan Africa, Latin America and the Middle East and Central Asia having slowed down much more markedly than Developing Asia. Within the Emerging and Developing Asia category, South Asia did not fare as well as East Asia, being at nearly 2 per cent lower for both the 1980–2000 and 2000–20 average growth rates (Appendix Figure 4.5). Performance has also varied between the regions in terms of the levels of per capita income and in terms of human development.

As of 2019, the last year before the pandemic, per capita income of the AEs was about US$46,500 ($52,000 in PPP terms), relative to an income of US$65,200 for the US, which is used as the benchmark with the same market and PPP income. AEs are followed by Emerging Europe with US$10,000 ($26,000 PPP); Latin America and Caribbean with US$7,900 ($15,500

PPP); Developing Asia with US$5,400 ($11,100 PPP); the Middle East and Central Asia with US$4,600 ($11,300 PPP); and Sub-Saharan Africa with US$1,600 ($3,900 PPP).

The relative level of PPP per capita income improved significantly in the case of the Developing Asia region, increasing from 9 per cent of advanced countries per capita income early in the century to 21 per cent in 2019. It grew from 32 per cent to 50 per cent for Emerging Europe, although the reduction in the gap is smaller in current terms.

Because these regions did well, they lifted the overall performance of the EMDEs as a whole relative to the AEs by 7 percentage points in PPP terms, and slightly less in current terms. In sharp contrast, the rest of the EMDEs (Latin America, the Middle East and Central Asia and Sub-Saharan Africa) saw a small increase in their relative position in current terms, and more strikingly almost no change in PPP terms for Africa, and a decline for Latin America and the Middle East. For the period since 2014 — the base period for *The World in 2050* — only Asia has reduced the gap in PPP terms, with all other regions showing a retreat, keeping the ratio for all EMDEs to AEs virtually constant. As discussed in Chapter 14, the losses may well reflect the relative behaviour of commodity prices.

These developments are reflected in terms of the share of world GDP. Latin America accounted for 8 per cent of global GDP in 1980 and 6.5 per cent in 2000. After rising to 8 per cent subsequently, it declined to about 5 per cent by 2020, losing significantly in importance in the world economy (Figure 4.3). Meanwhile, Emerging Asia's share of world GDP, while stable at somewhat more than 6 per cent in the last twenty years of the twentieth century, rose to 20 per cent in 2014 and to 26 per cent in 2020. All other emerging regions increased their participation (except in the 90s), partly driven by high demographic growth and improved terms of trade through 2014–15 but declined in relative participation since then. In contrast, the AEs saw their participation in world GDP (at market prices) decline from more than 75 per cent to 67 per cent in 2010 and to 61 per cent by 2020. Equivalent changes occurred in PPP terms, with the share of EMDEs rising from 37 to 56 per cent of the total in 2014–15 and to 58 per cent in 2020, mostly driven by Asia.

Figure 4.3: Regional share in global GDP — 2010 and 2020

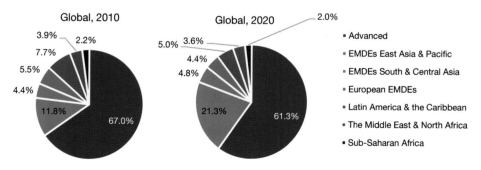

Source: Centennial Group 2021

Another way to highlight the divergence of performance within the EMDEs is to look at changes over time in the share of individual regions of EMDEs' total GDP. While Latin America accounted for 32 per cent of EMDEs' GDP in 1980, its share of total EMDEs' output had dropped to only 9 per cent in 2020. By contrast, Emerging Asia's share rose from 27 per cent to 57 per cent, led by China but reflecting high growth for India, South Korea, Taiwan and ASEAN countries. Emerging Europe rose slightly, but all other regions declined.

It is also important to note the behaviour of per capita income for the different regions relative to 2010—at the end of the Great Recession. Since then, Emerging Asia and to a much lesser extent, Developing Europe, have witnessed sustained increases in per capita income, even with a one- or two-year reversal in 2020–21—an event in common with all other regions (Figure 4.4). AEs saw modest but also steady increases. While the other three regions were characterized by declining or stagnant incomes, at least since the middle of last decade, Latin America has clearly been the worst performer during the period.

Figure 4.4: Per capita GDP by region (2010=100)

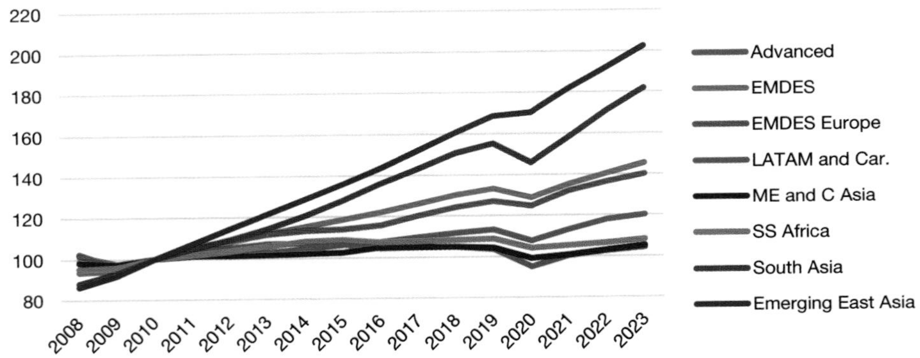

Source: Centennial Group 2021

Factors Affecting Regional Performance

Asia's strong performance can be explained by many factors, such as much higher savings and investment rates, greater openness, better human capital development, and other actions reflected in stronger global competitiveness and 'cost of doing business' rankings. However, in addition to relative weaknesses in these areas, Latin America, Africa and the Middle East have also continued to suffer from other structural weaknesses, a possible lack of a long-term vision, and a generally weaker macroeconomic policy framework, even as inflation has tended to be contained. All these factors have led to, amongst other indicators, relatively poor growth in total factor productivity (see Table 4.2), with particular concern regarding Latin America, the Middle East and, to a lesser extent, Sub-Saharan Africa, precluding rapid convergence.

Differences in the savings and investment rates are another important factor in explaining differing growth performance around the world. With the highest per capita income, the AEs are likely to have a greater propensity towards consumer spending, resulting in low levels of savings and investment. However, it can be observed that the emerging regions, with the clear exception of Emerging East Asia and, to a much lesser extent, the Middle East and North Africa, have also suffered from low savings and investment (Figure 4.5). These low investment rates, combined with poor productivity (TFP) growth, have resulted in sluggish growth rates compared to fast-growing East Asia.

The relative progress of different regions is again reflected in the behaviour of the Human Development Index produced by the United Nations Development Programme (UNDP), which considers economic, educational and health performance. In the last thirty years, all regions have improved; however, East Asia has done particularly well, in addition to Emerging Europe and Central and South Asia—these cases started from lower levels (Figure 4.6). The laggards in terms of improvement are again the Middle East and Latin America, with Sub-Saharan Africa in an intermediate position between the two other groups.[3]

Produced by the World Bank until 2020, the Ease of Doing Business (EDB) Index, while subject to controversy in terms of some of the countries' behaviour, provides a strong case for relative regional positions. While countries in the Latin American and the Middle Eastern regions benefit from relatively high income, their lacklustre performance is clearly associated with the low relative EDB ratings for the two regions, as is the case for Sub-Saharan Africa.

Table 4.2: Total factor productivity growth

Region	TFP
Advanced	0.79
EMDEs Asia	3.94
EDMEs Europe	2.36
LATAM CA	-0.06
ME & C Asia	0.56
Sub-Saharan Africa	1.22

Source: Centennial Group 2021

Figure 4.5: Savings and investment by region (2010–19)

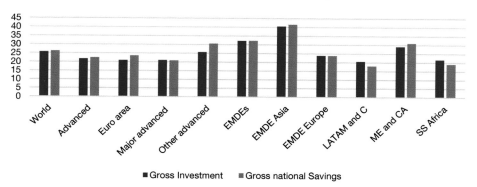

■ Gross Investment   ■ Gross national Savings

Source: Centennial Group 2021

---

3. The Human Development Index (HDI) is a composite statistic of life expectancy, education and per capita income indicators, which is used to rank countries into four tiers of human development.

Figure 4.6: Human Development Index (1990–2019)

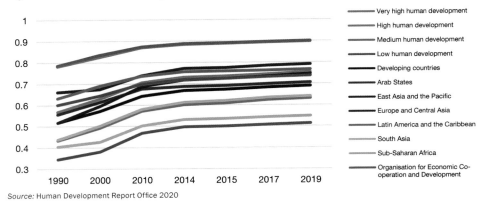

Source: Human Development Report Office 2020

Figure 4.7: Ease of doing business scores by region

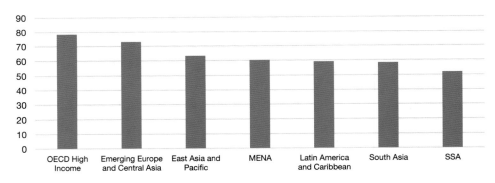

Source: World Bank 2021b

Equivalent resultscan be extracted from the Global Competitiveness Index for 2019 (the last index produced in that format) of the world Economic Forum, although with a different country classification, as it includes OECD countries in the geographical groupings. On that basis, East Asia comes first, being the most dynamic region, followed by Europe and North America, and in third place, Eurasia (Figure 4.8).

As was indicated in *The World in 2050*, while the pace and trajectory of different regions and countries in the EMDEs cannot be summarized easily because countries' economic and political conditions varied widely, there have been positive policy trends. In most cases by now, there has been a significant improvement in macroeconomic policies, even with some back-tracking; there have been robust financial systems, and, of equivalent and related importance, until recently, there was a sharp reduction in the prevailing rate of inflation, accentuated by the initial effect of the COVID-19 pandemic. While this is especially true for Latin America and the Middle East, patterns are observed in the other regions, including Sub-Saharan Africa, where countries were the last to embrace macroeconomic and structural reforms and to build modern

Figure 4.8: Global Competitive Index, median score (2019)

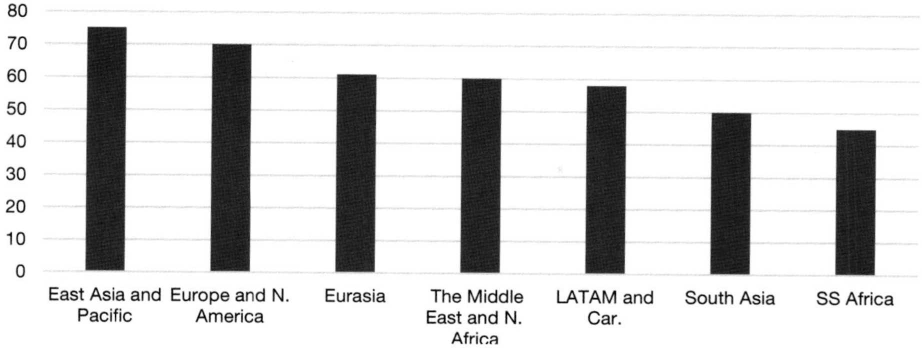

Source: World Economic Forum 2019

institutions. In 2021, however, there was a reversal in inflation on account of the disruptions in supply in the international value chain, unexpected shortages in the available workforce in advanced countries, and other structural difficulties, which resulted in a sharp price increase in many commodities, mostly metals and fuels.

Because of generally favourable conditions, countries appeared to have emerged from their previous pattern of non-convergence. As discussed, starting in the early 2000s, the average annual GDP growth rate of Emerging Asia, Africa, Latin America and the Middle East rose rapidly, in large part for the three latter regions due to the decade-long improvement in terms of trade, caused by the super commodity cycle that extended through 2012. As noted earlier, as the impulse coming from China weakened and terms of trade declined, growth in the emerging markets declined through 2019, while the rate of growth of AEs rose.

As a result, the growth rate differential of EMDEs with respect to that of the AEs narrowed from its peak of more than 5 per cent between 2007–09 to 2.5 per cent in the period 2013–19, a level comparable to the beginning of the twenty-first century. The differential is estimated to narrow significantly further, for the period 2020–22, to 1.4 percentage points. Even though the spread may increase somewhat subsequently, this may put in doubt the plausibility of continued significant changes in the relative shares of world output, at least in the near term. These developments, including the pandemic, raise questions about the long-term growth prospects of the global economy in general and of EMDEs more specifically.

One important consideration in terms of the capacity to adapt is that the increase in domestic public borrowing by AEs has and will continue to absorb significant resources. This, together with previous significant public borrowing and consequently higher risks among emerging economies, limits capital flows to these countries in the future. Furthermore, China's domestic spending revival is resulting in a narrowing of its current account surplus and thus, its ability to lend. These circumstances point to a problematic recovery in the medium term and increased poverty.

Even with these difficulties, several regions are converging. The average annual GDP growth rate of Emerging Asia—particularly Emerging East Asia—and Emerging Europe has remained strong, and convergence remains a strong possibility for those areas, but, as discussed, less so for the other regions. In any event, world GDP growth has decelerated and growth of most EMDEs has slowed in parallel. The performance of the AEs showed that their growth has recovered, albeit slowly, since 2010 (Figure 4.2), especially in the US, the UK, Germany and many northern European nations (plus Japan, though to a more modest degree and more unevenly).

In these circumstances, emerging economies will need to deal with several correlated but identifiable effects. AEs and some emerging economies have been able to counteract the sharp decline in activity through lockdowns and related business disturbances because of their deep fiscal resources, as well as through their robust financial markets. The ability of most EMDEs to take equivalent actions has been limited by both fiscal constraints and their narrow domestic and closed foreign financial markets. This has resulted in the reduced effectiveness of countercyclical actions, with possible inflationary and balance of payments consequences. The sharp initial decline in global demand has hit primary producers extremely hard, although there has been a recent strong recovery. All this brings to the fore questions about the plausibility of continued significant changes in the relative shares of world output, at least in the near term.

Medium- and Long-term Outlook

This section presents scenarios up to 2060, based on the global growth model that has been widely used by the Centennial Group.[4] This is a long-term model, and, therefore, its results and projections are stylized; they are not intended to predict the future exactly but rather to provide a context for policymaking and reform (Kohli, Alberto and Arnold 2012). Centennial Group's long-term models explore alternative scenarios for the global economy, with a focus on the outlook for EMDEs. The model has been adapted to reflect the developments described above and considers the fact that during the last few decades, there has been a decline in the growth of the global productivity frontier. The latest scenarios generated by the model suggest that, as result of the pandemic, the world economy will incur an accumulated loss of at least one year of output in the next twenty years and that, even with the strong growth revival of 2021, global GDP will not be on track to go back to the pre-pandemic trendline. Asia will remain the most dynamic region, and Latin America, the Middle East and Europe will suffer the most from the recent events. Finally, independent of the effects of the pandemic, there is a slowdown in the long-term global productivity growth, particularly for the commodity dependent regions, as discussed earlier.

The new growth model results consider the effect of the COVID-19 pandemic compared to an alternative no-COVID-19 exercise based on 2019 projections. It includes a significant convergence reclassification of countries, based on the indicators used in the model, plus consideration of the Resilience Index and the World Bank classification of states in high- or medium-intensity conflict. Based on the current run, summarized in the tables and figures of the next few pages, the world should recover relatively quickly, as supported by the projections of the WEO and others.

The study presents three scenarios—central, strong policy and poor policy—to allow for a simple and clear presentation, but are not intended to constitute definitive projections. The scenarios revolve around a 'central' scenario considered most plausible for the global economy, based on current circumstances. A crucial assumption under this scenario is that the global

---

4. The medium- and long-term projections are based on the October 2021 IMF WEO.

productivity frontier (the US economy) will improve at an average annual rate somewhat below 1 per cent. It had been about 1 per cent for the past 100 years or so, but has experienced a decline in more recent years. In that sense, it is far from certain that the US will remain the determinant of the productivity frontier in the next forty years, as some countries in Asia—China in particular—may take this role. The model further assumes that only the AEs that have performed well in the past twenty years will continue to move at the same pace as the US and similarly that EMDEs that have a record of successful convergence in the past will continue to converge in the future as well. The model presents another scenario for the EMDEs called 'strong policy'. Under the strong policy scenario, the global productivity frontier improves at a faster rate than under the central scenario. In all other aspects besides the increased productivity frontier growth, the advanced economies' performance remains broadly the same, but policy performance of EMDEs improves significantly. A third 'poor policies' scenario combines two simultaneous adverse developments: many EMDEs fall into the middle-income trap because of their inability to maintain a reasonable policy regime and the global productivity growth rate slows to only 0.6 per cent per year (as strongly argued by some cautious experts). While this scenario is defined as pessimistic, it cannot be ruled out. In fact, without progress towards addressing the climate crisis, and without a solution to income distribution issues, a pessimistic scenario may become more likely.

Central Scenario

The central scenario for the global economy suggests that there will be a continued increase in the participation of EMDEs in world GDP. Under the central scenario, post-COVID-19 annual GDP growth on average would be 2.9 per cent for the period 2022–40 and 2.75 per cent for 2021–60, about in line with the no-COVID-19 projections (Table 4.3 and Figure 4.10). Per capita income could grow at a rate of 2.1 per cent a year. Today's EMDEs would grow at an average annual rate of 3.6 per cent, in comparison to a rate of growth of 1.6 per cent for today's advanced economies. The average rate of growth for Sub-Saharan Africa would be in the order of 4.7 per cent, and that of Emerging Asia would be 4.0 per cent. Disaggregating Emerging Asia, growth in East Asia would begin to slow to 3.5 per cent and growth in South Asia would begin to recover from its previous poor performance and average 5.0 per cent (Appendix Figure 5). The rate of growth of GDP in Emerging Europe would be 2.2 per cent, somewhat above AEs, in Latin America 2.1 per cent, and in the Middle East 3.0 per cent. Except for Sub-Saharan Africa, and marginally Latin America, the world would experience a lower average annual growth rate during the period through 2060 than during 2001–20, characterized by the Great Recession and the pandemic (Table 4.4).

By 2060, the global economy will more than triple in size, reaching US$276 trillion at 2018 prices and market exchange rates (US$409 trillion in PPP terms). The world will be significantly wealthier, with the global per capita income averaging close to US$28,700 (US$41,000 in PPP terms) as compared to about US$12,200 (US$18,100 in PPP terms) in 2021. Additionally, there will be dramatic improvements in the income levels and living standards of people who live in countries currently referred to as 'developing'.

For today's advanced countries, GDP per capita in terms of PPP (at 2018 prices) would rise from US$56,800 in 2021 to US$104,100 by 2060, with a growth rate of 1.5 per cent per year. For EMDEs, per capita GDP would increase from US$11,400 to US$34,000; this entails an

Table 4.3a: Income and income per capita, PPP 2018

Region	Scenario	GDP (US$ mill PPP 2018)			Annual Percentage Change
		2020	2040	2060	2020–60
World	Central	127942	243950	409457	3.0%
	Strong Policy		287945	607778	4.0%
	Poor Policy		205226	253686	1.7%
Advanced Economies	Central	54020	79323	110109	1.8%
	Strong Policy		88213	130365	2.2%
	Poor Policy		73531	86121	1.2%
Emerging East Asia and the Pacific	Central	31213	71555	122089	3.5%
	Strong Policy		83488	167689	4.3%
	Poor Policy		54345	61655	1.7%
Emerging South and Central Asia	Central	13337	40224	93140	5.0%
	Strong Policy		48172	137905	6.0%
	Poor Policy		29308	40507	2.8%
European Emerging Economies	Central	10106	16742	23949	2.2%
	Strong Policy		18909	30458	2.8%
	Poor Policy		14588	16724	1.3%
Latin America & Caribbean	Central	9303	14934	20968	2.1%
	Strong Policy		20987	45367	4.0%
	Poor Policy		13801	16925	1.5%
The Middle East and North Africa	Central	6028	11389	19784	3.0%
	Strong Policy		14049	31330	4.2%
	Poor Policy		10458	14780	2.3%
Sub-Saharan Africa	Central	4069	10066	25951	4.7%
	Strong Policy		14359	64295	7.1%
	Poor Policy		9068	17435	3.7%

Source: Centennial Group 2021

average growth of 2.8 per cent. Latin America and the Caribbean would go from US$15,400 to US$27,8000. This would mean that the difference in income levels between the region and the rest of the EMDEs would be significantly narrowed. However, at market prices, income gaps would be maintained. In 2021, advanced countries are estimated to have a per capita

Table 4.3b: Income and income per capita, PPP 2018

Region	Scenario	GDPPC (US$ PPP2018)			Annual Percentage Change
		2020	2040	2060	2020–60
World	Central	16613	26891	40965	2.3%
	Strong Policy		31741	60806	3.3%
	Poor Policy		22622	25380	1.1%
Advanced Economies	Central	50654	71736	94019	1.6%
	Strong Policy		79775	118194	2.1%
	Poor Policy		66497	78083	1.1%
Emerging East Asia and the Pacific	Central	14748	32069	56684	3.4%
	Strong Policy		37417	77855	4.2%
	Poor Policy		24362	28626	1.7%
Emerging South and Central Asia	Central	6564	16708	36301	4.4%
	Strong Policy		20010	53749	5.4%
	Poor Policy		12174	15788	2.2%
European Emerging Economies	Central	25862	44013	67513	2.4%
	Strong Policy		50049	85861	3.0%
	Poor Policy		38613	47145	1.5%
Latin America & Caribbean	Central	14581	20543	27812	1.6%
	Strong Policy		28869	60174	3.6%
	Poor Policy		18984	22450	1.1%
The Middle East and North Africa	Central	16925	24500	35706	1.9%
	Strong Policy		30222	56543	3.1%
	Poor Policy		22497	26675	1.1%
Sub-Saharan Africa	Central	3837	5949	10737	2.6%
	Strong Policy		8487	26603	5.0%
	Poor Policy		5360	7214	1.6%

Source: Centennial Group 2021

income of US$52,000 and would move to US$89,000. EMDEs would go from US$5,400 to US$20,700, with Emerging East Asia going from US$11,000 to US$49,000 and South Asia going from US$2,000 to US$16,500.

Over time, the rate of growth of the global economy will decline as countries are expected to converge toward the global best practice and as population growth rates decline worldwide (with the exception of Sub-Saharan Africa) (Figure 4.9).

In 2060, as many as fifty-three countries will have GDP per capita higher than the average income of the AEs today, and eighty will be above the average income of France, Italy, Japan, Spain and the UK today, even though the list of richest countries will not be significantly changed. The distinctions between AEs and EMDEs that were so clear half a century ago, will have diminished radically. Perhaps even more importantly, as many as 5.5 billion, or 57 per cent of the world's expected total population of 9.6 billion in 2060, will live in these eighty countries; somewhat over 1 billion people, or 14 per cent of the world's population.

By 2060, Emerging Asia will account for just over half (52 per cent) of global output at market exchange rates (54 per cent on a PPP basis) under the central scenario. China, India and Indonesia will lead the way in this process. Asia's economic share will be more in line with

Table 4.4: Comparative GDP growth 2001–20 and 2021–60

Country Group Name	2001–20	2021–60
world	3.4	3.0
Advanced	1.5	1.8
EMDEs	5.2	3.5
Emerging East Asia and the Pacific	7.8	3.5
South & Central Asia	6.2	5.0
EMDE - Europe	3.4	2.2
Latin America and the Caribbean	2.0	2.1
The Middle East and Central Asia	4.0	3.0
Sub-Saharan Africa	4.5	4.7

Source: Centennial Group 2021

Figure 4.9: World GDP growth

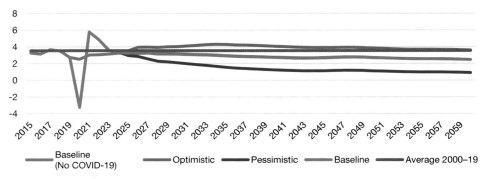

Source: Centennial Group 2021

its share of world population, though Emerging Asia's per capita income in 2060 will remain well below of that of the countries defined as advanced today.

Emerging East Asia will account for about 47 per cent of global growth between 2021 and 2060, today's AEs for another almost 25 per cent and South Asia for 15 per cent. The rest of the world will contribute only 13 per cent of global growth, unless the other regions step up their economic performance, particularly Latin America, the Middle East and Sub-Saharan Africa, as postulated in the strong policy (optimistic) scenario outlined below, or China and India decelerate, as presented in the pessimistic scenario. Even so, the shock from the COVID-19 pandemic and its traumatic human and economic effects are unlikely to disappear over time. However, based on the current run, with results summarized in the tables and figures of the next few pages, the world is recovering to pre-pandemic levels quickly.

Post-COVID-19 annual GDP growth on average would be 3.2 per cent for the period 2021–40 and 1.8 per cent for 2021–60, slightly above the no-COVID-19 run due to the recovery of output after 2020. However, output will remain lower in the post-COVID-19 period than what the scenarios suggested for a no-COVID-19 situation. On average, the level of GDP after COVID-19 for the period 2020–40 would be 1.4 per cent lower than in the no-COVID-19 scenario, and 1.6 per cent for the period 2020–60, with a catch up in 2022–24 (Figure 4.10).

Figure 4.10: World GDP (PPP)

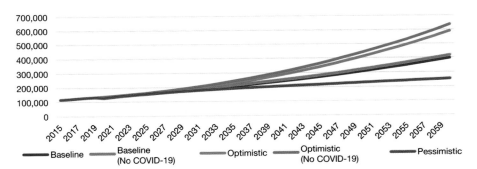

Source: Centennial Group 2021

As an example, in the baseline scenario, in 2021, GDP is 5.6 per cent less than in the no-COVID-19 scenario; whereas in 2030, it is just 1 per cent lower, and in 2040, it is 1.3 per cent lower. In any event, the cumulative loss will be significant. The present value of the loss of GDP over the period 2020–40 would be equivalent to 28 per cent of 2019 GDP, and 59 per cent over the period 2020–60, although considerably lower than estimates made earlier.[5]

The shares of each region in global GDP are not expected to change significantly with respect to no-COVID-19 projections. The largest economy is expected to be China in the baseline and the optimistic scenarios, with the US as the second largest economy, and India as the third largest. The US would remain the largest economy in 2060 under a globally more

---

5. Present value estimates have been carried out using the average rate of growth as the relevant (for simplicity) discount rate. Other discount rates can be used and would give similar results.

pessimistic scenario. Japan would be the fourth largest economy, except under the optimistic scenario, where Indonesia surpasses Japan and Brazil. Other emerging economies would tend to take higher positions in the optimistic scenario, while the more traditional rich countries would keep their relative positions under the more pessimistic scenarios (see Appendix Table 1 for GDP MkFX rankings and values).

Per capita income on a PPP basis does not show major surprises, with Ireland, Singapore, Luxembourg, Switzerland, the US, Malta and Norway showing very high levels of income. A surprise in the model is Guyana, which is currently benefitting from the identification of significant oil reserves[6] (the per capita GDP values can be found in Appendix Table 2 ranked by PPP levels).

GDP and TFP growth will be more marked (as expected) among both East and Southern Asian emerging economies (Appendix Figure 3a and 3b), including China, India, and Indonesia, among larger countries, even though at a lower rate than in the period 2001–20 for East Asia. Lower rates of growth of TFP would be expected for Central and Eastern Europe and Central Asia. The AEs will experience a somewhat higher growth of TFP from the first twenty years of the twenty-first century, as will be the case for the three commodity exporter regions. In the latter case, this may be on account of no implicit impact of lower terms of trade, as discussed in Chapter 14, and challenges confronting commodity-exporting countries. However, there is no catching up with the levels of TFP of the advanced countries, as was the case in the no-COVID-19 estimates. Regional per capita income ranking would experience some significant shifts in relative terms. East Asian EMDEs (mainly China and Southeast Asia) will have effectively surpassed all other EMDE regions. In turn, under the central scenario, they would surpass Latin America by the late 2040s and the Middle East by the end of the projection period (Figure 4.11).

Figure 4.11: GDP per capita (PPP) by region

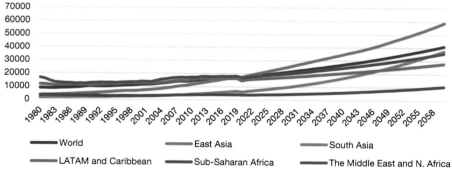

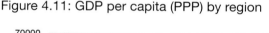

Source: Centennial Group 2021

---

6. There is a likely overestimation for the country, as the effect of the oil findings will not be expected for the full period of the scenarios.

Figure 4.12: Share of global GDP by region (2020)

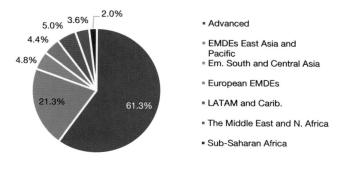

Source: Centennial Group 2021

Figure 4.13: Share of global GDP by region and scenario (2060)

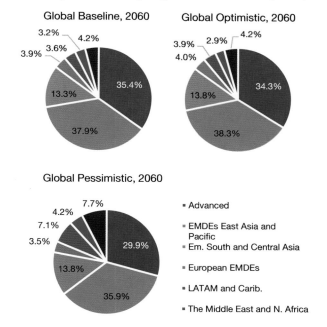

Source: Centennial Group 2021

Comparison of 2016, Pre-COVID-19, and Current Scenarios

A crucial issue that comes out of this exercise is that beyond the slowdown in growth caused by COVID-19, both the pre-pandemic and the post-pandemic projections show a significant decline in the prospective rate of growth for most of the regions of the world with respect to the projections incorporated into *The World in 2050*. Using a slightly different classification than the one used above to conform with the projections made at that time, we can see that all regions show a decline in the rate of growth for the period 2015–50, except for Emerging East Asia, which remains basically unchanged, and Emerging Europe, which shows an increase in more recent estimates (Figure 4.14). The regions with the largest negative adjustments are Latin America, the Middle East and North Africa and Sub-Saharan Africa, all hit by declines in terms of trade and thus in estimated TFP, as discussed in Chapter 14, with smaller projected declines for South and Central Asia and for advanced countries. To some extent, the difference in the projections reflects the actual performance of the world economy between 2015 and 2020 and the expected recovery from the pandemic in the next few years. To observe the possible differences in the scenarios in the medium- and long-term projections, we provide a comparison of the GDP growth rates for the period 2030–50, included in the 2016 scenario as well as the pre-COVID-19 and post-COVID-19 estimates (Figure 4.15). It can be observed that declines in the growth rates are observed for East Asia and for the three commodity-intensive regions, with a slight decline in the case of South and Central Asia; a slight increase after COVID-19 for the advanced countries can also be observed. Effectively, the current scenarios adjust for the terms of trade bias and provide a more realistic assessment, based on the newly available information. It should also be noted that the new projections incorporate a reclassification of several countries from 'convergers' and 'half-convergers' to lower categories, based on the experience in the last ten years.

Figure 4.14: GDP (PPP), projected growth rates: Projected 2016, projected pre-COVID-19 and projected post-COVID-19

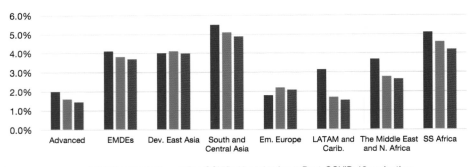

Source: Centennial Group 2021

Strong Policy (Optimistic) Scenario

The strong policy scenario differs from the central scenario by quantifying effects of three key 'what if' questions. The first is: what would be the outcome if most EMDEs became fast-growing 'convergers'? The second is: what would be the impact of this convergence occurring at a faster rate than that assumed under the central scenario? This, of course, assumes that the current 'non-convergers' will successfully adopt the adequate policies and institutional reforms

Figure 4.15: GDP (PPP), projected growth tates: Projected 2016, projected pre-COVID-19 and projected post-COVID-19 (2030–50)

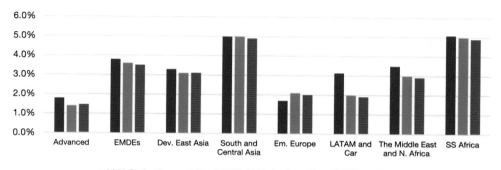

■2016 Projection ■ Pre-COVID-19 Projection ■Post-COVID-19 Projection

Source: Centennial Group 2021

needed to unleash a rapid catch-up process and accelerate productivity-driven growth. The third is: what would be the impact of faster global productivity frontier growth?

Under this scenario, the average rate of growth of the EMDEs group will increase from an average annual rate of 3.6 per cent in the central scenario to 3.9 per cent. By 2060, the difference for the relevant economies becomes highly significant. By the end of the period, the resulting global GDP will also be almost 59 per cent higher than in the central scenario. While GDP per capita in EMDEs will almost triple from its 2021 level under the central scenario (jumping from US$11,400 to US$33,900), it will increase nearly four-fold reaching US$55,500 under the strong policy scenario. The increase would be significant for the advanced countries, with an income of US$125,000 instead of US$94,000 under the baseline scenario.

Though the regional differences will remain significant, they will become less pronounced. This is because the largest contributors to growth in Asia are already 'convergers'—China, India, Indonesia, and others. By contrast, growth in the less-dynamic regions under the central scenario (Africa, the Middle East and Latin America) is much higher in this more optimistic scenario (Table 4.3, and Appendix table 3a). What is important to keep in mind is that this scenario is consistent with good policies throughout. More importantly, for this scenario to materialize, productivity and, more specifically, technological change, will be of the essence. Chapter 13, discussing the Productivity Conundrum, explores the current conditions and extraordinary prospects for the world if conditions allow. The chapter suggests that there has been an uptick in the global productivity growth. If this trend persists over the longer term, then the probability of the optimistic scenario being realized would increase, as global productivity growth has substantial influence on the overall world economic growth. However, not all regions will benefit automatically. Thus, country policies will remain critical. Otherwise, there may be even greater divergence between the innovators, for example, in East Asia, and the lagging EMDEs.

The Poor Policies and Low Productivity Growth (Pessimistic) Prospects

The global 2060 outcomes could be dramatically worse if domestic policies prove inadequate in most EMDEs (particularly in the cases of China, India and the rest of the Asian emerging economies) and if the rate of global productivity growth were to slow down dramatically. The latter would be the result of poor policies, climate change and the required offsetting investments, and the impact of conflicts related to inequality, not to speak of possible armed conflicts. Specifically, global warming already has and will continue to have destructive effects on the stock of capital and human well-being, that will require significant remedial spending and additional investment to preclude or reduce the potential losses in potential GDP in the world and particularly among emerging and poor economies. Events like a new pandemic or equivalent natural disasters are an additional cause of reduction in potential GDP growth. Moreover, these events can be envisaged to occur in the future, but cannot be predicted with any degree of certitude, thus increasing uncertainty. Moreover, there is the risk of increasing impediments to trade, regional tensions and financial crises, as have occurred in the past. Finally, global armed conflicts have been absent for three-quarters of a century, but there is no guarantee that a new one may not emerge, with catastrophic consequences, well beyond the scenarios presented here.

Under the pessimistic scenario, preliminary results suggest the average annual world GDP growth could be 1.5 per cent or 1/4 percentage points lower than in the central scenario (Table 4.3). The fall would be particularly harsh in the case of Asia, with a decline in the rate of growth by 2.7 percentage points, followed by a decline of 1.3 percentage points for Africa. However, all regions would suffer. In absolute terms, overall world GDP would be 38 per cent lower than in the central scenario and less than half of the estimate for the strong policy scenario. The range of possible results is a function of the assumptions about country policies and about the global productivity frontier, but it clearly shows the dramatically different impacts of good and poor policies as well as the importance of the rate of growth in global productivity. While this scenario is labelled pessimistic, existing trends in policies and political events, plus the deepening climate crisis, may make this outcome more likely than would have been expected in the past.

Concluding Remarks

The main message resulting from the new run is that the central scenario envisions a future where countries remain on a somewhat lower trajectory than they have followed in the past, but to remain on their trajectory, countries will need to work hard as they catch up with the more developed economies. The challenges of improving their underlying productivity and competitiveness are daunting. It will require overcoming significant obstacles—political, social and institutional—that have worsened with the COVID-19 shock and its structural consequences.

The strong policy scenario remains unlikely, given recent experience, except for possible progress in factor productivity. This scenario will require all developing regions to emulate the past record of East Asia, which is actually weakening for its more advanced countries. Achieving this scenario will require great discipline and dedication to economic development on a massive scale, particularly because over the long haul, commodity exporters cannot expect sustained improvements in their terms of trade—a key factor in their earlier and transient success. Still, the possibilities envisaged in the more optimistic scenarios are significant, and should be sought, subject to unexpected natural or human-caused disasters.

The likelihood of a more pessimistic outcome is high and is a warning that countries can also move in an adverse direction, failing to learn lessons and stagnating or even falling below their own record. In the end, success or failure is more dependent on domestic actions and inaction, and not the result of exogenous events—uncontrollable but expected, if positive, or excluded from the planning horizon, if negative.

Appendix 4.1: Additional Figures

Table A4.1a: GDP 2020–2040–2050

2020 - Baseline	GDP (MkFX)	World Share	2020 - Baseline	GDP (MkFX)	World Share
United States	20,283	24.6%	Brazil	2,583	3.1%
China	14,432	17.5%	France	2,548	3.1%
Japan	4,898	5.9%	United Kingdom	1,830	2.2%
Germany	3,731	4.5%	Russia	1,596	1.9%
India	2,631	3.2%	Korea	1,590	1.9%

2040 Baseline	GDP (MkFX)	%, World GDP	2040 - Optimistic	GDP (MkFX)	%, World GDP	2040 - Pessimistic	GDP (MkFX)	%, World GDP
China	41366	26.1%	China	47462	25.4%	United States	29530	22.6%
United States	31724	20.0%	United States	34635	18.6%	China	26697	20.5%
India	9083	5.7%	India	10604	5.7%	India	5939	4.6%
Japan	5741	3.6%	Japan	6809	3.6%	Japan	5335	4.1%
Germany	5189	3.3%	Germany	5860	3.1%	Germany	4829	3.7%
United Kingdom	4356	2.8%	United Kingdom	5102	2.7%	United Kingdom	4046	3.1%
France	3680	2.3%	France	4224	2.3%	France	3421	2.6%
Canada	2848	1.8%	Brazil	4058	2.2%	Canada	2659	2.0%
Korea	2706	1.7%	Indonesia	3829	2.1%	Korea	2248	1.7%
Indonesia	2587	1.6%	Canada	3252	1.7%	Italy	2197	1.7%

2060 Baseline	GDP (MkFX)	%, World GDP	2060 Optimistic	GDP (MkFX)	%, World GDP	2060 Pessimistic	GDP (MkFX)	%, World GDP
China	85593	31.0%	China	114570	27.4%	United States	36596	23.2%
United States	43772	15.9%	United States	51703	12.4%	China	28134	17.9%
India	28925	10.5%	India	41331	9.9%	India	8359	5.3%
Japan	6432	2.3%	Indonesia	13726	3.3%	Japan	5377	3.4%
Germany	6339	2.3%	Brazil	10150	2.4%	Germany	5306	3.4%
United Kingdom	5962	2.2%	Japan	9902	2.4%	United Kingdom	4972	3.2%
Indonesia	5736	2.1%	United Kingdom	8651	2.1%	France	3949	2.5%
France	4726	1.7%	Germany	8323	2.0%	Canada	3324	2.1%
Canada	3963	1.4%	Mexico	7623	1.8%	Indonesia	2972	1.9%
Nigeria	3892	1.4%	Nigeria	7434	1.8%	Australia	2774	1.8%

Source: Centennial Group 2021

Table A4.1b: GDP 2020–2040–2050

2020 - Baseline	GDP per capita (PPP)	2020 - Baseline	GDP per capita (PPP)
Luxembourg	114,550	United Arab Emirates	64,813
Ireland	94,239	Brunei	63,660
Singapore	92,934	Norway	63,483
Qatar	87,377	United States	61,272
Switzerland	70,703	Iceland	58,068

2040 Baseline	GDP per capita (PPP)	2040 Optimistic	GDP per capita (PPP)	2040 Pessimistic	GDP per capita (PPP)
Ireland	169106	Ireland	170959	Ireland	156430
Luxembourg	132902	Qatar	138514	Luxembourg	129441
Singapore	124989	Singapore	138263	Singapore	116858
Qatar	123138	Luxembourg	134854	Qatar	116208
Guyana	94725	Switzerland	99544	Guyana	94814
Switzerland	89837	Guyana	98300	Switzerland	83517
United States	86522	Norway	95623	United States	80540
Norway	85014	United Arab Emirates	95299	United Arab Emirates	79793
United Arab Emirates	84582	United States	94462	Malta	79016
Malta	83600	Brunei	92103	Norway	78986

2060 Baseline	GDP per capita (PPP)	2060 Optimistic	GDP per capita (PPP)	2060 Pessimistic	GDP per capita (PPP)
Ireland	233655	Ireland	209540	Ireland	194076
Singapore	162798	Singapore	190688	Guyana	143467
Qatar	146650	Qatar	189033	Singapore	136868
Guyana	145297	Luxembourg	152556	Luxembourg	128093
Luxembourg	141983	Guyana	145743	Qatar	124806
Switzerland	114202	United Arab Emirates	141506	Switzerland	95378
United States	111783	Switzerland	141010	Malta	95092
Malta	111749	Norway	140090	United States	93457
Norway	108960	Iceland	134972	United Arab Emirates	91968
United Arab Emirates	108258	United States	132035	Norway	90892

Source: Centennial Group 2021

Figure A4.1: Major countries GDP (MkFX) Global baseline 2012–15

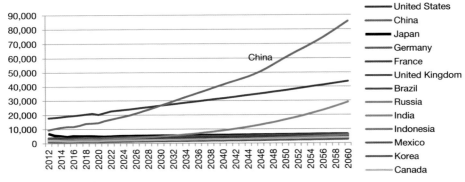

Source: Centennial Group 2021

Figure A4.2: Major countries, excluding USA, PRC and India GDP (MkFX)

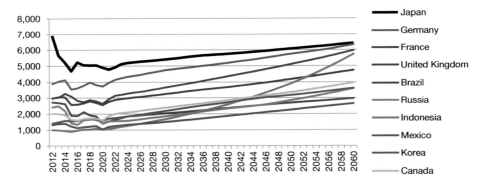

Source: Centennial Group 2021

Figure A4.3: Average GDP growth, 2001–20 and 2020–60 scenarios

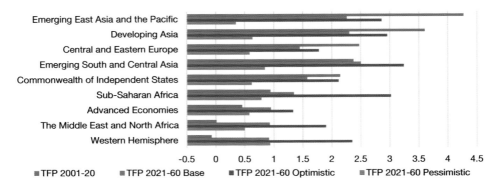

Source: Centennial Group 2021

Figure A4.4: Average TFP growth, 2001–20 and 2020–60 scenarios

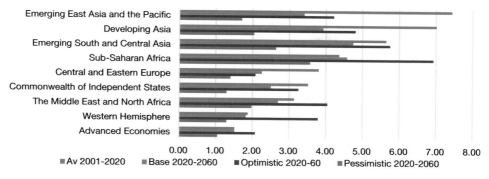

■ Av 2001-2020   ■ Base 2020-2060   ■ Optimistic 2020-60   ■ Pessimistic 2020-2060

Source: Centennial Group 2021

Figure A4.5: Asian sub-regions growth rate—GDP per capita

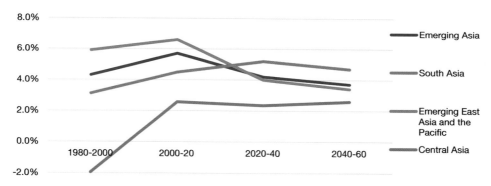

Source: Centennial Group 2021

Figure A6.: Asian sub-regions GDP per capita (USD 2018)

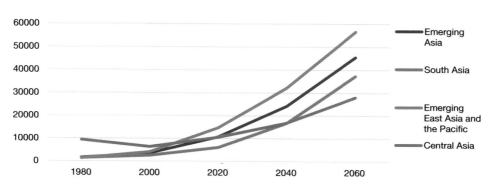

Source: Centennial Group 2021

Chapter 5: Governance—Critical for Sustainable and Just Development

Governance—Critical for Sustainable and Just Development

Chapter 5 Rajat Nag, Harinder Kohli and V. B. Tulasidhar

Introduction

Governance, the focus of this chapter, has become a key mantra of development, and rightly so. It is critical for sustainable and just development.

In our work and travels over the years around the developing world, be it in Asia, Africa, Central and Eastern Europe or Latin America, we have spoken to many of the intended principal beneficiaries of a country's development efforts: the poor and even the not so poor. What has been striking about these conversations is that they seldom talked about poverty or deprivations alone. Of course, they were concerns, but their stories were a very complex interplay of challenges they faced in the daily grind of their lives and indeed, their existence.

They talked about the violence and insecurities they faced in their daily lives. They talked about the powerful villager whose lands they tilled or houses of the rich they cleaned in the cities, and who threatened them with loss of livelihood, and the daily humiliations they, particularly women, suffered at the hands of these powerful men (yes, mostly men, but alas, often including women). They talked about the fears of losing their meagre properties because they did not have the necessary documentation to prove their ownership and even if they did: who cared? They recounted attacks from strangers (and even from neighbours) based on ethnicity, caste or religion. And they talked about gender-based domestic violence. They talked about the lack of jobs, even casual labour. They talked about the lack of money in hand to buy basic daily necessities. They talked about their dependence on the moneylenders and desperation and fear of how they would pay them back. They talked of the feeling of disempowerment and helplessness against those more powerful than them (almost everyone). They talked of the indignities they faced in their interactions with the police at street corners. They recalled the high-handedness of petty bureaucrats at the local administration offices where they would go to collect their dues, or of being ignored by the medical staff (if they were present to begin with) at the primary health centres to get some urgently needed healthcare. They talked about the unfairness of it all.

They talked of travelling for hours by bus and often on foot to collect the necessary papers and permissions to avail of government programmes due to them, only to be told to come back the next day as the 'dealing officer' was away, or, in this age of digital progress, 'the system was down'. They talked about their daily battles with rules and regulations and processes, which they did not understand but which ground them down. They talked of the feeling of being supplicants and at the mercy of others more powerful (official or otherwise), when, in fact, they were asking for no favours and nothing more than was already their due (access to health and education, for example).

RAJAT NAG, HARINDER KOHLI AND V. B. TULASIDHAR

5

And while there often was the unstated message that perhaps the system could work faster and, in their favour, if some money was offered, it was not necessarily always so either. The challenges were much deeper than 'corruption' alone: they were a combined effect of biases and prejudices, of processes and procedures not clearly defined and often not transparent so that the intended beneficiaries did not know (and would not be told) which pillars and posts they were supposed to run between. And even if known, poor and indiscriminate application of the rules ground them down. And worst of all, no accountability.

Essentially, it seemed to us that they all talked about various aspects of governance, or the lack of it. And in almost every instance, our conversations ended with some variation of a resigned closing sentence: 'There is no governance here.'

We have been struck at how often we have heard this refrain all over the world: 'There is no governance here.' Without necessarily defining what governance is or even actually using that word, people (be it the hapless citizen who has had to pay a bribe to get her papers, or the villager seeking redress from the petty [often not so petty] acts of harassment by the local officials or the local village elite) instinctively know and feel the effects of 'no governance' or the lack of good governance.

In a strikingly moving and powerful book, *Voices of the Poor: Can Anyone Hear Us?*, Deepa Narayan and her colleagues at the World Bank recount their conversations with over 40,000 poor women and men in fifty countries to hear the voices of the poor. They note the 'commonality of the human experience of poverty across countries. From Georgia to Brazil, from Nigeria to the Philippines, similar underlying themes emerged: hunger, deprivation, powerlessness, violation of dignity, social isolation, resilience, resourcefulness, solidarity, state corruption, rudeness of service providers, and gender inequity' (Narayan (ed.) 2000).

Our conversations and those presented by Narayan above, neatly encapsulate a failure of society. Failure to deliver on a set of fundamental development objectives, which can be assumed to apply to all societies: 'Freeing its members from the constant threat of violence (security), promoting prosperity (growth), and ensuring that such prosperity is shared (equity)' (World Bank 2017). And a common thread running through the failure to deliver on these objectives is the essence of lack of governance.

Governance is a broad, multidimensional concept meaning different things to different people. While many instinctively think of good governance as implying an honest government, that is, absence of corruption, it is only one of the many aspects of governance.

What Is Governance?

Governance is not a recent concern for society. Going back more than two millennia, Chanakya's *Arthashastra*, Plato's *Republic* or his disciple Aristotle's *Politics* all reflect wise ruminations and advice, simultaneously deeply philosophical and practical, on how a society could best govern itself to enhance its citizens' welfare. As a matter of fact, the word 'governance' derived from the Latin 'gubernare' is itself originally derived from the Greek word 'kubernaein', meaning 'to steer'. In its most basic sense, governance is the process by which a society governs (steers) itself. It is the process by which a society manages its affairs for the overall good of its citizens. It is not hard to imagine that even the first human habitants on Earth must have, even if instinctively, realized that they needed to evolve 'rules of engagement' with each other to coexist and 'steer' their affairs. Fundamentally, these rules of engagement define governance.

But it is not just a question of articulating the rules and regulations and laws and statutes, executive government orders, and fiats and policy declarations of aspirations and intentions, to ensure good governance. No doubt, the laws, rules, and regulations are important. But it is even more important to consider how a society applies them to enhance the welfare of its citizens.

Intrinsic and Instrumental Values of Governance

In his seminal work, *Development as Freedom*, Amartya Sen had distinguished between the 'intrinsic' (also called primary or constitutive end) and 'instrumental' (also called principal end) values of freedom. He argued that human freedom (to choose, express views, live as one wishes, for example) is of value by itself to be cherished as an important, indeed inevitable, metric of development itself. Freedom is intrinsic, a primary end of development in its own right. 'This fundamental point is distinct from the "instrumental" argument that these freedoms and rights may also be very effective in contributing to economic progress' (Sen 1999).

The value of good governance as discussed so far can be termed its 'intrinsic value'. Good governance is good in its own right. It recognizes and restores—even if partially—human dignity and gives people a sense of empowerment, which is of value on its own, irrespective of whether they lead to some other positive outcomes as well ('instrumental value'). However, the intrinsic value of good governance as a desirable end in itself does not in any way diminish the instrumental value of good governance in contributing to economic development.

Good governance can lead to sound development; bad governance will not. In all the examples cited above, good governance would have helped in achieving the desired effects of the economic reforms and changes, and improve the welfare of the intended beneficiaries (even if not perfectly), instead of leaving them feeling frustrated and helpless as we have reported. This is the instrumental value of governance since this alone can help achieve inclusive and sustainable development.

Governance in the Context of Social Justice: Niti and Nyaya

Furthermore, governance needs to be looked at through a wider prism of social justice. In this context, it is useful to draw on two Sanskrit words, which Sen often uses in his discourses on social justice. The first is *niti*, and the other is nyaya (Sen 2009).

Niti and nyaya both mean justice, in a sense, but the nuanced difference between the two is very important. Niti refers to organizational propriety, behavioural correctness, the rules and regulations—how you ought to behave. Nyaya, on the other hand, refers to realized justice. Nyaya recognizes the role of niti, the rules and the organizations, the importance of institutions, but considers the world as is.

The context in nyaya is the world we live in, not some idealized state of society. Nyaya recognizes the role of niti in shaping institutional framework, but focuses on implementation. It takes into account the context while using the rules, norms and legal measures to ensure justice is administered in a fair and just manner to govern society. Niti is a necessary condition to achieve nyaya, but ultimately, it's nyaya that a society aspires to achieve. Good governance must concern itself with both niti and nyaya. Niti alone is not enough.

In this context, there is another very relevant Sanskrit word, *matsyanyaya*, which means justice in the world of the fish. And justice in such a world allows a big fish to devour the small fish at will. Such a situation is obviously a fundamental violation of human justice, no matter how well laid out the rules, regulations, and institutional structures might be. Therefore, a key element of good governance is ultimately about assuring and ensuring justice, or at least the reduction of patent injustices, which many of the 'voices of the poor' passionately articulate in our introduction above.

Defining Governance

Interest in governance has increased dramatically in recent decades, be it politicians, policy makers, or bureaucrats; be it academic researchers or development practitioners; or be it the ordinary citizen. But how does one define governance? Is there any standard definition? As a matter of fact, there are multitudes of definitions and descriptions of governance, depending on who is defining.

It is perhaps equally important to ask, 'governance for what?' Governance for economic development (growth), of course. Societies aspire to be prosperous, of course, but if they only cast their aspirations on economic growth, it would be too limiting. Societies should aspire to see people living better lives, free from the scourges of income poverty but also of other social deprivations, such as ill health and illiteracy, and exploitation by others. Surely, societies would also want to be concerned with how such prosperity is shared. Chapter 2, 'The World We Live In,' has outlined the various debilitating deprivations in many emerging economies, characterized by serious income and human development inequities. And driving this all, there is the fundamental primordial concern for societies to be safe: free from the constant threat of violence (security), perhaps indelibly imprinted on the human DNA to preserve itself. As neatly encapsulated by the World Bank, 'Governance for what? Achieving the goals of security, growth, and equity' (World Bank 2017). In a nutshell, governance should be seen as society's capacity to deliver on these outcomes.

Francis Fukuyama defines governance 'as a government's ability to make and enforce rules, and to deliver services, regardless of whether that government is democratic or not' (Fukuyama 2013). Fukuyama's concern is about the government's economic management capacity, not its political form: 'Governance is thus about execution or what has traditionally fallen within the domain of public administration, as opposed to politics.'

Avinash Dixit considers governance in the context of a smoothly functioning market economy. He defines governance as 'the structure and functioning of legal and social institutions that support economic activity and economic transactions by protecting property rights, enforcing contracts, and taking collective action to provide physical and organizational infrastructure' to ensure efficiency of the market system (Dixit 2009).

M.G. Quibria captures well the challenges of defining governance. Recognizing that governance is a complex concept with many different dimensions, he observes that 'while some have used governance expansively to refer to the entire gamut of social, political, and legal institutions that have a bearing on the functioning of the government, others have used it to refer specifically to state capacity; and still others have used it as a code word for corruption and malfeasance of the government' (Quibria 2014).

Another perspective emphasizes legal aspects of governance: the laws, rules and regulations that would govern behaviour and the interactions between various members and groups in society—the citizens, businesses and the government; essentially the principals and the agents. Under this consideration, governance is about defining the 'rule of law', enforcement of contracts and securing property rights. This definition equally emphasizes the importance of 'rule by law' and the necessary institutional arrangements (an independent judiciary, for example) to ensure that.

Yet another grouping focuses on state capacity for efficient economic management, à la Fukuyama. Governance is about the ability of the performance of agents in carrying out the intentions of the principals, not how the principals are selected. Note that Fukuyama specifically adds in his definition the phrase 'regardless of whether the Government is democratic or not'. Governance from this perspective is about execution to improve the lives of its citizens: 'In improvement of the provision of public services and in efficacious economic management that helps avoid delays of execution, malfeasance and corruption' (Quibria 2014).

International development financing organizations (World Bank, Asian Development Bank, Inter-American Development Bank and African Development Bank, for example) can only consider economic aspects of development and are prevented by their charters from getting into political issues in any member country. These institutions have thus cast governance in the mould of sound development management and defined it as 'the manner in which power is exercised in the management of a country's economic and social resources for development' (Asian Development Bank 1995).

Good governance is to be valued because that would lead to sound development management and thus, contribute to 'creating and sustaining an environment which fosters strong and equitable development, and it is an essential complement to sound economic policies' (World Bank 1992).

In short, two basic messages stand out from the rich literature that has tried to define governance. First, that not only is governance multidimensional but it also involves multiple stakeholders (members of society), and they all have to somehow come together to decide and choose how they would like to steer themselves. Carcaba et al. (2017) thus define governance as being about 'the interaction between governments and other social organizations; the relationship with citizens, decision making, and accountability. Governments have a key role in this network, since good governance implies managing public affairs in a transparent, accountable, participatory and equitable manner'. And second that governance, in a very broad sense, is the process of how a society governs (steers) itself. Easily said, it is actually a complex amalgam of multidimensional and multidisciplinary considerations. Legal, political, social, anthropological and economic aspects all have a bearing on how we understand governance and how we define it.

Four Basic Elements of Good Governance

The various definitions of governance laid out above, all touch on one or more aspects of governance: political, economic, state capacity, legal and social justice. Each aspect is relevant in some way or another, but they can indeed get overwhelming in the breadth of their coverage. But a closer reflection on the various definitions reveals that four basic elements of good governance can be identified: predictability, transparency, participation and accountability (ADB 1995).

Members of a society need to know in advance the laws, rules and regulations that apply. They need to have the assurance that they will indeed be applied predictably and transparently to all, not capriciously and unfairly with irrelevant and pernicious considerations of a person's station in life or access 'to higher ups'. An oft repeated story in many poorly governed states (unfortunately, not apocryphal but true) is of miscreants caught speeding or doing worse, loudly demanding of the hapless policeman apprehending them: 'Don't you know who my father is?'

Just as the adage 'sunshine is the best disinfectant', transparency is a key enabler for good governance. The best designed and even perhaps intended rules of law will not mean much if citizens don't know about them or can't readily find out about them. If information is power, it needs to be widely disseminated and easily available to all so that this power is not cause for abuse by those in power, and instead becomes empowering for all.

Citizens must have the confidence that their participation in the efforts to expect and demand good governance as agents of change and development will be encouraged and not ignored, or worse. Nobody has a greater stake in the successful outcome of development efforts than the intended beneficiaries of such efforts themselves. But the intended beneficiaries, that is, the citizens, must not be seen only as passive recipients of such a process. Instead, they are also the agents of development. As such, they need to be actively involved in determining what the best development interventions, initiatives, programmes or projects might be.

Accountability pins responsibility. Who is responsible for what? And what are the consequences if such responsibility is not met? If a citizen has travelled for a day to visit the local administration office to collect her papers (or her pension) but doesn't find the concerned officer at his desk and no one else can help her, who is to be held accountable?

Good governance requires public officials to be answerable for their actions (or more often, the lack thereof). But to hold such officials accountable, there is a need for a clearly laid out and well-publicized criteria for their performance (predictable and transparent). A major factor that dramatically improved governance in Singapore since its establishment as a city state in 1965, was Prime Minister Lee Kuan Yew's laser focus on holding public officials to account.

Corruption: A Key Aspect of Governance

Corruption is not the only factor that impedes development. But, it is an important factor at play. It is important not to downplay how serious a scourge corruption is. It hurts the poor disproportionately and dampens the benefits of economic growth. Contrary to some misperceptions that corruption is a relatively recent phenomenon and is limited to the poor countries alone, corruption is a curse for all places and all times.

Around third century BCE, Chanakya (350–275 BCE) penned an extraordinary treatise in Sanskrit, the *Arthashastra*: a comprehensive guide to statecraft, and he wrote specifically about corruption. Ever the clear-eyed realist, he harboured no illusions that 'just as it is impossible not to taste honey or poison that one may find at the tip of one's tongue, so it is impossible for one dealing with government funds not to taste, a little bit, of the King's wealth' (Rangarajan (ed.) 2016).

The brilliant book *Bribes* traces in fascinating detail a 4,000-year-old history of bribes and corruption: from ancient Mesopotamia and Egypt to modern America; from the Code of Hammurabi (a Babylonian legal code enacted by King Hammurabi around 1754 BC) to the modern times (Noonan 1984).

Corruption, broadly defined as misuse of public office for private gain, is at the core of bad governance. Its pernicious effects are felt by all, though the incidence of such ill-effects is borne disproportionately by the poor. The ills of corruption and the economic costs (by some estimates exceeding US$6 trillion 'in poor countries between 2001 and 2010 with devastating impacts on the livelihoods of ordinary people') have been extensively documented in the literature (Kar, Dev, and Freitas 2010) and will not be repeated here.

Pranab Bardhan observes that economists tend to focus on efficiency, growth, institutions and incentives for fighting corruption and thus 'promote market-inspired solutions such as competition, liberalization, deregulation, and privatization' (Bardhan 1997).

But noting that there is little evidence that such anti-corruption measures have generally achieved much, Alina Mungiu-Pippidi argues that such actions fail 'because these initiatives are non-political in nature, while most of the corruption in developing countries is inherently political' (Mungiu-Pippidi 2006). Most assessments of corruption and the consequent design of anti-corruption strategies make an implicit assumption that corruption is a deviation from a norm of 'universal ethics'. The state is assumed to operate under some norm of universalism where all citizens are treated equally and fairly, which may occasionally be infringed by favouritism (because of connections or bribery, for example). Corruption in such a state is thus an exception, and anti-corruption strategies are designed on this assumption.

Unfortunately, the reality in many, if not most, societies is different. Rather than universalism, these societies may be considered to be practising 'particularism', where people are treated differently depending on their social status and economic power. Unequal treatment is the norm in particularistic societies: 'A culture of privilege reigns in societies based on particularism' (Mungiu-Pippidi 2006). The balance of power is so tilted in favour of the elite in such societies that they can easily subvert the rule of law, and thus negate the possible consequences of, say, anti-corruption legal measures.

Another feature of most anti-corruption strategies is their treatment of corruption as a typical 'principal-agent' problem. Under such a situation, it is the principal who has to be protected from the agent's possible nefarious activities since he (the agent) has the informational asymmetry in his favour. But the truth may be just the reverse. The principal, as an elite actor who holds the levers of power, benefits from the rent-seeking activities he indulges in and has all the incentives not to let anti-corruption measures work.

There is a rich literature which argues that corruption can instead be better understood as a 'collective action' problem rather than a 'principal-agent' relationship (Olson 1971).

In thinking of corruption, a similar phenomenon exists. Members of a society may all agree that corruption is bad. They also may know that, as a group, they are worse off with existing corruption, and it is, therefore, in their interest to support anti-corruption measures. Paradoxically, however, they will (individually) still slip the policeman a bribe to avoid being charged with jumping the red light. As Persson et al. (2012) note: 'the short-term costs of being honest are comparatively very high since this will not change the game. Hence: why should I be the sucker?'

This phenomenon of collective action has a very corrosive influence on society's attitude towards corruption. It dilutes trust within a society when, as Bo Rothstein says, 'Without norms of trust, the tragedy of the commons is unavoidable' (Rothstein 2000). Rothstein (2020) well captures the social dilemma that follows when trust is in short supply: 'I would pay taxes if I knew others were paying too, and the tax authorities were not corrupt; but since I cannot assume either of these two conditions to hold, I evade taxes, as do others, and all suffer:' a classic result of collective action pushing the system to a suboptimal equilibrium. Once the system gets there, it stays there (stable but suboptimal), caught in what is often referred to as a 'Corruption Trap'. The serious challenge for many societies is, therefore, how to nudge themselves out of the corruption trap.

5 Emerging Societal Pressures for Good Governance

We are persuaded that pressures for good governance will increase in the coming decades through a combination of rising societal pressures in most emerging economies (though not necessarily to the same degree in each).

These societal pressures fall in two general groups. The first group comprises many of the megatrends mentioned in Chapter 3, 'Ten Global Megatrends', which are gradually taking hold in more and more emerging economies as they become economically better off and the average citizens push harder for better governance; we call this group 'positive societal pressures for reform'. The second group—also highlighted in the megatrends—consists of the impending changes in the global, national and local economic, social and physical environment that calls for urgent joint actions by governments and societies, and which will make it impossible for countries to continue to operate on a business-as-usual basis. Major changes will become ultimately inevitable to tackle these second group of pressures. If governments and ruling elites in power do not voluntarily bring about the needed changes, they may be forced from power; chaos may be the result in some countries.

First, we would like to highlight five megatrends that could combine to become a powerful positive force for change in many societies, leading at least some emerging market economies to emulate past (positive) experience of advanced economies. Chapters 2 and 3 have discussed the expectation that during the next decades, emerging market economies in East Asia, South Asia as well as Africa would continue to urbanize rapidly; that income levels in most emerging economies would grow decently, and that this, in turn, would result in a massive increase in the size of the middle classes (as defined by the World Bank) around the world (leaving aside the issues of distribution and inequalities). The reality that the majority of the population in many emerging market economies will be both urban and middle class, will lead to their demanding better governance, even if nothing else changes. But other changes are at play too. The information technology revolution mentioned in Chapter 3 and discussed in more detail later in this book, is leading to a much more interconnected world—almost everyone already has or will soon have smartphones and access to the Internet and TV. With social media, news travels fast, and people are getting socially and politically active. Add to that the emergence of civic societies in most countries, which serve as powerful means to express people's views, file grievances and demand both transparency and accountability on the part of the elites.

In short, younger, urban, more affluent generations will be less tolerant of poor governance than their previous generations have been. They will expect and demand more honest, transparent, open and inclusive institutional arrangements and be willing to express such demands through the ballot box or other means.

Coming to the second group of pressures to improve governance, the list is indeed long, including economic management at the national and international levels, globalization, rising inequality, the need to adapt to the coming technological revolution (including the way we work) and, of course, the utmost urgency to fight climate change.

As individual economies grow and also integrate with the rest of the world, economic transactions become more complex and informal institutions have to yield space to more formal, structured institutions. Greater predictability, transparency, participation and accountability (that is, better governance) become necessary for robust and sustained economic growth. A new challenge highlighted by the pandemic is the constant need to refine (and periodically even redefine) the relative roles of the public and private sectors, even in the most sophisticated economies.

While globalization has obvious benefits (of seamless supply chains, enhancing global trade, taking advantage of varying comparative advantages of the trading nations and greater ease of sharing knowledge at a global scale), there are costs as well. Consumers in the developed countries benefit, for example, from cheaper goods now available from low-wage countries, but jobs—particularly in manufacturing in the high-wage countries—suffer. There are obvious asymmetries in the incidence of costs and benefits among the population and most countries have been less than fully successful in addressing such asymmetries and compensating the losers (through financial measures or retraining/reskilling initiatives, for example). Admittedly, there are some serious structural issues as well. How practical would it be, for example, to think of reskilling steel foundry workers to become software programmers? These asymmetries cause major governance and institutional challenges, and failure to adequately address them is, in part, responsible for the rise in populist and inward-looking regimes in many parts of the world, an issue that deserves serious attention at the national and global levels.

Inequality has become a major issue—both inequality between countries and within countries. While globally, inequality between countries remains big, it has been coming down gradually over the past fifty years or so. This cannot be said of inequality within countries, which unfortunately has been rising in many countries in the recent past (see Chapter 7, 'Two Faces of Development'). To some extent, it can be ascribed to poor domestic governance. In any case, there will be mounting societal pressures to reverse this recent trend. And a major part of the solution will be better governance.

Countries will also be under tremendous pressure to prepare for the unfolding technological revolution to remain competitive in the world economy, to protect jobs and to prepare the future workforce as well as the business sector. Similarly, as mentioned in Chapter 3 and elaborated later in Chapter 12, 'Future of Work and Jobs', fundamental changes are already underway in how work is being carried out—particularly in the services sector—in many advanced countries. These changes are bound to come soon to more and more emerging market economies. Smart governments and proactive institutions will be critical to helping their people and businesses adjust to this fast-changing world. Again, all this will require better and more effective governance.

Last, but not the least, is the urgent and existential challenge of climate change. Especially the younger, socially active, generations will be more demanding of themselves and their governments to face the multiple challenges of climate change. The young know they will have to live with the consequences. What was most striking as well encouraging was the large presence of civil society participants, especially the young activists, at the 2021 Glasgow Summit COP 26 pressuring national governments—developing and developed countries alike—and the international community to take actions. We should expect similar pressures to emerge increasingly at the national and local levels in emerging market economies, as they have in most advanced economies already.

Some Lessons from History

Improvements in governance—with institutional development at its core—is arduous and unpredictable; it cannot follow a 'how-to-do manual' with a streamlined cookie-cutter approach in all countries. Local context is critical. Reforms cannot be easily transplanted. However, experiences in various parts of the world and at various times have proven that 'history is not destiny'.

History need not be destiny. Lessons can be drawn from some historical experiences around the world as countries make the transition from limited access to open access institutional systems and improve their overall governance. Denmark is a positive example. Its institutions and governance at one time (in the 1600s) were in very poor shape; many things were indeed 'rotten in the state of Denmark' (Shakespeare 1992). But they improved. Great Britain and Japan are other examples of countries that moved from limited access to open access order, and prospered as a result. In more recent times, the experiences of Botswana, Georgia, Singapore, South Korea and Uruguay provide encouraging evidence that history is not necessarily destiny.

Enlightened national leaderships combined with national emergencies caused by external (or even internal) factors have often led to major institutional improvements. In other words, when unexpected opportunities arise, local leaders can make a huge difference: change can happen in nonlinear ways. Such opportunities combined with enlightened national leaders led to nonlinear changes in countries as diverse as Denmark, Japan, Singapore and South Korea.

Governance and Institutions

However, even if the right drivers, as noted above, are in place, they will result in good governance only if the right institutional framework is in place and national leaders truly leverage these drivers, rather than merely react to them. If a society has a growing young population, with high information and communications technology (ICT) penetration and integration into global value chains, it may be ripe for governance reform, but a country would need sound institutions in place to deliver such reforms. It is equally important to recognize that rising inequalities, increasing youth unemployment (particularly in Africa) and climate change could lead to social upheavals and weaken the credibility of existing institutions. Essentially, the thesis is that institutions matter in delivering good governance and thus ultimately in a country's quest for development. Chapter 6, 'Institutions and Prosperity', discusses further the critical role of institutions—formal and informal—in doing so and to that we now turn.

Chapter 6: Institutions and Prosperity—A Conceptual Framework

Institutions and Prosperity—A Conceptual Framework

Chapter 6 — Werner Hermann

'We plough and we scatter the seed on the land—but growth and prosperity are not in our hand.'
—Inscription on an archway in Gifhorn, Germany

Introduction

How to meet human needs and achieve general prosperity is one of the essential questions of economics. It is a concern of advanced nations as much as of developing countries. Leading economists have always tried to fathom what makes a prosperous economy. They have put forward a variety of promising hypotheses: free trade, the financial system, religion, climate, etc. They largely agree on what impedes prosperity—yet they fail to find a recipe for prosperity which is universally applicable and at the same time practical. This suggests that feasibility is overestimated. Uncontrollable factors may play a stronger role than observers are prepared to believe. It may be that prosperity cannot be actively brought about at all, and all that can be done is to remove obstacles so that prosperity hopefully arises spontaneously. Even if economics cannot provide a panacea, economic concepts can help to understand the mechanisms at work and offer starting points for improvement.

This chapter aims to present a conceptual framework that can help explore or evaluate measures to foster prosperity. Its main message is: one cannot engineer prosperity, but one can create better or worse conditions for prosperity to occur. The focus is on social rules (so-called institutions) and their role in the development of the economy.

Part I briefly touches on what renowned economists have written on safeguarding prosperity; Part II presents the effects of social rules on prosperity, their determinants and the possibility of controlling them. Part III discusses pragmatically selected approaches to adjusting the rules.

Part I: You Can't Engineer Prosperity

What Makes a Prosperous Economy?

Prosperity in this chapter is defined as real income per capita growing over generations. After more than 200 years of the most spectacular growth in much of the world, with marked differences from country to country in both the extent and the timing of growth, and intensive research into this development, some aspects of its causes have been understood. It is known what does not lead to growth or even stunts it, but little is known on how to ensure prosperity in the future. Acemoglu and Robinson put it pointedly: you can't engineer prosperity (Acemoglu and Robinson 2012, 446).

The signs that characterize prosperous societies include tremendous technological progress. The growth of the last 200 years would be unthinkable without it. Moreover, new technology usually requires increased investment in real and human capital combined with increased division of labour; this development is also undeniable. But innovations here and there without adoption by many others are not sufficient for broad growth—diffusion of technical progress is what makes the difference. Diffusion often takes place through trade. The division of labour and trade are also mutually dependent, and trade is facilitated and made cheaper by standardization. It allows products from different producers to fit and function together.[1] This can also be observed empirically; just think of the container ships that have become so large that they hardly fit into the ports anymore. According to De Soto, developing countries suffer from having a capital stock that it is not fungible (De Soto 2000). Recently, the view has also spread that sustainable prosperity requires an inclusive and open social order (North et al. 2009 and Acemoglu and Robinson 2012). In this context, the migration of rural populations to cities after disasters also plays a role (cf. Baumol and Strom 2010).

The idea that some places are favoured by nature, primarily by climate or geography, while others are unlikely ever to support a prosperous economy because they are disadvantaged by nature (i.e., the idea that nature largely explains the observed differences) is outdated. While resource abundance creates wealth in the short term and can trigger a boom, it is now seen as more of an impediment to long-term development. Max Weber's thesis that religion or culture are decisive is also outdated.

Additionally, a strategy of achieving prosperity through strength (cf. Seabright 2010) is not very promising in the long run in terms of leading to prosperity. The USSR barely lasted seventy years; the Roman Empire was one of the few exceptions where this strategy was successful for centuries. Economists such as Bauer, Easterly and Deaton have pointed out the aid illusion and shown that traditional development aid is mostly ineffective, often even harmful. The last big-name initiative, Jeffrey Sachs' Millennium Villages Project, is now regarded as a failure by many observers. The chances of success are poor when countries are administered recommendations of the so-called Washington Consensus (cf. Acemoglu and Robinson 2012) by international organizations, and they are reluctant to implement them. Governments seldom lack insight; they have reasons for their actions or inaction; the so-called ignorance hypothesis can be considered rejected.

Unfortunately, these findings do not go much further, a comprehensive model that reveals the direction of causality, not just correlations would be needed. One would need to know which independent root causes determine all the other variables and ultimately, prosperity.

Would understanding what determines prosperity be sufficient? Probably not, because explanations are not enough, the desire is to bring about prosperity where it has not happened by itself. Besides the lack of theory, there is another hurdle. It is not at all clear that one can actually influence prosperity. To do so, one would need to be able to freely control the influencing factors. But the very immunity of governments to the recommendations mentioned above suggest that this is often not the case.

Prosperity can be framed in macroeconomic terms. GDP, investment, consumption and the balance of payments are important indicators of prosperity. But one thing is clear: a lack

---

1. Interoperability cf. Kling and Schulz's 'From poverty to prosperity' (2009, 23).

of prosperity cannot be cured by macroeconomic measures; political economy is also critical. Presumably, prosperity depends on the behaviour of people, notably on the way they interact. Therefore, making certain assumptions about human nature, one could investigate what makes people behave in a way that fosters prosperity. Baumol (1990) finds that 'it may be possible to change the rules in ways that help to offset undesired institutional influences or that supplement other influences that are taken to work in beneficial directions.' That is the way this chapter intends to go. What this chapter is looking for are factors that influence prosperity that can also be controlled.

The next part draws from the economics literature of the last couple of decades and tries to develop a conceptual framework. This will help understand the mechanism of the system and hopefully hint at points where it can be influenced.

Part II: A Framework to Think about Prosperity

Cause of Diverging Developments

The example of Berlin and Germany after WWII can help explain what sparks prosperity. As is well-known, between 1945 and 1989, Berlin had a prosperous half in the West and a wanting half in the East. The two halves were initially very similar: both bombed out, the same population and the same climate. The main difference between the East and West was the economic systems by which their society functioned: capitalism in the West and communism in the East. There were admittedly some other differences: West Berlin was cut off from the FRG, but benefitted from Marshall Aid. Furthermore, some communists migrated to the East and entrepreneurs went to the West. But these differences can hardly explain the huge prosperity gap that emerged in just under fifty years. This strongly suggests the crucial role of social rules. Further evidence is provided by the difference between North and South Korea and the collapse of the USSR. Economists have argued again and again that the capitalist system is superior to the socialist one, their most prominent exponent being Hayek. In the twenty-first century, however, it is no longer necessary to prove the superiority of the capitalist system. The examples should merely illustrate that the design of social rules determines whether or not an economy prospers.

The next section discusses the rules of society, what they do and how they come about. In doing so, it should become clear why they are important for prosperity. In a nutshell, they are important for two reasons: because they determine incentives or behaviour and thus are a necessary, critical link in the causal chain leading to prosperity, and because they can be influenced.

Institutions

Every society adopts rules that facilitate living together. These social rules are referred to in the literature—going back to Jean-Jacques Rousseau—as institutional arrangements, or institutions for short. The term institution, as used here, does not correspond to the term in common usage; it therefore does not denote any established organizations or legal entities, but refers to written or unwritten social rules that determine what one is allowed to do and what one is not allowed in a given society, i.e. elements or procedures that constitute the social order; they say what is acceptable and what is not tolerated. The implementation of some institutions requires organizations to perform certain tasks; for example, the commercial register is traditionally kept by a government office. In the future, it would be conceivable to keep registers based on distributed ledger technology, on which bitcoin is also based. This chapter defines institutions as the rule, rather than the organization that implements it.

Institutions are often laid down in laws or contracts, but institutions can also exist as informal customs. And sometimes reality does not reflect the proclaimed convention. In this case, the relevant institution is the behaviour that actually passes, not what is proclaimed (actual social practices not de jure rules). If it is generally accepted that civil servants accept tips or that elites are treated differently from ordinary people, then these are the relevant institutions, no matter what is written in law.

A fundamental institution in any society concerns property, it has to specify how one acquires property and how far one can freely dispose of one's property. Other important modern institutions are political equality, freedom of trade and commerce and the independence of the courts. Taxation and government spending, and of course, the way the government is established, are institutional issues as well. The following section looks into property rights as an example.

Property Rights

The importance of property rights is emphasized regularly, usually by the wealthy, and the statement meets with broad approval—sometimes property is considered sacred and inviolable. With so much agreement on the importance of property rights, it may come as a surprise to learn that there are significant differences in the property rights between and within countries over time. Land ownership, for example, is more extensive in the United States than in Europe; in the United States, whoever owns the land also owns the oil, gas, coal and other minerals found below the surface.

Therefore, the statement that property rights are important and have to be protected is too general to be of any help, for it is often not clear exactly what is meant by property rights. What property rights can refer to needs to be clarified. Is property absolute and unrestricted, or is it sufficient to clarify in detail what rights property includes? Is land ownership, ownership of production goods or even serfdom and intellectual property allowed and are they actually protected by the legal system or not? Can or must one acquire regalia and licenses for certain trades? Can one do what one wants with property without restriction, can it be expropriated or restricted by courts and can one bequeath it to one's descendants? Is property or its transfer taxed? The answers to these questions vary widely in different countries and at different times, and it is often not obvious which answers are best. There is therefore no ideal property regime that is always the right one everywhere. Society needs to stipulate what can be owned and what rights ownership includes. It is also worth noting that property rights are established only when something becomes scarce; free goods are not worth the cost of establishing an institution.

The Impact of Institutions

It is generally agreed that a society needs institutions, but why are they actually needed? The purpose of rules is to guide and to clarify. Guiding implies constraints, clarifying lowers costs and both build trust. This cost reduction is the economic raison d'être of an institution. Beyond these direct effects, institutions can influence the behaviour of those concerned and increase their productivity.

Cost Reduction

Institutions reduce transaction costs. For example, the introduction of universally accepted money eliminates the need to find a partner in the market who wants what you have to offer and offers exactly what you want. In the higher stages of development, the institution of the clearing bank made it unnecessary to carry gold around and expose it to the risk of loss. The thrust of institutional development is to reduce transaction costs.

Building Trust

Institutions can also reduce transaction costs by establishing trust between people who would have every reason to distrust each other. Only on the basis of the institution can they cooperate, which is beneficial for both. A comparatively expensive institution is the pledge, which has to be deposited, especially if the pledge is a living being. A good and historically significant example of a cheaper institution to create trust is the community responsibility system (cf. Greif 2006). The community responsibility system was able to establish trust between merchants from different cities in Europe without an encompassing jurisdiction. The system worked like this: a local communal court held all members of another commune legally liable for the default of any member in contract with a member of the local community. If a defaulter's communal court refused to compensate the injured party, the local court acquired compensation by confiscating the property of the defaulter's commune members who were present within its jurisdiction. For a trader, therefore, worrying about the personal reputation of a particular trader from another community became a secondary issue.

Institutions Influence Behaviour

Everyone knows on which side to swerve to avoid an oncoming person or vehicle and, for their own benefit, adheres to the rule. The rules in road traffic are not only self-enforcing, they also have another special feature: they have no further-reaching effects on the behaviour of road users. In one half of the world, oncoming traffic is traditionally avoided to the right, and the other half, to the left. Since Sweden in 1967 and Iceland in 1968 joined the continental practice and switched to right-hand traffic, there has been no change in any country with a developed road network. It does not seem to matter much which applies.

In general, however, it does matter whether the rules are one way or another. William Baumol in *Entrepreneurship: Productive, Unproductive and Destructive* (1990) writes that 'entrepreneurial behaviour changes direction from one economy to another in a manner that corresponds to the variations in the rules of the game'. One example that is often cited is patent protection. Patent protection increases the production costs of patented goods and on the one hand, makes it more difficult to adopt patented production processes. This is a direct and economically undesirable effect. Advocates of high patent protection, however on the other hand, claim that the investment in patent development can only be made if the invention is protected from imitators; otherwise, the incentive to invent is too small and not worth the effort. Economic theory supports this argument, and the large number of patent applications show that it is valid. So, a high level of patent protection encourages development and also facilitates trade in intellectual property. Baumol considers trade in patents to be the decisive competitive advantage of capitalism (cf. Baumol 2004).

Another good example of a rule that can influence behaviour is the wage system. A piece-work wage delivers high output of minimally acceptable quality and attracts people who can work expeditiously. However, if the quality of the work is important and also difficult to assess, then piecework is not the appropriate form for a labour contract.

How companies are organized and how they make decisions is highly relevant for the prosperity of a community. A period of strong institutional innovation in business was the Commercial Revolution in the Middle Ages. Venice and Genoa took important steps towards the formation of modern businesses around the year 1000 with new forms of contracts such as the colleganza. The colleganza allowed people from different families to trust each other and enabled them to work together over long distances. In the simplest and most common form, a colleganza was an arrangement between two parties, a travelling merchant and an investor (or sedentary merchant). The investor provided wares to the travelling merchant who then boarded a ship with other merchants for an overseas destination. There, the travelling merchant sold the wares, used the proceeds to buy other wares and upon his return handed them over to the investor to sell them. Any profits were split as pre-agreed and the venture was ended. The colleganza was not yet permanent and was neither a legal entity in its own right (persona ficta); the merchant always acted in his own name. This meant that the conditions for trading in company shares had not yet been fulfilled. These development steps took place later. The first stock exchange opened in Amsterdam in 1602.

Behaviour Influences Prosperity

The claim that people's behaviour affects the prosperity of a country probably doesn't need a very long justification. 'If a society does not grow it is because no incentives are provided for economic initiative' (North and Thomas 1972). If people work hard, the argument goes, success follows, and the economy prospers. For this to hold, people's effort must be productive; simply redistributing income from others does not increase the size of the pie. Some observers attributed the weakness of the United States' economy, at times, cynically to the high number of lawyers relative to the number of engineers. Baumol (1990) writes 'the allocation of entrepreneurship between productive and unproductive activities, though by no means the only pertinent influence, can have a profound effect on the innovativeness of the economy and the degree of dissemination of its technological discoveries'. Thanks to technological progress, productivity increases and costs fall. With output and income rising for a given amount of input, the supply curve shifts to the right, which in turn can trigger growth effects.

The influence of institutions, in a nutshell, can be summarized as 'institutions played a necessary role in making possible economic growth and political freedom' (North and Weingast 1989).

How Do Institutions Come into Being?

One might expect that similar countries would feature very similar institutions; surprisingly this is not the case. Why are big differences in the design of institutions from country to country observed? Social factors such as tradition and population density, but also technology, plays a role—and so does chance.

Social Factors

A society establishes institutions according to its needs under the given circumstances. One of the influencing factors is likely to be population density. It is easy to imagine that life in crowded cities calls for different institutions than life in rural areas. North and Thomas (1973, 8) identify institutional innovations triggered by population growth as the main cause of the Industrial Revolution.

At first sight, one might believe that institutions would be designed to best serve society as a whole. Unfortunately, this is not the case, because several obstacles stand in the way: limited knowledge, divergent interests of different social groups, chance and the inertia of institutions, even when circumstances have changed and adjustments would be appropriate. Institutions are designed in such a way that they appear advantageous or at least acceptable to the relevant social circles. Again, property law may be cited as an example; it was written, of course, by the propertied class, not by the poor. The interests of large sections of society were often more clearly reflected in institutions during prosperous periods of history than in others; think of ancient Athens and the Commercial Revolution in medieval Venice, and later in England and the Netherlands.

Technology

One determinant of institutions is technology in its broadest sense (Allen 2012). Modern technology, with its ability to reduce dependence on external influences such as the weather and its means to specify and monitor the content of contracts, allows for very different arrangements than in the past. Just 100 years ago, it would have been completely unthinkable for anyone in a foreign country to be able to make contactless, on-the-spot payments in the local currency using a means of payment issued in their home currency. Less well-known, but perhaps more important, is the introduction of real-time gross settlement (RTGS) payment systems such as FEDWIRE, made possible by advances in information technology (IT). These ensure that only liquid banks make payments, thereby precluding the need to reverse payments already made after a participant in the payment system has turned out to be illiquid. Technical progress often provides opportunities to modify institutions.

Technology here refers not only to the possibilities of production, but is understood in a broad sense. How one can communicate over small and large distances; language, writing, units of measurement and standards, are all shaped by technology. Also, whether and how, and above all how quickly, one can get from one place to another is a question of technology—and also, whether it is possible to control traffic and levy charges or customs duties. The development from tally stick to writing, to double-entry bookkeeping, to printing, to debt registers, to computers and to block chain, are all technological developments.

Other Factors

There are certainly other determinants of institutions, some perhaps more profound than those mentioned above, but there is no need to explore them for the purpose of this essay. Mokyr, for example, also considers culture as a factor influencing institutions (Mokyr 2017). One determinant, however, cannot be ignored: chance. It shapes lives more than most are willing to admit. Humans try to find meaning and purpose behind events and therefore fail to recognize the role of chance. Institutions may emerge along the same principle as biological evolution: random variation and survival of the fittest. People often have no explanation or completely wrong explanations for their customs (Henrich 2016), which often result from cultural adaptation without anyone really understanding the forces at work and the processes going on. Man is known to often overlook the unintended consequences of his decisions. Thus, it is not to be expected that he can easily make his institutions purposeful and expedient. One can only hope that the probability of beneficial variation is higher than in biology. An example of detrimental variation is the ban on interest. The Church's justification at the time for money not yielding fruit, indicates that people did not understand the essence of a loan—nobody takes out a loan to let the money sit in a safe-deposit box.

An example of an institution that found its purpose via a detour is patent protection. Initially patent protection was not at all granted with the intention of providing an incentive to invent new techniques and inventors could not expect to cover their costs with patent revenues. In England, patents were initially granted to bring into the country techniques already existing abroad (North, Thomas in Baumol, Strom 2010). Apparently only later did it dawn on the leader of the Industrial Revolution that the institution of patents could be used to develop genuinely new techniques. The example also shows that the function of one and the same institution can change. Further, remarkable features of intellectual property are its spatial and temporal limits: it is only valid within certain jurisdictions, and even there it has an expiry date after which anyone can dispose of it. In other areas, an expiry date on ownership would be considered objectionable (contra bonos mores).

Institutions normally resist change once they are established, especially if they are morally or religiously dressed up. But they do evolve over time, and in crisis even abrupt institutional changes occur. A recent example of such a crisis is the collapse of the Eastern bloc and the USSR.

One can expect the influence of chance to be quite significant in the short run and to fade into the background in the long run. The fundamental relationships are therefore more easily visible when long periods are observed.

The Framework in Summary

Assuming a set of prevailing social conditions and a given technology, a society develops certain institutions (e.g. property rights and markets). The design of the institutions, in turn, influences people's behaviour; and that behaviour determines a society's economic success, its prosperity. Finally, this economic success allows, in a favourable case, technological progress, which closes a feedback loop and might allow a step forward in the evolution of institutions. In addition, the improvement in technology can directly feed and stimulate prosperity. It is important to note that time lags and random influences, large and small, blur the effect. Figure 6.1 illustrates the indirect relationship between institutions and prosperity.

It is difficult to advance technology and it is difficult to change behaviour permanently; presumably, it is easier to change institutions. If institutions can indeed be modified and the above model is able to describe reality adequately, then institutions are the key to prosperity. The opportunities to influence institutions may be restricted and arise only occasionally, but the chances of success seem to be highest with the institutions. With appropriate institutions in place, prosperity can arise spontaneously, or as Olson (1982) put it: 'it takes an enormous

Figure 6.1: Important influences on prosperity

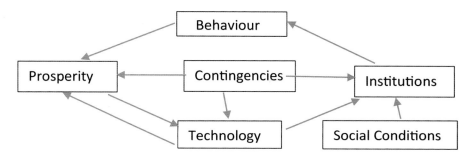

Source: Author

amount of stupid policies or bad or unstable institutions to prevent economic development'. The next part discusses possible starting points and directions for institutional reform.

Part III: Possible Starting Points for Institutional Reforms

Evolution tends to favour societies with appropriate institutions, but from this, it does not follow that the most appropriate institutions will spontaneously prevail. The general goal is to establish socially beneficial institutions. To achieve it, simply put, it would be necessary to design the rules in such a way that everyone bears all the consequences of their actions—the consequences for themselves and also those felt by others. In economic slang: the private rate of return has to be equal to the social rate of return.

Controllability

To some extent, institutions can be amended deliberately, but the scope for targeted design of institutions is limited. Olson (1982), for example, has pointed out that interest groups have a strong incentive to assert their particular interests at the expense of the general public. This explains why a small number of producers usually have a stronger lobby than a large number of consumers. To what extent can one design institutions selectively? Targeting institutions certainly requires a thorough understanding of what an institution does and whom it ultimately serves and how much. Some institutions do not actually serve those they pretend to serve. Alleged consumer protection sometimes hinders competition and serves producers or regulators more than consumers. With an understanding of the effects of an institution, one can assess how a modification would affect interest groups and whether it would be socially desirable. If this is the case, then the question of acceptance arises.

The evolution of institutions is also sluggish because those negatively affected by a change feel generally stronger than the potential beneficiaries. This could be due to the fact that man hates losses more than he loves gains of the same size.

Chances of Success

Where should one start, in practice, to increase opportunities for growth? Firstly, opportunities arise where institutions proven under similar circumstances can be adopted. Since there is always a danger that institutions are adopted merely as a sham, it is particularly important to check whether the conditions for success are in place. Obviously, it takes more than just holding elections to bring about democracy. Secondly, there are opportunities where conditions of life have changed. In particular, advances in technological progress, strong growth, globalization and urbanization call for a review of institutions. Third, opportunities exist where interests or the balance of power have shifted. England is an example where, since *Magna Carta*, ascending classes have increasingly succeeded in limiting the discretion of the king in favour of the general public. Today, the rise of the middle class in many countries raises hopes for a more inclusive society; but in others, the decline of the middle class is a reason for concern. Fourth, there is a prospect of change after positions have been filled with new people.

Under normal circumstances, a pragmatic approach in small steps is recommended. The exception to this are serious crises that have shaken up the entire social order. Then, for a short time, there is a small chance of the success of a big throw.

Selected Examples

The following sections highlight three broad areas of possible reform: the market, public goods and the government, a particularly important public good. After that, it addresses the obstacles that stand in the way and finally ask how to preserve reforms that have been achieved.

The Role of Markets

Markets are central institutions that contribute greatly to prosperity. Markets serve to direct goods to the most useful use and increase the efficiency of the economy. This mechanism is Adam Smith's famous invisible hand. The market is one of several ways of dealing with scarcity. Its attractiveness lies in its potential to meet above aspiration that people fully bear the consequences of their action and to charge the price of the second most valuable use of the traded item. Where the problem of allocating scarce goods is solved by other methods, such as queues, one has to wonder if the market can't do it better. Congestion pricing allows to move forward to those willing to pay in cash, it reduces pollution and brings money into the coffers, which can be used to expand capacity or compensate those who choose not to use the road. Waste charges based on quantity instead of flat rates have reduced waste in many places.

Ideally, society offers suitable institutions to its members so that markets can develop wherever the conditions for their functioning are passably met. Important preconditions for well-functioning markets are competition, a certain form of production costs and clear property rights. Markets can be developed along with property rights. Consider commons, an area where property rights by definition are absent. Sometimes commons are overused because individuals do not take into account that their use of the commons reduces the yield of all others (cf. Hardin 1968). To avoid overuse of commons, a community may, among other options, sell rights to use the common. Examples are fishing quotas, radio frequencies or taxi licenses. In doing so, a monopoly might be granted and the pros and cons should be considered. A further important consideration should be the duration period of the license. Should it be for an unlimited period of time or defined in advance? The value of the licence may fluctuate and trend upwards. A due date gives future generations a chance to reconsider. One example is the city of Zurich, which mainly grants sixty-five-year-long building leases on state-owned land instead of selling it outright. In Iceland, however, fishing quotas allocated in 1984 have in the meantime found new owners so that local residents are no longer allowed to fish along the coast.

Proposals for the evolution of markets are on the table. Posner and Weyl (2019) raise the idea of competitive common ownership of land. The proposal is indeed radical, but absolutely in the spirit of the market economy, and an unprejudiced discussion could inspire the debate.

The attractive thing about the market economy is that the overall welfare is maximized automatically if everyone acts in their self-interest. However, this is only the case under certain conditions, which are often violated. Then (and only then) one speaks of market failure. In these cases, regulatory intervention is required. Economic theory has long since developed appropriate prescriptions for the various types of market failure, so there is no need to delve into them here. What needs to be stressed here, however, is that technological breakthroughs have led to a general decrease in marginal costs of production with tendencies toward monopolization and widespread increase in external effects. This is particularly true of computer technology, which offers new opportunities for price differentiation. This calls for stricter regulation and adjustment of institutions.

Public Goods

There are significant areas of the economy where the market does not function and cannot be made to function by regulation. One of these is the increasingly important area of so-called public goods. Public goods are goods and services that, once provided, are available to everybody in an area, whether people pay for them or not. The textbook example of a public good is national defence, however, the establishment of a social order with its institutions is a less often mentioned but much more fundamental public good. Today, climate preservation may be the most elusive public good. It is symptomatic that there is a struggle to do enough to preserve the climate, and that it is questionable whether the endeavour will succeed.

One can ask whether roads meet the conditions for public goods. Traditionally, this was the case, and road tolls have a smack of robber baronism. With large investments in bridges, tunnels and motorways, to which access can be controlled at reasonable cost, user charges emerged in some places, and today some roads can hardly be described as public goods because of traffic congestion. The technology developed in recent decades offers new opportunities for road pricing, some of which are already being implemented.

In the case of public goods, the homo economicus fails because of the collective action problem. If everyone only maximizes his own egoistic benefit, then no one is willing to contribute to the community without compensation. But this is necessary, as without such a commitment, a community is dysfunctional because homo economicus tries to free-ride and the provision of public goods collapses. What is needed is a civil society made up of citizens with a sense of community who are prepared to do something for the public good. This idea corresponds to the model of the homo reciprocans, who is willing to return a favour or to punish antisocial behaviour. Fehr and Gächter (1998) show that many people behave as homo reciprocans and they consider it a key force that sustains social norms. An external threat, such as a virus, may help to bring this trait to bear in a good sense. Whether cooperation then becomes permanently established is another question. The introduction of homo reciprocans does not, however, solve the problem of public goods because it is by no means always clear that an action for the good of the community actually promotes the common good. It may be true in an extended family, but in a more complex community, it no longer is: good intentions and good behaviour do not guarantee a good outcome. The paradox of thrift is a case in point: if every individual saves a bigger share of income, the aggregate savings decline.

To date, no generally applicable procedure exists that would ensure an optimal supply of public goods; these exist only for rather unrealistic special cases. Public goods have to be procured by a political decision and paid for with public funds (tax money or soccage). The provision of public goods should maximize the social benefit. For two reasons, it is difficult to find out what utility a certain amount of a public good provides. First, many people do not want to reveal their needs truthfully, and second, it is unclear how the utility of different people can be aggregated into an overall utility. One method that gives reasonable results is the cost benefit analysis. Any use of public funds must be justifiable by a neutral observer as the procurement of a public good.

Political decisions often contain an element of redistribution, and sometimes, decisions are even deliberately politicized in order to make redistribution feasible. Redistribution entails the danger of efficiency losses and waste of resources—in the trenchant terminology of Jacobs (1984) 'transactions of decline'. However, redistribution can also increase efficiency and release constructive forces if it enables steps towards equality of opportunity. In the literature this goes under the keywords 'inclusiveness' and 'open access order' (cf. Acemoglu and Robinson 2012; North, Wallis and Weingast 2009). Moreover, primary distribution is not necessarily equitable, and humanitarian reasons can also justify (temporary) redistribution. The question of equitable distribution can only be posed here, it cannot be answered. Redistribution must certainly meet ethical standards and in principle, requires qualified majority. Transparency (publicity and clarity) with regard to the redistributive effects of decisions can establish trust. Therefore, the redistributive effects of political decisions should be disclosed.

The Government

The most important provider of public goods is the government. How it comes into power opens a wide array of institutional questions of capital importance that deserve particular attention. In a democracy, it has to be decided whether it should be a direct or an indirect democracy and how the government should be elected. Multi-stage election procedures with run-offs can easily lead to a winner the majority would reject. In ancient Athens, the majority could send an undesirable politician into exile through ostracism. The trouble of a minority dominating a majority can also occur in majoritarian voting, especially if the constituencies are conveniently gerrymandered.

Any form of democracy requires a civil society and a critical mass of citizens willing to take responsibility and make a personal contributions to the community. In direct democracy, this mass must be especially high and the contributions particularly big. Collier (2018) writes: 'an informed electorate is the ultimate public good . . . most public goods can be provided by the state, but this one can only be provided by people themselves'.

An important question is, at which level of a state should certain competencies be located? The answer depends not only on the size of the country. If many public goods and externalities have a local or otherwise limited character, for example, safety in the streets at night, a partial devolution or some degree of federalism is called for. Italy has been able to increase government efficiency by delegating powers from the central state to the regions (cf. Putnam et al. 1993). By contrast, if important public goods transcend national borders, then binding decisions would ideally be made at a supranational level. In principle, a decision should be taken at that political level which corresponds to the group of consumers of the public good in question. It is legitimate to ask whether it is necessary at all to make a decision at the political level. In Switzerland, a referendum was held in 2021, initiated by a citizen who wanted to abolish the election of federal judges by parliament and turn it over to professionals. This would have reduced the influence of political parties and given candidates who are not members of a party a higher chance of success. Political bodies often resort to quotas when filling vacancies. This suggests that loyalty is more important than competence in the office in question.

This chapter has looked at public expenditure. What must not be forgotten is government revenue, that is, taxes. What is taxed and how are as important as spending itself. Tax issues are not only about equity but also about efficiency, because taxes usually entail distortions that can lead to huge misallocations. These can be avoided with a poll tax, which is socially unacceptable, or by taxing so-called economic rents only, which is hardly possible. Economic rents are the difference between the price paid and what an economic agent would have been willing to pay or what a seller would have been satisfied with, e.g. windfall profits. The fact that the ideal of distortion-free taxation is unlikely ever to be achieved, need not be a worry, but the fact that there has been movement away from it in recent decades with ever higher tax rates, the spread of VAT and ever more complicated tax rules, should be a serious concern. Arnold Harberger (1974) made an illustrious proposal fifty years ago to drastically simplify wealth taxation; it looks frighteningly radical and has not yet been taken up seriously anywhere. As an aside, periodic auctions of licenses should also be considered as sources of government revenue.

Obstacles and Dangers

What are the obstacles and dangers standing in the way of improving institutions and how can good institutions be preserved? A society where patronage and clientelism prevail has a long road ahead of it to modern institutions. North, Wallis and Weingast (2009) claim that an open, democratic society, which they call open access order, is the end point of a long social development and suggest that it remains stable over time. After the experience of the last decade in quite a number of countries, one must have doubts about this claim. In history, a pattern can be observed again and again: that after decades—in a few cases, centuries—of upswing, relative or absolute decline sets in. What are the reasons for this pattern? It seems that after a period of prosperity, an upper class often manages to gain the upper hand at the expense of the general public. The so-called 'Serrata del Maggior Consiglio' of 1297 was the beginning of the decline of Venice brought about by the existing elite. It shut out major parts of society from the legislature. Switzerland has done comparatively well so far by carefully avoiding giving too much power to anyone. This has probably helped to include all relevant social forces and align interests, at the cost of a sluggish and delayed development of institutions. The greatest challenges are likely to keep the interests of the power elite in check and, if necessary, bringing in a 'blocking minority' demanding concessions to behave constructively.

Finally, a last obstacle should be mentioned. This chapter has often simply spoken of community, without specifying exactly which community is meant. Of course, there are many diverse communities that consume a public good, and these communities overlap. So, drawing boundaries is difficult. How are boundaries to be drawn between neighbourhoods, cities, local states, nations, linguistic communities, etc.? It is impossible to build a single hierarchy that reflects the relations between those communities, so how can their cooperation be ensured? These are important but very difficult questions, and addressing them is way beyond the scope of this chapter.

Recommendations to Emerging Markets

Can specific recommendations for emerging markets be derived from the above? That cannot be the purpose of a chapter as general as this; it is enough of a challenge to try to point out how and where to look for opportunities. An attempt to make recommendations can, of course, never do justice to the vastly different circumstances in emerging markets. Nor can it take into account the fact that opportunities for reform arise only occasionally. Of course, it would be important to take account of local circumstances and to time reform initiatives. With these caveats in mind, the following attempts to indicate the direction in which steps towards institutional reform should be read.

Emerging markets have high growth potential and if the growth does not materialize, one has to wonder what institutions are hindering production in the country. The reason is most likely that productive entrepreneurship is not worthwhile, whether because of state bureaucracy and corruption; because a mafia skims off the profits; or because young people in the country see no future and emigrate en masse. The only way to remedy this situation is to change the institutions in such a way that efforts are not directed towards redistribution and destruction, but towards increasing the size of the pie.

A common feature of many emerging markets is a split society, a concentration of power in the authorities and excessive bureaucracy. In such countries, people feel more like minor subjects of the powerful and less like citizens with rights and duties. Fighting bureaucracy is an uphill battle; bureaucrats love complicated and lengthy procedures. Bureaucrats are not led by an invisible hand, they do not earn the fruits of their deeds, nor do they bear the costs. Even with the best of intentions, they expand their activity beyond what is reasonable and have no incentive to shrink it when appropriate. They cannot be expected to find the thin line between insufficient and excessive fulfilment of tasks. For instance, if a certain activity, say driving a car, should be reserved to people with proven skills, then it may make sense to verify that candidates meet certain standards, but does it make sense to regulate by law the training to acquire those skills? Good bureaucrats have little doubts that it does.

Where private enterprise is hampered by red tape or petty corruption, people should be given incentives to take countermeasures. If bureaucratic procedures can be simplified so that people understand them and could apply them themselves, they can at least resist arbitrariness. One can also try to transfer control to those directly affected, they have the greatest interest in keeping bureaucrats in check. An institution with considerable success in protecting citizens' rights is the ombudsman.

In order to develop a civil society, the entire mindset of people has to change. It is easier to start this endeavour on a small scale with local self-government in a village or a town, and then extend it to a region and the whole country. When people are involved and see how their taxes are spent, and can perhaps even influence it, they are more likely to take responsibility for the community and shape it constructively. Inclusion is also helped when redistribution moves resources towards equality of opportunity and if the people are not simply tranquilized by bread and circuses. The modern equivalent of handing out bread would be, for example, subsidizing fuel. It should not be the task of the state to feed its inhabitants in normal times.

The worst case of a split society is a state captured by an oligarchy, the military, the secret service or religious group that has installed a charismatic populist leader. Then, grand corruption, government capture of parliament and the judiciary and a selective application of law are common. These countries can be considered lucky if they only remain stuck in the middle-income trap because it could be much worse. State capture can end in full-blown disasters, as the cases of the Third Reich and Venezuela show.

In emerging markets, the implementation of agreed measures sometimes seems to be difficult. There might be ways to secure implementation of reforms from the outside. The conditionality of international financial institution loans is one example, but its credibility is often questioned. A well-known means of preventing inflationary government financing through the printing press is a currency board, where money issued must be backed one-to-one by balances of the associated currency. The correct implementation of agreements between rival factions can also be guaranteed by external auditors or neutral administrators, such as the podestà in medieval Genoa. For example, from 1997 to 2004, the central bank governor of Bosnia Herzegovina was a foreigner, because the locals did not allow entrusting the post to a member of another ethnic group in their own country. Romer (2018) cites an example of how corruption was reduced in Hong Kong with the help of an authority that was independent of local political forces and accountable only to the British prime minister. Such mechanisms can only be about ensuring the implementation of agreements, never about pushing through reforms that are not fundamentally desirable.

Summary and Conclusion

In summary, it must be stated that there is no silver bullet for prosperity, one can only try to create better preconditions for a prosperous economy. Prosperity depends on the behaviour of people. If a society does not grow, it is because no incentives are provided for economic initiative.

The designing of institutions sets incentives and determines people's behaviour. Institutions are shaped by social forces according to the prevailing technical possibilities; in the process, their economic effects are often not foreseen, and even supposedly minor differences can have a massive impact over time. Institutions can be deliberately influenced, but politics constrain the scope of available choices.

To increase prosperity, one should start with institutions. There are opportunities in particular:
- when proven institutions can be copied,
- when circumstances have changed,
- when interests or the balance of power have shifted,
- after positions are filled.

The institutions should be developed towards promoting social interest. In many areas, free markets are the best precondition for prosperity. There, the state should not inhibit, but rather support trade. In the modern world, however, political decisions are increasingly needed to correct market failure and to procure the right quantity of public goods. A cost-benefit analysis is a useful indicator of social interest. Public goods should be decided at the political level that corresponds to the group of consumers of the goods in question. Where red tape hampers private enterprise, notably in emerging markets, the parties affected should be given incentives to take action.

The vagaries of life and uncertainty open up many opportunities for special interests to politicize decisions. Keeping them in check is the greatest challenge. Effort is therefore needed just to maintain the conditions; improving them requires insight, leadership and perseverance—for the emerging markets even more than for others.

Chapter 7: Two Faces of Development—Rising Incomes Combined with Increasing Inequities, and Policies to Address the Latter

Two Faces of Development—Rising Incomes Combined with Increasing Inequities and Policies to Address the Latter

Chapter 7

Jose Fajgenbaum and Ieva Vilkelyte

'No society can surely be flourishing and happy, of which the far greater part of the members are poor and miserable.'
—Adam Smith

Introduction

Since WWII, the world has experienced unparalleled economic prosperity, as evidenced by economic, social and political indicators. Since the 1980s, the faster growth rates of Emerging Market and Developing Economies (EMDEs) than those of Advanced Economies (AEs) contributed to this prosperity and resulted in a narrowing of the income per capita gap across countries. At the same time, income inequality within countries has risen significantly in AEs and many EMDEs, reflecting both a decline in the income share of the lowest 40 per cent of households and a large increase in the income share of the richest households. This increase in inequality reflects a new wave of major technological changes that started in the early 1980s, such as the technological and digital/communication revolution and the financial services reform. These technological changes benefitted the skilled and the risk-takers, while leaving behind large swathes of the population. Other developments such as globalization, reductions in safety nets and declines in income tax progressivity contributed to the increases in inequality.

The unprecedented and synchronized shock of the COVID-19 pandemic accentuated inequality within countries and reversed progress in reducing inequality between countries, as shown by the latest IMF WEO. Moreover, the AEs are recovering to pre-pandemic output levels rather quickly while most EMDEs (except China) are taking longer to recover to those levels. Using the baseline scenario of the Centennial Growth Model (CGM), the third section shows that the income gap between countries will come down as EMDEs, as a group, start to grow again faster than the AEs. It also shows the increase in the number of poor caused by the pandemic and estimates of how long it will take to eliminate such an increase, by income group and region.

With the above as background, and in response to the question why inequality and especially growing inequality should be a concern for policymakers, the fourth section briefly reviews the literature, which points to the adverse effects of inequality on, inter alia, economic growth, social fabric including wide dissatisfaction and crime and political stability.

The fifth section discusses policies that could help reduce inequality and build an inclusive society, recognizing that equity issues are complex and intertwined with social values and moral views of fairness and social justice, and suggesting that individual countries (or regions) may have different perceptions of what is equitable. The goal is that policies go beyond just supplementing people's income through government transfers, they should seek to increase access to opportunities and thereby equalize income or vice versa. The menu of possible policies goes from improving the quality and access to education and health, starting at an early age, to removing gender discrimination in education and labour markets, to the provision of targeted but conditional transfers (like Bolsa Familia in Brazil). To help finance some of these policies there is a need to enhance the efficiency of government spending and to increase revenue to ensure fiscal sustainability. The section ends with a brief discussion on the roles of the private sector and the international community, and the sixth section concludes the discussion.

Developments and Trends Pre-COVID-19 Pandemic

Global Inequality Trends

Multiple methodologies exist for measuring global and national income inequality, ranging from the GINI coefficient, a number between 0 and 1 (or 0 and 100 per cent) with zero representing perfect equality and 1 (or 100 per cent) indicating complete inequality, to comparisons of incomes shares of the top 1 or 10 per cent income earners versus the income earners at the bottom 10 or 50 per cent. This chapter primarily focuses on the GINI coefficient, utilizing data obtained from the World Income Inequality Database as it provides a comprehensive dataset covering 1950–2019.[1]

Inter-country Inequality

Using the GINI index as a key measure of income inequality, global overall inequality was relatively stable with very few fluctuations through most of the second half of the twentieth century and only began declining in the 1990s and has lasted through the first two decades of this century (Figure 7.1). This decline reflects a considerable drop in the disparity in per capita incomes

Figure 7.1: World GINI

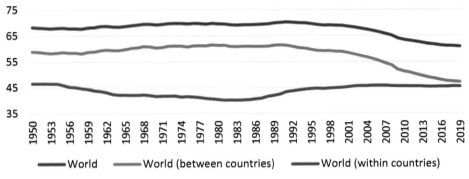
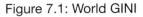

Source: UNU-WIDER 2021

---

1. Other sources include the World Bank's GINI Index, which utilizes PovcalNet data based on primary household survey data, and the World Income Inequality Database which utilizes a compilation of source data including the Luxembourg Income Study Database (LIS) as its main source, some regional sources (ECLAC and SEDLAC for Latin America and Eurostat for the EU), national sources and PovcalNet.

between AE and EMDEs that more than offset the growing trend in inequality within countries. Over most of these decades, EMDEs saw significant increases in their per capita incomes, with China and India having a particularly large impact. The beginning of a convergence of EMDEs per capita incomes with those of AEs has been key in the decline of the world GINI.

The high growth rates of EMDEs over the last several decades are reflected in the breakdown of world per capita income growth from 1980 to 2020 by income per centile group —the 'elephant chart'.[2] Globally, the bottom 50 per cent (mostly comprising the populations of EMDEs) had some of the highest rates of income growth during this period (Figure 7.2), translating into the large decline in inter-country inequality.

Figure 7.2: Total income growth by percentile, world, 1980-2020

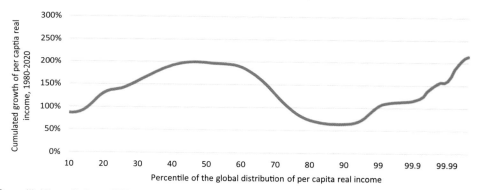

Source: World Inequality Report 2022

Within-country Inequality

In contrast to inter-country inequality, within-country income inequality, the inequality most people perceive, has been on an upward trajectory since the mid-1980s (Figure 7.1). This has occurred both in EMDEs and AEs. Notably, some of the largest economies, such as India, China, and the United States, have faced and continue to face increasing inequality (Figure 7.3). In addition, 'there is a growing gap between low- and middle-income households, which is particularly pronounced in Finland, Israel, Sweden, Spain and the US'.[3]

The fast-rising incomes of the top income groups have contributed to this trend in both AEs and EMDEs. The share of income of the top 10 per cent of earners has dramatically increased in several large AEs and EMDEs (including China, Germany, India, Indonesia, Japan, and the United States) (Figure 7.4). For example, the top 10 per cent of earners receive 45 per cent of national income in the United States and nearly 60 per cent in India, compared to 35 and 32 per cent, respectively, in 1980. This trend is also reflected by the top 1 per cent of earners.[4]

---

2. The 'elephant chart' was first published in 2013 (Lakner and Milanovic 2013) and has been since updated by multiple sources.
3. https://www.oecd.org/economy/growth-and-inequality-close-relationship.htm
4. Although, this chapter focuses on income inequality, it should be noted that these trends are also seen in wealth concentration, the share of wealth controlled by the top 1 and top 10 per cent of wealth holders has increased since the mid-1990s. In China, India, and the United States the wealthiest 10 per cent now hold 68, 65 and 71 per cent of wealth compared to 40, 55,and 65, respectively, in 1995 (WID 2021).

The global elephant chart (Figure 7.2) indicates that this trend is worldwide: the top 1 per cent of earners have had the highest growth rate during the past four decades and have captured almost 2.5 times as much growth as the bottom 50 per cent and have had significantly higher growth rates than the middle class of AEs, corresponding to those in the seventy-fifth to the ninety-ninth percentile, which fared the worst in terms of income growth (WID 2021).

Figure 7.3: GINI—Select countries

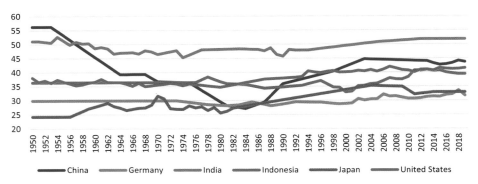

Source: UNU-WIDER 2021

Figure 7.4: Share of income earned by top 10 per cent of earners

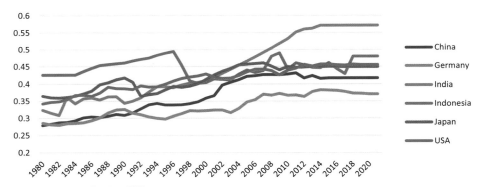

Source: World Inequality Database 2021

Income inequality impacts many economic and social trends, such as social mobility, education, and life expectancy. For example, countries with higher income inequality also tend to have lower intergenerational economic mobility, indicating that there is a lack of equality of opportunity in countries with high inequality (Corak 2012). Additionally, higher inequality rates are also tied to larger gaps in educational levels and shorter life expectancies for different income groups.

There is not one explanation for why inequality within countries has increased since the mid-1980s, but there are several interconnected factors that have contributed to the increase:

- Technological change, which has negatively impacted low-skill workers and at the same time increased the demand for high-skill workers and, therefore, higher earnings;
- Financial sector reforms that involved a major transformation of the sector a shift to highly skilled workers;
- Decreasing the share of labour in GDP (Autor et al. 2017) as wages have not kept up with GDP, including because of a decline in unionization—and the increase of firms with large market shares;
- Low taxation of multinational corporations (Tørsløv 2018);
- Fiscal policies became less progressive, including reductions in income tax progressivity and in safety nets;
- International competition due to globalization has kept wages of the low-skilled, low.

Regional Trends

Regional inequality trends followed the global pattern of staying relatively stable from post-WWII to the mid-1980s to early-1990s (Figure 7.5), after which they diverged.[5] East Asia and the Pacific experienced a significant decline, of nearly 30 per cent, in inequality over the last three decades. This can be largely attributed to declines in several populous countries in the region. Unlike the region as a whole, China has recently experienced an increase in inequality. While inequality had significantly declined in China from 1950 to the mid-1980s, these gains have been partially reduced in the past thirty-five years. The reduction has been attributed to 'widening of the rural–urban income gap, and the increase in income from property and assets, driven by the development of urban residential real-estate markets, the expansion of stock and capital markets, the growth of private enterprises, and other property rights' (Alvaredo and Gasparini 2015). Inequality in Latin America started a declining trend in the late 1990s with several reasons theorized as the cause, such as 'improved macroeconomic conditions that fostered employment, the petering out of the unequalizing effects of the reforms in the 1990s, the expansion of coverage in basic education, stronger labour institutions, the recovery of some countries from severe unequalizing crises, and a more progressive allocation of government spending, in particular monetary transfers' (Alvaredo and Gasparini 2015). The commodity boom during the 2000s to mid-2010s also played a key role, expanding labour and wages, and positively affecting other sectors of the economies (IMF 2018).

While having some of the highest inequality rates in the world, Sub-Saharan Africa has recorded a gradual decline in inequality since the 1980s, owing to improved macroeconomic performance and reforms, the impact of debt reductions under the HIPC and MDRI initiatives and the commodity boom mentioned above (Alvaredo and Gasparini 2015). South Asia has had lower income inequality compared to other developing regions; however, inequality has begun to gradually rise since the 1970s with various causes cited, including strong growth owing to structural reforms. The growing wage divide between rural-urban regions, industry-agriculture sectors, and low-skill and high-skill workers has contributed to increasing inequality in South Asia (Alvaredo and Gasparini 2015). Another important contributing factor is the educational attainment gap, which government policies have not sufficiently addressed.

---

5. Except for the Middle East and North Africa region, where inequality increased from 1950 through 1970, declined for the following two decades, and then was relatively stable.

Figure 7.5: Regional GINI

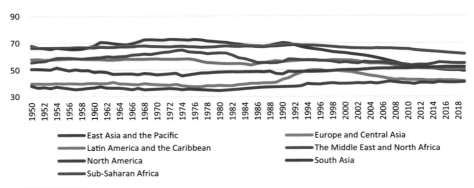

East Asia and the Pacific   **Europe and Central Asia**
Latin America and the Caribbean   **The Middle East and North Africa**
North America   **South Asia**
Sub-Saharan Africa

Source: UNU-WIDER 2021

The large increase in world inequality within countries in the early 1990s can partly be explained by the effect of the dissolution of the Soviet Union. Former Soviet States, particularly Russia and Ukraine, experienced significant increases in inequality in the early 1990s, which translated into the bump in Europe and Central Asia's GINI coefficient (Figure 7.5). This is also confirmed by PovcalNet data which indicates that the mean GINI 'grew from 26.4 in 1990 to 31.9 in 1996' and this increase was attributed to the 'process of privatization, which implied an increase in earnings dispersion in comparison to the more compressed wage structure of the state-owned firms' (Alvaredo and Gasparini 2015).

The sustained increase in global within-country inequality can also be attributed to the increase in inequality in AEs, particularly in North America and Europe. For example, 'all of the 9 advanced economies that are members of the G20 saw the GINI coefficient of disposable income rise between the early- to mid-1980s and 2013' (Dervis and Qureshi 2017). Several causes of this include 'globalization, technological change favouring higher-level skills and capital, structural changes in labour markets, the rising importance of finance, the emergence of winner-take-all markets, and policy changes such as shifts toward less progressive fiscal regimes' (Qureshi 2017).

Varying Methodologies, Similar Trends

Irrespective of the varying methodologies and data sources to measure inequality, they lead to similar conclusions and results regarding inequality—historical trends and its current state. Income share trends display similar trends to the GINI coefficient. For example, the income share of the global bottom 50 per cent has slightly increased since 1980 (Figure 7.6). Similarly, according to this indicator, Europe and North America have been the most equal (the bottom 50 per cent having the largest share of income compared to other regions) and Sub-Saharan Africa one of the most unequal.

Additionally, comparing the average income of the 10 per cent to that of the bottom 50 per cent shows globally that inequality has declined over the past two decades, similar to the decline seen in the global inter-country GINI index over the last three decades (Figure 7.7).

Figure 7.6: Income share of bottom 50 per cent

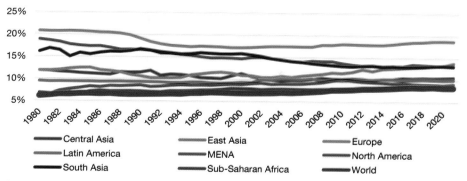

Source: World Inequality Database 2021

Figure 7.7: T10/B50 ratio between the global average income of the top 10 per cent and the average income of the bottom 50 per cent

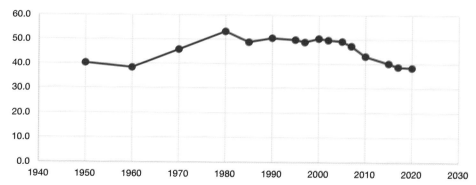

Source: World Inequality Report 2022

The Impact of the COVID-19 Pandemic on Inequality

The common perception is that the deep and synchronized shock of the COVID-19 pandemic accentuated global inequality because of its asymmetrical impact across and within countries.

The Pandemic and Inequality Across Countries

The IMF WEO (October 2021) shows that the COVID-19 pandemic has widened the income gap between AEs and the lower income countries, and that the gap would be larger than pre-pandemic times for a number of years, reversing temporarily the convergence trend of recent decades. The IMF WEO estimates that the output loss during 2020–22, compared with pre-COVID-19 projections, would be some 3.1 per cent for AEs, 3.9 per cent for EMDEs, and 6.0 per cent for low-income countries. To an extent, the varying output losses reflect the EMDEs' (and particularly the low-income countries) more limited space to mitigate the impact of the pandemic through fiscal[6] and credit policies than the AEs have had, and their more limited capacity to mobilize resources to stimulate the economic recovery. As a result, the recovery paths of these groups of countries will vary, with the former group taking longer than the latter.

To illustrate the significant longer-term differences in per capita GDP losses relative to the pre-pandemic baseline by income groups and by regions, the Centennial Growth Model (CGM) is used. Of course, the scenario is tentative at best, given the greatly uncertain path of the pandemic and its effects.

Even by 2030 the low-income countries will have lost 4.0 per cent of per capita GDP, nearly three times the loss of the EMDEs (excluding the low-income countries) and significantly higher than the loss of AEs (Figure 7.8). Figure 7.2, in turn, shows that by 2030 the loss in income per capita in Latin America and the Caribbean, the Middle East and Northern Africa, Europe and North America will be the lowest (less than 1 per cent) followed by the other regions (1–2 per cent), except for Sub-Saharan Africa which is expected to lose as much as 7 per cent. Eventually, EMDEs are expected to resume their faster growth rates than AEs, thereby return to the convergence process that prevailed prior to the pandemic.

Figure 7.8: Change (per cent) in GDP per capita PPP by 2030, 2040 and 2060 due to COVID-19 by income group

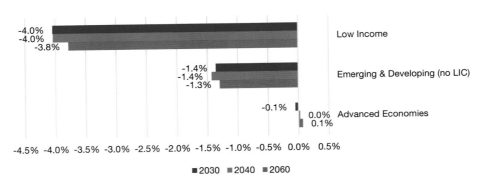

Source: Centennial Group 2021

The Pandemic and Inequality within Countries

A recent IMF study estimated that the impact of COVID-19 on income shares by quintiles (without reflecting any distribution policies or other factors) raised the average GINI coefficient of EMDEs by 2.6 per centage points to 42.7, broadly comparable to the level in 2018 (IMF 2020).

However, despite the absence of actual data such as GINI coefficients to assess the impact of the pandemic on income inequality within countries, there is a general perception that because of the COVID-19 pandemic most countries have seen a worsening of inequality,

---

6. The mitigation efforts, the decline in activity, and the already high public debt burden pre-pandemic are expected to cause EMDEs' public debt to rise to an all-time high of 65 per cent of GDP at end-2021. A large number of low-income countries is facing high risks of debt distress or is already in debt distress. This severe debt burden has the potential of further slowing these countries' recovery.

Figure 7.9: Change (per cent) in GDP per capita PPP by 2030, 2040 and 2060 due to COVID-19 by region

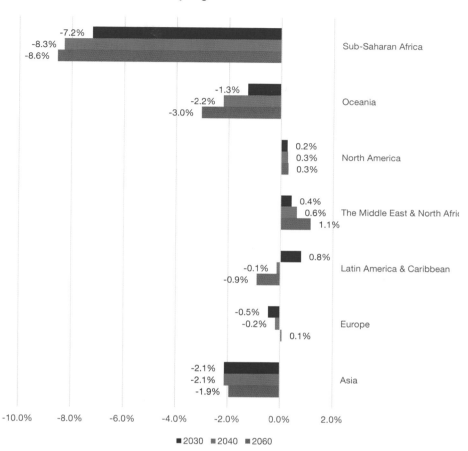

Source: Centennial Group 2021

halting or reversing the improvements achieved by EMDEs during recent decades. This perception reflects the considerable appreciations that benefitted holders of financial assets and real estate (partly owing to very low interest rates), and the differing impacts the cycles of lockdowns and containment measures have had on various income groups. For example, these measures have had limited adverse effects on the incomes of workers with skills and able to perform their jobs from home (activities that saw small rises in unemployment), while the majority of those that have not been able to work at home lost their jobs and livelihoods mostly because they are low-skilled or work in contact intensive activities (informal sectors, tourism and other services). Moreover, these measures have had considerable adverse effects on micro, small and medium sized enterprises, and on women and youth (a large number of them become unemployed or underemployed).

School closures have had a major negative impact on the build-up of human capital of the many students who have limited or no access to online education. The UNICEF estimated that 'school closures affected 253 million students, potential causing losses in learning' (UNICEF 2020) and human capital, hampering income earnings in the future. A recent study shows that online learning has caused a drop in academic performance and exacerbated the equity gap (Meckler and Natanson 2020). Keeping children out of school has pernicious effects—academically, socially, and mentally—with potentially lasting consequences. Anecdotal evidence from Zambia in 2020 suggests that being out of school six months raises the risk of students not returning to school, teen pregnancy, child marriage, and child labour, particularly for children from poor households or households economically impacted by COVID-19. Keeping children out of school has caused mothers to quit their jobs in the absence of childcare; in addition, with schools closed, children have not benefitted from school feeding programs, adding to the demand for food at home at a time when household income dwindled.

The World Bank's High Frequency Household Surveys, which have been conducted in low- and some middle-income countries, confirm the above and other broadly expected developments. For example, there has been a reduction in educational participation across the board, and many countries in Sub-Saharan Africa show that students in rural and lower income households have been less likely to engage in learning activities. In Vietnam, informal sectors have been substantially impacted by work disruptions, as have lower income households because of outright job losses; those in the top quintile were more likely to experience a reduction in wages. In Lao PDR, 17.8 per cent of workers with less than secondary education either have lost their jobs or have been forced to switch their jobs. In Indonesia, micro, small and medium size enterprises have reported difficulties in repaying loans, paying rents and wages. Lockdowns in South Africa affected equally the urban and rural areas, but the latter have taken longer to recover. Owing to restricted mobility of migrant workers (due to containment measures), households experienced sharp declines in domestic remittances (by as much as more than 50 per cent in Chad and Zambia). Similarly, international remittances also dropped sharply, disproportionately affecting low-income households. However, in Lao PDR, households with a head who completed secondary education were less likely to report a reduction in both domestic and international remittances.

As mentioned above, to mitigate the effects of the pandemic, most governments implemented measures that reinforced safety nets and supported incomes, such as cash transfers, food assistance and tax reduction, thereby avoiding major humanitarian crises. In the case of low- and low-middle-income countries, these measures were enhanced by the swift assistance of the international community. This assistance included the suspension of the debt service payments to bilateral creditors falling due from May 2020 to December 2021 (the Debt Service Suspension Initiative (DSSI) of the G20) and the provision of significant disbursements of concessional loans.

A recent study by the United Nations University World Institute for Development (Olivera et al. 2021) shows that tax benefits and mitigation measures were well targeted and did provide some income protection to poorest households in five Sub-Saharan African countries. Another study, by N. Lustig et al., used macrosimulation to estimate the (positive) distributional consequences of mitigation policies implemented in four Latin American countries, based on the economic sector in which household members work (Lustig et al. 2020). This study shows that the larger the mitigation package, the larger the positive results. However, given fiscal space constraints, most packages were likely insufficient to offset the increase in poverty. Moreover, as most assistance was focussed on the poorest households, many lower-middle income households fell into poverty.

To convey a sense of the impact and the lasting effect of the pandemic within countries, the Centennial Growth Model (CGM) estimates the increase in extreme poverty (both by regions and by country income groups) in 2020 and the lasting impact through 2040. While increases in poverty do not necessarily imply increases in inequality, it is generally known that the impact of the pandemic, lockdowns and measures to contain the pandemic, and the global recession disproportionately affected the lower income households, women and the young, and made them extremely poor. Based on the premise that the higher-skilled and wealthy retained their livelihoods or even experienced considerable gains, as indicated above, it could be assumed that increases in extreme poverty are a proxy to higher income inequality.

Compared to the pre-COVID-19 baseline, the CGM estimates that the pandemic pushed some 90 million people worldwide into extreme poverty in 2020 (Figure 7.10) under the threshold of US$1.90 a day treshold, 180 million under the US$3.10 a day threshold, and 220 million under the US$5.50 a day threshold. As noted above, these increases wiped out the progress made over the last five to ten years. Moreover, they suggest that the 2030 Sustainable Development Goals (SDGs) on Poverty and Inequality are unlikely to be achieved because the number of extreme poor due to the projected recovery will decline only gradually; reversing the increase in the number of poor globally, would take nearly forty years, under the thresholds just mentioned (Figure 7.10). Thereafter, as total factor productivity and thus long-term economic growth is

Figure 7.10: Change in number of people living in extreme poverty due to COVID-19

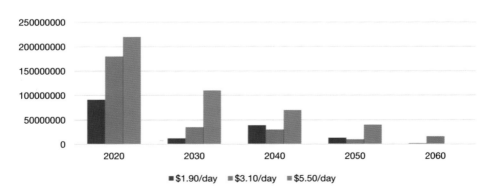

Source: Centennial Group 2021

JOSE FAJGENBAUM AND IEVA VILKELYTE

assumed to be higher than envisaged under the pre-COVID-19 baseline, the absolute number of poor worldwide starts to decline.[7]

The worldwide increase in the number of poor due to the pandemic masks large differences when looking at income groups of countries or regions. The change in the number of people living in extreme poverty due to COVID-19 by 2030 and by 2040, respectively, broken down by country income groups and by regions (Figures 7.11 and 7.12).

In terms of poverty, low-income countries, particularly those in Sub-Saharan Africa, are most negatively impacted by the pandemic through 2030. By 2040, the impact is lessened, however poverty rates are still considerably higher in Sub-Saharan Africa and Latin America and the Caribbean, compared to a no-COVID-19 scenario. Extreme poverty paths by income groups and regions persist through 2060, according to the daily US$1.90, US$3.10 and US$5.50 thresholds. After a sharp increase in the number of extreme poor in 2020, the number of extreme

Figure 7.11: Change in number of people living in extreme poverty due to COVID-19 by 2030

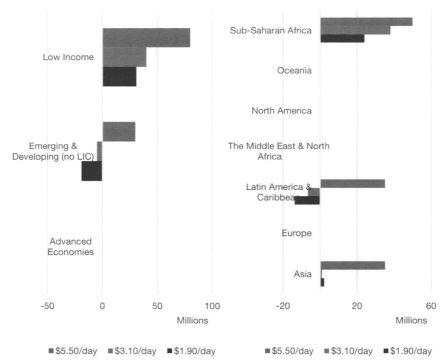

Source: Centennial Group 2021

---

7. Growth and recovery prospects are subject to considerable uncertainty and downside risks, such as emergence of new COVID-19 variants, availability of COVID-19 vaccines, persistent supply chain problems, soft commodity prices, rising interest rates and widening spreads, and severe climate events, with potentially different country impacts.

Figure 7.12: Change in number of people living in extreme poverty due to COVID-19 by 2040

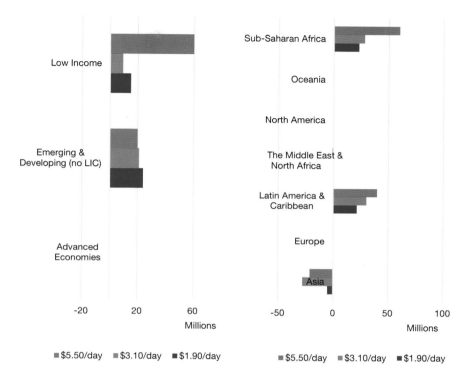

Source: Centennial Group 2021

7

TWO FACES OF DEVELOPMENT – RISING INCOMES COMBINED WITH INCREASING INEQUITIES AND POLICIES TO ADDRESS THE LATTER

poor (compared to a no-COVID-19 scenario) steadily decreases in all regions and country income groups. Figures 7.13 and 7.14 show that even by 2060 there will remain some 10 million extreme poor caused by the pandemic in low-income countries (mainly Sub-Saharan Africa), under the daily US$1.90 threshold, but no increase in the number of extreme poor caused by the pandemic in the other income groups or regions under the daily US$5.50 threshold.

Why Should Inequality, and Especially Growing Inequality, Be a Concern for Policy Makers?

With the previous two sections as background, this section briefly discusses why inequality or growing inequality should be policy makers' concern. In addition to ethical and solidarity considerations, the extensive literature on income inequality suggests several reasons, including adverse effects on economic growth; social fabric, including wide dissatisfaction and crime; and political stability. Underlying these effects is the fact or perception that the benefits of economic growth are not being shared equitably. In examining the channels through which inequality affects economic growth, research shows that inequality is associated with low human capital

Figure 7.13: Change in number of people living in extreme poverty due to COVID-19 by income group

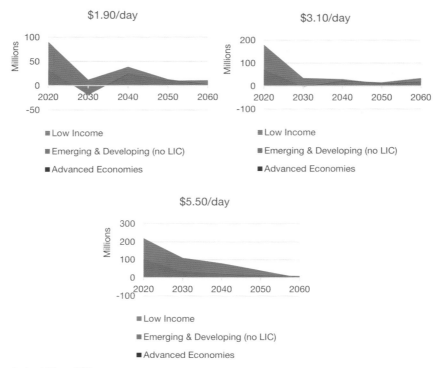

Source: Centennial Group 2021

formation and thus low growth. It also shows that very unequal societies tend to be politically and socially unstable, and have poor quality institutions, all of which are reflected in lower rates of investment and higher rates of corruption and cronyism (Easterly 2007). Although the adverse effects of inequality are discussed separately, many are closely linked and reinforce each other.

Economic Growth
After many studies with opposing findings regarding the relationship between income inequality and growth, the literature now leans more clearly towards the view that income inequality harms growth because of its association with poor human capital. Redistribution, inequality, and growth led to this change (Ostry, Berg, and Tsangarides 2014), as it identified human capital as the factor behind the negative relationship between income inequality and economic growth. The study finds that economic growth was slower, and periods of growth were shorter in developed countries with higher inequality and that human capital explains this process. Subsequently, based on a completed dataset that distinguishes between market and net (post tax and transfers) inequality, these authors together with Yakhshilikov (Ostry et al. 2018) confirm that lower inequality is robustly correlated with faster and more durable growth, that

Figure 7.14: Change in number of people living in extreme poverty due to COVID-19 by region

Source: Centennial Group 2021

redistribution appears benign in terms of its impact on growth, except when it is excessive, and that inequality seems to affect growth through human capital accumulation (OECD 2014). Along the same lines, Milanovic stresses the importance of human capital in development, and that human capital is now more important than physical capital (Milanovic 2011). Ravallion finds that a country with high inequality will take much more time to reduce poverty than one with low inequality. Interestingly, Herzer and Vollmer find that increased income inequality reduces economic growth, but growth itself increases income inequality (Herzer and Vollmer 2013). In this regard, *Forbes* finds that if country-specific effects were eliminated using panel estimation, income inequality has a significant positive relationship with economic growth (*Forbes* 2000), supporting Kuznets' theory that with economic development (especially due to technological changes and structural inter-sectoral reallocation of labour) (Milanovic 2016) inequality first increases and then decreases.

A study conducted by the OECD in 2014 compares the level of income inequality, economic growth, and education across its thirty-four member countries, and identifies education is a key pathway through which inequality affects growth adversely. Specifically, steep income disparities lead to lower educational achievement and lower quality of education for children of the lowest income households. Subsequently, in 2015, the OECD found that countries with decreasing inequality see faster economic growth than those with rising inequality (OECD 2015).

Education and Social Mobility

The just-mentioned study shows that large income disparities lead to lower educational attainment and lower quality of education for the children in the lower end of the income distribution (Perotti 1996), and that the higher income inequality is the higher are the chances that the economic status of parents be transferred to their children through lower education attainment, poorer skills and employment prospects. For instance, a child of a top quartile family is 45 percentage points more likely to complete college than a child of a bottom quartile family (Bailey and Dynarski 2011). The resulting lower human capital leads to lower social mobility. Put differently, many countries have seen an erosion of opportunities for lower income households, which hampers the potential for low-income parents to improve the economic and social position of their children. In turn, higher income parents have the resources to invest in the better education (and health) of their children and have better connections and superior job networks that improve their children's prospects. To a large extent, the endurance of this duality explains the view that inequality is highly persistent over time.

In 2012, Krueger developed the 'Great Gatsby Curve,' which plots a relationship between income inequality (as measured by the GINI coefficient) and intergenerational income immobility (as measured by the intergenerational income elasticity) in different countries of Europe or America (Kreuger 2012). The upward-sloping curve shows that whether you are rich or poor depends to a great extent on where you happen to be born. Corak confirmed that countries with more inequality at a point in time (e.g., Italy, the United Kingdom and the United States) experience less earnings mobility across generations than countries with lower inequality (e.g., the Nordic countries) (Corak 2013). He then discusses how the interaction between families, labour markets, and public policies structure a child's opportunities and determines the extent to which adult earnings are related to family background. Chetty et al. show a major decline in inter-generational inequality in the US: at age thirty, people born in 1940 had an near 90 per cent chance of out-earning their parents but for people born in 1980 this chance has declined to 50 per cent (Chetty et al. 2017). Hoff uses the relationship between inequality and mobility to estimate the number of generations that will take for a low-income family to reach the country's average income; of course, in countries with better upward mobility, the process will take fewer generations than in those with weaker upward mobility (Hoff 2020).

Health

Using data from twenty-three developed countries and the fifty states of the US, Wilkinson and Pickett found that health problems (e.g., obesity, mental illness, child conflict, drug use) and poor social indicators (e.g., life expectancy, educational performance, social mobility) are more prevalent in countries and states with higher inequality. This was based on an index of health and social problems derived from nine factors. They argue that inequality and social stratification can lead to depression, drug dependency, parenting problems, and stress-related diseases. A related study concludes that life expectancy (counting each person equally) in the top industrialized countries is lower in more unequal countries (r= -907) and in more unequal US states (r= -620) (Kaplan et al. 1996). Similarly, another study finds that national income inequality is positively related to the country's rate of schizophrenia (Burns, Tomita and Kapadia).While some researchers question the causality of these findings, there is a clear relationship. For example, the UNICEF index of child well-being in rich countries correlates with greater equality and not with income per capita (UNICEF 2007).

Social Cohesion

There is an inverse relationship between income inequality and social cohesion; put differently, equality and community are mutually reinforcing. People are more likely to trust each other in more equal societies. Indeed, Uslaner and Brown found a high correlation between the amount of trust in society and the extent of income equality (2005). Comparing the 1950s and 1960s with the period after 1965–70 in the United States, Putnam finds that in the first period social connectedness and civic engagement was at a high point as were equality and social capital (Putnam 2000). By contrast, during the last third of the twentieth century, inequality grew, and social capital eroded, and society became less connected socially and politically. This finding is consistent with Temple's conclusion that high inequality increases social and political instability, and therefore, lowers growth (Temple 1999). Stiglitz has argued that economic inequality has led to distrust of business and government (Stiglitz 2012). Inequality has adversely affected democracy, public policy, and the system of justice. The resulting disillusionment may lead to discontent and political instability.

Crime

Crime rates have been shown to be correlated with inequality. Homicide rates among US states and Canada provinces are highly and positively correlated with income inequality as measured by the GINI coefficient (Daly and Wilson 2000). Moreover, the temporal change in the GINI coefficient is a significant predictor of the temporal change in homicide rates. A World Bank study found a similar causal relationship worldwide (Fajnzylber, Lederman, and Loayza 2002). While these studies refer to violent crime or homicides, a study looking at the effect of inequality on property crime found a nearly zero relationship (Corvalana and Pazzonab 2019).

Environment

The effects of inequality on the environment are highly debated. While some argue that alleviating poverty can result in detrimental environment effects because, as poor people become wealthier, they increase carbon emissions. Others take the view that alleviating poverty will lead to progressions on the environment in terms of energy efficiency and urbanization. For instance, through urbanization, societies have a higher standard of living that can promote environmental health with better technology, education, etc. Research shows that biodiversity loss is higher in countries or US states with higher income inequality (Mikkelson 2007).

Political Outcomes

Following the Engermann and Sokoloff hypothesis, Easterly finds high inequality to be a significant barrier to prosperity, good quality institutions, and high-quality schooling, i.e., income inequality is a determinant of bad institutions and underdevelopment (Easterly 2007). It leads to poorer forms of social, cultural and civic participation. A recent study suggested that low social mobility reduces voter turnout among lower income groups (Wass and Hiilamo 2017). This may also allow the better off segments of society to capture legislation and institutions. Looking at interregional inequality, Ezcurra and Palacios find that inequality may lead to terrorism (2016). Milanovic finds that income inequality increases the likelihood of coups (Milanovic 2016), giving some credence to the argument that WWI was caused by inequality, as raised by J.A. Hobson, R. Luxemburg, and V. Lenin.

What Can Be Done to Build a Fairer and More Equitable Society?

Following the utilitarian principle of seeking the greatest good for the greatest number,[8] economic inequality is a problem that needs to be addressed. However, adopting policies to maximize the sum of individual utilities could harm the incentives to produce. This is a conflict, among others, that policy makers need to deal with when considering and implementing policies to reduce inequality and build an inclusive society. In addition, two further issues from the political economy point of view are critical: one is that some of policies to address inequality adversely affect the interest of important stakeholders and potentially influential interested groups, and the other, perhaps as important, is that many policies bear fruits in the medium to long run,[9] long after the term in office of policy makers. The idealists among them would go ahead and implement them anyway, while others are likely to wonder why they should spend their political capital on steps that would benefit their successors.[10] The complexity of these considerations and the difficult choices involved should not lead to inaction, especially because 'inequality is bad for everyone in society' (Ingraham 2018). The serious adverse effects of inequality discussed above suggest the need to address them without delay, even more so if they take long to bear fruits.

Equity issues are complex because they are intertwined with social values and moral views of fairness and social justice, including over inter-generational issues. In addition, individual countries (or regions) may have different perceptions of what is equitable (i.e., how much inequality is acceptable, given that some degree of inequality is desirable from the point of view of rewards to innovation and risk-taking), and which are the priorities and appropriate policies to promote equity depend on the initial circumstances (including institutional structures that create social barriers based on social status, gender, ethnicity, and age), preferences and needs of the individual country (region). There is no 'one-size-fits-all'. Thus, policy makers need to pay particular attention to these values and views when considering the mix of policies that would promote equity or fairer access to opportunities and income.

Key features of successful strategies include understanding the constraints to reducing inequality, building support from key stakeholders and across the political spectrum, sequencing the reforms to yield benefits early on, and preventing administrative and budgetary bottlenecks given government implementation capacity. In term of contents, strategies to promote equity vary greatly. Some countries have used inequality reducing policies, including public resources to raise transfers to the poor, while others have focussed on levying highly progressive taxes. Yet others have taken an indirect approach, seeking to help low-income families by stimulating overall growth (a high tide lifts all boats approach). This would allow the problems mentioned

---

8. According to the law of diminishing utility, the loss of economic welfare suffered by the rich when some of their resources are transferred to the poor is substantially smaller than the gain of economic welfare by the poor.
9. This raises inter-generational equity.
10. Another political economy issue is that politicians may agree on the need to tackle the inequality problem, but it may be difficult to find common ground on the solution.

in the fourth section to fester and lead to low and/or unsustainable growth; 'inequality and unsustainable growth may be two sides of the same coin' (Ostry and Berg 2014). Perhaps these diverging views are the reason why reducing inequality has proven to be so difficult; indeed, progress toward achieving SDG 10 has been limited. A combination of both approaches seems preferable because it would create a dynamic and more inclusive economy.

Irrespective of these circumstances, there is a growing need for countries (regions) to redouble their efforts at reducing inequality, particularly in view of the adverse effects and disruptions caused by the COVID-19 pandemic presented in the previous section, and the structural transformations being caused by the megatrends discussed elsewhere in this book. As bad as inequality had been before the pandemic, the post-pandemic world would experience greater inequality unless governments act (Stiglitz 2020). The goal is to address inequality at its roots, to implement policies that go beyond just supplementing people's income, they should equip them—starting from a very early age—with the capacity to access opportunities and prosper.

Following McCall (2016), there are three political and policy approaches to address problems of inequality and opportunity, each characterized by a particular mix of views concerning inequality of outcomes (i.e., income inequality) on the one hand and opportunity on the other.

- The equalizing opportunity approach places greater emphasis on equalizing opportunities rather than on equalizing incomes and goes so far as to actively oppose equalizing outcomes as a policy objective. Policies that promise or provide job opportunities to lift oneself by the bootstraps to achieve, for example, the American Dream (the idea that hard work is essential to get ahead). Samples of policies implemented in the US under this approach include universal education and affirmative action. This approach is identified with conservative parties.

- The equalizing outcomes approach places greater emphasis on equalizing outcomes than on equalizing opportunity. It typically sees the goal of equalizing opportunities as being met implicitly through government tax and transfer policies that reduce disparities in disposable income. Increasing taxes on the affluent as a method to divert funds from those that 'do not need' them to those who do, and thereby mitigate economic inequality; redistribution is too often seen as an end on itself. This approach is identified with liberal parties.

- The equalizing outcomes to equalize opportunity approach is in the middle of the political spectrum as it fuses concerns about both opportunity and outcome, it connects the problem of inequality to the problem of opportunity, seeing inequality as a barrier to opportunity. It takes the view that concerns about restricted opportunities appear to coincide with desires for less inequality. This approach moves from taxing for redistribution to taxing for opportunity. For example, by avoiding a diffuse set of social or public goods, Bill de Blasio (in the United States) campaigned successfully under the promise to raise taxes on the wealthy to fund universal preschool education. Similarly, President Biden's Build Back Better initiative in the United States includes raising taxes to fund opportunity enhancing programs. The recent so-called 'social investment' strategies in Europe call for a shift from the traditional outcomes-based agenda to one that seeks to harness the human capital potential of the entire population, regardless of social background.

This chapter broadly follows the latter approach, although many of the policies described below follow an equalizing opportunity to equalize outcomes approach. While the rest of this chapter focusses on the policies and measures that country and regional authorities could implement to address inequality, international cooperation plays an important role in assisting governments to achieve the SDGs, as well as in designing, implementing, and financing inequality reduction programs in areas such as education, health and infrastructure.

The following non-exhaustive list of potential policies does not imply a particular priority or order of policy implementation. As just noted, the priority given each of these policies should be carefully assessed and tailored to the circumstances and social values of the country or region; bearing in mind that many policies are mutually reinforcing, a multiprong approach is needed. As noted, policies addressing inequality and seeking inclusive growth need to go beyond just supplementing people's income through government transfers, they should seek increasing access to opportunities and thereby equalizing income.

- Invest in early childhood development. This is an essential policy to increase access to opportunities because 'the highest rate of return in early childhood development comes from investing as early as possible, from birth through age five' (Heckman 2012). Over this period the brain develops and builds the foundation of cognitive and character skills necessary for success in school, college, career, and live. Early childhood education raises cognitive skills and attentiveness, motivation, self-control, and sociability, all of which turn knowledge into know-how and people into productive citizens. Skill begets skill and motivation begets motivation. Early childhood development will give each child a reasonable opportunity to attain an economic place in society based on their talents, interests, desires, and efforts. Every child needs early childhood education, but those coming from disadvantaged environments, from families that lack education, need it the most to avoid the skill gaps that open early in life due to limited stimulus, poor nutrition, and health risks, which typically leads to social immobility. Heckman stresses that early childhood development is a cost-effective strategy to promote economic growth (thereby increasing fiscal revenue), and reduce the costs of remedial education, health, social services, and criminal justice (thereby lowering public spending).

- Enhance education quality and mitigate education inequalities. There is broad agreement on the importance of ensuring universal access to quality education. The required efforts deserve high priority because they translate into stronger human capital and access to opportunities, and thus greater social mobility. In 2019, G20 leaders restated its commitment to invest in human capital and promote inclusive and equitable quality education for all. To this end, key elements are strengthening the quality of education by bolstering teachers' quality and training and by removing any obstacles to education reform. Similarly, make public education free, including tertiary education for low-income families. These efforts take years to implement, and the productivity enhancing effects are seen with lags; their large economic and social effects could take decades.

  - Starting with early childhood development programs, as just mentioned, supplement them with universal pre-K. Develop support programs for at risk mothers and babies to address malnutrition and poor health. Support day care centres and pre-school programs to improve early development of cognitive and social skills, while stressing good nutrition and health.

- Strengthen primary and secondary education stressing the importance of quality of education in addressing the acute problem of learning poverty (World Bank 2019).[11] This calls for bolstering the quality and capacity of teachers and adopting policies to attract and retain them. Boost school funding to improve the availability of school inputs, especially in disadvantaged areas. This requires, in some countries, a reform of the current funding based on property taxes, which discriminates against schools in poor districts, where property values are lower than in affluent districts. Put in place a good system to track learning outcomes and assess the extent to which policies and programs contribute to students learning. These efforts should help close the gap in years of schooling between AEs and EMDEs (averaging three and a half and five and a half years) (IMF and World Bank 2020).
- Support appropriate tertiary education, as it provides high labour market rates of return. To this end, establish career guidance in secondary schools to ensure parents with low levels of education and their children understand the potential benefits of tertiary education; in addition, provide these students with means tested financial assistance (e.g., scholarships, grants such as the Pell Grants in the US, and reduced fees). Help raise completion rates by providing counselling and remedial instruction at an early stage. University-business partnerships could help design education programs that are well aligned with labour market needs.

While in many countries the much-needed quality improvement may not require additional spending,[12] in other countries there is a need to increase education spending, including school buildings, teaching material, and higher remuneration to attract good teachers, especially in remote, underserved areas. Additional resources may be needed to fund appropriately targeted assistance to disadvantaged students. In many countries, however, a better allocation of budgetary resources may also require shifting funding from tertiary to the earlier stages of education, as well as bolstering the capacity and efficiency of the ministry of education while improving its human management.

In a previous study based on the endogenous growth theory, the authors—together with J. Guzman—confirmed that concerted efforts to raise cognitive skills though improvements in the coverage and quality of education can have sizable long-term effects on both economic output and the distribution of income (Fajgenbaum, Guzman and Vilkelyte 2019).

- Improve health outcomes and reduce inequalities in health service delivery. Improving health outcomes is, together with enhancing education, a key factor in building human capital; it helps raise child learning and worker productivity. It improves growth prospects and income distribution by enabling continued access to opportunities. In fact, healthcare needs are highly unmet among low- and middle-income segments of the population in OECD countries (OECD 2018). In EMDEs coverage is very limited and inequitable, while its quality is poor (WHO and World Bank 2017). To address these problems, there is a need to boost the quality and capacity of health care facilities (especially in EMDEs), increase the number of healthcare professionals (promoting enrolment in medical education programs), encourage their supply to underserved

---

11. Defined as the inability to read and comprehend a simple text by age ten.
12. For example, Costa Rica spends more than 8 per cent of GDP on education, but students' attainment is rather poor.

areas, prioritize reliance on outpatient care (especially of expecting mothers, infants and young children), and enhance communication technologies. Focus on addressing major risks common but preventable among lower-income households through adequately funding research on microbial resistance, a key threat in most countries; intensify public and private efforts to eradicate communicable diseases, which are prevalent in EMDEs; and provide means-tested subsidies on medicines and boost competition among pharmaceuticals. Where appropriate, support comprehensive family planning programs.

- Broaden access to clean water and sanitation services. This is key to improving health, especially in poor urban and rural areas. Well targeted tariffs and subsidies would ensure equitable and sustainable service.

- Support vocational training and continuing education programs. These programs are critical to maintain workers' human capital that is competitive and up to date with new technologies, thereby raising workers' opportunities. They could include financial incentives, such as wage subsidies or sub-minimum wages, rebates of social contributions to employers so that they establish apprenticeship places and good quality adult training (earn-while-you-learn programs). Strong business-education partnerships should allow continuing education and other training programs to be well aligned with employer requirements.

- Provide lower income families with affordable but quality childcare. This could be government or privately provided, with means-tested subsidies. Ensuring that every working family can afford high quality childcare will facilitate an increase in labour force participation by women, and thereby raise the family's income and reduce inequality. Of course, it would also contribute to early children development.

- Promote gender equality in access to education and labour markets. There is plenty evidence of the important the role women play in health and education of their children that women's access to education would lead to better children education and health, and thus, on increased social mobility. In OECD countries, women's participation in the labour force is comparable to that of men, but they still earn 15 per cent less than mem for similar work. Gender disparities in middle- and low-income countries are grater, as women participation in the labour force is 49 per cent and 64 per cent, respectively, compared to 75 per cent and 77 per cent, respectively for men. The OECD estimates that a 50 per cent increase in the participation by women will increase output growth by 0.3 per cent reduce household inequality by about 2 GINI points (OECD 2015). 'The evidence suggests that greater gender equity and increasing female economic participation are associated with higher growth, more favourable development outcomes, and lower income inequality' (Jain-Chandra et al. 2015). Thus, there is a clear benefit from removing gender discrimination in education and in the labour market (amending laws and regulations to facilitate part-time, flexible work schedules, and gender-neutral family leave policies). These steps will help reduce the employment cost differential between women and men and enhance women's access to opportunities and income. Implementation of gender budgeting would help address gender inequality, including by ensuring funding for high quality childcare and parental leave policies.

- Provide means-tested conditional transfers. By increasing disposable income, these transfers help low-income communities to raise their economic activity while promoting human capital build-up. Conditional transfers have been effective in many countries—including Brazil, Jamaica, Peru and Mexico—in improving income distribution and reducing poverty, while encouraging steps to enhance human development. Typical conditions result in better nutrition, greater school attendance and better health, including through periodic check-ups and vaccinations. These transfers would be even more effective if the country's safety net were improved.

- Alleviate spatial disparities. Increased public support for significant investment in infrastructure and services would lower accessibility gaps in regions and cities. These gaps constitute important barriers in accessing jobs, housing, education and health services, especially for the low-income population; transport policies could ease geographical mobility and improve connectivity. For instance, building access roads would significantly improve living conditions of remote farmers. Public support in the form of investment aid or loan guarantees could promote small business and activity in depressed areas.

- Increase participatory decision-making. This policy seeks to include the voice and perspectives of the poor in the decision-making, monitoring and evaluating of public policy on inequality.

- Establish a universal basic income. In contrast to the means-tested conditional transfers, the universal basic income (UBI) is a cash transfer of an equal amount to all individuals in a country. This idea has revived in recent years in response to potential effects of automation and artificial intelligence on jobs in future. It could replace inefficient public spending, such as fuel subsidies. While the UBI may have a positive impact on inequality outcomes and poverty, it could involve a heavy budgetary burden, turning it unadvisable in countries with low taxing capacity. A more general drawback is UBI's potential adverse effect on incentives to work. Instead of the UBI, Anthony Atkinson proposed several measures with similar goals (Atkinson 2021). Guaranteeing a minimum wage to those who seek employment, establishing a capital endowment (minimum inheritance) paid to all at adulthood, paying a Child Benefit to all children at a substantial rate and subject to income tax, and introducing a national participation income that complements existing social protection. He also envisaged an eventual EU-wide child basic income.

- Improve the functioning of key markets. Reform labour market legislation and regulations to reduce the ability of employers to use their market power and anti-competitive practices to set wages below workers' marginal productivity, especially regarding low-income workers. Clemens and Strain show that reasonable increases in minimum wages in the US had no or moderately positive effect on employment, while large increases reduced it by just over 2 per cent in the short-run (Clemens and Strain 2019). Interestingly, faced with large unfilled vacancies in the aftermath of the COVID-19 pandemic, low-income workers in the US are demanding higher salaries and better working conditions through informal bargaining and massive resignations (the Great Resignation). Serious consideration needs to be given to removing regulations that promote informality with a view to reduce the informal sector, especially in developing countries where it accounts for some 70 per cent of 'employment' with virtually no safety net. Assistance with affordable housing has proven helpful for low-income families in searching and contracting rental housing and move from depressed areas to higher opportunity areas. A study on a large city in the US, conducted by Bergman et al. found that families benefitting from this assistance were 40 per cent more likely to move to high opportunity neighbourhoods than those that did not receive such assistance (Bergman et al. 2019). The study concludes that assistance to housing search could reduce residential segregation and increase upward social mobility. Addressing market power concentration, by reviewing mergers could benefit many stakeholders, including workers, buyers and suppliers.

- Ensure financial inclusion. This is critical to foster a more equitable income distribution. Evidence indicates that having access to saving accounts results in a higher degree of self-insurance against health and weather risks, and higher investment in education. These accounts help prevent theft and impulse-spending, and foster women empowerment (IMF and World Bank 2020). Greater small and medium enterprise (SMEs) access to financial services (e.g., digital payments, savings, credit, and insurance) tends to be associated with access to new technologies, increased employment, labour productivity and economic growth. Credit Bureaus could help reduce information asymmetries between borrowers and creditors and thereby improve SMEs access to credit. Introducing movable collateral registries would allow SMEs to borrow against their movable assets (which typically exceed their fixed assets). Reducing the cost of financial reporting by providing cost efficient accounting standards and training in simple financing management and information would encourage SMEs reporting (UNCTAD 2013).

  Fintech has been a major contributor to financial inclusion in recent decades, including rural households' access to payment services and SMEs access to small, short duration credit that financial institutions could not provide. The potential for further financial inclusion is large: about 100 million unbanked adults receive government payments and transfers in cash, while nearly seven out of ten of these adults have a mobile phone that could be used for digital payments. Improving connectivity infrastructure will help include the poor, women, and rural residents in the financial system.

- Address impact of climate change. Given that climate change hits the poor the hardest, it raises inequality further and hampers development. The World Bank estimates that climate change could push an additional 68 to 135 million people into poverty by 2030, and thus amplify inequalities (Guivarch et al. 2020). This suggests that policies to tackle climate change are urgently needed. For instance, policies to ensure that redistribution of the revenue from carbon prices would offset (or be higher than) the negative impact of climate change on the poor. Financial transfers between countries may reduce the burden of mitigation in poorer countries and increase participation in mitigation efforts.

- Boost fiscal space to reduce inequality. Some of the policies and measures discussed above require additional budgetary allocations. Although, preferably, the resources should come from improving expenditure efficiency and regressive spending, increasing revenue may be unavoidable to help achieve distributive objectives, consistent with fiscal sustainability. To cut or eliminate inefficient and regressive spending, consideration needs to be given to:

- improving the efficiency and efficacy of every expenditure line, including through strengthening public financial management (particularly transparency and accountability);
- replacing across the board subsidies that benefit more higher-income households (e.g., fuel or energy) by subsidies targeted at low-income ones; and
- restrain the growth of military spending.

To increase revenue, it is important to strengthen tax administration by modernizing the technology and raising the budgets and managerial autonomy of the respective agencies. Regarding tax increases, careful consideration is needed to avoid adverse effects on incentives to work and save. The same applies to corporate taxation in light of international competition.[13] Increasing the progressivity of personal income taxes (reversing some of the decline over the last decades) as well as broadening their base by taxing all types of incomes (e.g., fringe benefits) could lead to significantly higher revenue. This should be accompanied by rationalizing exemptions and deductions and removing tax loopholes. Increasing progressivity has the dual function of raising fiscal resources and reducing after taxes income inequality. IMF's Fiscal Monitor found that AEs with relatively low personal income tax progressivity have room to raise top marginal tax rates without adverse implications for growth (IMF 2017).[14] Furthermore, a recent study conducted by Lakner et al. shows that a relatively small reduction in the growth rate of the top earners is necessary to ensure that the income of the lowest earners grows substantially faster than the mean (Lakner et al. 2019).

Other tax measures include restricting the use of trusts to shelter assets and incomes, removing inefficient corporate income tax expenditures (some of which benefit high income recipients), removing tax avoidance and evasion opportunities, such as profit shifting, transfer pricing and interest stripping by multinational corporations (IMF), and raising taxation on goods with negative externalities (e.g., carbon emissions and cigarettes). Raising indirect taxes, such as the VAT, could be progressive when their proceeds are used to help reduce inequality, like financing conditional transfers or introducing or increasing an earned income tax credit. Taxation of natural resources also offers an efficient and equitable source of revenue. While many observers propose introducing or increasing taxes on assets, wealth, and estate, there is little consensus on the advisability of raising these taxes.

- Promote macroeconomic stability and structural reforms. Even if these policies are presented at the end, they are essential to sustain the growth of output and employment, lower poverty and improve income distribution. Ensuring economic stability is critical, as lower-income earners suffer disproportionality more than the rich during times of economic crises (typically accompanied by surges in unemployment). Thus, policies need to focus on maintaining low fiscal deficits consistent with debt sustainability, keep inflation low (as it affects the poor the most), implement strong prudential regulation and supervision of financial institutions, and attaining adequate fiscal space and international

---

13. Recent discussions and support of a minimum corporate income tax on multinationals are an important step in this direction.

14. However, the extent of the rise in top marginal rates should be carefully assessed because if progressivity were too steep it could cause unintended consequences, such as encourageing capital flight or lowering private investment and thus employment and growth.

reserves to help deal with potential adverse shocks. Important reforms could promote equality of opportunities and outcomes: for example, deregulating the economy, setting up strong and accountable institutions, including a well-functioning judiciary, removing discriminatory legislation, and curbing corruption. Moreover, '[b]road public support is likely to come for a wise and sustained course of adjustment and reform when the distribution of income and opportunities to attain economic advancement are seen as relatively 'fair' or at least not outrageously biased toward privileged groups' (Camdessus 1995).

While this chapter has so far focussed on what governments could do to build a fairer and more equitable society, there is significant potential role to play by the private sector. They include changing corporate managerial objectives toward (i) long-term profitability (rather the short-term increases in share values) with greater emphasis on investment and innovation; (ii) enhancing labour productivity by providing productivity-based wages and retention programs, while avoiding discrimination; and supporting the community, including by addressing negative externalities. In addition, the private sector could help build clinics, child daycare and education facilities, and finance their operations; it can also play an important role in the area of continuing education and training. Non-governmental organizations, through their activities, especially research and lobbying, help address important problems that affect the disadvantaged. And many charitable organizations like doctors without borders (MSF), the Bill and Melinda Gates Foundation, and the Carter Center do important work that helps address health and education problems, among others.

At the global level, bilateral and multilateral assistance should support recipient countries in these areas and by bringing awareness of policies that have been successful elsewhere. The recent SDR allocation could help finance the initial steps of these policies. The advanced and other rich countries could use part of the SDR allocation they received to help fund such policies; one way would be to capitalize the Multilateral Development Banks and thus increase their financing potential, perhaps by leverageing this capitalization.

Conclusion

The unprecedented and synchronized shock of the COVID-19 pandemic has intensified the increasing inequality within AEs, which started in the early 1980s, and within many EDMEs, which started subsequently. It has even reversed a declining trend in inequality within countries in other EMDEs. Moreover, in addition to the impact on health, the pandemic has led to an enormous increase in extreme poverty worldwide, despite major mitigation efforts, and it has led to school closures that have affected millions of students with limited or no access to online education, hampering human capital build-up and future earnings. The expected monetary policy tightening by the United States, and possibly soon after by the central bank of the UK, the ECB and the Bank of Japan is likely to further widen the inequality between AEs and EMDEs.

In these circumstances, policymakers need to act decisively and urgently to address inequality not only because of ethical and solidarity considerations, but also because inequality within countries may have risen to unsustainable levels (but masked by the ongoing pandemic). As already discussed, inequality leads to poor educational attainment and human capital formation among the lower income population, limited opportunity for social mobility, and poor health; hinders economic growth; weakens social cohesion, which could lead to dissatisfaction and mistrust, and increased violent crime rates; and tends to make societies politically unstable.

Equity issues are complex, as they are intertwined with social values and moral views of fairness and social justice, which suggest that individual countries (or regions) may have different perceptions of what is equitable (i.e., how much inequality is acceptable). Thus, the priorities and appropriate policies (and sequence) to promote equity depend on the initial circumstances of each country or region. Guided by the objective of equalizing opportunities to equalize incomes or vice versa and build an inclusive society, potential policies include early childhood development; enhancing education quality and health; promoting gender equality in access to education and labour market; providing vocational training and continuing education; providing means-tested conditional transfers; alleviating spatial disparities; ensuring financial inclusion; and addressing the impact of climate change. Clearly, many of these policies will require increased budgetary allocations. This could be achieved by raising the efficiency of government spending and by raising revenue through improvements in tax administration, a somewhat more progressive income tax, removing loopholes and exemptions, and raising indirect taxes.

The private sector should play an important role in reducing inequality, as should the international community, by supporting governments in their efforts to address inequality.

Chapter 8: Reforming the International Monetary and Financial System— More Urgent Than Ever

Reforming the International Monetary and Financial System— More Urgent Than Ever

Chapter 8 | Bernard Snoy

'As Jean Monnet used to say, politics is not merely the art of the possible. It is also the art of making possible to-morrow what still seems impossible.'
—Robert Triffin

Introduction[1]

The major shift in monetary policies that lies ahead is likely to focus renewed attention on the international dimension—both regulatory and systemic—of monetary and financial policies. During 2021, the dollar had already appreciated significantly against most Emerging Market Economies (EME) currencies, and financial conditions have tightened in most emerging markets. Entering 2022, the Fed is set to curb their bond purchases, and the funds rate is likely to begin rise. Global liquidity conditions seem likely to tighten, although the timing and extent of this are unknown.[2] Such a renormalization of benchmark dollar interest rates would bring to light the latent vulnerabilities of borrowers who have become over-extended during more than decade of near-zero interest rates. In addition, international regulatory attention is now focussed on non-bank financial intermediaries and on dysfunctions in international capital markets. The combination of tighter monetary policy and new financial regulations in the advanced economies over the next few years could have major implications for EMEs.

The last period of monetary tightening in the main financial centres (from mid-2004 to the end of 2006) revealed how earlier regulatory shortcomings (e.g., the blind spots of Basel II, inadequate oversight of short-term dollar exposures of non-US banks, the failure in the advanced economies to develop a macroprudential policy framework, and so on) had weakened the global financial system. Once the US housing market turned, dollar funding markets became illiquid, and several major banks faced the threat of insolvency.[3] It also showed that central banks were not prepared to ease monetary policy quickly enough to counter this shock. Nor were they prepared for the severity of the dollar liquidity squeeze, which would freeze capital markets and hit banks hard.

How the coming transition to higher interest rates will be managed at the international level matters greatly for the emerging markets. In December 2019, the Robert Triffin International (RTI) Association released a report of an RTI working party on 'Managing global liquidity as a global

1. The author is Chairman of Robert Triffin International (RTI), an association dedicated to the preservation and the promotion of the intellectual heritage of the Belgian-American economist Robert Triffin (1911–93). This chapter benefitted from very substantial comments and suggestions of Christian Ghymers, Vice Chairman of RTI and from Philip Turner, Member of the RTI Board.
2. Higher and higher rates of inflation during 2021 served to bring forward expected future monetary tightening. See also de Larosière and Marsh (2017) and de Larosière (2021).
3. For a summary analysis of these developments, see Turner (2021, 79–90).

147

public good' (RTI 2019). Using data from the BIS and the IMF, this report documented the scale of the expansion of global liquidity since the financial crisis. This extraordinary expansion has been driven by the international capital markets.[4] All this has been conditioned by domestic policies in both the monetary and regulatory spheres—especially policies in the advanced countries. But much of the impact has fallen on the emerging markets. As Alexandre Lamfalussy concluded in his Yale lectures, financial crises in the emerging market have so often been driven by 'the exuberant behaviour of lenders and investors in the developed world … which raises leverage and asset prices to levels that eventually become unsustainable'.

The report showed an unprecedented decade-long surge in international lending to the EMEs and especially to non-financial companies. Much of this lending has taken place through dollar bond markets. The dollar debts of EME companies have risen much faster than exports increasing their currency mismatches. The more heavily indebted companies tend to buy dollars whenever they fear a depreciation of their local currency, and this can destabilize forex markets.

As for other and more important policy shortcomings of the international monetary and financial system itself, the report expressed concern that the IMF's financial capacities had not kept up with the increased vulnerabilities that much greater dollar borrowing had created. And the role of the Special Drawing Right (SDR) had remained far too limited. While the extensive use of Fed swap lines after the financial crisis had defused potential dollar liquidity squeezes in the main financial centres, there was no lender of last resort (LOLR) in dollars.

A fundamental systemic problem is that interest rate policies suited for US economic developments may not suit other countries which use the dollar for a large proportion of their financial transactions (Bordo and McCaulet 2018).[5] Because the US economy in late-2019 seemed near full employment, the RTI report was concerned that increases in dollar interest rates would damage those economies (especially in the emerging markets) heavily dependent on dollar international financing. There were also worries that the Fed would be less forthcoming in dollar lending to central banks under pressure.

In recent events, however, the nature of the shock was totally unexpected—the spread of the COVID-19 virus. Since the US was itself directly threatened, the Fed rapidly eased monetary policy, took new measures to support private markets (notably for corporate bonds), and ramped up dollar liquidity support for central banks, including those not covered by swap agreements. The worry about a US-led tightening did not materialize.

But the result—a renewed and substantial expansion in dollar lending, notably to EME borrowers—has reinforced the underlying worries expressed in the RTI's December 2019 report. COVID-19 led to unexpected developments but made the fundamental imbalances ever more dangerous.

In particular, the need to identify the systemic dysfunctions in the international monetary and financial system was once again highlighted. What reforms could address such dysfunctions remains a live issue and is the essential subject of this chapter. It begins by summarising various proposals associated directly or indirectly with RTI over the past decade. It then considers

---

4. See Figures 5 and 6 in RTI (2019) for data on the scale of this development. Figure 7 shows that currency mismatches were concentrated in the private sector (notably because of dollar borrowing of non-financial companies) while the official sector built up a large stock of dollar assets.

5. This is perhaps the most general form of the Triffin dilemma.

other drivers of IMFS reform, including some new ideas, which now might seem impossible but which, as Monnet put it, may one day become possible.

8

Proposals to Reform the International Monetary and Financial System: The Palais Royal and Other RTI Supported Initiatives and Their Aftermath

Since the collapse of the Bretton Woods system in 1971, one of the great paradoxes about the reform of the international monetary system is that although so much has been said and written about it, for instance on the occasions of the seventieth and the seventy-fifth anniversaries of the Bretton Woods Conference,[6] little concrete action has taken place. Interest for the subject has waned as if the advent of a new international monetary system was an impossible endeavour, at least in the foreseeable future. Even the IMF, which should be the foremost institution dedicated to the advent of a reformed system, seems to carefully avoid touching on this sensitive subject. In his contribution to the book edited by the Reinventing Bretton Woods Committee (RBWC), Harold James, Professor of History and International Affairs at Princeton University, concludes, in a disillusioned way, that 'the sad lesson of Bretton Woods is that things need to be extremely dangerous before a political dynamic of reform develops. It may be that today's world, for all its anxieties, is simply not obviously dangerous enough' (James 2016).

Cross-border financial flows and international financial markets have received much more attention, particularly since the outbreak of the 2008 Great Financial Crisis. Regulation and supervision of financial institutions have improved, with, among others, the creation of a new international institution—the Financial Stability Board (FSB). The FSB, however, has no political authority. Its task is to coordinate national financial authorities and international standard-setting bodies as they work toward developing strong regulatory, supervisory, and other financial sector policies. It fosters a level playing field by encourageing coherent implementation of these policies across sectors and jurisdictions. The creation in 2008[7] of the G20 was also an important step. Questions related to the International Monetary and Financial System (IMFS) have been frequently on its agenda; there was progress on regulatory issues, but there was no significant advance towards addressing the systemic weaknesses in its architecture nor toward strengthening institutionally the IMF, the only embryo at the global level that can assert authority on the IMFS and play the most important role to ensure its stability, namely the role of global LOLR.

A major landmark for reflections on reform was the Palais Royal Initiative[8] (PRI) in 2011 (Boorman and Icard 2011). This was a very wide-ranging report, which brought many

---

6. See for instance: Uzan (2016); On the occasion of the French Presidency of the G7, Banque de France organized in Paris on 16 July 2019, a major conference on 'Bretton Woods: 75 years later—Thinking about the next 75', the proceedings of which are available on the Internet, and a virtual book was also produced on that occasion by Reinventing Bretton Woods Committee (RBWC) - *The Spirit of Bretton Woods: Past, Present and Future.*
7. The G20 has been working at Finance Minister and Central Bank level since 1999 but was upgraded at Heads of State and Government in November 2008 in the context of the global financial crisis on a joint proposal from France and the UK.
8. In October 2010, Michel Camdessus, former Managing Director of the IMF, Alexandre Lamfalussy, former General Manager of the BIS and Chairman of RTI, and Tommaso Padoa-Schioppa, former Minister of Economy and Finance of Italy and former Member of the Executive Board of the European Central Bank (ECB), convened a group of 18 former Ministers, Governors, Heads of International Institutions, and Senior Officials, which took the name of Palais Royal Initiative (PRI) to evaluate the international monetary system and to propose changes that might be needed to stabilize it and reduce the likelihood of future failures. The eighteen signatories of the PRI report included also eminent personalities such as Paul A. Volcker, former Chairman of the US Federal Reserve Board, Edwin Truman, former Assistant Secretary for International Affairs of the US Treasury, Xiaolian Hu, Vice President of China Society of Finance and Banking, Horst Köhler, former Managing Director of the IMF and former President of Germany, Andrew Crockett, former General Manager

perspectives to the analysis of this controversial issue. Two key messages can be identified. The first one is that the collective failure in establishing over four decades an IMFS truly worthy of this name had been one of the key factors of the 2007–08 crisis. The second is that if no credible responses were given to the absence of effective discipline, to weak and ineffective surveillance, and to excesses of all kinds, the increasingly integrated world economy would become all the more vulnerable as it simultaneously engaged in a process of transition toward a multicurrency regime. In addition, the report pointed to the lack of effective global governance. Suffering from a 'legitimacy deficit', the IMF has not been able to play its expected role of catalyst to ensure that major economic and financial policy decisions made nationally, including exchange rate policies, are mutually consistent and contribute to world stability.

The PRI report suggested that the IMF and the BIS should work together to develop a set of indicators to measure global liquidity. This led central bank governors to direct the BIS to develop an extensive set of Global Liquidity Indicators, which are published quarterly.[9] The Landau Report, which introduced these indicators, demonstrated that private liquidity was considerably larger than official liquidity. Of great systemic significance is the fact that the destruction of liquidity, related as it often is to the forced deleverageing by private institutions, can be sudden and brutally procyclical.[10]

In addition to advocating for stronger surveillance and benchmarks for globally consistent exchange rates and for a greater role for the SDR, the PRI made three main policy proposals:

- National macroprudential policies should take account of global liquidity conditions;
- capital flows need to be managed because they are key to the transmission of risks; and
- A permanent crisis financing mechanism akin to a global LLOR should be put in place, requiring also important changes in IMF governance.

There has been significant progress on the first two proposals. The development and improvement of macroprudential policies has been one of the successful policy innovations since the financial crisis; although, by focusing on banks, these policies contributed to the expansion of non-bank financial intermediation, especially through the repo market, which still escapes most regulations. There has also been progress on capital flow management. This had been a bone of contention between the IMF and the emerging markets. But over the past decade or so, the IMF has become more pragmatic about the adoption of such measures. Nevertheless, a recent review by the IMF Independent Evaluation Office (IEO) suggested that further movement was necessary. In particular, the pre-emptive and long-lasting measures should in some circumstances be allowed (IEO 2020). Unfortunately, there was no progress on the more important third one. The onset of the sovereign debt crisis in the eurozone in some ways led to a crowding out of discussions of reforms of the IMFS that would be of a more systemic nature.

As a follow-up to the PRI, the RTI Association set up in 2013 a working party under the leadership of André Icard in view of defining more specific proposals towards using the SDR as a lever to reform the international monetary system (RTI 2014). In view of enhancing the international public role of the SDR, the Working Party Report recommended that the IMF's accounts should be placed on an all-SDR basis, requiring an amalgamation of the General

---

of the BIS, Sergey Aleksashenko, former Deputy Director, Central Bank of Russia, Y. Venugopal Reddy, former Governor of the Reserve Bank of India, and Guillermo Ortiz, former Governor of Banco de Mexico, among others. RTI was indirectly involved in the initiative.

9. See BIS (2011).

10. The IMF and BIS indicators are summarized and assessed in RTI (2019, 12–17).

Resources Account with the SDR account and that future lending would all be in SDRs. It suggested that the IMF resume SDR allocations and be enabled to issue SDRs at last resort in a crisis situation. The SDR should be made more attractive, and the composition of the basket should reflect more closely the relative importance of economies in international trade and financial transactions. The report proposed an orderly diversification of reserves, which would be facilitated through a mechanism allowing their conversion into SDR-denominated claims. In particular, periodical substitution account facilities should be offered to member countries, and currency exchange operations against the SDRs should be organized between the IMF and its members. Another important set of proposals relates to the promotion of a private SRD market. Official support (e.g., significant private SDR operations by the public sector) is needed to jumpstart the private SDR market, in the same way that public policy actions helped the private ECU bond market reach a critical mass in the 1980s and 1990s before the advent of the euro. The official sector should take the lead in providing appropriate structures suited to the functioning of an active SDR market. A multilateral clearing of SDR operations should be set up on the model of the former ECU clearing operated in the past by the BIS. To enable central banks to use their official holdings directly on private markets, it is necessary to create a link between private and official SDRs. This could be achieved either by allowing private banks to hold SDRs or by allowing the official SDRs to be converted into claims that central banks and private banks could hold.

In a subsequent contribution entitled Reforming the IMS—A sequenced agenda prepared in 2016 for the Emerging Markets Forum, Michel Camdessus and Anoop Singh[11] (2016) proposed the following sequenced agenda in three critical steps:

- IMF Reforms in several major areas: Reinforcing the IMF's surveillance function, developing guidelines of acceptable imbalances, broadening the surveillance of the capital accounts, and developing a statutory mechanism for sovereign debt resolution; making countries' obligations of exchange rate policies more specific through the use of benchmarks; adjusting IMF quotas and voting rights to reflect the increasing importance of emerging countries and entrusting final decision-making power to a Ministerial Council or to the existing IMF's International Monetary and Financial Committee (IMFC), comprising ministers and central bank governors rather than the present Executive Board of senior officials; and reforming the make-up of the G20, restructuring it along the lines of the IMFC, based on the twenty-four Bretton Woods constituencies, to ensure that the full membership of the IMF is represented.

- Introduction of a reliable mechanism to monitor and manage global liquidity:[12] This would involve the development of measures for calibrating global liquidity and the creation of a high-level group able to monitor movements in global liquidity. One aim would be to ensure that SDR allocation could be used much more flexibly, responding as needed to the global liquidity situation. This high-level group, which could, for instance, include the governors of the central banks whose currencies are included in the SDR

---

11. Anoop Singh is a former Director, Western Hemisphere and Asia Pacific at the IMF and more recently Member of the Indian fifteenth Finance Commission
12. See RTI (2020), which addresses the serious vulnerabilities in the way global liquidity is managed and makes a few specific recommendations addressed in particular to the IMF, the BIS, and the FSB. See also sub-section A in Section 4 below.

currency basket, would periodically submit to the IMFC a report on global liquidity and measures for calibrating global liquidity.

- Convening of a Bretton Woods II Conference, completing ongoing negotiations on the reform of the IMF, concluding parallel work on the governance and collaboration with other organizations in the IMFC (such as the World Bank, the FSB, the BIS, the WTO, etc.): The ultimate ambition would be that the IMF become the 'supranational bank that would have similar relations with the national central banks to those that exist between each central bank and its subordinate banks' envisaged by Keynes in the 1930s and proposed again by him at the Bretton Woods conference of July 1944. As national central banks issue their national currency, the IMF would issue a multilateral currency—the revamped SDR becoming the Multilateral Drawing Right—a liquid liability that would not be a debt of any individual country. The IMF would be empowered to become a genuine global LOLR.

Reactions to the reform proposals of the PRI have been mixed. A prominent US intellectual figure, Joseph Stiglitz, former Chief Economist of the World Bank and Chair of the International Commission of experts on Reforms of the IMFS appointed by the President of the UN General Assembly in the aftermath of the 2008 crisis has come up with conclusions very close to those of the PRI, asserting, among others, that a global reserve system is doable (Stiglitz 2016, 349). Another important academic figure, John Williamson, Senior Fellow at the Peterson Institute for International Economics, who passed away in 2021, endorsed broadly in his last book the PRI conclusions, placing emphasis on three key ingredients of IMFS reform: (i) giving the IMF unlimited possibilities of bail out in extreme situations; (ii) introducing a mechanism capable of disciplining surplus countries by limiting the freedom to set exchange rates; and (iii) making the SDR a vibrant private sector asset, benefitting from public support for clearing and conversion into official SDRs (Williamson 2018). Other prominent figures, coming from EMEs such as Raghuram Rajan (2016), former Governor of the Reserve Bank of India, or Jose Antonio Ocampo (2016a; 2016b), former Minister of Finance of Columbia, have called for new rules of the monetary game or proposed their own version of a program of reform of the IMFS.

These issues have frequently been on the agenda of the G20. As a result of a momentum created under Chinese chairmanship of the G20 in 2016, the ensuing German chairmanship launched in 2017 the G20 Eminent Persons Group (EPG) on Global Financial Governance chaired by Tharman Shanmugaratnam, Deputy Prime Minister of Singapore. The EPG' report submitted in October 2018 tackled several important but controversial issues. First, and echoing a major theme in the PRI report, it noted several shortcomings in international surveillance. It therefore proposed that the surveillance efforts of the IMF, the FSB, and the BIS be integrated into a coherent global risk map, a proposal endorsed by the IEO of the IMF. But it warned that any joint process' must avoid converging on a diluted consensus.' Secondly, taking account of the views of many EMEs on the need to manage capital flows, it concluded that the IMF should be ready to countenance measures needed to contain the financial risks from capital flows. Thirdly, the EPG recognized the critical need to plug the gap in the Global Safety Net for systemic crises in the future. The international community needs mechanisms to be able to quickly access a large amount of liquidity to ensure or restore financial stability. Disappointingly, members of the EPG could not agree on the specific mechanisms through which this could be achieved, nor did they dare to consider any institutional transformation of the IMF that would make it a genuine global LLOR. In particular, there was no consensus on possible innovative options for IMF funding in large and severe global crises, including on-lending of unused SDRs from member country savings, market borrowing by the IMF, and replenishing and expanding the New Agreements to Borrow (NAB). What was particularly puzzling was that this 2018 report did not even mention among the options a significant SDR allocation as was decided by the IMF in 2009 and now in 2021.

- Just before COVID-19 struck, a working party of RTI took stock of a key issue in the IMFS—the management of global liquidity. Its report, released in December 2019, argued that there was an immediate need to establish some pragmatic global liquidity framework. Building on existing arrangements, it proposed that the FSB brief the G20 Ministers and Governors about the systemic vulnerabilities coming from global liquidity developments. It recommended paying particular attention to the risks generated by the growing activities of non-bank financial intermediaries (NFBIs). Regulatory reforms after the financial crisis concentrated on banks, which had the effect of driving international financial intermediation into bond markets.[13] The report also highlighted the inadequacy of the Global Financial Safety Net; adding many elements together, it estimated that the official capacity of international support amounted to only one-fifth of outstanding international credits.[14]
- A string of episodes of instability in core and normally liquid markets—notably in September 2019, March 2020, and February 2021—has set alarm bells ringing. The further growth of the dollar debts of non-US borrowers has drawn more attention to these issues by the G20, by EME authorities, and by the FSB.[15] By the summer of 2021, the FSB had completed their long and very comprehensive consultation process. The huge international expansion of credits, especially dollar credits, via bond markets represents a major threat to global financial stability. Bond funds, often leveraged and disguising substantial liquidity mismatches, have been a major driver of this development. But the FSB did not yet agree on any global minimum standards for such funds. National regulators, however, are preparing new rules. The outgoing chairman, Randal Quarles, then-vice president of the Federal Reserve, said it was not just 'jurisdiction-specific circumstances' but also 'cross-border spill overs', and he stressed the need to avoid regulatory arbitrage.
- Shortly later, in an unusual and well-publicized step, the head of the BIS, Agustin Carstens (2021),[16] used the *BIS's Quarterly Review* of December 2021 to warn in strong terms about the financial stability risks created by NBFIs. Such institutions, he noted, have been the main cause of several episodes of extreme market dysfunction, and the regulatory framework governing them is not 'fully fit for purpose'. What happens to NBFIs could have a first-order impact on EMEs. In particular, the combination of new regulations aimed at constraining risky bond issuance and Fed monetary tightening will alter the international financing possibilities for EME non-financial companies. Liquidity and credit risks may rise, perhaps appreciably.

---

13. See Turner (2021, 90–100) for why bond market exposures constitute at present the greatest risk to global financial stability. See also Hung Tran (2019).
14. Details of this calculation are found in RTI (2019, 26).
15. A good summary is provided by Hinge (2021).
16. See also Lewrick (2021).

In the meantime, the new global economic and financial crisis linked to the COVID-19 pandemic has prompted the IMF to react through the establishment of several new facilities, and the advent of the Biden Presidency made it possible for the G20 to agree on a substantial SDR allocation equivalent to US$650 billion, which is a very positive step. But neither IMF management nor any member G20 dared to put the broader issue of IMF reform and IMF potential LLOR role on the agenda.

The Mutations of the Triffin Dilemma and the Worsening Unsustainability of the Present IMFS

In 1960, the Belgian–American economist Robert Triffin (1911–93) shed light on the inadequacy and the unsustainability of the Bretton Woods system, based on the US dollar, convertible into gold, and on fixed exchange rates, that could nevertheless be adjusted under the supervision of the IMF (Triffin 1960). He explained that if a national currency is used as a global currency, there is an irremediable contradiction between the issuing country's internal domestic requirements and the external requirements of the world using it. In the context of growing US public expenditures, associated with the Vietnam War and the financing of the Welfare State, Triffin formulated as follows his famous dilemma.

Either the United States controls its budget and current account balances by restricting domestic consumption and the world runs the risk of a recession, or it finances on credit its growing deficit and the abundance of dollars thus created will one day show the impossibility to ensure the convertibility of the dollar into gold. It was the second branch of this alternative that came about, and, on 15 August 1971, the United States put an end to the gold convertibility of the dollar. Shortly thereafter, the international monetary system gave up the system of fixed exchange rates.

Did the new system, with flexible exchange rates and theoretically more freedom for sovereign countries to conduct independent fiscal and monetary policies, bring about a more sustainable framework? Surely not when one observes its dominant features: massive global indebtedness, generating a succession of ever more severe financial crises; serious and persistent misalignments of the exchange rates among the major currencies; continued asymmetry in the burden of adjustment between deficit and surplus countries; a preference for holding liquid assets rather than long-term investments so badly needed; maintenance of the 'exorbitant privilege' of the dollar—US deficits remain the central element supplying the world with reserves, and the richest country in the world, the US, continues to live on credit being financed even by the poorest countries; diminution of the authority of the IMF, concentrating on developing countries and endowed with insufficient resources to play a genuine role of LOLR; dominance of private over public liquidities; and absence of any mechanism to ensure that global liquidity would be managed as it should, namely as a global public good.

In the meantime, the fiscal dimension of the Triffin dilemma has worsened. In a world characterized by huge uncertainties and strict limits to the capacity of the IMF to bail out countries in sudden difficulties, there is, particularly in EMEs, an unsatiable appetite for safe assets, the satisfaction of which depends on the constant increase of liabilities issued by the US Treasury. Demand for safe and liquid assets is rising faster than the capacity of the United States to supply them, where that capacity is limited by the ability of the US government to raise taxes and service the government debt securities that are held as reserves and used in cross-border transactions by other countries. How long will confidence in the dollar be compatible with the illimited expansion of US indebtedness?[17] According to Andrew Sheng (2021), the net external liability of the USA is equivalent to 65 per cent of US GDP and to 16.7 per cent of world GDP.

It was also Robert Triffin (1991), who, at the end of his life, foresaw the development of a vicious circle of disequilibria, which he named a 'built-in destabilizer', relying upon two inter-twined mechanical channels—(i) the weakening of the external constraint on the issuer of the reserve currency, exacerbating macroeconomic imbalances and pushing down its saving rate and (ii) the 'spill overs' to the rest of the world of the monetary conditions prevailing in the United States. EME central banks are threatened with destabilizing inflows and outflows of short-term capital unless they align themselves on the US monetary policy. To avoid excessive inflows, these central banks are inclined to pile up additional reserves, resisting appreciation of their currency and reinjecting their dollar reserves in the international capital markets, thus creating a multiplier effect and driving down interest rates. All this contributes to the endogenous gen-eration of pro-cyclical monetary waves and growing monetary instability with boom-and-bust episodes. In this context, we can view the Great Financial Crisis (GFC) of 2008–09 as a result of the system's inability to address the Triffin Dilemma and the related 'built-in destabilizer.' Of course, international policy coordination might theoretically make up for the policy spill overs, but experience shows that coordination attempts of the past were not only ineffective but asymmetric, carrying much more weight in countries having to rely on IMF assistance—gener-ally emerging markets or developing countries—while authorities of countries issuing reserve currencies were paying scant attention to the IMF recommendations.

Triffin's 'built-in destabilizer' must also be seen in the light of the hypotheses developed by Hyman Minsky and Michel Aglietta concerning financial markets' intrinsic propensity to insta-bility (see explanations in Annex 1). It is true that, in view of limiting this instability, there was major progress in international banking regulation and supervision since the GFC. Nevertheless, as shown in the previously mentioned recent RTI (2019), a number of new vulnerabilities have emerged, namely an increasing and opaque part of intermediation on global capital markets is taking place through NBFIs and greater reliance on international bond markets, through bond funds active in the supply of global credit, has created new, opaque risks (liquidity illusion) that largely escape regulation. Any unexpected shock could create a dollar liquidity crunch. Furthermore, only recently has the FSB begun a wide consultation on how to address these issues (FSB 2020). There has also been an aggravation of the second major failing of the current international monetary system, namely the absence of a genuine and clearly designated Global LOLR. The firepower (quota plus pre-arranged agreements to borrow), the authority and the legitimacy of the IMF, as it stands today, for taking this role did not keep pace with the continuing explosion of global liquidity and risks. As explained by Christian Ghymers (see Annex 2), the increased role of non-banks has two other systemic implications—(i) the pro-cyclical behaviour of Repo markets affects the monetary policy tools, especially when a liquidity crisis disrupts the intermediation capacity of the repo markets, in which case conventional monetary policies

---

17. See Eichengreen, Mehl, and Chitu (2018, 197), which formulates as follows the twenty-first century version of the Trif-fin Dilemma: Either the United States will limit its issuance of debt securities, in which case other countries will be starved of international liquidity, or the US government will increase issuance along with foreign demand, in which case confidence in its ability to service that debt, and therefore the safety and liquidity of the latter, will be cast into doubt.

cannot prevent fire-sales on the repo markets and (ii) a huge structural increase in the demand for 'safe assets' as collaterals, leading to a global shortage of USD safe assets, which might be the new form of the Triffin Dilemma.

The global deflationary effect of the mercantilist policies pursued by surplus countries and their refusal to pursue expansionary fiscal policies has induced the most important central banks to adopt unconventional quantitative easing policies, leading to an exponential increase of their balance sheets and of global liquidities that compounded the above structural changes in global capital markets. With the advent of a genuine inflationary threat, the same central banks will find themselves obliged of tapering their assets buying programs, which creates a dangerous context of instability, with what Mohamed El-Erian (2021), President of Queens' College, Cambridge and Adviser to Allianz and Gramercy, calls 'pockets of illiquidity amid generalized liquidity' that could degenerate into a global liquidity crisis. 'Until now, episodes of sudden illiquidity amid liquidity have proved to be temporary and reversible, and for good reason—the Fed's constant flooding of financial markets with liquidity reinforced the market's conditioning to buying the dip for "fear of missing out". With such high market confidence in the "Fed put", every bout of localized illiquidity encouraged the private sector to extend its leverage to take advantage of a reversible market drop.' But of course, no one knows when the bubble might burst.

In the farewell speech he gave on 23 August 2019 at the annual Jackson Hole Symposium, Mark Carney (2019), Governor of the Bank of England and former Governor of the Bank of Canada, focussed on how the nature of the IMFS challenges monetary policy. Without referring to Triffin's 'built-in destabilizer', he talked about a growing

> 'destabilizing asymmetry at the heart of the IMFS' and the increasing risk of a global liquidity trap. In his view, 'the IMFS is structurally lowering the global equilibrium interest rate, r^*, by—(i) feeding a global savings glut, as EMEs defensively accumulate reserves of safe US dollar assets against the backdrop of an inadequate and fragmented global financial safety net; (ii) reducing the scale of sustainable cross border flows, and as a result lowering the rate of global potential growth; and (iii) fattening of the left-hand tail and increasing the downside skew of likely economic outcomes.
>
> In an increasingly integrated world, global r^* exerts a greater influence on domestic r^*. As the global equilibrium rate falls, it becomes more difficult for domestic monetary policy makers everywhere to provide the stimulus necessary to achieve their objective.' (Carney 2019)

Further to this lucid diagnosis, Mark Carney examined what could be done in the short term, for instance, asking those at the core of the IMFS to incorporate spill overs and spillbacks in their flexible inflation targeting. But in the medium-term, he saw no other solution than having the policymakers 'reshuffle the pack', that is improve the structure of the current IMFS and rebuild an adequate global safety net. 'In the longer term,' says Mark Carney (2019), 'we need to change the game. There should be no illusions that the IMFS can be reformed overnight or that market forces are likely to force a rapid switch of reserve assets. But equally blithe acceptance of the status quo is misguided. Risks are building, and they are structural. As Rudi Dornbusch warned, "In economics, things take longer to happen than you think they will, and then they happen faster than you thought they could."' Mark Carney is also probably the first senior central banker to come out with a view of what the alternatives might be: 'When change comes, it shouldn't be to swap one currency hegemon for another. Any unipolar system is unsuited to a multi-polar world. We would do well to think through every opportunity, including those presented by new technologies, to create a more balanced and effective system'

Other Drivers of Reform of the IMFS

A. Structural Change Needed in the IMFS to Finance the Ecological Transition

Is the current IMFS suitable for the mobilization of the huge amounts of capital required to achieve the ecological transition, in particular the move of the global economy towards carbon neutrality? The financial dimension of the challenge of moving to carbon neutrality is indeed daunting. For example, the International Energy Agency (IAE) (2017) estimates that the low-carbon transition could require US$3.5 trillion in energy sector investments alone every year for decades—twice the rate at present. Climate-resilient infrastructure could reach an estimated US$90 trillion of infrastructure expected between 2015 and 2030. Furthermore, EMEs and less developed countries would need a higher volume of investments as they are less advanced in their development. This means that advanced nations need to expand the scope of their financing farther than the limits of their own nations. Economic development in the twenty-first century can be sustainable only if it is inclusive.

The experience so far is disappointing as the COVID-19 crisis has considerably reduced global energy and infrastructure investment volumes while the world's richest nations have so far failed to make good on a US$100 billion-a-year commitment they took in Cancun in 2010 and reaffirmed in Paris to help developing nations cope with climate change.

Several structural or systemic features, including in the current IMFS, make it particularly difficult to implement the commitment taken by the Parties in Article 2 of the Paris Agreement, namely making finance flows consistent with a pathway towards low greenhouse gas emissions and climate-resilient development.

In addition to what Mark Carney calls the tragedy of the horizon, namely the short-sightedness prevailing in financial markets and electoral cycles and the classical environmental problems of the tragedy of the commons and of free riders, the financing of the required huge capital-intensive investments is made difficult by the instability of the IFMS caused by the 'built-in destabilizer' in the absence of solution to the Triffin dilemma, global over-indebtedness, and the liquidity trap into which the global financial markets have fallen. The systemic evolution in financial markets, with the emergence of non-bank intermediation, the predominance of the dollar repo markets and the insatiable appetite for the safest of the safe assets are creating an unfavourable environment for raising funds of the magnitude required. Refinancing existing debts on a short-term basis or speculating in the stock market might always be more attractive to investors and assets managers. This constitutes an emergency situation. How quickly can responsible investing replace the dominant mentality of the asset management profession aiming at making money with money? Behind all the above obstacles, stands the persistent infeudation of the Western elites to the neo-liberal ideology, with its obsession about shareholders value and its excessive confidence in the efficiency of financial markets, as if the market value of a commodity, an asset, or a currency was always right.

The reduction of GHGs being a public good and the returns to investments being by definition long-term, uncertain, and subject to political risks, a large part of the investments will have to be made by public actors (Griffith-Jones 2020), many of whom are already overindebted and would need to issue long-term bonds on an unprecedented scale (Griffith-Jones 2020). A very high degree of international cooperation will be needed, and a much more important role will be expected from multilateral financial institutions. As pointed out by Aglietta and Coudert (2019), this will imply, in the long-term if not the short-term, a key role for the IMF, a bigger role for the SDR, and ultimately, the move to a multilateral currency. The strategy proposed by the IMF (2021) to help its members address climate change-related policy challenges by incorporating them in Article IV consultations and into financial stability assessments and by channelling additional resources to developing countries using the Poverty Reduction and Growth Trust and the recently established Resilience and Sustainability Trust are all valuable initiatives but remain insufficient. In fact, as pointed out by Aglietta and Coudert (see Annex 3), the change of energy paradigm could lead us to a corresponding change in the international monetary system.

B. Geopolitical Changes Pointing in the Direction of International Monetary Reform

Robert Triffin and his successors underestimated the resilience of the dollar and the willingness of central banks and private banks and non-banks worldwide to accumulate dollar-denominated assets despite the severe and persistent imbalances in the US budget and current account balances and the exorbitant privilege this entailed. The dollar crash never materialized. During the 2007-08 crisis, which originated in the US, the world still viewed the dollar as a safe haven and the pivot international currency. The US dollar has appreciated in recent years despite the imbalances.

Nevertheless, we must examine, in a prospective way, the geopolitical shifts at work in today's world. There is a weakening in the theoretical and practical justifications in the status of the USD as hegemonic key currency. The Trump presidency raised doubts on the benevolent nature of the US hegemony. There has been unease and sometimes outright indignation at the way in which the US instrumentalized the dollar for geopolitical purposes. Uncertainty is expressed about the continued capacity and willingness of the Federal Reserve to play the role of LOLR in future global USD shortage. More profoundly, there is a lack of intellectual leadership. The US does not appear to have a long-term vision on how the international role of the dollar should evolve. In a nutshell, the status quo does not serve anybody well.[18] There is an aspiration for change despite the inertia or stickiness supporting the continued dominance of the dollar.

What about the evolution, which appears inescapable, towards a multi-reserve currency system? Already, today, the euro is the second most important international payment and reserve currency. The international role of the euro is set to increase. The Juncker Commission launched in 2018 a strategy 'Towards a stronger international role of the euro' (European Commission 2018). There are nevertheless significant risks involved in the internationalization of the euro, in particular unwanted currency appreciation and tensions between the ECB's domestic mandate and the international consequences of its monetary policy decisions (Hudecz et al. 2021). Similar considerations could be developed with emerging economies currencies, which, given the increasing weight of their economies in the world, would aspire to share the USD's

---

18. See Tett (2019, 9), which comments a recent seminar on this subject organized in Zurich by the IMF and the Swiss National Bank.

international currency status and possibly one day replace it. If we take a long-term perspective, China looks set to become the dominant economic and political power of the twenty-first century. The question is how quickly it would be able to internationalize its currency and how responsibly it would handle the resulting exorbitant privilege and exorbitant burden.

Of course, a multipolar reserve currency world could be combined with a network of regional or inter-regional safety net arrangements, such as the European Stability Mechanism (ESM) in the EU, the Chiang Mai Initiative Multilateralization (CMIM), the Fondo Latinoamericano de Reservas (FLAR), the Arab Monetary Fund (AMF), the Eurasian Fund for Stabilization and Development (EFSD), and the BRICS Contingent Reserve Arrangements (BRICS-CRA). These Regional Financial Arrangements (RFAs) are surely useful for regional crises. Their respective strength[19] depends largely on their funding strategies, their capital structures, and their resulting creditworthiness and lending capacity. In a serious global crisis, there is no doubt that their effectiveness would depend on their capacity to coordinate their actions with the global safety net, which can be provided only at the global multilateral level. The alternative is the fragmentation of the globalization into regional blocks, relying on specific reserve currencies and regional safety nets. This would entail a huge cost to the global economy and global welfare.

In fact, a multiplicity of national currencies playing the role of global currency does not solve the Triffin dilemma, leaving alive problems of asymmetry in balance of payments constraints, the 'built-in destabilizer' and monetary policy spill overs, and the differences in perceived 'money-ness' in times of crisis, as explained by Christian Ghymers (see Annex 2).

Furthermore, history tells us that risks to global stability are greatest in periods of transition when economic leadership passes from one country to another. There are indeed reasons to believe that the transition would not be smooth, and the US would offer a strong resistance (Rickards 2011).

China gave the impression in 2009 it could support a multilateral currency system,[20] but recently, it has shown less enthusiasm for the SDR cause—a circumstance that can be interpreted as revealing that its 2009 proposal was mostly motivated by the protection of the value of its huge stock of dollar-denominated reserves. In the meantime, the renminbi has been incorporated in the SDR basket, and a few international bond issues in SDRs have been placed in China.

The internationalization of the renminbi, although still in an early phase, is part of a long-term strategy of international opening and liberalization of the Chinese economic and financial system adopted by the Chinese authorities at the highest level in 2014 for both internal and geopolitical reasons.[21] The Chinese government is determined to enhance its international financial influence as an instrument to integrate commercially and financially East Asia around the Chinese economy, to guarantee its security of supply in raw materials, and to structure its trade flows

19. See interesting study by Cheng and Alvise Lennkh (2019).
20. The President of China's People Bank, Governor Zhou Xiaochuan (2009), strongly chastised a system based on nationally issued reserve currencies, stating that the frequency and increasing intensity of financial crises … suggest the cost of such a system to the world may have exceeded its benefits. He referred to Robert Triffin. More specifically, he envisaged an international reserve currency with three characteristics: an international reserve currency should first be anchored to a stable benchmark and issued according to a clear set of rules to ensure orderly supply; second, its supply should be flexible enough to allow timely adjustment according to the changing demand; and third, such adjustments should be disconnected from economic conditions and sovereign interests of any single country. These are indeed the characteristics of the SDR as envisioned by Triffin.
21. For a detailed account of this new strategy, see Aglietta and Valla (2021).

with Europe and other parts of the world. This new phase of reform, destined to re-establish China's historical place in the world, that of the Middle Kingdom, implies a decoupling of the renminbi from the USD. At the same time, Beijing is reinforcing the institutional framework allowing the internationalization of the renminbi and presenting itself to emerging countries as an alternative to the Fed in the case of a new liquidity crisis (SWIFT 2019).

A new important development is the progress achieved by China towards developing its own Central Bank Digital Currency (CBDC), allowing it potentially to challenge the US-dominant influence on the SWIFT payment infrastructure and to bypass the sanctions imposed by the US through its de facto control of the SWIFT payment rails (Bansal and Singh 2021). China could become the standard setter in the CBDC relatively new technology, which would have significant geopolitical implications.

Unless emerging conflict can be defused, the world could see a rise of geopolitical forces analogous to those that destroyed the first globalization at the beginning of the twentieth century.

It is essential to prevent the US and China from falling into the so-called Thucydides trap,[22] under which trade and currency wars could lead to a fully-fledged arms race and a military conflict. Such an outcome would doom global efforts towards implementing the Paris climate agreement.

A reform of the IMFS, involving a new power sharing in the IMF and the World Bank between the US, the EU, China, and other advanced or emerging countries, as well as the subsuming of currency rivalry through the move to a genuine multilateral currency, could be part of a global package deal, involving other advances in multilateralism, including shared responsibilities in moving to carbon neutrality. For such a win-win solution, there is no need to create a new institution. The IMF exists but needs to recuperate the monetary role it lost since the Jamaica Agreement to become the linchpin of global monetary governance and multilateral cooperation. The multilateral currency exists already in embryonic form through the SDR created in 1969. The blueprint for reform of the IMFS and for a sequenced agenda leading to it are already available and as argued in the final section, the new climate created by the recent SDR allocation opens a window of opportunity for it.

Towards the Urgent Reform of the IMFS: A Silver Lining

After a difficult start in 2020, the global response to the pandemic has involved a higher degree of multilateral cooperation than earlier. It led, after the election of President Joe Biden, to an unprecedented SDR allocation equivalent to US$650 billion. Despite its big global size, the SDR allocation will send only about US$55 billion directly to 82 highly debt-vulnerable developing economies, which is equivalent to only about 1.8 per cent of their gross public debt stock, but the allocation has placed the SDR in the limelight. The need to find a way to channel part of the advanced countries' shares of the SDR to developing countries has led to several innovative

---

22. Graham Allison coined this expression in a 2012 article for the *Financial Times*. It is based on a quote by ancient historian and military general Thucydides in his *History of the Peloponnesian War* positing that 'it was the rise of Athens and the fear that this instilled in Sparta that made war inevitable', Allison used the term to describe a tendency towards war when a rising power (exemplified by Athens) challenges the status of a dominant power (exemplified by Sparta); Yet, stressing that war is not inevitable, Allison also reveals in her book *Destined for War*, London, Scribe, 2017, how clashing powers have kept the peace in the past—and what painful steps international leaders can and must take to avoid disaster. More specifically, he recommends clarifying vital interests, understanding what the rival power is trying to do, to 'do strategy', and making domestic challenges central, i.e., to grasp the seriousness of the problems both rivals face on the home front, e.g. failures of governance, and the ways to address them.

proposals, which are steps in the right direction.[23] This channelling of SDRs raises a number of issues (Sobel 2021) pointing in the direction of an overhaul of the SDR legal framework, with the potential to transform it into a much more effective instrument in the IMFS. Paradoxically, the current unsatisfactory intermediate situation is bound to stimulate the reconsideration of previous proposals that had not received sufficient attention[24] and the formulation of new ones,[25] enhancing the SDRs' impact and using them as a lever to reform the IMS. Finally, the SDR could be used much more proactively in support of regional integration, particularly in Africa,[26] underpinning regional monetary unions, 'payments union' agreements similar to those implemented in Europe after WWII and promoting the choice of the SDR as a 'unit of account'.[27]

As has been seen, the blueprint for a comprehensive reform of the IMFS has been on the table since the publication of the PRI Report in 2011—complemented by several RTI reports— and a roadmap to achieve the reform, step by step, has also been available for more than five years. Neither the features of the blueprint, nor the relevance of the sequenced agenda have been seriously challenged. What has been lacking has been the political will to move ahead, as the G20 has remained blocked by its internal divisions. Nevertheless, the recent SDR allocation and the cooperative climate of the negotiation about its distribution look like a silver lining at a moment when a fundamental reform of the system appears more urgent than ever. Indeed, the present depressing situation could evolve due to several interconnected drivers for change:

The Triffin dilemma is no more an academic concept; it is an increasingly unsustainable situation that sooner rather than later will oblige global decision makers to act. Even for the US, the dangers of inaction exceed now by far the more and more dubious advantages of the status quo, as US monetary policy might become hostage of the world's insatiable appetite for the safest of the safe assets, namely the USD Treasury bills. The worsening of the 'built-in destabilizer', linked to the structural changes in financial markets under the present system, might at any time trigger a new financial crisis of unknown magnitude, with potentially catastrophic consequences for the real economy as well as for the survival of democratic regimes.

The status quo would likewise not allow the IMFS to mobilize, on a timely basis, the long-term resources to finance the huge investments required to address Climate Change and adaptation, which are becoming the most threatening global challenge for the survival of human civilization. A new currency paradigm will be needed based on the adoption of a common global price for carbon reduction.

Although the world appears to move in the direction of a multipolar system of reserve currencies, competition among currencies could lead to dangerous instability and currency wars.

---

23. For a preliminary global assessment of the response before the change in the US Administration, see G30 Working Group on Sovereign Debt and COVID-19 (2020). In 2020, the IMF mobilized and almost immediately exhausted its concessional lending capacity, which was not designed for a global shock of the magnitude of the pandemic or for countries prone to large scale capital outflows. It increased disbursements to low-income countries through the concessional Rapid Credit Facility (RCF) and covered payments on existing IMF loans to the poorest low-income countries through the Catastrophe Containment and Relief Trust. However, the RCF is designed to support a steady-state lending capacity of only between US$1.5 billion and US$2 billion a year, not for widespread shocks and large-scale outflows. Also, the IMF's non-concessional capacity has remained underutilized, with the IMF disbursing in 2020 only US$30 billion, i.e., less than a third of its US$100 billion envelope for pandemic-related financing through the Rapid Financing Instrument (RCI).
24. Such as RTI Working Party (2014).
25. Such as Ocampo (2021).
26. See Masini (2021), in which the author suggests that the EU member States should consider pooling part of the SDRs recently received to launch Next Generation Africa, a major investment plan, of both grants and loans, aiming at triggering endogenous growth in Africa and at strengthening African integration. See also (Flor 2020).
27. See (De Rambures, Iozzo and Viterbo 2020).

The exacerbation of the Sino–American economic rivalry could find a solution in the context of the negotiation of a package deal involving the move to a multilateral currency system, acknowledging the upgraded status of China and of other EMEs, combined with their agreement to cooperate fully in the ecological transition.

The old Triffin-Keynes plan aimed at establishing a rational system for global liquidity management could become feasible, based on a more ingenious use of the SDR to face the world multiple financing challenges and pave the way for the transformation of the SDR into the principal reserve asset in the international monetary system, as foreseen under Article XXII of the IMF Articles of Agreement.

The situation is not hopeless. Both the dangers we have identified for the world monetary and fiscal stability and the opportunity for a negotiation on new terms create a window of opportunity. The purpose of this contribution is to stimulate the debate, putting on the table concrete reform proposals. The US, the EU, Japan, Canada, Australia, and the other OECD countries, as well as China and the other EMEs have all huge stakes in a successful comprehensive reform of the IMFS as an indispensable underpinning to sustainable globalization and the achievement of the United Nations Sustainable Development Goals.

Annex 1: The Financial Instability Hypothesis of Minsky and Aglietta

The 'built-in destabilizer' effect has to be seen also in the light of the financial instability hypothesis—combined with the preponderance of the financial cycle hypothesis—as developed by economists such as Hyman Minsky[28] and Michel Aglietta (2019). The key reason for financial instability is that the pivot of financial markets is not fundamental value: it is liquidity but liquidity, by acting upon both demand and supply of credits, generates self-fulfilling fluctuations that impede free financial markets to ensure inner stability. Financial markets do not operate like ordinary markets. In the latter, the two sides of the market have opposing interests regarding prices, which guarantees a supply curve that rises with prices and a demand curve that falls. In financial markets, any actor can be seller or buyer any time, alternating euphoria and panic, whereby the demand and supply curves are not independent and move up or down with asset prices.

Annex 2: The New Form of the Triffin Dilemma According to Christian Ghymers: How the Increasing Role of the Repo Markets Contributes to a Global Shortage of USD Safe Assets

As explained in this chapter, a key feature of the recent structural changes is the shift from bank loans to borrowing from the wholesale money markets, i.e., the relative growing importance taken by the non-bank intermediaries (or the so-called 'shadow banks'), which are less or not regulated and therefore do not have direct access to refinancing by their central bank. The consequent higher liquidity risks are individually covered by an intensive use of collateral assets (repo and asset-backed commercial papers) whereas the co-variation of collaterals with the cycles raises a global systemic risk. This increased role of non-banks has two other systemic implications: (i) the pro-cyclical behaviour of repo markets affects the monetary policy tools, especially when a liquidity crisis disrupts the intermediation capacity of the repo markets, in which case conventional monetary policies cannot prevent fire-sales on the repo markets; and (ii) a huge structural increase in the demand for 'safe assets' as collaterals that constitute the basis of the reversed pyramid of global liquidity.

As shown by Christian Ghymers (2019 and 2021), such a basis is necessarily pro-cyclical and submitted itself to an unstable, reversible multiplier in the present working of the IMFS because it does not benefit from a multilateral LOLR but only from national LOLRs whose efficiency is decreasing. In normal times, in the case of liquidity squeeze, banks can feed this wholesale market by borrowing reserves from their central banks and intermediate this liquidity to non-banks on their repo-market, which is able to create additional safe assets. However, the value of these collaterals used to co-vary more with the financial cycle triggers a dangerous

---

28. Hyman Philip Minsky (1919–96) was an American economist, a professor of economics at Washington University in St. Louis, and a distinguished scholar at the Levy Economics Institute of Bard College. Minsky proposed theories linking financial market fragility in the normal life cycle of an economy with speculative investment bubbles endogenous to financial markets. Minsky stated that in prosperous times, when corporate cash flow rises beyond what is needed to pay off debt, a speculative euphoria develops, and soon thereafter debts exceed what borrowers can pay off from their incoming revenues, which in turn produces a financial crisis. As a result of such speculative borrowing bubbles, banks and lenders tighten credit availability, even to companies that can afford loans, and the economy subsequently contracts. Minsky opposed some of the financial deregulation policies popular in the 1980s, stressed the importance of the Federal Reserve as a lender of last resort and argued against the over-accumulation of private debt in the financial markets. Minsky's economic theories were largely ignored for decades, until the subprime mortgage crisis of 2008 caused a renewed interest in them.

global liquidity crisis according to the following scenario: bigger 'haircuts'[29] lead to downgrading, especially of non-dollar collaterals, disrupting the intermediation of the repo, as they are unable to feed the non-bank with liquidity from banks received through the national monetary policies. These haircuts make suddenly visible the effective scarcity of the genuine basis of the inversed pyramid of global liquidity, which is narrowing under the discrimination created by a 'Gresham law' among collaterals, favouring a run to the higher quality of dollar safe assets at the detriment of non-dollar ones.

Ghymers explains this fragility by the impossibility of ensuring a stable liquidity basis for this inversed pyramid with only safe assets issued in national currencies because, not only their volume is endogenous with the cycle, but essentially because safe assets in USD enjoy a higher quality of liquidity than those of non-dollar safe assets. The destabilizing factor comes from the pro-cyclical amplification of the difference in the degree of 'moneyness' across currencies: during the upward phase of the cycle, this difference is minimized and hidden, but is suddenly amplified when the cycle turns downwards, exposing the global liquidity reversed pyramid to boom-bust cycles in private liquidity. In case of stress, a run to dollar safe assets provokes an abrupt narrowing of the liquidity basis, which destroys private liquidity with a multiplicative impact. He shows that this structural shortage of dollar safe assets is nothing else than the present form of the Triffin Dilemma and his 'built-in destabilizer' — the logical impossibility for the liquid debt of a national economy to ensure a stable basis for global liquidity while respecting domestic stability criteria.

The combination of these new unsustainable features of large and long-term uncertainties and of the higher returns of speculation has led to the global liquidity trap witnessed today. The large scale injection of liquidities is not achieving its objective of stimulating long term investment in the real economy; rather, they are massively invested in short term instruments, driving interest rates further down, driving stock exchanges and real estate prices up, and worsening social inequalities. Meanwhile, the world remains direly short of long-term investments, such as those required to fund the environmental transition and attain the UN Sustainable Development Goals (SDGs).

Annex 3: Could the Change of Energy Paradigm Lead Us to a Corresponding Change in the International Monetary System?

According to Michel Aglietta and Virginie Coudert (2019), relying themselves on analysis by Timothy Mitchell (2011), there has been a link in the two eras following the Industrial Revolution between the key currency system and the primary source of energy. In the age of classical capitalism up to 1913, the sterling gold standard prevailed as the key currency system with coal as the most important source of energy; in the Bretton Woods system, it was the dollar standard with oil as the dominant energy source. The dominant source of energy being the most traded commodity worldwide, it is not surprising that its price be denominated in the key currency, becoming the anchor of the international price system. Exporting countries recycle revenues for investment in the most secure financial system — that of the country issuing the key

---

29. The haircut is loss of value of the collateral (or the risk-premium spread in term of yield), representing the lower degree of moneyness (liquidity) of the internally generated collaterals by the Repo dealers with respect to the value of the external 'first-quality' collaterals.

currency. The reasoning of Aglietta and Coudert is that the shift to renewables and electricity, which are also much more diversified geographically than coal and oil, might give rise to a new international payment system. In the new ecological era, the anchor will be the social price of mitigation action, i.e., the tutelary price required to undertake massive, long, and risky investments. As carbon pricing would be the most important variable of this mitigation action, one might expect this price to replace the price of oil as the anchor of the new economy. This price would express what the collective is prepared to pay to restore an ecosystem of common interest (Carbon Pricing Leadership Coalition 2017). This price should be the outcome of a global agreement and be expressed in an international currency, which logically should be the SDR.

Chapter 9: Climate Change Policy for Developing Countries

Climate Change Policy for Developing Countries[1]

Chapter 9 | Montek Singh Ahluwalia[2] and Utkarsh Patel[3]

Introduction

This chapter attempts to take stock of what has been achieved in the COP 26 meetings held in Glasgow in November 2021 and suggests the course of action that developing countries should follow in subsequent negotiations. Ultimately, there was progress in several areas, but many critical issues remain unresolved. Developing countries need to evolve a constructive approach that can carry the dialogue further and fill in the remaining critical gaps.

The chapter is organized as follows. Section 1 presents a brief review of climate change negotiations to show that despite apparently irreconcilable differences between developed and developing countries in the early stages, the negotiations were successful in narrowing these differences very considerably over time. Section 2 summarizes the findings of the Intergovernmental Panel on climate change (IPCC) on the impacts of a rise in global temperature of 2°C and above, which was a critical input into COP 26. Section 3 reviews the outcomes of COP 26 and indicates the areas where more remains to be done. Section 4 presents an assessment of what developing countries have to do to implement their COP 26 commitments. Section 5 discusses the scale of financial support developing countries will need to achieve climate-related goals. Finally, Section 6 gives recommendations on how developing countries should now proceed.

Narrowing Differences over Time

Scientists have been worrying about climate change for well over a century.[4] However, it was only in 1988 that the issue first surfaced on the international stage when the UN General Assembly recognised it as a global problem and set up the IPCC to provide scientific guidance in this area. This was followed by the Earth Summit in Rio in 1992, which discussed several aspects of the environment and sustainability and formally acknowledged that global warming, which is caused by rising concentration of CO_2 and other greenhouse gas (GHGs) in the atmosphere, was a threat to life on

1. The work on this paper has been carried out at the Centre for Social and Economic Progress (CSEP), New Delhi. An earlier version of this chapter was published as a CSEP working paper. We are grateful for very helpful comments received from Amar Bhattacharya, Anne O. Krueger, Harinder Kohli, Jagadish Shukla, Laveesh Bhandari, Lord Nicolas Stern, Raavi Aggarwal, Rahul Tongia, Rajat Nag and Rakesh Mohan. Needless to say, the errors that remain are entirely ours.
2. Distinguished Fellow, CSEP, and former Deputy Chairman of the erstwhile Planning Commission of India.
3. Associate Fellow, CSEP, New Delhi.
4. Irish physicist John Tyndall was the first to demonstrate in 1859 the absorption of heat by certain gases—what is now known as the greenhouse effect. Swedish scientist Svante Arrhenius claimed in 1896 that fossil fuel combustion may eventually result in enhanced global warming. One half of the 2021 Nobel Prize in Physics was jointly awarded to two climate scientists, Syukuro Manabe (US) and Klaus Hasselmann (Germany) for work done in the 1960s and the 1970s, respectively, on models linking weather with climate.

earth. The Rio Summit formally launched the UN Framework Convention on Climate Change (UNFCCC) as a negotiating forum on climate change issues for all countries of the world.

Developing countries originally took the view that since the higher concentration of GHGs in the atmosphere was primarily due to the burning of fossil fuels by developed countries as they industrialized, the burden of reducing emissions to halt global warming must fall on them. Developing countries were beginning their development process, which would involve an increase in energy use and therefore emissions. They should not be restrained from doing so, but they could be encouraged to undertake voluntary mitigation actions, for which they must be supported financially. In addition, developing countries would also need financial assistance to meet the costs of adapting to climate change which was not caused by them.

The Kyoto Protocol (1997)

The first international agreement on reducing emissions was the Kyoto Protocol signed in 1997. It enshrined an asymmetric approach, imposing emission reduction targets only on developed countries. The principle of financial assistance to developing countries was conceded, though no amounts were quantified.

The Kyoto Protocol was not successful. The first commitment period (2008–12) had very modest targets: a 6–8 per cent reduction in GHG emissions from 1990 levels. The US did not ratify the Protocol and other developed countries withdrew later, citing non-participation of developing countries as the reason. The Protocol never went beyond the second commitment period (2012–20).[5]

The Copenhagen Accord (2009)

COP 15 in Copenhagen in 2009 was an important step forward in climate negotiations. It was the first time the international community adopted the target that global warming should be limited to below +2°C. Developing countries as a group remained unwilling to commit to reducing emissions, but some developing and developed countries agreed that the way forward was for developing countries to adopt some mitigation measures that would reduce the 'emissions intensity of GDP'[6] and for developed countries to provide financial assistance reaching US$100 billion per year by 2020 for developing countries' mitigation and adaptation. This agreement, which was called the Copenhagen Accord, was finally adopted by over 130 parties in COP16 at Cancun (Mexico) in 2010.

The Paris Agreement (2015)

COP21 in Paris in 2015 was the next major advance. It saw progress in three critical areas:
- First, the global warming objective was restated to limit global warming to 'well below 2°C and ideally to 1.5°C'. This was a concession to small island nations reflecting the fact that a sea-level rise resulting from a +2°C global temperature increase would pose an existential threat to their inhabitants;
- Second, all parties, including developing countries, made commitments in the form of Intended Nationally Determined Contributions (INDC) to reduce emissions and mitigate

---

5. The US committed to a target but did not ratify it; Canada withdrew from the Agreement in 2011; Japan, New Zealand and Russia did not make further commitments beyond the first commitment period.
6. That is, keep the growth of emissions less than that of GDP.

climate change. This was the first time that all developing countries took on commitments on mitigation, although they were limited to reducing the emissions intensity of the GDP; and,

- Developed countries extended the promise of *additional* climate finance of US$100 billion per year by 2020 for developing countries, to continue up to 2024. The finance would be a mix of private and public flows, but neither was the composition specified nor were the criteria for determining the additionality stated.

- The universal acceptance of some mitigation obligations by all developing countries was seen as a positive outcome, even though they made no commitment to any reduction in absolute levels of emissions. However, it soon became evident that the totality of the commitments made by all countries was not sufficient to limit global warming to the level targeted. UNEP reported that even if the Paris commitments were achieved in full, global temperatures could rise by 3°C or more by the end of the century (UNEP 2016a).

The failure to ensure achievement of the global warming target was a direct consequence of relying only on voluntary commitments, with no overarching mechanism to ensure that the prospective CO_2 emissions would remain within the 'carbon budget'.[7] The decision to stay with voluntary commitments appears understandable in retrospect since developing countries until then had been unwilling to undertake any commitments.

The first reliable estimate of the carbon budget was provided by the IPCC Special Report on Global Warming of 1.5°C in 2018.[8] The report quantified the differences between warming of +1.5°C and +2°C and highlighted the adverse effects associated with +2°C, calling for lowering the global warming target to +1.5°C. It also indicated that given the limited size of the CO_2 budget available, global CO_2 emissions must reach net zero to halt the progression of global warming.

The Consequences of Global Warming of 2°C

The findings of IPCC (2021) on the consequences of allowing global warming to exceed +2°C are deeply disturbing. They need to be much more widely understood to develop public support for measures to combat climate change. The main point to note is that all regions of the world will experience global warming, but the extent of warming will vary across regions, with very different outcomes in terms of changes in precipitation, local temperature, and vulnerability to extreme weather events.

In a +2°C warming scenario, the average annual temperature in the northern regions, i.e., Europe and North America, could rise by 2.5°C and 3.1°C, respectively, by the end of the century. The rise in the warmer regions of the South would be in the range of 1.8–2.2°C (Figure 9.1). The increase in temperature is higher in Europe and North America than in Asia, Africa, and Central and South America, but since the latter are already at warmer temperatures, they would suffer more damage.

---

7. The carbon budget is the volume of net CO_2 emissions that can be released in the atmosphere which will keep its total atmospheric concentration at a level consistent with the warming target.

8. The IPCC's Fifth Assessment Synthesis Report (SYR AR5) in 2014 mentions the carbon budget, but the value was revised substantially in the IPCC Special Report in 2018 using more accurate methods that ensured that uncertainties in the model from the historical estimates do not get accumulated into future projections.

Figure 9.1: Rise (°C) in near-surface temperatures in a +2°C warmer world

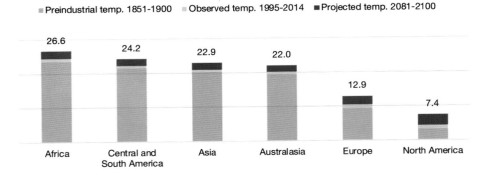

Note: Asia excludes the Russian sub-continent of Serbia and Artic, Europe excludes Greenland.
Source: IPCC 2021

Impact on Productivity and GDP

The effects of climate change on GDP and income levels in different parts of the world are not easy to estimate. Several economic models have produced estimates, but the results differ depending upon the assumptions used, which are difficult to validate based on available empirical evidence. It is important to note that the extent of global warming currently being predicted takes us outside the realm of human experience, and non-linearities could make outcomes much worse than made out by naïve economic models so far.

Burke, Hsiang, and Miguel (2015) find that economic productivity increases with warming up to an optimum temperature and then starts to decline at an increasing rate with each unit rise in temperature. They estimate that climate change will reduce projected global output by at least 23 per cent by the end of the century, compared to a world without climate change.

A recent study by the Swiss Re Institute (2021) suggests that if no corrective action is taken and the temperature by mid-century increases to 2°C above pre-industrial levels, expected GDP in 2050 for the world as a whole will be 11 per cent lower than in the base case of no climate change. North America and Europe stand to lose 7–8 per cent of their expected GDP, while countries in the southern continents will lose in the range of 11–15 per cent. The report finds that the countries in Southeast Asia will be the hardest hit—losing nearly 17 per cent of their expected GDP (Swiss Re Institute 2021).

As expected, the agriculture sector would be the worst hit by rising temperatures and changing precipitation. Ortiz-Bobea et al. report that increased temperatures have reduced global average agricultural productivity by about 21 per cent since 1961 with impacts more pronounced in warmer areas like parts of Africa, Latin America and Asia (Ortiz-Bobea et al. 2021). Since a large share of the poor in these countries depend upon agriculture and manual labour for their livelihoods, the projected change is likely to reduce the pace of poverty reduction and widen income inequality.

Health- and Welfare-related Impacts

Climate change will also have adverse effects on health through various interactions. The WHO projects that between 2030 and 2050, approximately 250 thousand additional deaths per year, from malnutrition, malaria, diarrhoea, and heat stress could be attributed to climate change (WHO 2021). Frequent forest fires in many parts of the world have caused wild animals to move to new places in search of habitats, threatening an increase in zoonotic infections. Melting of polar ice caps due to global warming poses the danger of pathogens, that existed in the past and were long isolated or thought of as extinct, being released from the permafrost.

The ongoing COVID-19 pandemic is an example of the large economic and human cost of diseases spread by new pathogens. Climate change will only increase the probability of such outbreaks with low-income countries, which have weak public health infrastructure and lack the resources to strengthen it, severely hit.

The UN High Commissioner for Refugees (2021) has estimated that between 2008 and 2016, an average of 21.5 million people were forcibly displaced each year due to weather-related events linked to climate change. Bangladesh, for example, is witnessing a movement of people from high-risk coastal areas and rural regions where agricultural lands have turned barren due to salinisation from rising sea levels, towards urban centres seeking safety and better livelihoods, which is putting pressure on cities that already lack access to public services (*The Economist* 2021).

The World Bank (2018) estimates that without concrete mitigation action, around 143 million people in Sub-Saharan Africa, South Asia, and Latin America—approximately 2.8 per cent of the combined population—would be forced to migrate internally to escape floods or drought-prone areas. This would exacerbate poverty and could trigger spontaneous cross-border movements which can potentially cause conflicts and regional instability.

The consequences mentioned above relate to a +2°C rise. By most projections we are likely to cross that threshold by the middle of the century and reach even higher levels of global warming by 2100. Developing countries will be the worst hit which means they have a strong interest in avoiding this outcome. However, they can only do so much on their own to affect the pace of climate change. They must work together with developed countries to produce an agreement on collective action that can moderate and ultimately halt global warming, while taking care of their interests.

Outcomes of COP 26

The IPCC (2021) report, which warned that global warming was 'widespread, rapid, and intensifying' and would have potentially catastrophic consequences if not checked set the tone for the COP 26 meetings. UN Secretary General, Guterres, described the report as signalling 'Code Red'. There was unprecedented participation by civil society groups, environmentalists, philanthropic organisations, and private investors. The meetings were widely described as 'the last chance to save the planet'.

The hype was such that it is not surprising that the results fell short of the hopes raised. Many climate change activists described the meeting as a failure. Developing countries also expressed disappointment at the failure of developed countries to deliver on the financial assistance that was promised in the Paris Agreement. Despite this, one can argue that there was substantial progress.

The scale of the challenge facing COP 26 is summarized in Figure 9.2 which presents the IPCC's assessment of the prospects for global warming if the recent trend in CO_2 emissions continues (dashed curves) and compares it with what is needed to prevent global temperatures

Figure 9.2: Atmospheric CO_2 concentration and global surface temperature since 1850

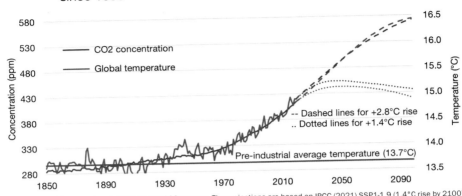

Note: Pre-industrial temperature implies 1850-1900 average. The projections are based on IPCC (2021) SSP1-1.9 (1.4°C rise by 2100) and SSP2-4.5 (2.8°C rise) scenarios.
Source: Authors' calculations based on NOAA 2021, GCP 2021, and IPCC 2021.

from exceeding +1.5°C (dotted curves). It is clear that if global warming is not to exceed 1.5°C above the pre-industrial level by 2100, then atmospheric CO_2 concentration must peak by 2050 and subsequently decline. Peaking CO_2 concentration by 2050 implies that total emissions must be net zero by then. Furthermore, since the peak CO_2 concentration level projected for 2050 actually exceeds the threshold for +1.5°C, it is necessary to reduce the concentration level after 2050, by going net negative in terms of CO_2 emissions thereafter.[9]

Faced with this challenge, what did COP 26 come up with? The results of the negotiations, in terms of agreements reached, are summarized below.

- The global warming targets were tightened to 'not exceed +1.5°C' in recognition of the high costs of warming up to +2°C, indicated by the IPCC;
- 136 countries, representing 88 per cent of the total annual CO_2 emissions, including many developing countries, announced programmes to reduce emissions to net zero over time. Earlier unwilling to commit to reducing emissions, developing countries for the first time accepted the need to reduce the absolute level of emissions and to achieve net zero. The change in their position reflects a recognition that technology has made renewables—solar and wind—an alternative source of energy that could allow them to meet their increasing energy demands without emitting GHGs;
- Most countries have opted for 2050 as the target date, but some have announced later dates. Russia and many large developing countries like China, Indonesia, Nigeria, and Saudi Arabia have declared 2060 as the target year for net zero. India, which has much lower per capita emissions than other large emitters, has declared 2070 as its target year. Some developed countries have opted for target dates earlier than 2050: 2045 for Germany and Sweden, 2040 for Austria and Iceland, and 2035 for Finland. Nepal has announced 2045, making it an exception among developing countries for choosing a target earlier than 2050;

9. Net negative emissions imply removing CO_2 from the atmosphere by means of forest carbon sequestration, and carbon capture and storage technologies which are assumed to be viable at large scale by then.

- In addition to committing to reach net zero in the future, most countries have also indicated intermediate shorter-term targets for 2030, though not all on the same dimension (Box 9.1);
- The Glasgow Pact acknowledged that the promise to deliver additional financial assistance reaching US$100 billion per year by 2020, which was offered in Copenhagen in 2009 and was a key part of the Paris Agreement, has not been met. According to the OECD (2021a), the delivery reached only US$79 billion by 2019, though others have said it was lower (Roberts et al. 2021). Part of the reason for the disagreement is because it was never spelt out what would qualify as 'additional'. An OECD (2021b)

Box 9.1: Latest INDCs of the top emitters

China
- 65 per cent reduction in the emissions intensity of GDP from 2005 levels by 2030
- Peak emissions by 2030/reduce coal consumption starting 2025–30
- Increase the share of non-fossil fuels in primary energy consumption to ~25 per cent by 2030
- Increase the forest stock volume by 6 billion cu. metre from 2005 level
- 1.2 TW wind and solar electricity generation capacity by 2030
- Net zero by 2060

US
- 50–52 per cent reduction in emissions from 2005 levels by 2030
- Carbon pollution-free power sector by 2035
- Net zero by 2050

EU
- 55 per cent reduction in emissions from 1990 levels by 2030
- Net zero by 2050

UK
- 78 per cent reduction in emissions from 1990 levels by 2035
- Net zero by 2050

India
- 45 per cent reduction in the emissions intensity of GDP from 2005 levels by 2030
- 500 GW of non-fossil fuel electricity generation capacity by 2030; 50 per cent electricity generation capacity to be renewables-based by 2030
- Reduction of 1 Gt-CO_2e emissions over 2022–30
- Net zero by 2070

Russia
- 30 per cent reduction in emissions from 1990 levels by 2030
- Net zero by 2060
- Under discussion: peak emissions by 2030, 79 per cent reduction in emissions from 2019 levels by 2050

Japan
- 46 per cent reduction in emissions from 2013 levels by 2030
- Net zero by 2050

Indonesia
- 29 to 41 per cent reduction in emissions from BAU levels by 2030
- Peak emissions by 2030
- Net negative CO_2 emissions from the forest and land-use sector.
- Net zero by 2060

Brazil
- 50 per cent reduction in emissions from 2005 levels by 2030
- End illegal deforestation by 2028
- Net zero by 2050

analysis suggests that the full amount of US$100 billion would only be reached by 2023. The Pact has targeted doubling the amount for adaptation finance from 2019 levels by 2025 (UN Climate Change Conference UK 2021), but since this is part of the total financial commitment, it only affects the composition of the assistance;

- The pact also approved rules on government-led international carbon markets to implement Article 6 of the Paris Agreement, superseding the UN Clean Development Mechanism. The new rules would allow countries to partially meet their climate targets by buying offset credits that represent emission reductions by others, such as via forestry, and avoid double counting of credits. This is expected to financially benefit developing countries with large forest covers and also reduce deforestation; and,
- In addition to CO_2, the pact emphasized reducing non-CO_2 GHG emissions. Over a hundred countries have pledged to act on reducing methane emissions by 30 per cent by 2030, over the 2020 levels.

The willingness of developing countries to target an actual reduction in emissions reaching net zero at some future date must be counted as a major advance from the Paris Agreement. However, the new country targets announced in Glasgow remain inadequate to limit global warming to +1.5°C. Early assessments by the UNEP show that even if all countries met their targets in full—clearly an optimistic scenario given the record—we may still end up with global warming of +1.8°C (UNEP 2021). A more realistic assessment, which makes allowances for possible slippages in performance, suggests that the more likely outcome is a rise of up to +2.4°C.

The situation after COP 26 is therefore better than it was after Paris, but it is certainly not good enough. Recognizing this problem, the Glasgow Pact has asked all parties to raise their climate targets by the time of COP 27 in Sharm El-Sheikh in Egypt in 2022, instead of after five years as originally planned.

Modification of Country Trajectories

Since the emissions trajectories emerging from Glasgow are to be reviewed in COP 27, developing countries need to prepare for this review carefully. If total emissions must stay within the fixed carbon budget, it is necessarily a zero-sum game in the sense that high emissions by some countries must be offset by lower emissions by others.

In theory, the best way of solving the problem would be to divide the available carbon budget in a demonstrably fair manner into individual country budgets and then leave it to each country to define its own emission trajectory respective to its carbon budget.[10] The date by which a country reaches net zero is not important in this framework since the critical requirement is that countries stay within their budget. However, this approach requires some agreement on what a fair basis would be for distributing the budget, and this issue has never been discussed thus far.

This was not discussed in the run-up to COP 26, because developed countries focussed their efforts on getting all countries to commit to reaching net zero by 2050. This simple formula appeared to be justified by the 2018 IPCC report, which asserted that limiting global warming

---

10. The UK, for instance, under its 2008 climate change Act, sets for itself a five-year statutory cap on total GHG emissions. The carbon budgets are set twelve years in advance to provide sufficient time for businesses to align their activities. The emission targets are set per the UK's long-term goals of emission reduction—earlier 80 per cent below 1990 levels by 2050, and now net zero by 2050. See for reference the 6th Carbon Budget report of the UK climate change Committee (2021). Accessible at https://www.theccc.org.uk/publication/sixth-carbon-budget/

to +1.5°C will require global CO_2 emissions to reduce to 55 per cent of 2010 levels by 2030 and reach net zero by mid-century (IPCC 2018). Many developing countries were unwilling to accept a common goal of net zero by 2050, which was often criticized by developed countries and other critics as unreasonable. The subsequent announcement of net zero dates later than 2050 by many developing countries has also been criticized as being too weak.

This criticism must be viewed against the proposition that a common target date for net zero for all countries does not lead to an equitable outcome. It would have been so if all countries were at the same level of per capita emissions to begin with, but since the starting points are vastly different, in terms of both per capita incomes and development needs, pushing all countries to reach net zero by 2050 is highly inequitable. This can be seen in Table 9.1, which presents estimates of the net CO_2 emissions of the eight largest emitters, responsible for almost two-thirds of the annual emissions, under alternative assumptions.

Column 3a of the table shows our estimates of the outcome of the net CO_2 emissions associated with the Glasgow targets. The total claim of the top eight countries adds up to 113 per cent of the available carbon budget. Many of these countries end up claiming a share in the carbon budget nearly twice or more than their current population share. These trajectories are clearly not acceptable since they imply that if the carbon budget for +1.5°C is to be respected,

Table 9.1: Alternative estimates of prospective CO_2 emissions of the eight largest emitters

	Share in global emissions since 1990 (per cent)	2020 population share (per cent)	Estimated share in the CO_2 budget* (per cent)		
			Glasgow pledges	Common targets for 2030 and 2050	Popula-tion-weighted CO_2 budget distribution
	(1)	(2)	(3a)	(3b)	(3c)
China	18.9	18.5	50.4	25.5	19.8
US	16.8	4.2	13.2	14.1	4.5
Europe †	12.0	6.8	9.1	9.4	6.9
India	4.3	17.7	20.9	5.6	17.8
Russia	3.5	1.9	6.3	2.5	2.7
Japan	3.7	1.6	3.2	3.1	1.8
Indonesia	3.5	3.5	6.2	2.8	4.0
Brazil	4.2	2.7	3.5	3.9	2.9
Combined	67	57	113	67	60

* This relates to the CO_2 budget (starting 2021) for a 50 per cent probability of limiting temperature rise to +1.5°C. If a higher probability is chosen then the budget will be lower, and the emission rights appropriated get significantly larger.
† Europe comprises the EU-27, plus the UK and EFTA nations
Source: Authors' calculations, WRI Climate Watch 2021, Global Carbon Project 2021, UN Population Division 2019, IPCC 2018, and IPCC 2021.

the other countries, accounting for 43 per cent of the world's population, would have to collectively contribute negative emissions.

Column 3b of the table shows the outcome of having all eight countries follow the common targets as given in the IPCC 2018 report. The resulting projections respect the carbon budget, but the outcome is clearly inequitable across countries.

The high emitting nations—China, the US, Europe, Russia and Japan—which together account for 33 per cent of the world's population, would claim almost 55 per cent of the carbon budget. The low emitters in the table—India, Indonesia and Brazil—which have 24 per cent of the world's population, would be limited to only 12 per cent of the available budget. Since these are countries with high growth potential, restricting them to low carbon budget shares is particularly inequitable.

The other countries not listed in the table are a mix of developed and developing nations. They account for 43 per cent of the population and would be left with only a 33 per cent share in the carbon budget. Since this group also includes African countries whose population share is expected to increase sharply, denying them even their existing population share cannot be justified.

Column 3c in the table presents modifications in the emissions trajectories emerging from Glasgow to bring each country's claim on the carbon budget much closer to its population share. For example, the US should aim at a sharper reduction in net emissions by 2030 and advance its net-zero date to 2040. Europe as a whole could follow the German/Swedish example and aim at net-zero by 2045, as should Japan.

China has announced that it intends to increase its emissions up to 2030 and then reduce them to net zero by 2060. But, as shown in column 3a of Table 9.1, this trajectory would lead to China pre-empting more than 50 per cent of the carbon budget—the largest absolute deviation from a country's population share among those analysed. Instead, it should be persuaded to keep net emissions at their current level for a few years and then rapidly reduce them to zero by 2050. Similarly, Russia with 1.9 per cent of the population is projected to pre-empt 6.9 per cent of the budget. It should be persuaded to stabilize the rising trend of net emissions and start declining thereafter to reach net zero by 2050.

The three other countries included in the table—Brazil, Indonesia and India—would also need to tighten their targets but to a comparatively lesser extent. For Brazil and Indonesia, 50 per cent of their emissions are caused by land-use change and forestry. Thus, they could make a substantial improvement by acting on this front. Indonesia has already set some ambitious targets conditional to the availability of adequate international finance. In the case of India, emissions would need to peak by 2035, instead of around 2040 as currently projected (Mint 2021).

The impact of the recalibration described above for each country can be seen in Figure 9.5 in the Appendix, which compares the recalibrated trajectory for each country (in green curves) with the trajectory based on the Glasgow commitments (in red). The cumulative carbon emissions from these recalibrated trajectories fall to 60 per cent of the budget, much closer to the 57 per cent population share of the eight countries in question. This raises the question whether approximating the population share is fair. Determining fairness is a complex issue and one can imagine that considerations other than population share should be relevant, but there is no doubt that population would be a very important consideration (Budolfson et al. 2021; Raupach et al. 2014; Tongia 2021).

Pushing developed countries to reach net zero before 2050 (including through measures of negative emissions, i.e., withdrawing CO_2 from the atmosphere) will impose additional costs. But these are precisely the countries that can bear those costs. Besides, there are developed countries that have opted to get to net zero well before 2050. Others should be willing to do so if saving the planet is at stake.

An important co-benefit of pushing developed countries to decarbonize faster is that it will accelerate the development of technologies that could help others achieve their own decarbonisation targets. Developing countries need to work towards evolving the criteria that could guide future negotiation on modifying the Glasgow trajectories.

What Developing Countries Must Do to Decarbonize

Setting an end date some decades ahead is only the beginning. The next step is defining an operational plan to achieve that target and then implementing it. Having committed to reducing emissions to net zero, it is thus logical for developing countries to take the next step of conceiving a specific plan of action. In this context, the plan of action for the next ten years should be spelt out in detail, while that for the subsequent years can be kept flexible at this stage.

In general, any developing country wishing to decarbonize would need to push forward in four areas:

- Increase energy efficiency in the economy;
- Electrify final energy consumption by substituting direct use of fossil fuels with electricity where possible, and replace fossil fuels in rest of the areas with synthetic or biofuels;
- Shift electricity generation from fossil fuels to non-fossil fuel-based sources, mainly renewables. This is an essential complement to (ii) above, since shifting from the use of fossil fuels to electricity in a particular sector will not reduce emissions unless the production of electricity is emissions free; and
- Deal with emissions from hard-to-decarbonize sectors by increasing the stock of forests and through carbon capture and storage technology, which will hopefully become economical in future.

The rest of this section discusses the scope for action in each of these areas along with a suitable elaboration of the complexities involved.

Increasing Energy Efficiency and Rational Energy Pricing

Increasing energy efficiency reduces the amount of energy needed by the economy without impacting output. Where the energy saved is derived from fossil fuels, there will be a corresponding reduction in emissions. If the energy saved comes from renewables there is no reduction in emissions, but higher efficiency is still desirable because the reduced demand for renewable energy implies lower energy costs.

One way of increasing energy efficiency is to impose mandatory energy efficiency standards that must be met before any product can be sold. The other is to ensure rational energy pricing. Both are important, and developing countries need to examine the scope of both.

Statutory minimum standards of energy efficiency help to raise the demand for energy efficient electrical appliances such as refrigerators, air conditioners, electric pumps, and petrol/diesel vehicles, etc. Since more efficient appliances/equipment tend to be costlier, government bulk procurement and distribution programmes and finance schemes can help to lower prices and raise adoption rates of such products.[11] Similarly, building standards incorporating energy efficiency considerations will help to reduce energy consumption on account of lighting and heating/cooling. Developing countries are set to experience rapid urbanization in the next few decades, and this will involve a massive expansion in buildings. In India, for example, it is estimated that more than half of the building stock that will be needed by 2050 is yet to be built. Steps to incorporate energy efficiency standards provide a huge opportunity to leapfrog.

Standards set by law only establish the minimum level of efficiency required. They can be supplemented by a multi-star labelling system to signal products with higher levels of efficiency hoping that it will persuade consumers to move up the efficiency chain. However, more energy-efficient appliances and building designs are typically also more expensive. Thus, consumers will have to weigh the higher up-front cost against the lower running cost due to energy savings. This is where rational energy pricing comes in. If electricity is underpriced, as it is in many countries for certain categories of consumers, it will weaken the incentive to choose more energy-efficient products.

Rational energy prices can induce a behavioural change in consumers by incentivizing them to choose more energy efficient products, leading to very substantial energy savings. Ensuring rational energy prices requires removing subsidies on fossil fuels which are very common. The Glasgow Pact has endorsed a 'phase-out of inefficient fuel subsidies', but there is ambiguity over what subsidies would qualify as 'inefficient'.

Subsidies can be narrowly defined to refer to situations where the price charged for the fuel does not cover the full market cost of its supply. The difference is called an explicit subsidy, and this has fiscal costs either on the government budget or on suppliers (typically public sector entities in many countries) that are forced to bear the burden. There is also a wider definition based on whether the price charged covers both the market cost and the external cost in terms of the damage to the environment from using such fuels.

The IMF has estimated that on the narrow definition of energy subsidies, lower middle-income countries spent an equivalent of 2 per cent of their GDP in 2020 on subsidizing the supply costs of energy (Parry, Black and Vernon 2021). If the wider definition is used, the subsidy in these countries increases to 12 per cent. High-income countries also have the subsidies, but at 0.3 per cent and 3.1 per cent of GDP, respectively. The much higher share of subsidies in developing countries on the wider definition is because they are heavily dependent upon coal, whereas developed countries use natural gas which is much less polluting.

Raising energy prices is easier said than is politically done, and that is true not only in developing countries but also in developed countries.[12,13] One of the arguments often made in developing countries against raising energy prices is that it will hurt the poor. The point is certainly relevant, but not entirely correct. The poor do benefit from electricity subsidies, but the bulk of the benefit goes to better-off households which consume most of the subsidized energy. The poor could be easily compensated for the withdrawal of fuel subsidies through means such

---

11. See for example the UJALA LED bulb distribution scheme of the Government of India.
12. The Greens party in Germany contested the last election on an explicit platform of ensuring that energy prices will be made to reflect true carbon costs. The party is part of the government today, but there is no indication yet that its promise will be implemented.
13. The federal excise taxes on petrol and diesel in the US are ¢4.86/L and ¢6.45/L, respectively. These specific rates have not changed since Oct 1993 on the argument of not hurting the poor consumers.

as direct cash transfers, while allowing energy prices to be raised to a suitable level. These alternative mechanisms are being tried and have shown positive results.[14]

Political difficulties notwithstanding, developing countries would be well-advised to take on the challenge of eliminating energy subsidies, at least as narrowly defined, by 2030. The fiscal costs of these subsidies are substantial and even if the impact on the poor is offset by direct cash transfer, the net savings will help to support much-needed investments in other areas required to achieve the energy transition. Developed countries could lead the way by eliminating fuel subsidies of the wider definition in the same period, thus prompting developing countries to move in the same direction.

Promoting Electrification

Shifting from the direct use of fossil fuels to electricity is critical for decarbonization and the scope for electrification is considerable.

The industrial sector is the largest consumer of energy in most countries. Electricity generation, which is considered part of the industrial sector, is heavily reliant on coal in many developing countries. Shifting from electricity generation using fossil fuels to renewable sources is an important part of the transition and is discussed separately below. Excluding electricity generation, much of the energy demand in other industrial subsectors is met through electricity even today. However, there are certain industrial sectors, usually large industries, where fossil fuels continue to be used. This includes industrial processes requiring very high-temperature heat (e.g. smelting and cracking), involving chemical reactions which emit CO_2 (e.g. in cement manufacturing), or needing fossil fuels as chemical inputs (e.g. for steel and fertilizer production).

High-temperature heat needed in some processes can be generated using electric arc furnaces to replace coal-fired furnaces. However, in some other processes, fossil fuels cannot be replaced at present. This problem could be addressed effectively in the future as green hydrogen and CO_2 capture and utilization/storage becomes cheaper.

Transport is the second largest consumer of energy in the economy and is heavily dependent on fossil fuels such as petrol, diesel, and natural gas. Fortunately, the technology for switching to hybrid or pure electric vehicles (EVs) is now well-developed and two- and three-wheeler vehicles, passenger cars, light commercial vehicles, small industrial trucks, and city-buses, running partly or fully on electric batteries, are a reality. Hybrid EVs offer a pathway to drastically cut transport sector emissions in the short term and enable a transition to pure EVs subsequently.

Governments in developing countries can accelerate the switch to EVs in many ways. These include:

- Mandating that all government purchases of vehicles in the future will be only of hybrid or pure electric type (depending on national circumstances). These may be more expensive initially, but prices could be negotiated for bulk purchases;
- Accelerating the adoption of electric city-buses and urban metro railways for public transport and prescribing that eventually taxi licences will be given only to more efficient vehicles, including hybrid vehicles and pure EVs;
- Promoting public transport (both electric buses and urban railway/metros), with complementary measures to disincentivize private vehicle use through appropriate parking

---

14. See for example the PAHAL scheme of the Government of India, which provides direct cash transfers to cooking gas (LPG) consumers in India.

and congestion charges, will take some private cars off the road. This will help to reduce emissions and decrease traffic congestion and particulate matter pollution which has become a major problem in many developing countries;

- Announcing that from some date in the future, domestic manufacturers/importers will not be allowed to sell any internal combustion (IC) engine vehicles. If one wants the full automobile fleet to be electric by, say 2050, it would be necessary for all automobile sales to be of EVs much earlier, say by 2035, to ensure that the existing IC engine vehicles are fully phased out by 2050. An early announcement of the planned switch gives manufacturers sufficient advance notice of the change to ensure that production capacity is restructured to meet the EV demand. It is also necessary that an EV-charging network is developed in anticipation;
- Standardizing chargers and batteries to make them compatible across the different EV models would help in achieving the scale needed for mass adoption of EVs and bringing down the costs;
- Offering fiscal incentives to reduce the upfront cost of shifting to EVs. This can take the form of reducing or waiving registration charges, reduced toll fees, concessions or exception from sales tax, cheaper rates of financing, etc.

We cannot at present do without fossil fuels in areas such as long-distance road freight, earthmoving machinery, aviation, and shipping. However, there is considerable scope for reducing emissions from freight transport by shifting from road to rail or water, where possible, both of which have significantly high energy efficiency on per tonne-km basis. Besides, rail transport is already electrified in many cases and is anyway easily electrifiable. Technological advancements involving biofuels or green hydrogen-derived e-fuels, and hydrogen fuel-cell engines or high-density batteries may offer a solution to completely eliminate emissions from this sector in the future. Technology is developing rapidly in this area and the prospects seem brighter than they did even a couple of years ago. The fact that developed countries have strong interests in these developments increases the prospect of rapid technological development.

Shifting to electricity for transport would imply a gradual phasing-out of fossil fuels from the transportation sector. Taxes on petrol and diesel contribute disproportionately to the total government revenues in most developing countries and their elimination will adversely affect government budgets. However, in many cases, petroleum products are also imported, and a fall in consumption would save foreign exchange of the countries. Since developing countries can be expected to retain robust economic growth, it should be possible to offset foregone tax resources through other sectors of the economy. But this would need a restructuring of the tax system in anticipation of the decline in revenues from petroleum sales.

Buildings, both residential and commercial, already rely almost entirely on electricity for both lighting and cooling. Heating in colder regions often involves use of fossil fuels and wood, but this could be substituted by electricity over time, along with a shift to more energy efficient building designs mentioned earlier. The promotion of rooftop solar generation would further help in decarbonization, and the pace at which this occurs can increase greatly if suitable feed-in tariffs are fixed for the electricity supplied from these systems to the grid.

Cooking, especially in parts of Sub-Saharan Africa and rural areas of South Asia, is currently dominated by biomass, charcoal and kerosene, which have adverse health effects, especially for women and children. Households in India, for example, are currently moving towards using liquefied petroleum gas as a safer and more reliable cooking fuel, and those in African countries are switching to modern biomass cookstoves which are more efficient and less harmful. As electricity access improves, whether through rural grid connectivity or decentralized micro-grids (based on solar photovoltaics (PV) modules and battery storage units), switching to electricity for cooking would be possible.

Shifting to Electricity Generation from Renewables

The push to electrification must be combined with shifting, as rapidly as possible, towards electricity generated from renewables. Hydropower and nuclear generation are two important methods of generating non-polluting electricity, but each has limitations. Capacity expansion in hydropower is limited by geo-physical factors, irrigation requirements, environmental concerns with submergence, and problems with displacing people in and around reservoir areas. Nuclear energy in developing countries has a very low share in total electricity generation compared to developed countries, and the scope for capacity expansion is limited due to the high cost of construction and concerns about the safety of nuclear waste disposal.

Solar and wind power are the most promising sources for clean electricity and their generation capacity is being expanded in many parts of the developing world. The ASEAN countries have set a combined target of achieving a 35 per cent share of renewables in total installed electricity generation capacity by 2025. India has set a renewable energy capacity target of 450GW by 2030, which will be half the projected total capacity by then.[15] South Africa aims at sourcing 25 per cent electricity from wind and solar sources by 2030.

Both solar and wind power pose problems of intermittency. Solar generation has large variations within the day. Wind also has intraday variation but also seasonal variations, which differ with location. Intermittent supply makes grid management difficult since the demand and supply of electricity in the grid must be always balanced. This is not a very serious problem in the initial stages when renewables account for a small share in total electric supply, because the rest of the system can be ramped up or down to offset intermittency. However, as the share of electricity from renewables rises, as it will to meet the target of net zero, special efforts would be needed to help manage the grid.

There are several ways of dealing with intermittency. Optimising the solar-to-wind capacity ratio to moderate the degree of variation in total supply is one option. Spatially spreading out wind turbine installations to locations that complement inter-seasonal peaks in wind is another. Strengthening cross-border interconnections and transmission networks can also help to trade power across regions as needed. Pumped-hydro projects that combine renewable generation with hydro-storage capacity, where available, can be a cost-effective power storage and balancing solution. Conventional hydropower projects can usually be upgraded with a facility to pump and recharge water and discharge as needed, however, the scope for expanding hydro capacity is limited for reasons mentioned above.

Battery storage at grid-scale could be the most viable solution in the longer run, with excess power generated at peak times being stored in a battery for use when generation tapers off. Grid scale battery storage is in operation in California and Australia, and similar experiments are underway or proposed in China, India, Morocco, and Saudi Arabia.

---

15. The share of renewable electricity in the total electricity mix will be lower than 50 per cent since the capacity utilization of wind and solar power plants is much lower due to their intermittent nature.

Green hydrogen, produced through electrolysis of water using renewable electricity, provides another solution. It can be safely stored and used to produce electricity by fuel cells when needed. Energy storage via hydrogen is likely to be costlier than batteries.[16] However, the cost of green hydrogen is expected to fall. A Bloomberg analysis of the levelized cost of green hydrogen in 2030 forecasts that Brazil, India, and many other developing countries would have the lowest cost of green hydrogen production in the world, thanks to falling costs of renewable electricity production in these countries (Bloomberg 2021a).[17]

Intermittency in supply can also be handled by efforts to shift demand patterns to align better with supply. Shifting agriculture load to solar peak hours, for example, is a low hanging fruit and this has already been done in some states of India.[18] Looking further ahead, time-of-day metering with sufficient variation in intraday prices, could discourage consumption of electricity during peak demand hours. This calls for sophisticated regulation aimed at developing an effective market for wholesale trading in electricity. Smart metres can optimize domestic electricity demand by triggering devices to operate when prices are low. Such options may be many years away in developing countries, but the transition to net zero is also long-term.

The shift to renewables will need to be supported by reforms in the functioning of wholesale electricity markets to facilitate expanded and flexible trading of renewable electricity at regional level. Electricity markets would need to allow for high frequency spot and futures trading of electricity from both renewable and conventional sources. Further, offering term-ahead contracts at energy exchanges will allow small private developers to sell power directly in open market, without entering into long-term power purchase agreements, making new investments in the energy sector more favourable. Market regulators in developing countries will have to gain the necessary capacity in order to plan for developing such practices.

Is Renewable Energy Cost Competitive?

In the end, a strategy of shifting to electricity generation based on renewables will only succeed if the electricity is cost competitive. Costs per unit of both solar and wind electricity have fallen drastically over the past ten years making them competitive with new coal-based plants. With the costs expected to fall further, they will soon be competitive even with older thermal power plants that generate electricity at marginal costs. This can be seen in Figure 9.3 where the shaded region represents the range of costs from different vintages of existing coal power plants.

Developing countries such as India have been able to attract highly competitive low-cost bids from private sector generators of renewable power. But these bids are for variable (or intermittent) power and not for a steady supply over a longer period supported by an energy storage system. If the costs of storage needed to produce a steady supply are included, renewable electricity is not competitive, especially with electricity from older coal power plants.

16. Green hydrogen-based energy storage has poor round-trip efficiency—in the process of converting electricity into H_2 and back, nearly two-third of the energy is lost with the current technology (Sepulveda et al., 2021).

17. There are several large-scale green hydrogen projects planned or being constructed around the world including in developing countries such as Brazil and India.

18. This is possible by having segregated feeder systems for rural agriculture consumers. Starting first in the Indian state of Andhra Pradesh in 2001, electricity supply feeders for agriculture and non-agriculture consumers in rural regions were separated by phase to regulate the amount of power supplied to farmers for irrigation (which is usually free) while ensuring uninterrupted supply to non-agriculture consumers. Many states (e.g. Gujarat, Karnataka) have implemented the system since by having completely separate feeders.

Figure 9.3: Global average cost (US¢/kWh) of electricity from variable RE and coal

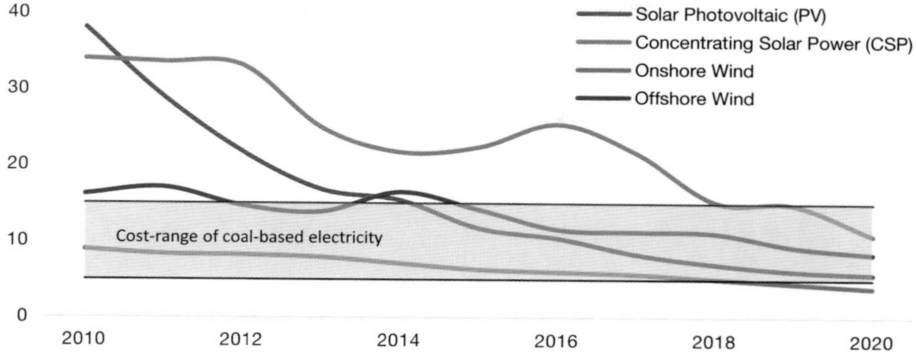

Source: IRENA 2021

CLIMATE CHANGE POLICY FOR DEVELOPING COUNTRIES

9

This is because grid-scale battery storage is expensive at present, but costs are falling (Cole, Frazier and Augustine 2021). It is difficult to be certain about future trends in costs because much of the available mineral sources and refining capacity worldwide have been pre-empted by China, and reserves of many of these metals are also in conflict-prone regions of the world (e.g. Democratic Republic of Congo (DRC) and Afghanistan).[19] However, if the world is going to need much more battery storage, one can expect intensification of efforts at finding more reserves of these minerals in the years ahead.[20]

The competitiveness of renewable power will change dramatically if carbon pricing, in the form of a tax on fossil fuels to reflect the social and environmental cost of CO_2 emissions, is introduced. A recent IMF staff paper proposed a carbon price floor for the world's top emitters, differentiating by income levels—US\$75 per tonne of CO_2 for high-income countries (e.g. the US and the EU), US\$50 for upper middle-income countries (e.g. China), and US\$25 for lower middle-income countries (e.g. India) (Parry, Black and Roaf 2021). Low-income countries are exempted from any such tax under the proposal.

India already has a tax on coal which was meant to promote the transition towards renewables,[21] but it is currently levied at the rate of US\$3.5 per tonne of CO_2 (INR 400/tonne-coal). Indonesia has also taken a step towards carbon taxation by mandating that coal power plants emitting above 1 tonne of CO_2 per megawatt-hour of electricity have to purchase offsets or pay a tax of US\$2.1 per tonne CO_2e (IDR 30 per kg of CO_2e).[22] They plan to raise the price to US\$5.2 per tonne CO_2e, and to include the forestry sector by 2025 (Bloomberg 2021b).

Raising the existing carbon taxes to the levels recommended by the IMF would raise electricity prices considerably, and this is bound to be resisted by domestic consumer groups. There could be less resistance if developed countries also impose the taxes at the higher rate

19. See for reference, in the context of India, Chadha and Sivamani (2021).
20. We can also count on technological progress in identifying possible alternatives (such as cobalt-less Li-ion batteries), along with recycling. Redox flow batteries, for example, may be a potentially cheaper option than Li-ion batteries for long-duration grid-scale storage (Mongird et al., 2020).
21. Earlier clean energy cess, under the National Clean Energy Fund created in 2010; rebranded as a GST compensation cess since 2017.
22. CO_2e or carbon dioxide equivalent.

proposed by the IMF. Unfortunately, there is no evidence at present to suggest that developed countries are considering this option, though attitudes could change.

A factor that may lead developing countries to consider some form of carbon taxation is the legislation introduced by the EU to impose a Carbon Border Adjustment Mechanism (CBAM) by 2026 on imports to the EU from countries that do not have a carbon pricing mechanism comparable to what is in place in the EU (European Commission 2021). If duties are imposed on imports from developing countries to offset the effect of the implied tax on carbon in developed countries, it may make sense for exporting nations to levy an explicit carbon tax on the consumption of fossil fuels and avoid the border adjustment duty. Developing countries should be willing to engage in discussions to evolve an internationally accepted approach to carbon taxation in order to forestall moves that impose protectionist duties on them.

Phasing Down Coal-based Power

A contentious issue that was intensely discussed in COP 26 was phasing out unabated[23] coal-based power plants. Coal is the most polluting of all fossil fuels and developed countries argued strongly that coal power plants should be phased out. Their position is understandable since they have almost graduated out of coal power, though they remain highly reliant on natural gas for power generation. Several developing countries not dependent on coal-based power also took the same stand. However, there are many developing countries that are heavily dependent on coal for electricity generation (see Figure 9.4), and they could not agree to a phase-out. Since coal is expected to remain the cheapest base-load source of electricity in the short-term, a premature phase out also poses serious threat to energy security of many countries. The implications of any such decision must therefore be thoroughly studied by the electricity planning authorities before committing to decommissioning of coal power plants by a certain date.

The unwillingness of many developing countries to agree to a phase out was also because much of the coal-based generation capacity in developing countries is relatively new. The

Figure 9.4: Share of coal in electricity generation mix (per cent), 2020

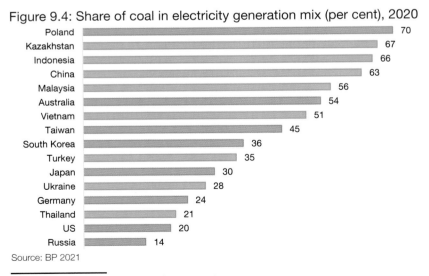

Source: BP 2021

---

23. That is, without a CO_2 capture and storage system.

median remaining life of operational coal power plants in low- and middle-income countries is twenty-six years, compared to only five years in high-income countries (Global Coal Plant Tracker 2021). In these circumstances, phasing out coal power plants before the end of their life would incur a substantial economic burden on developing countries.

In the end, there was a compromise, based on a suggestion from India, whereby the Glasgow Pact called for a 'phasing down' rather than 'phasing out' of unabated coal-based power. This was seen in some quarters as weakening the pact. However, getting agreement on the need to phase down coal-based power was in fact a substantive step forward. Since coal power plants have a life of about forty years, any country aiming to reach net zero in the foreseeable future should not set up any more plants beyond the ones already under construction. All future electricity demand, that cannot be met by the presently operational coal plants plus those under construction, should be met by renewables. Implementation of this decision would prevent countries from getting locked into highly carbon intensive infrastructure.[24]

The gradual phasing down of coal-based power capacity also implies a phasing down of future coal production in coal-producing countries (e.g. China, Indonesia, India, South Africa, etc.). This has implications for future employment in coal mining and allied businesses. The loss of employment in coal mining could be offset by larger and better employment opportunities in the renewables sector, but since coal production is regionally concentrated, some compensatory measures would be required to ease the burden of the transition on the affected communities. It would also be necessary to re-skill the labour force for the new jobs demanded in the renewables sector, and this will be a major challenge that must be planned for well ahead.

Even though existing coal plants need not be retired prematurely, countries that expect to have coal plants operating for the next few decades should take steps to upgrade these plants through anti-pollution/emission control measures to mitigate some of the social costs involved. Strict enforcement of such measures may lead to situations where upgrading more inefficient or polluting plants may be uneconomical. It would then make sense to decommission such plants well ahead of their end of life.

Afforestation

Forests are natural carbon sinks that reduce the net CO_2 emitted by a country. Unfortunately, deforestation is occurring in many developing countries at a pace that makes the land use change and forestry (LUCF) sector a net emitter of CO_2. Brazil, DRC and Indonesia are respectively the most rainforest-covered countries in the world and are also the top three emitters in terms of LUCF emissions. Much of the deforestation in these countries is happening illegally.

There is a very strong case for reversing this process through afforestation. Leaders of 141 countries, covering more than 85 per cent of the world's forest area, pledged to do so in COP 26.[25] Several developing countries, including Brazil, India, China and Indonesia have plans for afforestation as part of their climate NDCs (see Box 9.1).

Protecting forests would pose a special challenge for countries that depend on the exploitation of natural resources. Indonesia, for example, is the world's largest exporter of palm oil and

---

24. This decision can be reviewed if the technology for carbon capture and storage, which has so far not yielded very encouraging results, sees some breakthroughs that will make it economical to set up coal-based power plants that do not emit CO_2.
25. Previous such declarations, notably the 2014 New York Declaration on Forests which aimed at halving deforestation by 2020 (and end by 2030), have failed to realize.

has planned to expand its nickel mining industry for EV batteries. All these activities require clearing of the forests (Reuters 2021). On the other side there are also substantial numbers of indigenous peoples and rural communities whose livelihoods depend on forests and are endangered by deforestation. Forest conservation initiatives should involve these communities in afforestation and forest protection through suitable modes of engagement with the government.

Estimating the Investment Requirement of the Transition

The strategy for decarbonization outlined above will require large investments in energy and in many other sectors in the economy. The need for such investments has been much discussed and several figures of the investment amount needed have been estimated by international institutions. Major developing countries would be well-advised to come up with their own estimates of the investments most urgently needed over the next ten years.

The major focus must be on quantifying the investments needed in electricity-related sectors to achieve the shift to renewable energy that is implied by net zero. It is particularly important to identify the public sector and private sector components of this investment. Since the electricity sector is subject to regulations, it is important to consider whether the incentive structure emerging from the regulatory system, including especially payment risk from unviable distribution companies and unexpected actions by governments, is consistent with stimulating private investment as much as would be needed.

In addition to the electricity sector, it would also be desirable to identify the investment needs of the following other areas:

- Developing new energy sources such as hydrogen and biofuels and creating relevant transport infrastructure for hydrogen. Industries like steel and fertilizers will also need to restructure to replace fossil fuel feedstocks with alternatives like hydrogen. The investments in all these areas will be largely private, though some government funding may be desirable to encourage the development of green hydrogen production;
- Restructuring the automobile sector to become fully electric by mid-century. The investment in manufacturing these vehicles, where there is a large domestic manufacturing sector, has to come from the private sector, but there may be a need for extending some public support for creating the EV charging and battery-swapping infrastructure, which will not yield returns in the short or even medium term, but which is essential for the transition to take place. Public sector oil companies could think of diversifying into these new areas to remain in business and utilize their public assets such as urban land;
- Building mass transit systems such as metro railways and electric bus systems. The investment involved in this transition could be largely public, or some combination of public and private, much of which will happen at sub-national/city levels;
- Agricultural research to develop crop varieties that are better able to cope with heat and water stress arising from climate change. This will involve public funding, though it could be combined with private resources where the private corporate sector is keen to get into research and development (R&D).
- Efforts to mitigate methane emissions from certain forms of crop production, e.g. introducing the system of rice intensification or direct-seeded rice cultivation instead of flood irrigation. Similarly, popularising special cattle feeds to reduce methane emissions from cattle. Both will likely involve public resources.

- Improving systems of water management in rural areas to deal with water stress, which is already evident in many areas and may increase because of changes in precipitation levels due to climate change. This will involve substantial public investment at the sub-national levels. It will also require rethinking on water pricing. At present, there is no willingness to charge for water even though it is increasingly a scarce resource. If pricing is not politically acceptable, it has to be replaced by some form of quantitative rationing but that is in many ways even more difficult.
- Forest development and protection to increase the area under forests, is by all accounts a very cost-effective way to reduce net CO_2 emissions for tropical countries. This needs additional public resources.
- Creating climate resilient urban infrastructure to deal with exceptional precipitation leading to floods and to protect against the likely rise in sea levels in coastal cities. This is another area which will require additional public investments, mainly at sub-national levels.

Planning for the structural change implied by net zero requires developing countries to get a good sense of the total volume of investment needed and how much of it must come from the public sector. Most developing countries have severe fiscal constraints, and they would be keen to shift as much of the funding requirement as possible to the private sector. But in that case, they should work in parallel to develop policies that will attract the private sector into these areas.

Since the transition envisaged involves large scale adoption of new technologies, like solar PV and wind turbines, batteries, EVs, hydrogen electrolyzers and fuel cells, the larger developing countries with significant domestic manufacturing capability will want to reorient their industries to produce many of the new products domestically. Encourageing domestic production capacity to meet the changing demand is logical, but it should be ensured that this does not lead to the development of inefficient production capacity, sheltered from competition behind tariff walls. The energy transition will involve new areas subject to rapid technological evolution, and it will be important to avoid getting locked into outdated production methods that are being replaced globally by better and more cost-effective technologies. Designing an industrial cum trade policy that avoids this problem while also encouraging R&D of efficient production methods in these new areas will be essential.

It is evident from the above that planning for net zero calls for wide-ranging transformation, not just of the energy supply sectors but also of all energy-consuming sectors. This has been described as a 'whole of the economy approach'. It calls for the coordinated effort of many different ministries and, in a federal structure, also the active involvement of sub-national governments. It would also require the active involvement of independent regulatory agencies, such as those involved with fixing electricity tariffs, notifying building laws, granting automobile permits, etc.

Developing countries aiming for this transition should also keep in mind that the same is also taking place in the rest of the world simultaneously. This would make the transition easier because new technologies will evolve much faster. This would also increase the rate of transition as trade policies and policies enforced on private corporations will force a change in the supply chains.

Financing the Energy Transition in Developing Countries

Providing financial assistance to developing countries for mitigation and adaptation has long been a part of the agenda of climate change negotiations, and it is in fact a practical way of ensuring 'climate justice'. The Paris Agreement promised delivery of US$100 billion per year by 2020 and the failure to do so has been a source of much disappointment among developing countries, contributing to a considerable erosion of trust.

The full amount is now expected to be reached only by 2023. The Glasgow Pact has urged developed countries to act urgently to reach the promised US$100 billion and has also acknowledged that the level of assistance after 2025 will have to be much higher. It is important for developing countries to start working on determining the scale of financial support that will be needed and to make realistic assessments of what is feasible, with clarity on what is expected from different groups.

Investment Needs of the Transition

The first step must be to get a sense of the investment needs of the energy transition in developing countries. There is a variety of estimates to choose from. The IPCC (2018) estimated that to limit global warming to +1.5°C, the world (as a whole) would need to invest a total of US$2.8 trillion in 2020, or 2.5 per cent of the global annual GDP.[26] The IEA (2021) has made an even larger estimate of US$4 trillion annually by 2030, but this relates not just to energy but also to other related infrastructure. These are estimates for the entire world and the investment needed in developing countries will obviously be smaller.

There is also a need to recognise that the case for international financial assistance must be related to the additional investments required to make the energy transition, above the amount that would be spent on a business-as-usual basis. It is often difficult to determine what exactly is the additional requirement. For example, if a country shifts future electricity capacity from conventional to renewable sources, it is only the additional capital cost of such capacity compared with the cost of conventional capacity for the same amount of electricity that should be called additional. Financing for the conventional electricity capacity can be assumed to come anyway from the usual/existing sources.

McCollum et al. (2018) had estimated that the additional investments in the energy sector arising from mitigation efforts in non-OECD countries for a +1.5°C outcome would be around US$600 billion per year up to 2050 (in 2020 US$). Adding the cost of adaptation, which UNEP (2016b) had estimated as US$300 billion per year by 2030 and rising to US$500 billion by 2050, would suggest a combined additional cost of both mitigation and adaptation of about US$1 trillion per year.

Bhattacharya and Stern (2021)[27] have estimated that developing countries, excluding China, would need an additional US$800 billion per year by 2025, rising to US$2 trillion per year by 2030. This includes investments in energy and other infrastructure and the adaptation and restoration of natural capital. More recently, the McKinsey Global Institute (2022) has estimated that global capital spending on energy and land-use systems infrastructure would need to increase by US$3.5 trillion per year, over the period 2021–50, for achieving the transition to net zero by 2050.

---

26. The figure is updated from the original IPCC (2018) estimate of US$2.4 billion in 2010.
27. The paper was circulated during the COP 26 meetings.

These alternative estimates vary considerably but the important point is that the additional investment estimated in all cases is clearly enormous compared to the US$100 billion per year that has been promised for 2023. International estimates of investment needed could be usefully supplemented by country specific studies of the type recommended in Section 4 of this chapter. However, for the rest of this chapter we proceed on the assumption that US$1 trillion per year is a reasonable working estimate of the additional investment that needs to be made for the rest of this decade by developing countries excluding China. This would amount to approximately 4 per cent of the GDP of these countries.

Sources of Climate Finance

The gap between US$1 trillion and the estimated delivery of only US$80 billion in 2019, which is expected to increase to US$100 billion by 2023, highlights the extent of the gap in this area. The global community needs to jointly evolve credible targets of what can be expected, with greater clarity on the roles of different groups.

Developing countries will have to accept that some portion of the additional investments would have to be mobilized domestically, while the rest is sought from external sources. Assuming about 40 per cent of the US$1 trillion needed must be mobilized domestically (that comes to US$400 billion per year or about 1.6 per cent of the GDP of these countries), that leaves US$600 billion to come from external sources.

Is US$600 billion per year from external financing at all realistic? As in the past, external financing will have to consist of a combination of public and private flows. However, unlike in the past, separate targets should be set for these two components. Developed country governments can only be held responsible for ensuring that public flows, which consist of bilateral and multilateral flows, come up to the level targeted. Private flows will obviously depend upon market conditions and on government policies in developing countries seeking investment. Countries counting on large private investment flows must be willing to subject the appropriateness of their policies to critical review.

We also need to recognize that low-income countries are unlikely to be able to access private flows on commercial terms and they will have to depend almost entirely upon grants or near-grant flows such as International Development Association (IDA) credits. Greater clarity is needed on the extent of availability of such funds from bilateral and multilateral sources.

Middle-income countries do not need grant or near-grant funding. They can absorb long-term debt at reasonable interest rates and can also hope to attract non-debt private investment flows. The potential for private financing viewed purely in terms of available supply is very large. Private corporate investors present at COP 26 created the Glasgow Financial Alliance for Net Zero (GFANZ), a group with combined assets under management worth US$130 trillion. Investor sentiment among these institutional investors also favours 'green financial investments' and it is often pointed out that even if a small proportion of the managed assets could be redirected to climate financing in developing countries, it could contribute massively to the financial assistance expected for the required energy transition over the next ten years.

In reality, the flow of private capital to emerging markets is very limited and even that is disproportionately concentrated in a few countries. OECD estimates show that of the US$80 billion climate finance mobilized in 2019, private flows accounted for only about US$16.5 billion (inclusive of export credits). Investors point out that this is because there are not enough well prepared projects and the risks associated with such investments are also unmanageably large.

The lack of 'shovel ready' projects is a genuine problem, but one can imagine that this can be overcome by special efforts at identifying projects at appropriate locations. The issue of risk perception is much more difficult. Energy projects can suffer from a variety of risks during construction and operations, and due to regulatory uncertainties. In addition, there are political risks because of unpredictable actions by government and these are magnified by poor legal redressal for non-performance of contract, especially if the disputes are with the government itself.

There is no doubt that these are genuine problems, especially if the investments envisaged are in highly regulated sectors, such as energy or transport, where governments may be compelled to take actions that are politically motivated. One can take the view that these deficiencies have to be addressed by developing countries themselves and countries that want to tap into the very large pool of global capital available must take the steps needed to overcome investor fears. However, this is also an area where, as Jeffery Sachs (2021) put it, there are market failures and expanded public financial flows can help correct these. Multilateral Development Banks (MDBs) can do a great deal in this area.

The Role of Expanded MDB Lending

Expanded MDB lending to climate change-related sectors could be structured to leverage a larger flow of private finance into these sectors than would happen otherwise. One way of doing this would be through co-investment in the same project. In that case, the involvement of an MDB would give comfort to private investors, especially passive investors like sovereign funds and pension funds, on both the extent of project preparation and the likelihood of the government taking a constructive approach in dealing with problems as they arise during development and operation stages. Apart from co-investments, MDBs can also leverage private finance in such projects by innovative forms of financing like offering first loss guarantees to private lenders.

MDBs can also leverage private flows into climate change-related areas by undertaking sectoral lending, which is linked to sector-specific reforms that will promote the economic viability of the sector and reassure investors. This is particularly important in the energy sector where governments in developing countries are heavily involved.

India, for example, has seen a surge of private investment in renewable electricity generation, but distribution is largely in the hands of state-owned companies which suffer from large losses for a variety of reasons. These include the inability to invest in the distribution system to reduce technical losses because of poor finances, the inability to collect bills because of political interference, and the toleration of unduly low consumer tariffs often encouraged by political leaders 'persuading' the utility not to revise tariffs. The financial condition of the distribution companies translates into a serious payments risk which would discourage private investors from investments in generation. Distribution companies must be sufficiently financially strong for generators to invest in new capacity without needing any guarantees.[28]

---

28. The Government of India has tried to solve the problem for investors in renewable generation capacity by setting up the Solar Energy Corporation of India, a public trading corporation which buys bulk power from generators and sells it to distribution companies, thus insulating investors from payments risk. This cannot be a sustainable solution in the long-term.

Mexico presents another example where there may be a reversal of the energy reforms of 2014, which opened the Mexican energy sector to private investment. The proposed reversal would restore the monopoly of the state electricity company to sell power to final consumers and allow it to prioritise purchase of electricity from the state-owned generation companies instead of going by the merit order. Large consumers that generate captive power or buy electricity directly from the private market would no longer be able to do so. If these changes are made, it would deter investment by the private sector in renewable power generation projects and perpetuate the dominance of natural gas in Mexico's electricity mix. An NREL analysis suggests that the proposed bill could potentially increase Mexico's annual GHG emissions by up to 65 per cent, derailing its climate ambitions, and raise electricity generation costs by up to 54 per cent (Bloomberg 2021c).

Institutional and political problems such as these can only be overcome by a systematic sectoral push for reforms. MDBs can help in doing this by lending conditional to policy reforms in the sector.

It is worth noting that developing countries have not pushed for larger flows from the MDBs because their climate change negotiators have traditionally preferred getting such flows routed through the Green Climate Fund (GCF).[29] This is possibly because MDB lending is seen to be associated with conditionality. However, the scale of financing available via the GCF is very limited. The latest funding available over a five-year period is only around US$10 billion, which is much less than could be channelled through the MDBs. GCF has the advantage of not prescribing the more onerous conditions associated with the MDBs, but on the other hand it is precisely the reforms related conditionality of MDB lending that will make investment in these sectors more attractive to private investors.

Bhattacharya and Stern (2021) have called for doubling bilateral finance between 2018 and 2025 (from US$32 billion to US$64 billion) and tripling multilateral finance (from US$30 billion to US$90 billion) in the same period.[30] These proposals would increase public funding by US$90 billion per year by 2025. That is certainly impressive, but it is unlikely that additional public flows of this magnitude could leverage private flows sufficient to yield a total of say US$600 billion in external financing per year for climate change.

Perhaps the aim should be at additional lending of about US$250 billion per year provided by all MDBs (the World Bank, IFC and the regional development banks). These institutions will be able to raise the sums required in international markets at much lower costs than individual private investors or even middle-income country governments. The proposed expansion in lending would require a substantial expansion in the capital of these institutions. This may be resisted because of the fiscal cost involved, but the cost in terms of paid-up capital would be a fraction of the increase in authorized capital and it would also be spread over time. The increase in capital needed would be even lower if it could be combined with higher leverage ratios enabling much larger volumes of lending for the same amount of authorized capital.

---

29. Proposed at COP 15 in Copenhagen, and established at COP 16 in Cancun, the Green Climate Fund is designed as an operating entity of the UNFCCC's financial mechanism to fund climate change mitigation and adaptation projects in developing countries.
30. Based on OECD (2021a).

Using SDRs for Climate Finance

Public funding from the MDBs can be supplemented by innovative use of the recently allocated special drawing rights of about US$650 billion (SDR 456 billion) to all IMF members. About US$375 billion (SDR 263 billion) of this allocation was to developed countries, and they are not likely to need it for balance of payments purposes. These SDRs could be transferred to a fund that would be used to channel resources to developing countries on the condition that they use it to undertake climate-friendly investments. Since SDRs do not have to be repaid within any pre-determined period, these resources could be lent for long-term at the relatively low interest rate that applies to the use of SDRs.

The finite availability of SDRs limits their contribution to international public flows over a longer period, but they can supplement MDB lending over the next few years until action is taken to expand the capital base of these institutions.

To summarize, the scale of financial flows needed to finance the energy transition developing countries have to make is very large. If the flow of climate finance from bilateral sources plus the MDBs can be expanded to US$250 billion per year for the rest of this decade (from about US$63 billion at present), about US$350 billion would still need to be mobilized from private flows to reach the target of US$600 billion. This would represent a massive expansion in private flows from a base of only US$16.5 billion in 2019. As pointed out above, the total availability of private capital is indeed huge, but it will require Herculean efforts to mobilize capital on the scale required from this source. Without the leveraging effect of MDB lending, a response on the scale required is unlikely.

Looking Ahead: An Agenda for Developing Countries

We now summarize our recommendations on what developing countries should do to come up with a credible global compact for managing climate change which protects their interests.

Managing Climate Change Requires Action in Multiple Areas

A central feature of managing climate change is that it requires interventions not in just one or two areas, but in many sectors like energy, including development of green hydrogen and other alternative fuels, industry and manufacturing, especially automobiles and associated sectors like battery production and charging infrastructure, buildings, public transport, agriculture, water management, forestry, etc. In other words, it calls for a 'whole of the economy approach'.

The ministries involved in the COP negotiations are typically the ministries of environment and foreign affairs. However, the evolution of a credible country strategy and its subsequent implementation will require the active involvement of many other ministries dealing with the sectors mentioned above. It will also require the active involvement of governments at sub-national levels. Developing countries need to keep this consideration firmly in mind.

Defining Domestic Strategies for Getting to Net Zero

Having committed to reaching net zero by a certain date, each developing country must define a domestic strategy to get there. It is not necessary to work out all the details of the longer-term strategy up to the end date because there is merit in retaining flexibility for later years as new technologies will develop and experience will be gained. However, it is important to outline what needs to be done in the next ten years in sufficient detail to allow constant monitoring of progress.

The ten-year strategy would inevitably include some combination of the various measures listed in Section 4, though the exact mix will vary from country to country, depending upon country circumstances and endowments. While spelling out these components, the strategy should provide an indication of the time by when emissions are expected to peak and then start declining.

The respective roles of the public and private sectors in the energy transition over this period should also be clearly spelt out as this will help define the fiscal cost of the transition. Governments that are fiscally stressed may wish to rely on private investors to undertake some of the investments needed, and therefore, the policy environment should be one that is attractive for private players.

The progress of large developing countries in this ten-year period will be of interest to all developing countries. It should be closely watched so that successful efforts can be emulated by others. Keeping pace with what is happening in other developing countries would be an important indicator of competitiveness in a world determined to reduce emissions. Major corporations in particular would be keen to look good on these indicators both to attract investments and to gain global recognition.

Modifying the COP 26 Emissions Trajectories

An immediate challenge facing developing countries is the review of the COP 26 emissions trajectories to find ways of bringing them in line with what is needed to limit global warming to +1.5°C. Developing countries should resist any simplistic push to solve the problem by getting all countries to reach net zero by 2050. As demonstrated in Section 3 of this chapter, the approach of getting all countries to net zero by 2050 is not consistent with fair burden sharing.

An ideal way to proceed would be to tighten country trajectories of all the major emitters that claim much larger shares in the remaining carbon budget than their respective population share. The US, China, Russia, Japan, Australia, Canada, many European nations and rich countries in the Middle East are the most obvious cases that qualify on this criterion. These countries need to be persuaded to (a) accelerate the pace of emissions reduction up to 2030, and (b) advance their net zero dates. Concrete steps taken by these countries could be the prelude to a more comprehensive renegotiation of the net zero dates for all countries at a later stage.

Regional Cooperation

Climate change issues are normally discussed at the global level in COP meetings, but there may be instances where regional consultation can help. Interconnection of electricity grids is an obvious area of potential interest. Marine R&D is another area that would be of interest.

There are several regional and sub-regional cooperation arrangements already in place across all continents, which can take up climate-related issues. They could be used to forge common positions on global issues allowing the constituent nations to negotiate jointly on global platforms. They could also provide a useful forum for sharing experiences.

Penalizing Non-performance

The current framework of negotiations does not envisage any means of penalizing countries that fail to adhere to their promises. However, if we ever get to a global compact based on some agreed burden-sharing in the matter of emissions reductions, we will also need a mechanism to incentivise countries to honour their commitments. This is especially relevant because defaults on the part of developed countries are just as likely to arise as those on the part of developing countries.

This is not an urgent problem currently, as we have yet to come to an agreed set of trajectories consistent with the global warming target, but it will surface once we get to such an agreement. Perhaps a working group should be set up, representing both developed and developing countries, to recommend alternative ways of institutionalizing this problem.

International Finance to Assist Developing Countries

The financial assistance needed by developing countries to achieve the decarbonization envisaged is a major, and as yet unresolved, issue. Section 5 of this chapter elaborated that it is reasonable to plan for financing additional investment of about US$1 trillion per year for both mitigation and adaptation for developing countries excluding China. This is an order of magnitude larger than the US$100 billion that has been discussed so far and is now expected to be reached only by 2023.

Developing countries should consider carefully what is a realistic expectation in terms of international support for this target. A suggested 40 per cent of this amount may need to come from domestic sources, in which case the balance to be raised through international transfers is reduced to US$600 billion. Even this is several times larger than the flows achieved thus far.

The total international transfer will have to be a mix of public and private flows, but separate targets should be set for the two components. Developed country governments can then be pressed to deliver on the public component of the financial assistance through some combination of bilateral and multilateral flows.

The potential scale of private flows is much larger than public flows, but actual flows of private funds thus far have been much lower. This is because of the perception among investors that there are not enough viable projects on offer in developing countries and that the risks with undertaking the investments are too high. Section 5 argues that this problem can be dealt with by creative use of public bilateral and multilateral flows to leverage larger private flows into climate finance for middle-income countries.

The MDBs such as the World Bank, IFC, ADB, AfDB and the European Investment Bank could be particularly useful in this context. Expanded lending by the MDBs will require an increase in the authorized capital of these institutions which will allow them to lend a multiple of the capital contribution. These multilateral flows could be supplemented by innovative use of the SDRs allocated to developed countries, which these countries are not likely to need. capital increases would impose a fiscal burden on developed countries, but it would be small because only a portion of the authorized increase in capital has to be paid-in, which can also be spread over several years.

Combined bilateral and multilateral lending for climate finance can be raised from around US$63 billion at present to say US$250 billion a year over the next ten years, and it could be used to leverage US$350 billion of private flows to make up the US$600 billion of international finance that is needed.

Activating the G20

The real constraint to expanding MDB lending on the scale that is needed is not the fiscal cost but the lack of political enthusiasm among developed countries for a greater role of multilateral institutions. This reflects a deeper move, in recent years, away from the earlier conviction on the merits of globalization and multilateralism, combined with the effect of growing geopolitical tensions. These trends have encouraged greater insularity and a fragmentation of global solidarity, which is evident in many areas. It is particularly ill-timed as the world tries to address climate-related challenges that call for much greater global cooperation.

For all the frustrations expressed by many participants, COP 26 negotiations have succeeded in getting developing countries to accept the need to reduce emissions and reach net zero sometime around mid-century. The major developing countries are in a position where they should start spelling out a more specific ten-year strategy consistent with their longer-term emissions reduction targets. They would be best encouraged in this effort by reasonable assurance of international financial support.

The logical forum to provide this assurance is the G20. The group includes all the major developed and developing countries, and it is also the forum for taking decisions on policies relating to the MDBs. It was set up precisely to deal with issues of international economic cooperation. It performed very well at the time of the global financial crisis in 2008. However, since then, it failed to come up to expectations on saving the Doha Round and it has also failed in generating cooperation in ensuring equitable access to COVID-19 vaccines during the pandemic. It could perhaps take on the challenge of restoring its reputation on the issue of multilateral finance for sustainable development in a world of climate change.

The agenda of the G20 thus far has been set largely by developed countries. However, the next three G20 Summit meetings offer a unique opportunity for developing countries to set the agenda: Indonesia has the G20 presidency in 2022, followed by India in 2023 and Brazil in 2024. These three developing countries should not only collaborate closely in the upcoming COPs, but also work together within the G20 to (a) get a broad acknowledgement of the substantial steps that developing countries are proposing to take to help limit global warming, (b) ensure that there will be a sufficient scale of public funding, both bilateral and multilateral, available to support this effort, and (c) structure the increased flow of public finance to ensure a much larger flow of private finance to meet the climate related goals.

The G20 works on two tracks—the Finance Ministers Track and the Summit Track. The troika, which will comprise only developing countries in 2023, should cooperate to get the Finance Ministers Track to work on these ideas expeditiously so they can be considered later at the Summit.

Appendix: Figure 9.5: Committed versus required trajectories (Gt-CO₂/year)

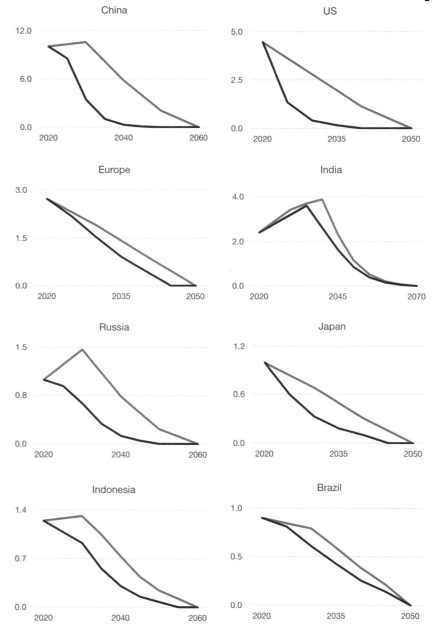

Note: Green curves represent the trajectories as per the latest commitments of the countries. Purple curves represent population-weighted trajectories.

Source: Authors' calculations, WRI Climate Watch 2021, Global Carbon Project 2021, UN Population Division 2019, IPCC 2018, IPCC 2021

Chapter 10: Agriculture, Employment, and Climate Change—With Specific Reference to Developing Countries

Agriculture, Employment and Climate Change—With Specific Reference to Developing Countries

Chapter 10 | Kevin Cleaver

Abstract and Introduction[1]

This chapter is intended to: i) describe the evolution of global agriculture over time, and up to the present, ii) explain the reasons for variations in agricultural performance between regions and within regions, iii) assess the potential for the agriculture sector to expand employment opportunities in developing countries, iv) assess the impact of climate change on agriculture and v) undertake a preliminary analysis of the impact of the COVID-19 pandemic on global agriculture.

The chapter finds agriculture production to have expanded globally prior to the COVID-19 pandemic. The year 2019 saw the total value of global agricultural production achieve a record. However, there are significant differences in performance between regions. Generally, East Asia, South Asia and North America have agricultural sectors that have been flourishing. Africa and West Asia continue to lag, with Latin America in between. Within each region, there are vast differences in performance between countries. COVID-19, however, has had an important negative impact on agriculture, at the farm level and in terms of domestic and international trade.

A major proximate explanation for a country's agricultural performance is the amount of private and public expenditure on agricultural research and development, rural infrastructure, fertilizers, and farm mechanization. Government agricultural policy is important in determining agricultural performance, including by influencing the amount of investment in R&D, infrastructure, and farm inputs. Policy that effectively taxes agriculture and over-regulates, inhibits performance.

The chapter finds that the potential for agriculture to expand employment opportunities is limited. However, at the margins, governments can slow the exit of labour from agriculture by switching subsidies away from direct payments to farmers into the support of public goods, such as agricultural R&D, education, infrastructure and territorial development.

The chapter summarizes the literature on the impact of climate change on agriculture, predicting significant impacts, mostly negative in the tropics, though sometimes positive in northern climes (such as Russia, Canada and Scandinavia). However, the latest data suggests that up to the present, the negative impact of climate change on agriculture in the tropics has been offset to date in many countries by successful farmer adaptation. The question is whether further increases in temperature, reduction in rainfall and other climate changes can continue to be adapted to by farmers as these events become more severe. The latest publications on this subject almost

---

1. Harinder Kohli, Amnon Golan, Martin Raine, Adolfo Brizzi and Iqbal Sobhan, all made valuable suggestions, including editing suggestions, for this report. An agriculture database was created, held by the Centennial Group, consisting of agricultural data from the World Bank, Food and Agriculture Organization (FAO), United States Department of Agriculture (USDA), International Food Policy Research Institute (IFPRI) and the Organization for Economic Co-operation and Development (OECD).

all predict very negative impacts on agriculture, which will be difficult to adapt to. Increased funding for agricultural adaptation will, therefore, be important. Switching agricultural subsidies from farmer and crop support to the support of measures to assist farmers to adapt to climate change, and to measures to mitigate the impact of farming on CO_2 and methane emissions is essential, though politically difficult.

Based on the analysis, recommendations are provided for consideration by governments on how to reform agricultural policy to stimulate better agricultural sector performance, including in employment creation and adaptation to climate change. It is found that there is considerable room for additional financing of developing country agriculture. This is more difficult than it may first appear, as many long-standing donors continue having difficulty funding effective agricultural projects and policies, and there will be resistance to shifting funding and subsidies towards climate change adaptation and mitigation in agriculture.

The impact of the novel coronavirus pandemic on agriculture was beginning to be felt as this report was being **prepared**. By October 2021, reports had emerged in the international press and among institutions, which monitor agriculture performance, that the pandemic had negatively affected the supply and demand for agriculture products. Supply has been curtailed worldwide resulting from labour shortages on farms (reduced numbers of migrant workers in North America and Europe), disruption of agricultural and farm input supply chains due to increased transport bottlenecks, and the closing of food processing plants and plants producing farm inputs. This, in turn, was negatively impacting farm production. The World Food Programme (WFP) recently reported a negative impact on food aid provided to food deficit countries, particularly in Africa. A rigorous analysis of the impact of the pandemic on global agriculture remains to be done since the pandemic is still rageing as this is being written.

The State of Global Agriculture and Regional Differences

What Is Included in 'Agriculture'?
Nearly every government defines agriculture to include primary agricultural production. Most often, agriculture also includes livestock, forestry, and fisheries. It sometimes includes agro-industry, farm input supplies, and agricultural marketing. For the purpose of this report, agriculture will refer to primary production, livestock production, fisheries, and forestry. Agro-industry, farm input supply, and agricultural marketing will be treated separately and lightly.

The Long-term Trends in Agricultural GDP, and World Agricultural Prices, Broken Down by Region

Table 10.1 shows considerable variation in agricultural growth rates between both countries and time periods. This huge variability reflects the vagaries of weather, changing government policies, changing agricultural trade patterns, and changing directions of agricultural aid. Differences in growth rates are also affected by agricultural endowments (available land and labour, and available capital). Growth rates of 4 per cent per annum or better are exceptional for agriculture, while growth rates lower than 2 per cent per annum reflect poor performance. In the most recent period, agricultural value added has grown best in the Middle East and North

Table 10.1: Agriculture, forestry and fishing, value added (annual growth, %)

	1982–1986	1987–1991	1992–1996	1997–2001	2002–2006	2007–2011	2012–16	2017–21
Africa - Eastern and Southern	1.0	2.9	3.6	2.6	2.8	3.2	3.3	2.5
Africa - Western and Central	4.2	3.4	2.8	3.6	11.7	4.8	4.2	3.3
Central Europe and the Baltics	-1.1	-1.4	1.7	0.5	0.7	0.5		
Caribbean small states	0.0	3.3	3.7	-0.8	-1.1	2.2	1.7	-0.2
East Asia and Pacific	5.9	3.5	3.2	2.4	3.4	3.7	3.0	2.8
Europe & Central Asia	-3.1	-1.6	1.3	1.4	2.2	1.1	1.3	
European Union		3.4	0.6	0.3	1.5	0.3	0.6	
Fragile and conflict affected situations	2.7	2.6	4.2	2.9	7.6	3.5	2.2	2.7
Latin America and Caribbean	1.1	2.2	3.7	2.5	3.6	2.4	2.0	2.4
The Middle East and N. Africa	6.3	4.4	3.4	1.9	4.7	1.8	1.3	3.4
North America			5.9	2.9	-2.1	5.4	2.7	
Sub-Saharan Africa	2.2	3.1	3.3	3.0	6.7	4.0	3.8	3.0
World	4.0	3.0	2.4	2.5	3.1	2.8	2.7	2.8

Source: World Bank 2021b

Africa, Sub-Saharan Africa and East Asia, in that order. The poorest performances have come from the Caribbean, the European Union, and Central Europe and the Baltics.

Per capita food production indexes prepared by the FAO are another useful indicator of agricultural performance. This data differs from agricultural GDP (which includes more than food, relative prices affect GDP figures but not food production indexes, and per capita food production indexes are adjusted for population growth). Per capita food production indexes show the most rapid increases occurring in South Asia and South America, followed by West Asia. Africa and North America show declines. The problem in Africa is that population growth has outstripped food production. Population growth in East Asia and South Asia has been much less rapid than the growth in food and non-food agricultural production (World Bank 2021b).

Another way to look at agriculture performance is through trade balances (net agricultural export value minus agricultural imports). Table 10.3 shows Africa and Asia to be major net agricultural importers, while the Americas are major net agricultural exporters. Europe has transitioned from a major importer to an exporter.

The implication of these three ways of looking at agricultural performance (agricultural GDP growth, growth in per capita food production, and net agricultural trade balance) are that Africa and Asia have started with a major agricultural production deficit, reflected in the negative trade balance and poor agricultural performance historically. However, in much of Asia (particularly East Asia), growth of food production and agricultural GDP have been higher than population growth. In Africa, since 2004–06, food production growth is slower than population growth. Per capita food production is improving in South America (with, of course, variation between countries).

World prices are a good indicator of global supply and demand balances, as the market for agricultural products has become globalized. World prices fluctuate constantly, as world

Table 10.2: Gross per capita production index

	1990	2000	2010	2015	2019
World	94.3	99.85	101.97	44.64	69.8
Africa Total	97.52	100.55	99.26	57.7	80.63
North America	88.53	94.81	95.42	97.04	98.98
South America	62.26	72.88	93.2	101.93	107.28
Asia Total	62.61	78.32	93.27	99.98	103.75
Central Asia	N/A	65.46	86.3	100.51	101.47
Eastern Asia	50.37	73.54	91.81	100.71	102.29
Southern Asia	75.4	80.82	92.75	98.44	107.31
South-Eastern Asia	62.91	73.29	94.48	100.15	104.16
Western Asia	119.58	110.83	101.74	100.82	104.29
Europe	106.53	91.23	91.35	99.77	101.79
Oceania	98.27	107.58	93.01	100.13	88.11

Source: FAO 2022

Table 10.3: Net food (excluding fish) trade (USD million)

Region	2000	2010	2018
Africa	-7398	-26789	-30672
Americas	23546	101828	105194
Asia	-46161	-102888	-191420
Europe	-192	-14724	31821
Oceania	13332	25866	42722

Source: FAO 2020

demand and supply conditions vary constantly. Cereal prices have, over the long term, tended to be relatively depressed compared to meat and dairy prices, in particular, but also compared to prices of fruits and vegetables as well. This reflects the rapidly rising demand for meat and dairy, fruits and vegetables, with slower increase in demand for cereals (FAO 2020).

Crop Yields (Production Per Hectare)

Because agricultural GDP involves both production and relative prices, it is dependent in part on the crop mix in a country's agriculture. A country that is a major coffee producer, for example, can suffer an agricultural GDP decline as a result of a decline in the real export price of coffee, even when its production increases dramatically. For that reason, it is useful to look at performance in terms of physical production per hectare of major agricultural products.

Table 10.4 shows that with few exceptions, crop yields in Africa have been below those in Asia and South America, and far below crop yields in Europe and North America. They also show slow growth in crop yields in Africa (except for wheat and to a lesser extent, cotton), suggesting that this region is not catching up with the rest of the world. Increases in agriculture

Table 10.4: Crop yields (tons/hectare); and per cent increase 2000–18

	Maize 2000 2018	Wheat 2000 2018	Seed Cotton 2000 2018	Rice Paddy 2000 2018	Green Coffee 2000 2018
Africa	1.8 2.0	1.8 2.9	0.9 2.1	2.3 2.3	0.4 0.4
Per cent increase	11	61	24	0	0
Asia	3.6 5.4	2.6 3.4	1.7 2.1	3.9 4.8	0.8 1.1
Per cent increase	50	31	24	23	38
Europe	4.7 7.5	3.3 4.0	3.2 3.0	5.2 6.4	
Per cent increase	60	21	-7	23	
South America	3.2 5.3	2.4 3.0	1.9 3.7	3.6 6.1	.8 1.4
Per cent increase	66	25	95	69	75
North America	3.5 11.7	2.7 3.2	1.8 2.7	7.0 8.6	
Per cent increase	234	18	50	23	

Source: FAO 2020

productivity, as measured by crop yields, are occurring in South America, North America, Asia and to a lesser extent, Europe.

Agro-industry, Agricultural Marketing, and Farm Input Supply

Most agricultural products are marketed and processed, and the processed products are marketed again. Think of cocoa, for example, which is processed into a myriad of chocolate products. All farm production of raw cocoa is in the tropics: tropical Africa, Asia and Latin America. Cocoa goes through an elaborate collection by private, public or cooperative companies, depending on the country. These companies do the initial processing, consisting of weighing, sorting, drying, bagging, aggregating and shipping. Most is sold to European and American buyers who combine the cocoa with other products (notably sugar, milk and preservatives) into chocolate products. These chocolate-producing countries import the cocoa from tropical countries. The tropical countries that produce most of the high-quality cocoa for export only produce chocolate for domestic consumption. It is difficult for companies from developing countries to break into the European and American markets with processed chocolate products, while it is easy for them to export raw cocoa. This is because of high transportation costs, quality issues, marketing costs and, in most cases, trade barriers erected by importing American and European countries. Most of the sales prices of final chocolate products goes to the big European and American chocolate-makers, not to the farmers and marketing enterprises in developing countries.

Many agricultural products have some variant of the above situation (tea and coffee, for example). Cotton is more widely grown than cocoa (India, several Sahelian African countries, China and Uzbekistan are major cotton producers, for example), while its eventual processing into cotton clothing is done all over the world. Maize and rice are widely produced, processed and consumed in many countries.

Despite the obvious advantages of domestic agro-industry, the data suggest that most developing countries have not seen large increases in agro-industrial growth, and are still largely dependent on primary agricultural production. The exceptions are some countries in Asia, particularly China, and for some commodities. Cotton is an exception with much of the industry producing cotton products having moved to developing countries.

The World Bank's most recent World Development Report found evidence that participation in global supply chains (including agro-industry) results in a boost to agricultural productivity, income, and employment (World Bank 2020b). A major policy objective in developing countries with important primary production should, therefore, be the encouragement of agro-industry investment.

Policies that boost value chain development include, most importantly, those which attract foreign investment as well as domestic investment. These include trade liberalization, contract enforcement, investment in human capital investment, and policies that improve business climate (World Bank 2020b). Foreign direct investment in the agricultural and food sectors of Africa, Asia and Latin America has grown from US$790 million in 1993 (in constant 2005 dollars) to US$8.3 billion in 2010 (2005 dollars). Most of this has been for agro-industry.

Box 10.1: Côte d'Ivoire's cashew value chain

Cashews are Côte d'Ivoire's third-ranking export after cacao and refined petroleum products, and they are an important source of cash for smallholders and processors. Although Côte d'Ivoire produces 23 per cent of the world's cashew supply, fewer than 7 per cent of raw cashew nuts are processed domestically. In 2017, a government programme provided training, access to inputs, and market information, along with processing demonstration units. The programme was supported with access to new sources of finance for smallholders, notably through the introduction of a warehouse receipts system that enables processors to use unprocessed nuts as collateral for working capital loans. About 225,000 cashew farmers are expected to benefit from the upgrading and improved value chain integration.

Source: Adapted from World Bank 2020a

Box 10.2: Rwanda's coffee value chain

The coffee sector was historically Rwanda's main export crop and a major source of earnings for up to half a million rural Rwandans. But at the end of the 1990s, fallout from the civil war helped put the sector on the verge of collapse because of the low quantity and quality of its product. To address this challenge, the country put in place a strategy, completed in 2002, to upgrade technology, increase production, and boost skills and improve quality. The result has been more skilled farming techniques, better use of technologies, and higher productivity. Private investment in coffee washing stations grew by an average of 120 per cent a year in locations with the highest cherry (the fruit that contains the coffee bean) availability, water supplies, and road linkages. The total number of coffee washing stations rose from just two in the entire country in 1998 to 299 in 2015. Meanwhile, the higher-quality coffee began to merit higher prices, with Rwandan coffee now fetching a premium in international markets.

Explanation for Regional Differences in Agricultural Performance

Factors Contributing to Differences in Agricultural Growth and Performance between Regions and Countries

Why are agricultural yields and productivity in Europe and North America so much better than that of Africa, the Middle East and Latin America, and why is Asia catching up while most of the rest of the developing world is not?

The proximate causes for the difference in agricultural productivity and growth between regions, and indeed between countries within regions, is well-known and involves differences in fertilizer use, water use (and irrigation), mechanization, farm-level investment, rural energy, rural infrastructure, changes in rural land use, changes in rural labour availability, labour skills and, most importantly, R&D.

Expansion of agricultural land would be a relatively easy way to increase agricultural output, though not of productivity. However, agricultural land declined globally since 1990, with continuous decline in Europe and North America. There has been a modest expansion in Africa until 2010, with a slight decline thereafter. A similar pattern has been followed in South Asia. East and West Asia have a relatively stable amount of land under agriculture. The causes for decline in agricultural land include urbanization and suburbanization, conservation efforts (putting land into parks and public land into forestry) and pollution (salinization of irrigation areas, saltwater intrusion) (FAO 2022).

Agricultural growth is nowhere propelled by an expansion in agricultural land. On the contrary, the modest decline in agricultural land has probably contributed negatively to agricultural production.

Chemical fertilizer use is expanding across the entire globe, but has started at a much lower level in developing countries. Fertilizer use has caught up in East Asia. South Asia is rapidly expanding the use of chemical fertilizers. Sub-Saharan Africa barely uses chemical fertilizer, and the Middle East, North Africa and South America are way behind Asia. However, the figures look starker than the reality because farmers in many developing countries use on-farm fertilization techniques, including the use of animal manure and crop residues as fertilizers. Nevertheless, the lack of use of chemical fertilizers is an important proximate cause of lower crop yields in much of the developing world outside of Asia.

Table 10.5: Fertilizer use (kg per hectare of arable land)

Region	2002	2015	2018
East Asia and Pacific	253.2	326.5	293.5
Latin America and the Caribbean	101.4	139.6	171.2
South Asia	102.5	164.4	170.1
The Middle East and North Africa	93.4	74.0	76.5
Sub-Saharan Africa	13.8	15.5	20.0
World Average	108.2	135.8	136.8

Source: World Bank 2021b

The use of farm machinery follows a slightly different pattern than that of fertilizers. The proxy used to measure the use of farm machinery is tractors per 1,000 farm workers. The use of tractors in Sub-Saharan Africa is miniscule and not growing significantly. It remains low in East Asia and South Asia, but is growing rapidly. It is higher in the Middle East and North Africa, and growing. It is higher still in South America and growing (FAOSTAT 2022).

Water is critically important for agriculture. Where rainfall is deficient in quantity, or comes at the wrong time, supplementing it with irrigation is important. The percentage of cropland under irrigation is the typical measure of its degree of development. This is not a very good indicator because the need for irrigation varies considerably. Where rainfall is adequate and spaced adequately, irrigation is not needed at all. In very dry areas, agriculture is impossible without it. The data suggests, however, that Africa is most poorly served by irrigation. The per centage of Sub-Saharan African cropland under irrigation is tiny, and not growing. In Latin America, it is small and growing very slowly, but outside of a few areas, less necessary. Asia has more than 14 per cent of cropland under irrigation, while Africa has less than 2 per cent. The significant use of irrigation in Asia has contributed to good agricultural performance in terms of growth and crop yields.

Table 10.6: Share of area equipped for irrigation in land area (per cent)

Region	2000	2015	2018
World	5.9	7	7.1
Africa	1.2	1.4	1.4
Americas	4.1	4.7	4.7
Asia	11.8	14.2	14.3
Europe	5.5	5.6	5.7
Oceania	0.6	0.9	0.9

Source: FAO 2020

The use of modern varieties of crops is important in agricultural growth, as these varieties confer great advantage in terms of yield, resistance to pests and diseases, and adaptation to climatic conditions. There has been a remarkable spread of modern varieties of cereals in East and South Asia. The use of modern varieties of cereals in Sub-Saharan Africa, though starting late, is beginning to catch up albeit with a long way to go. Sub-Saharan Africa in the 2010–2014 period reached the level of use of modern varieties in Latin America in the year 2000. The Middle East and North Africa had 69 per cent of their area sown to wheat using modern varieties by the year 2000, which has resulted in expanded crop yields (FAO 2019).

This brings us to labour, which is of special interest to this report. Available data suggests that agriculture is shedding labour throughout the world, except for Sub-Saharan Africa, North Africa, and West Asia (which includes the Middle East). Available data shows the growth of cropland per worker; namely, each worker is increasingly operating on more land (US Depart- ment of Agriculture Economic Research Service 2018).[2] This is because, globally, labour use is declining, while land under cultivation is changing very little. Expanding labour use is, there- fore, not a factor behind agricultural growth anywhere. Most remarkable is the movement of

2. Measures the number of adults economically active in agriculture.

labour out of agriculture in China. The rapid growth of agricultural production in China, and indeed throughout Asia, has occurred despite a reduction in the use of labour, largely due to the introduction of improved crop varieties, mechanization, irrigation and the use of chemical fertilizers, as well as productivity improvements not represented by these inputs, but reflected in the total factor productivity figures presented in Table 10.7. The much slower introduction of modern agricultural improvements in Africa and the Middle East has resulted in lower productivity gains and continued dependency on the use of labour.

This takes us to the remaining source of growth, namely total factor productivity, which represents the portion of growth in output over and above that obtained by expanding inputs of the types described above. Productivity is measured as value added, divided by indexes measuring the various inputs. This data show that total factor productivity growth is remarkably high throughout Asia. Contrary to the data on inputs, growth of agricultural total factor productivity is also relatively high in West Asia and North Africa. Latin America is doing less well, and Sub-Saharan Africa is far behind in total factor productivity growth.

Table 10.7: Growth in total factor productivity (annual per cent growth, 2001–15)

China	2.8
South Asia	2.7
Southeast Asia	2.5
West Asia/North Africa	2.3
Sub-Saharan Africa except Nigeria	0.6
World	2.5

Source: FAOSTAT 2018 (Database)

Since 2015, data shows total factor productivity declining in Sub-Saharan Africa and Oceania, and increasing only very slowly in North America. Asia continues to be the champion, with Europe and Latin America improving (USDA 2021).

The most important input into total factor productivity is research and development. It is the intangibles, such as the use of digital technologies, improved farmer skills, better intellectual property rights, removal of government policy barriers to agricultural innovation, introduction of risk management tools, improved land tenure systems, better rural infrastructure, and freer international trade, that matter here. Behind these factors lie government policy and investment. Pro-agriculture policy measures include, among other things, greater investments in agricultural research, agricultural schools, farmer education, land tenure security, farm risk management tools, rural infrastructure, and rural finance. The return on agricultural R&D was estimated in 2008 by the World Bank at an astounding 43 per cent (World Bank 2008). Good policy will not only affect total factor productivity but will also affect the quantity of agricultural inputs and machinery, fertilizer use, labour use, and land use. It is to these policies that we now turn; the more fundamental causes of agricultural growth versus stagnation.

Agriculture Policy and Investment of OECD countries

Beyond the proximate causes for differences in agricultural performance described above are a set of less obvious causes. Among these are agricultural policy and investment of OECD countries, including foreign aid to developing countries. Early foreign assistance programmes aiding developing country agriculture were modelled on the internal agricultural policies and programmes of OECD countries. After all, OECD countries, for the most part, had highly productive agricultural sectors and had developed sophisticated agricultural production and trading systems. Movement of agricultural products to agro-industry, and to market, worked well in all OECD countries.

Government policy in OECD countries was highly supportive of agriculture, involving substantial aid to farmers. This support was direct in the form of payments to farmers, and indirect through border protection against competing imports and financial support for public goods related to agriculture. The myriad of schemes introduced over time, and the shifting emphasis is too voluminous to describe here. In a nutshell, direct payments to farmers included price support schemes for various crops, public sector-supported crop insurance and mandates (such as the ethanol mandate in the US requiring gas at the pump to contain a mandated percentage of ethanol, sourced from maize). Indirect subsidies included the implicit subsidy accruing to farmers as a result of tariff and non-tariff barriers to farm products from other countries, and subsidized credit to farms and to agro-industry. In addition, there are a myriad of government expenditures on public goods, such as irrigation infrastructure, rural roads, agricultural research, agricultural schools and universities, food safety measures, veterinary services, forest services, and fish and wildlife services. All OECD countries provide these public goods, though to varying levels. The total value of OECD agricultural subsidies to their own country farmers was at about US$210 billion in 2015, according to the OECD.[3]

Most of the literature on the impact of the above policies and programmes suggests that the public goods expenditures in OECD countries have been remarkably effective in stimulating improvements in the use of farm inputs and generating farm-level productivity gains. R&D is a public good, and good public institutions, such as the agricultural universities in OECD countries, have been successful at educating farmers and others working in the sector. Agricultural extension, irrigation investment, and rural road and rural energy investment are highly effective in the OECD. These public goods are increasingly being provided as part of public–private partnerships in which the private sector is mobilized to provide a service, with public funding.

More controversial has been the direct and indirect payments to farmers, which in Europe and North America, go primarily to large industrial farms. The payments are often captured by the most politically astute farmers groups (such as sugar, cotton, dairy and cereals producers in the US), and bypass the less politically connected (such as vegetable growers and producers of organic produce). Because these direct subsidies are usually captured by large farms, they may inadvertently result in a decline in the number of small family farms throughout the OECD, and the consolidation of farmland into large industrial farms. These payments and protection from imported agricultural products also discriminate against agricultural imports from developing countries, which, in many cases, have a basic competitive advantage in comparison to OECD country production (due to cheaper labour), but can't compete due to the subsidies and the protection.

The above issues have been increasingly recognized in the academic, aid and government communities. Progress has been made in the OECD in reducing the direct and indirect

---

3. FAOSTAT monitors this data, which is prepared by the OECD (OECD/FAO 2020).

subsidies to farms (World Bank 2020a). Unfortunately, there has also been some reduction in government expenditures for the public goods of agricultural R&D, and agricultural education. It is likely that for most OECD countries, agriculture itself would be better off if direct subsidies to farmers and protection from agricultural imports were reduced, and public expenditure increased for agricultural R&D, agricultural extension, food safety, support to veterinary services, fisheries and forest services, and investment in rural infrastructure.

OECD countries have provided considerable aid to developing country agriculture, in part compensating, though unintentionally, for the negative impact of their domestic protectionism. Official Development Assistance (ODA) fluctuated over time. It was flat in current dollars, and declined in real dollars, during the period 1995–2006, despite warnings from the FAO, IFPRI, and International Fund for Agricultural Development (IFAD) that declining aid was adversely impacting developing countries (IFAD 2016). One example is the Asian Development Bank that began decreasing its aid to agriculture much earlier than other development partners, from nearly US$2.7 billion in the 1982–86 period to about US$1.8 billion in the 1987–91 period. This decline continued in the 1997–2001 period, picking up slightly in the 2002–06 period. Total ODA to agriculture, according to the FAO aid monitor, amounted to US$2.5 billion in the year 2000, growing to about US$11 billion in 2017.

In addition to ODA, multilateral development banks have provided loans at near commercial rates to agriculture. There was a decline in lending in the 2000s, though with ups and downs. The decline was driven by poor performance of projects in the sector and changing donor priorities in terms of sectors and instruments (for example, moving towards policy-based loans) (ADB 2019).

Agriculture Policy and Investment of Developing Countries

The developing world is diverse; there is no one pattern of agricultural policy and investment characterizing all developing countries. However, up until about 2005/2007, contributing factors to many developing countries' poor agricultural performance were found by academic and aid agency researchers to lie largely in macroeconomic and agricultural policies inimical to agriculture growth. Such ineffective policies often included the following (ADB 2007 and World Bank 2008):

1. Many developing countries had a weak enabling policy environment for private investment in agriculture, input supply, agricultural marketing and processing that resulted in limited private investment in the sector. Financial market distortions resulted in limited availability of rural credit.
2. Agricultural policies and a regulatory and institutional framework often permitted or caused harm to the natural environment (pollution of water, land degradation, over-fishing and excessive forest and wildlife loss).
3. There was, in many developing countries, an effective taxation of agriculture through price controls dampening farmgate prices. The purpose was usually to subsidize consumers or to support parastatal marketing and processing enterprises. Controls on the movement of agriculture products, often in the attempt to direct supplies to urban centres, also often served to reduce farmers' income. Border controls preventing or curtailing agricultural imports from neighbouring countries, reduced export possibilities within regions.

4. Low prioritization of agriculture was typical in nearly all developing country government budgets. This demonstrated a lack of interest in agriculture by many developing countries, and was reflected in low public investment in agricultural research, extension, education, infrastructure, livestock and forestry services. Figure 10.1 below shows the declining share of public expenditure going to agriculture in most of Asia up to 2012 (ADB 2019). Africa shows a worse pattern, with the share of public investment going to agriculture hovering in the 2 per cent range (ADB 2019).

Figure 10.1: Agriculture share in government expenditureby region, 2001–19

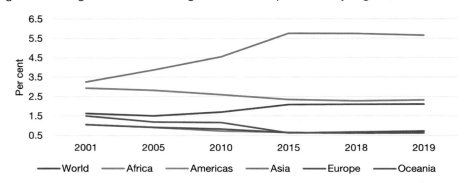

Source: FAO 2021

The Connection between Nutrition, Health and Agriculture

Agriculture and Nutrition

Discussions of agriculture now go hand-in-hand with discussions of nutrition, and the health consequences of food choice. This is because not all foods provide the same nutrition results. Too much processed food, for example, may satisfy calorie requirements (the traditional way of assessing hunger), but may lead to significantly worse nutritional and health outcomes than, say, the consumption of fresh foods or a mixture of cereals, vegetables, fish and livestock products. Individuals eating too much food, especially of processed food and sugar, become overweight and possibly obese. More food for the individual is, therefore, not necessarily better. In fact, much of the world has seen a shift from a problem of lack of calories (lack of sufficient quantity of food), to excessive consumption of high calorie/low nutritional value food, and a resulting increase in rates of obesity, and the health problems associated with it. Much of the problem lies in phenomena outside of primary production, such as processing technologies and demand (and advertisement), but some of the problem lies in the composition of production.

The numbe of undernourished people in the world declined, from 947 million in 2005, to its low point at 785 million in 2015. The number has increased since 2015, to 822 million at the end of 2018, according to the FAO (FAO et al. 2019). The increase in undernourishment since 2015 is attributed by the FAO to civil wars in some countries, economic slowdown in 2016 and beyond, poverty, and continued problems of access to water and sanitation, health services, education and food. The COVID-19 pandemic has worsened the problem. Access to food is itself a function of local production, imports, poverty and levels of violence, including war. The regional distribution of undernourishment is shown in Table 10.8.

The prevalence of undernourishment increased everywhere in 2019, except Asia and Europe. Undernourishment is high in Sub-Saharan Africa and is not decreasing there, although

Table 10.8: Prevalence of undernourishment (per cent of population)

Region	2005	2010	2017	2018	2019
World	12.3	9.4	8.2	8.3	8.9
South Asia	20.6	15.9	13.4	13.5	14.5
East Asia & Pacific	9.6	5.6	4.4	4.3	4.3
The Middle East & North Africa	8.8	9.1	10.4	10.4	10.7
Europe & Central Asia	3.1	2.7	4.4	4.3	4.3
Sub-Saharan Africa	23.3	20.0	18.5	18.8	20.3
Latin America & Caribbean	9.4	7.2	6.9	7.1	7.7

Source: World Bank 2021b

there is considerable variation between African countries. The overall situation in Latin America is worsening slightly (again with huge variation between countries). Asia has seen the most dramatic declines in undernourishment, especially between 2005 and 2010 and at much slower decline thereafter.

According to the WFP, the current pandemic has exacerbated the undernourishment problem. *The Washington Post* reported on 15 May 2020, that 1.6 billion of the world's 2 billion informal workers had lost their jobs (citing the International Labor Organization). The resulting loss of income was propelling about 50 million additional people into poverty (World Bank data was cited). The United Nations (UN) estimated at the time that 580 million people could become impoverished. The WFP projected that 265 million people would be at risk of starvation. The most recent data from the World Bank (December 2021) stated that 2.37 billion people lacked adequate access to food in 2020 (World Bank 2021a).

Obesity

Obesity is increasingly emerging as a worldwide phenomenon, with no region being exempt. According to the FAO, obesity contributes 4 million deaths per annum (FAO et al. 2019). Around 207 million adolescents and 2 billion adults were overweight in 2016. Obesity is estimated by the FAO to cost US$2 billion per annum in loss of productivity and increases in healthcare. Causes for the dramatic rise in obesity cited by the FAO include the expansion of the quantity and reach of low-cost, high-processed and often sweetened foods, advertisement and lack of nutrition education, stimulating an increased demand for low nutritional quality foods. Much of the developing world has considerably lower rates of obesity than do North America and Europe, but rates of obesity are increasing everywhere (FAOSTAT 2022).

Food Waste

Ironically, with widespread nutritional and food security problems, up to 30 per cent of food is lost to waste, from the farm to the fork. In most developing countries, the problem of food waste is concentrated on the farm and in primary marketing. Farms and marketing agents typically have poor storage facilities (including an absence of cold storage), poor transport facilities, and poor retail marketing outlets. In more developed countries, which have fewer of the above problems, the main source of wastage is at the supermarket, restaurant, and consumer levels. A reduction of waste in developing countries would require significant investment in the deficient items listed above. In developed countries, the problem is at least conceptually more difficult to resolve, as it would require significant behavioural changes. This could be accelerated by education.

Agricultural Employment and Migration

In practically every country, labour is leaving the agricultural sector. At the same time, agriculture is a huge employer of labour throughout the world. The FAO published a document in 2018, entitled 'The State of Food and Agriculture in 2018: Migration, Agriculture and Rural Development', which provided data on this issue (FAO 2018). There are 608 million farms in the world, according to FAO, of which 90 per cent (550 million) are family farms, occupying 70–80 per cent of farmland, and producing 80 per cent of the world's food in value terms (Lowder et al. 2019, 13). The remainder of the farms are industrial farms owned by companies. However, not all family farms are small (FAO's definition of small farms includes farms less than two hectares). Small farms account for 84 per cent of all farms worldwide, operate on 12 per cent of agricultural land and produce 36 per cent of the world's food (Lowder et al. 2019, 13). This means that some family farms are big.

In geographical terms, 43 per cent of the world's farms are located in East Asia and the Pacific, 30 per cent in South Asia, 12 per cent in Sub-Saharan Africa, 6 per cent in low-income Europe and Central Asia, 4 per cent in Latin America and 2 per cent in high-income countries. The largest 1 per cent of farms operate on 70 per cent of the world's farmland (Lowder et al. 2019, 8–13). Hence, the political and economic clout of the large farms.

This brings us to farm labour. Family labour exceeds hired labour on most farms worldwide. The ratio of household members to hired permanent workers in agriculture averages five (Lowder et al. 2019, 67–70).[4] The data in the FAO study, which is the source of this information, suggests that worldwide there are on average 0.54 permanent workers per farm (not including family members). Large industrial farms will have many hired workers, while small family farms often have none. With 608 million farms of all types worldwide, this suggests that some 330 million people are permanent farm workers, not including household members. Agricultural household members are estimated at 2.3 billion people (Lowder et al. 2019, 67–70).[5]

Modern history in both industrial and developing countries is one of movement of rural peoples to towns and cities, and to more developed countries. The literature suggests that in many, if not most, cases, rural-urban migration has been beneficial to the migrants themselves

4. This is based on a review of agricultural census material from fifty-one countries, and then extrapolated to the world. The margin of error is huge. These numbers are approximations only.
5. Calculated from the data available from fifty-one country agricultural censuses and extrapolated to the world. These are very crude approximations.

(who improve their own standard of living and that of their families), beneficial to the towns and cities to which they move (by bringing needed labour) and to the rural areas from which they came (through remittances back to family members remaining in the rural areas, which improve the well-being of those left behind). The positive effects are most characteristic of demand-pull migration in which higher productivity and higher-wage jobs in cities attracts lower productivity and lower-income farm labour. This migration has helped reduce poverty, particularly in parts of Asia (China, Taiwan, South Korea and Vietnam) as well as in North America and Europe. The positive impacts on rural areas occur not only through remittances but also by enabling land consolidation and by stimulating farm modernization. Farm modernization occurs through greater investment in labour-saving technology and productivity improvements in the rural areas left behind by the migrants.

Rural-urban migration can, however, also have negative consequences, most frequently when the reasons involved are push factors, such as social breakdown in rural areas, forcing rural people to seek refuge in other countries or in the big cities (examples abound from Somalia, Sudan, Congo, Syria, parts of the Sahel, Afghanistan and parts of the Middle East and Central America). Push migration often overwhelms the receiving cities and countries, with migrants encountering joblessness and social ostracism. The rural areas from which they come may receive little in the way of remittances (this varies; in Central America, for example, the remittances are substantial), and conditions on the farms they have left behind are often too disrupted to benefit in terms of land consolidation and investment. In these cases, the decline in the rural labour force is much faster than it would have been without such disruption. The answer lies outside of agricultural policy in these cases; it is rather one of conflict-resolution.

There are situations in between the above extremes, where demand pull from urban areas combined with poor agricultural policy and investment results in an excessive rate of rural-urban migration, which cities and foreign countries cannot absorb. Parts of Asia, Latin America and parts of Africa are in this situation.

The outcomes of these forces on labour use can be seen in the rate of change in the ratio of land to labour in agriculture. This ratio is growing very fast in China as labour departs agriculture and agriculture modernizes. Chinese agricultural growth has not been compromised, and its agricultural sector has supplied much-needed labour to urban areas. The ratio of land to labour is also increasing in Southeast Asia, though at a lesser rate than in China. Urban areas are absorbing this labour, and agriculture is growing quickly. The same phenomena, though much less rapid, is occurring in South Asia. However, in the Middle East and in Sub-Saharan Africa, the size of farms is shrinking, and the land-labour ratio is declining. Labour is migrating off the farms in Africa and the Middle East/North Africa. But the growth of rural populations and the lack of employment opportunities in most African and Middle Eastern cities means that there are an increasing number of agricultural labourers per hectare despite the migration. Because agricultural productivity growth is low in most African and Middle Eastern countries, this expansion in agricultural labour is occurring along with a decline in average farm incomes. Labour would migrate off these farms even faster if there were adequate employment opportunities in the cities, or easier access to foreign countries.

The literature suggests that the dream of developing countries' agricultural sectors absorbing the large rural populations is unlikely anywhere near to being accomplished. A thriving agro-industry can help, but even where agriculture is thriving, for example, in North America, parts of Europe, Australia and New Zealand, there continues to be rural-urban migration. Rapidly growing agricultural sectors in China and South Asia are shedding labour the fastest. Slow-growing agricultural sectors in Africa and the Middle East are absorbing labour, but into low productivity farms and only because the opportunities elsewhere are so limited.

The objective of absorbing more labour in agriculture can be at least partly achieved in countries characterized by push factors (pushing labour out of agriculture and out of rural areas) due to civil war, civil strife, extreme rural poverty, drought, etc., by attacking the cause of the push (end to civil strife, drought mitigation, etc.). On the opposite extreme are countries such as China and those in Southeast Asia, where there is no need to take explicit measures, as the movement out of agriculture is positive—for the people who move, the industries to which they move, and for the farmers left in rural areas who receive remittances, have bigger farms and are modernizing more rapidly than would otherwise be the case.

In the intermediate cases, where rural-urban migration is too fast for cities to absorb, more aggressive rural development measures are appropriate. In these situations, improved agricultural and rural policy and investment to make rural areas more attractive is the answer. These policies include territorial investment, rural infrastructure, rural health and education, improved agricultural R&D and often improved land tenure regimes. Greater focus on rural development, including greater public investment, should generate rural jobs (particularly in agro-industry and service industries, including public services), in turn slowing migration. Such investments are, of course, desirable everywhere, even in advanced industrial country agriculture because the continued growth in agriculture and agro-industry helps stimulate overall economic growth. But in the countries which are shedding agricultural labour too quickly for cities to absorb, these proactive rural and agricultural development policies and investments take on added importance.

On the margins, there are policies that can slow the rate of out migration from the farm, if desired. For example, in the United States, the bulk of agricultural subsidies go to large grain farms, sugar estates and cotton farmers. Organic farming and vegetable growing receives much less. But organic farming and vegetable production uses more labour per hectare than the highly mechanized grain, cotton and sugar producers. Switching the subsidies to the former would tend to be labour-using, though likely to have only a small effect on agricultural employment.

Climate Change and Agriculture

The Intergovernmental Panel on climate change's (IPCC) Sixth Assessment report, 'Climate Change 2021' (2021) says that 'Global surface temperature in the 2001–20 period was .99 degree centigrade higher than the average temperature during 1850–1900.' The report finds that this, along with other human influences, has already resulted in melting of the Greenland ice sheet, a shift in mid-latitude storm tracks poleward, a global sea level increase by 0.2 metres between 1901 and 2018, hot extremes more frequent and more intense, a greater frequency of more intense precipitation and storm events, and more severe drought. Climate change is already here.[6] IPCC's Sixth Assessment Report has modelled various scenarios, with

---

6. IPCC AR5; 'Climate Change 2014: Impacts, Adaptation and Vulnerability', Part A; 'Global and Sectoral Aspects', IFPR; 'Climate Change, Impact on Agriculture and Costs of Adaptation'; Food Policy Report 2009, Washington DC, October 2009. Union of Concerned Scientists; 'Climate Change and Agriculture', 20 March 2018. FAO, 'The State of Food and Agriculture; climate change', Agriculture and Food Security, Rome, 2016.

an intermediate scenario suggesting a 2.1 to 3.5°C average temperature increase by the year 2100. This would bring even more extreme changes of the type listed above.

Although the most recent IPCC report on the impact of climate change on agriculture is not yet out (expected in February–March of 2022), there is now a significant literature on this subject.[7] The literature overwhelmingly finds that the impacts of agriculture on climate change, and the impact of climate change on agriculture, are significant, and will continue to grow as climate change evolves.

Generally, agriculture in the tropics is found to have already suffered from climate change and is projected to suffer more. The 2007 synthesis report of the IPCC stated: 'By 2020 in some African countries, yields from rain-fed agriculture could be reduced by up to 50 per cent. This would further adversely affect food security and exacerbate malnutrition' (IPCC 2007). The literature since then shows vast ranges of possible effects of climate change on agriculture (Muller et al. 2011; Aydinalp and Cresser 2008). Most show severe negative effects, but some show positive effects for some countries. A 2011 US National Academy of Sciences study on climate risks for Africa projected a range of from 100 per cent to 168 per cent decline in agriculture production from climate change in the long run, based on econometric studies (Muller 2011). A recent study found that 'flood shocks, defined as annual rainfall higher than one standard deviation from the 50-year average, is associated with a 35 per cent decrease in food per capita consumption and a 17 per cent point increase in extreme poverty in Sub-Saharan Africa' (Azzarni and Signorelli 2020). On the other hand, in northern climates, such as those found in Russia, Canada and Scandinavia, rising temperatures combined with CO_2 fertilization can increase crop yields and permit cultivation in areas previously uncultivated.

The difference in impact is due to the variation in the nature of climate change. Where rainfall declines or becomes more variable (more deluge followed by longer periods of drought), and where temperatures are already high but get warmer, agriculture of all kinds suffers. Changes in temperature and rainfall also bring new pests and diseases, cause rising sea levels and hence sea water intrusion in coastal agricultural areas. These changes also cause stress on forests and on fisheries.[8]

Rainfall has been declining, and temperature has been increasing in Sub-Saharan Africa since the 1950s, hence the dire IPCC prediction. As predicted by the IPCC, rainfall has shown a long-term decline, and temperatures a long-term increase in Sub-Saharan Africa.

In 2016, the FAO predicted net crop yield decreases in the tropics by 16 per cent for wheat and 6 per cent for maize due to a two-degree temperature increase (FAO 2016). This was before taking into account changes in rainfall, impact of new pests and diseases, etc., and not accounting for the impact on livestock. A recent World Bank study found that 'for every degree centigrade increase in temperature, average global cereal yields are expected to decline 3 per cent to 10 per cent' (Fugli 2020). An IPCC study in 2014 projected negative impacts on agricultural yields double the positive effects in the period 2020–49. For the period 2016–29, IPCC 2014 projected that the negative and positive effects globally would be equal and offsetting (IPCC 2014).

---

7. Ibid.
8. For further information see the Union of Concerned Scientists, 'Climate Change and Agriculture', The World Bank: Climate Smart Agriculture (2020), 20 March 2019; and IFPRI, 'Climate Change: Impact on Agriculture and Costs of Adaptation', Food Policy Report 2009, Washington DC, October 2009.

It is now 2022, and we can see to what extent the initial projections have materialized. The answer is that globally, they have not. Global agriculture has continued to grow, as has agriculture in most of the developing world, including the tropics; in fact, 2019 was a record year for global agriculture production. How has this happened, since the agricultural science is clear that the physical impact of less rainfall, higher temperature, new pests and saltwater intrusion must be negative? The answer is that agricultural adaptation to climate change has worked so far, and on aggregate. The IPCC, the World Bank, and the FAO all explained that the negative impacts could be mitigated, and in those circumstances where the impacts were positive, they can be further promoted, through adaptation of agriculture to the new circumstances.

Adaptation includes actions, such as modifying planting times, changing crops (in the tropics to more drought- and temperature-tolerant crops), new cultivars which are drought- or temperature- or salt-tolerant, improving soil and water management, expanding irrigation, introduction of a myriad of conservation agriculture techniques, and on-farm crop and livestock diversification.[9] This widespread adaptation in developing countries has been assisted by agricultural research and foreign assistance, including new agricultural climate adaptation funds. It is almost certain that agriculture would have grown even more in the absence of climate change. But it appears that so far, with the climate impacts already occurring, farmers in most countries are adapting. This does not mean that all farmers are adapting; many have not been able to adapt, and many of them have dropped out of farming. Given the pressure on the land, it is also likely that in many of these cases, other farmers have taken over this land. The global picture also hides considerable variation by country. Many countries in the Sahel region of Africa, for example, will face difficulties in adapting enough to offset the negative effects of climate change (IPCC 2018).

The next question is: what is the likelihood that agriculture will continue to successfully adapt globally, as temperatures continue to rise, rainfall patterns continue to change and additional pests and diseases continue to appear? Is there a limit to farmers' ability to adapt? In answer, it is likely that many places in the tropics will reach a limit, as parts of the Sahel region in Africa appear to have already reached. Rainfall may become too constrained and erratic, irrigation possibilities exhausted, new pests and diseases so devastating that agriculture and/or raising livestock becomes so difficult that farming collapses.

Indeed, the IPCC report on climate change 2014 undertook a substantial review of the literature on climate change and agriculture, resulting in dire warnings for the future. It predicted particularly severe and negative climate impact on wheat and maize, globally. It stated that 'for major crops in tropical and temperate regions, climate change without adaptation is projected to negatively impact production' (IPCC 2014, 17). This underlines the need to greatly expand on the efforts at adaptation, and that agriculture become a major promoter of climate change mitigation.

Adaptation will continue to require its inclusion in agriculture education, and then agricultural research and extension. Predicting changes in agricultural situations likely to occur due to climate change will be critically important. Developing new tools to help farmers to adapt must be a continuous process (different planting and harvesting dates, tools to combat new pests

---

9. Adaptation measures include, most importantly, better management of rice paddies, which are major CO_2 emitters, zero or minimum tillage, mulching, direct seeding, better water management, reduction in mineral fertilizer use, more poultry and pigs and less cattle and buffalo, better treatment of animal waste, solar drying of crops and reforestation.

and diseases, improved irrigation and improved livestock handling are examples). Individual farmers and farmer associations generally do not have the tools to undertake this type of research and development. Their job will be to master, and apply, these new tools as climates change. Governments and international aid organizations will have the more important role to play in this type of policy and investment. Countries able to do this well may thrive under current projections of climate change, while those not adapting at all will face important agricultural and hence rural challenges.

Agriculture continues to contribute over 20 per cent of CO_2 emissions (including the impact of livestock and deforestation) (FAO 2016). Conservation agriculture (such as no-till farming) can reduce this. Reduction in deforestation and conversion of cropland to tree crops can lessen this impact, but probably not by much. More radical measures, such as reducing livestock production, massive forest planting and use of algae as food, could do more and are possibilities. Many of these measures are also good from the standpoint of nutrition. But it is unlikely that in the absence of these radical measures, requiring enormous changes in dietary patterns, that agriculture and livestock production will contribute significantly less to climate change.

As indicated above, OECD countries, China, Brazil, India, among others, support their farming sectors, with subsidies totalling several hundred billion dollars per annum. Switching some of these subsidies, particularly those consisting of direct subsidies to farmers, to investment in climate change adaptation and mitigation, could supply the additional funds needed for these latter purposes. The constraints to this obvious solution are many. Current recipients of subsidies tend to be politically powerful farm lobbies, which will resist. Some farming and agro-industrial activities (ethanol production in the US, for example) are totally dependent on subsidies, and will likely collapse in their absence (OECD 2020c). A phase-in of subsidies for adaptation and mitigation measures, and a phase-out of direct and indirect payments to farmers will be needed. This should start now.

Prognosis for the Future of Global Agriculture

Projections by the OECD and the FAO (prior to the pandemic) indicate a future in which rising production matches rising demand, resulting in a 'low real price environment' continuing for the next ten years (OECD/FAO 2019). The OECD/FAO analysis suggests that per capita food demand and global biofuel demand are levelling off, meaning that increased demand is coming largely from areas where populations are growing (Sub-Saharan Africa, India, the Middle East and North Africa). Demand for animal products is continuing to increase rapidly, as is the demand for animal feed (maize and soybeans particularly). Fish production from aquaculture is growing rapidly while that from capture fisheries is declining. Relative world prices of these commodities will adjust accordingly, with prices for meat, dairy, fruits and vegetables increasing relative to those of cereals.

The global prospects hide regional differences. Production constraints in Sub-Saharan Africa and the Middle East and North Africa, combined with higher population growth, mean that these regions are likely to be increasingly dependent on food imports and food aid, as well as subject to higher relative food prices. This is already reflected in high food import growth. Latin America, North America, Europe and Oceania were projected to have expanded agricultural trade balances (exports-imports).

The impact of the COVID-19 pandemic has so far been negative on agricultural supply chains, on agricultural production, and on food aid. The FAO/OECD projections were thus too optimistic, largely because they predate the pandemic. Agricultural prices have increased almost everywhere in early 2020–21. The very latest summary of the impact of COVID-19 on agricultural prices globally (29 October 2021) stated that domestic food price inflation remains highest in Africa, followed by Latin America and the Caribbean and South Asia. In most regions, including Africa, food price inflation has picked up in recent months. Rising energy, fertilizer and transport costs pose further risks to global food markets.

However, moving to a more disaggregated level, there is, and will continue to be, great variation in country performance. Within Africa, we already see dramatic differences in performance between countries, with some now achieving very good agricultural growth and growth of agro-industry (Rwanda, Ghana are the champions), while others are going backwards (Congo, Sudan, Egypt, Zimbabwe, Ethiopia and parts of the Sahel). Within Asia, there is a similar pattern of very mixed performance, with China, Taiwan, South Korea and Vietnam continuing to outpace the rest of Asia, while Central Asia is stagnating. This can change with policy and investment of the types recommended below. This requires, in many cases, political and institutional changes. The ability to deal with the rural-urban migration equation and climate change will become increasingly important as migration continues, and climate change becomes even more daunting. The impact of future climate change on agriculture is very dependent on the world's ability to change policy and investment in response. Agriculture could be disastrously affected or, on aggregate at least, adapt depending on the global policy and investment response.

New Directions Needed in Agricultural Policy and Investment

Desirable and undesirable policies and approaches to agriculture development have been described above. New approaches which need to be added to the mix include the following.

Agriculture, and the enterprises which provide its inputs and market, and process its outputs, are increasingly viewed as a private sector, not a public sector. Even in developing countries with strong public sectors, such as China and Vietnam, the essential private sector nature of agricultural production, processing, and marketing is recognized in policy and investment. Major development partners are expanding their assistance to private agri-business, often through equity investment and non-sovereign lending,[10] while development institutions such as International Fund for Agricultural Development (IFAD), which do not have a non-sovereign lending instrument, are channelling more of their funds through projects involving public-private-producer partnerships. The World Bank and International Finance Corporation (IFC) have been undertaking joint projects in the sector through their plan to maximize financing for development in agricultural value chains by crowding-in private investment and optimizing the use of scarce public resources (World Bank 2020a).

Project investments and policy advice are increasingly viewed within the framework of the 'value chain'. The idea is to view agricultural products as commodities and to develop related investments and policy advice, beginning with the inputs required, and including farming,

---

10. Such as by ADB, African Development Bank, European Bank for Reconstruction and Development, European Commission, UK's Department for International Development (DFID), the Agence Française, United States Agency for International Development and the World Bank.

marketing, processing and consumption. Value chain support for basic staples, such as maize, rice and wheat, would, therefore, consider inputs such as seed supply, fertilizer needs, land use, water and farm equipment. It would then focus on farming techniques appropriate to the location, storage and marketing of the product, processing into different products, and finally retail and consumption. Included in this analysis would be environmental issues, nutritional concerns, gender aspects and finance. This new approach has led to the realization that the value chains of different commodities (for example, tea or coffee) have different requirements. Further, the value chains for the same commodity will differ across countries. In most value chains, the requirements of private farmers and agri-business (or cooperatives in some cases) are likely to dominate. However, government policy changes and public investment in infrastructure, education, and agricultural research and extension are almost always present. Access to finance is also important. The involvement of both private and public investment often requires private-public linkages and partnerships in value chain development.

In many parts of the developing world, ecological damage is evident in the form of growing biodiversity loss, water scarcity, water and air pollution, ocean acidification, fisheries depletion and wetland degradation. In 2008, Asia and the Pacific recorded the world's highest number of threatened species, with Southeast Asia experiencing the most serious cases (UNDP 2010). In South Asia, water security is already low and these areas may be disproportionately affected by more frequent and intense droughts and other stresses on water management (ADB 2013). In the Asia region, many rivers and lakes are dead or dying, groundwater aquifers are over-pumped and some species of aquatic life have been driven to extinction. Agriculture has contributed to this situation through soil degradation and fertilizer and pesticide run-off. There is a decline in forest cover as a per cent of land area for many Asian countries. The conversion of forest land and protected areas to agricultural purpose is happening in Indonesia, Myanmar, Nepal, and Sri Lanka. Bhutan, China, India, Lao PDR, Vietnam and the Philippines have expanded areas under forests. For China, India and Lao PDR, this is particularly remarkable, given the rapid growth in agriculture. This type of damage is less evident in Africa, though forest destruction is important.

It follows from the above that there is a need for much more environmentally sustainable and climate-friendly farming systems. The world's agriculture currently uses 11 per cent of the world's land, accounts for 70 per cent of its freshwater withdrawals, causes 80 per cent of deforestation, 30 per cent of energy consumption, and emits 10 gigatons of CO_2 per annum. There is growing recognition of the need to use limited water and land resources more efficiently and to reverse the environmental degradation. In addition, climate change and climate variability poses large, but regionally differing, threats to agriculture and food security in Asia and Africa through higher temperatures, more extreme weather events, drier conditions in large parts of the region, sea-level rise and flooding, which can impact on crop patterns and yields, and cause crop damage (ADB 2017). This will compound already observed pressures, such as decreasing soil productivity, groundwater depletion and declining water availability, as well as increased pest incidence and salinity. As indicated above, switching of agricultural subsidies from direct and indirect payments to farmers, to the support of measures to help farmers adapt to climate change, mitigate climate change and protect the rural environment will be necessary.

Food safety is a growing issue throughout the developing world. China, for example, while doing very well in terms of agricultural production, has relatively low sanitary and phytosanitary standards for its agricultural goods, but has incorporated food safety as a priority in its most recent five-year plan. Excessive pesticide residues, low food hygiene, unsafe additives, contamination with heavy metals and other contaminants and misuse of veterinary drugs have all led to trade restrictions with Japan, the United States and the European Union. Similar issues have been widely publicized in Thailand and Vietnam. Other Asian countries and all African countries face similar problems, though the degree of severity is less well-studied (IFPRI 2017).

A related issue is food waste, which is substantial. Waste occurs along the entire supply chain, from the farm, to marketing and processing, to the household. Solutions include more investment in storage and transport at all levels of the supply chain, and consumer education.

As described above, nearly all African countries need productivity-inspired agricultural growth, which expands output per unit of investment, land and water. This is because these three ingredients are in short supply everywhere in Africa. The only ingredient not in short supply is labour. As a result, labour-using productivity improvements will be particularly beneficial. Private investment in agro-processing, marketing and input supply will be beneficial both to stimulate productivity improvements and to expand agro-industry. Governments will have a major role, not in investing in farming and agro-industry directly but by moving to a policy environment, which encourages private investment in these activities (that is, macroeconomic policy, regulation and institutional development). Expanded public and private investment in rural infrastructure, rural education, rural health, rural energy and rural telecommunications will also be important for a healthy agriculture and agro-industry, as well as helping in the adaptation to climate change and in slowing rural-urban migration (which is too rapid in Africa).

Much of Asia requires the same agricultural productivity focus as Africa does, given land and water constraints. Investment constraints in large parts of Asia (especially China) are much less severe, so the rural investments required should be easier to finance; a great part of these investments could come from domestic resources, as these countries are considerably less aid-dependent than Africa. Likewise, the need to retain labour in Asian agriculture is much less important than in Sub-Saharan Africa and the Middle East, as industry has been able to better absorb rural migrants. Government-sponsored or induced R&D to adapt agriculture to climate change and to discover and adapt productivity-enhancing technology will continue to be important. Introduction of better food safety and quality standards and more environmentally benign agricultural technology (due to high levels of water and soil pollution, and negative impacts on human health) are particularly important for the more advanced agricultural sectors in China, Taiwan, South Korea and Vietnam.

Box 10.3: India's agriculture

Indian agriculture is a good example of both the successes of agricultural development and the issues facing developing country agriculture. India is the world's biggest producer of milk, pulses and jute, and the second largest producer of rice, wheat, sugarcane, groundnuts, vegetables, fruit, and cotton. Agriculture is the largest source of livelihood for 70 per cent of Indian households. 82 per cent of India's farmers are 'small and marginal'. India has achieved food self-sufficiency, but has 25 per cent of the world's hungry people, and 190 million Indians are undernourished (FAO 2022). Despite remarkable production gains, Indian agriculture faces significant hurdles, already constraining production, which may become even more daunting in the future. There is considerable stress on water resources, in part due to huge subsidies for energy use in irrigated agriculture, leading to overuse of groundwater, poor irrigation maintenance and management, and coastal intrusion of salt water. Desertification and land degradation are widespread. Government policy subsidizes the production of cereals and water-intensive crops (rice and sugarcane), while not subsidizing more nutrition-rich foods, such as vegetables and fruit. Subsidizing water-using crops also encourages groundwater mining. Underinvestment in on-farm storage and handling, and in-market infrastructure, has led to enormous food waste. The IPCC predicts a significantly negative impact of future climate change on Indian agriculture. The recommendations made above, all apply to India, particularly the need to de-regulate the sector, reform farm subsidies, invest in rural infrastructure, invest in climate change adaptation, protection of the rural environment, and dealing with food safety and waste. Given the political nature of these reforms, a careful phasing in of reform will be needed.

Box 10.4: Getting policies right: Lessons from the People's Republic of China

As arguably the best recent agricultural performer in the world, the case of the People's Republic of China (PRC) is informative. The PRC has been remarkably innovative in its agricultural policy, and its private sector has invested effectively in agriculture and agro-industry. The PRC invests a greater share of its public expenditure in agriculture than almost any other country in the world. In particular, it invests more in agricultural research and development than any other country, with growth in agricultural research and development at nearly 10 per cent on average in the 2000–09 period. Notable policy changes in the past decade have included the PRC's expansion of farmers' land rights by allowing land transfer through the rental market. The PRC has also invested heavily in rural areas in infrastructure, irrigation, rural education and health and improved environmental management. The Chinese government also provided agricultural tax exemptions, granted subsidies for agricultural production, and higher prices for government procurement of agricultural commodities. There has been some domestic and international trade liberalization, and expansion of social as well as environmental protection, and social security coverage in the PRC. There have been failures, however, particularly in environmental protection. Much of China's water and soil is significantly and dangerously polluted. China will need to deal with its severe rural environmental problems, water conservation, and distortions due to farmer subsidies. Switching subsidies to supporting farmer adaptation to climate change and mitigation of climate change will be important in China.

Chapter 11: Technology in our Post-pandemic Future

Technology in Our Post-pandemic Future

Chapter 11

Dr R. A. Mashelkar, FRS

Unprecedented Speed and Scale of Change

The present COVID-19 pandemic stands out not only because it brought about a change but also because of the unprecedented speed of the change and the massive scale and scope of the change.

In a strange way, history repeated itself when the virus moved from Wuhan, China, to Italy in the fourteenth century and then in the twenty-first century.

In the fourteenth century, it took sixteen years, that is, from 1331 to 1347, for the bubonic plague to spread from Wuhan in China to Italy (Kanga 2020).

In 2020, it took only sixteen weeks for the coronavirus to move to Italy.

It was not only the speed but also the scale that was massive.

In the first three months of the pandemic, besides millions getting infected and several thousands dying, 1.6 billion children from 192 countries (Psacharopoulos et al. 2020) had to resort to online learning. Almost one-third of them were digitally deprived and, therefore, had no access to education. The world saw the worst economic recession after the Great Depression of 1930s (BBC 2020).

As the terms 'pre-war' and 'post-war' are commonly used to describe the twentieth century, pre-COVID-19 and post-COVID-19 eras will be discussed in the same way.

Interestingly, pandemics do damage as well as some good. They induce new technological changes. The 1918 pandemic inspired research in microbiology, infectious diseases, and public health. Quick adoption of e-commerce in China after the SARS epidemic in 2005 is yet another example.

Acceleration of Technology Deployment and Development

The COVID-19 crisis has sped up the acceptance and deployment of technology. In the past, it took a decade or longer for game-changing technologies to evolve from novel findings to productive gains in the field. Here, the transition in several areas was from years to months and, in some cases, even weeks.

Here are some major examples of speed, scale, and scope of change.

COVID-19 accelerated adoption of digital technologies across industries by several years and many of these changes will stay for the long term. In the early days of the pandemic, Microsoft CEO Satya Nadella said, 'We've just seen two years' worth of digital transformation in two months' (Tottoc 2021).

Telemedicine saw exponential growth during the COVID-19 crisis. A McKinsey study suggests that overall telehealth utilization has stabilized at levels 38X higher than before the pandemic (Bestsennyy et al. 2021).

The e-commerce sector has witnessed an unprecedented ten years' growth in just three months. Online sales in the US hit US$791.70 billion in 2020, up 32.4 per cent from US$598.02 billion in 2019 (Digital Commerce 360 n.d.).

During the COVID-19 pandemic, consumers preferred contactless payment methods. With over 1.2 billion registered accounts across ninety-six countries (Michaels 2021), mobile money transfer platforms have witnessed exponential growth during the pandemic. It took the industry a decade to reach 100 million active users. About 136 million accounts were added in 2020 alone. Tap-to-pay transactions grew more than 30 per cent in 2020 (Michaels 2021).

Coursera, one of the largest online learning platforms in the world, registered over 650 per cent usage growth globally (Majumdar and Pathak 2020).

This pandemic has been not only a great accelerator of usage of many technologies but also that of technology development and deployment. It made decades of progress happen in a few weeks.

The most accelerated technological change took place in biotechnology, especially when one witnessed the development of safe and effective vaccines (90 per cent efficacy) in just ten months instead of the ten years it used to take (Wellcome 2021).

Having reviewed the unprecedented acceleration of technology development and deployment during the pandemic, we will now look at the way the technology landscape will change in the post-pandemic era and the impact it will have on the future society.

New Biology in Our Future

We've seen multiple trends come to fruition at the intersection of biology and digital exponential technologies, which is causing a bio-revolution. It will have a significant impact on economies, our lives and livelihoods. This is tantamount to a new Industrial Revolution in human history.

Confluence with AI, automation and DNA sequencing has created a revolution that promises the development of gene therapies, hyper-personalized medicines and genetics-based guidance on food and exercise.

The origin of this exponential change was triggered before the pandemic. The Human Genome Project for sequencing human genome was set up in 1991 and finished the task in 2003, for around US$3 billion. Now, it would cost US$300 (Mullin 2020). That's an exponential decay in cost.

There is Moore's Law for biology, thanks to the rising power of computation; machine learning and AI are transforming many areas of bio-pharma and healthcare; the ability to not just 'read', but 'write', to bio, including CRISPR (even in just a decade) has been truly disruptive.

CRISPR: The Game Changer

Emmanuelle Charpentier and Jennifer A. Doudna won the Nobel prize in 2020 for CRISPR, the 'scissors' (NobelPrize.org 2020). CRISPR stands for Clustered Regularly Interspaced Short Palindromic Repeat. The CRISPR system is a sophisticated defence that bacteria evolved to disarm invading viruses, similar to the way fungi developed penicillin to protect themselves against bacterial infection.

The CRISPR system is empowering scientists to alter human and other genomes with great benefits, such as repairing gene mutations that cause damageing diseases like cystic fibrosis.

CRISPR has fundamentally changed the thinking about what's possible. For example, it took more than thirty years to develop the first effective vaccine for malaria and that too with an efficacy of only about 50 per cent in the first year, dropping in subsequent years (Mandavilli 2021). The CRISPR system will make it possible to develop many more effective vaccines in the next five years. Indeed, CRISPR can lead to a new suite of tools called programable medical therapies; it could greatly accelerate the development of therapeutics for new viruses and prevent the damage due to future pandemics.

CRISPR can lead to breakthroughs in creating plant varieties that can withstand the effects of climate change. It may also create a cure for blood diseases like sickle cell anaemia and beta thalassemia. A recent breakthrough, elegantly described by Elizabeth Finkel, also shows how the newly found CRISPR-Cas 13 will allow us to beat viruses at their own game and create anti-COVID-19 therapeutics (Finkel 2021).

But there are risks involved in the unethical use of CRISPR. The Chinese scientist He Jiankui created a controversy (Cyranoski 2019) by using genome editing for the first time in human embryos in 2018. This led to legal and ethical controversies, resulting in Jiankui's indictment along with two of his collabourators.

He Jiankui started a project to help people with HIV-related fertility problems. He used the CRISPR technology for editing embryos' genomes to remove the CCR5 gene in an attempt to confer genetic resistance to HIV. His work raised wide-ranging controversies. He was imprisoned by the Chinese authorities for three years (Cyranoski 2019).

After the fallout of Jiankui's work, the World Health Organization (WHO) issued a call to halt all work on human genome editing, and launched a global registry to track research in the field.

CRISPR has potential to do good. Maybe one day CRISPR can change the gene in the embryo, so that the child born to parents with sickle cell doesn't have sickle cell. But its misuse is a matter of concern.

The ethics of CRISPR's use are not clear. There are moral and ethical issues, especially the potential for genetic editing to exacerbate inequality.

The Magic of Messenger Ribonucleic Acid (mRNA)

Just as impactful as CRISPR is the phenomenon of mRNA, whose true potential was realized as a result of the pandemic challenge.

Moderna's vaccine, which was designed in two days, was further developed, tested, and deployed within a year—a record time (Clifford 2021). This vaccine is based on the messenger RNA, called mRNA, which is a piece of ribonucleic acid that carries information about the amino acid sequence of a specific protein from the DNA (where all that information is stored) to the ribosome, where, in the cell, different proteins are synthesized. To explain it in simple words, one can view mRNA as a USB device that cells use to pass information from the computer (DNA) to another device, such as the printer (ribosome).

The virus sequence was published in January 2020 (Institut Pasteur 2020). Then the race began to create a vaccine, which enabled the development of proteins that would bind to the spikes of the virus. The goal was to prevent it from binding to human cells, thus rendering the virus harmless. mRNA technology won the race.

Essentially, this revolutionary mRNA technology instructs the human body to make the vaccine itself. The magic of mRNA technology may bring a paradigm shift in the pharma industry. Its potential is being examined to treat heart diseases, cancer and other infectious diseases. While transformative, mRNA technology has been in the making for over twenty years, it took a pandemic for it to be adopted successfully.

The potential of the bio-revolution is expected to go much beyond health. As much as 60 per cent of the physical inputs to the global economy could theoretically be produced biologically (Chui et al. 2020). Examples include agriculture (genetic modification to create heat- or drought-resistant crops or to address conditions such as vitamin A deficiency), energy (genetically engineered microbes to create hydrogen from biomass or even biofuels), and new materials (artificial spider silk and self-repairing fabrics). Those and other applications feasible through current technology could create trillions of dollars in economic impact over the next decade.

As with artificial intelligence, facial recognition and other digital technologies, society should play an active role in drawing the ethical lines in new biology and its applications. Only then can we ensure that the world maximizes the potential of these remarkable innovations for the good of humanity.

Digital Transformation of Our Life and Livelihoods

There is a general agreement that there are as many as twenty-five technology trends that will shape the decade of 2020s and beyond (Marr 2020; Daugherty 2021; UNCTAD 2021; Fleming 2021).

These include 5G, affective computing, artificial intelligence (AI) and machine learning, autonomous vehicles, big data and augmented analytics, block chains and distributed ledgers, cloud and edge computing, computer vision, cryptocurrency, cyber security, digital platforms, digital tweens, digitally extended realities, drones and unmanned aerial vehicles, edge computing, facial recognition, genomics and gene editing, intelligent spaces and smart places, Internet of Things (IoT), mass personalization, nanotechnology, natural language processing, new materials science, quantum computing, robotic process automation, robots and collaborative robots (cobots), voice interfaces and chat bots, wearables and augmented humans and 3D- and 4D-printing.

It is not possible to deal with each of these in detail. However, here is a highlight of some key features.

First and foremost are the enablers which will help accelerate the digital transformation progress. The key enablers are:

Rising Power of Networks: 2G to 6G

The 2G and 3G eras were all about human-to-human communication through voice and text. 4G heralded a fundamental shift to the massive consumption of data, while the 5G era has turned its focus on connecting the Internet of Things (IoT) and industrial automation systems. In the 6G era, the digital, physical and human world will seamlessly fuse to trigger extrasensory experiences (Nokia 2021).

5G is a new generation of wireless connectivity that supports a 100-fold increase in the number of simultaneous connections while improving speed (100 times faster than LTE/4G), latency and reliability (an improvement from 20 milliseconds to less than 1 millisecond with 99.99 per cent reliability) (McKinsey & Company n.d.).

Faster digital connections, powered by 5G and the IoT, have the potential to unlock economic activity. Adoption of 5G in mobility, healthcare, manufacturing and retail could increase global GDP by US$1.2 trillion to US$2 trillion by 2030 (McKinsey & Company n.d.).

6G (sixth-generation wireless) will pave the way for always-on and zero-lag communications at a potential rate of 1 terabyte per second (Nersesian 2021). For 6G wireless to become a reality, it must overcome several technical hurdles, such as connecting terahertz spectrum to hard, optical transmission lines, etc.

Web 3.0: A Game Changer

Web 1.0 (1990–2005) was about open protocols that were decentralized and community-governed with most of the value accruing to the edges of the network, namely users and builders (Mersch and Muirhead 2019).

Web 2.0 (2005–20) was about centralized services run by corporations with most of the value accruing to a handful of companies.

Web 3.0 will combine the decentralized, community-governed ethos of Web 1.0 with the advanced, modern functionality of Web 2.0. Web 3.0 will be built largely on three new layers of technological innovation: edge computing, decentralized data networks, and artificial intelligence. Web 3.0 will be the Internet owned by the builders and users, orchestrated with tokens (Mersch and Muirhead 2019).

Web 3.0 is a fundamental disruption. It is a leap forward to open, trust-less and permission-less networks. 'Open' in that they are built from open-source software created by an open and accessible community of developers. 'Trust-less' in that the network itself allows participants to interact publicly or privately without a trusted third party. 'Permission-less' in that anyone, both users and suppliers, can participate without authorization from a governing body. Web 3.0 will be spreading the data centre out to the edge, and often right into our hands.

Web 3.0 and Hyperconnected Global Village

So much for the technology, but what difference will this make to individuals and society as a whole?

With Web 3.0, people, machines and businesses will be able to trade value, information, and work with global counter-parties they don't know or explicitly trust yet, without an intermediary.

This entails huge benefits for society.

First, societies can become more efficient through disintermediating intermediaries, and returning value directly back to the users and suppliers in a network.

Second, enterprises and machines can share more data with more privacy and security assurances.

Third, we can future-proof entrepreneurial and investment activities by virtually eradicating the platform dependency risks we observe today. We can own our own data and digital footprints by using provable digital scarcity of data and tokenized digital assets.

Fourth, organizations can become more resilient to change through their new mesh of more adaptable peer-to-peer communication and governance ties between participants.

Web 3.0 will go far beyond the initial use case of cryptocurrencies and lead to the rise of fundamentally new markets and associated business models.

The result is akin to a 'return to the global village', in other words, return to highly personified human-centric interactions like in the good old times in a village. But it will be a 'global' village, as it will be delivered at the 'global' scale of the Internet and fuelled by the ever-increasing power of human-machine interaction-enabling technologies.

Major Digital Transformations

Applied Artificial Intelligence (AI)

AI is one of the biggest and fast-changing and all-encompassing tech trends. It is changing so fast that by 2024, AI-generated speech will be behind more than 50 per cent of people's interactions with computers (Fleming 2021).

An upcoming explosion in AI applications is set to augment nearly every aspect of human-machine interaction and power the next level of automation, both for consumers and businesses. Applied AI will further disrupt research and development through generative models and next-generation simulations.

There is a word of caution though. We must ensure that we control AI and not the other way round. Therefore, it is important to develop techniques for AI systems to learn what humans prefer from observing their behaviour. We must make sure that the interests of super intelligent systems are fully aligned with human values. We must make AI systems explain their decisions to humans. We must keep AI-driven weapon systems under meaningful human control. Finally, AI for all is a good goal, but ethical AI has to be a way of life.

Process Automation and Virtualization

Around half of all existing work activities could be automated in the next few decades, as next-level process automation and virtualization become more commonplace. This will spur powerful changes to the future of work, labour costs and public policy.

The McKinsey report predicts that by 2025, more than 50 billion devices will be connected to the Industrial Internet of Things (IIoT) (McKinsey & Company n.d.). Robots, automation, 3D-printing, and more will generate around 79.4 zettabytes of data per year.

As advanced simulations and 3D- or 4D-printing continue to dematerialize processes and make them virtual, dramatically shorter development cycles will become possible, for example, by the integration of design and product development through visualized simulations of optimised prototypes.

Next-generation Computing

Next-generation computing will help find answers to problems that have bedevilled science and society for years, unlocking unprecedented capabilities for businesses. It includes a host of far-reaching developments, from quantum AI to fully autonomous vehicles.

Quantum computing uses quantum mechanics to solve computational problems more efficiently. Quantum-computing hardware is in early development, with progress depending on solutions to technical bottlenecks, including scalability of the number of quantum bits (qubits) available for computing, substantial decrease in error rate, and the development of quantum random access memory (RAM).

Next-generation computing will enable further democratization of AI-driven services, radically fast development cycles and lower barriers of entry across industries.

Trust Architecture

It is reported that in 2019, more than 8.5 billion data records were compromised (IANS 2020). Trust architectures will help in the fight against cybercrime. Trust architectures both mitigate risk and, for companies in certain industries, increase it.

Blockchain, which uses distributed ledgers, is emerging as a powerful approach to building a trust architecture. Blockchain is a type of Distributed Ledger Technology (DLT), a public network with a shared ledger without a central authority controlled by economic incentives for nodes to update the ledger.

This will reduce the cost of complying with security regulations, lower the operating and capital expenditures associated with cybersecurity and enable more cost-efficient transactions, for instance, between buyers and sellers.

Zero-trust security is an approach to preventing data breaches by eliminating the concept of trust from an organization's network architecture and instead following the principle of 'never trust, always verify'. In contrast to perimeter-based security models, zero-trust security uses segmentation to control access even within a network by verifying the user, the system and the context for accessing data.

Cyber risk goes down as companies use zero-trust security measures to reduce the threat of data breaches.

Augmented Humanity

In the years ahead, societies and businesses will look at disruptive technologies to change the way we live, work, interact and indeed transform human existence.

In the future, human capabilities will be elevated by a mix of established, emerging technologies, what is now being referred to as 'Augmented Humanity'.

Augmented humanity, through interaction between the digital and physical worlds, allows 'technologically enabled humans' to unleash their full potential and perform at levels they could not reach without technology.

Such humanized interactions between humans and machines will be leveraged by technologies such as ingestibles, implantables, injectables, biometrics, brain-computer interfaces, affecting computing, wearables, augmented reality (AR) and virtual reality (VR) and smart devices.

How will augmented humanity techs disrupt the world? Here are just a few illustrative examples.

AR and VR will revolutionize the traditional mental health industry by allowing professionals in the industry to deliver an immersive experience to their patients.

VR technology will enable professionals to learn new things about human cognitive functions while leading health providers toward better treatments and outcomes. As the technology becomes more accepted and accessible to people, individuals lacking time or financial resources will use VR for self-therapies and personalized mental health treatments delivered at home.

Psious delivers VR software that helps deliver virtual environments, combining sensory stimulation with custom-designed situations to help healthcare providers treat anxiety disorders. By examining traditional cognitive theories, Psious uses VR to allow health professionals to relearn patients' psychological experiences from first-person observation (Psious n.d.).

Smart wearables have enabled the 'quantified-self' phenomenon, in which end users and tech makers share an interest in self-discovery through datafication.

The wearable industry is transitioning from activity trackers to health platforms. By quantifying our sleeping pattern, the Oura ring instigates actionable insights for health improvement through datafication, which can avoid health conditions linked with diabetes, cardiac disease, or Alzheimer's (Psious n.d.).

Brain-computer Interfaces

Brain-computer interfaces (BCI) will engage in cerebral activity and support human functions.

BCI is a communication pathway between the brain and an external device. It translates human brain activity into an external action via neural commands, enabling humans to control machines without the physical constraints of the body, just by using their minds.

BCI can help restore functional impairment in people with illnesses such as motor system disorder, intellectual developmental disorder, memory loss and mobility deficits.

In the future, amputees can directly control sophisticated prosthetic limbs and people with impaired movement may be able to use integration between exoskeletons and BCI to restore their movement functions.

It will be possible to better understand human emotions expressed in their voices, faces, text, and other behaviours to micro-target individuals in extremely highly personalized ways.

Affective Computing

Affective computing is emerging as a disciplinary field that interfaces computer science, psychology and cognitive science. Through this, the study and development of systems and devices that can recognize, interpret, process and simulate human affects will be possible.

Unlike artificial intelligence, affective computing is still not widely adopted, but platforms capable of recognizing and responding to users' emotional states will be used to enhance experiences and safety in the automotive industry, optimize in-store shopping experiences in retail, detect fraud in banking or insurance, produce real-time diagnosis in healthcare or measure student effectiveness in education.

BMW worked with Affectiva to examine the emotional in-cabin experience and understand how automotive companies can realize if drivers are falling asleep or are attentive. Affectiva helps automotive companies ensure road safety and enhance the driving experience by gaining insight into driver interactions and recognizing drivers' levels of drowsiness, distraction and anger (Psious n.d.).

Ingestible Technologies

Ingestible tech will innovate healthcare services and although approval from medical bodies and scepticism will be among the strongest barriers to adoption, hospitals are trialling capsuled cameras to replace endoscopies with less invasive techniques by turning invasive in-hospital screening into at-home medical care.

By swallowing a capsule camera, patients can go about their day as normal and access routine screening services from home. The imaging technology will provide a diagnosis within hours and will help decrease patient stress, while also decreasing pressure on healthcare, bringing technology-driven disruption and transformative alternatives to traditional medical screenings.

An unprecedented capsule camera trial of 11,000 patients is taking place in England. Patients will trial Pillcam Colon 2 technology, provided by Medtronic, which aims to replace traditional endoscopies (Psious n.d.).

Implantable medical devices will create connected self-monitoring humans.

The road to full integration between different smart devices is long, but in the future, we will use integration between smart devices to create autonomous experiences that will help us in our private and work lives.

Climate Change and Getting to Net Zero

Sense of Urgency

It is obvious that the steps taken in the decade ahead will be crucial in determining whether or not we avoid runaway climate change. An average global temperature rise above 1.5 or 2°C would create risks that will have disastrous consequences. At an emission rate of 40 to 50 gigatons of CO_2 per year, the global economy has ten to twenty-five years of carbon capacity left (Pinner, Rogers and Samandari 2020).

For getting to net zero, three questions are important.

First, for the world to maintain public support for climate action it is important to make sure that the costs of energy transition be affordable. Decarbonizing energy use in time to avert catastrophic climate change requires intensified international cooperation, financial mobilization, strengthened institutions and broad policy cohesion.

Second, emerging economies like India, Brazil and South Africa—which have done much less to contribute to climate change than the rich countries but are affected the most—must continue to reduce poverty without emitting greenhouse gases. Again, it comes down to affordability, so they don't have the challenge of a trade-off between growth and a liveable climate.

And third, the current generation will have to adapt to a warmer climate. The effects of higher temperatures—frequent droughts and floods, the desiccation of farmland and the spread of crop-eating pests—will hit farmers hard, especially those in low-income countries. So, in addition to making green energy affordable, we need to accelerate innovations like high temperature-resistant seeds that will help the poorest farmers grow more food through breakthrough technologies by using the likes of CRISPR technology that we earlier alluded to.

Progress and Challenges Ahead

The year 2020 was a record one for renewables. Globally, 260 gigawatts of renewable energy capacity were added in 2020, exceeding expansion in 2019 by close to 50 per cent—and breaking all previous records (Ingram 2021). More than 80 per cent of all new electricity capacity added last year was renewable, with solar and wind accounting for 91 per cent of new renewables (Ingram 2021).

In the book *The World in 2050* (ed. Kohli 2016), the author predicted the rapid expansion of solar power. This prediction has come true.

According to the International Energy Agency (IEA), solar power will be the new king of electricity supply and looks set for massive expansion (Masterson 2021). Projects with low-cost financing that tap high quality resources, solar PV is now the cheapest source of electricity in history. This includes being more cost-effective than coal and gas in many countries today, including in the largest markets—the United States, European Union, China and India (Masterson 2021).

Solar power will reach, in many parts of the world, a levelized cost of energy that will be so affordable that it will become unbeatable when compared to fossil fuels.

But we must continue firmly on the innovation path, even in solar PV. In that sense, it is heartening to see a shift from first-generation to second- and third-generation solar technologies. Perovskite solar cells are third-generation solar technologies.

Conventional silicon solar cells are most effective at using the photons in the red, lower energy end of the solar spectrum. Perovskite solar cells, however, effectively utilize the high energy photons at the blue end of the solar spectrum.

The first perovskite solar cells were announced just ten years ago in 2009. But those early lab prototypes were incredibly unstable and had an efficiency of just 3.8 per cent (Kumagai 2019). The current efficiency record for Perovskite Silicon Tandem Solar Cells is 29.52 per cent, held by Oxford PV (Oxford PV 2020).

Though perovskite solar cells have become highly efficient, several challenges such as stability, efficiency degradation, life-cycle cost, etc., need to be addressed for making it a competitive commercial technology.

The other important innovation is around how best to integrate solar into our homes, businesses, and power systems. This means better power electronics and a greater use of low-cost digital technologies.

New technologies addressing the rapidly growing need for clean energy generation will include systems for smart energy distribution in the grid, energy storage systems, carbon-neutral energy generation and fusion energy. These new technologies will have broad applications in the power sector, transport and buildings and infrastructure.

The transition to renewables, efficiency and electrification can drive broad socio-economic development.

Jobs in renewables would reach 42 million globally by 2050, four times their current level, through the increased focus of investments on renewables. Energy efficiency measures would create 21 million and system flexibility will create 15 million additional jobs (IRENA 2021).

Socio-economic measures to maximize the benefits of the energy transition include industrial policies, labour market interventions, educational and skills development and social protection programmes.

Besides the government, the private sector has a huge role to play, not just by participating in the entire supply chain of production, distribution and usage of green energy but also in fuelling disruptive and game-changing innovation.

At the 2015 United Nations Climate Change Conference in November 2015, Bill Gates announced that a coalition of twenty-eight high net-worth investors from ten countries had committed to the Breakthrough Energy initiative (Banerjea 2020). In December 2016, a group of investors collectively worth US$170 billion announced more personal commitment to funding the efforts of a US$1-billion fund 'focussed on fighting Climate Change by investing in clean energy innovation'. The fund is named Breakthrough Energy Ventures fund (Delaney 2016). The rationale was simple. The Breakthrough Energy invests primarily in businesses where the risk of failure is high and the timeframe for return on investment is twenty years. Traditional venture capitalists look for a return on investment in five years, which may not be enough for the special challenges of the energy sector.

Green Hydrogen for Our Green Future

Hydrogen (H_2) is the lightest and most abundant element in the universe. It was given new impetus in the 1960s by space travel, which relied heavily on hydrogen as an energy store, and in the 1970s as a consequence of the energy and oil price crises, when the search began for alternative energy concepts (Shell Deutschland Oil GmbH 2017).

Hydrogen technology is now gathering strong momentum as a key energy vector after decades of false starts and debate about its safety and viability. Key drivers for this are: falling production costs, technological improvements, a global push toward decarbonization and expanding potential end-markets. The global shift toward decarbonization backed by government financial support and regulation is supporting this momentum.

There has been an exponential growth in H_2 deployment globally in the last few years. Around 93 countries have net zero carbon ambitions and around thirty-nine countries have formulated national H_2 strategies (Hydrogen Council 2021).

As of November 2021, 522 large-scale projects have been announced worldwide, totalling about $160 billion direct investment (Hydrogen Council 2021). Europe remains the centre of hydrogen development, accounting for 80 per cent of new project announcements. Total estimated investment by 2030 for the hydrogen value chain (including OEMs and government targets) amounts to ~US$700 billion (Hydrogen Council 2021).

Hydrogen production varies in terms of raw materials and end products. Over 99 per cent of hydrogen is currently made using fossil fuels (Petrova 2020). Grey hydrogen produced from natural gas is the most widely used method to produce hydrogen today. It produces carbon dioxide as a by-product. Blue hydrogen captures and stores most of the carbon dioxide output. Green hydrogen is produced by water electrolysis with various types of electrolyzers, in which zero-carbon electricity is used to split water molecules into hydrogen and oxygen molecules.

Current renewable technologies, such as solar and wind, can decarbonize the energy sector by as much as 85 per cent by replacing gas and coal with clean electricity (Carbeck 2020). Other parts of the economy, such as shipping and manufacturing, are harder to electrify because they often require fuel that is high in energy density or heats at high temperatures. Green hydrogen has a great potential in these sectors. Green hydrogen and fuels derived from it (for example, ammonia, methanol and aviation fuels) can replace higher-carbon fuels in some areas of the transportation sector, industrial sector and power sector. H_2 as an energy buffer or storage can potentially solve intermittency problem of large-scale renewables.

Long-distance and heavy-duty transportation, industrial heating and heavy industry feedstock together comprise roughly 15 per cent of global energy consumption (Hydrogen Council 2020). Adoption of hydrogen, a clean energy source, in these sectors will be a game changer.

The Hydrogen economy has the potential to generate US$2.5 trillion in direct revenue. Total market potential could reach US$11 trillion by 2050 (Bank of America 2020).

What should be the technological advances to realize the potential of green hydrogen? Again, affordability is the key bottleneck for mainstream adoption of green hydrogen, since it is not yet cost competitive, at US$3–7.5/kg in comparison with traditional carbon-intensive methods of hydrogen production that cost as little as US$1/kg at the low end.

Recent technological advances and early demonstration projects (IRENA 2020) are changing the cost dynamics significantly. With hydrogen production costs falling, transmission and distribution costs are the next frontier when it comes to reducing delivered hydrogen costs, and we need technology breakthroughs here.

There are aspirational targets that are being set up by both nations and corporates.

For instance, '10-10-10' is Europe's Energy Ministerial Target, which implies 10 million Fuel Cell Electric Vehicles (FCEVs) and 10,000 H_2 fuelling stations over the next 10 years (Hydrogen Council 2020).

'H_2 under 2' is Australia's hydrogen strategy, which stands for production cost of below AUD US$2/kg of hydrogen (Australian Government Department of Industry, Science, Energy and Resources n.d.).

'1-1-1' from US Department of Energy (DOE) is the first Energy Earthshot, launched on 7 June 2021. Called the Hydrogen Shot, it seeks to reduce the cost of clean hydrogen by 80 per cent to US$1 per 1 kilogram in one decade (US DOE n.d., a).

Reliance Industries chairman Mukesh Ambani has set a 1-1-1 target for green hydrogen in India, meaning India to become the first country in the world to produce green hydrogen at less than US$1 per kilogram in a decade (Pathak 2021).

All such aggressive targets augur well for not only the development of new breakthrough technologies that will shift the price performance envelope but also deployment with speed and scale.

Energy Storage: The Holy Grail of Clean Energy

Increased adoption of renewable energy also poses several challenges. Intermittency is the key challenge. Solar and wind power is not available when it gets dark, or the wind stops blowing.

Typically, most utility grids do not store energy because it is very expensive. Some utilities rely on fossil fuel burning plants to meet energy demand during peak hours, which have higher carbon footprint. Therefore, interest in grid-scale energy storage has grown significantly in recent years. Energy storage offers a potential solution to the variability of certain forms of renewable energy generation. It also offers a low-carbon alternative to natural gas peaking plants that provide the grid with a fast-ramping, flexible resource.

A wide array of technologies has been developed for energy storage. Pumped hydro-power, batteries, thermal energy storage and mechanical energy storage are widely used technologies for energy storage.

Lithium-ion batteries are currently the most preferred and have a wider range of applications when compared to other rechargeable battery types due to benefits such as higher energy density, negligible issues of loss in storage capacity on continuous usage, and minimal self-discharging.

Flow batteries, liquid metal batteries, compressed air and liquid air have been considered promising for long-duration storage.

Declining costs in available technologies have propelled interest in energy storage forward like never before. The price of lithium-ion batteries has fallen by about 80 per cent over the past five years (Hicks 2020).

Long-duration energy storage systems can store energy for more than ten hours. It is considered as the Holy Grail of clean energy. In July 2021, the US DOE launched an effort to push down costs of long-duration energy storage by 90 per cent by 2030 as part of its Energy Earthshots Initiative (US DOE n.d., b).

A McKinsey study suggests that Long Duration Energy Storage (LDES) deployment could result in the avoidance of 1.5 to 2.3 gigatons of CO_2 equivalent per year, or around 10 to 15 per cent of today's power sector emissions (McKinsey & Company 2021). In the United States alone, LDES could reduce the overall cost of achieving a fully decarbonized power system by around US$35 billion annually by 2040.

Frontier Technologies and the Developing World

We now consider an important question. How do we ensure that the developing nations will 'ride' on the wave of frontier technology and not 'sink'? What policies and institutional reforms should developing countries undertake to take advantage of these exciting frontier technological developments, tackle their economic challenges and avoid getting left behind in the global race?

Frontier technologies could indeed transform jobs and labour markets with profound implications for societies as a whole. In particular, low-income countries cannot afford to miss this new wave of technological change. But where do they stand today in terms of readiness to embrace the change?

To assess the national capacity to equitably use and adapt the frontier technologies, the United Nations Conference on Trade and Development (UNCTAD) developed a 'readiness index' for 158 countries (UNCTAD 2021). The index comprises five building blocks: ICT deployment, skills, R&D activity, industry activity and access to finance.

Based on this index, the countries best prepared are the obvious ones, like the USA, UK, Switzerland, Sweden, Singapore, South Korea, etc. The list also has high rankings for some transition and developing economies—such as China, Russian Federation, etc.

India figures in much higher than its GDP per capita might predict. However, most of the least-ready countries are in Sub-Saharan Africa, and in the developing countries generally.

What are the challenges that the developing countries face in not only moving up the ladder on the readiness index but also enjoying the huge benefits that the frontier technology can bring?

They include the demographic changes (with expanding and younger populations, increasing demand for jobs, and a reluctance to adopt automation of jobs), lower technological and innovation capabilities (especially with shortage of those skilled in STEM, meaning science, technology, engineering, and maths), weak research and innovation financing mechanisms (with very little private funding of industrial technologies for productive applications), and finally, and very importantly, the digital divide due to lack of digital infrastructure, without which the benefits of frontier technology cannot accrue.

If these challenges are not dealt with, then the lack of readiness will persist and the waves of frontier technological changes may also create fresh risks. Frontier technologies could disrupt labour markets. A well held view has been that innovations in processes increase productivity and thus destroy jobs, while innovations in products generate new markets and thus create jobs. But for frontier technologies, the situation could be different because the change is so rapid that they could outpace the capacity of societies to respond.

What it all means is that speed is of essence. We need energetic public policy—devising plans, raising awareness and creating incentives within a national innovation ecosystem while also encouraging investment and community participation.

The developing countries should set up twin technology targets to catch up and forge ahead. In other words, they will need to adopt frontier technologies while continuing to diversify their production bases by mastering existing technologies. They need to keep to both targets in sight.

Strengthening innovation systems, while aligning science, technology and innovation (STI), and industrial policies, should attract firms into the core sectors of frontier technology development and deployment. This would enable traditional production sectors to benefit from multiple channels of diffusion, covering foreign direct investment, trade, intellectual property rights, patents and the exchange of knowledge and know-how.

Indeed, the governments should engage a wide range of actors who can help build synergies between STI and other economic policies—industrial, trade, fiscal and monetary, as well as educational policies.

The government should use innovative public procurement processes to embed exponential technologies that will stimulate economic development while also bringing social benefits to poor households.

Innovations are products of creative interaction of supply and demand. We also need aggressive demand side initiatives. With large procurement budgets, the governments cannot only be the biggest but also the most influential and demanding customer.

As suggested by Mashelkar, government approach could be based on three pillars (Mashelkar 2018).

First, government could act as the 'first buyer' and an 'early user' for small, innovative firms and manage the consequent risk, thus providing the initial revenue and customer feedback they need to survive and refine their products and services so that they can later compete effectively in the global marketplace.

Second, the government can set up regulations that can successfully drive innovation either indirectly through altering market structure and affecting the funds available for investment or directly through boosting or limiting demand for particular products and services.

Third, government can set standards that can create market power by generating demand for innovation. Agreed standards will ensure that the risk taken by both early adopters and innovators is lower, thus increasing investment in innovation. The standards should be set at a demanding level of functionality without specifying which solution must be followed. By not prescribing a specific route, innovation is bound to flourish.

What about the role of private sector? The private sector has been increasingly asked to show corporate social responsibility (CSR), which can take many different forms, including what is referred to as compassionate capitalism. Corporate houses, from Tatas in India to Ford and

Rockefeller in the US, have done this through self-motivation. Governments have begun to provide legislations to increase the scale and impact. For instance, the Indian government has mandated that corporates to spend 2 per cent of net profit on CSR.

In his K.R. Narayanan Memorial Oration, titled 'Dismantling Inequalities with ASSURED Innovation', Mashelkar has proposed a new categorization of corporate social responsibility (Mashelkar 2018).

The first belongs to the case where a corporate house becomes highly profitable and then sets aside a sum of money to create a trust or foundation—the Bill and Melinda Gates Foundation being the most notable example in recent times. In a sense, this is 'doing well AND doing good' (Mashelkar 2018).

But then there is CSR 2.0, which means 'doing well BY doing good' (Mashelkar 2018). This means doing good itself constitutes a good business. Mashelkar exemplifies this by Reliance Industries in India setting up Jio, a telecom company, which provides high-quality 4G LTE mobile services most affordably to almost one-third of India today. The voice is free and the data is priced at just 2 cents per GB, the cheapest in the world. The company is highly profitable, too. This is an example of giving access to a frontier mobile Internet technology to the masses and doing well, while doing good. In other words, creating value for money and also for many.

The transition from traditional to transformational frontier technologies has to be managed well. There is always the risk that rapid technological change will perpetuate or accentuate inequalities. There has to be public response to strengthen social protection and easing workforce transitions. In addition to encouraging training and re-training through the public and private sectors, government agencies should also support workers with personal counselling, improved job matching and placement services.

Finally, one needs to emphasize the importance of creating high readiness level, despite being at a relatively low part of the economic ladder. It is instructive to consider the case of India, whose readiness level was higher than its relatively low GDP may indicate, which helped it accelerate impressively during the pandemic.

Take online learning. The use of Coursera learning platform grew by over 1,400 per cent in India during first half of 2020, twice that of the global average (Mashelkar 2018).

Take e-commerce. COVID-19 accelerated India's e-commerce adoption by at least three years. India's e-commerce market is expected to grow by 21 per cent annually over the next four years (Business Standard 2021).

In India, unified payment interface (UPI) was started in April 2016. It facilitates money transfer through a mobile device round the clock. It took more than three years to reach the 1 billion UPI transactions milestone before the pandemic (Manikandan 2020). During the pandemic, in less than a year, UPI transactions crossed 2 billion (Manikandan 2020). UPI transactions stood at 4.21 billion in October 2021 (BFSI 2021).

Take telehealth. As per the report published by the Telemedicine Society of India (TSI) and Practo, India recorded a 3X increase in the number of people using online consultations between March and November 2020 (Ganguly 2020). Non-metro cities recorded a growth of 7X in online consultations in the same period as compared to last year (Ganguly 2020).

In short, the pandemic saw unprecedented acceleration of the use of digital technology, simply because the readiness levels were high. One can draw an inspiration from this for other parts of the developing world, especially the low-income countries.

Frontier Technologies and Productivity Growth

Let us examine the likely impact of all these technological breakthroughs and developments on the global productivity frontier over the longer term. It is well known that in the past twenty to thirty years, global productivity growth has slowed down compared to its growth over the past several decades.

'Productivity isn't everything, but, in the long run, it is almost everything. A country's ability to improve its standard of living over time depends almost entirely on its ability to raise its output per worker,' said Paul Krugman, Professor of Economics and International Affairs Emeritus at Princeton University (Colford 2016).

Technology-enabled innovation is often considered as a major boost for productivity growth. Yet, paradoxically, productivity growth has slowed as digital technologies have boomed in the last two decades (Qureshi 2020).

Declining productivity growth has various possible explanations. This includes the challenge of measurement of real productivity growth itself, the challenge of 'sectoral stagnation' with shortage of demand and investment opportunities, essentially affecting negatively the productivity growth, the impact of technological innovation, either today's innovations not being as transformational as those in the past or the other being Solow Paradox of the 1980s, with the slowdown really being a lag in the realization of productivity benefits following the introduction of new waves of technologies (McKinsey Global Institute 2017).

These four are not mutually exclusive—each may play a role in unlocking the solution to the puzzle.

Technological innovation has played an important role in increasing productivity growth throughout history. Take, for instance, the US productivity growth between the mid-1990s and early 2000s.

The first wave of ICT investment starting in the mid-1990s was using technology to deliver supply-chain, then back-office, and later front-office efficiencies. Today we are experiencing a new way of digital change that entails a more fundamental transformation of entire business models and end-to-end operations.

To give an analogy, whereas previously the transformation meant creating a given caterpillar into a faster caterpillar, the new digital transformation is like a true transformation of a caterpillar to a butterfly.

Today's digital technology, such as mobile Internet, cloud computing, artificial intelligence, machine learning, Internet of Things, etc., is fundamentally transforming business models, altering value chains, and blurring lines across industries.

The breadth and diversity of innovations is such that beyond improving existing business operations, the innovations are creating new digital products and features, introducing new ways to deliver them and also enabling the creation of game-changing new business models. The scale is still at an early stage in many industries.

Many digital technologies are relatively new and most companies and sectors are still at an early stage of adopting them.

It is a fact that digitization has not yet reached scale, with a majority of the economy still not digitized. It has been shown that Europe overall operates at only 12 per cent of digital potential, and the United States at 18 per cent (McKinsey Global Institute 2016).

In the past, several factors have dampened the pace of digital adoption, including consumer preferences for digital versus traditional products and services. That is no more the case as we have seen in terms of the way speed and scale have been achieved, something that we enumerated at the beginning of the essay. The risks associated with major business model changes, including fear of cannibalization, capability gaps and concerns about technological obsolescence, had held the companies back. Today, digital transformation has been considered essential for both survival and success. Large existing legacy businesses are realizing this, especially watching the success of new digital-only businesses.

How has the pandemic affected the productivity growth so far and how will it affect it in the next few decades? A new McKinsey Global Institute report shows that during the pandemic, companies shifted rapidly to online channels, automated production tasks, increased operational efficiency and sped up decision-making and innovation of operating models (McKinsey Global Institute 2021). The pressures of the pandemic also forced many businesses to become more efficient, to rethink their product, business, and operating models, and become more agile, all of which could potentially drive faster productivity growth.

The McKinsey report estimates that this could potentially more than double the rate of annual productivity growth observed after the global financial crisis (McKinsey Global Institute 2021).

Further, it finds that there is potential to accelerate annual productivity growth by about 1 percentage point in the period till 2024. That would be more than double the pre-pandemic rate of productivity growth, which will have a huge impact. In terms of actual numbers, it has been shown that achieving 1 percentage point of additional productivity growth per year in every country to 2024 would imply an increase in per capita GDP ranging from about US$1,500 in Spain to about US$3,500 in the United States (McKinsey Global Institute 2021).

In summary, the rate of technological diffusion, a maturation of global supply chains, a shift to services, changing industry structure and dynamics, and secular stagnation have played a role in the past. However, this can be changed through policy measures.

Take, for instance, technology diffusion. Policies can be developed to enhance the technology diffusion substantially by influencing four key factors. First, global connections, via trade, foreign direct investment (FDI), participation in global value chains, and the international mobility of skilled labour. Second, innovation by firms with new ideas, technologies, and business models. Third, the efficient reallocation of scarce resources to underpin the growth of innovative firms. Fourth, investments in R&D, skills, and organizational know-how—particularly managerial capital—that enable economies to absorb, adapt, and reap the full benefits of new technologies.

Finally, frontier technologies hold considerable potential to lift the trajectory of productivity and economic growth, and to create new and better jobs to replace old ones. As much as two-thirds of potential productivity growth in major economies over the next decade could be related to the new frontier technologies.

A Step towards Our Assured Future

This chapter is essentially focussed on the post-pandemic scenario vis-à-vis the emerging technology and its potential socio-economic impact.

We also have seen that in terms of technology deployment during the pandemic, what could be achieved in years has been achieved in months and even weeks. Further, the magic of designing, developing, testing, and deploying the mRNA vaccines ten times faster shows that it is possible to create rapid and radical change.

Can we institutionalize the process of such radical yet sustainable transformation? The answer is provided in the book that the author co-authored with Ravi Pandit. The title of the book is *Leapfrogging to Pole Vaulting: Creating the Magic of Radical yet Sustainable Transformation* (2018). The book is replete with case studies, where such feats have been achieved in the past.

The idea of the book is as follows: why does the frog leap? Because he is afraid of the predators, and the frog jumps a few feet, reactively and defensively. Instead, one should pole vault over the wall of obstacles, not reactively but proactively, also aggressively. The size of the pole will be the size of the aspiration.

The book focuses on three key areas of global concern—the three Es, namely, environment, energy and employment.

It shows that two keywords are critical in achieving success. The first is STEP and the second is ASSURED.

The book shows that for success, there are four levers that must work in tandem with each other, in STEP with each other. STEP comprises social engagement, technology, economics, and policy.

In this essay, we have mainly looked at technology, but whether the technology will make a difference in the field sustainably or not depends critically on the other three factors.

Look at social engagement. The emergence of many great technologies listed in this essay can be halted due to several societal-related factors.

These would include the fear of impact of technology on employment (AI and hyper automation), risks to moral values (gene editing), human health (genetically modified foods) and environmental safety (nuclear technology). Calestous Juma (2016) shows that technological tensions are often heightened by perceptions that the benefits of new technologies will accrue only to small sections of society while the risks will be more widely distributed. Similarly, innovations that threaten to alter cultural identities tend to generate intense social concern. As such, societies that exhibit great economic and political inequities are likely to experience heightened technological controversies.

Further, how do we ensure assured success in the journey from mind to marketplace or ideas to impact? For this, the authors propose an ASSURED framework. ASSURED comprises seven important attributes, namely, being affordable, scalable, sustainable, universal (user-friendly), rapid, excellent and distinctive. These parameters can be semi-quantitative or quantitative (Malshekar and Pandit 2018).

They are interlinked. What is not affordable will not be scalable. Solar PV scaled once it became affordable. Green hydrogen will not scale if its price is not brought down to make it competitive.

ASSURED is a dynamic matrix. The fact that one is ASSURED today does not mean that one will be ASSURED forever.

Napster is a classic example. It allowed fans to upload and share music files for free. It had 80 million users. But it doesn't exist today. Why? Because the music creators did not allow free download of music, and failed the sustainability test in terms of societal acceptance.

Blackberry was a big hit at one time with 50 million users, but it failed to anticipate the smartphone revolution. They failed to cash in on the emergence of the app economy and the evolution of smartphones as a full-fledged mobile entertainment devices rather than just communication devices. So they failed the 'user-friendly' test as also the 'distinctive' test.

Mashelkar and Pandit have elaborated on the power of the ASSURED framework by showing its application in a wide range of business failure areas, including General Motors' EV-1, an electric car that was launched in 1996, which was well ahead of its time.

Final Thoughts

The focus of this chapter has been on technology and its role in transforming the post-pandemic world. In fact, the pandemic has been a big learning for the entire world. It is said that one's best teacher is your last mistake, provided one learns from it.

Whereas the world is focusing on post-pandemic recovery, this has given us an opportunity, not just to look at recovery and rethink, but reimagine and reinvent the post-pandemic world.

So, what are the biggest learnings from the pandemic?

The current pandemic provides us with a foretaste of what a full-fledged climate crisis could entail in terms of simultaneous exogenous shocks to supply and demand, disruption of supply chains, and global transmission and amplification mechanisms.

There are big lessons to be learned from the similarities between pandemics and climate risks. They both represent physical shocks, which then translate into an array of socio-economic impacts. Both are systemic, with their knock-on effects propagating fast, both being nonlinear—in that their socioeconomic impact grows disproportionally and even catastrophically once certain thresholds are breached (like in the second wave, hospitals running out of ICUs)—and then, being regressive—in that they affect disproportionally the most vulnerable populations and subpopulations of the world. There are three big learnings that can be highlighted.

The first big learning is that pandemics and climate risk will require the same fundamental shift, from optimizing largely for the shorter-term performance of systems to ensuring equally their longer-term resiliency.

The second learning is that the massive devastation caused by the coronavirus outbreak indicates that the world at large is equally ill-prepared to prevent or confront either the pandemic or the fallout of climate change. The trillions of dollars of losses during the pandemic also indicate the cost of lack of unpreparedness and the potential cost of inaction for battling the climate change challenge.

The third learning is that the same factors that mitigate environmental risks—reducing the demands we place on nature by optimizing consumption, shortening and localizing supply chains, substituting animal proteins with plant proteins and decreasing pollution—are likely to help mitigate the risk of pandemics.

The fourth learning is that of the incredible ability of the human to convert an adversity into an opportunity. So, we end where we began this essay—by highlighting not only the change but also the amazing speed, scale, and scope of the change that was brought about through the instrument of technology. Can we then think of a rapid, radical yet sustainable transformation into a NextGen society?

We have moved from the hunting society (Society 1.0) to agricultural society (Society 2.0) to industrial society (Society 3.0), to an information society (Society 4.0).

We now have a great chance to rethink, reimagine and build a human-centric Society 5.0, where the powerful revolutionary technologies described in this essay are used to not only create 'augmented humanity' but also 'augmented humanism', a society, which will see a smile on the faces of not just a privileged few but every citizen of this world.

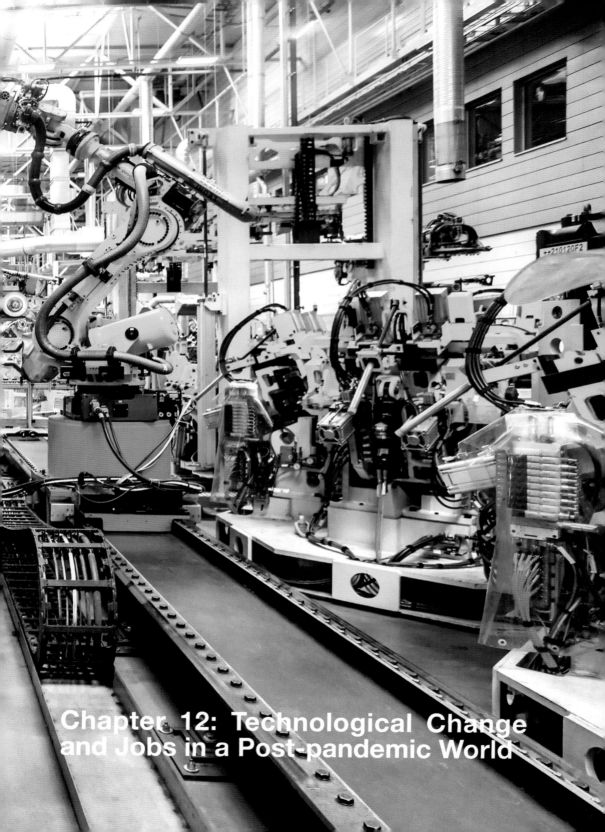

Chapter 12: Technological Change and Jobs in a Post-pandemic World

Technological Change and Jobs in a Post-pandemic World

Chapter 12 | **Soumitra Dutta**

The COVID-19 pandemic has been a global tipping point in the adoption of technology. In a matter of a few weeks in the first half of 2020, practically all countries—both developed and developing—were forced to adopt lockdowns and required most businesses and educational institutions to shift to remote working and learning. The world witnessed a global digital acceleration of a scale and magnitude that few would have imagined possible, barely a couple of years ago.

The COVID-19 virus has not yet been defeated but the successful roll-out of vaccines and greater knowledge about the virus has certainly allowed for a gradual 'return to normalcy' in most parts of the world. Many countries have allowed businesses and schools to reopen with some conditions in place to assure the health of the local population. There is also a greater recognition of the fact that it is likely that the COVID-19 virus will never be truly eradicated. The world will have to learn to live with the COVID-19 virus endemic in society much like it has learned to do with various version of the flu virus.

Businesses and society at large are at the same time beginning the journey to realize the full impact that the pandemic has had on both personal and professional lives of the people. While more than a year of mandated remote working has led to more flexible attitudes towards hybrid workplaces, the full impact of the pandemic along with its accompanying digital acceleration on work, jobs, and professional lives is yet to be understood. This chapter explores these themes in more depth below.

The Great Acceleration

McKinsey has estimated that the pandemic has accelerated the digitalization of customer and supply-chain interactions of companies and of their internal operations by three to four years (Laura LaBerge et al. 2021). Further McKinsey estimates that the 'share of digital or digitally enabled products in their portfolios has accelerated by a shocking seven years'. The sheer scale of acceleration of digitalization during the pandemic is also reflected in some of the amazing growth of the tech giants. *The New York Times* has noted that that the five tech superpowers—Amazon, Apple, Google, Microsoft and Facebook—had combined revenue of more than US$1.2 trillion in 2020 (Ovide 2021a; Ovide 2021b). While the big tech companies thrived during the pandemic, smaller businesses such as restaurants also adapted their processes to fit the new demands of web orders and deliveries. This success of technology companies can also be observed in emerging markets where local players such as Tencent and Alibaba in China, Jio/Reliance and Flipkart/Walmart in India, Mercado Libre in Latin America and Jumia in Africa, have all thrived during the pandemic.

It is not COVID-19 alone, though, that accelerated the pace of digital transformation of the workplace. The pandemic arrived at a crucial time when new digital technologies had matured to a point that they could be deployed on a large scale rapidly. Consider, for example, the challenges of transitioning to remote working and learning. Education has traditionally been a laggard in adopting new technologies. Faculty and students in many institutions remained stubbornly wedded to an in-person format of learning that is almost as old as humanity itself. Looking back, it is remarkable how smoothly most educational institutions around the world transitioned to remote learning during the pandemic. The core technology of video conferencing (via Zoom, Webex and other systems) had matured to a point that it was easy and reliable enough for mass adoption. Parents and students could easily run video-conferencing systems on their home computers and laptops. With some support from their home institutions, faculty overcame challenges to adapt their learning process and move them online. Students who had gotten used to online collaboration and sharing on social media could rapidly and successfully adapt to the norms of online collaboration and learning.

A similar story played out in professional work environments. Remote teams had become common as companies globalized their operations. Flexible office practices had started to be implemented in many organizations with open office plans to support collaboration and flexible hours to support work-life balance. Once the pandemic arrived, it was relatively easy for many businesses to move to a fully remote or hybrid work environment. The technology was ready and mature (enough) and employees had enough experience with collabourative software systems, such as Slack. Many organizations reported no loss of productivity due to remote working during the pandemic period. 94 per cent of 800 employers surveyed by Mercer, an HR and workplace benefits consulting firm, said that productivity was the same as or higher than it was before the pandemic, even with their employees working remotely (SHRM 2021). This is particularly remarkable, as employees have not only had to deal with the challenges of remote working but also with health and well-being related stresses of isolation from their families and friends.

The great digital acceleration has been a boon for emerging markets as it has pushed forward the digitalization of their economies by several years. While the COVID-19 pandemic has adversely affected several groups, including women and minorities, the increased reliance on digital technologies has forced businesses in emerging markets to move their businesses online and has spawned an explosion in digital start-ups and unicorns in emerging markets. In September 2021, Goldman Sachs estimated that India has more than sixty-six unicorns with around twenty-six unicorns created in the first nine months of 2021 alone (Business Today 2021). Other emerging markets that historically lagged in digitalization have also progressed, such as Brazil now boasting thirteen unicorns. Digital companies now make up a significant part of the equity markets in emerging markets—for example, new economy companies now make up more than 60 per cent of the China MSCI index.

In a study of digitalization in companies, McKinsey Global Institute noted that the benefits of digitalization begin to percolate only when companies fully absorb digitalization, a process expected to be complete only by 2045, when automation and AI technologies have spread more broadly and deeply around the world (Bughin et al. 2020). In 2018, according to McKinsey, only 26 per cent of worldwide sales were through digital channels and only 25 per cent of supply-chain interactions were digitized. This situation was ripe for change when COVID-19 spread around the world.

Forced digitalization is now changing industries that have been resistant to adopting digital technologies. For example, the healthcare sector had been slow to digitize. As the pandemic took hold, many healthcare companies were required to change and prioritize vaccines and remote delivery of healthcare. This was done through large-scale digitalization, by adopting virtual research and development platforms, remote patient monitoring for clinical trials, and virtual health consultations (Licholai 2020). The insurance industry also transformed quickly. For example, a study by JD Power in 2018 showed that only 11 per cent of consumers in the US reported a loss through a digital channel. In April 2020, Allstate Insurance estimated that 90 per cent of claims were through virtual channels (Ryan 2020).

Back to the Future or a New Future?

It is hard to predict the long-term impact of technology. There are numerous examples of predictions made about technology that went so wrong with the benefit of hindsight (Szczerba 2015):

- 1995: 'I predict the Internet will soon go spectacularly supernova and in 1996 catastrophically collapse.' —Robert Metcalfe, founder of 3Com.
- 2005: 'There's just not that many videos I want to watch.' —Steve Chen, CTO and co-founder of YouTube expressing concerns about his company's long-term viability.
- 2007: 'There's no chance that the iPhone is going to get any significant market share.' —Steve Ballmer, CEO of Microsoft.

Each of the above technologies have gone on to have a far-reaching impact on the world and changing our lives—both professional and personal. Why is it that it is so hard to predict the long-term impact of new technologies? The answer is complex, but a simple framework helps.

When a radical new technology arrives, the first order impact of the new technology is substitution of the old technology by the new. For example, when the automobile was invented, people relaced travelling by horse carriages with travelling by car. Similarly, when the cell phone was invented, people replaced fixed line calls by cell phone calls. The second order impact of new technology is diffusion. This happens because usually the new technology is better, cheaper, and more effective, meaning more and more people start using it. This can be seen with the increased adoption of cars and cell phones a few years after their invention. The final and third order impact of new technology is transformation—when ways in which people live and work is fundamentally changed due to the widespread adoption of the new technology. So, to continue with the car example, shopping malls and suburbs came into existence in many developed economies because most families had cars which they could use to drive to shops or to commute from home to their workplace. Similarly, cell phones have changed so many aspects of the way of life and work in society today. Few of these far-reaching transformational changes could have been predicted initially when the technologies were first invented.

During the COVID-19 pandemic, remote working pushed organizations rapidly up the first two stages of the above framework: substitution and diffusion. As the pandemic eases, the question before organizations is simple but important: go back to the old normal of in-person work or create the new normal of more flexible jobs. Current plans across organizations vary and while there is no consensus on the way forward, many are 'forcing' a return to the old normal or a 'back to the future' scenario. These organizations have mandated employees to return to the office and have often put compulsory vaccination plans in place. However, this return has not always been smooth for both employers and employees. While many employees have expressed a preference for more flexible work arrangements, there is also a realization that more must change in the work environment than simply to allow people to call in remotely from home.

Creating a new future of jobs will require a strategic intent to experiment, to learn, and to iterate. Organizations will need to not just move existing work processes to a digital medium but to design entire new approaches and frameworks that take advantage of new technological possibilities. While the flexibility of remote working can improve employee motivation and be beneficial to employers by opening new, geographically dispersed talent pools, such as in emerging markets, there are important human resource policies to be rethought such as on compensation and travel. Also critical are new approaches to ensuring that teams stay connected and that the culture of the organization is nurtured. Lessons from organizations such as Gitlab highlight the importance of transparency and structured approaches to curating online conversations as being vital to building and sustaining organizational culture (Herbst 2021).

It is hard to develop a unified perspective of the impact of technology on the world. Over time, technology affects business, people, government and society differently. Some of these effects are easy to see, initially, but the deeper and more fundamental impacts play out over a longer period, sometimes over several decades. A lot of experimentation is needed, which presents a challenge, especially for rapidly advancing digital technologies.

Changing generations of technology also opens the possibility for emerging markets to leapfrog and move forward rapidly in the adoption of new technologies. Several examples of this exist in emerging markets. Software firms in India leapfrogged with the adoption of advanced software quality methodologies and innovated with offshore software development practices to gain a strong position globally. Internet firms in China have rapidly moved from initially copying business models from Silicon Valley to becoming innovation leaders by building a leadership position in new technologies such as facial recognition and by leveraging the widespread adoption of mobile technologies and gaming in local populations. For example, TikTok surpassed Google as the most popular site in the world in 2021 (Gold 2021). Leapfrogging can also be witnessed in Africa, where adoption of mobile payment systems such as M-Pesa started ahead of most developed nations, and countries such as Rwanda are setting the frontiers in the application of advanced drone technologies.

Based on an analysis of over a decade of innovation data from the Global Innovation Index,[1] some nations are able to invest more successfully in technological innovation and benefit from faster development as measured by higher GDP per capita growth rates (Dutta and Luo 2021). These nations have an overall better performance due to greater sophistication of their business sectors, which is driven by the presence of higher management capability, greater ability to absorb new knowledge, and a greater focus on labour force skilling. Moreover, the study finds that besides investing in the sophistication and capabilities of their businesses, innovation accelerators in the low-income group also perform well at supporting and encourageing sophisticated markets. This encompasses dimensions such as ease of getting credit, the presence of venture capital investors, and the diversification and scale of domestic markets. The findings also show that the two aspects of innovation linkages and trade, competition and market scale,

---

[1]. The Global Innovation Index is a series of annual studies of the state of innovation in the world. It provides an excellent set of longitudinal data to study technological leapfrogging amongst emerging markets. (https://www.globalinnovationindex.org/Home)

are outstanding in innovative low-income countries, while the aspects of knowledge worker, political institutions and research and development stand out in innovative high-income countries. These findings are consistent with recent research findings at the micro-level that less developed countries should focus more on trading, while developed countries should invest more in research and development.

The Rise of the Flexible Economy

In recent decades, people change more jobs during their lifetimes and/or do multiple jobs. More people freelance in their jobs, choosing or rejecting work depending on their interests. The widespread prevalence of remote working and work-from-home during the COVID-19 crisis has accentuated many of these shifts. It is now more easily possible through appropriate technology and more accepted by employers to work from home and to divide time flexibly across multiple commitments.

The changing nature of work is one of the reasons why jobs have become so fluid. As countries develop their economies, jobs shift from manufacturing to services, a sector amenable to job-hopping and flexible work. Since the services sector provides greater flexibility, employees have more opportunities to combine their skills and aspirations with their life goals and pressures. The second change in the sector is digitalization. In the 1980s, digitalization allowed outsourcing of work, which was then moved to low-cost nations, such as India. While outsourcing and offshoring began four decades ago, other benefits of digitalization began showing up in the last two decades, aspects that allowed flexible work. Digitalization allows tasks to be broken down and regrouped in different ways, which could then be outsourced in flexible ways for both employer and employee. The proliferation of digital devices and widespread use of the cloud for data storage let workers connect from anywhere, thus allowing remote and flexible working.

Along with digitalization, companies shifted more to project-based work than permanent jobs. Like in filmmaking, teams assembled to do a project and then disassembled after the project. Digitalization has allowed companies to transform their workflows into projects. For individuals, digital technologies have provided an opportunity to work at will, to work according to convenience, and to switch work easily. These developments allowed for the rise of flexible work.

More recently, the rise of platform technologies had a big impact on the nature of work in many countries. Jobs using technology platforms are not necessarily temporary, but platforms have given rise to the so-called gig economy, where people work on temporary projects in flexible ways. Surveys have indicated substantial willingness within the workforce in many countries to work as freelancers. The Indian newspaper, *The Hindu*, estimates that India has 15 million freelancers, a group that is growing at very fast pace annually, second only to the USA (Sheth 2020). Many emerging market governments are also encourageing the growth of gig workers to drive the overall growth of their economies. For example, *Forbes* reports that the Malaysia Digital Economy Corporation, a government entity, has set up several programs to get underemployed Malaysians onto gig economy platforms, including eRezeki and eUsahawan (Loo 2017). The former is a website designed for Malaysians to make money completing tasks online (e.g. reviewing images, writing content, filtering out spam, editing databases, inputting data, checking tagged photographs, etc.). Overall, the programs target people from households in the bottom 40 per cent of income.

While the rise of the flexible economy has been positive on many fronts, it has also increased insecurity and created difficult living conditions for many. When employed as flexible part-time workers, people rarely obtain the health, education and other benefits that regular employees take for granted. The high costs of some of these advantages, such as proper health coverage, puts financial pressures on workers. Without appropriate health coverage, workers and their families are often subject to the high risks of unforeseen medical emergencies. Workers in the gig economy often do not make living wages from any one job and thus must work multiple jobs to make ends meet. With little free time after working multiple jobs, many workers do not have the time to invest in their own education and development. Hence, they frequently get stuck at certain levels of employment and fail to benefit from wage growth and social mobility. This divergence in living standards can also lead to increased divergence in political views and reduced political stability in countries.

These are not insurmountable problems. Business and government leaders can address these needs and help workers in the flexible economy that is being created because of the increasing digitalization of the economy. Policies for supporting quality affordable education and providing adequate healthcare for all are good starting points. Many governments are also now pushing firms to share some of the benefits of digitalization with their workers by increasing minimum wages and providing other labour benefit conditions. For example, there are movements in many emerging markets to provide more government protection to the rights of gig workers. Employers are being asked or encouraged to also invest in the future skilling and development of their gig workers and this is good for the overall development of the entire country also. *Forbes* reports that 'certain digital employment platforms—like Kazi Connect in Nairobi and Andela in Lagos—offer skills development opportunities as well as actual gigs. Ideally, this will help gig economy workers bulk up their resume and move up the employment ladder, rather than simply filtering out spam forever' (Loo 2017).

Digital Taylorism and Algorithms at Work

The first serious study on technology and people on the shop floor was done by Frederick Taylor, who was responsible for formulating the theory of scientific management and starting the efficiency movement in production. Taylorism, the term by which his methods came to be known, consisted of breaking a production process into a series of small steps and then analysing every step for maximum efficiency. Taylor wanted to make sure that each task was executed efficiently. For this, he separated planning from execution, the former to be done by managers and the latter by workers. Among several other things, he also introduced the practice of basing management decisions on precise measurements rather than instinct. His overarching aim was to optimize work output by minimizing the skill and time necessary for a person to do a job. The nature of shop floor work changed after Taylorism was adopted by companies. Each factory worker began to specialize in a specific task rather than a collection of tasks. Taylorism was widely adopted in the US after he published *Principles of Scientific Management* in 1911, and it was responsible for the rapid increase in US industrial output and the rise of America as a major world power.

Taylorism has been used by several companies across sectors. For example, McDonald's has used the principles of scientific management to set temperatures, cooking times and other parameters in making hamburgers and French fries. Call centres require workers to follow strict guidelines. Even some schools follow these principles to develop teaching methods that are uniform across different kinds of teachers. These principles of production remain relevant in the twenty-first century, even as the workplace and education change rapidly.

Taylorism had a big impact on jobs by increasing their number and reducing the skill necessary to perform each task. Likewise, new digital technologies are creating a more sophisticated version of Taylorism that some call digital Taylorism. For one, it has become easy to monitor task-level performance of employees through the introduction of tracking digital tools which leverage the power of digital innovations including IoT (Internet of Things), micro-device level sensors, Bluetooth/5G and other local communication modes. Researchers at MIT have also created the sociometer that can be worn around the neck to monitor a range of gestures and moods of people in human-to-human communication (Choudhury and Pentland 2002). More recently, many tracking apps deployed for COVID-19 give governments the ability to monitor the locations and contacts of individuals on a real-time basis.

There are many more examples, and it is evident that digital Taylorism has only just started. In contrast to the adoption of Taylorism on the factory floor, digital Taylorism allows the same principles to be applied to a broad range of workers, including white-collar employees. The performance of skilled professionals, such as doctors and lawyers, at a task level, can be monitored within digital Taylorism. An important question in digital Taylorism is whether this actually aids the worker to improve and develop themselves further or makes them less skilful. Critics argue that technology monitors analyse every aspect of work, and ultimately, technology dehumanizes and deskills the worker. The situation is much more complicated, as digital technologies can also be used to aid workers. As evidenced from the large-scale adoption of work-from-home during the COVID-19 crisis, digital technologies do indeed allow the breakdown of work into tasks that can be easily done by people anywhere. The information generated by digital tools can also help develop worker skills.

Rising digitalization and digital Taylorism have also facilitated the widespread use of algorithms for defining and executing work. Algorithms are widely used in many contexts—both personal and professional. Algorithms deployed by social media sites decide what we read in the news. Search algorithms decide what is displayed on individual Google or Amazon pages. Algorithms decide, or strongly influence, the credit score of a person and whether they are eligible for a new loan or mortgage. As algorithms have become more intelligent, so too have the sophistication of their application. Today, algorithms powered by big data and AI decide the probability of a person succumbing to a fatal disease and influence the amount of healthcare provided to the patient. Algorithms are also used by some human resource departments to judge employee engagement and estimate the probability of that person leaving the organization. Many organizations also use algorithms to judge the possibility of fraud or criminal behaviour and to take appropriate action.

As the use of algorithms has become more widespread, people's unease with them has also increased. In research conducted by the Pew Institute in November 2018, about 60 per cent of surveyed respondents felt that algorithms would always reflect the biases of people who designed them (Smith 2018). The concerns around the use of algorithms covered a range of issues. For example, people felt that personal financial scores determined by algorithms would invariably be incomplete and biased, as algorithms would be unable to capture the complexities of the financial histories and the specific individual contexts. Further, many surveyed participants felt that such algorithms reflected an invasion into their personal privacy and would deter people from freely making purchases or conducting activities online.

The combination of digital Taylorism and the rising use of algorithms has also raised concerns about the loss of human agency. As algorithms become more complex, especially with the use of AI models, the ability of humans to understand and control the results of these algorithms would decrease. As corporations pursue profits and efficiencies, they may have increased incentives to create algorithms to manipulate people and outcomes—such as the use of techniques by many social media sites to increase their addictiveness for people. There is concern that even if algorithms are well-intentioned, they may be based on incomplete data, and it may be impossible to remove the ethical and other systemic biases embedded in their conclusions. Also, if algorithmic systems are increasingly used to automate decision making, they may have a negative impact on jobs and may lead to increased redundancies.

New Skills for the Age of Mobility

Digital technologies are having a profound impact on the workplace and consequently on the skills required for success (Arregui Pabollet et al. 2019). Take, for example, the rise of virtual teamwork. COVID-19 has firmly put remote teams at the centre of a corporation's work processes. Success in virtual collaboration now requires knowledge for connecting smoothly to different technology platforms, basic skills for assuring security and privacy of the discussions, successfully sharing documents online, and integrating work outputs from a virtual meeting into other corporate technology systems. As AI systems such as chatbots are deployed, knowledge is required about how they impact sales and marketing, and how the data and smart analytics provided by these technology systems can be used to strengthen customer relationships.

The challenge with skills required for success in the digital age is that they change rapidly as technology evolves. Few in middle to senior management positions studied remote collaboration or AI chatbots as subject areas when they were in college. It is not surprising then to find them challenged when they need to engage with technology-intensive processes and projects. The traditional way was to finish school, receive a college education and then start working. Few people went back to the university after they started working unless they had unfinished degrees. On-the-job training was sparse, except in a few organizations. With the increasing need for digital skills, learning in the twenty-first century must continue on a lifelong basis.

In a dynamic world, the ability to adapt quickly is valuable, as important as experience and knowledge. The ability to work with technology is a fundamental skill. Also important are critical thinking, leadership skills, project management and the ability to work with people, and creative and communication skills. In a fast-changing world, the ability to learn on a continuous basis becomes the most important skill for a good career. Unfortunately, the world faces a serious skill gap. The Global Talent Competitive Index (GTCI) report notes that more than one in ten people face long-term unemployment due to lack of basic work skills (Lanvin and Monteiro 2021). According to Hays PLC, a human resources services company, 30 per cent of Chinese companies are not confident of finding enough talent for technology jobs within the country to meet their requirements (Bloomberg 2019). Aspiring Minds, a global skills credentialing company, found that, in a 2019 survey, 80 per cent of Indian engineering graduates are not immediately employable (SHL 2019).

To reduce this skills gap and to remain relevant in the twenty-first century, schools, universities and companies are now rethinking education and training. The old classroom, where students assembled for lectures and wrote tests, has given way to online and blended learning. With the COVID-19 pandemic, technology is widely used in the classroom, and many of the new features of online and blended learning are expected to stay after the pandemic is over. But there are other changes in education as well. Teaching is richer with the use of data and media, more centred on the learner and more practical. Universities, schools and education specialists have recognized that lifelong learning is the essence of the modern workplace and are trying to teach lifelong learning skills. Countries that nurture an environment for lifelong learning generally have a better-equipped workforce. In the GTCI, the top performing countries all perform well in the lifelong learning sub-index.

Human beings are migratory animals by instinct, willing to move across geographies for improved opportunities. Human mobility has played a key role in shaping the twentieth century economy, as major regional and national economies have benefitted from mobilizing talent from across the world. There is data to prove that countries that encourage mobility also do well in innovation and economic growth. In the Global Talent Innovation Index, top countries like Switzerland, United States, and Singapore have all had open immigration policies for a long time. They rank among the top nations in the ability to attract and retain talent, although there has been more than a murmur of protest in these countries.

Improvements in digital technologies have brought a new dimension to mobility, providing people with the ability to move work without really moving physically. Now, with the COVID-19 pandemic, mobility is being rethought. Companies are facing increasing pressures to reduce costs, and many are allowing greater flexibility for their employees to work from home. With remote working becoming the norm in many sectors, organizations can cast a wider net globally for accessing talent while obviating the need to relocate talent. Talent no longer needs to reside at the location of work. This flexibility is helping companies to both reduce costs and, in many cases, to support their strategy to diversify their supply chains. Numerous questions are also arising with respect to regulations for these changes in the global talent pool. For example, under current regulations, New York State levies income taxes on employees of New York companies who work remotely in other states. Avoiding double taxation for remote work is one of the many changes that will be needed to integrate remote work into global talent pools.

There are also important issues around strengthening company cultures when all or a major part of the workforce is remote. Gitlab is a fully remote organization of more than 1,500 employees, and it has openly shared some of the challenges in managing a globally remote workforce (Herbst 2021). Gitlab emphasizes extreme transparency across its organizations and has also put into practice a formal set of informal communication processes to share and build a common company culture (GitLab 2022). Many of these informal communication processes are themselves digitally enabled, such as Zoom-based watercooler meetings. GitLab's employees are encouraged to document virtually everything. Due to GitLab's asynchronous work style, meetings are optional. Meetings are recorded and often live streamed publicly on the GitLab Unfiltered YouTube channel. Attendees take notes in a standardized format, and those who miss meetings are encouraged to read through them and add appropriate context later (Grindle 2015).

The Young Will Drive Change

Millennials, or those born between 1981 and 1996, tend to be generally more educated and better informed than their parents, and they seem to be more optimistic about the future. A recent Pew Research study showed that young adults up to their late twenties are more optimistic about their own future than their parents, a trend that is also reflected in other countries both developed and emerging (Stokes 2017). Millennials show, in global studies, as being more responsible and more willing to do their bit to improve the state of the world. A 2015 survey by Global Tolerance showed that 84 per cent of millennials considered it their duty to make a positive difference to the world through their lifestyle (Global Tolerance 2015). Half of the millennials surveyed said that they would choose work with a purpose over that with a high salary. A survey in 2016 by Deloitte showed that 87 per cent of millennials evaluate the success of companies based on parameters beyond financial performance (Deloitte 2016). The same survey showed more young people focussed on their own success in alignment with societal progress.

Generation Z, or those born between 1997 and 2015, are the first digitally native generation. Amazon went public on the stock market on 15 May 1997, heralding the start of the digital economy as we know it today. Imagine what the world has looked like for Gen Z. From birth, they have had access to the Internet, and they have grown up in a world that is real-time, interactive, transparent and global. They did not have to learn about the Internet. They grew up with it. Gen Z came to age as social media prospered globally, as Facebook was started in February 2004. Social media and the digital world have defined the 'normal' world that they have grown up in. Gen Z has little recollection of the world before smartphones. A study by McKinsey noted that Gen Z had four core characteristics: they are analytical, they avoid labels, they believe in working for causes and they consider dialogue as the best way to resolve conflicts (Francis and Hoefel 2020). Gen Z is more conscious of their consumption and are also keen to drive changes in businesses.

There are broad similarities in the attitudes and characteristics of millennials and Gen Z. This represents a reordering of priorities as compared to their parents—the baby boomers—who were more concerned with discipline, hard work and orderly progress in the work environment. The younger generations are more concerned about values, less concerned about money (even in a more uncertain context), and keen to contribute towards building a better world. Being more informed, they are aware of the dangers of a lifestyle that harms the environment. The pandemic and their recent experiences with the lockdown and remote work has only increased their support for small businesses and is making them spurn companies with values differing from their own. Seeing the rapid and positive changes in nature after lockdowns, they have also become less pessimistic about climate change.

Millennials and Gen Z are both more digitally savvy, as well as more aware of the potential of technology to solve global problems. A Pew Research survey in 2018 showed that 95 per cent of teens in the US have access to a smartphone, and 43 per cent were online almost constantly. In 2019, Pew Research did another survey on millennials and found that they stood out for their technology use (Vogels 2019). Compared to 68 per cent of baby boomers, 92 per cent of millennials said that they owned a smartphone and nearly 100 per cent of them used the Internet.

These two generations, as they grow and become a large part of the workforce, are driving changes in government and business priorities, and they are helping build a more sustainable and inclusive world. More than any other preceding generation, they are using technology to create positive change. For example, the Internet makes it easy for people to volunteer for a range of social goals. VolunteerMatch.org connects volunteers with causes and roles that suit them. RLab's JamIIX matches troubled youth anonymously to counsellors through a series of text messages (Grindle 2015). Internet message boards and social media posts make it easy to exchange ideas and concerns with others. Through an active online presence, the younger generations can build an engaged, worldwide network of volunteers, activists, donors, and concerned citizens. Indiegogo provides a platform for organizations and individuals to create 'family and friends' fundraising campaigns around causes that they care about or are involved in. It is no longer necessary to rent out community space to bring people together. One can easily do so online (Walden University 2021).

The Great Resignation or a Chance to Reimagine?

There has been much talk in recent months about the Great Resignation, or the phenomenon of large numbers of people willingly leaving the workforce, especially in the USA and developed economies of Europe. The *BBC* notes that in the US, 4.3 million Americans left their jobs in August 2021, or about 2.9 per cent of the national workforce—the highest number on record (Lufkin 2021). In the UK, the number of open jobs surpassed 1 million for the first time ever in August. According to Politico Europe, there are 20 million fewer people at work in the thirty-eight member countries of the OECD (Taylor 2021). Of these, 14 million have exited the labour force and are classified as 'not working' or 'not looking for work'.

China is witnessing a similar reduction in the workforce, especially as the younger generations shy away from the hard grind of factory jobs (Sun 2021). The situation is similar in number but grimmer in other emerging markets. The International Labour Organization (ILO) notes that 26 million jobs were lost in Latin America and the Caribbean. Most of these job losses were not willing choices made by the population but rather hardships imposed on them by the closure of businesses and reduction in economic growth during the pandemic.

The real reasons for many people quitting their jobs are hard to decipher accurately, as data collection is both recent[2] and spotty. Academics and labour market observers agree that there are a multitude of reasons why people seem to be quitting jobs. Some have had no choice but to quit as their employers' shut doors or the economy contracted, as was the case for many who were employed in the hospitality sector prior to the pandemic. Some others quit their jobs out of exhaustion and the stresses of their role—as was the case for many employed in the healthcare sector. Yet others have quit their jobs to wait for and seek better wages. The rebounding of the global economy and the decrease in available workers has put pressure on jobs in the developed markets, and there is evidence to show that job switchers are gaining higher wage increases. However, this is not true for many Latin American and Caribbean countries where low-skilled workers have lost their jobs, have had to take on additional debt to survive during the pandemic, and are now forced to accept lower wages to re-enter the workforce.

Regardless of the reasons behind people quitting their jobs, the continued impact of the pandemic and the accompanying digital acceleration has provided an opportune moment for employers to stop and rethink their views on jobs and the expectations of their employees.

---

2. The USA has been collecting data about resignations since 2000 only.

Many employees have now experienced working from home for an extended period and are more appreciative of the positive impact of remote work on their work-life balance. While some mothers have had to quit their jobs to look after their children, many parents have realized that they were missing, in the pre-pandemic world, the value of being able to enjoy meals with their children and to spend quality time on activities with them daily. Many road-weary workers now value the benefits of reduced travel and appreciate the fact that a lot of the tasks and meetings they travelled for earlier—at both a financial cost to the firm and to their own health—can now be performed well remotely.

Employees, especially those engaged in many white-collar and knowledge-based tasks, today, have a renewed set of expectations from their jobs. Rather than try to force-fit their employees into the pre-pandemic model, this is an opportune moment for all to rethink and reimagine the future of jobs. People's expectations have changed, technology has become more powerful and we owe it to society to redesign jobs to support work-life balance and create a more sustainable future. The situation is more complex and still more urgent in many emerging markets. While a rethinking of white-collar jobs is needed in those markets also, there is a greater urgency to revive the economy and get workers, especially those in blue-collar jobs and in factories, back to work. Businesses and governments need to collaborate to reduce the debt burden on the poor and to invest in skills to prepare them for better and more future-orientated jobs. According to the World Economic Forum, only 21 per cent of businesses report being able to make use of public funds to support their employees through reskilling and upskilling (World Economic Forum 2020). There needs to be more incentives for investments in the markets and jobs of tomorrow.

Chapter 13: The Productivity Puzzle— Increasing Divergence between Regions

The Productivity Puzzle—Increasing Divergence between Regions

Chapter 13 | Laura Shelton and Hasan Tuluy

Introduction

The world economy witnessed output increases of nearly 5 per cent average annual rate for the three decades between 1950–80. Some of this growth was the result of increases in the factors of labour and capital, though an even larger share—explaining around half of the growth rate—was due to growth in productivity of 2 per cent or more per year, and an expanding productivity frontier through better efficiency and reallocation of factors, product and market innovation and improvements to quality, and new ways to organize production.

While there were—and are—considerable differences among regions and countries, several rapidly growing emerging economies began to converge with advanced economies, pulling large segments of the global population out of poverty. A sense of optimism prevailed during these years that such gains in productivity and economic growth were to be expected and would be sustained.

After this sustained period of growth in productivity, however, productivity and GDP growth slowed down considerably during the decade of 1980 subsequently followed by many countries by a similarly low growth period in early 1990s. The reason for this slowdown is not well-understood, with many potential explanations offered but without a shared agreement on a definitive explanation that can explain the pattern across all regions and countries. Although productivity growth briefly recovered to above 2 per cent per annum again, the 2008–09 global financial crisis and its aftermath once again dampened productivity growth. These events led to concern that these slowdowns might portend a more permanent erosion of productivity, and that the frontier of productivity had peaked.

Although it is premature to label it a trend, there is some evidence of a pick-up in productivity growth, and an acceleration of technology adoption and diffusion triggered by the shock of the global COVID-19 pandemic, with significant changes in modes of production, trade and work.

This paper summarizes these stylized periods: the period of sustained productivity growth between 1950 and 1980, the period of slowdown in productivity growth from 1980–2010 and some early signs of an expanding productivity frontier and an apparent return to productivity growth. We conclude with a brief discussion of possible, speculative considerations in what countries might want to focus on to increase productivity and growth.

The Miracle of Productivity (1950–80)[1]

Between 1950–80 the world economy experienced a rapid, average growth of nearly 5 per cent per annum. While increases in the quantity factors of production—capital and labour—contributed to the growth, increase in inputs only partly accounts for of the overall growth.[2]

The labour force is estimated to have grown at an average annual rate of 1.8 per cent between 1950 and 1980, nearly doubling from 1.26 billion in 1950 to 2.15 billion in 1980. The growth in the labour force was augmented by the increased participation of women into the workforce following WWII.[3] Towards the end of the period, the integration of the baby boomer generation into the workforce in advanced economies likewise spurred growth in labour force. In addition to growing in size, the quality of the labour force also improved over the period with better education and health. Whereas the world population aged fifteen and above had an average of 3.2 years of education in 1950, the years of education had risen to 5.3 years in 1980 (Barro and Lee 2010). A better educated workforce brought greater skill and adaptability to new technologies and contributed positively to economic activity (Dieppe 2021). Advances in medicine extended life expectancy and contributed to a healthier, more productive workforce.[4]

During the period from 1950–80, capital stock also grew considerably, with the level of global capital stock increasing from 27.2 trillion USD to 88.0 trillion USD, in PPP terms.[5] Public investment increased the capital stock in core infrastructure like roads, ports, bridges and electricity. The growing capital stock and improvements in the quality infrastructure served as 'horizontal' (typically untargeted to firms or sectors) incentives to grow productivity, allowing firms to increase connectivity, specialize and decrease operating costs. This positive relationship between long-run growth and investment rates has been observed by several growth models (Dieppe 2021). Furthermore, evidence has shown an association between investment rate and greater labour productivity (Beaudry, Collard and Green 2005).

Notwithstanding the additional mobilization, labour and capital contributed a declining share to growth over the period. Labour's contribution to output per worker declined from around 30 per cent in the late 1950s to around 25 per cent in 1980 (Gallardo-Albarrán and Inklaar 2020). capital's contribution similarly declined from around 20 per cent in the 1950s to around 15 per cent in 1980. By 1980s labour and capital together explained less than half of growth rate.

As the factors themselves do not explain the magnitude of growth experienced during this period, some other factor must contribute to growth—productivity, or how efficiently the inputs of labour and capital are being used. Total Factor Productivity (TFP), calculated as the residual

---

1. There is an extensive literature on growth and productivity, which we will not attempt to summarize here. Rather, this section draws on the work by Yusuf (Productivity Matters, unpublished), Maloney and Cuselito, Dieppe, Goldin et al. and Gordon.
2. Gallardo-Albarrán and Inklaar et al. (2020), using development accounting, show that produced capital, human capital and productivity all contribute to output; however, the relative importance that each of these factors has in determining output per worker has changed over time, with productivity gaining in relevance.
3. The difference between the labour force participation of working-age (between twenty-five and sixty-four years of age) men and women narrowed from around 30.9 in 1950 to 23.8 by 1980.
4. Life expectancy has dramatically improved since the 1950s driven by medical innovations such as vaccinations and antibiotics as well as improvements to public health in the form of improved sanitation and the introduction of publicly funded healthcare (Roser, Ortiz-Ospina and Ritchie, 2019).
5. Capital stock here is measured in constant 2010 PPP US dollars. The measure of capital stock presented here comes from the Centennial growth model. Initial capital stock is calculated as initial investment divided by ten-year average annual GDP growth plus 6 per cent depreciation. Subsequent years are calculated based on capital stock growth, which is calculated as capital investment from the previous year divided by the previous year's capital stock all minus 6 per cent depreciation.

of the labour force, capital stock, and historical GDP, is a measure of productivity that represents the 'excess growth' in output compared to growth in input factors.[6] For the purpose of this chapter, TFP will be used as a proxy for country productivity. Whereas the relative contribution of capital and labour to per capita GDP declined over the period, the importance of productivity rose, with the relative contribution to growth of productivity, capital, and labour remaining at relatively constant/comparable levels from the end of WWII to 1980.

Table 13.1: Average growth rates 1950–79

	GDP Growth	TFP Growth
World	4.74	2.23
Advanced Economies	4.54	2.50
Emerging and Developing Economies	5.23	2.27
Latin America and the Caribbean	5.45	1.52
The Middle East and North Africa	7.73	-1.12
Sub-Saharan Africa	4.20	1.17
East Asia and Pacific	6.77	1.20
South Asia	4.05	0.72
Europe and Central Asia	4.57	3.30

Source: Centennial Group 2021

Some of the early gains in productivity were obtained from resources—in particular labour—moving from lower productivity sectors like agriculture and from rural areas, toward higher productivity sectors of industry and manufacturing and to urban agglomerations. The period saw two major transitions away from the domination of the agricultural sector. First, in the 1940s, the economic value generated by industry and services surpassed that made by agriculture, forestry, mining and fishing (Satterthwaite, McGranahan and Tacoli 2010). Second, around 1980, the labour force employed in industry and services exceeded that in agriculture, forestry, mining and fishing. In 1950, less than 30 per cent of the world population lived in urban settings, compared to over 55 per cent in 2020, a trend that is projected to continue.[7] This shift to urban settings improved economies of scale and created agglomeration clusters, enhancing productivity. A recent study found that a 10 per cent increase in residents in an area corresponds to 0.4 per cent increase in productivity, through more efficient spread of knowledge, ideas and innovations, more efficient use of infrastructure as a larger number of users shares the same facilities, and due to employers' ability to find workers from a larger labour pool that better match their skills need (Ahrend, Lembcke and Schumann 2017). This reallocation of resources first began in advanced economies has been followed with some lag, by all emerging economies across the world.

---

6. TFP presented in this paper comes from the Centennial Growth Model. It is calculated as $GDP/K^{\alpha}L^{1-\alpha}$ for 2011 and all years prior. Subsequent years are projected based on the following country criteria: rich or developed, converging, non-converging and fragile countries.

7. The Centennial Growth Model estimates that by 2060 over 70 per cent of the global population will be living in urban areas.

Importantly, the period also witnessed a rapid and broad diffusion—at least among the advanced economies—of new technologies, materials, and innovative products such as electricity, telephone, personal vehicles, airlines, pharmaceuticals and medical products, plastics, etc. and new ways of organizing and delivery, such as modern management methods. Deepening global trade, initially in goods but subsequently also in capital flows, accelerated the diffusion of technologies and innovation across the globe.

Figure 13.1: 5-year global growth rates—GDP, TFP, labour and investment

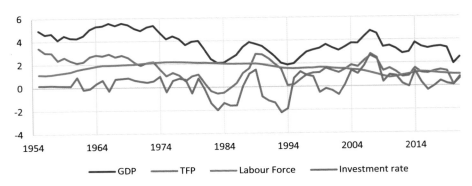

Source: Centennial Group 2021

This overall pattern where productivity and growth closely track each other, masks significant differences between Advanced (AE) and Emerging and Developing economies (EMDE). From 1950 to 1980, AE GDP grew by 4.5 per cent with TFP (growing at 2.5 per cent) contributing 55 per cent to growth. EMDE during the same period grew faster at 5.2 per cent with TFP (2.3 per cent) contributing 43 per cent.

The regional[8] differences are even more prominent: Europe and Central Asian (ECA) GDP grew 4.6 per cent driven by strong TFP growth (3.3 per cent) that contributed nearly 70 per cent to growth. GDP for Latin America and the Caribbean (LAC) increased faster at 5.4 per cent but with TFP contributing 21 per cent, significantly less than the world average. Similarly, while realignment of oil markets propelled the Middle East and North Africa (MENA) GDP to grow at 7.7 per cent, nearly 50 per cent faster than EMDEs, TFP growth was actually negative at -1.1 per cent for the period, suggesting less than efficient and effective deployment of resources. Sub-Saharan Africa's (SSA) GDP on the other hand grew more slowly at 4.2 per cent with similarly low but positive contributions from TFP growth (1.1 per cent). GDP in East Asia and Pacific (EAP) grew rapidly at 6.8 per cent but with also modest contributions from TFP growth at 1.2 per cent. South Asia GDP growth of 4.0 per cent with TFP growth of less than three-quarters of a per cent at 0.72 per cent. Regional trends in TFP growth shown in Figure 13.2.

What might account for these differences? Many reasons emerge, with each region telling a somewhat different story, though with some common elements. Clearly the quality of human capital and the level and quality of core infrastructure critically matters (Barro and Lee 2010).

---

8. Using World Bank regional classifications. See https://datahelpdesk.worldbank.org/knowledgebase/articles/906519

The extent of openness to trade and to FDI allows for gains in productivity while dominance of state actors such as state-owned enterprises tends to pull down productivity. Finally, commodity dependence often challenges productivity growth.

Figure 13.2: 5-year TFP growth, (a) by economy level and (b) by region

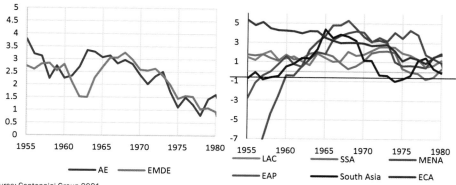

Source: Centennial Group 2021

Looking into Regional Disparities

ECA, which showed a strong performance during the period, benefitted from a mature, educated population and considerable public investment in infrastructure and R&D; however, growth was pulled down by central planning and SOEs. Commodities with strong price cycles slowed productivity growth in LAC and MENA, though growth in MENA was bolstered by high oil prices for part of the period. In SSA, where TFP growth was consistently one of the lowest across regions, reliance on commodities, low levels of human capital due to poor quality in education and gaps in access to health, a weak and costly infrastructure sector (water, electricity, roads, communication technology), low investment and low trade integration with little trade openness constituted significant barriers to growth. EAP began transitions from rural economy with a massive shift in China after opening up to global markets. South Asia, although facing a still dominant state sector and SOEs and closed markets, saw consistent improvement to TFP growth though from a low base and with a significant dip in the early 1970s.

Notwithstanding these differences, this period broadly coincided with optimism that countries could build human capital, grow their core infrastructure and capital base, and adopt technology and innovation, thereby spur productivity and growth, lift population out of poverty and begin to catch up.

A Period of Stagnation and Doubt (1980–2010)

The optimism experienced in 1950–80 was however called into question as productivity growth—especially among advanced economies—declined by half to hover around 1 per cent and even turning negative for several years as recessions and crises in the early 1980s and throughout the 1990s buffeted the world economies, stifled growth and slowed productivity.

While productivity growth rallied from 1995 until the global financial crisis of 2008, thereafter it once again steadily declined.

Figure 13.3: 5-year TFP growth 1970–2010 against relevant economic crises

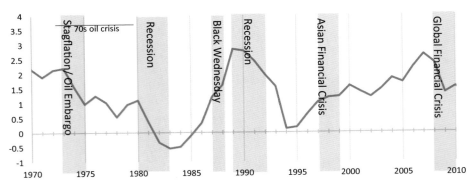

Source: Centennial Group 2021

There have been many attempts to better understand the reasons behind the decline of productivity growth. These explanations include the effects of external shocks, the size of labour force and diminishing returns to education, declining returns to R&D, slower adoption of technology and measurement issues.

- *External Shocks and Recessions.* The period between 1975 and 2008 experienced series of recessions and crises that stunted growth and impacted global value chains. As seen in Figure 13.3, many of these events coincide with dips in productivity growth. During such deep recessions TFP growth deteriorates as high productivity sectors such as ICT and trade tend to contract relatively more than lower productivity sectors such as social services and real estate, resulting in a misallocation of resources (Furceri, Kilic Celik, Jalles and Koloskova 2020).
- *Labour Force and Declining Return to Education.* In times of technological transformation, a higher labour force growth contributes to a faster adoption and implementation rates of new technologies, thereby ensuring those countries pull out of periods of slowdown faster compared to low labour force growth countries (Beaudry, Collard and Green 2005).[9] The impact of declines in labour productivity has predominantly been felt through TFP growth—due to labour hoarding, barriers to mobility though non-compete clauses, historic mismatch of skills to occupation due to social barriers/discrimination.[10] Gordon points to stagnating returns to education and changing demographics

---

9. Under the assumption that investment in old technology ends with the introduction of the new technology, depreciating old technology physical capital stock with a faster growing labour force means a more rapid decline of the old technology capital per worker and, thus, a more rapid decline in the relative importance of the old technology in those economies, creating a greater incentive to learn the new technology. Thus, in high labour force growth economies, more workers are engaged in learning and fewer engaged in production in the early stages of the transition and subsequently the economy can adopt the new technologies faster as more skilled labour becomes available.

10. Better allocation of human resources was estimated by Goldin et al. (2021) to account for 20 to 40 per cent of increase in output per person between 1960 and 2010.

as causes for the labour productivity decline, although returns to education may vary by the type and quality of education received (Gordon 2016).[11]

- *Inequality, the Gig Economy, and a Surge of Informality.* The rise of the gig economy has increased opportunity, especially for unskilled labour; however, this rise in short-term and sometimes informal work may have resulted in lower rates of investment in skill accumulation compared to longer-term contractual labour (Goldin 2021). Gordon argues productivity growth is held back further by challenges such as the rise in inequality experienced since the late 1970s and rising debt levels. Especially in EMDEs, the informal sector has expanded; these firms tend to be less efficient and relatively less productive compared to firms in the formal sector (Dieppe 2021).

- *Declining Returns to R&D.* Another explanation lies in decreasing returns to R&D. Cowen and Southwood (2019) note that 'scientific progress and innovativeness per capita had declined although patenting volume continued to grow worldwide'. This finding is similar to Bloom et al. (2020) that 'productivity of research is falling by as much as 5 per cent [per annum] in US since 1930s'.[12]

- *Slower Adoption of Technologies.* A declining pool and rising costs of technological innovations could also explain the slowdown in productivity. Gordon argues that the productivity slowdown dates back considerably to earlier than 1980, that the adoption of technological improvements such as electricity, the WASH sector, the combustion engine, and telecommunications had run their course by 1970. He argues the boons of the digital revolution experienced in the late 1990s and early 2000s will not continue as a basis of future growth, and that more recent digital technologies (such as AI, Cloud technologies, and 'Big data') have not delivered the 'productivity windfall' that followed earlier innovations. However, while this finding may hold for AEs, the slowdown of technological innovation should not affect productivity growth in emerging countries still below the productivity frontier. The reasons for slower productivity growth in these countries is likely to be found misallocation of resources in less productive sector, or less effective use of resources due to lack of competition, poor policies and regulations that hold back adoption of new technologies and the growth of efficient firms.

- *Measurement Issues.* Goldin posits that productivity measure are impacted by mis-measurement in capital deepening caused by the procyclical nature of investment and the increase in intangible capital, which is typically underestimated and difficult to accumulate by its nature.[13]

11. Barro and Lee (2010) estimate that the rate of return is higher at the secondary (10.0 per cent) and tertiary (17.9 per cent) levels than at the primary level. Thus, although many countries may have achieved almost universal primary education, the real returns come from quality, higher education.

12. Yusuf reports that 'countries that are investing heavily in R&D such as Israel and Korea (both expending well over 4 per cent of GDP) and other like Finland and Sweden (over 3 per cent of GDP) have failed to arrest a decline in already low TFP growth since the turn of the century' (Shahid Yusuf, Productivity Matters: The Big Picture, May 2021 p13, unpublished).

13. Goldin et al. (2021) explains that intangible capital is typically (1) scalable, and therefore prone to creating economies of scale and concentration, (2) more sunk, in that it is typically linked to the firms that create it making it bad collateral, (3) conducive of spillovers and thus less attractive investment and (4) has strong synergies with IT capital, explaining the long lags in diffusion.

Explaining Regional Trends

The slowdown in GDP and productivity growth was not experienced uniformly across income groups and geographic regions.

advanced economies experienced a gradual decline in productivity growth since the 1980s—from around 2 per cent in the 1980s to around 1 per cent in 2010—with a substantial decrease due to the declining contribution of capital to productivity. EMDEs on the other hand experienced an increase in productivity, on average, of around 2 per cent, peaking at almost 5 per cent in 2003–08.

Table 13.2: Average growth rates 1980–2010

	GDP Growth	TFP Growth
World	3.09	1.21
Advanced Economies	2.49	1.04
Emerging and Developing Economies	3.89	2.04
Latin America and the Caribbean	2.68	0.09
The Middle East and North Africa	2.65	-0.69
Sub-Saharan Africa	3.41	0.53
East Asia and Pacific	5.60	2.70
South Asia	5.88	2.17
Europe and Central Asia	1.80	1.80

Source: Centennial Group 2021

Differences in GDP and productivity growth between regions became more prominent over the period 1980–2010[14] (Table 13.2). EAP and South Asia experienced strong GDP growth at above 5 per cent, while LAC, SSA and MENA GDP grew by 2–3 per cent for SSA, and ECA by only 1.8 per cent. Productivity growth likewise varied. EAP, and to an extent SA experienced sustained TFP growth—of 2.7 per cent for EAP and 2.2 per cent for SA—that outperformed other EMDEs and the world. Productivity growth at 0.5 per cent remained sluggish in SSA; LAC productivity was merely 0.1 per cent, while in MENA productivity growth declined by -0.69 per cent during this period. Notably, for LAC and SSA, reductions to TFP played a large role in productivity decline between the two periods.

What Contributed to These Different Outcomes between Regions?

High productivity growth in EAP was supported by long-term investment in human capital and quality educational outcomes. According to the World Bank's Human Capital Index (2019), EAP led EMDEs in expected years of schooling (13.1 years) and was converging with AEs in learning-adjusted years of schooling (9.4 versus 11.5 years).[15] EAP economies aggressively

---

14. All regional groups experienced a decrease in productivity from the period 2003–2008 to the period 2013–2018, though the magnitude of this decline varied across regions. LAC, MENA, and SSA experienced the greatest per cent change between the two periods, 79 per cent, 161 per cent, and 74 per cent declines respectively.
15. The World Bank's Human Capital Index is offers 'a summary measure of the amount of human capital that a child born today can expect to acquire by age 18, given the risks of poor health and poor education that prevail in the country where she lives'. Learning-adjusted years schooling is a composite part of the overall index. It provides a measure for the years

moved to reallocate labour and capital towards more sophisticated and higher productivity sectors and pursued policies that encouraged trade, FDI, and integration into global value chains (Dieppe 2021). Furthermore, EAP invested heavily in core infrastructure; roads, ports, airports, electricity and the Internet, which strengthened domestic and global connectivity of clusters and development corridors.[16]

SA on the other hand experienced a later start to the shift from lower productivity rural activities to urban, manufacturing and industrial activity. Countries in the region were likewise of latecomers to the policies that foster productivity.[17] However, despite this late start, the shift away from agriculture bolstered SA productivity—agriculture accounted for over 30 per cent of GDP of the region in 1980, which declined to 17.6 per cent by 2010.[18] By comparison, the SSA region roughly maintained broadly the same level of agriculture around 20 per cent from 1980 to 2010.

ECA experienced a rise in TFP growth in the late 1980s and early 1990s as liberalization and transition to markets freed up/released/unleashed pent-up productivity as resources shifted from low productivity state-dominant sectors. Toward the end of the period, productivity dropped off as opportunities for reallocation toward more productive sectors diminished, and regional conflicts, volatility in commodity prices, and spillover effects from the EU debt crisis slowed progress (Dieppe 2021). Those that were able to insulate themselves—some central European and central Asian countries—were able to do so by integrating into the supply chains of Western Europe or China.

Growth in LAC, MENA and SSA was challenged by their dependence on commodities; they suffered from the cyclical nature of commodity prices.[19] Furthermore, these regions faced other constraints and burdens. For LAC, sluggish growth arose from poor business climates and burdensome regulations which in many countries allowed unproductive firms to continue operations, as well as periods of extended political instability (Dieppe 2021). Those LAC countries which experienced higher productivity growth, including Dominica, Costa Rica and Dominican Republic, often undertook reforms that encouraged openness, FDI, greater 'formalization' of the economy, and fostered diversification away from rural sector (Dieppe 2021). MENA experienced poor productivity growth even before the period of slowdown, due to excessive reliance on the oil and gas sector. Resource rich MENA were caught in the resource curse developing dominant public sectors and public employment, unable to diversify and shift resources to the private and non-commodity sectors (Dieppe 2021). In SSA, low savings and investment rates, poor quality of human capital and the relatively small size of the individual economies hindered productivity growth. Commodity reliant SSA countries witnessed periods of rapid growth spurred

---

of schooling expected in a country adjusted for the quality of that education.

16. East Asia and Pacific had achieved near universal access to electricity by 2000 with 93 per cent of the population having access. Likewise, EAP saw considerable progress towards access to Internet, jumping from near zero access in 1990 to 34 per cent in 2010, one of the frontrunning EMDE regions.

17. South Asia as a region has the second lowest learning-adjusted years of schooling at 5.9 years suggesting relatively low investment in human capital. For infrastructural improvements that foster productivity, South Asia has a mixed performance with around 57 per cent of the population having access to electricity in 2000. The region has also faired somewhat poorly with regards to access to Internet with only 7.16 per cent access in 2010. (World Bank, Human Capital Index and World Development Indicators).

18. Data from World Bank, World Development Indicators.

19. Although these commodity dependent regions experienced periods of higher productivity, this is likely an overestimation due to the interaction of TFP with Terms of Trade, a notion that is further developed/elaborated in Chapter 14 on Commodity Prices, Terms of Trade and Productivity.

Figure 13.4: 5-year TFP growth 1980-2010, a) by economy level and b) by region

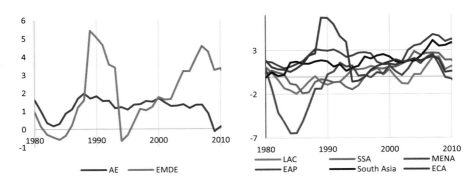

Source: Centennial Group 2021

by expansion of oil, metal and mineral investments and exports, but with limited backward linkages to the rest of the economies (Dieppe 2021).

While productivity slowed down in all regions but EAP and SA, paradoxically the 1980–2010 period also saw widespread technological progress such as adoption of personal computing,[20] invention of the Internet, and vast expansion of global trade, GVCs and financial integration. Despite these notable advances, the period of volatile growth and productivity slowdown led to pessimism that sustained growth had run its course, with investment, education, innovation, and R&D having reached diminishing returns. It raised questions whether the world would see continued social and economic convergence, as many had hoped for following the period of high productivity.

Signs of Pick-up

After the Global Financial Crisis, GDP and Productivity growth began to pick up around the world. Global average annual GDP grew at 3.35 per cent and TFP grew at 1.24 per cent for the period 2011–18. The social and economic shock triggered by the COVID-19 pandemic arrested progress, caused GDP growth to plummet by -3.4 per cent and TFP growth to decline sharply to -4.7 per cent in 2019–20. Despite this abrupt interruption, the pandemic and early recovery period also have evidence of 'green shoots' that may provide grounds for optimism. Rebounds, especially by the East Asia and South Asia regions, suggest rapid GDP and productivity growth is still feasible.

AEs did not return to the high productivity growth experienced in the 1950–80 period but were able to sustain growth around 1 per cent from 2010–18. At the same time, EAP and South Asia saw high, sustained levels of productivity growth over the period realizing an average TFP growth around 3.1 per cent and began to separate from other EMDEs. Productivity and growth in commodity dependent regions—MENA, LAC and SSA—on the other hand, remained

---

20. However, as Solow (1987) famously said: 'We see the computer age everywhere but in the productivity statistics'.

Figure 13.5: 5-year TFP growth 2010–20, (a) by economic level and (b) by region

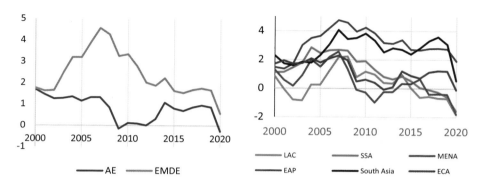

Source: Centennial Group 2021

Table 13.3: Average GDP and TFP growth rates, 2010–18

	GDP growth	TFP growth
World	3.60	1.49
Advanced Economies	2.09	1.03
Emerging and Developing Economies	5.06	2.05
Latin America and the Caribbean	2.15	0.28
The Middle East and North Africa	3.11	0.03
Sub-Saharan Africa	3.88	0.20
East Asia and Pacific	5.74	3.16
South Asia	6.84	3.14
Europe and Central Asia	2.06	1.24

Source: Centennial Group 2021

sluggish over the period, with a near-zero average TFP growth (0.03 per cent, 0.28 per cent, and 0.2 per cent respectively) (Table 13.3).

What Explains This Growth and Renewed Optimism?

This re-emerging optimism is centred on two emerging trends: the adoption and diffusion of existing technologies and the emergence of new innovations. The contribution of these trends to growth is largely corroborated by the insights expressed in Chapters 17 by Manu Bhaskaran, Chapter 12 by Soumitra Dutta, and Chapter 11 by Dr Mashelkar. And for now, this optimism is confined to two regions: East Asia and South Asia.

- *The acceleration of adoption and diffusion of several existing technologies.* There remains considerable potential for countries to exploit the existing technology and productivity frontier. There are many known technologies and applications which have yet

Figure 13.6: Value added by services, per cent GDP

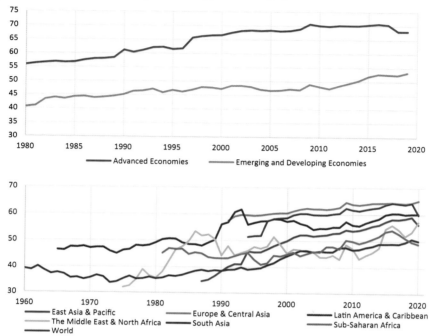

Source: World Bank 2021 and IMF 2021b

to gain wide scale traction, including use of the Internet which was adopted slowly before rose accelerating geometrically.[21]

In the 1980s services sector represented 35 per cent of GDP in EAP, SA and MENA and around 45 per cent of GDP in LAC and SSA.[22] By 2020 services accounted for around 50 per cent of GDP in SA, MENA and SSA, and 60 per cent in LAC and EAP. Despite the economic weight the services sectors have been relatively protected and slow to adopt new technologies and applications.

Crises such as the Global Financial Crisis and the current COVID-19 crisis have the potential to shift the speed and breadth of transformation, including in services. As explored further in Chapter 12, the pandemic heralded a paradigm shift in how we work—jumpstarting rapid digitalization across sectors as firms grappled with continuing operations in the face of the public health restrictions. ICT and digitization, once a luxury, have become vital to operations. COVID-19 compelled a rapid pivot to on-line distance education and to telehealth. Digitization provided a pathway to greater productivity in banking and finance, in retail and other white-collar professions. It has been integrated

---

21. Justin Rowlatt (2021) describes the S-curve path of adoption and mainstreaming of personal computers and the Internet—from the invention of the Internet in October 1969 to initial adoption by the tech savvy in 1990s to its exponential growth between the mid-1990s to the early 2000.

22. Data from World Bank World Development Indicators. Services accounted for around 57 per cent of ECA GDP in 1991; comparable earlier data are not available.

into municipal and central government services through e-government services. It has also played a key role in improving the efficiency of production processes, especially in determining the optimal use of water, fertilizer and pesticides in agriculture. McKinsey (2021) found that the industries most likely to be at the forefront of productivity following the Pandemic are healthcare, construction, ICT, retail and pharmaceuticals (Mishke et al. 2021). ICT capital is estimated to have three to seven times the impact of non-ICT capital, which can allow countries realize higher growth rates without substantially increasing capital spending (Yusuf 2021a).

Within the ICT sector, there is considerable scope to build on existing technologies. The examples of the Republic of Korea, China and India show that as technological capabilities improve, countries build upon existing innovations and repurpose them for their own markets (Yusuf 2021b). The Republic of Korea has had considerable success on this front in the multimedia sector in the production of Massive Multiplayer Online Roleplaying Games—leveraging its research and talent pools and bolstered by a strong electronics industry. China and India have similarly found success in modifying existing fintech, online commerce, and ride hailing services, adapted to the context of their markets.

- *New technologies, innovations, processes.* In addition to accelerating the spread of existing technologies, by adopting and adapting these technologies, there is potential to expand the frontier outward, as what was done for the mRNA COVID-19 vaccines, the breakthroughs in renewable energy and developments in storage batteries. The US experience of technological transformation in the ICT sector during the 1990s and 2000s shows how innovation can spur productivity, with ICT computing improving the efficiency of both front- and back-office operations.[23]

However, new technologies may take considerable time to see productivity gains to become mainstreamed. Public policy can play an important role in altering the pace of diffusion and adoption of new technologies. Commitments to address climate change for instance, have, and will continue to, spur the diffusion and adoption of technologies in the renewables sector. Renewable technologies such as photovoltaics, more-efficient batteries, green hydrogen technologies and electric vehicles, have been developed but remain in the early phases of their diffusion path. Declining costs for these technologies will allow them to become competitive with traditional technologies, leading to an accelerated uptake especially in countries with fewer stranded assets.

While technological innovation and digitization provide an important avenue for increasing productivity, they also enable shifts in the way production, services, trade, and firms are organized with considerable opportunities for integration of digital technologies into back office and front-line customer interface business processes.

What Makes East and South Asia Stand Out?

Given the remarkable performance of EAP, and in more recent years of South Asia, compared to that of the other regions, it is important to consider what makes these regions different. Other

---

23. This idea is further elaborated by Dr Mashelkar in Chapter 11.

regions—LAC, SSA and MENA—also operate well below the productivity frontier yet have not been able to reach sustained GDP and productivity growth rates of EAP and SA.

Clearly most countries in EAP had invested heavily in building their core infrastructure and developing their human capital. EAP countries on the whole also ensured that public policy favoured savings and investment, and their economies were integrated into global trade, open to FDI and competition. As discussed in Chapter 17, East and South Asia benefitted from existing manufacturing and industrial clusters, domestic competitiveness in emerging sectors, and start-up activities. These elements were foundational to adopt, adapt and leverage maturing technologies to facilitate accelerated growth. An example of this is Vietnam which since the late 1990s followed in the footsteps of the East Asian Tigers, and pursued economic openness, a focus on export-led industrialization, dismantling of rural collectives, providing incentives for foreign investors, investment in physical and human capital, increased participation in the regional economy and integration with thriving cross-Pacific global value chains (Yusuf 2021c).

Through a series of prior investments, many countries in EAP and South Asia were able to create the 'right' environment for innovation to flourish, a necessary factor to promote increased productivity. Many have done so through the introduction of multinational anchor firms (FDI), which can be a great source of technological spillovers. Firms such as Nike, Samsung and LG in Vietnam, the major automotive companies and Foxconn in China, and others operating in Singapore built domestic ecosystems of suppliers and enabled domestic firms to gain a firm foothold in advanced global value chains (Yusuf 2021b). But, these innovation ecosystems did not arise spontaneously. These connections were often created by public agencies that work in partnership with multinational companies and business associations to identify and groom domestic firms that can meet the specific needs.[24]

The essential conditions that allowed EAP and SA to respond and accelerate adoption of available technologies to boost productivity—core public infrastructure, quality human capital, constructive partnership between public sector, industry, academia and above all, a stable, permissive and competitive economic and trade policy—are not yet or are not universally present in LAC, SSA and MENA. These regions face the additional burden of being commodity dependent, which makes sustained progress in productivity growth even more challenging.

The Way Forward?

Over the past decades there have been broad shifts in GDP and productivity growth rates and expansion of the frontier. The extended period of robust expansion of the productivity frontier was followed by much more modest growth, and indeed to periods of volatility and decline, accelerating then slowing convergence of emerging economies with AEs.

The most recent episode of productivity gains seen during, and perhaps triggered by, the pandemic points to a potential new phase of productivity growth. It raises the question of whether and what countries could undertake in priority to spur productivity growth and build foundations for future growth? What lessons are offered by experiences of more successful countries? Could the forthcoming years present an opportunity for countries to leapfrog and accelerate their progress towards the frontier?

---

24. For example, EDB in Singapore forged these linkages through its Local Industry Upgrading Program (LIU) See M. Perry, T.B. Hui (1997) Global manufacturing and local linkages in Singapore. https://citeseerx.ist.psu.edu/viewdoc/download?doi=10.1.1.871.4921&rep=rep1&type=pdf

Although the set of priority actions will necessarily differ by country and their specific context, the following six considerations should factor into long-term planning for countries to increase their productivity:

1. *Promote Shift to Digitalization and New Technologies.* All countries will need to facilitate adoption of digital technologies and the shift to digitization.[25] This particularly important for the services sector now accounting for over 60 per cent of GDP, a sector that in the past has suffered from relatively low productivity. Widespread integration of digitization, AI and machine learning in a broad range of services such as distance education, telehealth, trade, e-government and fintech has transformed these core service sectors. This is similar to what Singapore has done, which experienced a meteoric rise in its services sector with services now accounting for 161 billion USD of exports in 2018.[26] Digitization has also begun to be integrated much further into agriculture, manufacturing and industry to increase sector productivity. There is likewise considerable opportunity to invest in frontier sectors with positive spillover effects such as Renewables. Many EMDEs could replace dissuasive trade and price policies regarding digital investments and equipment, and instead use tax and trade policy to facilitate and accelerate transitions. Many of the ASEAN and so-called Asian tigers have been successful in augmenting productivity by fostering openness and providing incentives for foreign investment.

2. *Ensure Policy Stability and Economic Openness.* There is considerable evidence from countries that have outperformed their regional cohorts, that predictable and stable macroeconomic policies, and openness to trade and Foreign Direct Investment (FDI) are key for long-term investment and raising productivity (Dieppe 2021). Openness to trade and FDI facilitate development of new products and markets, and mobilization of finance and knowhow—positive spillovers that contribute to improved productivity. Further, countries that do not have the advantages of size and location, should pursue regional cooperation and development with neighbours, aligning policy and regulatory regimes, and strengthening infrastructure along trade corridors, increasing mobility of labour and capital.

3. *Invest in Core Infrastructure.* Upgrading the quality of green, climate resilient, and inclusive infrastructure—especially around agglomeration clusters and trade corridors—is a key public good, as evidenced from the EAP experience. Solid infrastructure encourages dynamic firms to achieve greater domestic and global connectivity, to operate more efficiently, and competitively.

4. *Upgrade Human Capital.* Countries need to strengthen the education systems with a focus on quality of outcomes. Special attention to STEM and vocational and technical skills which have been linked to the ability and speed to adopt new technologies and innovations is warranted. Partnerships between government agencies, private sector, and academia have proven valuable to shape the education system and link

---

25. Dieppe projects that if EMDEs were able to close the technological gap with AEs by at least half, they could increase their annual growth rate by a tenth of a percentage point.

26. https://oec.world/en/profile/country/sgp?exportServicesYearsSelector=ServiceYearFlow219&yearSelector1=export-GrowthYear6

it to dynamic skills needs going forward.[27] These partnerships have also given rise to knowledge and innovation clusters that support and facilitate R&D.

5. *Create Supportive Environment for Private Sector Development.* Support private enterprises, especially to SMEs through knowledge and finance, to encourage greater adoption of good management practices and innovations in products and markets. For larger firms, it is important to encourage digitization and FDI for better knowhow, market access and finance. Evidence indicates that larger and fast-growing private firms are better at translating research findings into innovation and are on balance more productive than SOEs (Goswami, Medvedev and Olafson 2019; Yusuf 2021b). It is equally important to foster entrepreneurship which is the link between R&D findings and commercial viability (Yusuf 2021b).

6. *Anticipate and Proactively Deal with Dislocation of Labour and Capital.* Beyond these actions to enable change, countries will need to prepare for the fact that new technologies and innovations will necessarily lead to dislocation and 'creative destruction'. As transitions occur, not fully depreciated but viable investments will become stranded assets, with similar loss of employment in a number of industry segments. Countries can and should develop fair bankruptcy laws to ensure smooth exit and pre-emptively strengthen safety nets to help population—both labour force and communities—likely to be adversely affected by the more productive new technologies (Trebilcock 2014).

These six considerations will inevitably have to be tailored to best take account of specific country circumstances depending on their distance to their productivity frontier, their scope for intersectoral allocation and dispersion of adoption within sectors. EMDEs at greater distance from the productivity frontier, with fewer stranded assets than mature AEs operating close to the frontier, for instance will want to be more aggressive and accelerate reallocation of resources toward more productive sectors. Smaller countries with narrow domestic markets may want to seek greater trade openness and join in regional cooperation and development arrangements. Countries may particularly encourage FDI to innovate in products and markets, gain know-how and obtain financing to sustain productivity growth.

The extended period of rapid GDP and productivity growth from 1950–80 gave way to a period of slower growth, lower productivity and greater volatility, raising doubts that the earlier, optimistic—what some may call deterministic—period could be replicated/sustained. The decidedly more mixed period from around 2011 to today, has opened a window into possibilities—not guarantees—that the path toward growth, greater productivity and higher incomes can be altered. One fact remains; convergence and sustained income growth require continued gains in productivity—unless changes such as highlighted here are adopted vigorously and consistently, some countries are unlikely to be on track for the 'optimistic' scenario presented in Chapter 4.

27. Examples include the 'triple helix' created between universities, industry and government in South Korea (Park and Leydesdorff 2010); the relationship between Japanese automakers and suppliers with the US automotive industry in promoting innovation (Sasakawa Peace Foundation 2021); public-private partnerships for innovation in Austria (OECD 2004); and the Automotive Manufacturing Technical Education Collaborative in the United States (Lorenzo 2012).

Chapter 14: Commodity Price Cycles—Impact on Productivity and Growth Rates

Commodity Price Cycles—Impact on Productivity and Growth Rates

Chapter 14

Claudio Loser, Laura Shelton and Harpaul Kohli

The process of globalization has had a strong positive effect on emerging economies. Many countries changed their structure of production based on their legacy-resource and dynamic comparative advantages. Emerging regions developed their commercial links with the rest of the world based on exports of commodities and other primary products. Over time, different countries moved up the technology scale with more complex industrial and higher value-added and integrate value chain exports, among them China, India, Malaysia and Taiwan R.C. in Asia and Mexico in Latin America.

Nonetheless, commodities, whether they are agricultural products, metals and minerals, or oil and gas, continue to be critical exports of the Emerging Markets and Developing Economies (EMDE) of Latin America, Africa and the Middle East. As of 2019, commodities represented about 44 per cent of Latin America and the Caribbean's exports, 72 per cent for Sub-Saharan Africa and 59 per cent for the Middle East (as approximated by Western Asia and North America) (UNCTAD 2020). By contrast, for Developing Asia and for high-income OECD countries, exports of commodities represented 21 per cent and 22 per cent of total exports, respectively (Loser 2013).

The increase in commodity prices at the beginning of the twenty-first century resulted in a marked improvement in exporters' terms of trade, largely in response to the rapid growth in Asia, in particular China. Terms of trade declined subsequently; although, by 2019, they were still higher by some 20 per cent compared to 2000 for Latin America and for the Middle East and North Africa, and 43 per cent for Sub-Saharan Africa. In contrast, terms of trade for Advanced Economies (AEs) and Developing Asia were about the same as in 2000. In 2020, terms of trade declined for all commodity exporters, but prices recovered strongly in 2021, as the world economy pace improved, and is expected to remain at the new levels in 2022.

As prices increased early in the century, Latin American, African and Middle Eastern countries experienced strong growth and prosperity until the break of the super commodity cycle in 2012–13. The subsequent sharp decline in commodity prices broke the assumption that these countries were at a safe level of security and that they were on the way to a prosperous future.

The new reality became evident during the period 2013–19, particularly in the case of fuels and metals. A slowdown in the advanced and emerging world caused major shocks. Reversals of commodity prices had a major impact on the incomes of all commodity exporters, including through the multiplier effects of a decline in export income, as prices reverted to 2005 levels or even earlier for some metals and fuels (Figure 14.1). Rising prices for raw materials in 2021 generated a perception that the previous difficulties of commodity dependent countries were going to ease considerably. However, historical experience suggests such change may reflect shorter-term circumstances, rather than sustained structural changes.

Figure 14.1: Commodity prices and terms of trade goods

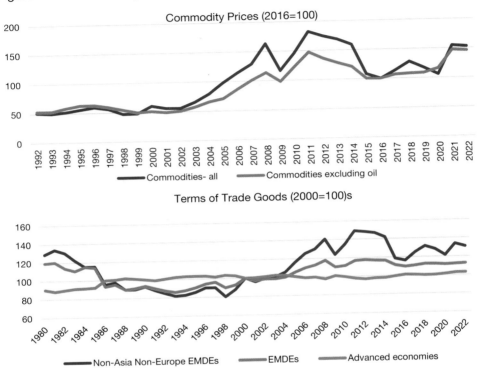

Source: IMF 2021b Centennial Group 2021

Evidence shows that throughout the past sixty years, terms of trade for commodity-exporting countries have presented a highly cyclical pattern. In addition, the terms of trade of these regions were much more volatile than those of the AEs, Emerging Asia and Europe, as suggested by the standard deviation in growth rates (Table 14.1).

A related issue in reviewing the performance of various regions in the last several years is that major commodity-exporting regions were considerably lagging behind Asia, the advanced countries and Emerging Europe. Of equal importance: the growth trajectory for these regions as envisaged at the time of previous studies was much higher than the actual trajectory. In contrast, for the advanced countries, Asia and Emerging Europe, the growth path was very much in line with what was projected at that time. This can be observed in Figures 15.2a and 15.2b, which show the expected path of GDP as of 2015 compared to the actual numbers through 2020, with the most marked decline experienced in regions that depend heavily on commodities. In part, this phenomenon may also be related to the retreat from globalization as

Table 14.1: Regional average change in terms of trade 2000–20

Region	Average per cent change	Standard deviation
Advanced	-0.09	1.46
EMDEs	0.83	3.22
EMDEs Asia	-0.28	2.95
EMDEs Europe	1.33	6.60
LATAM and CA	1.28	4.10
ME and C. Asia	1.86	11.61
Sub-Saharan Africa	2.14	6.97

Source: IMF 2021b Centennial Group 2021

reflected in a shortfall in the volumes of trade with respect to the 2014–15 projections, despite world GDP remaining broadly in line with expectations through 2019, as observed in Figure 14.3. In this regard, an important factor comes into the picture—the interaction between terms of trade and the estimate of total factor productivity, discussed in the next section, which suggest that total factor productivity, excluding effects from terms of trade, has been much lower than previously estimated. The process of globalization, opening of trade opportunities and reduced import restrictions through the beginning of this century have resulted in a major increase in the importance of trade transactions in total GDP. Export and import prices have, therefore, taken on a growing importance in determining nations' real incomes. In particular, the effect of changes in terms of trade is central to the measurement of available resources to a specific economy.

In summary, gains in terms of trade have been a source of unprecedented prosperity in Africa, Latin America and the Middle East. However, it is clear that these trends were reversed in many cases. The impact of lower terms of trade can be staggering—a decline in GDP of half a percentage point for each per centage point change in terms of trade. With the certainty that in the future, prices will continue to fluctuate and that they will not easily reach the levels observed a decade ago on a sustained basis, it is essential that EMDEs prepare proactively for the lower price contingencies. Otherwise, volatility will take over and hinder future growth.

As commodity-importing EMDEs like China, India, and other Asian countries mature demographically and economically, and as new technologies and concerns about climate change are expected to lead to calls for conservation of natural resources, the sharp increase in demand for commodities observed in the last few decades may not be repeated other than for cyclical factors as is the case at present. Moreover, a significant increase in output is taking place for many products in response to the high prices of recent years (oil and gas production through hydraulic fracturing). Exporters have to adapt to these new realities. Complacency among policymakers reflecting a benign view of the future, may prove inimical to their long-term national interest. The past may repeat itself in terms of periods of growth and prosperity followed by times of crisis and needed reform, unless actions are taken.

CLAUDIO LOSER, LAURA SHELTON AND HARPAUL KOHLI

14

Figure 14.2: GDP projections since 2015 (2015=100)

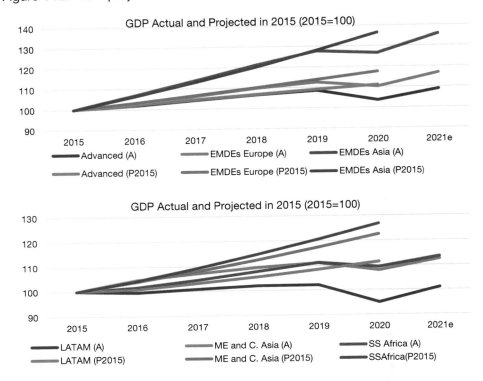

Source: IMF 2021b Centennial Group 2021

Figure 14.3: GDP and trade volume actual and projected in 2015 (2015=100)

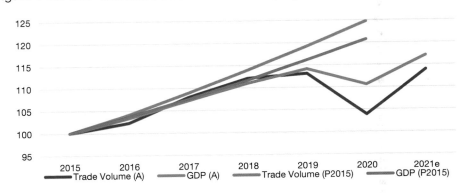

Source: IMF 2021b Centennial Group 2021

Terms of Trade and Total Factor Productivity

The process of globalization, opening of trade opportunities, and reduced import restrictions through the beginning of this century have resulted in a major increase in the importance of trade transactions in total GDP. Export and import prices have, therefore, taken on a growing importance in determining nations' real incomes. In particular, the effect of changes in terms of trade is central to the measurement of available resources to a specific economy.

Over longer periods of time, terms of trade have fluctuated markedly, as discussed above. This has affected the level of prosperity of commodity exporters in Africa and Latin America in the last ten years, and in the Middle East over an even longer period. When the terms of trade change, there is a significant divergence between the movements of GDP in output terms and real income. The difference between the change in GDP in volume terms and real income is generally described as the 'trading gain' (or loss). The differences between movements in GDP in volume terms and real GDP including price effects, may be large. In measuring the contributors to growth in GDP, as is applied in the Centennial model, these are divided into two variables—labour force and capital increase, measured by investment minus depreciation— and, as a residual, the gains in productivity, measuring implicitly technological and institutional change, improved levels of education and, by default, the impact of terms of trade.

Work conducted by Centennial Group suggests a significant correlation between the estimates of total factor productivity (TFP) and movements of terms of trade. The work consists of an econometric analysis linking the estimate of TFP with terms of trade as an independent variable, together with capital stock as a trend variable, and with the understanding that most of the changes in total factor productivity not associated with human capital generally reflect improved technology, normally embodied in new investment. A supplementary analysis, presented below, analyses the effect of terms of trade on GDP growth, distinguishing commodity dependent and nondependent countries.

The regression formulation is as follows:

Log 10TFP= intersect + a*log 10Terms of Trade + c*log 10 capital Stock

Where log TFP is the estimated rate of growth of total factor productivity, as a function of the rates of change in the capital stock and the level of terms of trade plus a constant.

The regression analysis is based on historical information for six key regions—the advanced countries, Emerging and Developing Asia, Emerging Europe, Latin America and the Caribbean, the Middle East and North Africa and Sub-Saharan Africa. The data on total factor productivity and capital stock accumulation are obtained from the Centennial Growth Model, updated as of April 2021. Data on terms of trade of goods is obtained from the IMF WEO database. The data for the regressions generally start in 1979, with data for Sub-Saharan Africa starting in 1985 and for Emerging Europe in 1989. The results for the regressions are presented in Table 14.2. It includes for each variable the regression coefficient, t, and p statistics, R^2 and the number of annual observations.

From these results, it can be observed that terms of trade are a significant explanatory variable of measured TFP, even though slightly less so in the case of Emerging Europe. Capital accumulation is also a strong explanatory variable, with the exception of the Middle East.

Because of the significant changes and standard deviation of the variable (see Table 1.51), the effect of terms of trade changes tends to be significant in the case of the three recently

Table 14.2: Regression analysis—Total factor productivity, terms of trade and capital accumulation

Region	Intercept	Terms of trade	Capital accumulation	R^2	Observations
Advanced Countries	0.697	0.234	0.411	0.979	42
t stat	4.287	2.707	36.781		
p stat	0.000	0.010	0.000		
Emerging and Developing Asia	1.777	-0.313	0.421	0.995	41
t stat	4.287	2.707	36.781		
p stat	0.000	0.010	0.000		
Emerging Europe	0.389	0.195	0.561	0.831	32
t stat	2.514	1.856	6.771		
p stat	0.018	0.074	0.000		
Latin America and Caribbean	1.469	0.201	0.054	0.745	40
t stat	27.575	5.705	3.276		
p stat	0.000	0.000	0.002		
The Middle East and North Africa	1.436	0.223	0.015	0.568	41
t stat	21.057	6.164	0.649		
p stat	0.000	0.000	0.520		
Sub-Saharan Africa	1.091	0.280	0.175	0.938	36
t stat	19.468	6.885	8.852		
p stat	0.000	0.000	0.000		

Source: IMF 2021b Centennial Group 2021

Table 14.3: Average annual per cent change in TFP, total and net terms of trade

Region	Average annual per cent change in TFP	Change net of T of T	Average estimated per cent change in TFP	Change net of T of T
Advanced Countries	0.840	0.825	1.062	1.047
Emerging and Developing Asia	3.126	3.113	3.314	3.301
Emerging Europe	2.474	2.214	2.107	1.848
Latin America and Caribbean	-0.213	-0.216	0.126	0.123
The Middle East and N. Africa	-0.677	-0.960	-0.039	-0.322
Sub-Saharan Africa	0.572	0.424	0.694	0.546

Source: IMF 2021b Centennial Group 2021

lagging regions: Latin America, Sub-Saharan Africa, and the Middle East and Central Asia, with a much smaller effect on Asia and the advanced countries.

Table 14.3 shows the average annual and the average estimated TFP growth for all the regions. The estimates include the numbers for unadjusted TFP and those numbers where the effect of the terms of trade has been subtracted, that is, measuring non-terms-of-trade TFP changes. The rates of change, well described by the Centennial Model, show particularly high rates of growth for Asia, the advanced countries and Emerging Europe (the last case is a reflection of the collapse of the Soviet Union and the integration of the region with Advanced Europe). The TFP growth rates for Sub-Saharan Africa are relatively low, while those for the Middle East and North Africa, and for Latin America and the Caribbean, are negative or extremely low for the period under consideration. Looking at the path of commodity prices and terms of trade in the last forty years, it is possible to distinguish two clear periods: first, from the early 1980s to the mid-1990s and second, from the late 1990s to the mid-2000s. For the first period, when commodity prices and terms of trade were falling, TFP may have been underestimated historically, while they were overestimated subsequently in the second period, as terms of trade increased for the commodity-exporting regions. For the advanced, Asian, and emerging European countries, the impact was likely the reverse, but the movement of relative prices was considerably narrower for these countries, with limited impact on TFP.

As terms of trade turned against the commodity exporters in the three lagging regions in more recent years, unadjusted TFP growth rates declined, impacting actual GDP in comparison with what was projected in 2014–15 on the basis of a previously overestimated TFP (although, at the time, serious warnings had already emerged with respect to the growth prospects of commodity dependent regions). The regression analysis indicates that if the effect of terms of trade is subtracted from movements in TFP, the rate of growth attributable to all other factors is much lower than the measured values for the period 2000–19. The difference in growth rate of TFP for emerging economies, including and excluding the terms of trade effect, could be as high as two percentage points for the period. This is consistent with the results for the commodity exporters, although less marked for Africa.

The analysis of the results shows that in the cases of the advanced and the emerging Asian countries, the impact of terms of trade on the measurement of TFP is negligible, and both regions show strong innovation. This is also the case, although to a lesser degree, for Emerging Europe. In the case of Latin America and Sub-Saharan Africa, the effect of terms of trade in the unadjusted measurement of TFP is significant, and, as suggested above, it is clear that TFP was underestimated initially and overestimated subsequently, with little trend growth at all. Probably the most dramatic case in terms of mismeasurement is that of the Middle East, where total factor productivity is estimated to have grown at a slow rate once the effect of the energy prices is subtracted from the estimate. Figures A1–A6 in Appendix A show for each region the measured and estimated TFP, the TFP (net of terms of trade), and the effect of terms of trade.

The Growth Behaviour of Commodity Dependent and Non-dependent Country Groups

A separate but complementary analysis reinforces the results presented above. Again, based on the Centennial Growth model, additional econometric analysis shows the high sensitivity of economic growth of primary commodity dependent countries to changes in prices. Again, the results are based on an econometric analysis, in this case, working with groups of countries classified on the basis of their dependence on commodity exports, by type of commodity (agricultural, fuels, minerals and metals), in comparison with countries with diversified exports. Furthermore, a distinction is made between countries currently defined as advanced and those defined as EMDEs. As with the previous analysis, this analysis links the estimate of TFP with terms of trade as an independent variable, together with capital stock as a trend variable, and with the understanding that most of the changes in total factor productivity not associated with human capital generally reflect improved technology normally embodied in new investment. The universe of this exercise consists of 104 commodity dependent countries and eighty-seven non-commodity dependent countries. Within these, there are thirty-five agricultural EMDEs and two agricultural advanced countries, thirty-two fuel-dependent EMDEs and two fuel-dependent advanced countries, and thirty-two metal-dependent EMDEs and one metal-dependent advanced country. Among non-commodity dependent countries, in turn, according to the current UNCTAD classification, there are thirty-three advanced countries and fifty-four EMDEs (UNCTAD 2019).

The statistical analysis links GDP with a commodity price index as an independent variable, together with capital stock accumulation and changes in the labour force as tend variables, and again, with the understanding that changes in total factor productivity reflected in GDP growth will be influenced by both these variables. A dummy variable is included for the years 2009 and 2020 to account for two major and unusually disruptive events—the Great Recession and the COVID-19 pandemic. In this case, the regression formulation is as follows:

Log 10 GDP= intersect + a * log 10 employment + b*log 10 capital Stock + c*log 10 Real Commodity Price Index + d*log 10 Dummy for Major Shocks

Where real commodity indices are estimated using IMF commodity price indices, deflated by the manufacturing export price index for advanced economies (IMF 2021b),[1] and the historical data on GDP, capital stock and employment are obtained from the Centennial Group Growth Model database.

The regression analysis is based on information for five broad country groups—commodity dependent countries, agricultural commodity dependent countries, fuel commodity dependent countries, mineral commodity dependent countries and non-commodity dependent countries. For each group, the analysis focuses on all countries, as well as advanced and EMDEs countries separately within each group. In addition, among non-commodity dependent EMDEs, calculations are conducted excluding China and India, by far the most important countries in the group. The data for the regressions start in 1992. The results for the regressions are presented in Annex A, Table A1. It includes for each variable, the regression coefficient, the t- and p-statistics, and the R^2.

From these results, it can be observed that commodity prices are a significant explanatory variable of GDP behaviour, though less so in the case of commodity dependent advanced countries, and more specifically, advanced mineral exporters. Capital accumulation and labour, to a lesser degree are also strong explanatory variables, particularly when analysing all commodity

---

1. For each group of specific export dependence, the commodity price index for that group is used. For broader groups, namely, commodity dependent and non-commodity dependent countries, the general all-inclusive deflated commodity index is used.

dependent countries. The dummy variable for major shocks is particularly relevant for advanced countries, but not for EMDEs, mainly because the crises of 2009 and of 2020 were transmitted through commodity prices and exports for those countries and not directly to their economic activity. In addition, for non-commodity dependent EMDEs, this variable had limited explanatory power beyond the predictive value of the other variables that are considerably less insulated from shocks than in advanced economies.

Because of the significant importance of commodities in EMDEs exports, the impact of prices changes over time has tended to have very significant effect on economic growth. While commodity price behaviour is generally cyclical, during the period under analysis (1992–2020), there was an upward trend. In other words, even after the sharp decline in commodity prices after 2012–13, prices in real terms remained significantly higher than prior to the boom of the first twelve years of the century. On this basis, a key question is the effect of these high prices on economic growth, answered in a somewhat different framework in the previous section.

The key issue is whether the average economic growth did not fully reflect increases in labour, capital and factor productivity. For that purpose, Table 14.4 shows the effect of eliminating the impact of commodity prices from the estimated equations—that is, assuming that there is no change in prices by either keeping them at the base value or at the average for the period. The table shows the average annual and average estimated growth for each group of countries.

Table 14.4: Average percentage change (1992–2020)

	Actual GDP	Estimated GDP	Estimated net of comm. prices
Commodity Dependent	2.25	2.48	1.97
Commodity Dependent EMDEs	2.32	2.59	1.99
Commodity Dependent Advanced	1.83	1.81	1.87
Agricultural Dependent	2.68	2.80	2.42
Agricultural Dependent EMDEs	2.53	2.70	2.22
Agricultural Dependent Advanced	3.24	3.23	3.36
Fuel Dependent	2.02	2.31	1.87
Fuel Dependent EMDEs	1.79	2.12	1.64
Fuel Dependent Advanced	1.30	1.46	1.25
Mineral Dependent	3.55	3.79	3.63
Mineral Dependent EMDEs	3.88	4.22	3.94
Mineral Dependent Advanced	3.00	2.84	2.73
Non-commodity Dependent	3.24	3.34	3.35
Non-commodity Dependent EMDEs	5.45	5.60	5.29
Non-commodity Dependent Advanced	1.83	1.81	1.87
Non-commodity Dependent EMDEs, except China	4.00	4.23	4.02
Non-commodity Dependent EMDEs, except China and India	3.89	3.60	3.35

Source: IMF 2021b Centennial Group 2021

Figures A7–14 in the Appendix show for each group of countries, the actual and estimated rate of economic growth, as well as estimated growth net of commodity prices. They clearly show the marked effect on growth, of maintaining constant real prices among EMDEs. No significant deviations are observed for other groups, although individual countries may behave differently and thus deviate from the broad averages presented here.

Table 14.5 presents the possible effect of commodity prices on future performance. Using a fifteen-year horizon, the table shows the estimated average rate of growth, according to the newest Centennial Growth Model run. The first column shows the average rate of growth for the various country groups under the Baseline Scenario of the model, presented in Chapter 4,. The second column presents the projections under the regression model presented above, with the capital and labour values from the Centennial Model and with no change in commodity prices. As the growth estimates under the Centennial Model may implicitly contain a TFP estimate that includes the historical commodity price trend, an alternative corrected series is presented in column three. The estimate is simply the Centennial Model estimates, corrected for the difference between the trend commodity price increase and an assumption of no change in

Table 14.5: Average percentage change (2020–35)

	Estimated GDP (Centennial model)	Estimated net of Commodity Price Effect	Commodity Prices Regression
(No price change)	2.25	2.48	1.97
Commodity Dependent	3.03	2.51	1.41
Commodity Dependent EMDEs	3.15	2.55	1.28
Commodity Dependent Advanced	2.21	2.27	2.34
Agricultural Dependent (EMDEs)	3.03	2.46	2.08
Agricultural Dependent EMDEs	3.12	2.39	2.34
Agricultural Dependent Advanced	2.09	2.33	3.02
Fuel Dependent	2.61	1.79	0.54
Fuel Dependent EMDEs	2.73	1.85	-0.32
Fuel Dependent Advanced	1.92	1.46	-0.27
Mineral Dependent	3.85	3.62	3.37
Mineral Dependent EMDEs	4.50	4.05	3.71
Mineral Dependent Advanced	2.41	2.21	1.82
Non-commodity Dependent	3.52	3.31	2.79
Non-commodity Dependent EMDEs	4.71	4.38	3.99
Non-commodity Dependent Advanced	1.97	2.04	1.11
Non-commodity Dependent EMDEs, except China	4.72	4.43	3.67
Non-commodity Dependent EMDEs, except China & India	3.74	3.40	3.06

Source: IMF 2021b Centennial Group 2021

commodity prices.[2] As expected, the scenario based on the regression presented here shows a sharp correction in the rate of growth for all regions—most likely an over-correction. In turn, the third column shows a somewhat lower downward adjustment for all EMDEs regions, with actual higher estimated rates of growth for commodity dependent advanced countries, except for a few fuel- and metal-dependent countries.

Conclusions and Main Policy Implications

1. With regard to total factor productivity on a geographical basis, for the advanced and the emerging Asian countries, the impact of terms of trade on the measurement of TFP is negligible, and both regions show strong innovation. This is also the case, although to a lesser degree, for Emerging Europe.

2. In the case of Latin America and Sub-Saharan Africa, the effect of terms of trade in the unadjusted measurement of TFP is significant. TFP was underestimated late in the twentieth century and overestimated subsequently, with little trend growth at all. The mismeasurement may have most significant effects in the Middle East, with a very slow growth in productivity when adjusted.

3. When analysed in terms of the effect of export composition on GDP growth, non-commodity dependent EMDEs show a much higher rate of average growth than commodity dependent groups. In contrast, there is no difference among advanced economies.

4. Among commodity dependent countries, metal and mineral exporters have shown a higher rate of GDP growth, followed by agricultural exporters. Exporters of fuels, the third category, show by far the lowest average growth rate.

5. Non-commodity dependent exporters excluding China and India, by far the largest countries in the group, show strong economic growth. While commodity specialization plays a role, most likely, the results suggest weakness of policies in response to commodity-dependence more than the variability of prices itself. There are no significant differences in performance among advanced countries.

6. When the effect of commodity prices is subtracted, the corrected average rate of growth is much lower for commodity dependent EMDEs. No such effect is observed for nondependent countries. In fact, there is a slight upward correction among advanced economies or only a small decline. The downward correction for EMDEs is more marked for agricultural exporters and fuel exporters, with a much more limited impact among mineral-dependent exporters.

7. The high impact of commodity prices on exporters strongly suggests that total factor productivity has been far lower than normally assumed, and that as prices declined, the alleged improvement in productivity vanished to a large extent, mainly in Latin America, the Middle East and Africa, consistent with the findings in previous sections.

8. For the future, if average commodity prices show no trend increase, growth for the commodity dependent countries could well be lower than the Centennial Model suggests. There will likely be considerable variability in prices with boom-and-bust periods, which

---

2. The correction is estimated as the difference between the projected results in the regressions in this section assuming a growth rate in prices equivalent to the trend for the historical period (1992–2020), and the results assuming no change in prices. The difference in growth rates is then subtracted from the Unadjusted Growth Model, thus preserving the non-price TFP effect.

again calls for improved countercyclical and expenditure evening policies over time, as consistently highlighted through this and other chapters.

Based on the experience of the last quarter century and on the assumption that terms of trade will not change in the future, new estimates of future growth within the Centennial model suggest a lower growth path, as discussed in Chapter 4. It is important to note in this regard that terms of trade today are well above the levels observed in the last part of the last century and earlier this century.

At present, there are no expectations of sharp increases in commodity prices other than those of a cyclical nature, due to changing demand patterns, like slowing growth in China and the advanced countries, concerns about global warming, movement away from fossil fuels and towards renewables (as suggested by the Net Zero growth strategies) even if in an uneven fashion, and a changing technological landscape.

Except for the Asian EMDEs, convergence to the current advanced countries is less likely than had been expected previously, based on corrected TFP change. Recent disappointing performance of the commodity exporting EMDEs means they need high TFP growth, even higher than what the Centennial Model predicts in its Central Scenario. Major structural changes will be necessary, beyond macroeconomic stability, if they want to improve on their relative performance, and overcome the so-called resource curse, and converge again.

Appendix 14.1: Additional Figures

Figure A14.1: Total factor productivity for advanced countries

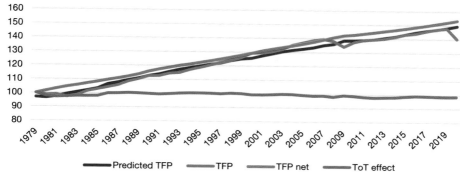

Source: IMF 2021b Centennial Group 2021

Figure A14.2: Total factor productivity for Emerging Asia

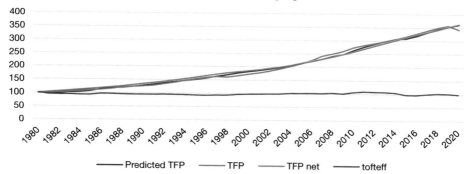

Source: IMF 2021b Centennial Group 2021

Figure A14.3: Total factor productivity for Emerging Europe

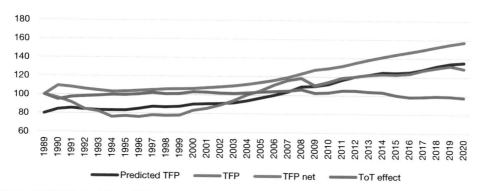

Source: IMF 2021b Centennial Group 2021

Figure A14.4: Total factor productivity for LATAM

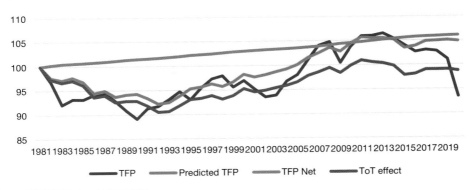

Source: IMF 2021b Centennial Group 2021

Figure A14.5: Total factor productivity for Sub-Saharan Africa

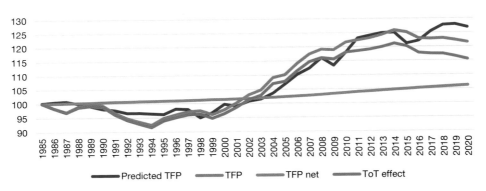

Source: IMF 2021b Centennial Group 2021

Figure A14.6: Total factor productivity for the Middle East and North Africa

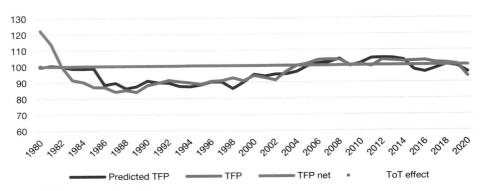

Source: IMF 2021b Centennial Group 2021

Table A14.1: Regression analysis: GDP growth, real commodity indices, capital accumulation, labour growth and major economic shocks (logs, 1992–2020)

Regression	Intercept	Labour	Capital accumulation	Real commodity prices	Dummy (2009 and 2020)	R²
Commodity Dependent EMDEs						
Coefficient	0.41	-0.09	0.62	0.26	0.00	0.99
t stat	2.34	-0.54	7.25	9.92	-0.11	
p stat	0.03	0.60	0.00	0.00	0.91	
Commodity Dependent Advanced						
Coefficient	-3.21	2.16	0.47	-0.03	-0.02	0.99
t stat	-2.27	2.34	2.17	-1.72	-4.05	
p stat	0.03	0.03	0.04	0.10	0.00	
Agricultural Dependent						
Coefficient	-0.80	0.99	0.10	0.31	-0.01	0.99
t stat	-6.97	5.57	0.76	5.03	-1.00	
p stat	0.00	0.00	0.45	0.00	0.33	
Agricultural-dependent EMDEs						
Coefficient	-1.27	1.07	0.17	0.39	-0.01	0.99
t stat	-7.30	6.00	1.69	5.62	-0.87	
p stat	0.00	0.00	0.10	0.00	0.39	
Agricultural-dependent Advanced						
Coefficient	-0.10	0.66	0.51	-0.12	-0.02	1.00
t stat	-2.24	7.09	6.07	-3.14	-2.61	
p stat	0.03	0.00	0.00	0.00	0.01	
Fuel Dependent						
Coefficient	1.14	-0.50	0.72	0.20	0.01	0.98
t stat	3.28	-1.74	6.47	8.48	0.50	
p stat	0.00	0.09	0.00	0.00	0.62	
Fuel-dependent EMDEs						
Coefficient	1.79	-0.92	0.79	0.22	0.01	0.98
t stat	4.76	-3.25	8.10	8.69	0.64	
p stat	0.00	0.00	0.00	0.00	0.53	
Fuel-dependent Advanced						
Coefficient	-2.56	2.04	0.11	0.11	0.02	0.94
t stat	-5.65	9.00	1.20	4.44	1.40	
p stat	0.00	0.00	0.24	0.00	0.17	

Source: IMF 2021b Centennial Group 2021

Table A14.1: Regression analysis: GDP growth, real commodity indices, capital accumulation, labour growth and major economic shocks (logs, 1992–2020) (cont.)

Regression	Intercept	Labour	Capital accumulation	Real commodity prices	Dummy (2009 and 2020)	R²
Mineral Dependent						
Coefficient	-0.95	1.24	0.19	0.04	-0.02	1.00
t stat	-8.58	7.90	1.80	2.85	-2.25	
p stat	0.00	0.00	0.08	0.01	0.03	
Mineral Dependent EMDEs						
Coefficient	-1.04	1.06	0.36	0.08	-0.02	0.99
t stat	-8.45	7.02	3.99	3.80	-1.83	
p stat	0.00	0.00	0.00	0.00	0.08	
Mineral Dependent Advanced						
Coefficient	3.08	-2.77	2.22	0.04	0.00	0.99
t stat	4.64	-4.47	7.90	1.64	-0.38	
p stat	0.00	0.00	0.00	0.11	0.71	
Non-commodity Dependent						
Coefficient	-1.35	0.95	0.68	0.04	-0.01	1.00
t stat	-8.25	8.72	24.19	3.86	-3.84	
p stat	0.00	0.00	0.00	0.00	0.00	
Non-commodity Dependent EMDEs						
Coefficient	-1.82	1.06	0.72	0.14	0.00	1.00
t stat	-8.53	8.16	31.74	8.10	-0.51	
p stat	0.00	0.00	0.00	0.00	0.61	
Non-commodity Dependent Advanced						
Coefficient	-3.21	2.16	0.47	-0.03	-0.02	0.99
t stat	-2.27	2.34	2.17	-1.72	-4.05	
p stat	0.03	0.03	0.04	0.10	0.00	
Non-commodity Dependent EMDEs, except China						
Coefficient	-1.13	0.73	0.73	0.09	-0.01	1.00
t stat	-6.83	5.66	16.18	4.63	-1.02	
p stat	0.00	0.00	0.00	0.00	0.32	
Non-commodity Dependent EMDEs, except China & India						
Coefficient	-1.08	0.69	0.74	0.11	0.00	1.00
t stat	-6.17	4.17	10.08	4.84	-0.12	
p stat	0.00	0.00	0.00	0.00	0.90	

Regression Format: log GDP= intersect +a*log Labor +b*log capital Accum +c*Commodity Prices +d*log Dummy
Source: IMF 2021b Centennial Group 2021

Figure A14.7: Commodity dependent EMDEs GDP (1991=100)

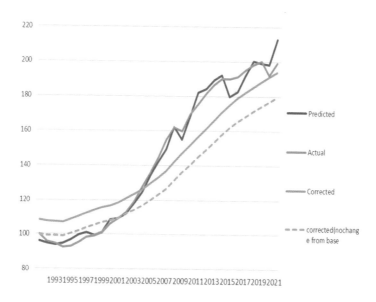

Source: IMF 2021b Centennial Group 2021

Figure A14.8: Commodity dependent advanced GDP (1991=100)

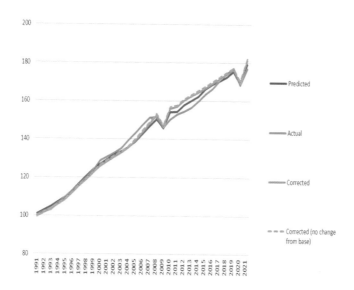

Source: IMF 2021b Centennial Group 2021

Figure A14.9: Non-commodity dependent EMDEs GDP (1991=100)

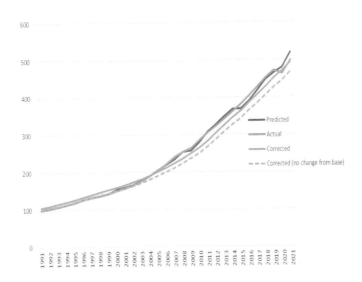

Source: IMF 2021b Centennial Group 2021

Figure A14.10: Non-commodity dependent EMDEs (excluding China and India) GDP (1991=100)

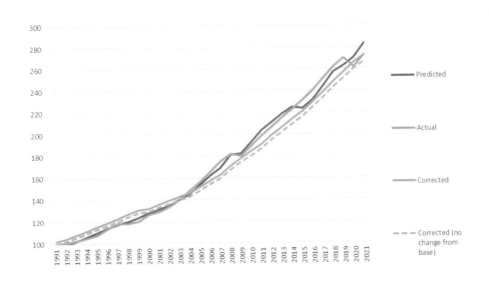

Source: IMF 2021b Centennial Group 2021

Figure A14.11: Non-commodity dependent advanced GDP (1991=100)

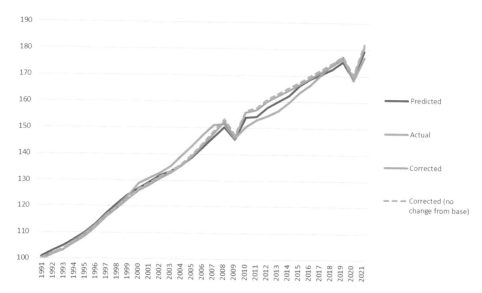

Source: IMF 2021b Centennial Group 2021

Figure A14.12: Agricultural commodity dependent GDP (1991=100)

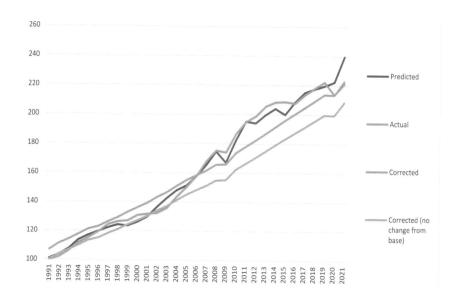

Source: IMF 2021b Centennial Group 2021

Figure A14.13: Fuel dependent GDP (1991=100)

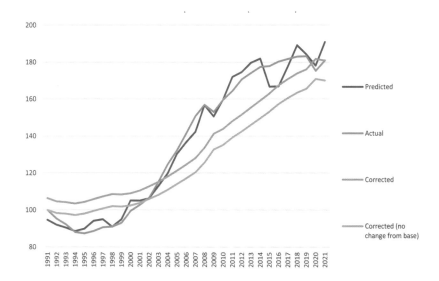

Source: IMF 2021b Centennial Group 2021

Figure A14.14: Metal dependent GDP (1991=100)

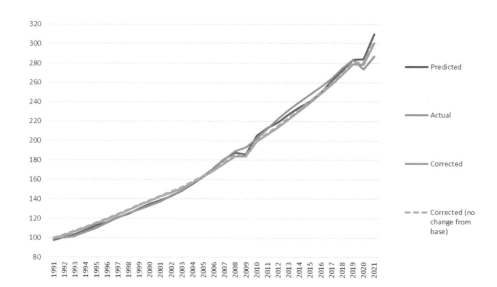

Source: IMF 2021b Centennial Group 2021

Chapter 15: Future Prospects of Africa—The Final Development Frontier and a Global Common

Future Prospects of Africa—The Final Development Frontier and a Global Common

Chapter 15 | Jean-Louis Sarbib, Celestin Monga and Katie Ford

When the Emerging Markets Forum published *Africa Reset: A New Way Forward*[1] in 2017, the book presented two scenarios: a continuation of prevailing trends or convergence with the rest of the world in terms of per capita income. Convergence would require an 'average per capita GDP growth of 3.5 per cent or more starting in 2017' (Ahlers and Kohli 2017). Up until the end of 2019, only a few countries south of the Sahara were on the convergence path (Ethiopia, Ghana, Mozambique, Rwanda, Sierra Leone and Tanzania). Many more remained mired on the less hopeful trend. Overall, the countries south of the Sahara (SSA) were plotting an uneasy middle path between the two scenarios, while the long-term trends that have hampered SSA's transformation continued to prevail as the COVID-19 pandemic struck.

This chapter will take a comprehensive look at Africa and its prospects in a changing world. Part I briefly reviews the status of Africa (north and south of the Sahara) before the pandemic, highlighting the progress made and factors that have contributed to the continent's relative improvement over a period of about twenty-five years. It also discusses the persistent challenges on the path to transformation. Part II assesses the pandemic's impact on Africa—from macroeconomic shocks to consequences for the social sectors and poverty. Part III outlines Africa's long-term economic prospects under three scenarios (basic/central, strong policies, and poor policies) and identifies four interconnected threats that should be the focus of public policies (climate change, very rapid population growth, deteriorating security in several regions, and heightened geo-political tensions). For the continent to achieve the African Union's vision of Africa 2063 and take its rightful place in the world as a major source of global demand, stability and peace, Africa's leadership must be bolder, govern better, and deliver results. In addition, the current mostly asymmetric cooperation between Africa and its traditional partners in the West (many of them former colonizers) must evolve to become a balanced and mutually beneficial partnership, enhanced by a faster deepening of cooperation across the Global South (South–South cooperation).

Part I. Africa Before the Pandemic: A Quick Stocktaking[2]

Africa is the world's second largest continent, home to a rapidly growing population of 1.2 billion in 2020 that is the youngest in the world with a median age of 19.7 years and 40 per cent of the population is fifteen years and younger. Of the continent's fifty-four countries, sixteen are landlocked, and all vary in population size from the largest, Nigeria, with 206 million inhabitants, to the smallest, Seychelles, with 99,000. The people of Africa speak between 1,250 and 2,100 native languages

---

1. The book was focussed on Sub-Saharan Africa (SSA).
2. A more detailed version of this chapter will be available online at www.emergingmarketsforum.org

(Heine 2000), with strong allegiances to their nation and pride in their ethnic and cultural heritage. While it is important to keep such diversity in mind with regard to Africa, some broad similarities exist, mostly in the inability of many, if not most, African countries in SSA to radically transform their economies and to converge with the rest of the emerging and developing world.

Since independence, the story of Africa's economic development is one of broad swings largely linked to commodity price cycles between periods of rapid growth (the 1960s and the 1970s) and periods of stalled progress (the 1980s and the first half of the 1990s), with a return to more hopeful prospects since the mid-1990s. Overall, however, with a GDP per capita of about US$2,000 (constant 2018 prices), Africa continues to trail the emerging and developing world, with significant differences between the countries north and south of the Sahara (Figure 15.1). The countries of North Africa have more diversified economies and stronger links with advanced economies, especially the European Union and the United States. They can constitute a bridge between the two sides of the Sahara, facilitate SSA's reach into richer markets and provide a source of experience and dynamism, especially under the Africa Continental Free Trade Area.

Figure 15.1: Real GDP per capita as per cent of world per GDP (in 2018 prices)

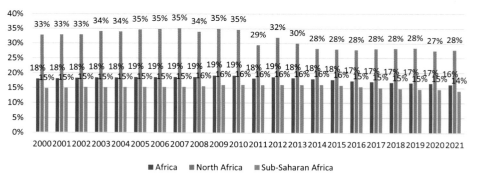

Source: Centennial Group 2021

Many Factors Have Contributed to Africa's Relative Improvement over the Last Twenty-five Years

Since the mid-1990s, the countries of Africa have, with some notable exceptions, expanded at a robust average (4.5 per cent in terms of GDP for SSA till 2015). They improved and stabilized their policy environment, diversified their sources of development finance and participated more fully in the global economy. The results have been a reduction in the rate of poverty in SSA from 54 per cent of the population in 1990 to 41 per cent in 2015, even though the poverty headcount has increased from 278 to 413 million due to rapid demographic growth (Beegle and Christiaensen 2019).[3]

- Policies have improved. When comparing the World Bank Country Performance and Institutions assessments for SSA with that of the world and East Asia and Pacific (EAP)

---

3. Note that the numbers apply to Sub-Saharan Africa. Poverty is most acute in rural areas and the Sahelian zone.

—the most dynamic region, the broad performance trends of Africa have followed the rest of the world (with Africa doing better than EAP on structural policies in 2018 and 2019 and consistently on social inclusion/equity) but with the biggest performance gap vis à vis EAP in public sector management and institutions.

- More domestic resources for the economy. Domestically, governments in Africa raise taxes equivalent to 16 per cent of the GDP, a figure that has been increasing steadily since 2010. The inclusion of natural resource revenue raises that figure to 18 per cent, which is still short of the levels needed to meet development needs and requires additional efforts on domestic resource mobilization. To finance the economy, African banks are now generally well-capitalized, liquid, solvent and resilient to liquidity and credit risk. While micro- and large enterprises have good access to credit, there is still a lack of proper long-term finance for small and medium enterprises. Credit to the private sector varies across the continent with Western and Central Africa trailing behind Eastern, Southern, and North Africa. Overall, across Africa, credit remains well below the levels in OECD countries or in East Asia. In some sectors, such as banking, telecommunications, mining, construction, air transport and agribusiness, large African firms have emerged and expanded beyond their countries of origin and are also participating increasingly in global value chains. They are concentrated in South Africa, Nigeria, Kenya, Morocco and Egypt (Abreha et al. 2020).

- More external sources of finance. After roughly three decades (1960–95) of relying mostly on official assistance (ODA), Africa, especially SSA, has diversified its sources of external finance. Today, the combination of public private partnerships, FDI, sovereign borrowings and remittances from the diaspora dwarfs official development assistance (Figure 15.2). The overall volume of external financing remains, however, well below Africa's needs. FDI has grown but remains relatively small by global standards. The more diversified economies, as well as those doing better regarding reforms, are the main destinations. In 2019, while extractive industries attracted 36 per cent of the total volume of investment, the largest number of projects were in telecommunications, media, technology, consumer products and transport and automotive (EY 2019).

Figure 15.2: External resource flows to Sub-Saharan Africa 1990–2022

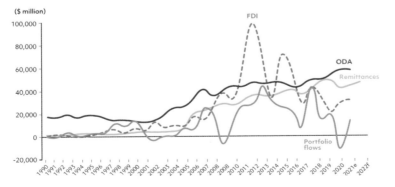

Source: Ratha et al. 2020

JEAN-LOUIS SARBIB, CELESTIN MONGA AND KATIE FORD

- The growing role of China. Over the period 2016–20, China was the largest source of FDI with a total of US$70.6 billion compared to US$23.8 billion from the UAE, 23.7 billion from the US, US$19.5 billion from France and US$16.3 billion from the UK (EY 2021). China, the world's largest bilateral creditor, holds at least 21 per cent of African debt with around 30 per cent of 2021 debt service being payments to China (Acker et al. 2021). In addition to economic and social infrastructure throughout the continent, China has invested in low-skill manufacturing in Ethiopia.
- Renewed interest from North African countries. North African countries (Morocco, Algeria, Tunisia and Egypt)[4] are showing an increasing interest in SSA for a variety of reasons: geopolitics, economics, security and migration. Another incentive to look south was the lack of progress in regional integration across the countries of the Maghreb due to the continuing tension between Algeria and Morocco that paralyzes the Arab Maghreb Union. Between 2003 and 2017, Moroccan FDI in Africa totalled roughly US$10 billion, making up around 60 per cent of the country's overseas investment. By 2017, Morocco had become the leading African investor in West Africa and was second only to South Africa in being the largest African investor across the continent. Tunisia starts from a low base: in 2018, only 3.1 per cent of Tunisian exports went to SSA, representing little increase from a share of 2.8 per cent just ten years earlier (Berthaud 2019, 6). Long focussed on the Middle East, Egypt is taking a fresh look at Africa. The shift reflects the changing nature of the security risks that Egypt faces with the spread of jihadist groups across North Africa and the Sahel, and continued turmoil in Libya and Sudan. Most significantly, Ethiopia's decision in 2011 to begin building the Grand Ethiopian Renaissance Dam (GERD) on the Blue Nile, close to its border with Sudan threatened Egypt with the disruption of the water supply, on which it overwhelmingly depends.[5]
- Sovereign borrowing on private markets. Except for South Africa and the Seychelles, SSA countries had not issued sovereign bonds in international capital markets until 2007. As of July 2021, this financial instrument has reached US$136 billion with twenty-one SSA countries now holding one or more outstanding Eurobonds. The pandemic has so far not slowed demand. In 2021 alone, African sovereigns issued US$11.8 billion worth of Eurobonds. While some of this US$11.8 billion was issued by Egypt ($3.75 billion issuance), most of it was issued by SSA economies. These borrowings remain necessary at least in the medium-term, given the time needed to improve domestic resource mobilization further and to broaden the tax base in the face of pressing development needs. However, they need to be made carefully and prudently, as they are often more expensive and create more difficulty for their inclusion in debt reduction initiatives, if and when needed. The tightening of monetary policy in rich countries to mitigate inflationary pressures creates additional risks for servicing this kind of debt.
- Remittances. Migration out of Africa is significant (40 million Africans left their countries of origin in 2019) and the African diaspora has become an important source of external finance. The flow of remittances has grown steadily from about US$50 billion in 2010 to an estimated US$90 billion in 2021, after a smaller than expected dip in 2020 because

---

4. Since the fall of Muammar Gaddafi, Libya has been focussed on its internal problems even though the country's troubles have played a major role in the security issues affecting its southern neighbours, particularly in the Sahel.
5. This section draws from Dworkin (2020).

of the COVID-19 pandemic. These flows help meet basic needs and smoothen household consumption and welfare, often for the most disadvantaged groups.

- The decreasing importance of ODA. After long being the main source of external financing for SSA, ODA is playing a lesser role, with many countries often seeking other sources that limit transaction costs and sometimes, conditionality. ODA remains, however, important for the poorest countries, where it continues to represent a significant proportion of GNI (7.5 per cent of GNI in Burkina Faso, 6.3 per cent in Chad, and 11.1 per cent in Niger compared to 3.2 per cent in Kenya, 1.4 per cent in Ghana, and 2.1 per cent in Côte d'Ivoire) (World Bank 2021b).

Significant Challenges Remain for a True African Transformation

Despite the progress outlined above, true economic transformation and convergence with the rest of the world will require addressing the long-standing structural constraints that continue to limit Africa's prospects. The principal constraints are well known and include deficient economic infrastructure, a poorly educated workforce, low productivity, continued dependency on primary commodities, limited intracontinental trade, growing debt distress, lack of dynamism of the largest economies and weak governance. These issues have been thoroughly analysed in the literature, thus only the most salient points are mentioned here.

- Deficient economic infrastructure. The AfDB Infrastructure Development Index provides a composite assessment of four main infrastructure clusters—road transport, electricity, information and communication technology and water and sanitation. It shows great disparities among the continent's sub-regions, with Central Africa trailing, and small improvements over the period 2016–18.
- Access to electricity. Progress has been made but significant gaps still exist both in overall access to electricity and between urban and rural areas. In 2019, 46.8 per cent of the population in SSA had access to electricity, but only 28.1 per cent in rural areas. In addition to supply deficiencies, there are also demand impediments, as many poorer

Table 15.1: Africa Infrastructure Index evolution 2016–18 (100 is maximum)

Rank	Subregion	2016	Rank	Subregion	2017	Rank	Subregion	2018
1	North Africa	71.63	1	North Africa	71.62	1	North Africa	72.96
2	Southern Africa	33.47	2	Southern Africa	34.97	2	Southern Africa	35.46
3	West Africa	18/92	3	West Africa	19.76	3	West Africa	20.47
4	East Africa	13.52	4	East Africa	14.00	4	East Africa	14.60
5	Central Africa	10.69	5	Central Africa	10.78	5	Central Africa	11.04
	Africa	27.12		Africa	27.75		Africa	28.44

Source: African Development Bank

households cannot afford the still high costs. Further reforms are needed to improve the efficiency of utility companies.

- Access to Internet. About 25 per cent of SSA's population had access to Internet in 2019, half of the global rate. The average hides considerable differences between

North and Sub-Saharan countries and among different income groups. Although mobile phones are widely available, only a small proportion provides access to the Internet. In addition to limited access, the cost of Internet services remains unaffordable for many, often due to lack of competition among providers. Massive investments in connectivity are needed as well as the right supportive policies (e.g. sufficient market competition, better entrepreneurial and worker human capital and better physical infrastructure).

- Reducing learning poverty and improving human capital. African countries have made significant progress in enrolling children in primary school since the late 1990s and met the quantitative SDG goal of universal primary education enrolment. This achievement came at the expense of quality. Recent figures (2019) estimate the rate of learning poverty in SSA at 87 per cent (Azevedo 2020)[6] resulting from poor early childhood development, the challenge of language of instruction in early grades, the high proportion of untrained teachers (around 60 per cent in SSA), the inadequacy of teaching materials and the lack of relevant curricula. Less progress has been made for secondary school enrolment, especially for girls. The demand for higher education has been increasing faster than funding capacity. Most public universities and colleges are currently understaffed, underfinanced and in poor operating condition. Many of the students who go on to complete secondary and tertiary education face another challenge—the mismatch between the skills they acquire and the needs of the economy. The education challenge is made even more urgent by the rapid demographic growth and the need to provide skills that will allow the large cohort of youth entering the workforce to find jobs.

- Can digital technologies help? The rapid development of mobile telephones and its impact on financial and other services has shown the potential impact of digital technologies. A small but increasing proportion of youth have become entrepreneurs using digital technologies to create new ways of delivering services, the most successful to date being in fintech, with a positive impact on financial inclusion and the reliability of social transfers (M-PESA in Kenya is a well-known example). If governments and businesses can correctly harness digital technologies by proper policies and investments, the World Bank foresees the possibility of cost reductions and productivity increases in various activities (e.g. small-scale agriculture, the informal sector, in addition to industry, commerce, and services) using innovative digital applications (Choi, Dutz and Usman 2020). Real as it is, the promise of digital technology must, however, be tempered by the situation that continues to prevail in many countries in terms of both access and connectivity.

- Low productivity. In Chapter 13, Hasan Tuluy and Laura Shelton show the relationship between adequate infrastructure, good human capital and productivity. They note that in SSA, during the period 1980–2010, low savings and investment rates, poor quality of human capital, and the relatively small size of individual economies hindered productivity growth. Commodity reliant SSA countries witnessed periods of rapid growth spurred by expansion of oil, metal and mineral investments and exports, but with limited backward linkages to the rest of their economies. The relative growth of services where

---

6. The World Bank and UNESCO have introduced the concept of learning poverty to mean children being unable to read and understand a simple text by age ten.

considerable productivity gains can be expected, particularly from innovations in digital technology and e-services, could lead to increases in productivity on the continent and help accelerate growth.

- Lack of economic diversification. While many Asian countries managed to diversify their exports during the last decades, export diversification stagnated or declined in SSA (Figure 15.3). Several Asian countries, such as Indonesia, Malaysia, Thailand and Vietnam, which started from a level of export diversification that was close to Africa's, managed to diversify their export base significantly. African oil-producing and mineral-rich countries suffered from a declining export base. Examples in Africa of successful export diversification include Mauritius and Morocco. Periods of high commodity prices have too often led to complacent policies rather than to the transformation of natural capital into human and produced capital.
- Limited intracontinental trade and fragmented markets. The volume of trade among the countries of the continent represents 17.8 per cent of its total trade, with North Africa having the lowest at 5.4 per cent. This figure, which compares poorly to Europe and Asia, is the result of many factors, including the importance of export of primary

Figure 15.3: Export diversification by region

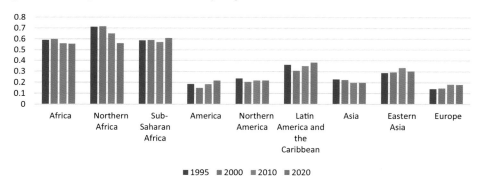

Note: The diversification index is computed by measuring the absolute deviation of the trade structure of a country from world structure. A value closer to 1 indicates greater divergence from the world pattern.
Source: UNCTADSTAT 2021

commodities to the rest of the world by a minority of countries (e.g. oil from Nigeria and Angola); the weight of trade outside Africa, of the largest economies (e.g. Egypt with market access to the EU or South Africa for historical reasons); and the fact that official trade statistics do not account for the large informal cross-border trade (Mold and Chowdury 2021). Greater intracontinental trade is, however, widely viewed as a potential contributor to both diversification and accelerated growth. Regional trading groups have been established over the years to facilitate regional integration and facilitate the movement of goods and people (Tuluy 2017), but their impact has been limited. Some examples exist of privileging trade corridors to facilitate investment and trade across countries (the Maputo Development Corridor that links Eswatini and the landlocked regions of South Africa to the port of Maputo in Mozambique, shows the promises and challenges of this approach).

To boost intracontinental trade, the leaders of Africa agreed in 2018 to create the African Continental Free Trade Area (AfCFTA). As of the end of 2021, after twenty-two countries had ratified the agreement, the AfCFTA came into force. The pact connects 1.3 billion people across fifty-four countries with a combined GDP valued at US$3.4 trillion, with significant upward potential for economic and social development, provided proper policies are put in place, especially for trade facilitation and behind-the-border issues (World Bank 2020c).

- Debt Sustainability. SSA's debt is estimated to have risen by 6.3 per cent of the GDP in 2020 to 57.8 per cent because of declining economic activity and fiscal measures to mitigate the effects of the pandemic. External debt rose by nearly 5 per cent of GDP to 27.8 per cent in 2020, with an expected decrease to 26.7 per cent in 2021 (IMF 2021b). These factors raise concerns about debt sustainability in the region. The thirty-eight African countries eligible for DSSI owed US$25 billion in 2021 repayments (Acker et al. 2021), and thirty-one of those have requested DSSI relief.
- Poor dynamism of the largest economies of SSA (Angola, Ethiopia, DRC, Nigeria, and South Africa). Apart from Ethiopia, before the recent conflict, the largest and better-endowed countries in SSA that could have a positive impact on their sub-regions have not performed well over the last five years with low or negative per capita GDP growth, and all have suffered further from the economic consequences of the COVID-19 pandemic.
- Improving governance and fighting corruption. The Mo Ibrahim Foundation's 2020 *Ibrahim Index of African Governance* report notes that after continuous improvement over the past decade, the overall governance score fell in 2019. While the indices on economic opportunity and human development are showing improvement over the decade (with a slight deterioration in human development in 2018), security and rule of law have deteriorated, and participation, rights and inclusion have declined even more. Corruption remains a major concern in Africa, damaging the availability of resources for development, the trust of citizens in their government, and access to affordable public services by the poor (UNCTAD 2020). Significant funds that could be devoted to economic and social development are leaving the continent in the form of illicit flows that include pure theft of public resources, tax avoidance, or tax evasion. First calculated by the Mbeki commission in 2015, illicit flows have been estimated at US$88.6 billion in 2020, an amount equivalent to half of the estimated SDG financing gap (UNCTAD 2020),[7] and close to the diaspora's remittances. Illicit flows involve not only the exporting countries but also the service providers in the recipient countries (law, accounting, banking, real estate, art dealers, etc.) that allow these funds to be dissimulated and profitably invested, as evidenced recently by disclosures of the Panama papers and others (Vogl 2021). Tax policy has also allowed large corporations (especially, but not exclusively, in extractive industries) to lawfully shift profits or avoid taxes through leonine clauses in often opaque concession contracts. Initiatives for greater transparency (for example, the Extractive Industries Transparency Initiative) and tax reforms are underway

---

7. UNCTAD (2020) includes a full analysis of the definition of illicit flows and the legal issues it entails.

under the aegis of the OECD, to reduce budget base erosion and profit shifting (BEPS). The recent agreement for a minimum tax for multinational corporations is also promising, provided it is implemented as intended.

Part II. The Pandemic's Impact on Africa

A Quick Institutional, Organizational Response to Health

The COVID-19 pandemic is having a profound and potentially lasting impact on Africa. Based on the continent's experience of previous viral epidemics (HIV/AIDS and Ebola), the African Union (AU) reacted quickly on the institutional front. The African Centre for Disease Control (ACDC) prepared the Africa Joint Continental Strategy for the COVID-19 outbreak, which was adopted by the AU. ACDC created the Africa Task Force for Novel Coronavirus, and WHO named six global special envoys to advocate for Africa around the world. At the onset of the pandemic, the poor state of Africa's health infrastructure, especially SSA, created concerns for a rapid and devastating spread of the virus. While the pandemic left a significant toll, it did not reach the feared levels for reasons that are still to be fully analysed.

Mobilization for fighting the pandemic accelerated the creation of the Africa Medicine Agency, a project with a long gestation period. The treaty creating the agency was signed in 2019 and came into force in November 2021. Once vaccines were available, the AU created the African Vaccine Acquisition Task Team (AVATT) to ensure the availability of vaccines for the continent.

Macroeconomic and Growth Impact

Africa experienced its first recession in decades, with negative GDP growth of 2.1 per cent, in 2020. Tourism-dependent economies in SSA faced permanent income losses up to 15 per cent of the GDP. Initial lockdowns and containment measures affected transport, retail trade and other services, and hampered activity in the large informal sectors of the African economies and the livelihood of large swathes of their population. Outside of the service sectors, the pandemic has less severely impacted capital-intensive extractive sectors in the region (IMF 2021a). Economic contraction reflected major declines in consumption and investment, caused by considerable consumer and investor uncertainty, lockdowns and containment measures and disruptions in supply chains (domestic and external), which affected manufacturing and other activities. Commodity prices have now surpassed pre-pandemic levels in SSA, although continued low oil production in SSA has caused the oil prices to 'remain buoyant' (IMF 2021a), expected to return to pre-pandemic levels towards the end of 2022 (World Bank Group 2021a). Tourism-based economies are likely to continue to face difficulties, given an expected slow normalization of cross-border travel.

Further, the region has experienced declines in exports due to lower oil and non-oil commodity prices as well as lower volumes caused by the synchronized fall of the global economy and associated drop of global trade (estimated at 8.5 per cent). The WTO annual report, published in November 2021, noted that it 'expects the volume of world merchandise trade to increase by 10.8 per cent in 2021 and by 4.7 per cent in 2022' (WTO 2021).

Figure 15.4: Volume merchandise trade in Africa

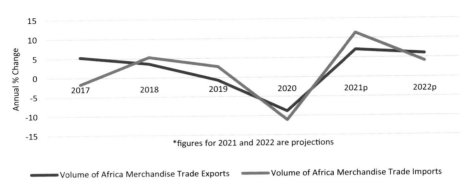

*figures for 2021 and 2022 are projections

━━━ Volume of Africa Merchandise Trade Exports   ━━━ Volume of Africa Merchandise Trade Imports

Source: WTO 2021

Globally, the pandemic's impact on jobs is greater than initially expected, with disproportionate impacts on women, youth and the poor. SSA had a 7 per cent decrease in working hours in 2020.

COVID-19 had a severe impact on FDI in Africa. FDI declined by 16 per cent in 2020, to US$40 billion. The decline in Africa, which is higher than that of the developing country average, came on top of an existing stagnant trend, with FDI on the continent having remained almost unchanged in 2019 compared to 2018. Egypt remained the largest recipient, and while Morocco saw no significant drop in FDI, FDI to South Africa was cut in half. Greenfield project announcements, an indication of investor sentiment and future FDI trends, dropped by 62 per cent to US$29 billion, while international project finance, especially relevant for large infrastructure projects, plummeted by 74 per cent to US$32 billion. An expected rise in demand for commodities, new opportunities due to global value chain (GVC) restructuring, the approval of key projects, and the impending finalization of the African Continental Free Trade Area (AfCFTA) agreement's Sustainable Investment Protocol, could lead to investment picking up greater momentum by 2022 (UNCTAD 2021).

With the COVID-19 shock, African central banks were forced to loosen the often-strict limits on credit to governments and grant macroprudential regulatory reliefs to ease liquidity constraints within the financial sector. To a large extent, these supportive policies, together with stringent supervision and regulation, ensured that the banking sector remained sound and well-capitalized with strong growth in total assets, investments and deposits. Despite the challenging economic issues posed by the pandemic, profitability in the African banking sector has remained strong.

The macroprudential policy measures and regulatory relief measures implemented by African central banks to mitigate the economic effects of the pandemic helped most governments weather the storm. However, the expected boost to private sector credit growth has been sluggish, amid relatively sticky lending rates in the banking sector. Across the continent, these rates have remained very high and have constrained the private sector credit expansion that was expected from the regulatory relief. Annual growth in private sector credit was about 10 per cent or less in end-2021, lower than in previous years.

Around half of the public debt in SSA is due to domestic commercial borrowing sources, which have shorter maturities and higher interest cost (IMF 2021a). One study conducted by the Brookings Institution found that domestic sovereign debt has increased because of limited access to international capital markets (Heitzig, Ordu and Senbet 2021). They found that 'the value of outstanding domestic bonds more than doubled from 2019 to 2020 ($34 billion to US$73 billion), the value of Eurobonds declined over this period ($47 billion to US$45 billion)'.

In addition, inflation has trended up in 2021, with rates creeping above the medium-term target band of most African central banks, due to both supply (food prices) and demand (petroleum price pressures) shocks. To prevent the potential risk of worsening inflation expectations and undermining the price stability objective of the central banks, monetary policy committees have raised interest rates, which limit even more drastically, access to credit by the private sector.

Rating agencies have reacted with harshness and pessimism to Africa's negative growth performance in 2020; in just the first year of the COVID-19 pandemic, eighteen of the thirty-two African countries rated by at least one of the 'big three' agencies (Fitch Ratings, Moody's, and S&P Global Ratings) suffered a downgrade. These rating changes exacerbated the fears and the immediate crisis of higher debt payments and other macroeconomic challenges (low growth, fiscal revenue and weak governance) and will make access to international capital markets more difficult and more expensive at a time when debt distress is already high.

The post-COVID-19 widening of Africa's sovereign bond spread after years of successful bond issues reflects investor sentiments and their assessment of the continent's fiscal risks—they perceive the fiscal and balance of payments deficits in some countries as unsustainable, and doubt that bold and decisive measures from governments will be effective in re-anchoring fiscal consolidation and stabilizing public debt. Investors' assessment of government budgets also suggests doubts about the ability of governments to increase in domestic revenue. In some countries, the widening spread triggered investor sell-offs and created a large financing gap, which put pressure on some local currencies.

Market access countries have the burden to demonstrate the viability of their post-COVID-19 policy frameworks to avoid the unravelling of their development finance strategies and the erosion of the macroeconomic gains made over the past decade. This calls for more than new economic and financial decisions; a new social contract is required to set and manage common aspirations between the government, the private sector and civil society. It is also an important condition for boosting the economic recovery.

The Impact on People

The pandemic had a major impact on people, especially in SSA, where health systems are weak, social safety nets fragile and human capital low. The countries north of the Sahara fared better.

- *Weak health systems in Sub-Saharan countries.* Africa's poorest countries entered the COVID-19 pandemic with significant vulnerabilities in the management of a health emergency, reflected in low health coverage, inadequate government spending on health, and elevated out-of-pocket health payments by citizens. Overall, countries in SSA have severe weaknesses in their ability to prevent, detect and respond to health emergencies. They also display severe gaps in healthcare systems, such as health care capacity in clinics and hospitals, medical personnel deployment, access to health care and infection-control practices (Figure 15.5).

Figure 15.5: Global Health Security Index, 2019

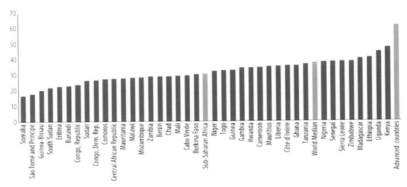

Source: NTI and the Johns Hopkins Center for Health Security 2021

Figure 15.6: Share of population fully vaccinated against COVID-19

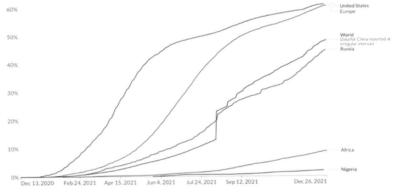

Source: Our world in data 2022

Weak health systems are also limiting testing for the COVID-19 and hampering efforts to address the pandemic while attending to other serious diseases, such as AIDS, TB and malaria. In its 2021 Results Reports, the Global Fund to Fight HIV, TB and malaria wrote '. . . over the last year [2021], the impact of the COVID-19 pandemic has been devastating. For the first time in the Global Fund's history, key HIV, TB, and malaria program results declined. To regain this lost ground and end HIV, TB, and malaria, we must also fight COVID-19-and we must urgently reinforce the systems for health needed to defeat today's pandemics and prepare for tomorrow's' (The Global Fund 2021).

As of the beginning of January 2022, 14.14 per cent of the population was partially vaccinated, 9.47 per cent was fully vaccinated, and 0.35 per cent had received a booster dose (Africa CDC 2021). The African continent imports 99 per cent of the vaccines its populations use. The dangers of this have magnified during the pandemic, as forces outside the continent left its countries without adequate supplies of lifesaving COVID-19 vaccines. The promises of the international community to provide vaccines to the developing world through COVAX have fallen short with G20 countries keeping the vaccines for their own populations and pharmaceutical companies fighting to stop the decentralization of manufacturing that could have been made possible with modifications of intellectual property rules, despite WHO's efforts to move the issue forward. By November 2021, only 399 million doses of vaccine had been shipped to Africa out of the 1.8 billion promised,[8] and by January 2022, the financing gap for the Access to COVID-19 Tools (ACT) Accelerator was US$23.4 billion.

Africa CDC launched the Partnerships for African Vaccine Manufacturing in April 2021, which has a long-term vision of building up the vaccine manufacturing capacity across the continent so that by 2040, 60 per cent of all vaccines used on the continent are produced within African nations—with interim goals of 10 per cent by 2025 and 30 per cent by 2030. Algeria, Egypt, Morocco, Rwanda, Senegal and South Africa have either signed agreements or memoranda of understanding for COVID-19 vaccine manufacturing or begun production. Côte d'Ivoire, Ghana, Kenya and Nigeria have also expressed interest in vaccine manufacturing (Jerving and Ravelo 2022).

- *A further weakening of education*. Prior to the pandemic, most SSA countries were unlikely to reach universal basic education by 2030 for the reasons explained above. The impact of the pandemic could delay this by years. The closing of schools added to the already difficult situation in the education sector with an estimated 32 million out of school because of the pandemic in Eastern and Southern Africa alone, compounding an already dire situation. This means that at least one-third of SSA's youth will be illiterate in the 2030s and that two in five children would be born to illiterate mothers. Less than one-third of adults have completed primary education. The pandemic's long-term negative impacts in delaying education progress include setbacks in improving the status of women, equity and labour productivity. This will impede much-needed progress in accelerating SSA's very slow demographic transition and economic transformation, reinforcing the rapid growth in youth unemployment. Given that SSA's share of the global population aged fifteen to twenty-four is projected to increase from 18 per cent in 2020 to 30 per cent in 2050—a more than 80 per cent increase for SSA compared to a decline by 5 per cent for the rest of the world—this will have wide-ranging global implications, including for global labour force growth and migration.

- *Increased poverty.* Despite having some of the highest inequality rates in the world, SSA had recorded a gradual decline in inequality, specifically in the GINI index, since the 1980s, owing to improved macroeconomic performance and reforms, the impact of debt reductions under the HIPC and MDRI initiatives, and the commodity boom (see Chapter 7 on inequality). However, using poverty as a proxy indicator, the pandemic has most likely increased inequality in Africa. In terms of poverty, low-income countries, particularly those in Africa, are likely to be most negatively impacted by the pandemic through 2030. By 2040, the impact is likely to be lessened; however, poverty rates are

15

FUTURE PROSPECTS OF AFRICA—THE FINAL DEVELOPMENT FRONTIER AND A GLOBAL COMMON

---

8. Data from the Mo Ibrahim Foundation based on Duke Global Health Information Center Update 12 November 2021.

still considerably higher compared to a no-COVID-19 scenario. The Centennial Group Model estimates that, compared to the pre-COVID-19 baseline, the pandemic pushed some 40 million people in Africa into extreme poverty in 2020 under the threshold of US$1.90 a day and over 50 million under the US$3.10 a day threshold (Centennial Group 2021). Children and women were the most severely affected, and weak safety nets compounded the negative impact of the pandemic.

Part III. Long-term Perspectives: Africa in a Post-COVID-19 World

A new world order is emerging that will define the twenty-first century. The economic order and the global institutions that had dominated the last seven decades are now under stress. In many advanced countries, people left behind by globalization are losing trust in their leaders and turning to populism, leading to more inward-looking and divisive policies. The COVID-19 pandemic has bolstered these trends. Tensions between the US and China, the two leading world economies, are reshaping alignments and alliances. The European Union, the third largest economic bloc, is undergoing an existential moment. These massive shifts, whose final shape is still unclear, will force other nations to make difficult choices. Amid such profound changes, Africa must be proactive and exert agency to define its role and place in the emerging new order and safeguard its long-term strategic interests while sharing its culture and wisdom with the world.

Africa must do so in a way that will help the continent meet the challenges of a true economic transformation. Over the next four decades, Africa's population will double, and the continent will remain the youngest part of the world. Providing jobs to cohorts of young people will require rapid, broad-based and sustainable growth, based on good domestic policies and strategic alliances that reflect changing geopolitical realities.

The most concerned actors are obviously the Africans themselves; government, private actors and civil society need to build trust (domestically and internationally), implement reforms, and mobilize large resources (nationally and globally) in ways that are commensurate with the challenge of sustainable and equitable growth. The challenges are huge and will require bold, long-term actions, where Africa has a strong voice in the concert of nations and controls its future, and where partners make significant contributions in mutually responsible ways that are consistent with Africa's own vision. Celebrating the fiftieth anniversary of the creation of the Organization for African Unity (OAU), African leaders adopted:

'Agenda 2063 to refocus and reprioritize Africa's agenda from the struggle against apartheid and the attainment of political independence for the continent, which had been the focus of the OAU; and instead to prioritize inclusive social and economic development, continental and regional integration, democratic governance and peace and security amongst other issues aimed at repositioning Africa to becoming a dominant player in the global arena' (African Union 2021).

Long-term Projections

The Centennial Group's Global Growth Model for Africa through 2060[9] projects the continent's GDP under various scenarios. This is a long-term model, and therefore its results and projections

---

9. The medium- and long-term projections are based on the October 2021 IMF WEO.

are stylized; they are not intended to predict the future exactly but rather to provide a context for policymaking and reform (Kohli, Szyf and Arnold 2012), see Chapter 4 for more information on the model. For this study, three scenarios were prepared:

- Under the 'central' scenario, the global productivity frontier (the United States economy) improves at an average annual rate somewhat below 1 per cent (similar to its historical average). The scenario assumes that only the advanced economies (AEs) that have performed well in the past twenty years will continue to move at the same pace as the United States and similarly that the emerging markets and developing economies (EMDEs) that have a record of successful convergence in the past will continue to converge as well.
- The 'strong policy' scenario assumes that the global productivity frontier improves at a faster rate than under the central scenario. In all other aspects besides the increased productivity frontier growth, the advanced economies' performance remains broadly the same, but policy performance of EMDEs improves significantly.
- The 'poor-policies' scenario assumes that many EMDEs fall into the middle-income trap because of their inability to maintain a reasonable policy regime and the global productivity growth rate slows to only 0.6 per cent per year.

Some of the above results may be a surprise, particularly that Africa's share of EMDEs is greater in the poor policies scenario than in the central one. This can be explained by the relative movement of the policies of various country groupings compared to the central scenario. Poor policies reduce the performance of EMDEs compared to the central scenario more than Africa's, where policies are already comparatively weak. The policies performance (up or down) of AEs does not vary much across the scenarios. Good policies have a comparatively greater impact on Africa than on EMDEs and AEs, given the greater distance from the policy frontier of Africa's central scenario policies. This illustrates, if need be, the importance for Africa to improve its policy environment and increase total factor productivity, or at the very least, to maintain the current performance.

Figure 15.7: Africa GDP per capita

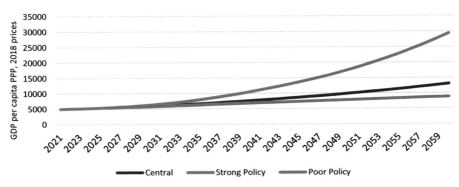

Source: Centennial Group 2021

Table 15.2: Africa GDP PPP per capita in 2060 compared to others (per cent)

	Poor policies	Central	Good policies
Africa as per cent world	34.8	31.8	48.3
Africa as per cent EMDE	47.9	38.4	55.2
Africa as per cent AE	11.3	13.8	24.8

Source: Centennial Group 2021

To reach the good policies scenario, significant progress must be made on the structural obstacles analysed above. In particular, productivity must be improved through a combination of factors that require adequate policies: improved human capital (education and health, with an emphasis on gender equity), green and resilient infrastructure, renewed focus on the rural economy, more conducive and stable business climate and improved governance. Fostering the use of digital technology and accelerating regional integration are key to achieving progress. Highlighted below are some ways in which African leaders and elites can move forward, based on lessons from successful EMDEs.

Four Interconnected Threats

As an additional set of challenges, four interconnected threats must be kept in mind and managed by all stakeholders within and outside the continent, and their implications factored into the design of policies and projects.

1. Adapting to climate change

   Africa is the most vulnerable continent to cimate change impacts under all climate scenarios above 1.5°C. Despite having contributed the least to global warming and having the lowest emissions, Africa faces exponential collateral damage, posing systemic risks to its economies, infrastructure investments, water and food systems, public health, agriculture, and livelihoods, threatening to undo its modest development gains and slip to higher levels of extreme poverty. Seven of the ten countries that are most vulnerable to climate change are in Africa (AfDB n.d.).

   SSA has 95 per cent of rain-fed agriculture globally (AfDB n.d.). The large share of agriculture in GDP and employment adds to vulnerability, as do other weather-sensitive activities, such as herding and fishing, leading to income losses and increased food insecurity. Warming temperatures are slashing crop yields. WMO projects a reduction in yields of 13 per cent in West and Central Africa, 11 per cent in North Africa and 8 per cent in East and Southern Africa (Fick 2020). In drought-prone areas including the Sahel, the number of undernourished people has jumped by 45 per cent since 2012. Climate change is compounding problems such as conflict that drive growing hunger. In the Horn of Africa, below-average rainfall in 2018 and 2019 led to the worst cereal harvest in Somalia since records began in 1995, and to crop failures in neighbouring Kenya. Floods followed. Somalia, Kenya, Ethiopia and Tanzania recorded at least double their average seasonal rainfall in late 2019. The rain helped crops grow but also fuelled the locusts that have devoured hundreds of thousands of hectares of land in those countries. Warmer and wetter weather is also more suitable for insects that transmit dengue fever, malaria and yellow fever. More severe weather events and rising sea levels threaten an already inadequate infrastructure.

Climate change will add to migration with up to 86 million Africans migrating within their own countries by 2050, according to the World Bank (2021b). The data on countries in West Africa and the Lake Victoria Basin show that climate migration hot spots could emerge as early as 2030, and highlight that without concrete climate and development action, West Africa could see as many as 32 million people forced to move within their own countries by 2050. In Lake Victoria Basin countries, the number could reach a high of 38.5 million (World Bank Group 2021b).

Proper policies of adaptation and investment in sustainable and resilient infrastructure can turn the climate crisis into an opportunity, especially given the gap in infrastructure that can be filled with climate-friendly and resilient investments using the latest technologies. The climate financing needs for Africa are huge, estimated at over US$7.8 billion per year. In 2009, the international community committed to provide US$100 billion yearly to EMDEs by 2020 for climate change activities. This commitment has fallen short by about US$20 billion.

2. A young and rapidly growing population, struggling to find sustainable employment and livelihoods

Africa is and will remain the continent with the youngest and fastest growing population with a median age of 19.7 years. As of 2021, around 40 per cent of the population is aged fifteen years and younger, compared to a global average of 26 per cent. The demographic challenge is primordial and difficult to address for social, cultural and religious reasons, especially in the countries with the fastest demographic growth where fundamentalism is tying the hands of policymakers. In addition, Africa shows unique characteristics compared to other regions that have achieved their demographic dividend; the youth share of the working age population is expected to decline slowly. The world's ten highest fertility countries are now in Africa, and these countries, which have not even started the transition, will keep the regional fertility averages and youth shares up at least until 2050 (Fox 2019).[10] Combined with the improvement in life expectancy and weak safety nets, this reduces the prospects for poverty reduction.

A large proportion (52.6 per cent in 2020) of the population lives in rural areas, where the lack of employment is leading to massive rural-urban migration. Productivity in agriculture is limited, inter alia, by the lack of irrigation (only 5.4 per cent of agricultural land is irrigated) in a largely arid region with uncertain rainfall (made even more so by climate change), poor storage facilities and access to markets, low use of fertilizers and tractors. As noted by Kevin Cleaver in Chapter 10, Africa's food production will not keep up with demographic growth, making large numbers of people subject to food insecurity. Young people are not interested in agriculture as it is still practiced with primitive technology and is back-breaking work, and educated youth are not prepared for farming. Youth interest in digital technology may, however, lead them over time to create applications that would modernize agriculture, increase its productivity and renew their interest in the sector.[11]

---

10. The fertility decline in SSA was two children in 35 years, from its maximum of 6.9 children per woman in 1975–80 to 4.7 children in 2015–20. At present trends, the fertility transition might take at least sixty years in many SSA countries in May and Guengant (2020), which provides a fascinating analysis of long-term demographic trends in SSA and their impact on emergence.

11. For a full and rich discussion of African agriculture, see ACET (2017) and Chapter 10 of this book.

Although Africa has the lowest unemployment rate globally on paper (ILO 2020) among youth aged fifteen to twenty-four (10.6 per cent in 2021), most of Africa's youth work informally, and many are underemployed or remain in poverty despite working, due to low wages and the lack of a social safety net. The African Development Bank estimates that 10 million to 12 million youth enter the workforce in Africa each year, but only 3 million formal jobs are created annually. AfDB estimates that in 2015, one-third of Africa's then 420 million young people between fifteen and thirty-five years old were unemployed, another third were vulnerably employed, and only one in six was in wage employment (AfDB 2016).

The relatively small number of youths coming of age who find employment in formal activities, often in the public sector, is largely due to the mismatch between the skills they acquired during their education (for those who completed secondary or tertiary education) and the skills required by private employers. Unemployed youth are an easy prey for jihadist recruiters in the Sahel or drug and arms traffickers (see below).

For many young Africans, migration offers a last recourse solution to their employment problem. Dramatic stories of migrants drowning or parked in camps at the doors of Europe make headlines. However, the 2019 IOM report on Africa migration shows that most of the migrants in Africa move between African countries (Adepoju, Fumagalli, and Nyabola 2020). In 2019, according to the IOM, 53 per cent of the 40 million African migrants moved within Africa with Europe being the second most common destination (26 per cent). Within Africa, 30 per cent of the migrants go to Eastern Africa, 28 per cent to Western Africa, 14 per cent to Middle Africa, and 11 per cent to North Africa. Economic migration combined with population movements due to climate change exacerbate social tensions in the receiving countries both within and outside the continent.

3. Keeping peace and ensuring security

In his book, *Africanistan: Development or Jihad*, Serge Michailof (2018) sent a dire warning about Africa: 'The continent is, in fact a powder keg. The powder is demographics. And the detonator is unemployment.' There were 168 million people living in internal displacement because of conflict and violence in Africa as the end of 2018, the highest recorded figure for the continent and about 40 per cent of the world's total (iDMC 2019). In 2020 and 2021, eighteen of the thirty-nine countries on the list of Fragile and Conflict-affected States were in Africa.

The civil war in Côte d'Ivoire (2020–11), the jihadist attacks in Mali that started in 2011 and have since led to the weakening of the Malian state and multiple coups, the ability of Boko Haram and various jihadist groups to defy the armies of many countries—these are a threat not only to the Sahelian countries (the impact on Burkina Faso and Niger is already severe) but also to the northern regions of the coastal countries of the Gulf of Guinea and the countries themselves. Continuing unrest in the Kivu region of DRC, persistent instability in South Sudan and at the borders between Chad and Libya and Chad and Sudan, the long-standing threat of the Lord's Resistance army in Uganda and Kenya, the civil war in Ethiopia, uncertainty in Guinea cast a shadow on development prospects, to name a few hot spots. The Early Warning Project (2021) Statistical Risk assessment shows that seventeen of the thirty highest risks countries are in Africa.

Security threats deter investors (foreign and domestic), and addressing them requires government to divert scarce domestic resources from economic development. Insecurity also creates environments where illegal activities can proliferate, and offers unemployed young people avenues for gaining status and livelihoods not offered by their societies. Sadly, owning a Kalashnikov in many parts of the Sahel offers a better livelihood and more social status than having graduated from a poor education system. While international assessments and conferences reaffirm that there can be no development without security, few, if any, resources are devoted by the international community to help strengthen the institutions in charge of ensuring justice, peace and security, and a gap persists between humanitarian and development assistance that must be bridged. To make progress, many issues would have to be solved, especially for multilateral organizations, but solutions can and must be found to allow financial and technical assistance to the security sector. Serge Michailof (2018) offers avenues that can be explored, underlining that the cost/benefit ratio in some Sahelian countries would be quite favourable, not only to the countries themselves but in the longer term to Europe as well.

4. Navigating geo-political tensions

Long-term observers of Africa remember the negative consequences of the Cold War on the continent, with the competing superpowers of the time (USA and USSR) intent on keeping countries in their camp, regardless of their governance or economic performance, with the Zaire of Mobutu or the Ethiopia of the Derg as tragic examples of the consequences on development outcomes.

After the Fall of the Berlin Wall, the US interest in Africa waned only to be revived during the 'War on Terror' and the spread of Islamic extremism in Africa (Combined Joint Task Force to the Horn of Africa, Pan Sahel Initiative, setting up the Africa Command in 2007, etc.), but African countries had few partners, except their traditional ones in the West and the multilateral institutions they controlled.[12]

Today, China has become the main trading partner of Africa and is investing heavily into the Belt and Road initiative. The Eighth Meeting of the Forum on China–Africa Cooperation was held in Dakar at the end of 2021, with the Chinese president making significant promises on vaccines and investment in poverty reduction and green development. China is also expanding its soft power though training of African elites and military cooperation.

Russia has recently signed military agreements with Nigeria and Ethiopia and is involved in conflicts in Libya, Mali and CAR (Smith 2021). As France reduced its military presence in Mali, Russian advisers and mercenaries came to assist. The first Russia–Africa Summit was held in 2019, with the Russian President offering to engage in competition for cooperation with Africa. Turkish drones were key in helping government forces during the recent Ethiopian conflict. In addition to financial and military cooperation, these new partners are selling their models of governance, which has appeal to many autocrats in the region.

---

12. This section draws from Hisham Aidi (2021).

While having more numerous and new partners is increasing the freedom of negotiation of African governments and increasing their leverage with their traditional development partners, the dangers of choosing a camp and reproducing the results of the Cold War must be kept in mind by Africans and be avoided.

African Policymakers and Elites Must Lead

Notwithstanding the setbacks and potential new difficulties caused by the COVID-19 pandemic and the challenges of its lingering effects, the time is right for African countries to assert themselves on the global economic scene. After the shock of the pandemic, international trade, which is the main engine of growth for the continent, is back to its positive, long-term trend, largely the result of the strong recovery in global demand due to subsiding pandemic restrictions, economic stimulus packages adopted in advanced economies, and increases in commodity prices.[13]

Moreover, the emergence of several large middle-income countries (most notably, China, Indonesia, Vietnam, etc.) as new growth centres offers an unprecedented opportunity to all developing economies with income levels currently below theirs—including those in Africa. By becoming important contributors to global demand, emerging economies, such as China, are also major potential importers of African goods and services—and thus, new potential markets for the continent. And because these countries have recorded dynamic growth and climbed the industrial ladder, they are on the verge of 'graduating' from low-skilled manufacturing jobs. They must keep moving up the value chain and relocate many of their existing labour-intensive manufacturing industries to countries where wage differentials are large enough to ensure competitiveness in global production networks. The 'graduation' of these large middle-income countries from certain types of manufacturing will free up an estimated 85 million jobs (Lin 2012) and open market niches, and new possibilities for industrialization and employment creation to African countries, where manufacturing jobs are currently estimated to be less than 20 million in total.

To seize these potential growth and employment benefits, African countries must strengthen macroeconomic management and improve productivity and external competitiveness. They should also focus on private sector development, industrialization (including in cultural and creative industries) and employment-creation in modern services.

Maintaining a sound and predictable macroeconomic framework—including exchange rate policies ensuring external competitiveness—is essential, and much has been written on the topic that need not be repeated here. The same is true of economic infrastructure. Actions must also be taken to provide new dynamism to the economy and especially the private sector. These include the revamping of national and regional development finance institutions; skills development for employment generation; and the creation of special economic zones and industrial parks (enclaves of excellence) to boost competitive industries. All of them require the implementation of effective programs for stronger governance.

- Development banks. Well-functioning development banks help countries meet two objectives simultaneously. They provide much-needed long-term financing to

---

13. UNCTAD (2020) estimates the value of world imports and exports of goods at US$28 trillion for 2021—an increase of 23 per cent in 2020 and 11 per cent compared to pre-COVID-19 levels. But trade's overall strong performance masks that the recovery has been uneven across countries and sectors.

economies, contributing to expanding and modernizing infrastructure, and they maintain sustainable fiscal balance. Reinforcing such banks' financial and economic role would not require African governments to substantially increase their borrowing. Rejuvenating public investment and development banks would stimulate confidence by supporting large-scale, regional investment projects and programmes that create employment opportunities. But those investments would be made by the private sector or by some local governments, with the necessary funding borrowed or raised by the investment and development banks—not by governments.[14]

Revitalizing these financial institutions would go a long way toward addressing the short-term market failures in private capital markets that prevent poor economies from getting funding for their development projects. By making long-term finance available for sound investment, investment and development banks could support new export industries that reduce dependence on foreign borrowing to finance foreign products. Governments could use them to secure special credit lines and to provide incentives to commercial banks to offer in turn more favourable borrowing terms to firms in potentially competitive industries and sectors. This would also open new possibilities for the development of new products and services by commercial banks (including insurance facilities against exchange rate risks).

Although development and public investment banks have a poor track record across the developing world, it must be noted that these failures could again be traced to the blind pursuit of capital-intensive (modernization) projects that were not economically viable in the first place or were poorly managed and not upgraded to reflect changes in the economy's endowment structure.

Learning from past failures and successes, the new development finance institutions would borrow on the capital markets to finance economically viable projects in potentially competitive industries and sectors. They would offer partial or full guarantee of repayment of bonds issued by investment projects by bearing the risk and therefore reducing substantially the cost of funding. Newly revamped development finance institutions working with a rigorous, professional and transparent operational framework would also issue their own long-term bonds with a modest premium over US T-bills to raise money and finance large-scale projects directly. Good institutional and governance strategies would allow development and public investment banks to fund major infrastructure projects while consistently avoiding losses and maintaining a very low delinquency rate.

- Skills development and employment creation. Skill mismatches are prevalent and costly features of African labour markets. Yet, in industries where there is demand for skilled labour, investors also often point to skill shortages, weak human capital, and rigid labour laws as constraints to firm performance. Meanwhile, governments devote increasingly larger amounts of the countries' meagre resources to finance public schools, colleges, and universities. Families also use their savings to support their youth and ensure that they receive good education and training.

---

14. The 2021–25 Strategic plan of BOAD 'Le Plan Djoliba' offers an illustration of this approach.

There is a need to complement improvements in the education curricula in academic institutions with better-targeted skill and capacity development programmes to directly respond to the market demand for labour. To carry out this broader and more practical agenda, African countries should support private-sector-led skills enhancement zones, where governments collaborate with firms, academic institutions and non-governmental organizations on the design and implementation of medium- and long-term workforce development plans for selected industries with strong competitive potential (mainly agroindustry, light manufacturing and tourism). They are public-private centres where (mostly) young people are exposed to a wide set of skills across sectors, connected to industrial clusters and prepared for entrepreneurship.

The main goal of these skills enhancement zones should be to develop practical skills and implement programmes to quickly build the workforce needed in all the critical segments of the value chains of the country's competitive industries. Their strategies should be tailored to build human capital in specific groups:

- For existing workers, the focus could be to address shortfalls in skill-specific technical areas, and to provide pathways into agro-industry, manufacturing, and services.
- For new labour force entrants, the focus could be to improve the effectiveness of high school-to-work pathways—the type of basic assembly work in many light manufacturing activities that only requires high school-educated workers. By expanding pre-employment and prevocational places, the strategy would provide firms with work-ready new entrants and help them face less difficulty in attracting new entrants.
- For women, whose contribution to effective poverty reduction strategies in developing countries has been shown empirically, specific tasks and a more flexible and positive work environment should be created to attract them in large numbers into labour-intensive industries.
- For the many unemployed youth in rural areas where modern agriculture and light manufacturing industries can emerge, the skill enhancement zones would provide opportunities for training and employment.

African countries should also use these centres to refocus their vocational training on industries in which their economies have clear or latent comparative advantage. The launch of vocational institutions is generally a major step in the drive to produce skilled workers in high demand in booming industries. But such vocational institutions are often costly and depend on donor funding, which can be volatile. Training could be provided both on the job (especially for agriculture/agribusiness, light manufacturing, and tourism) and in training schools. With the provision of knowledge and skills linked to acquiring the necessary job experience, trainees would learn to cope with the job's constantly changing demands and to acquire precious 'soft' skills.

- Building enclaves of excellence. All African countries will need time to successfully undertake all the reforms necessary to make their business environments, infrastructure quality, governance institutions and regulations and national systems for delivering public policies that meet the standards of Singapore or Switzerland, while maintaining social peace. Time is also a requirement to address the capacity deficit and to solve the issues making the business environment unattractive. Today's top-performing economies in the World Bank Doing Business rankings did not get there overnight. Yet, time is of the essence for developing country political leaders.

Under such circumstances, the more pertinent strategy for growth and job creation is to devote the country's limited financial and administrative resources to the implementation of reforms in policy and geographic areas, where visible 'quick wins' can be achieved. Observable positive results in the creation of labour-intensive industries would also open up the political and policy space to gradually implement even the most difficult reforms.

Special economic zones (SEZs) are the most effective institutions for generating decent employment in potentially competitive industries (while taking the often extensive time necessary to identify and address the truly binding constraints to an improved business climate), especially industrial parks (IPs), and other closely related institutions, such as special agro-processing zones (SAPZs). They can be used effectively to gradually address many difficult economy-wide constraints on job creation.

SEZs and IPs provide special policy incentives and infrastructure in a circumscribed geographic location to firms that can attract foreign direct investment, create jobs, develop and diversify exports (even when economy-wide business environment problems and protective barriers are not yet resolved), increase foreign exchange earnings and serve as 'experimental laboratories' for new pricing, financial or labour policies. SEZs and IPs are more likely to produce increasing returns (economics of agglomeration), arising from localizing industries. These increasing returns, mainly in the form of localized external economies, allow for large-scale production.

A large-scale shift has occurred in global commerce which has not yet been integrated into economic thinking, development policies and private business operations. OECD research shows that tariff reductions and market access have become much less relevant for economic growth than was the case a generation ago. Trade is no longer about manufacturing a product in one country and selling it elsewhere but cooperating across boundaries and time zones to minimize production costs and maximize market coverage. Policymakers should spend less time talking about market access, although that remains important—especially for African agricultural exports—and more on developing well-targeted infrastructure that can connect developing economies to global value chains.

Effective programs for stronger governance. Africa has a long way to go on governance, and efforts at improving it must be sustained. With an average score of 33 out of 100 in the 2021 Transparency International Corruption Perception Index, SSA shows no significant improvement.

Weak and ineffective leadership has had devastating consequences. In Mali, poor governance and corruption have hampered the government's ability to deal with the jihadist rebellion, reducing the state's presence and authority in large parts of the country (The Economist 2021b). The entire sub-region is now under threat. Ineffective governments and leaders are also contributing to insecurity in many parts of the continent: Central African Republic, Eritrea, Somalia, South Sudan, the East of DRC and Nigeria, to name some. Improving governance will require the implementation of three types of measures:

1. Improve public expenditures management and revenue mobilization

- Implement a robust program for systematic, strict and independent public expenditure reviews (perhaps financed by a trust fund) to better target public investment and bring current expenditures in line with structural revenues.
- Establish an independent National Budget Committee (whose members would be a small number of independent and well-respected experts) to review draft budget bills before they are submitted to Parliaments and issue advice to the government on the quality of the budget.
- Increase domestic revenue mobilization, by shifting from commodity taxation and towards more neutral, broad-based value-added or sales taxes and personal income tax.

2. Improve transparency

- Improve transparency in budget management, including commitment by governments to release in real-time, all data on old and new debt from all sources. This will require efforts to standardize data-gathering practices, develop data collection systems, address data gaps, notably in the accounting of SOE-related liabilities and consolidate government accounts, across regional levels, agencies, ministries and institutions.
- Strengthen auditing and oversight systems through independent fiscal commissions.
- Release systematically, all auditing reports with trigger mechanisms for monitoring of further action.
- Strengthen an independent and professional judiciary system.

3. Foster civil society participation and the role of civil society organizations (CSO)

- Consult and involve CSOs in the budgetary process, building on the lessons on the example of the International Budget Partnership, and in policy reforms.
- Involve CSOs in the design of projects affecting their constituencies.
- Allow third party monitoring by CSO of governments commitments and flow of funds to increase accountability.

- Projecting Africa's image: The potential of cultural and creative industries. Africa has strong comparative advantage in cultural and creative industries (CCI) — defined broadly as the creation, industrial reproduction and mass distribution of cultural goods and services, and the use of new technologies to produce and trade valuable works of imagination. CCIs include art, crafts, visual and audio-visuals, design, digital fabrication, new media, performing arts and publishing.

Africa's CCIs were growing at a rapid pace before the COVID-19 pandemic. For instance, the market for African visual arts, which includes paintings, sculpture and photography, had become a vibrant global business and a highly debated source of meaning, and former colonial European countries, such as Germany, the Netherlands, France and Belgium, returned looted art to their former colonies, acknowledging their high economic and symbolic value.

Film and television production have been recognized as a major contributor to economic growth in Egypt, Nigeria, South Africa, Kenya, Ghana, Morocco or Côte d'Ivoire. The sector creates and supports employment for millions of people in Africa directly (in front of and behind the camera) but also indirectly (through the many related industries and services emerging around it), while generating a valuable global export. Leading fashion designers have inspired a new generation whose works attract some of the world's most influential entertainment figures and international investors during fashion weeks and various global flagship events. Game development from small but effective studios are on the rise across Africa and enhance technological competitiveness. Top game developers and digital animation professionals have emerged in Nigeria, Kenya and South Africa.

Together, these sub-sectors of CCIs could eventually hold a sizeable share of the global market and contribute substantially not only to export earnings but to more inclusive development and to changing Africa's image in the rest of the world.

The World Must Support Africa's Efforts: A Call for Symmetrical Cooperation[15]

Africa will have over 2 billion people in 2060 and, unless significant progress is made along the lines outlined in the preceding parts, long-term projections show that its share of the world GDP will still be the lowest in the world and, even more so, when looking at per capita GDP. Africans, aware of the disparities, will try to improve their lot. They can do so by being more demanding of their leaders and holding them accountable within existing rules, but they can also lose hope and join extremist groups (religious or other), engage in other forms of lawlessness to make a living, or migrate. Lack of hope can lead to desperate remedies. In addition, unless growth is green, it will exacerbate the climate challenge and accelerate the movement of people. For these reasons, the rest of the world ought to look to Africa as a global public good which, without proper cooperation, could turn into a global public bad.

But the nature of cooperation must continue to evolve with a more symmetrical form of cooperation between Africa and its traditional partners in the West (many of them former colonizers) and a faster deepening of the cooperation across the Global South (South–South cooperation). For too long, priorities and initiatives about Africa have originated outside the continent with Africans being asked to 'own' these initiatives to benefit from assistance in an asymmetrical form of cooperation laden with historical connotations. Progress has been made toward a more equal partnership, but much remains to be achieved to reach a truly symmetrical cooperation, where the contributions of each side are equally heard and valued.

Earlier, this report described the growing links between the two sides of the Sahara and the competition in Africa between traditional and new partners. Lessons can be drawn from these developments. Many groups are also rethinking the way in which development is done: the Doing Development Differently network argues for more adaptable approaches; others are rethinking the very concept of development, given the growing similarities in the problems faced by different countries formerly neatly split between developed and developing. No consensus has emerged yet, but these developments show the need for a rethinking of the very meaning of development and cooperation. The interconnectedness of the world economy, even if it is being rethought somewhat after the pandemic, and the global impact of climate change,

---

15. While the term may appear redundant, the intent is to signal the need for and importance of a more balanced power relationship between African countries and their partners, to overcome the lasting historical legacy of colonialism and its modern mutations.

make such reassessment even more urgent. Africa has a keen interest and a key role to play in making it happen.

Chapter 16: Latin America—Facing the Challenges of the Post-pandemic Era

Latin America—Facing the Challenges of the Post-pandemic Era

Chapter 16

Enrique García

Introduction

The dramatic global impact of COVID-19 in the economy with negative implications on the quality of life of the population and the stability of democratic institutions is indicative that the world is confronting a dynamic process of change, where the technological and institutional transformations generated by the fourth Industrial Revolution have accelerated the widening of economic and social gaps, intensified nationalistic attitudes and racial conflicts, as well as tensions among the main global powers. Global leaders have scrutinized and even attacked globalization and multilateralism in recent years. This is particularly evident for leaders of countries that were the founders, promoters and defenders of open markets, free trade, integration and multilateralism. In fact, international relations have moved from a cooperative spirit to a competitive one, weakening multilateral institutions and regional integration mechanisms. A clear illustration of the change in the global geopolitical scenario is the tension and growing rivalry between the United States and China.

Considering future scenarios is implicit in the challenging megatrends identified in this book; it is urgent that leaders around the world undertake a profound process of responsible reflection on the importance of designing and implementing renewed long-term holistic strategies at the global, regional and national levels, that respond to the trends and realities of the existing new era. With this purpose in mind, strengthening multilateralism becomes, no doubt, a fundamental instrument to restore a genuine and constructive international collaborative atmosphere, consistent with world peace and genuine progress for most of the population.

Latin America in the Global Scenario

From a regional perspective, Latin America is an interesting case to be analysed, not only because it has withstood some of the hardest impacts of COVID-19, imperilling both its health and its development in the 2019–21 period but for the fact that it has lost relative importance at the international level. In fact, considered the most successful developing region of the world in the first half of the twentieth century, it has fallen behind in recent decades; a victim of the so-called 'mid income trap', the phenomenon of developing economies getting stuck at a certain level of income. In this regard, even before measuring the dramatic negative impact of COVID-19, indicators clearly show that the region has diminished its relative importance in comparison to the industrialized countries of the world and the successful Asian emerging economies, as highlighted below (WBG, IMF and CEPAL 2021).

- Average GDP growth of Latin America in the 1961–2019 period was 3.6 per cent compared to 8.1 per cent and 7.4 per cent of China and South Korea in the same period. By the same token, while Latin America had an average rate of growth of 2.36 per cent in the 2000–18 period, the Asian Emerging Countries had an average rate of growth of 7.36 per cent.

- Because of low and volatile rates of growth compared to other dynamic emerging regions, Latin America has stagnated in a 5–6 per cent range of global economic output since 1960. By comparison, while China's GDP represented 62 per cent of Latin America's GDP in 1960, it was three times higher than Latin America's GDP in 2020.
- In purchasing parity terms (PPP), per capita GDP of Latin America compared to the United States has remained in the 23–26 per cent range in the last five decades. At the same time, while Latin America's per capita GDP was four times higher than China's in the early sixties, it was 14 per cent lower than China's in 2020. A more dramatic reversal corresponds to South Korea, since its per capita GDP has moved from being three and a half times lower than Latin America's per capita GDP in 1960, to two and one-third times higher than Latin America's in 2020.
- The participation of Latin America in world trade has been reduced from 11 per cent to less than 6 per cent in the period between 1950–2020. By comparison, China's participation in world trade has increased from 1 per cent in 1950 to 14 per cent in 2020.

The Impact of COVID-19 in Latin America

As was mentioned before, Latin America, is the region most severely hit by COVID-19. With 8 per cent of the world population, contagions and diseases in the region represented 28 per cent and 34 per cent of the world totals in 2020. Furthermore, in 2020, the region had a negative rate of GDP growth of 6.4 per cent, the most drastic reduction in output compared to all regions in the world. Notwithstanding a rebound of 6.7 per cent in 2021, projections for 2022 and 2023 indicate rates of GDP growth of 2.6 per cent and 2.7 per cent respectively, which are lower than the rates projected for most of the regions in the world (World Bank 2022). According to CEPAL, in addition to the closure of business and the increment of unemployment and informality, a worrisome evolution in the last three years is the increment of 23 million people in the extreme poverty category, which represents 13.8 per cent of the total population of Latin America (ECLACL 2021).

Structural Factors Affecting Latin America

In order to have an adequate analytical platform to project the future, it is fundamental to go beyond the pandemic's negative impact and objectively recognize the main factors that have influenced the region's mediocre and volatile economic and social performance in the last six decades. For this purpose, the following six factors should be highlighted (WBG, IMF and CEPAL 2021).

Export Concentration in Raw Materials and Low Technology Products

The lower and volatile rates of growth of Latin America compared to other successful emerging regions can be explained, in part, by the fact that most of its countries, have a high dependence on the production and export of raw materials and low technology-based manufactures. Exports in the region, apart from Mexico, which has a relative low participation in commodities (11 per cent), are characterized by a high concentration in commodity exports (35 per cent). In

South America, with 50 per cent of total regional exports, commodity exports represented over 55 per cent of the total in 2017. At the same time, Latin America has a very low level of intra-regional trade (17 per cent compared to 38 per cent in Asia and above 60 per cent in Europe).

Because of the traditional volatility of international commodity prices, economic performance in Latin America has been closely tied up to the continuous changes of those prices. While high commodity prices have been the catalysts of growth and social improvements in a context of macroeconomic stability, low prices have been the trigger to generate high inflation, fiscal and monetary imbalances and excessive external debt. An additional negative factor has been the insufficient efforts made by the region to accelerate a process of productive and technological transformation and export diversification that would generate higher value added.

All these factors have forced countries to periodically adopt severe adjustment programs to re-establish macroeconomic equilibrium, with the consequent recurrent periods of negative or low growth, unemployment and negative social and political effects.

Low Savings and Investment Ratios
In the 2000–16 period, Latin America had an average internal savings ratio of 19 per cent in relation to GDP (savings of governments, enterprises and households). This coefficient compares to 43.3 per cent in emerging Asia. By the same token, total investment (public and private) was on average, 21.9 per cent of GDP in Latin America, compared to 42 per cent in Emerging Asia, in the same period.

Insufficient Productivity Growth
Total factor productivity (TFP) average growth in Latin America has had a marginal rate of 1 per cent growth in the 1960–2019 period compared to 5 per cent in China and 3.5 per cent in Eastern Asia and the Pacific. Similarly, in the 2000–18 period, Latin America's average was 0.33 per cent compared to 2.93 per cent in all emerging and developing countries and 4.0 per cent in emerging Asia.

Low Competitiveness 4.0 Index
The 2019 World Economic Forum Competitiveness 4.0 rankings (WEF 2019) indicate that out of 142 countries included in the survey, Latin America ranked on average, at position 82. Only two countries were below position 50 (Chile 33 and Mexico 48) and eight countries were above position 90. Furthermore, in the twelve pillars assessing competitiveness, that include economic, infrastructure, technology, innovation, education, health, market and institutional criteria, out of a possible maximum 100 per cent performance index for each pillar, the average for all pillars in Latin America was 56.8 per cent, compared to 71.2 per cent in Europe and North America and 69.9 per cent in Eastern Asia.

Wealth and Income Disparities
As was mentioned previously, notwithstanding the substantial reduction in the levels of poverty and extreme poverty as well as the considerable improvement in social indicators in the last three decades, Latin America still presents levels of poverty and extreme poverty above 30 per cent and 10 per cent of the population, respectively. In terms of income distribution, Latin America presents the least favourable indicators worldwide. In fact, the average GINI coefficient

in 2019 was 0.48 for Latin America compared with the OECD countries average of 0.33, 0.42 in the Asian developing countries and 0.45 in Sub-Saharan Africa.

A Fragile and Unstable Institutional Framework

The recurrent political instability and institutional weaknesses observed in Latin America in the last six decades, characterized by dogmatic extreme positions of both democratic and autocratic governments—from the Left or the Right—on issues such as the definition of priority sectors, the role of the state and the private sector, the relevance of foreign investment and the definition of key areas and policies in international relations and regional integration. The lack of continuity and consistency in most countries of the region has been, no doubt, an important obstacle to stimulating the process of development and to close the prevailing economic and social gaps. An additional negative factor has been the high level of corruption that has seriously affected the stability of governments to such an extreme that many heads of State were impeached or forced to resign and many of them, including high-level members of their administrations, are or have been in prison.

The Road Towards a Renewed Long-term Development Strategy

Considering the structural weaknesses and bottlenecks described in the preceding sections and the world's geopolitical, economic, social and environmental scenario generated by the fourth Industrial Revolution and the pandemic, it is crucial that countries of Latin America, recognize that in order to promote actions to overcome those obstacles, it is imperative and unavoidable to make some necessary institutional adjustments. This will provide the platform to advance in political dialogues conducive to a negotiated, pragmatic and non-dogmatic consensus on the nature of the fundamental pillars of a long-term sustainable development strategy. For this purpose, the main political actors and representative sectors of society should be aware that non-dogmatic and flexible positions are required.

The following scheme illustrates the holistic approach required to design a sustainable long-term strategy of development (Figure 16.1). In essence, it implies linking economic, social and environmental objectives, sectors, and priorities in an integral and comprehensive way. This

Figure 16.1 A holistic approach for development

Source: Author

avoids the analysis of issues, challenges, and priorities in an individual and isolated way, as is common practice, not only in Latin America but at the international level. Cases in point are the ambitious goals (SDGs) in reduction of poverty, hunger and other social and environmental issues set for 2030 in the United Nations Sustainable Development Agreement signed in Paris in 2015 and ratified in 2017 by over 170 countries. In fact, there is no clear linkage between the social and environmental goals to be accomplished by 2030 and the feasibility of counting on the necessary financial resources and institutional mechanisms that would be required.

A Holistic Approach for Development

Main Priorities

A key element in the suggested holistic strategy is the urgency for the region to implement policy and institutional actions that, in addition to controlling COVID-19 in the immediate future, proceed to design a solid-long term development strategy that would accelerate the transition from a traditional comparative advantage model, highly dependent on the production and export of raw materials and low technology, to a model of dynamic comparative and competitive advantage. This implies the productive transformation of the economy triggered by technology, digitalization, innovation and solid principles of environmental sustainability. The central idea is to develop sectors and competitive activities that would have the capacity to generate relevant value added and insert the region to international production and trade value chains.

With this purpose in mind, the region should give high priority to the following key areas:

Control of COVID-19

Governments of the region, as governments around the world, will have to continue financing the necessary actions to control the pandemic. This implies the temporary generation of fiscal deficits, monetary expansions and public internal and external debt. Access to multilateral and bilateral financing with favourable long-term conditions, becomes a fundamental requirement for successfully accomplishing the following short- and medium-term objectives:

- Speed up vaccinations, particularly in the rural areas;
- Expedite universal access to vaccines and medicine;
- Strengthen logistic for emergencies and vaccination campaigns;
- Improve hospital facilities and provide the necessary medical equipment;
- Compensate unemployed and more seriously impacted social sectors.

Macroeconomic Equilibrium and Financial Stability

Considering the delicate and risky macroeconomic scenario generated by COVID-19 that might jeopardize the implementation of a successful long-term development strategy, governments of the region must adopt progressive coherent actions in the fiscal, monetary, exchange rate, debt and institutional areas to re-establish macroeconomic equilibrium, in a maximum period of two to three years. The preservation of sound and stable financial systems is an important component of this effort. The IMF, World Bank, Inter-American Development Bank, CAF-Development Bank of Latin America and other regional and sub-regional multilateral financial institutions can play very important technical and financial roles in this process.

Product Transformation and Trade Expansion

For Latin America to thrive, it will need to accelerate the transition toward a higher value-added paradigm. This implies an effective process of productive transformation that would expand natural resource manufactures and other medium- and high-technology exports, not only to traditional markets but also to new destinations.

As part of this strategy, intra-regional trade should be expanded to serve as a catalytic vehicle to support small- and medium sized enterprises that produce low and medium technology goods and services. This would make it possible to insert the region in value chains with a global perspective.

The decoupling of the USA–China in recent years and the pandemic-related acceleration of the digitalization of business, is an important example of a new window of opportunity for Latin America to substitute some Asian countries as the main suppliers for USA by near shoring economic activity for better regional coordination under changing production and supply dynamics. Unfortunately, Latin America, as the best positioned region in the world, is the least prepared to turn this moment to its advantage.

In terms of global production and trade value chains (GVC), Mexico and Costa Rica's experiences in recent decades illustrate two different approaches that should be taken as reference for the future (García and Méndez 2021). Mexico, as part of the trade agreements with the USA and Canada (UMCA and its predecessor NAFTA) has stirred its productive and trade strategy fundamentally to the automotive industry, following a more traditional labour-intensive productive process that is not taking full advantage of the opportunities implicit in the new digital era. On the contrary, Costa Rica has followed a strategy that connects much better with the realities of the fourth Industrial Revolution. In fact, it started by becoming a hub of electronic assembly and innovation after 1996, when it won a world competition to host INTEL's semiconductor operations by offering qualified human resources, tax incentives and stable rules of the game. One step further, in 2014, Intel moved assembly and testing to Asia, leaving design and engineering in Costa Rica, repositioning it up the value chain by increasing domestic value added to exports, raising average wages, productivity and linkages to innovation and expertise spillover to other sectors. This is, indeed, the approach that should be taken by Latin America in the future.

Infrastructure and Logistics

Latin America suffers from an important gap in economic and social infrastructure. On average, it invests around 3 per cent of GDP in this sector, compared to over 7 per cent in Asian emerging countries. Considering the key role of infrastructure in stimulating development, it is critical for the region to at least duplicate the level of investment in infrastructure. This effort requires the coordinated participation of both the public and private sectors and the support of multilateral and bilateral institutions, capital markets, wealth funds and other relevant actors at the international level. The introduction of innovative financial instruments, that go beyond the more traditional forms of financing, is something that must be stimulated.

The definition of sectoral and individual project priorities, the elaboration of comprehensive feasibility and design studies, and the transparent procurement and financing mechanisms, are elements that are necessary to ensure a positive impact of infrastructure in development. Furthermore, care must be taken to ensure that in the process of selection and implementation of specific projects, not only in infrastructure but in all sectors, a holistic appraisal methodology is applied. This means that starting at the pre-feasibility and feasibility stages, technical, financial, economic, social, environmental and institutional aspects are considered simultaneously. Particular attention must be given to the early evaluation of the environmental impact of alternative technical options so that the one chosen is coherent with the sound principles of sustainability.

In logistics, priority must be given to solve some critical administrative bottlenecks, especially those related to the existing high freight and duty costs and cumbersome administrative procedures. With this objective in mind, countries should make the necessary corrections to create an efficient and friendly administrative platform that would facilitate trade.

Technology and Digital Platforms

Investment in the creation, expansion and strengthening of information and communication technologies (ITC) and digital platforms, is a key component of the strategic approach required for Latin America to accelerate the process of productive transformation to facilitate the transition from the prevailing comparative advantage model—anchored in the production and export of raw materials—to a model of competitive advantage not so dependent on low salaries and other labour costs. It is also necessary to incorporate technological and logistic systems that are compatible with the principles of environmental sustainability, as those contemplated in circular economy processes.

Education and Skills

The weak link between the abilities demanded by potential employers and the actual skills of workers looking for a job, is an obstacle for the insertion of young generations in the labour market and clearly a factor that introduces a high degree of uncertainty around job stability at firms in many sectors.

Looking ahead, it will be necessary for countries to revolutionize the human resource, education and training systems in order to adapt to the demands of the new era. The strategy should be to go beyond the traditional educational framework of universities and technical schools. This implies implementing innovative schemes of continuous specialization and training, both at formal educational institutions and at the workplace itself. This change would have the positive effect of creating a qualified labour force, capable of responding to the profound transformations that are taking place in the productive, logistics and distribution processes.

Reduction of Greenhouse Carbon Emissions

The continuous rise in temperature worldwide is affecting all aspects of human life. Latin America, with abundant fossil energy resources—oil, gas and carbon—and rich in tropical forests, must act responsibly to advance in the reduction of greenhouse carbon emissions, as agreed at the United Nations Sustainable Development Summit in Paris in 2015 and in the Climate Change Summit that took place in Glasgow in 2021.

To this effect, concrete actions must be taken to transit to a renewable energy matrix that would substitute fossil-generated energy with hydroelectricity, renewable natural gas (RNG) and wind and solar panel energy systems. Similarly, deforestation—that is advancing in a disorderly manner—must be managed and regulated by governments in a way that is consistent with sound environmental principles. Priority should also be assigned to the introduction of circular economy technologies and practices in production and distribution processes.

Regional Integration and Cooperation

If countries in the region take the necessary actions to increase quality investment, accelerate productive and technological transformation and advance in renewed bilateral and regional trade negotiations, it would be possible to diversify exports, both in products and destinies. In this scenario, regional integration is, no doubt, an important instrument to increase intra-regional trade and to insert the region into production and trade value chains at the hemispheric and global levels. This approach has the additional benefit of opening opportunities for small- and medium-sized firms to participate in international production and trade schemes and contribute effectively to employment creation and other development externalities.

With this purpose in mind, now is the time to restore the excellent regional cooperation attitude that existed during the last decade of the twentieth century and the first one of this millennium. That positive scenario permitted advancing in the consolidation of workable cooperation schemes in the region.

An example of this trend is the high level of cooperation that was accomplished in South America between the two relevant sub-regional groups at that time—the Andean Community and Mercosur. In this context, the South American Infrastructure Integration Program (IRSA), launched in 2001 in Brasilia during the first Summit of Heads of State of South America, was successfully implemented in the first decade of this century with the main technical and financial support of CAF-Development Bank of Latin America and the Inter-American Development Bank (IDB). Other positive events that should be highlighted are the creation of the Union of South American Countries (UNASUR) and, on a broader regional geographic scenario (South America, Central America, Mexico and the Caribbean), the founding of the Community of Latin American and Caribbean States (CELAC).

All these events illustrate what is possible to accomplish when regional leaders have the will and non-dogmatic attitude that facilitates the construction of regional mechanisms, independently of their political and ideological differences. Unfortunately, this constructive spirit has been lost in recent years with the consequence of weakening these institutions and trying, instead, to substitute them with new institutions and mechanisms, integrated by group of countries, based on ideology. The Bolivarian Alliance for the Peoples of Our America (ALBA), the Forum for the Progress of South America (PROSUR), the Group of Lima and the Group of Puebla are specific examples of this trend. The consequence has been deepening regional fragmentation and the consequent loss of relevance of the region in the global scenario.

Thinking in terms of the future, it must be recognized that restoring the friendly and cooperative attitude of the late nineties and first decade of this millennium is an essential condition to re-launch viable regional integration and cooperation mechanisms. This is, no doubt, one of the preconditions for Latin America to regain a relevant and unified voice internationally, and to avoid being affected by the tensions between China and the United States. In this regard, it is of the utmost importance for the region to preserve a balanced and prudent geopolitical and economic relation with the main world powers.

External Financing and Direct Foreign Investment

Access to diverse sources of external financing and direct investment is crucial, considering the relatively low internal savings capacity of Latin America (below 20 per cent of GDP and reduced to below a 15 per cent average because of the pandemic), compared to a minimum investment ratio of 25 per cent of GDP that is required to sustain a reasonable and stable rate of GDP growth above 5 per cent to 6 per cent. These rates are necessary to reduce and eventually close the existing economic and social gaps that separate the region from the advanced and more dynamic emerging economies of the world.

To move in that direction, countries must have a permanent and constructive non-ideological relationship with the International Monetary Fund (IMF), the World Bank Group, the Inter-American Development Bank (IDB), CAF-Development Bank of Latin America, the other sub-regional financial institutions, the bilateral mechanisms worldwide and with the international capital markets. The role of the multilateral financial institutions is quite relevant, not only for the long- and medium-term financial resources they can provide to the region at favourable terms, but for the catalytic role they can play in attracting additional resources from bilateral and private financial sector institutions, international capital markets, wealth funds and other private investors. This catalytic role is possible thanks to the strict criteria applied by multilateral financial institutions in project appraisal, follow-up during the implementation phase and subsequent ex post evaluation to measure objectively the holistic impact of the financed programs and projects. Of special relevance are the transparent and competitive procurement and bidding procedures applied by these institutions.

It is also quite important that countries make the necessary efforts to establish and maintain adequate ratings, investment grade or close to it, from the main international rating agencies (Standard and Poor's and Moody's and Fitch), to ensure competitive access to international capital markets.

Finally, direct foreign investment is an area that deserves special attention not only for the financial resources it can bring to the region, but for the relevant role it can play in productive transformation, technological innovation, logistics and improvement of management and marketing practices. Moreover, it can be an important trigger to expand and diversify exports and stimulate a more relevant presence of the region internationally. China, an example of successfully attracting foreign investment in the last fifty years, is clear evidence of the remarkable positive impact foreign investment can have on a country's development.

It is required that countries maintain an efficient and transparent institutional framework with clear and long-lasting policies and procedures in order to attract good quality foreign investment.

Strong Democratic Institutions

Evidence shows that historically, Latin America has had a relatively weak and unstable institutional framework. It is of the utmost importance for the region to undertake the necessary reforms and policy actions to correct, this weakness, considering that it has been one of the main causes for the region falling behind, compared to other successful regions of the world.

To move in the right direction, the reforms should include measures that ensure the effective adoption of the following democratic principles:

- Transparent democratic elections;
- Limits on terms for heads of State;

- Separation of powers between the executive, legislative and judiciary branches;
- Clear definition of roles and responsibilities of the public and private sectors;
- Selection of public servants based on merit and not on political affiliations;
- Fair and stable policies for the attraction of foreign investment;
- Strict policies, norms and sanctions to fight corruption.

Concluding Remarks

The analysis presented in this chapter corroborates that economic and social disparities worldwide are one of the main causes of the political, racial and migration tensions and of the weakening of democracy, particularly in Latin America. This is a clear message to political leaders on the urgency of undertaking the necessary reforms to consolidate a solid and transparent political and institutional setting as a condition to overcome the structural bottlenecks responsible for the relatively mediocre performance of the region in recent decades. In this regard, triumphalism, dogmatism, revisionism, corruption and weak democratic institutions are some of the critical issues that must be corrected in order to facilitate the implementation of long-term strategies, that go beyond the four- to five-year electoral cycles and, in this way, become instrumental in reversing past negative trends and opening the door for a positive and stable regional future.

An important condition for this to happen is for leaders of the region to recognize the importance of renewing the existing social contract. This means, in essence, creating mechanisms of dialogue between the main representative sectors of society—government, political parties, private sector, labour and civil society—to establish a constructive atmosphere that would permit setting principles and norms to define holistic strategies and priorities that are consistent with economic, social and environmental sustainability criteria. Transparency and the adherence to ethical values are critical conditions to ensure satisfactory results in this process.

The strengthening of multilateralism and, more concretely, the world and regional monetary and developmental multilateral institutions is, no doubt, another high priority area that demands urgent actions at the global and regional levels.

Chapter 17: Emerging Asia and the World—Upside Scenarios

Emerging Asia and the World— Upside Scenarios

Chapter 17 | Manu Bhaskaran

Executive Summary

Major advances in diverse areas of technology are unfolding simultaneously, paving the way for transformational changes in the world economy. Consequently, substantial opportunities will be created which emerging Asian economies[1] can exploit to accelerate their own development (Statistic Times and IMF 2021b). With reforms and policy initiatives progressively strengthening their economic fundamentals, these economies are better able to manage the potential downsides that may accompany such major technological changes. If they can indeed manage the potential perils, the emerging Asian region could become the pre-eminent pole of dynamism in the world economy.

Groundbreaking Technological Changes Creating a Fertile Environment for Emerging Asia

The technological transformations that create these huge economic opportunities will be seen not only in the information-communications area where exciting changes such as artificial intelligence, robotics, the Internet of Things and Cloud computing are well-known. Many other sectors are also likely to enjoy revolutionary changes, including renewable energy, bio-medical sciences, new materials and even defence technology.

The pace of progress is likely to accelerate for two reasons. First, each of these separate technologies will tend to feed off advances in each other, thus helping to facilitate each other's progress. Second, the promise of high returns in these areas is likely to trigger a burst of growth-stimulating investments. Over time, these investments can help boost productivity and economic growth, which would feed back into more innovation.

Periods of Rapid Change Are Usually Accompanied by Dislocations

Even as the coming decades bring great opportunities, historical experience tells us that such revolutionary changes tend to cause dislocations. Rapid technological advances probably will displace jobs and render some segments of the economy irrelevant. That would mean job losses but also capital destruction, given the likelihood, for example, of stranded assets that will need to be written off. The surge of new investment will come with a substantial re-allocation of capital and structural changes that will create winners and losers.

---

1. When this chapter discusses the emerging Asian region, our focus will be on India and Southeast Asia. China's substantial transformation in the past two decades places it in a conceptually separate category of economies, since it has its unique dynamics. While smaller than China, India with a share of world output of 3.1 per cent in 2020 and the core ASEAN economies with a share of around 3.2 per cent are still large enough to be material to global economic prospects (Statistic Times and IMF 2021b).

Why Emerging Asia Is Well-positioned to Benefit from These Technological Revolutions

There are several reasons why the parts of the emerging Asian region being focussed upon, India and Southeast Asia, are set to benefit from these transformations despite the above-mentioned risks.

- These economies start off with a fairly developed economic base, comprising globally competitive niches in manufacturing and services, sound macroeconomic frameworks, growing synergistic linkages with other parts of the world economy and an improving level of human capital development. Most of all, the people in the region are hungry for success and their energies are set to be unleashed.
- Recent years have seen several of these countries put in place initiatives that can boost economic growth. A major infrastructure push is underway. New forms of economic partnership are being put in place. Reforms have been brought in to address deficiencies in the labour market and business ecosystem. Governments are also facilitating the development of urban agglomerations which could amplify economic synergies.

The track record of emerging Asian economies is not perfect, but they have made progress in creating the resilience and flexibility needed to be in a good position to seize advantage of the opportunities presented by the global economy, while weathering the potential dislocations and downsides.

Technological Revolutions

Technological Revolutions Are Unfolding Simultaneously in Multiple Areas

Much of the commentary on technology is focussed on Information Communications Technology (ICT) or areas where the rapid progress in computing power combines with stunning improvements in communication speeds through high-speed computer networks to generate new products and services or new business models and platforms. Compressing more and more computing power on even smaller chips reduces the unit cost of computing power, enabling a range of new products and services that would not have been feasible earlier. Similarly, when these are integrated with progress in communications technology such as 5G networks, even more capabilities can be created.

This leads the way to a range of ICT-related spinoffs such as big data, Cloud computing, artificial intelligence, robotics, autonomous vehicles and the Internet of Things which are just beginning to impact our lives and will soon be ubiquitous in our lives. These changes then create opportunities for new business models, such as ride-hailing or e-commerce or social media platforms or even snazzier video games.

However, technological progress goes well beyond the info-comm-related areas. Revolutionary changes are being witnessed in many, many other areas which are likely to have as consequential an impact on our lives as the advances in the info-comm space. The following is just a sample of the game-changing progress in a range of areas:

- *An energy revolution*: In renewable energy, for example, solar and wind power can now hold their own in terms of economic viability against conventional sources of electric power (IRENA 2016). These alternative energy sources will see explosive growth in coming years. And soon, even more forms of alternative energy such as hydrogen might be added to this list (Motyka et al. 2021).

- *A medical revolution:* In the course of the COVID-19 pandemic, progress in bio-medical sciences has enabled vaccines to be developed against COVID-19 in record time. That progress is probably only the tip of the iceberg of breakthroughs in medical care. In coming years, artificial organs, new and more effective drugs and therapies for cancer and diabetes, as well as better medical devices (KPMG 2018) that will enable better and less invasive treatment of ailments are likely to be seen.
- *An agricultural revolution:* The technology of developing meat substitutes using 'alternative proteins' has been improving the quality of meat substitutes so much that these meat substitutes are getting closer to tasting like the real thing. The market for meat substitutes is set to grow exponentially. Some analysts project that the share of alternative proteins in the global meat market will increase at least five-fold in the coming decade, from less than 1 per cent in 2020 (Witte et al. 2021). At the same time, production costs could be cut by half or more as a result of better techniques.
- *A revolution in materials:* The headway made in nanotechnology had led to the invention of nano-materials which can make all kinds of equipment much lighter, including aircraft, automobiles, luggage and power tools. Scientific progress is allowing for more uses of graphene, a super-lightweight material that is 200 times stronger than steel (Barkan 2021). Another newly discovered material, Perovskite, a light-sensitive crystal, will allow the efficiency of solar panels to double (Bellini 2021).

The Economic Implications Are Being Underestimated

This series of technological revolutions could provide an uplift to global economic growth that is likely to be well above what most forecasters have estimated, for a number of reasons. That means their impact on consumer behaviour, business models and costs will become much more visible, and therefore the spillovers into economic growth will be all the more powerful.

First, the pace of change itself is likely to accelerate.

Several of the technologies described above are reaching their take-off points: after many years of slow progress and adoption, the stage is now set for explosive growth, whether it is in renewables or quantum computing or nano-materials or meat substitutes. For example, quantum computing is set to drive rapid improvements in computing speed and power. Last year, IBM outlined a roadmap (Gambetta 2020) for developing a quantum computer with 1,000 qubits (a measure of computing power) by 2023, hugely up from its current largest quantum computer which has just 65 qubits. And that will help spur accelerated growth in a range of other areas, such as smart automation, fintech and blockchain.

Second, as these technologies reach critical mass, each of them will need new ecosystems that in turn require growth-promoting investments in many ways.

- New physical infrastructure will be needed. One example is in renewable energy, where the infrastructure that serves conventionally generated electricity will not suffice for renewables. That is why China is spending billions in constructing ultra-high voltage electricity grids (Wong 2020). Other countries will have to follow suit very soon or risk being left far behind China.

- The new industries will also need entirely new supply chains of their own. Take electric vehicles as an example—the components used are different from cars that use the internal combustion engine. That explains why battery technology has suddenly come into focus with a huge effort to build 'giga' factories to assemble the batteries that electric vehicles will need, and which are also needed to support solar and wind power.
- Moreover, each of these new industries will need an entirely new set of overhead services. As the Internet of Things connects more and more devices in almost every piece of equipment in our daily lives, for instance, the risk of hacking or other cyber-mischief will grow (Sobers 2021). So, the cyber-security industry will have to expand massively to ensure that the IoT roll-out is not marred by extensive damage caused by hackers.

In other words, these new technologies will boost investment spending substantially while creating new supply chains and generating demand for a range of new overhead services and support mechanisms.

Third, some new technologies are enablers that speed up progress in other areas.

Take 3D printing as an example. The basic technology has been known for decades but it is only now that 3D printing is gaining a more extensive foothold in manufacturing because enhanced computing power and advances in new materials have enabled costs to plunge. So, prices of 3D printers have fallen from US$20,000 when it was first introduced to the industry (Joel 2021), to around US$700 in 2020. Another example is in agriculture—new farming techniques will utilize advances in other areas, such as robotic technology and the development of sensors (Arrow 2020) for temperature and moisture as well as aerial images and GPS technology to produce a revolutionary leap in productivity.

In other words, there is a series of new technologies whose benefits feed into other new technologies, producing the kind of positive feedback loop that leads to unexpectedly rapid acceleration. Technological adoption is going to be much, much faster than most of us expect and that means much more rapid economic growth. The pandemic has galvanized businesses into exploring new ways of doing things and that will further hasten adoption of new technology.

Profound Implications for the World Economy and, by Extension, Emerging Asia

First, positive impacts on economic growth could offset the known headwinds

In recent years, many observers have been concerned about the proliferating headwinds to economic growth. They talk about ageing and more slowly growing populations that would limit labour supply; or the massive load of debt that, by burdening the balance sheets of corporations and governments, would limit investment. And there is the growing protectionism and inward policies that have diminished the synergies created by globalization.

With the right policies in place, technical progress can offset these headwinds, allowing post-COVID-19 growth in the emerging Asian region to accelerate, not decelerate. New technologies will open up bountiful new business opportunities for the daring. Higher productivity will reduce unit costs and raise profitability (Edquist 2021); the expectation of higher returns will spur a new surge of investment.

Second, the downside of accelerating growth will be more dislocations

Faster-than-expected development of new industries will mean faster-than-expected displacement of incumbent industries and companies. Power generation companies will be left with conventional power generation assets that have less or no value—the so-called stranded assets problem. The same could happen to automobile companies that have been slow to switch to electric vehicles. Many of these companies could go bust. Workers in the dislocated industries will lose jobs and may not be flexible enough to be re-skilled for the new jobs that are being created at a rapid pace. At the country level, there could be disruptive changes in the structure of competitiveness. For example, 3D printing could make production of currently labour-intensive items such as shoes and toys competitive in developed countries, and cause production to be relocated from developing economies.

Third, difficult questions will be posed to policy makers requiring good policy solutions in response

Some might argue that transformational changes such as these advances in technologies could cause prices to fall and produce deflation. But higher growth could also cause markets for labour and intermediate goods and services to tighten and so, cause costs to rise.

Another question is whether automation and other labour-saving technologies undermine the case for basing manufacturing production in low-cost emerging economies. It is unclear right now whether re-shoring—the relocation of production currently outsourced to low-cost regions back to developed economies—becomes so substantial as to hurt developing economies.

To all these difficult questions and many more that are likely to arise over time, the answer hinges critically on the economic fundamentals of each country and the quality of policy responses in each. The fundamentals of the emerging Asian economies are studied in the next section.

Emerging Asia's Fundamentals

The Starting Point: A Promising Economic Base to Start From

India and Southeast Asia have been developing rapidly. Thus, they have existing economic capacities to leverage off as they face the changes that the global economy offers in coming decades.

First, there are existing clusters of manufacturing competence. India has made progress in areas such as autos and engineering goods, with large industrial clusters centred around the Greater Delhi area, the Mumbai–Pune corridor, Chennai and Ahmedabad. Malaysia has three great clusters around the Penang–Kulim corridor, the Klang Valley and the Iskandar Region bordering on Singapore. And Thailand has its Eastern Seaboard region. While India's industrial development has been less export-oriented, ASEAN's has been led by foreign investment in export-processing industries, giving it a share of world exports of around 10 per cent.

Second, there has been encouraging progress in securing a competitive positioning in emerging new sectors. India has two clusters which have secured global standing as centres for software and related information technology services—Bengaluru and Hyderabad.

Third, the region is beginning to generate a large number of start-ups in emerging areas of technology. For example, Nikkei Asia (Koyanagi 2021) reported that fifteen Indian start-ups became unicorns in January–June this year and a further nine reached that status in July and August. In other words, India created more new unicorns in July–August this year than in all of 2020, when eight had emerged. India now boasts a total of fifty-seven unicorns, below China's 160 unicorns but clearly beginning to close the gap with China. The ASEAN region has thirty-five unicorns, of which fifteen are in Singapore and eleven in Indonesia (Ting 2021).

The Region Can Leverage Off Several New Trends in the World Economy

First, demographic trends provide an advantage to the late developers in Emerging Asia. India, Indonesia and the Philippines will continue to have youthful populations and growing workforces for the next few decades. Malaysia and Vietnam have supporting demographics currently, which will last through the rest of this decade. As China, South Korea, Singapore, Taiwan and Thailand, however, suffer the consequences of low fertility rates, declining workforces and ageing populations, their demographic predicament will open up opportunities for the countries with better demographics.

Second, rising costs in China coupled with geopolitical tensions will prompt a faster pace of supply chain reconfiguration. Southeast Asia stands to benefit, with Vietnam leading the list of winners. With the appropriate reforms, India and Indonesia can also benefit, while Malaysia and Thailand are likely to win some of this production relocation.

Prior to the pandemic, a process of production relocation was underway, as seen in Table 17.1. Southeast Asian economies have been significant beneficiaries where continued offshoring of production is sought (Table 17.1). That process has been interrupted by the dislocations caused by the pandemic, but the process will resume once the global economy stabilizes and returns to normal.

Undertaking Reforms and Implementing Initiatives That Boost Economic Potential

Countries are moving at different speeds to address supply-side weaknesses to better prepare their economies for the opportunities and challenges presented by the global economy. The responses come into broad areas: first, reforms to address deficiencies in the policy environment and, second, new initiatives to restructure the economy.

Reforms

There have been several groundbreaking reforms in the emerging Asian region. Some of these are meant to improve the business ecosystem so as to encourage higher levels of domestic and foreign investment, which in turn would help accelerate economic growth. Others are designed to improve macroeconomic stability so that the growth process is not interrupted by external or fiscal shocks. Many of the reforms noted below refer to India and Indonesia, for the simple reason that it was in these two countries that distortions existed that required reforms.

- *Regulatory reforms to improve the business ecosystem*: India and Indonesia, both economies that have been difficult ones for businesses to navigate, have made strides in reducing red tape. As a result, both have seen their ranking in the World Bank's Ease of Doing Business report improve impressively. India's rank improved from hundred and sixteenth in 2006 to the sixty-third in 2019, while Indonesia's improved from hundred and fifteenth to the seventy-third in the same time period (World Bank 2020). Similarly,

Table 17.1: Collation of media reports on companies relocating production out of China

Company	Sector	New production site	Notable comments from media report
American/European firms (n = 8)			
Google	Smartphones	Vietnam	Google 'seeks to build a low-cost supply chain in SEA'
Apple	Smartphones	Mexico, Southeast Asia	Apex of supply chain; major suppliers to evaluate ideal locations for relocation
Dell	PCs	Taiwan, Philippines, Vietnam	Dell to move 30 per cent of laptop production out of China
HP	PCs	Thailand, Taiwan	'20-30 per cent of production to a new supply chain in either Thailand or Taiwan'
Nike, H&M, Gap	Apparel and garment	Vietnam	Halting expansion plans for fear of pushing up factor input costs
Japanese/Korean firms (n = 15)			
Kyocera	Consumer, enterprise electronics	Vietnam	Chinese factories to produce for Europe; Vietnam facility to serve US demand
Nintendo	Gaming devices	Vietnam	Firm was considering diversifying production before trade tensions flared
Ricoh	Consumer electronics	Thailand	US-bound models shifted to Thailand, Chinese factory to continue serving Asia
Fast Retailing	Apparel and garments	Bangladesh, Vietnam	Still reliant on China for raw materials; may have to pass on costs to consumers
Kasai Kyogo	Capital goods (automotive)	Japan	Previously ships straight to US; now sends to Japan for processing first
Yokowo	Industrial electronics (sensors)	Vietnam	Full relocation of production of US-bound exports by end-2019
Konica Minolta	Printers	Malaysia	Increasing manufacturing footprint in Malaysia; reducing it in China
Nidec	Automotive electronics	Mexico	Will retain investments in China due to new growth engines in electric vehicles
SK Hynix	Semiconductor (memory chips)	Korea	Moving production of certain chip components—not factories - back to Korea
Sharp	Consumer electronics	Indonesia, Vietnam, Mexico	Sees opportunity in the trade war by shifting production to lower cost locations
LG	Consumer electronics	Indonesia	Further contingency plans are being made
Komatsu	Capital goods (construction)	Japan, US, Thailand	Re-shoring

Table 17.1: Collation of media reports on companies relocating production out of China (cont.)

Company	Sector	New production site	Notable comments from media report
Toshiba Machine	Capital goods (plastics)	Japan, Thailand	Re-shoring
Sumitomo Heavy Industries	Robotics	Japan	Re-shoring
Mitsubishi Electric	Capital goods (precision engineering)	Japan	Re-shoring
Asian/Taiwanese firms (n = 6)			
Li & Fung	Consumer goods, retail	Diversified across SEA	CEO: 'there is a trend to be less dependent on China'
Delta Electronics	Consumer electronics	Thailand	Shift production to Thailand via M&A
Inventec	Consumer electronics	Taiwan	Routing goods to Taiwan for final assembly before shipping to the US
Foxconn	Original design manufacturer (ODM)	India, Vietnam	Behemoth says it has the capacity to make all US-bound goods outside of China
Pegatron	Original design manufacturer (ODM)	Indonesia, India, Vietnam	New facility in Taiwan to make non-Apple products, to offset trade war costs
Wistron	Original design manufacturer (ODM)	Taiwan, Philippines	Already has existing facilities in the country
Chinese firms (n = 4)			
TCL	Consumer electronics	Mexico	Failed bid to acquire US tech firm on national security grounds (CFIUS)
Goertek	Advanced electronics	Vietnam	Expansion of existing facility in Vietnam
Zhejiang Hailide New Material	Chemicals	Vietnam	Setting up additional production centres outside China to "stabilize supply"
Hisense	Television	Mexico	Seeking closer proximity to the US market

Source: Centennial Asia Advisors 2019

the Philippines has also managed to cut red tape, which saw its position move up twenty-nine notches from hundred and twenty-fourth to the ninety-fifth spot.

- *Improving fiscal position*: India brought in a goods and services tax, replacing a plethora of state-level taxes that produced a single, unified market in its wake. Both India and Indonesia have also taken steps to reduce fuel subsidies and so improve the quality of spending. Indonesia intends to raise the VAT in April 2022, which is no mean feat, considering that there is never a good time to raise taxes, much less during a pandemic. In the Philippines, tax reforms enacted by the Duterte administration early in its term helped bolster the tax take by a full percentage point before the pandemic hit, providing useful fiscal space for the authorities to crank up social and growth-boosting infrastructure spending.

- *Reforms to facilitate foreign direct investment:* In 2015, for example, India brought in new procedures for automatic approval of foreign investment in some sectors. A single window for investment approvals has also been introduced in both India and Indonesia. Indonesia has also revised the negative investment list in a major push for liberalization and greater foreign involvement to spur growth. The Philippines has tinkered with a constitutional amendment to wind back some of the legal restrictions on foreign involvement, and while not much has been achieved to date, the fact that lawmakers are now more cognizant of the self-imposed constraints on growth is still a step forward, more so considering the inward-looking protectionist and statist policymakers. In fact, the restrictions are considered the most onerous in the Philippines, according to an index compiled by the OECD.

- *Tax incentives:* Emerging Asia has slashed the statutory corporate tax rate to bring down the cost of doing business in this part of the world. In the Philippines, the corporate tax rate came down 5 percentage points to 25 per cent (10 percentage points to 20 per cent for domestic investors). India also slashed its corporate tax rate to 22 per cent from 30 per cent, and to 15 per cent from 25 per cent for manufacturing firms. This comes on top of the litany of Production-Linked Incentives (PLIs) that serve to attract more manufacturing FDI into India as part of the government's quest to turn the South Asian behemoth into a manufacturing powerhouse, as well as to ride on the coattails

17

EMERGING ASIA AND THE WORLD – UPSIDE SCENARIOS

Figure 17.1: Infrastructure spending in Indonesia and Philippines

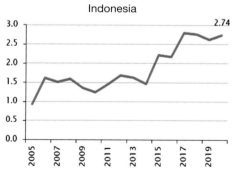
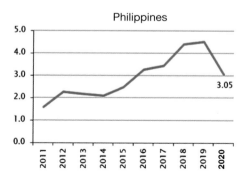

Source: Centennial Asia Advisors 2021

of China amid the wave of production relocation moving out of the middle kingdom. It is known for a fact that Singapore has also made use of tax incentives to attract more high value-add investment activity, even though exact details are lacking.

- *Labour laws:* Indonesia passed a series of bills called the Omnibus Bills in 2021, which pertained to a number of policy areas. But the critical change was in the labour laws, addressing some of investors' biggest gripes such as large redundancy payments and arbitrary increases in minimum wages. The reform would essentially halve severance pay and increase Indonesia's attractiveness to foreign investors, particularly as labour costs in the hinterland of Java province remain low vis-à-vis China. India, too, has introduced changes to its archaic labour laws, both at state level as well as at the central government level. For instance, firms hiring less than 300 workers will be allowed to let workers go without having to seek the green-light from the government, up from 100 under the previous law. These rules were clearly stifling and anathema to investors who favour flexibility in the labour market, and had prompted firms to remain small, at the expense of scale.

- *Corporate and financial sector reforms:* An example is India's bankruptcy reform under the Insolvency and Bankruptcy Code of 2016, which attempted to speed up the process of dealing with failed corporations and, thereby, to make it easier for banks to clean up their non-performing loans. This has improved the pace of resolution of such cases but because it has been dogged by problems such as a shortage of bankruptcy court judges, is likely to be further revamped soon. An earlier amendment extended the maximum duration permitted for the resolution of cases from 270 to 330 days, but the backlog of cases is still a key bone of contention that will be tackled by the government in the near-term.

Major Economy-boosting Initiatives

The past decade has seen a stepped-up effort by governments to address long-standing constraints on growth as well as growth-enhancing initiatives.

First, a huge push for infrastructure in India and Southeast Asia is evident. The trajectory of public sector investment in infrastructure in Indonesia and the Philippines, for example. Despite the recent setback caused by the ravages of the pandemic, infrastructure spending should resume growing in earnest again in 2022 (Figure 17.1).

India has also been ramping up infrastructure construction while Thailand and Malaysia, already blessed with relatively good infrastructure, are expanding road, rail, port and airport networks.

Second, countries in Southeast Asia have sought protection from protectionism through regional free trade agreements or broader economic partnership agreements. The Southeast Asian economies implemented the ASEAN Economic Community integration effort in January 2016. More recently, all ten ASEAN countries together with China, Japan, South Korea, Australia and New Zealand, agreed to create the Regional Comprehensive Economic Partnership (RCEP), which will take effect in January 2022. A smaller sub-set of ASEAN countries, viz., Brunei, Malaysia, Singapore and Vietnam, have signed onto the Comprehensive and Progressive Trans-Pacific Partnership (CPTPP) agreement. Vietnam and Singapore, in particular, have been prolific in negotiating bilateral free trade agreements. Another example of a successful

Figure 17.2: Long-term growth performance in India and Southeast Asia

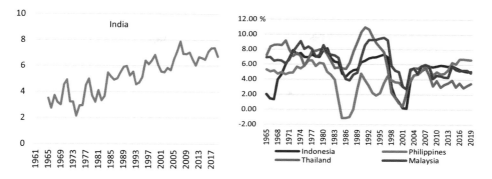

Source: World Bank 2021b

effort at regional integration is the Greater Mekong Sub-Region Initiative which brings together Myanmar, Laos, Thailand, Cambodia, Vietnam and the two southern-most provinces of China into a single region, where policies have been introduced and infrastructure built to enhance connectivity—which has resulted in a greater flow of goods, services, labour and capital.

These various agreements bring many benefits. One is that, in a time of growing trade protectionism and inward-looking policies being pursued by large economic powers, it helps to lend some momentum to continued trade opening. Another positive is that, by reducing tariffs and other obstacles to trade, they will help intra-regional trade grow. Finally, further trade integration in the region enhances the region's attractiveness to foreign investors.

Third, countries in the region are adjusting their economic models in order to create new engines of growth. One example is Thailand's Eastern Economic Corridor (EEC) plan. This aims to create a large urban-industrial services agglomeration, integrating the Greater Bangkok area with the successful Eastern Seaboard region of large industrial and port complexes. A massive US$650 billion infrastructure programme will be combined with the creation of new clusters of activity including innovation hubs (Reuters 2020). The EEC plan has attracted more than US$50 billion of investment commitments since its launch.

In Indonesia, the administration of President Joko Widodo is also adjusting its economic growth model. It is pushing for raw materials to be processed domestically rather than exported in unprocessed form. Initiatives in this area with crude palm oil and nickel have had some successes, which has encouraged the government to expand the initiative to other commodities. In tourism, the administration has launched the Ten New Balis Project to diversify its tourism offering away from the current excessive reliance on Bali.

What Can Go Wrong?

The upbeat tone of the foregoing discussion may come as a surprise to many analysts who have become concerned about the prospects for rapid economic development in India and Southeast Asia. After all, it is a fact that India's economic growth has slowed since the global financial crisis. Figure 17.2 (left side) shows how India's steady acceleration in economic growth over the years appears to have stalled since the mid-2000s. Similarly, Figure 17.2 (right side) shows that the Southeast Asian 'tiger economies' do not seem to have regained the extraordinary vigour they demonstrated in earlier years, especially in the 1980s until the onset of the Asian Financial Crisis in 1997. Their growth rates have decelerated following that crisis.

This pattern of growth is a reminder of that there are always external shocks or domestic political stresses or policy misjudgements that could throw once-successful economies off high-growth trajectory. Consideration for what could go wrong is needed as a prelude to assessing whether these economies have the wherewithal to overcome the challenges that are almost certain to emerge every now and then.

Indeed, there are potential pitfalls in the post-pandemic global economy which could hurt growth prospects in the emerging Asian region.

- There are increasing geo-political tensions in the neighbourhoods of India and Southeast Asia which could precipitate conflicts that disrupt the growth process. India has a long and contentious border with China where there have been occasional, though small-scale, clashes. The Southeast Asian region straddles the South China Sea, where territorial disputes have led to serious frictions among the claimant countries from time to time. Indeed, the South China Sea and Southeast Asia as a whole have become an arena for big power contestation involving the United States and China in recent years.

- Assuming that the worst case of outright conflict is avoided, worsening geo-political tensions could still lead to the various protagonists adopting aggressive measures in the spheres of trade, technology and finance, that could damage the productive integration that the world economy has benefitted from for many decades. While an outright decoupling of, say the United States and Chinese economies, does not seem likely, growing protectionism and inward-looking policies regarding the creation of domestic supply chains for strategic products could sever some synergistic economic linkages, and thus cause a slower expansion of global markets that Emerging Asia depends on for growth. The same could happen in the technology space if contending groups of countries cannot agree on common standards for new technologies. In the financial realm, it is possible that contending parties use regulation to reduce the flows of capital among countries.

- Apart from geo-political stresses, there are megatrends in the world that could make for a highly turbulent period, a period when exogenous shocks could erupt to disrupt the economic development process in poorer countries. Climate change appears to be accelerating, resulting in a higher frequency of unpredictable extreme weather events, higher average temperatures and rising sea levels. The extremely easy monetary conditions since the global financial crisis of 2008 through the pandemic crisis could possibly precipitate higher inflation or other financial imbalances that crystallize into more crises.

- A fourth set of dangers is related to technology itself. History tells us that the advent of revolutionary new technologies can cause dislocations. If innovations accelerate as rapidly as possible, some parts of the economy could lose relevance, resulting in companies shutting down, workers losing jobs and the banks and financial institutions that funded those companies, sitting on large losses. If the pattern seen in recent years of a few companies and individuals seizing a disproportionate share of the upside from such scientific progress, then inequality would worsen and there could be political backlashes that create instability.

Figure 17.3: Trends in economic resilience in Emerging Asia

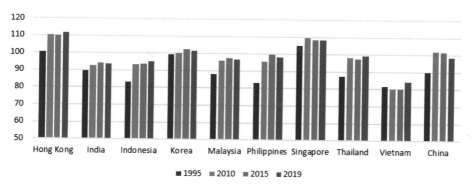

Source: Centennial Group 2021b

In the next section, the view that well-structured policy responses will be critical to ensuring that Emerging Asia is able to overcome these challenges and fully realize its potential is expanded upon.

The Policy Challenge: Key Responses for Emerging Asia to Succeed

The keys to the successful embrace of change will be for countries to develop resilience and flexibility.

- Resilience will be needed in the face of the financial and other shocks that are likely to fall upon the global economy in coming decades—countries with the capacity to absorb the shocks and bounce back will do better.
- Flexibility will be another critical requirement. This refers to the capacity to smoothly adjust economic structures to accommodate the potentially disruptive structural changes that tend to accompany such groundbreaking changes.

In the recent two decades, emerging Asian economies have endured their own financial crisis (1997–98). The lessons learnt were put to good use. The reforms that resulted helped the region to keep growing through the many other crises and shocks that erupted after that—the dot-com bubble bursting, the global war on terror, the global financial crisis and the ensuing debt shocks in Europe and other developed economies, a trade war and most recently, the pandemic.

Consequently, the emerging Asian economies have come out of this period of extraordinary stress. They have improved their capacity for adjustment and adaptation and so, have emerged as a tried-and-tested region. This might help them contain the dislocations that are imminent in coming years, opening the way for them to enjoy rapid economic transformation.

Resilience

The key to resilience is to ensure that shocks are not amplified, rather that shocks are absorbed, enabling an economy to rebound reasonably quickly from a setback. In short, this capacity for resilience is derived from the following:

- A diverse economic base with multiple engines of growth rather than an over-reliance on a single driver such as oil or other commodities, is important. Diversity in the geographic direction of exports and in the range of exportable products and services would provide a country with greater resilience.
- A robust external position such as strength in terms of current account balances, sources of funding current account deficits and foreign exchange reserves.
- A well-regulated financial sector so that the balance sheets of financial institutions, corporations and households can absorb the strain of an exogenous shock.
- The capacity for fiscal, monetary and other policy responses which are effective and credible.

The Resilience Index reflects these factors (Figure 17.3). It demonstrates that Asian economies have fared well in terms of resilience. Over time, the overall economic resilience of the region has improved materially, which gives confidence in the look ahead.

The challenge for policy makers is to maintain and build on this improvement. The most important point here is that the institutional reforms that helped improve resilience need to be preserved and enhanced. Central banks must be allowed to conduct sufficiently independent monetary policy so that financial markets find them credible. They need to be provided the resources and autonomy to develop their toolkits as financial sectors can evolve over time, often creating new sources of potential shocks. Legislative arrangements to entrench sound fiscal policies would be another area of priority for policy. Malaysia's recent commitment to a Fiscal Responsibility Act is an encourageing example.

The Capacity for Flexible Adjustment to Structural Changes

The factors that shape how economies adapt and adjust successfully to structural changes that unfold over the long-term are varied and are often the product of top-down policy efforts as well as the more spontaneous bottom-up responses of firms and workers. From the perspective of what public policy should address, the critical need is to create a business ecosystem in which firms and workers are best able and incentivized to undertake the adjustments needed. And that means the government providing these public goods is critical to successful adaptation.

This is a big topic but the short answer to the question of what public policy should aim at, is the following:

- The right regulatory environment will be one where government regulates with a deft touch what needs to be regulated, while not intruding into other areas where the private sector is best left alone. The key areas where regulation will be needed to address the challenges posed by the changes discussed in this chapter would be in the financial sector, since threats to financial stability are likely to persist, and in the area of competition policy, since there appears to be a tendency for new technologies to favour the emergence of large and powerful monopolies.
- The provision of physical infrastructure, such as roads, airports, ports, power generation and social overhead facilities.
- Human capital development, in a world of rapid technological change and innovation, has to go beyond getting schooling and higher education. Lifelong learning will have to become an ever-present component of the education policy.

- The soft infrastructure of a well-functioning community so as to address potential political backlashes to the dislocations that the post-pandemic era will bring. Since it is possible that some segments of the workforce may be displaced and some within these segments may be too old to be retrained for other growing sectors, enhanced social safety nets—unemployment insurance and early retirement benefits—that need to be built into existing social welfare schemes. Another component of the soft infrastructure would be creation of civil society groups undertaking community work where government agencies may not be best-equipped.
- Policies to ensure the optimal engagement of the domestic economy with the global economy. At a time of rising protectionism and where the World Trade Organisation is under stress, governments need to find ways to protect their economies from potential unruly developments in the global trading system, while doing what is possible to preserve synergies from trade and other forms of economic integration. Regional trade and economic partnership agreements are one way, while another approach might be to expand smaller-scaled economic integration through agreements to expand cross-border partnerships.
- Judicious interventionist policies may be needed in some countries to nudge economic development in the right direction. The success of economies such as Singapore, Malaysia and Thailand, for example, highlights how well-resourced and empowered investment promotion agencies can contribute greatly to accelerated economic development by attracting the right kind of foreign investment into the country.

Conclusion

The View on India

It is recognized that several observers have reservations about India's capacity to pull off a rapid transformation of its economy. In brief, this view is more positive, that India will soon put behind its recent period of relatively mediocre growth:

First, India is accumulating improvements in key areas which, over time, will compound and provide a vigorous impetus to economic growth. Even with some setbacks, there have been sufficient improvements in physical infrastructure, the business ecosystem, reforms such as labour laws and the introduction of the goods and services tax to allow higher growth.

Second, India's demographic advantages are more salient today as ageing and slower growth in workforces become more entrenched in developing economy competitors such as China and Thailand, for example, and in future years, Vietnam as well. A new generation of younger Indians are hungry for prosperity and could provide the energy and political force for progress.

Third, external trends could favour India. The reconfiguration of supply chains in response to geo-political tensions involving China could result in the relocation of production in some sectors to India.

Two reservations remain about India. One is the risk that the political elite becomes distracted from the laser-like focus on economic development by religious or communal issues. The successful experience of countries such as China and Korea show how vital it is for the leadership to be single-minded about development. Another reservation is what seems to be

India's growing aversion to economic integration with the dynamic regions of the world. India's withdrawal from the Regional Comprehensive Economic Partnership was a disappointment in our view. Without a balanced framework to drive such partnerships, India will be cutting itself off from the synergies provide by such integration, the competition that spurs efficiency gains, and the flow of ideas and external talent that nourishes innovation and adaptation of the sort that is critical for success in the post-pandemic world.

The View on Southeast Asia

There is a strong positive case to be made for Southeast Asia regaining some of the dynamism that has been missing since the Asian financial crisis of 1997–98. In short, a confluence of positives is beginning to fall into place including:

- A massive infrastructure push,
- Substantial deregulation that is improving the business ecosystem,
- Growing synergies from the various free trade agreements and economic partnerships that have recently been implemented;
- Production relocation from China to Vietnam and other parts of the region is likely, once the crisis related to the pandemic eases.

There is one concern, however, and that is domestic political risk. As seen via tragic events in Myanmar, economic potential can be squandered through unfortunate political developments.

Chapter 18: Reviving Multilateralism and Improving Global Governance— Responding to New Global Challenges

Reviving Multilateralism and Improving Global Governance— Responding to New Global Challenges

Chapter 18

Suma Chakrabarti and Ieva Vilkelyte

Introduction

The multilateral system, since its establishment after the Second World War, has been a leader in many of the most critical global issues of the twentieth century, including poverty reduction, economic prosperity and peace and security. However, the effectiveness of multilateralism and global governance has increasingly been questioned because, for a growing number of emerging market and developing economies (EMDEs), the system and the underlying institutions no longer address their needs in relation to today's most pressing issues such as inequality, trade, jobs, health, climate and technological change.

This chapter attempts to explain the diminishing effectiveness of the multilateral system and its corresponding institutions by:

1. Defining multilateralism and global governance, providing a brief overview of the history of the multilateral architecture and clarifying its purpose and objectives.
2. Investigating the effectiveness of the current global governance system by attempting to answer whether the most pressing issues for emerging market and developing economies are being addressed. To answer these questions, a sample of some of the most pressing global challenges/topics highlighted in this book will be examined through a global governance lens: inequality (Chapter 7), climate change (Chapter 9), technological progress (Chapter 11), jobs and the future of work (Chapter 12) and productivity (Chapter 13).
3. Assessing the voice of emerging markets in the global governance system and providing recommendations for loudening their voice.

Defining Multilateralism/Global Governance, Its History and Purpose

For the purpose of this chapter, multilateralism is defined as 'operating through architectures of organizations, institutions, and bespoke mechanisms, often based in treaties and international law, and grounded, fundamentally, in the UN Charter' (Moreland 2019). It is generally seen as a system or an architecture to promote coordinated action by several countries (three or more). Examples of multilateral institutions that make up the multilateral system include:

- International financial institutions such as the World Bank Group (International Bank for Reconstruction and Development [IBRD], International Development Association [IDA], International Finance Corporation [IFC] and Multilateral Investment Guarantee Agency), International Monetary Fund, regional development banks—African Development Bank (AfDB), Asian Development Bank (ADB), Development Bank for Latin America (CAF), Inter-American Development Bank (IADB) and European Bank for Reconstruction and

Development (EBRD)—and the European Investment Bank (EIB), Islamic Development Bank (IsDB), Asian Infrastructure Investment Bank (AIIB) and New Development Bank (NDB).

- UN entities such as the United Nations (UN), United Nations Development Programme (UNDP), United Nations Environment Programme (UNEP), United Nations Children's Fund (UNICEF) and World Health Organization (WHO).
- Special Purpose institutions such as Gavi, the Vaccine Alliance (GAVI); Global Fund to Fight Aids, Tuberculosis and Malaria (GFATM); Global Environment Facility (GEF); Green Climate Fund (GCF); and Network of Central Banks and Supervisors for Greening the Financial System (NGFS)
- Intergovernmental organizations such as OECD, World Trade Organization (WTO) and the G7 and G20.

This chapter concentrates heavily on those multilateral institutions—the international financial institutions, the UN development organizations and special purpose vehicles—that are most focussed on thematic and country policy work and lending programs in EMDEs.

The end of World War II (including its closing months) saw the establishment of multilateral institutions that continue today to make up the bedrock of the current multilateral system. The first organizations making up the current system, the IMF and IBRD, were established in 1944 at the Bretton Woods Conference (Figure 18.1). Soon after, in 1945, the United Nations was established. As new development needs arose, new organizations came into being in the following decades. These included, as part of the World Bank Group, the IFC, which focuses on the private sector in developing countries, and the IDA, which lends to the poorest developing countries. Several regional development banks were established in the following decades starting in 1959 with the creation of the IADB, then the AfDB in 1964, the ADB in 1966, and then, following the fall of communism and rejection of the command economy model in Eastern Europe and the Soviet Union, the EBRD in 1991. The increasing economic influence of emerging markets and their desire to have corresponding influence in the multilateral systems has led to the more recent establishment of the AIIB and the NDB.

Figure 18.1: MDB establishment timeline

Source: Authors

For this chapter, global governance is defined as 'the totality of institutions, policies, norms, procedures and initiatives through which states and their citizens try to bring more predictability, stability and order to their responses to transnational challenges' (UN Committee for Development Policy 2014). The general purpose of the multilateral system has been to provide leadership in many of the most critical global issues of the twentieth century, including poverty reduction, economic prosperity and peace and security. The evolution of the multilateral system and organization reflects the changing needs and influence of different countries.

Effectiveness of the Current Global Governance System

This section assesses the effectiveness of the current global governance system. It does so by further looking at five topics highlighted in previous chapters—inequality, jobs, climate change, technological progress and productivity—and seeks to answer the question 'is the multilateral system working?' in regard to each of these issues. For each of these topics, judgements are based on discussions with and commentary by those knowledgeable about the multilateral system around the questions of:

- the extent to which these trends are embedded in dialogue with shareholders;
- the extent to which global/multilateral institutions are tackling these in coordination with EMDEs;
- the extent to which multilateral institutions operate as a system (within the current multilateral/global governance architecture) and the corresponding business model; and
- the extent to which the needs of most countries and people are being met.

Inequality

The two facets of inequality, within country and between countries, have experienced diverging trajectories since the mid-1980s. Within-country inequality has been rising in both advanced and emerging economies, while cross-country inequality has been decreasing. The focus of MDBs and the UN on decreasing poverty, represented by the Millennium Development Goal (agreed by UN member states in 2000) of ending extreme poverty, has corresponded to rising incomes in emerging economies and lower inequality between countries. However, the multilateral system has been less successful in influencing within-country inequality but has recently increasingly emphasized its importance. Both the UN and MDBs have in recent years adopted goals to reduce inequality, for example:

- one of the World Bank's twin goals adopted in 2013 was to boost shared prosperity (World Bank 2015);
- Sustainable Development Goal 10 aims to reduce inequality within and among countries (UN 2015);
- AfDB, ADB, IaDB and EBRD all include reducing inequality or promoting inclusive growth as key strategic priorities.

Inequality is not only a concern for ethical reasons, but also for its negative impact socially, economically, and politically. Chapter 7 discusses inequality's detrimental effects on economic growth, education, social mobility, health, social cohesion, crime, environment and political stability, and emphasizes that it is and should be a concern of policy makers at the national and global level. National political will for some of these policies is low, as the results take decades to be seen, hence sustained support from multilateral institutions is key. Chapter 7 also provides an extensive list of policies to reduce inequality, many of which could be (or already are) supported by multilateral institutions, such as support for early childhood development, improved education quality and access, water and sanitation, increased accessibility to infrastructure and services, at all levels, and healthcare capacity and quality. The recent SDR allocation could be used to fund some of these policies. As inequality is a concern for developed and developing countries, it is well-suited for multilateral coordinated action.

Climate Change

As the climate is a global public good relevant to both developed and developing countries, climate change can only be addressed through a cohesive and coordinated global approach as discussed in Chapter 9. The global governance system has attempted to tackle climate change through many initiatives and agreements:

1. The 1997 Kyoto protocol was the first international agreement on reducing emissions.
2. The 2009 Copenhagen accord adopted by over 130 countries established the target that global warming should be limited to below +2°C.
3. The 2015 Paris Agreement was an important step in addressing climate change with both developed and developing countries agreeing to reduce emissions and mitigate climate change. It also established that financial assistance from developed countries to developing countries should increase by US$100 billion a year through 2024.
4. COP 26 established a target of limiting global warming to +1.5°C.

Unfortunately, this approach has not been successful in reaching the targets to reduce global warming or cut emissions: (i) the Kyoto Protocol did not achieve its target for reduced emissions; (ii) developing countries did not agree for many years to reduce their own emissions; (iii) the Paris Agreement's targets corresponded to +3°C global warming, well above the target of +2°C (UNEP 2016), relied on voluntary commitments for countries, and the US$100 billion target in additional financing was not met; and (iv) country targets are still not sufficient overall for meeting +1.5°C global warming.

The authors of Chapter 9 estimate that US$1 trillion per year is required for climate mitigation and adaptation, and believe that MDBs should play a crucial role in financing and leverageing private financial flows by:

- increasing the authorized capital of MDBs to help achieve the US$1 trillion target;
- providing comfort to private sector investors by co-investing in projects; and
- utilizing recent additional developed country SDR allocations for climate finance in developing countries.

The lack of a coordinated approach has been attributed to the different positions of advanced and emerging economies and their inability to reach a consensus within the multilateral system.

Jobs, Technological Change and Productivity

Chapters 11, 12 and 13 focus on the future of work, technological change, and productivity, which are increasingly linked. How these are addressed by EMDEs and the multilateral system will determine if EMDEs grow faster than or at least as fast as advanced economies, or face stagnation. Adopting new and frontier technologies and training a labour force that is adept with these new technologies will hopefully translate into continued productivity growth. Policies to improve jobs, technology and productivity directly impact one another.

Technological change is an important influencer in how people work and what kinds of jobs they have. Digitalization of work had been slowly progressing for years, but now has been accelerated due to the COVID-19 pandemic. The ability to adopt these new technologies is fairly high in advanced economies. However, according to UNCTAD's technological readiness index, the least 'ready' countries are located in developing countries (UNCTAD 2021). Although, multilateral institutions are well-placed to assist developing countries in creating policies that promote technological readiness, based on successful experiences elsewhere, this has not been central to their agenda.

Technological growth and changes can disrupt how people work. One effect of recent technological changes is the growth of the 'gig economy' which has resulted in more part-time work with limited access to healthcare, continuing training and education, and other benefits. These workers also fail to benefit from wage growth and social mobility. In addition, technological change can make some jobs obsolete.

Productivity growth is key to economic growth, a priority area for many MDBs. The period from 1950 to 1980 saw sustained productivity growth. However, the last three decades have experienced much lower productivity growth rates. Chapter 14 provides details on the trends in productivity and potential causes for its recent stagnation, including: external shocks and recessions, labour force size and declining returns to education, inequality and increase in informal/gig economy, declining returns to R&D and slow adaptation of technologies. MDBs are well-suited to address many of these areas. Multilateral support for education, focusing on STEM fields, promotion of digitalization and new technologies and policies to address dislocation of labour and capital due to technological change will impact jobs, technological growth and productivity.

Reasons for Lack of Effectiveness

As seen in the analysis of the five above topics, the multilateral and global governance system has room to make significant progress in effectively tackling the issues most relevant to EMDEs and their citizens. The relative lack of effectiveness in these areas thus far can be attributed to: (i) weak mapping between multilateral institutions and the needs of EMDEs; (ii) insufficient embedding of issues currently relevant to EMDEs and anticipation of new ones in the dialogue with multilateral shareholders; and (iii) minimal support of coordination on these topics between EMDEs and multilaterals. The reasons for these shortcomings, particularly the lack of mapping between multilaterals and the agenda of EMDEs today, may tell us something about the drivers of the work of multilateral institutions. Is this lack of mapping because those that are most interested in development issues in advanced economies are usually non-governmental organizations (NGOs) and their supporters, those that are most focussed on outdated ideas of development (one focussed only on basic needs) as represented by the older MDGs, and consequently that their governments, which provide the bulk of the capital of the MDBs, are essentially responding to that domestic pressure when influencing the policy and lending programs of multilateral institutions?

Western Standards and High Transaction Costs Driving Global Governance and Multilateral System

The influence of advanced economies in determining the standards of multilateral institutions generally, and development banks specifically, has increased the financial and non-financial costs for emerging markets and developing economies in working with MDBs and other institutions. The 2009 Report of the High-level Commission on Modernization of World Bank Group Governance recommended that 'these costs will have to be contained and reduced' and 'to make the non-financial costs of borrowing from the Bank less onerous while observing environmental and social standards'. Although high transaction costs at the largest MDBs have been criticized for years, no progress has been made in reducing them. Rather, they have increased.

The long history of multilateral development banks has resulted in their advanced economy shareholders becoming increasingly 'risk averse to stories of corruption, waste, human rights abuses, and environmental injustices' (Center for Global Development 2016). This has translated into rules and processes and increased bureaucracy that attempt to control for these factors. And yet, the effectiveness of these rules and processes has not been established. Rather, borrowers from the World Bank and other MDBs have criticized them for their long approval times, delays and high transaction costs (Humphrey et al. 2015). This is particularly noted as an issue with infrastructure projects (Center for Global Development 2016). This has been cited as a reason, alongside its relatively rapid appraisal and approval process, for the success and growth of CAF in Latin America (Humphrey et al. 2015). It was one of the reasons behind the desire to create the AIIB and NDB, although the former largely adopted the same due diligence practices of the legacy multilateral development banks.

Voice of Emerging Markets in the Global Governance System

Influence of EMDEs in Global Governance Entities Compared to Their Relative Economic Size and Population

Advanced economies continue to lead multilaterals and have outsized influence primarily because the shareholding structure of the majority of global governance entities has not materially changed since their establishment. Among the eight largest multilateral banks and financial institutions established in the twentieth century (IDA, IBRD, IMF, ADB, AfDB, EBRD, IADB and EIB), advanced economies accounted for over 50 per cent of the voting shares in six of them at the time of establishment; and advanced economies continue to hold the majority of voting power in 2021. Managements of these institutions, not surprisingly, give greater weight to the views of those shareholders that provide the majority of the institutional financial capital. The only two institutions in which emerging markets and developing countries, the borrowers, hold the majority of the voting shares, are IADB and AfDB.

Not only do the voting shares of most of these institutions skew toward advanced economies, but so does their leadership. The heads of five of the largest institutions—IBRD, IMF, ADB, EBRD and EIB—have always been from advanced economies. This not only reflects their large voting shares, but also the outdated 'understandings', between the advanced economies upon the establishment of these institutions. Although not set out in the IMF or World Bank's articles of agreement, there exists an informal understanding that the World Bank President will be an American (decided by the United States) while the IMF Managing Director will be a European (a single candidate increasingly decided by the EU). This informal agreement has been followed since the establishment of both institutions (Patrick 2019). Similarly, since its establishment, there exists an understanding that the ADB President will hail from Japan. Such understandings and the fact that they continue to be upheld also undermine efforts by emerging market and developing economy leaders to increase their role and influence at these institutions.

The shareholding and leadership nationality deficits in these institutions do not reflect the relative size of emerging market and developing economies globally, either in terms of GDP or population (Figure 18.2). As noted in Chapter 3, emerging economies already account for over half of global GDP in PPP terms, a share that is expected to continue to increase through to 2060. In seven of the ten MDBs reviewed, emerging market and developing economy members would have a much higher share of votes if voting shares were reflective of their GDP weight. The picture is similar if voting share were to reflect population weight. Nearly 85 per cent of the world's population lives in emerging and developing economies. In all of the MDBs, emerging market and developing economy members would have a significantly higher voting share if it reflected their population size.

Figure 18.2: EMDE voting share compared to population and GDP share

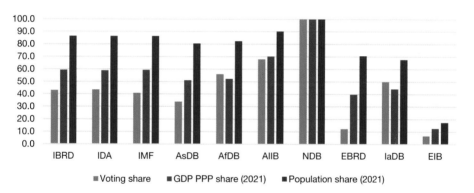

Source: World Bank 2021b and shareholding documents of included multilateral institutions.

Creation of Special Purpose Multilateral Institutions and New MDBs

There is a growing sense in many EMDEs that the current multilateral system is increasingly losing legitimacy because of its failure to address fully the issues of concern to EMDEs, an excessive focus on satisfying the needs of Western interest groups and a growing mismatch between actual economic weight of EMDEs and historic voting shares. This is a central reason behind the creation of, first, special purpose multilateral institutions, and then more recently, new emerging market-led multilateral development banks, specifically the AIIB and the NDB.

Special purpose institutions were established to address specific concerns that were not being (sufficiently) addressed by established multilaterals, most particularly in the health field. Due to a stalling in vaccination rates, Gavi, the Vaccine Alliance was created in 2000 to provide immunization to some of the poorest countries (Gavi, the Vaccine Alliance n.d.). The Global Fund for AIDS, TB and Malaria (GFATM) was created in 2002. In both of these bodies, the voice of emerging market and developing economies is much greater than in the traditional multilateral institutions.

New institutions were also created in the environment and climate change field throughout the 1990s and 2000s, largely because it was felt that the existing all-purpose multilateral institutions were falling to prioritize this agenda over other demands and falling short of providing the coordinated action that is urgently needed:

- The Global Environment Facility was created in 1991 to address environmental problems (GEF n.d).
- The Green Climate Fund (GCF), founded in 2010, is 'a dedicated financing vehicle for developing countries within the global climate architecture, serving the Financial Mechanism of the UNFCCC and the Paris Agreement' (GCF n.d.).
- The Network of Central Banks and Supervisors for Greening the Financial System (NGFS), created in 2017, aims to scale up central banks' green financing and work on the implications of climate change for banking systems.

Although advanced economies are prominent in all of these entities, and provide the majority of the financing—and thus far the leadership for GEF, GCF and NGFS—it is commonly held that the voice of emerging market and developing economies in these forums is quite influential.

New MDBs have also been established with the goal of giving an increased voice to emerging markets. The AIIB was founded in 2015 and NDB in 2014, and are headed by emerging market countries—China in the case of AIIB and the BRICS nations on a rotating basis in the case of NDB. Both are headquartered in China. They also have the highest voting shares held by emerging market and developing economy countries of any of the MDBs. In the case of NDB, 100 per cent of the voting power is held by EMDEs. A fundamental reason given by supporters of the creation of these two institutions was the failure of the established MDBs to recognize formally the growing economic weight of EMDEs in their shareholding structure.

Recommendations for Loudening EMDE Voice

The shortcomings of the multilateral system, particularly regarding EMDEs, could be addressed by: (i) reorienting their policy work and lending programs to match more closely the issues of current concern to EMDEs rather than the interests of development lobbies in advanced economies; (ii) reducing the transaction costs for EMDEs in the work of the multilateral system; and (iii) giving a louder voice to EMDEs in the multilateral system.

Setting a relevant agenda

The focus of the multilateral system is very largely set by developed economies, both because most of these organizations are led by those from advanced countries and because they represent the largest proportion of shareholding. A more inclusive and equitable system needs to be created in the agenda-setting process. One option would be to reform internal rules, without even amending founding articles, to take global policy agenda setting out of governance structures where advanced economies have the ultimate say and into forums where all voices are equal.

There is hope on this front. Compare and contrast the Millennium Development Goals (MDGs) with the more recent Sustainable Development Goals (SDGs), both in process and content. The MDGs were created very much under the control of advanced economy governments and ended up as a shortlist of basic needs goals that reflected the concerns of development lobbies in rich countries. They spoke partially but more clearly to the development condition in low-income countries. Even then, in 2000, when the MDGs were adopted, many middle-income countries argued that these were being imposed on them by bilateral donors and the MDBs despite the different development challenges that they faced. The creation of the Sustainable Development Goals shows the multilateral system can learn and was a more inclusive process in which all countries took part and led to a longer and more comprehensive list of desired development outcomes that are a far better description of the challenges across EMDEs.

The UN system therefore showed good adaptive behaviour in moving from MDGs to SDGs. Can the MDBs do the same? One way to build a more inclusive and relevant agenda for the policy and lending programs of the MDBs would be to make more proactive use of the Development Committee of the World Bank, on which all shareholders sit and where the chairmanship has often been provided by EMDEs. The Development Committee could come together twice a year to ensure the MDBs were focussed on an agenda that is relevant to all its borrowing countries and that the institutions were working as a system, and that work in each institution was truly reflective of its business model and expertise, so that the sum impact is better than the parts.

Reducing the transaction costs

In order for the multilateral system to function successfully for EMDEs, the latter have to view multilateral institutions as desirable partners. Fewer and fewer emerging economies will want to engage with multilateral institutions if the transaction costs are too high and prohibitive. Some institutions such as the AIIB, NDB and CAF have taken steps to reduce these costs such as:

- minimizing approval times;
- having a non-resident board; and
- raising the cut-off for financing that requires board approval.

There is a strong case for the legacy multilateral development banks to follow suit. A new initiative—a modern 'bonfire of regulations' within the MDBs—needs to be initiated. For this to happen, the MDB presidents, allied with their EMDE borrowers, need to form a cross-institutional initiative and set themselves a target, not necessarily to reduce the number of diligence areas, but to take on a more proportionate approach and adopt a target to reduce by half the time taken from project concept to effectiveness.

A louder voice for EMDEs in the multilateral system

Expanding the multilateral system to include additional emerging market-led institutions is one method to provide emerging markets with a louder voice. However, the current multilateral system can also be reformed to provide emerging markets and developing economies with louder voice and greater participation.

One straightforward, but probably still politically difficult, method would be to increase the voting shares of emerging markets in multilateral institutions, to more closely match their shares of global GDP (or even population shares). This would, of course, require significant support from current advanced country members. (In a similar vein, reforming the United Nations Security Council's Permanent Five Membership system would benefit emerging economies, but would likely face significant opposition.)

If experience suggests such a reallocation of shares in MDBs is politically impossible, then EMDEs should press for lowering the voting threshold for approval of country strategies and greater delegation of project approvals to management. Both actions would circumscribe the powers of the advanced economy shareholders on MDB boards to control the strategic policy and lending agendas of these institutions.

Outside of the MDBs, the EMDEs can become more influential in setting the global policy agenda if the OECD were to create an 'associate' status for EMDEs wishing to join the OECD (or other membership bodies) in the longer term. This is likely to face less resistance from advanced economies as it would also be a way to drive up standards within potential candidate emerging markets.

Another possibility for providing a greater voice to emerging markets and developing economies is promoting and supporting increased alliances between EMDEs in order to take advantage of their collective voice and voting power. Importantly, this would require no changes or reforms in any of the current multilateral institutions, increasing the likelihood that it would be successful. One has not seen this happen often enough, cf. the failure of EMDEs to agree on a common candidate for World Bank President and IMF Managing Director posts. If all other means fail, then strength in greater unity among EMDEs has to be one of the fastest ways of increasing their influence and role in the multilateral system.

Conclusion

This chapter presents the diminishing effectiveness of the multilateral and global governance system in addressing key concerns of EMDEs: inequality, climate change, jobs, technology, and productivity. Reasons for this include the high transaction costs of working with certain multilateral institutions and the inability of EMDEs to influence the agendas of these institutions.

The significant challenges faced by the world, the failure of the current multilateral system in addressing these challenges, and the distrust of the current global governance system require a rethinking of the multilateral and global governance architecture. The world has significantly changed since the establishment of the original Bretton Woods Institutions. The economic weight of the advanced economies at that time has diminished, and weight of emerging economies has grown. One option to capture these changes in a new system is to hold another Bretton Woods Conference—Bretton Woods 2.0. This will take a monumental, coordinated effort and may be a triumph of hope over experience, given the quality of leadership in G7 and G20. However, it is clear that the multilateral and global governance system must change very significantly to remain relevant.

Chapter 19: Towards a Missing Link: The Contribution of Cultures, Wisdoms and Spiritualities

Towards a Missing Link—The Contribution of Cultures, Wisdoms and Spiritualities

Chapter 19

Michel Camdessus

Considering at the end of the last century, the long-term perspectives of the world, we would have certainly joined the eminent economist Sir Nicholas Stern in concluding that 'if we faced properly the challenges at our hands, the twenty-first century could be the best of the human history; it will be the worst if we fail'. Twenty years later, the COVID-19, still with us, has strongly affected our scenarios and continues generating a climate of universal vulnerability and uncertainty, if not a sense of discouragement.

Facing these worldwide changes, the authors of the earlier chapters of this book have emphasized the fact that a global and coordinated responses at an unprecedented degree of multilateral cooperation will be needed for the international economy to remain on a trajectory slightly lower than but compatible with the central scenario we envision. But will the countries be ready for such an effort at a time of a rising nationalism in the USA, Europe and several other parts of the world? Will men and women of today and tomorrow be prepared to face the new realities requiring more than a marginal change in their ways of life: a universal change in their present mentalities and usual approaches, strengthening their ethics and opening their minds to different relationships to nature and to the universal? Doubts are in order. In spite of the universalization and unprecedented enrichment of the global culture over the last decades, our cultures remain basically that of yesterday. The profound cultural change which is required is the missing link in our reflections. So, it is urgent to identify where the cultures from yesterday continue generating a spirit of mistrust, division, fear and even hatred, and, simultaneously, to promote a climate of openness, stability and harmony as an essential step towards a new culture and better human conditions in the future.

Culture of Yesterday, Culture of Tomorrow

There is an abyss between the culture we have received, generation after generation, following the Industrial Revolution and the Enlightenment, and the culture which would be necessary to generate the universal harmony and a better human life in the years to come. So, let's try to identify the needed transformations.

Since the post-war boom, the advanced countries—increasingly imitated by emerging countries—have allowed profit and consumption to become the dominant mobile of their societies. The collective ethics have been deteriorated deeply. The man has been reduced, degraded to its economic contributions, life has become more and more meaningless and consumption, destiny. Greed can been seen as politically correct, if not a virtue according to President Trump's rhetoric. No wonder then if in many countries, the economic and financial spheres have become a fertile ground for corruption and all kind of abuses, creating the ethical vacuum in which the world economy rushed in 2007–08 and, with it, part of what made the economic strength and civilization of the West.

Efforts have been made during the last decade to get rid of the most evident and pernicious aspects of this economic system, but a lot remains to be done to address, with a deeper sense of solidarity, poverty and inequalities in the world. At the same time, our mindsets remain at odds with the changes required in our relationship with nature. The evidence, today, of the finiteness of the planet's resources leaves us distraught, as we are used to considering it in a deeply utilitarian way. This vision leads so far to an unscrupulous exploitation, often with devastating effects instead of the contemplation of nature as a gift to be received with gratitude and to be carefully taken care of. This cannot last longer. An inner transformation is needed in this area, too.

The same is true of the narrowness of our conception of the common good. We used to limit it to our villages or to the borders of our countries, sanctified by our mistrust and prejudice against migrants.

A last trait of the dominant old culture of the world hinders its encounter with that of men and women of the next generations: the deep and persistent impregnation of the international order by Western ways of thinking, more oriented towards action rather than towards being. As the world unites in erasing colonial eurocentrism, our old culture must open up to the cultures which took root in the East, Asia, Africa or in Latin America. It is crystal clear that a world universalized will not find the harmony to which it aspires, if it is not in the framework of a widely diversified cultural context, drawing from all its sources and no longer only from Jerusalem, Athens, Rome . . . or Hollywood.

The global common good must now inspire our choices and broaden our horizons to the entire world. Our collective survival is at stake. Suffice it to say that we need to change our cultures.

How to Change Our Cultures?

Cultural change is no small feat. To restore the ethics recognizing the universal connexions between the human beings and between them and nature, as the foundations of a new civilization are being set, is a sine qua non.

All political leaders know it: they cannot govern the mindsets of people as long as there is macroeconomic equilibria or the armies in the battlefield. The last attempt at a 'cultural revolution' at the end of an immemorial history was that of Mao Tse-tung's China. The Chinese today prefer to forget about it. Culture is the sovereign domain of the human mind and of its freedom. It changes, of course, permanently—but rarely as one would like. It can experience dazzling advances, sometimes regressions. We perceive today some clues of such risk with the craze for outdated nationalism and protectionist withdrawal, not to mention here and there, the return of a certain attraction for dictatorial modes of government. Even if we resist the idea that we could be there in some time, Aldous Huxley's *Brave New World* and the *Legend of the Grand Inquisitor* by Fyodor Dostoyevsky come to mind, reminding us of the periodic temptation of human societies to allow themselves to be gently channelled towards regimes offering them, 'the best of possible worlds', the quiet and mediocre comfort of irresponsibility in servitude. This risk is still with us. It is the honour of democracies to resist it, relying on all the resources of the reason and experience. The tragic history of twentieth century, nevertheless, reminds us that we have no absolute weapon in our hands to face such dangers. Our responsibility today is to stand ready to resume this fight and to make sure that the access of every man to culture is effectively recognized everywhere as an imprescriptible right.

We need to go further in our work for the advent of a new culture, encouraged by the fact that the difficulties of this challenge do not demoralize our contemporaries who, at ground level in all corners of the world, enact the values of brotherhood, solidarity and care for the nature, through thousands of modest but creative initiatives expressing their dream of a better world.

These experiences, often looked at with a degree of complacency (when not with scepticism), are basic cornerstones of the culture and of the society of tomorrow. This is how, in the ranks of the civil society, a culture of democracy, ecology, solidarity and the sense of universal citizenship is taking root and has the potential to facilitate the emergence of a new governance. Everything must therefore be made to allow these initiatives to protect the most vulnerable and nature to sustain their momentum, as they are always threatened by vested interests. It will then be of great importance that effective support be given to it at the global level, provided by an institution qualified and equipped to achieve this end. This should be the task, in particular, of the UNESCO, so contributing to make globalization into a chance for human conviviality. Their superb constitution of 1946 invites it. We will remember in particular the following paragraph:

> '… the States Parties to this Constitution, believing in full and equal opportunities for education for all, in the unrestricted pursuit of objective truth, and in the free exchange of ideas and knowledge, are agreed and determined to develop and to increase the means of communication between their peoples and to employ these means for the purposes of mutual understanding and a truer and more perfect knowledge of each other's lives' (UNESCO 2020).

Based on such a mandate, UNESCO could take the initiative for a global renewal of the education of the youth. Beyond knowledge sharing, it will be about helping the youth to recognize the universal and ecological dimension of their life, to take the measure of their responsibilities, of the chances and risks they will have to face in full respect of the universal ethics. Everywhere, this will imply a major pedagogic effort to revive education in otherness, 'Do to others what you want them to do to you'. The fundamental solidarity of man and nature will have to be taught, and children will have to learn that the quality of their lives will depend on their efforts to protect and cherish nature. Why not, to facilitate in practice this initiation, create a 'world body of volunteers for the environment' to which, in each country, local associations bringing together volunteers willing to devote time to catering degraded natural sites would be attached? This work is already in process in many places. To emphasize its global scope would make a lot of sense.

This educational renewal must become a great global cause justifying, at all levels—local, national and continental—much deeper and lasting efforts than those that have been led so far. All players in the cultural sphere: teachers from schools and universities, researchers, journalists, writers, artists, NGO managers, politicians, etc., should be involved. This will be for them a very exciting task; as observed by Professor Dutta, the young adults seem to be more optimistic, more responsible than their parents, and more willing to do their bit to improve the state of the world (see Chapter 12).

At a later stage, one might imagine that UNESCO could be recognized as the place of excellence where the fundamental issues emerging periodically in our societies would be debated.

19

TOWARDS A MISSING LINK—THE CONTRIBUTION OF CULTURES, WISDOMS AND SPIRITUALITIES

On the occasion of COP 21, many delegations, have time and again referred to this major document which was the Pope Francis' encyclical letter Laudato s'i. Whatever the importance of this contribution, it would have been most appropriate that, in the years preceding this conference, UNESCO be invited to proceed to a similar reflection. This work wouldn't have made the encyclical irrelevant, but it would have brought to the conference and those that will follow it, a precious intellectual and ethical foundation reflecting all world cultures. We can imagine that, over the next few years, questions arise of similar importance — the huge ethics questions raised, for instance, by technological advances such as those concerning the human genome or artificial intelligence. They will justify that the highest universal competences be invited to debate them in a renewed UNESCO, and to propose policies recommendations of a universal scope about them. The institution would thus fully respond to the visionary project of its founding fathers, who understood so well the importance of culture for the peace and happiness of humanity.

What Is the Contribution of Wisdoms and Spiritualities?

Daunting task, that of those who endorse the mission of contributing to the restoration of the ethics and to broadcast throughout the world, the culture of the universal! We can expect them to be numerous. As a matter of fact, everywhere, men and women silently aspire to it. A lot of young people recognize already this culture in themselves. More than the previous generation, they reject the vanity of 'earning more to consume more' and are looking for meaning and solidarity commitments across the borders. For those committed to such values, wisdoms and spiritualities should be now active supports after having been frequently all along history at the origin of the world cultures. 'Humanity is entitled to expect more from religions than we are currently giving', the Patriarch Bartholomew I of Constantinople declared on 27 April 2017, as he was guest of the Grand Imam Sheikh Ahmed Al Tayeb at the Al Azhar University in Cairo.

In reality, it would be difficult to imagine a deep restructuring of the current system of values without the contribution of those accompanying all populations of the world, training and supporting them in their spiritual life.

It would then become important to encourage all of them to remind their followers that dialogue, and respect for the nature are not 'optional matter', but are at the very heart of the ethics of their faith.

Together, the main wisdoms and spiritualities have basically the same common enemy: the perverse forces that set men against their brothers. Nothing of what tends to a real progress of humanity is far from the heart of their message. Difficult as it may be, in intensifying the dialogue between them and multiplying together their humanitarian initiatives, they would offer to the world, living examples of brotherhood and then contribute to the rapprochement between their faithful and with other believers.

Even if wisdoms and spiritualities have different cultural foundations, they all invite their faithful to practice brotherhood, truth, justice, the sense of the universal and choosing quality of life over the accumulation of material goods. These fundamental values could naturally unite them for tasks such as:

- the protection of the dignity of human beings, whatever their conditions;
- the promotion of peace;

- the construction of a sharing economy, by promoting disinterestedness and a sense of responsibility in all consumers and producers;
- a responsible management of the environment becoming more fragile every day, by inviting a more frugal economy, and of the recognition of our solidarity with the cosmos;
- a joint development of a proposal of global ethics inspired, for instance, by the project initiated by Hans Küng in the 1990s, in the framework of the Parliament, but of religions.

Who would be better placed, finally, than wisdoms and spiritualities of the world speaking jointly, to open minds and hearts, of the need to support, encourage and demand implementation of a profound reform of global governance? Who would do it if they don't?

No doubt, theological reasons could also powerfully stimulate their contributions. Far from being locked into their traditional teachings, religions discover today—as Claude Geffré, one of the greatest contemporary French theologians, liked to point out—that 'the plurality of languages and cultures is necessary to express the multiform wealth of the mystery of God'.

This implies a wonderful and powerful invitation to each of them to stand humbly before the others, developing between them without fear nor excessive diplomatic precautions a constant and brotherly dialogue, and looking forward to be mutually enriched by each others' questions and comments.

As a matter of fact, it cannot be ruled out that, in circumstances where so many threats weigh on peace, many believers come to be indignant at the timidity of their religious leaders to commit to fraternal dialogue and common actions, whatever the criticism they might have to endure.

Fraternal behaviour between these leaders of world spiritualities could also be of great importance. Far from the distance which, too frequently, separates them, it is encouraging to see more and more of them sharing their openness and readiness to contribute to advance the spiritual, moral and socio-cultural values of other religions. All this will certainly vivify local people's wisdoms and spiritualities, help them to communicate much better with each other and orient them more towards the horizon of all mankind.

The advent of a culture in phase with the world that takes shape now could be long to materialize. Cultures evolve at their own pace, often despairing of slowness, sometimes overwhelmingly rapid. Discouragement will not spare from, time to time, anybody. Leaders of the world of culture, wisdom and spiritualities, will have then a special responsibility not to spare any effort to help their fellow citizens to understand the deep meaning of the changes taking place and to convince them that a better world and the emergence of a new civilization are in their hands, provided that they comply with the only obligation defined for all human beings by the first article of the Universal Declaration of Human Rights of the United Nations, 'to act towards one another in a spirit of brotherhood'.

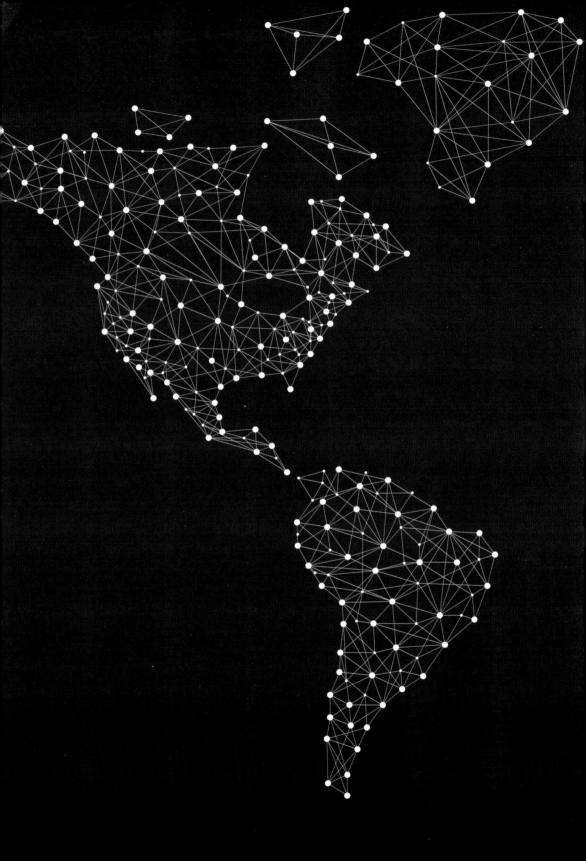

Chapter 20: Conclusions

Conclusions

Chapter
20

Harinder S. Kohli

The book presents two contrasting scenarios of how the world may look like in 2060—some forty years from now. At one end is an upbeat scenario, should most countries around the world seize fully the opportunities before them in order to benefit the vast majority of their people. At the other end is a pessimistic one, if many are unable to tackle effectively the critical issues highlighted in this book and, as a result, many countries and people—outside the currently advanced economies and East Asia—miss the opportunities so tantalizingly in front of them today.

It is up to the current generation of leaders—of political parties, civil societies, faiths, as well as youth groups, to shape the future in which their children and grandchildren will live. Time is of the essence.

The Potential of What Is within Reach: A More Affluent, Inclusive and Sustainable World

The potential within reach, and the desirable outcome, would be based on the upbeat scenario for 2060 described in Chapter 4[1] and possible synergies between the positive megatrends such as urbanization, rise of massive middle classes and rapid technological progress highlighted in Chapter 3. Further, it will be driven by the increasing calls for a better world from youth and civic societies around the world. Human ingenuity combined with unfolding technological developments make realization of this potential eminently conceivable.

Under this upbeat scenario, the next forty years will see the (current) emerging markets continue to build on the astonishing progress made by them during the past seventy years (Chapter 2) that will transform the current EMDEs, allowing many of them to replicate, in a sustainable way, the living standards and other social attributes associated with most advanced economies today. Indeed, by 2060, the number of advanced economies—by today's definition—could more than double and include much of East Asia, thus encompassing over 6 billion people worldwide, well over half of the world population at that time.

In 2021, just under 1.1 billion people lived in forty advanced economies. Their per capita income was US$53,000 (in 2018 PPP terms), while their total GDP was some US$57 billion (in 2018 PPP terms). The total global population classified as middle- and upper middle-class in advanced economies as well as EMDEs was 3.76 billion. In the upbeat scenario, by 2060, as many as 102 nations with a combined population of 6.4 billion people could have per capita incomes equal to

---

1. Chapter 4 defines this as the 'optimistic scenario'.

or higher than that of the advanced economies in 2021. By today's standards, 94 per cent of the world population would then be classified as middle- or upper-class. This will represent a five-fold increase over 2021, totally transforming the economic and social landscape of the world. The vast majority of these much more prosperous people will live in urban areas. In addition to higher incomes, they will have access to clean water, sanitation, electricity, better health and education services, and they would be constantly connected to each other through social media. Technological changes will have transformed the way people work and live. The global community will have found ways to contain climate change.

The Missed Opportunities Scenario: An Even More Divergent, Unequal and Unstable World

There are plausible reasons to be concerned that the world may fail to achieve the above outlined desirable scenario for 2060. Unless the issues highlighted below are managed adroitly and the global community acts with a sense of urgency, much worse outcomesl may become a reality, not only in terms of total GDP and per capita income levels, but also in terms of equity, broader social indicators and sustainability of the planet. Peace and security in many parts of the world may be at increased risk.

Apart from black swan events like the pandemic, three risks stand out.

First, as highlighted in Chapter 4, is the inability of countries to continue to pursue policies required to improve total factor productivity—especially in the services sectors—and to make other major reforms outlined in this book to achieve the GDP levels projected under the desirable scenario.

Second, there is always the risk that some of the economies that have been most successful in the recent past, such as in East Asia and Eastern Europe, stumble. Given their weight in the global economy, a major slowdown in these economies would have global implications.

Third, based on the past performance, two major divergences are even more likely to occur in the next four decades. At the global level, many emerging economies of East Asia are likely to converge with the advanced economies and become classified as advanced economies as well. On the other hand, much of Latin America and the Caribbean, Sub-Saharan Africa and the Middle East—comprising some 100 countries and by 2060, home to some 4 billion people (more than 40 per cent of the world total)—could continue to stagnate in terms of per capita income, have their fortunes tied to the ups and downs of commodity cycles as they remain mired in the so-called resource curse, fall further behind Asia and lose relative prominence in the world economy. Equally critically, global inequality and inequities within the countries could remain high, while their populations continue to be restless. Finally, climate change could have a devastating impact, adding to these existing problems. As the countries around the world move ahead with implementing their 'net zero emissions' pledges to fight global climate change, it is highly likely that within a few years, global demand for fossil fuels and perhaps some other commodities, could peak, and many energy reserves could become stranded. While these actions to wean the world from fossil fuels are critical to protect the planet, they will also be a major further blow to many countries in these three lagging regions. Such a divergent and unequal world can only increase social and political tensions, leading to further insecurity and failed states. Such potential developments in almost half the countries could lead to a much more unstable world. And this in an era of rising tensions between the superpowers could be a major threat to world peace and security.

This dire outcome is unacceptable both at national and global levels. Unfortunately, the risk is high of this outcome becoming a reality unless the following eight issues are tackled proactively and with a great sense of urgency—at the local, national, as well as global levels.

Eight Overarching Issues That Will Make the Most Difference

1. Climate Change

Chapter 10 has described so vividly the risks to the entire world resulting from the too slow pace of change, as far as climate and environment are concerned. Ahluwalia and Patel have described convincingly that even though emerging market economies were not responsible for causing the underlying problems (i.e., current stock of carbon emissions), they do have the most to lose from climate change. It is also most critical to them whether global warming is limited to 1.5°C, goes as high as 2.0°C or exceeds even that dangerous threshold. Given this, EMDEs cannot be mere bystanders or followers in discussions related to the steps necessary to contain climate change. They need to think of taking a lead, where practical. Remedial actions—going beyond pledges made at COP 26—need to be taken right away. As Ahluwalia and Patel suggest, Indonesia, India and Brazil, who fortunately hold the presidencies of the next three G20 meetings, should try to develop some initiatives under which emerging market economies can take a lead in developing and coordinating joint climate change actions that go beyond what can be accomplished during global deliberations under the COP process.

Absent more rapid progress that will ensure global warming stays within the critical 1.5°C threshold, potential developments in more than 150 countries of the world that are home to 60 to 70 per cent of the world's population could lead to a much more unstable world, with potentially hundreds of millions of environmental refugees alone. This is because climate change will aggravate all the other problems—including social and political tensions (for example, migration within and across regions, even without climate change, it is already a major global issue)—and lead to further insecurities and failed states, especially in the context of an era where rising tensions between the superpowers may pose a major threat to world peace and security.

2. Bridging the Gap between Different Regions: Transformation of Africa, Latin America and the Middle East

The only way to head off the dire outcome portrayed above would be by finding ways to prevent the emerging widening of divergence between different regions, and instead bridging these gaps. The solution lies in the type of continent-wide transformation proposed for Africa by Sarbib, Monga and Ford in Chapter 15, and the four-pronged, more balanced, approach to achieve long-sought transformation of Latin American economies proposed by García in Chapter 16 (he recommends adding social equity and sustainability considerations to the traditional economic growth and macroeconomic stability objectives, plus much greater attention to governance and institutional development). Similarly, steps tailor-made to its circumstances will be needed in the Middle East to wean its economies away from their current excessive reliance on export of fossil fuels and low-cost expatriate labour; increase their productivity and international competitiveness; significantly improve their domestic human capital; open the economies to more competition; and promote innovation and entrepreneurship. In most countries, there will also be a need to increase domestic resource mobilization, raise private investment rates, and attract more FDI (both to get more capital but also to obtain managerial knowhow and access to export markets). Only through these measures, over a sustained period, would these regions begin to catch up with the more dynamic parts of the world and meet the high aspirations of their (currently) restive populations. National leaders must also address the underlying causes of inequity and inequalities internally present in so many countries, a major global problem which we shall discuss below.

3. Reducing Inequality and Inequities within Countries

Persistent—and in many cases, rising—inequality and inequities are the Achilles' Heel of many economies, both developed and emerging. As convincingly demonstrated by Fajgenbaum and Vilkelyte in Chapter 7, even as inequalities between countries have gradually come down during the past thirty plus years, they have risen significantly within the countries. Latin America and Sub-Saharan Africa remain the most unequal regions of the world. Given their tepid growth in per capita incomes, their internal inequities are being increasingly noticed by the public, making it a major social and political problem. Clearly, inequality is bad for economic growth, in addition to being a serious social and political issue. Indeed, many social scientists ascribe the recent decline of liberal democracies, lack of trust in legacy institutions (including traditional political parties, police, the press etc.), and the rise of populism worldwide to increased inequalities. Without concerted actions to tackle inequality and inequities, it will not be possible for countries to maintain political stability over the long term and thus realize the desirable scenario visualized above. To achieve that scenario, countries should seriously consider the menu of actions out-lined in Chapter 6. While not all countries need to take every single policy action listed, there is an urgent need to reverse the recent trends everywhere and show positive results as soon as possible to win the trust of the public.

4. Improving National Governance and Institutions

This book makes obvious that major improvements in domestic governance and strengthening of institutions at all levels is crucial in almost all countries, if they are to make the progress envisioned by us. The case for these improvements is made at two levels. As Chapters 5 and 6 explain, economic history teaches us that better and credible governance anchored in strong and independent institutions has been the hallmark of countries that progressed steadily and became advanced economically and socially. With each stage of development, rule of law, transparency and accountability of public officials and institutions become more and more important. Today's emerging economies will have to follow the same trajectory for their economies to thrive and for their people's fast-rising aspirations to be satisfied. At the more practical level, this book presents a daunting action agenda that needs to be tackled nationally—at the local, regional, and national levels—by governments, businesses, and civic groups. For this agenda to be executed effectively and with the urgency necessary, countries will need strong policy formulation as well as implementation capacity. Good governance and strong (and credible) institutions will be essential. They are also a prerequisite for the private sector and entrepreneurs to thrive and become engines of economic development. These points are emphasized throughout the book, including by Tuluy and Shelton in Chapter 13, while explaining the success of the regions' that are leading the world in productivity growth; by García in Chapter 16 in highlighting the keys to triggering the transformation of Latin America, and similarly, by Sarbib, Monga and Ford in their recipe for turning around the fortunes of Africa.

5. Preventing Global Monetary and Financial Crises

It has been well-known for a long while that the present global monetary and financial system is outdated and ill-suited to meet the needs of the present-day global economy. It is all the more certain that it will be unable to perform its proper role and functions as the world economy becomes much larger, even more globalized, and much more complex by 2060. Professor Snoy has so convincingly made the case for urgently agreeing on a new architecture for the global monetary and financial system to replace the one which was essentially conceived more than seventy-five years ago, at Bretton Woods, in 1945 in the aftermath of World War II. The proposals in Chapter 8 are logical and deserve immediate attention at the highest levels. Indeed, while they may appear radical to some, they are neither new nor so different from what many knowledgeable personalities have proposed in the past. Past efforts include high-level commissions, including the Palais Royale Initiative sponsored by EMF. Twice, such proposals reached the G20 heads of states, but for a variety of reasons, the political leaders failed to act. But continued delays in acting would have a tremendous cost. The world could suffer a major financial and economic crisis, wider and costlier than the 2007–08 financial crisis. So, another high-level attempt must be made. The first best solution is convening of a Bretton Woods 2.0 Conference. Such an extraordinary step is necessary to prevent a global crisis and it deserves a serious consideration. This extraordinary conference should have the mandate to put in place the foundations of a robust and longer-lasting system that will meet the needs of the entire world economy for the next fifty years. The mandate must be given by the G20 Heads of State directly.

The above proposed steps are defensive in nature—preventing inequalities between and within countries, fighting climate change, ensuring political stability of countries and preserving stability of the global monetary and financial system—to ensure that the world avoids catastrophic outcomes and stays on track for a better future. However, to realize the desired scenario—the upside scenario—additional focus on two longer-term positive strategies is also needed to fully reap the potential benefits of ongoing technological developments: helping people and businesses adopt new work patterns that are already underway in many advanced economies; and harnessing these twin developments to trigger a new era of higher productivity growth and greater well-being, worldwide. Finally, a revamped global multilateral and governance system will provide the necessary platform for international cooperation and financial support for developing a more inclusive and sustainable world (see point 8 below).

6. Mastering Rapid Technological Changes and Adopting New Work Patterns

Professor Dutta has provided a glimpse into how future work patterns may look in the post-pandemic world in economies that master the ongoing technological changes. The new work patterns he describes—in office work, medical services, education, hospitality, retail industry and so on—are truly transformational. They allow a very different balance between work and family life and give much greater freedom to where people live, by working remotely. It will obviously raise productivity of those who successfully adopt to these changes and leave behind who cannot. But it also means that there is an urgent need for countries, businesses, and individuals to have the necessary technological infrastructure (e.g., computers, fast Internet, reliable 24/7 power supply, etc.). Basic literacy, not only in traditional subjects, but also in information and communication technologies, as well as science, math and STEM-related fields, will be essential. Otherwise, the world faces the danger of another divide: between countries that master the ongoing rapid technological changes and adopt new work patterns to remain competitive and countries that suffer from the digital divide and are unable to make the transition to the new world that is unfolding rapidly elsewhere.

7. Triggering Renewed Productivity Improvements (at Global and National Levels)

As Loser and his colleagues have demonstrated in Chapter 4, the biggest difference between their optimistic and pessimistic scenarios are the assumptions made about the future path of the global productivity frontier. Some comfort comes from Tuluy and Shelton, who witness in Chapter 13 green shoots of an uptick in global total factor productivity since 2008, driven perhaps by new technological developments. These positive developments are especially evident in East and South Asia. In that context, Bhaskaran's upbeat perspective on Emerging Asia (even excluding China), reinforces the view that at least Asia may see renewed productivity improvements. If such improvements can be replicated globally—that is including in Africa, Latin America, and the Middle East—a much more prosperous world can be foreseen, as well as a more equitable community of nations.

Achieving such an outcome will require not only facilitating new technologies to spread throughout the world—while ensuring ethical aspects and personal security—but also following national economic and trade policies that allow constant development and diffusion of new ideas and technologies within and across countries.

8. Revamping the Multilateral and Global Governance System

The significant challenges faced by the world outlined above, the failure of the current multilateral system in addressing these challenges, and the distrust of the current global governance system require a revamping of the multilateral and global governance architecture. The world has significantly changed since the establishment of the original Bretton Woods institutions in 1944. The economic weight of the advanced economies at that time has diminished and weight of emerging economies has grown tremendously, and yet their influence in the legacy multilateral institutions remains marginal. Given the quality of leadership in G7 and G20, one option to capture these changes in a new system is to hold another Bretton Woods Conference—Bretton Woods 2.0. This will take a monumental, coordinated effort. Whatever the mechanism to bring about the reforms, it is clear that the multilateral and global governance system must change very significantly to remain relevant.

In addition, there will be the need to revamp on an ongoing basis, the global governance framework as well as the multilateral development institutions to reflect the realities of a new global economy and respond effectively to the above challenges.

Final Remarks

It is evident throughout the book that change—often fundamental—will be a constant during the next forty years. Indeed, major changes have occurred periodically in the past and have normally been associated with economic and social progress. However, what is striking here is that the pace of change foreseen by various authors is different in three respects, this time: its speed is likely to be much faster; it is expected to occur on multiple fronts simultaneously; and it will spread geographically much quicker than in the past.

It is also clear that most actions must be taken at national (and local) level. While the international community (including development assistance agencies) can help (technically and financially), countries themselves must be in the lead for conceiving, designing, and implementing the major changes needed to tackle the above daunting issues, and setting priorities between them. They must exercise the agency for making and acting on difficult decisions. Leadership at the national level will be at a premium and will be of the essence everywhere.

This book has identified extraordinary opportunities for progress, daunting challenges, and, above everything, the critical responsibility that this generation carries for the future of the world: for the well-being of future generations as well as for the care of the planet. History will be the judge.

Epilogue

Epilogue

Michel Camdessus

Once again, but this time in the midst of the greatest uncertainties, the excellent team of researchers from the Emerging Markets Forum (EMF) shares with us its reading of the future, its analytical tools and its strategic recommendations so that the formidable risks that obscure the horizon can be contained and undeniable opportunities can be seized.

Never, throughout the twenty years during which these works have followed one another, has the world horizon appeared to us so blocked; so uncertain the outcome of the decisive fight for the future of humanity, which opposes the culture of yesterday and tomorrow. Our too rapid inventory of the cultural resources and the wisdoms and spiritualities of the world could not fully reassure us. We may be asked if their admirable messages will be able to reverse the powerful regressive thrust that is manifesting itself in so many places: will they be able to generate forces of openness and generosity sufficient for at least one silver lining to come timidly to illuminate our horizon? Our work does not allow us, objectively, to remove these doubts.

Our book therefore concludes simply with an appeal to the lucidity, intelligence, courage and disinterestedness of all men of good will and, particularly, of those in charge of the public and private destinies of the world.

Without claiming to speak in the name of solidly supported scientific knowledge, I would like to try to respond to Harinder Kohli's invitation, suggesting that, in adding to that wise conclusion, I share my personal conviction. Indeed, as he knows, I believe that in the midst of all the kind of difficulties, convulsions and setbacks imaginable, humanity is nonetheless moving towards a better future.

Is it optimism in the evening of a professional life enlightened by the joy of working in friendship, in the service of the global public good, alongside men and women driven by the same passion for man and the advance of humanity? Maybe…at least in part! Would it be rather a stubborn refusal to see called into question the efforts of man so far to broaden his horizons and his progress towards a fraternal unity of the world? Maybe also! But I believe there is more than that.

I could, for example, base myself on my international experiences and my encounters with men or women who have been able, in their country or at the head of multilateral structures, to change the lazy or dangerous march of history. Many names come to mind: those of Nelson Mandela, Kofi Annan, Benjamin Mkapa, Joaquim Chissano, Fidel Ramos, Manmohan Singh, Anwar Ibrahim and his wife Azizah, Kim Dae Jong, or those of Angela Merkel or Michael Gorbachev and those of Jacques Delors or Enrique Iglesias. But will providential men or women of this calibre be there at the critical moment? Let us not exclude it but, in the absence of certainties, let us turn instead to the lessons of two kinds of enlightening encounters that helped me get rid of the temptations of scepticism.

These are firstly meetings with many men and women around the world who, without even being able to name it, work in the service of the common good, even amid the backdrop of a deafening media silence. It is also the stimulating exchanges all over the world with young people, on the threshold of their active life, ardently in search of an alternative to the lure of profit, to the culture of overconsumption and to the withdrawal into oneself, who shared with me their concerns, their dreams and their vocation.

These two kinds of encounters have a striking common feature: a convergence between the sense of the admirable work of the first, often in the greatest destitution and the resolution that is expressed in the dreams and life choices of others. On both sides, there is an energy, a force of commitment that can become powerful levers for renewal. Let us stop there for a moment.

Let us first observe the work to which, in the poorest countries as well as in the pockets of misery of the most advanced countries, so many men and women who, far from resigning themselves to it, fight the thousand faces of misery. These experiences are most often ignored or viewed with complacency tinged with scepticism. They are, however, highly significant; they are building blocks for the culture and the ethics of the societies of tomorrow. I met them all over the world, wherever my international responsibilities took me—Madagascar, Zambia, Ethiopia, Mozambique, the Democratic Republic of Congo, India, Chile, Brazil, Cambodia and elsewhere. Their list could be much longer. In their astounding diversity, they share common traits. Among those who launch them or participate in them, there are many women.

It is always about the fight for human dignity and confidence in the capacity of the victims to take themselves in hand and to find strength, dynamism and courage to open, when necessary, the dialogue with the public authorities and carry their decisions. These initiatives are most often democratic and participatory. They ensure the dignity of working conditions and the fairness of remuneration. They carry very high concern for popular education: for the oldest, because it is a path to greater dignity and freedom, for the youngest, so that future leaders emerge from their ranks. Every opportunity is good for them to add flavour, conviviality and beauty to the human settlements they undertake to create or renovate. They take care not to leave anyone on the side of the road, including those who, too quickly resigned, would give up. They end up achieving what they might have thought impossible. Their success serves as an example to others, sometimes beyond the borders of their country. They are points of irradiation of a new culture. Let us just say it, these men and women are planting the milestones of a new collective ethic in human becoming.

Let us turn to the generation now approaching adulthood. Professor Dutta described it admirably. I, for my part, was fortunate enough to meet many of these young people and to observe that their dreams, their resolutions for the future and the way of life they choose are stingingly in line with the behaviour of many poor members of the civil society that I have just described. There is no doubt that most of them, who will take on the responsibilities tomorrow, will seek to refer to it; they will thus contribute to the cultural and ethical renewal essential to the success of the strategies we recommend. The essential features of these new approaches could be summed up in a few points:

- The absolute primacy of the human person and respect for his rights;

- The sense of a universal interconnection of the living, fundamentally surpassing that brought to us by the prodigious advances in digital technology. It invites us to recognize that every human is linked to all dimensions of the world for better and for worse;
- The sense of everyone's universal responsibility, even more evident in a world that is constantly closing in on itself, even more so than when Dostoyevsky was already proclaiming: 'The responsibility of all, before all.';
- The centrality of poverty reduction at a time when inequalities continue to worsen. This is where humanity must place the tip of its lever to have the best chance of finding its way into the future. A world that would be more open to those who are excluded, threatened by hunger, who are homeless, landless or jobless, would in turn benefit from this wisdom that the poor hold and which is perhaps, with the solidarity of one discovers among them, a key to accessing a more habitable and fraternal world;
- The critical importance of economically and socially transformed and politically stable as well as self-confident Africa and Latin America taking their rightful place in the global community of nations. Their much-needed transformations must be led by their countries themselves so the continents' relations with the rest of the world become more symmetrical.
- Respect for our environment and the cosmos, of which our century is finally discovering the organic solidarity with the destiny of humanity itself. Climate change is the biggest threat to humanity and the planet that our generation is destined to confront. This should be accomplished by a return to frugality, to self-discipline, to living in harmony with nature, which our ancestors practiced and which Professor Ramgopal Agarwala, in *The World in 2050*, saw 'a blessing in disguise';
- The renewal of education methods and the increase in the means allocated to it. It would be a question both of ensuring strict equality between girls and boys, and of replacing the bookish increase in knowledge with the concern to awaken the imaginations and creativity, as well as a sense of freedom, teamwork and discernment, and finally of guaranteeing access to lifelong learning.

Guided by these landmarks, the human community would renew today's fledgling relationships between the local and the global. As it engages from above in the reform of its structures of global governance, it would help to establish, at ground level, a universal network of micro-communities of immense diversity linked to each other by innumerable exchange links free to find its place and where a world citizenship could truly take root.

What to conclude from this? The 'weaker forces' that carry the elements of this new collective ethics are among us. In recent decades, there has been excessive emphasis on materialism, short-term gains and self-satisfaction at the cost of moral values and ethics. This must be reversed. We can hope that the so-called weaker forces and their idealism will start this process. And that they will be more vigorously represented by the generation that follows us. Would it, then, be unreasonable to expect that it will succeed in triggering a kind of spiritual new deal and thus curb the trend of history towards the success of the policies necessary to make the world a better place?

These weak forces are, perhaps, derisory in the eyes of cynics; however, a quick overview of history is enough to show us that if progress is constantly disturbed by perverse forces, the silent push of the forces of good often succeeds in straightening its course. So, let us not rule out this possibility, as so many young people cannot imagine the future to be built any other way.

Would this be sheer optimism? No, rather the convictions of a Christian who readily agrees with the immemorial wisdom of the Buddha proclaiming that 'Pessimism is a let-go' and that 'You have to want to be happy'. And for it, as reasonable people, we must unite to give ourselves the modest means, which are required for it.

References

Abreha, Kaleb, Emmanuel Lartey, Taye Mengistae, Solomon Owusu, and Albert Zeufack. Africa in Manufacturing Global Value Chains: Cross-country Patterns in the Dynamics of Linkages. Policy Research Working Paper No. 9439. Washington DC: World Bank, 2020.

Accenture. Tech Vision 2021. Accessed 8 December 2021. https://www.accenture.com/us-en/insights/technology/technology-trends-2021.

Acemoglu, Daron and Pascual Restrepo. The Race between Machine and Man: Implications of Technology for Growth, Factor Shares, and Employment. NBER Working Paper #22252, June, 2017.

Acemoglu, Daron and William Robinson. Why Nations Fail: The Origins of Power, Prosperity, and Poverty. New York: Crown Publishers, 2012.

ACET. African Transformation Report 2017: Agriculture Powering Africa's Economic Transformation. Accra: The African Center for Economic Transformation, 2017.

Acker, Kevin, Deborah Brautigam, and Yufan Huang. The Pandemic has Worsened Africa's Debt Crisis: China and Other Countries Are Stepping In. Washington Post, February 26, 2021.

ADB. Governance: Sound Development Management. Manila: ADB, 1995.

ADB. A Region At Risk: The Human Dimensions of Climate Change in Asia and the Pacific. Manila: ADB, 2007a.

ADB. Rural Poverty Reduction and Inclusive Growth. Manila: ADB, 2007b.

ADB. Asian Water Development Outlook 2013. Manila: ADB, 2013.

ADB. Evaluation of ADB Agricultural Assistance. Manila: ADB, 2019.

Adepoju, Aderanti, Corrado Fumagalli, and Nanjala Nyabola, eds. Africa Migration Report: Challenging the Narrative. Addis Ababa: UN International Organization for Migration and African Union, 2020.

AfDB. Climate Change in Africa. Accessed 12 December 2021. https://www.Afdb.org/En/Cop25/Climate-Change-Africa.

AfDB. Jobs for Youth in Africa: Catalyzing Youth Opportunity Across Africa. Abidjan: African Development Bank Group, 2016. https://www.Afdb.org/Fileadmin/Uploads/Afdb/Images/High_5s/Job_Youth_Africa_Job_Youth_Africa.Pdf.

Africa CDC. Africa CDC Vaccine Dashboard. Accessed 2 January 2022. Accessed At: https://Africacdc.org/Covid-19-Vaccination/.

African Union. Agenda 2063: The Africa We Want. Accessed on 13 December 2021 at https://au.int/en/agenda2063/overview.

Aglietta, Michel and Natacha Valla. Le Système Monétaire International: De La Devise Clé Au Multilatéralisme. In Le Futur De La Monnaie. Paris: Odile Jacob, 2021.

Aglietta, Michel and Virginie Coudert. The Dollar and the Transition to Sustainable Development: From Key Currency to Multilateralism. CEPII Policy Brief No 26. Paris: CEPII, 2019.

Aglietta, Michel. The Preponderance of the Financial Cycle and the Persistence of Financial Fragilities in Neo-Liberal Capitalism. Presentation for RTI Working Party on Managing Global Liquidity as a Global Public Good, March 2019.

Ahlers, Theodore and Harinder S. Kohli, eds. Africa Reset: A New Way Forward. New Delhi: Oxford University Press, 2017.

Ahrend, Rudiger, Alexander Lembcke, and Abel Schumann. The Role of Urban Agglomerations for Economic and Productivity Growth. International Productivity Monitor, Centre for the Study of Living Standards, No. 32 (Spring 2017): 161–179, 2017.

Aidi, Hisham. Africa and the Decline of American Primacy. Policy Brief PB-55/21. Policy Center for the New South, December 2021.

Allen, Douglas W. The Institutional Revolution, Measurement and the Economic Emergence of the Modern World. Chicago and London: The University of Chicago Press, 2012.

Arregui, Pabollet, Eskarne, Margherita Bacigalupo, Federico Biagi, Marcelino Cabrera Giraldez, Francesca Caena, Jonathan Castano Munoz, Isabel Clara Centeno Mediavilla, et al. The Changing Nature of Work and Skills in the Digital Age. Luxembourg: Publications Office of the European Union, 2019.

Arrow. Agriculture Sensors: Top 5 Sensors Used in Agriculture. 16 April 2020. https://www.Arrow.com/En/Research-and-Events/Articles/Top-5-Sensors-Used-in-Agriculture.

Atkinson, Anthony. The 15 Proposals from Tony Atkinson's Inequality—What Can Be Done? Accessed: 7 December 2021. www.tony-atkinson.com.

Australian Government Department of Industry, Science, Energy and Resources. Growing Australia's Hydrogen Industry. Accessed 28 November 2021. https://www.industry.gov.au/policies-and-initiatives/growing-australias-hydrogen-industry.

Autor, David, David Dorn, Lawrence Katz, Christina Patterson, John Van Reenen. The Fall of the Labor Share and the Rise of Superstar Firms. Cambridge, MA: National Bureau of Economic Research, 2017.

Aydinalp, Cumhrev and Malcom Cresser. The Effects of Climate Change on Agriculture. American-Eurasian Journal of Agriculture and Environmental Science, 3 (5): 672–675, 2008.

Azevedo, João Pedro. Learning Poverty: Measures and Simulations. Policy Research Working Paper No. WPS 9446. Washington, DC: World Bank Group, 2020.

Bailey, Martha J. and Susan Dynarski. Gains and Gaps: Changing Inequality in US College Entry and Completion. NBER Working Paper No. 17633, 2011.

Bakhshi, Hasan, Jonathan M. Downing, Michael A. Osborne, and Philippe Schneider. The Future of Skills: Employment in 2030. London: Pearson and Nesta, 2017.

Baldwin, Richard. The Globotics Upheaval: Globalisation, Robotics and the Future of Work. New York: Oxford University Press, 2019.

Banerjea, Aparna. RIL to Invest up to $50 mn in Bill Gates-owned Breakthrough Energy Ventures. Livemint, 12 November 2020. https://www.livemint.com/companies/news/ril-to-Invest-up-to-50-mn-in-bill-gates-owned-breakthrough-energy-ventures-11605195386475.html.

Bank of America. Game Changer: How Green Hydrogen Could Fuel Our Future. Bank of America, no date. https://www.privatebank.bankofamerica.com/articles/green-hydrogen-climate-change.html.

Bansal, Rajesh, and Somya Singh. Chinas Digital Yuan: An Alternative to the Dollar-dominated Financial System. Washington, DC: Carnegie Endowment for International Peace, 2021.

Bardhan, Pranab. Corruption and Development: A Review of Issues. Journal of Economic Literature 35(3): 1320–1346. 1997.

Barkan, Terrance. Taurus Invests in R&D to Incorporate Graphene into Their Weapons. The Graphene Council. Accessed 6 December 2021. https://www.thegraphenecouncil.org/Blogpost/1501180/373087/Taurus-Invests-in-R-D-To-Incorporate-Graphene-into-Their-Weapons.

Barro, Robert and Jong-Wha Lee. Educational Attainment in the World, 1950-2010. Last Modified 18 May 2010. https://Voxeu.org/Article/Educational-attainment-World-1950-2010#:~:Text=in%202010%2C%20the%20world%20population%20aged%2015%20and,From%20 2.1%20to%207.1%20years%20in%20low-Income%20countries.

Baumol, William J. and Robert J. Strom. Useful Knowledge of Entrepreneurship: Some Implications of the History. In David S. Landes, Joel Mokyr, and William J. Baumoll: The Invention of Enterprise. PrInceton, NJ: PrInceton University Press, 2010.

Baumol, William J. Entrepreneurship: Productive, Unproductive and Destructive. Journal of Political Economy, Vol. 98(3), Pp. 893–921. 1990.

Baumol, William J. The Free-market Innovation Machine: Analyzing the Growth Miracle of Capitalism. PrInceton, NJ: PrInceton University Press, 2004.

BBC. Coronavirus: Worst Economic Crisis Since 1930s Depression, IMF Says. BBC, 9 April 2020. https://www.bbc.com/news/business-52236936.

Beaudry, Paul, Fabrice Collard, and David A. Green. Explaining Productivity Growth: The Role of Demographics, International Productivity Monitor, Centre for the Study of Living Standards, No. 10 (Spring 2005): 45–58. 2005.

Beegle, Kathleen and Luc Christiaensen, eds. Accelerating Poverty Reduction in Africa. Washington DC: World Bank, 2019.

Bellini, Emiliano. Korean Researchers Achieve 25.8% Efficiency for Single Junction Perovskite Solar Cell. PV Magazine, 2021. https://www.pv-magazine.com/2021/10/25/ Korean-Researchers-Achieve-25-8-Efficiency-For-Single-Junction-Perovskite-Solar-Cell/.

Bergman, Peter, Raj Chetty, Stefanie DeLuca, Nathaniel Hendren, Lawrence F. Katz and Christopher Palmer. Creating Moves to Opportunity: Experimental Evidence of Barriers to Neighborhood Choice. NBER Working Paper No. 26164. 2019.

Berthaud, Fabrice. Le Commerce Extérieur De La Tunisie. Tunis: Ambassade De France En Tunisie, Service Économique Regional De Tunis, 27 December 2019. https://www. Tresor.Economie.Gouv.Fr/Articles/9f6ec321-6e45-4f20-B797-0496af428e9b/Files/ Ced54ace-D3d4-411b-9bb1-63fdb4657375#Page=6.

Berthene, April. Coronavirus Pandemic Adds $219 billion to US Ecommerce Sales in 2020–2021. Digital Commerce 360. Accessed 15 December 2021. https://www.digitalcommerce360. com/article/coronavirus-impact-online-retail/.

Bestsennyy, Oleg, Greg Gilbert, Alex Harris, and Jennifer Rost. Telehealth: A Quarter-trillion-dollar Post-COVID-19 Reality? McKinsey, 9 July 2021. https://www.mckinsey.com/industries/healthcare-systems-and-services/our-insights/telehealth-a-quarter-trillion-dollar-post-covid-19-reality.

BFSI.com. UPI Transactions More Than Double in a Year on COVID-19 Shift. BFSO.economictimes.indiatimes.com, 2 November 2021. https://bfsi.economictimes.indiatimes.com/news/fintech/upi-transactions-more-than-double-in-a-year-on-covid-19-shift/87476752.

Bhattacharya, Amar and Nicholas Stern. Beyond the $100 Billion: Financing a Sustainable and Resilient Future. London: LSE - Grantham Research Institute on Climate Change and the Environment, 3 November 2021.

BIS. Global Liquidity: Concept, Measurement, and Policy Implications. CGFS Papers No. 45. Basel: Bank for International Settlements, 2011.

Bloomberg. China Needs Gamers to Reach Next Level. Bloomberg.com. Bloomberg, 4 July 2019. https://www.bloomberg.com/Opinion/Articles/2019-07-04/China-Needs-To-Bridge-Growing-Labor-Skills-Gap.

Bloomberg. The Price Is Right (Levelized Cost of Hydrogen in 2030). Bloomberg, 1 November 2021a. https://www.Bloomberg.com/Toaster/V2/Charts/76729d8ffe6f47ababe8fe4c-ca6e1796.html.

Bloomberg. Indonesia Takes Low and Slow Path to Carbon Tax and Trade. Bloomberg, 15 November 2021b. https://www.bloomberg.com/News/Articles/2021-11-14/indonesia-Takes-Low-and-Slow-Path-To-Carbon-Tax-and-Trade.

Bloomberg. U.S. Energy Departments NREL Sees AMLO Bill Pushing Up Emissions and Costs. Bloomberg, 27 October 2021c. https://www.bloomberg.com/News/Articles/2021-10-27/Mexico-Power-Bill-Would-Raise-Carbon-Emissions-U-S-Agency-Says.

Boorman, Jack T. and andré Icard, eds. Reform of the International Monetary System: The Palais Royal initiative. New Delhi: Sage Publishing, 2011.

Bordo, Michael D. and Robert N. Mccauley. Triffin: Dilemma or Myth? NBER Working Paper No. 24195, 2018.

BP. Statistical Review of World Energy 2021. BP, 2021.

Budolfson, Mark B., David Anthoff, Francis Denning, Frank Errickson, Kevin Kuruc, Dean Spears, and Navroz K. Dubash. Utilitarian Benchmarks for Emissions and Pledges Promote

Equity, Climate, and Development. Nature Climate Change 11, No.10 (September 2021): 827–33. 2021.

Bughin, Jacques, Eric Hazan, Eric Labaye, James Manyika, Peter Dahlström, Sree Ramaswamy, and Caroline Cochin de Billy. Digital Europe: Realizing the Continent's Potential. McKinsey, 29 June 2016. https://www.mckinsey.com/business-functions/mckinsey-digital/our-insights/digital-europe-realizing-the-continents-potential.

Bughin, Jacques, James Manyika, and Tanguy Catlin. 2020. Twenty-five Years of Digitization: Ten Insights Into How to Play It Right. McKinsey & Company. Last Modified: 13 February 2020. https://www.mckinsey.com/business-functions/mckinsey-digital/our-insights/twenty-five-years-of-digitization-ten-insights-into-how-to-play-it-right.

Burke, Marshall, Solomon M. Hsiang, and Edward Miguel. Global Non-linear Effect of Temperature on Economic Production. Nature 527, No. 7577 (October 21, 2015): 235–39. 2015.

Burns, Jonathan K., Andrew Tomita, and Amy S. Kapadia. Inequality and Schizophrenia: Increased Schizophrenia Incidence in Countries with High Levels of Inequality. International Journal of Social Psychiatry. 60 (2): 185-196. 2014.

Business Standard. Indian E-commerce to Grow 84% in 4 years, Helped by Covid-19 Impact: Study. Business Standard, 10 March 2021. https://www.business-standard.com/article/economy-policy/indian-e-commerce-to-grow-84-in-4-years-helped-by-covid-19-impact-study-121031000846_1.html.

Business Today. India Adds 28 Unicorns in 2021 to Take Total to 66; Over 3.3 Lakh People Employed: NASSCOM. Business Today, 28 September 2021. https://www.businesstoday.in/Entrepreneurship/News/Story/india-Adds-28-Unicorns-in-2021-To-Take-Total-To-66-Over-33-Lakh-People-Employed-Nasscom-307845-2021-09-28.

Camdessus, Michel and Anoop Singh. Reforming the International Monetary System: A Sequenced Agenda. In the World in 2050: Striving for a More Just, Prosperous, and Harmonious Global Community, Edited by Harinder Kohli, 61–72. New Dehli: Oxford University Press, 2016.

Camdessus, Michel. Opening Remarks At the Income Distribution and Sustainable Growth: The Perspective from the IMF at Fifty. 1995. https://www.imf.org/en/News/Articles/2015/09/28/04/53/spmds9509.

Carbeck, Jeff. Green Hydrogen Could Fill Big Gaps in Renewable Energy. Scientific America, 10 November 2020. https://www.scientificamerican.com/article/green-hydrogen-could-fill-big-gaps-in-renewable-energy/.

Carbon Pricing Leadership Coalition. Report of the High-level Commission on Carbon Prices. Washington, DC: World Bank, 2017.

Cárcaba, Ana, Eduardo González, Juan Ventura, and Rubén Arrondo. How Does Good Governance Relate to Quality of Life? Sustainability 9(631). 2017.

Carlo Azzarni and Sara Signorelli. Climate and Poverty in Africa South of the Sahara. World Development 125 (January 2020): 104691. 2020. https://doi.org/10.1016/j.worlddev.2019.104691

Carney, Mark. (De)Globalisation and Inflation. 2017 IMF Michel Camdessus Central Banking Lecture. London: Bank of London, 2017. https://www.Bankofengland.Co.Uk/Speech/2017/De-Globalisation-and-inflation.

Carney, Mark. The Growing Challenges for Monetary Policy in the Current International Monetary and Financial System. Jackson Hole Symposium 23 August 2019. London: Bank of England, 2019. www.Bankofengland.Co.Uk/News/Speeches.

Carstens, Agustin. Non-Bank Financial Sector: Systemic Regulation Needed. BIS Quarterly Review. BIS, December 2021.

Centennial Group. Unpublished Data. 2021.

Center for Global Development. Multilateral Development Banking for This Century's Development Challenges. Last Modified 5 October 2016. https://www.cgdev.org/publication/multilateral-development-banking-for-this-centurys-development-challenges.

Chadha, Rajesh and Ganesh Sivamani. Critical Minerals for India: Assessing their Criticality and Projecting their Needs for Green Technologies. Working Paper. New Delhi: CSEP, 2021.

Cheng, Gong, and Rudolf Alvise Lennkh. RFAs Financial Structures and Lending Capacities: A Statutory, Accounting and Credit Rating Perspective. Working Paper 44. Luxembourg: European Stability Mechanism, 2020.

Chetty, Raj, David Grusky, Maximilian Hell, Nathaniel Hendren, Robert Manduca and Jimmy Narang. The Fading American Dream: Trends in Absolute Income Inequality Since 1940. Science Vol.356, Issue 6336, P398–406. 2017.

Choi, Jieun, Mark A. Dutz, and Zainab Usman, eds. The Future of Work in Africa: Harnessing the Potential of Digital Technologies for All. Africa Development Forum. Washington DC: World Bank, 2020. Doi:10.1596/978-1-4648-1444-0.

Choudhury, Tanzeem, and Alex Pentland. The Sociometer: A Wearable Device for Understanding Human Networks. MIT Media Lab. Last

Modified 1 November 2002. https://www.Media.Mit.edu/Publications/The-Sociometer-A-Wearable-Device-For-Understanding-Human-Networks-2/.

CIO. Cyber threat: 8.5 bn Records Compromised in 2019, Says IBM. CIO.econmicatimes.indiatimes.com, 13 February 2020. https://cio.economictimes.indiatimes.com/news/digital-security/cyber-threat-8-5-bn-records-compromised-in-2019-says-ibm/74109649.

Clemens, Jeffrey. and Strain, Michael R. Minimum Wage Analysis Using Pre-committed Research Design: Evidence Through 2017. IZA Discussion Paper No. 12388. Bonn: IZA, 2019.

Clifford, Catherine. How the Moderna Covid-19 mRNA Vaccine Was Made So Quickly. CNBC, 3 July 2021. https://www.cnbc.com/2021/07/03/how-moderna-made-its-mrna-covid-vaccine-so-quickly-noubar-afeyan.html.

Cole, Wesley, A. Will Frazier, and Chad Augustine. Cost Projections for Utility-Scale Battery Storage: 2021 Update. Golden, CO: National Renewable Energy Laboratory (NREL), 2021.

Colford, Christopher. Productivity for Prosperity: 'In the long run, it is Almost everything'. World Bank Blogs, 15 November 2016. https://blogs.worldbank.org/psd/productivity-prosperity-long-run-it-almost-everything.

Collier, Paul. The Future of Capitalism: Facing New Anxieties. New York: HarperCollins, 2018.

Corak, Miles. Income Inequality, Equality of Opportunity, and Intergenerational Mobility. Journal of Economic Perspectives, 27(3), 79–102. 2013.

Corvalana, Alejandro and Matteo Pazzonab. Does Inequality Really Increase Crime? Theory and Evidence. 2019. Accessed At: http://www.ecineq.org/ecineq_paris19/papers_EcineqPSE/paper_122.pdf.

Cyranoski, David. The CRISPR-baby Scandal: What's Next for Human Gene-editing. Nature, 26 February 2019. https://www.nature.com/articles/d41586-019-00673-1.

Daly, M., Margo Wilson, and Shawn Vasdev. Income Inequality and Homicide Rates in Canada and the United States. Canadian Journal of Criminology, 43(2), 219–236. 2001.

De Larosière, Jacques and David Marsh. Central Banks Need to Change Gear. OMFIF, 17 February 2017. https://www.omfif.org/2021/02/central-banks-need-to-change-gear/.

De Larosière, Jacques. Central Banks Must Change Course to Avoid Possible Financial Crisis. OMFIF, 7 July 2021. https://www.omfif.org/2021/07/central-banks-must-change-course-to-avoid-possible-financial-crisis/.

De Rambures, Dominique, Alfonso Iozzo, and Annamaria Viterbo. A Safety Net for Africa: Towards an African Monetary Fund. RTI and Centro Studi Sul Federalismo, 2020.

De Soto, Hernando. The Mystery of Capital: Why Capitalism Succeeds in the West and Fails Everywhere Else, New York: Basic Books, 2000.

Delaney, Kevin J. Bill Gates and Investors Worth $170 Billion Are Launching a Fund to Fight Climate Change through Energy Innovation. Quartz, 11 December 2016. https://qz.com/859860/bill-gates-is-leading-a-new-1-billion-fund-focused-on-combatting-climate-change-through-Innovation/.

Deloitte. Millennials Want Business to Shift Its Purpose. Deloitte United States, 2016. https://www2.Deloitte.com/Us/En/Pages/About-Deloitte/Articles/Millennials-Shifting-Business-Purpose.html.

Dieppe, Alistair. Global Productivity: Trends, Drivers, and Policies. Washington DC: World Bank Group, 2021.

Dingel, Jonathan I. and Brent Neiman. How Many Jobs Can Be Done at Home? NBER Working Paper No. 26948, National Bureau of Economic Research, June. 2020.

Dixit, Avinash. Governance Institutions and Economic Activity. American Economic Review, 99 (1): 5–24.DOI: 10.1257/Aer.99.1.5. 2009.

Dutta, Soumitra, Bruno Lanvin, Lorena Rivera Leon, and Sacha Wunsch-Vincent, eds. The Global Innovation Index 2021: Tracking Innovation through the COVID-19 Crisis. World Intellectual Property Organization, 2021.

Dutta, Soumitra and Xueyun Luo. Accelerating Innovation in a Post-Covid World: Evidence from the Global Innovation Index. California Management Review Insights, 2021. https://Cmr.Berkeley.edu/Assets/Documents/Pdf/2021-06-Accelerating-Innovation-in-A-Post-Covid-World.Pdf.

Dworkin, Anthony. A Return to Africa: Why North African States Are Looking South. European Council on Foreign Relations, 2020. https://Ecfr.Eu/Publication/A_Return_To_Africa_Why_North_African_States_Are_Looking_South/.

Early Warning Project. Countries at Risk for Mass Killing 2021–22: Statistical Risk Assessment Results. US Holocaust Memorial Museum, Simon-Skjoot Center for the Prevention of Genocide and Dartmouth, 2021. https://Earlywarningproject.Ushmm.org/Storage/Resources/2207/Early-Warning-Project-Statistical-Risk-Assessment-2021-22.Pdf.

Easterly, William. Inequality Does Cause Underdevelopment: Insights from a New Instrument. Journal of Development Economics. 84 (2): 755–776. 2007.

Edquist, Harald, Peter Goodridge, and Jonathan Haskel. The Internet of Things and Economic Growth in a Panel of Countries. Economics of Innovation and New Technology 30 (3): 262–83. 2021. https://Doi.org/10.1080/10438599.2019.1695941.

Eivhengreen, Barry, Arnaud Mehl, and Livia Chitu. How Global Currencies Work, Past, Present, and Future. Princeton: Princeton University Press, 2018.

El-Erian, Mohamed. Investor Appetite to Be Tested When Fed Pulls Support. Financial Times, 10 December 2021.

European Commission. The EU Carbon Border Adjustment Mechanism 2021. Brussels: European Commission, 2021. https://ec.europa.eu/taxation_customs/green-taxation-0/carbon-border-adjustment-mechanism_en.

European Commission. Towards a Stronger International Role of the Euro. Communication from the Commission to the European Parliament, the European Council (Euro Summit), the Council of the ECB, the European Economic and Social Committee and the Committee of the Regions, COM(2018) 796/4, Brussels: European Commission, 2018.

EY. How Can Bold Action Become Everyday Action? Africa Attractiveness Program 2019. Ernst & Young, 2019. https://Assets.Ey.com/Content/Dam/Ey-Sites/Ey-Com/En_Gl/Topics/attractiveness/Ey-Africa-attractiveness-Report-2019.Pdf.

EY. Reset for Growth: Fast Forward—EY Attractiveness Report. Ernst & Young, November 2021. https://Assets.Ey.com/Content/Dam/Ey-Sites/Ey-Com/En_Za/Topics/attractive-ness/Reports/Ey-Aar-Reset-For-Growth-Final.Pdf.

Ezcurra, Roberto and D. Palacios. Terrorism and Spatial Disparities: Does Interregional Inequality Matter? European Journal of Political Economy. 42: 60–74. 2016.

Fajgenbaum, Jose, Harpaul Alberto Kohli, Ieva Vilkelyte, and Laura Shelton. COVID-19 and Inequality. Presentation, Emerging Markets Forum, 27 April 2021.

Fajgenbaum, Jose, JorgeGuzman, and Ieva Vilkelyte. Addressing Income Inequality: Key Issues, Policy Recommendations and Long-term Scenarios. Washington, DC: Emerging Market Forum, 2019.

Fajnzylber, Pablo, Daniel Lederman, and Norman Loayza. Inequality and Violent Crime. The Journal of Law and Economics, Vol 45, Number 1. 2002.

Fankhauser, Sam, Stephen M. Smith, Myles Allen, Kaya Axelsson, Thomas Hale, Cameron Hepburn, J. Michael Kendall, et Al. The Meaning of Net Zero and How to Get It Right. Nature Climate Change 12, No.1 (December 2021): 15–21. 2021. Doi:10.1038/S41558-021-01245-W.

FAO, IFAD, UNICEF, WFP, and WHO. The State of Food Security and Nutrition in the World 2019. Safeguarding Against Economic Slowdowns and Downturns. Rome: FAO, 2019.

FAO. The State of Food and Agriculture, Climate Change, Agriculture, and Food Security. Rome: FAO, 2016.

FAO. The State of Food and Agriculture: 2018, Migration, Agriculture and Rural Development. Rome: FAO, 2018.

FAO. World Food and Agriculture: Statistical Yearbook. Rome: FAO, 2020.

FAO. Government Expenditures in Agriculture 2001–2019. Global and Regional Trends. FAOSTAT Analytical Brief Series No 24. Rome: FAO, 2021.

FAO. FAOSTAT Statistical Database. Rome: FAO, 2022.

Fehr, Ernst and Gächter, Simon. Reciprocity and Economics: The Economic Implications of Homo Reciprocans, European Economic Review 42 (1998) 845–859. 1998.

Fick, Maggie. Climate Change Poses Growing Threats to Vulnerable Africa, UN Says. Reuters, 26 October 2020. https://www.Reuters.com/Article/Us-Climate-Change-Un-Africa/Climate-Change-Poses-Growing-Threats-To-Vulnerable-Africa-U-N-Says-Iduskbn27b1lj.

Finkel, Elizabeth. Learning from Vaccines: The Race to Make Antiviral Drugs. Cosmos, 22 November 2021. https://cosmosmagazine.com/health/covid/race-to-make-rna-antiviral-drugs./

Fleming, Sean. Top 10 Tech Trends That Will Shape the Coming Decade, According to McKinsey. WEF, 12 October 2021. https://www.weforum.org/agenda/2021/10/technology-trends-top-10-mckinsey/.

Flor, Elena. Monetary Aspects of the African Continental Free Trade Area. In Alberto Majocchi ed., Africa and Europe: A Shared Future. Brussels: Peter Lang, 2020.

Forbes, Kristin. A Reassessment of the Relationship between Inequality and Growth. The American Economic Review. 90 (4):869–887. 2000.

Fox, Louise. Three Myths about Youth Employment in Africa and Strategies to Realize the Demographic Dividend. Foresight Africa Series. Brookings, 7 February 2019.

Francis, Tracy, and Fernanda Hoefel. True Gen: Generation Z and Its Implications for Companies. McKinsey & Company. Last modified 16 December 2020. https://www.McKinsey.com/industries/Consumer-Packaged-Goods/Our-insights/True-Gen-Generation-Z-and-Its-Implications-For-Companies.

Friedlingstein, Pierre, Matthew W. Jones, Michael Osullivan, Robbie M. Andrew, Dorothee C. E. Bakker, Judith Hauck, Corlnne Le Quéré, Glen P. Peters, Wouter Peters, Julia Pongratz, Stephen Sitch, Josep G. Canadell, Philippe Ciais, Rob B. Jackson, Simone R. Alin, Peter Anthoni, Nicholas R. Bates, Meike Becker, Nicolas Bellouin, Laurent Bopp, Thi T. T. Chau, Frédéric Chevallier, Louise P. Chini, Margot Cronin, Kim I. Currie, Bertrand Decharme, Laique Djeutchouang, Xinyu Dou, Wiley Evans, Richard A. Feely, Liang Feng, Thomas Gasser, Dennis Gilfillan, Thanos Gkritzalis, Giacomo Grassi, Luke Gregor, Nicolas Gruber, Özgür Gürses, Ian Harris, Richard A. Houghton, George C. Hurtt, Yosuke Iida, Tatiana Ilyina, ingrid T. Luijkx, Atul K. Jain, Steve D. Jones, Etsushi Kato, Daniel Kennedy, Kees Klein Goldewijk, Jürgen Knauer, Jan Ivar Korsbakken, Arne Körtzinger, Peter Landschützer, Siv K. Lauvset, Nathalie Lefèvre, Sebastian Lienert, Junjie Liu, Gregg Marland, Patrick C. Mcguire, Joe R. Melton, David R. Munro, Julia E. M. S. Nabel, Shin-Ichiro Nakaoka, Yosuke Niwa, Tsuneo Ono, Denis Pierrot, Benjamin Poulter, Gregor Rehder, Laure Resplandy, Eddy Robertson, Christian Rödenbeck, Thais M. Rosan, Jörg Schwinger, Clemens Schwingshackl, Roland Séférian, Adrienne J. Sutton, Colm Sweeney, Toste Tanhua, Pieter P. Tans, Hanqin Tian, Bronte Tilbrook, Francesco Tubiello, Guido Van Der Werf, Nicolas Vuichard, Chisato Wada, Rik Wanninkhof, Andrew Watson, David Willis, Andrew J. Wiltshire, Wenping Yuan, Chao Yue, Xu Yue, Sönke Zaehle, and Jiye Zeng. Global Carbon Budget. Preprint, Submitted in 2021. Earth System Science Data Discuss. https://Doi.org/10.5194/Essd-2021-386.

FSB. Policy Proposals to Enhance Money Market Fund Resilience: Consultation Report. Basel: Financial Stability Board (FSB), 2021.

Fukuyama, Francis. What Is Governance?. Washington, DC: Center for Global Development, 2013.

Furceri Davide, Sinem Kilic Celik, João Tovar Jalles, and Ksenia Koloskova. Recessions and Total Factor Productivity: Evidence from Sectoral Data. Economic Modelling, No. 94 (October 2021): 130–138. 2021. https://Doi.org/10.1016/J.Econmod.2020.09.025.

G30 Working Group on Sovereign Debt and COVID-19. Sovereign Debt and Financing for Recovery After the COVID-19 Shock: Preliminary Report and Recommendations. Washington, DC: Group of Thirty, 2020. https://Group30.org/Publications/Detail/4799.

Gallardo-Albarrán, Daniel and Robert Inklaar. The Role of Capital and Productivity in Accounting for Income Differences SInce 1913. Journal of Economic Surveys, No. 35 (June 2020): 952–974. 2020. https://Doi.org/10.1111/Joes.12374.

Gambetta, Jay. IBM's Roadmap for Scaling Quantum Technology. IBM, 2020. https://Research.Ibm.com/Blog/Ibm-Quantum-Roadmap.

Ganguly, Shreya. India Recorded 3X Increase in Online Consultations between March and November 2020: Report. Yourstory, 22 December 2020. https://yourstory.com/2020/12/india-recorded-3x-Increase-online-consultations-practo-report/amp.

García R, Enrique. América Latina: La Urgencia De Una Estrategia Renovada De Desarrollo. Desenvolvimento E Cooperação Na América Latina: A Urgência De Uma Estratégia Renovada. Enrique García (Coord.). São Paulo: Editora Da Universidade De São Paulo, 2020.

Garcia R, Enrique. Economic and Trade Challenges in a World in Transition. Shaping a Multi-conceptual World. World Economic Forum (WEF). Cologny/Geneva, Switzerland, 2020.

García R., Enrique and Mendez, Alvaro. Mañana Today: A Long View on Economic Value Creation in Latin America. Global Policy/Volume 12, Issue 3. Durham University and John Wiley & Sons Ltd, 2021.

Gavi. About Our Alliance. No Date. https://www.Gavi.org/Our-Alliance/About.

GCF. About CGF. No Date. https://www.Greenclimate.Fund/About/Timeline#:~:Text=GCF%20was%20established%20under%20the,UNFCCC%20and%20the%20Paris%20Agreement.

GEF. Who We Are. No Date. https://www.Thegef.org/Who-We-Are.

Gentilini, Ugo, Mohamed Almenfi, Ian Orton, and Pamela Dale. Social Protection and Jobs Responses to COVID-19: A Real-Time Review of Country Measures. Washington DC: World Bank, 2020. https://Openknowledge.Worldbank.org/Handle/10986/33635.

Ghymers, Christan. The Systemic Instability of the Ballooning Global Liquidity as a Symptom of the Worsening of the Triffin Dilemma. Unpublished Paper, October 2021.

Ghymers, Christian. Some General Remarks on Global Liquidity: Is There a Pilot in the Plane? Contribution to RTI Working Party on Managing Global Liquidity As a Global Public Good, RTI, 2019.

Gitlab. Informal Communication in an All-remote Environment. Gitlab, 2022. https://About.Gitlab.com/Company/Culture/All-Remote/informal-Communication/.

Global Coal Plant Tracker. Global Energy Monitory. San Francisco, CA. 2021. https://Globalenergymonitor.org/Projects/Global-Coal-Plant-Tracker/Download-Data/.

Global Tolerance. The Values Revolution. 2015. https://go-positive.co.uk/resources/Documents/The%20Values%20Revolution.pdf.

Gold, Ashley. Tiktok Surpassed Google as Most Popular Site in 2021. Axios. Last modifed 22 December 2021. https://www.Axios.com/Tiktok-Surpassed-Google-Traffic-2021-05bd-be31-B559-4479-B7c8-6df560d2c00e.html.

Goldin, Ian, Pantelis Koutroumpis, François Lafond, and Julian Winkler. Why Is Productivity Slowing Down? MPRA Paper 107644, University Library of Munich Germany, 2021. https://Mpra.Ub.Uni-Muenchen.De/107644/.

Gordon, Robert. The Rise and Fall of American Growth: The US Standard of Living Since the Civil War. The Princeton Economic Series of the Western World. Princeton: Princeton University Press, 2016.

Goswami, Arti Grover, Denis Medvedev, and Ellen Olafson. High Growth Firms: Facts, Fiction and Policy Options for Emerging Economies. Washington DC: World Bank Group, 2019. https://Openknowledge.Worldbank.org/Handle/10986/30800.

Greif, Avner. Institutions and the Path to the Modern Economy: Lessons from Medieval Trade. Cambridge: Cambridge University Press, 2006.

Griffith-Jones, Stephany. A Public Investment Bank Would Help the US Prosper. Financial Times, 12 November 2020.

Grindle, Abe. 6 Ways Technology Is Breaking Barriers to Social Change. Fast Company. Last modified 17 March 2015. https://www.Fastcompany.com/3043761/6-Ways-Technology-Is-Breaking-Barriers-To-Social-Change.

Guinet, Jean, Byung-Seon Jeong, and Gernot Hutschenreiter. Public-Private Partnerships for Research and Innovation: An Evaluation of the Austrian Experience. Paris: OECD, 2004.

Guivarch, Celine, Nicolas Taconet, and Aurelie Mejean. Policies Aimed At Slowing Worming Could Be Better Designed to Reduce Inequality. Washington, DC: IMF, 2020.

Harberger, Arnold. Taxation and Welfare. Boston, MA: Little, Brown, and Company. 1974.

Hardin, Garrett. The Tragedy of the Commons. Hardin, Garrett. Science, New Series, Vol. 162, No. 3859 (Dec. 13, 1968), pp. 1243–1248. 1968.

Heckman, J. J. Invest in Early Childhood Development: Reduce Deficits, Strengthen the Economy. The Heckman Equation. No Date,

Retrieved 27 January 2022, from https://Heckmanequation.org/Resource/Invest-in-Early-Childhood-Development-Reduce-Deficits-Strengthen-The-Economy/.

Heine, Bernd, ed. African Languages: An Introduction. Cambridge University Press, 2000, Quoted in Wikipedia At https://En.Wikipedia.org/Wiki/Languages_of_Africa.

Heitzig, Chris, Aloysius Uche Ordu, and Lemma Senbet. Sub-Saharan Africas Debt Problem. Mapping the Pandemics Effects and the Way Forward. Africa Growth initiative, Brookings Institute, 2021. https://www.Brookings.edu/Wp-Content/Uploads/2021/10/COVID-and-Debt.Pdf.

Henrich, Joseph. The Secret of Our Success. Princeton: Princeton University Press, 2016.

Herbst, Julia. Gitlabs Radical Vision for the Future of Remote Work. Fast Company, 24 April 2021. https://www.Fastcompany.com/90548691/Extremely-Transparent-and-Incredibly-Remote-Gitlabs-Radical-Vision-For-The-Future-of-Work.

Herzer, Dierk and Sebastian Vollmer. Rising Top Incomes Do Not Raise the Tide. Journal of Policy Modeling 35 (4): 504–519. 2013.

Hicks, Wayne. Declining Renewable Costs Drive Focus on Energy Storage. NREL, 2 January 2020. https://www.nrel.gov/news/features/2020/declining-renewable-costs-drive-focus-on-energy-storage.html.

Hinge, Daniel. Fixing Market-based Finance: Duct Tape or Deep Reform? Central Banking, 23 August 2021. https://www.centralbanking.com/central-banks/financial-stability/7866926/fixing-market-based-finance-duct-tape-or-deep-reform.

Hoff, Madison. Here's Where the US Falls on the Great Gatsby Curve, a Damning Chart Economists Use to Track Inequality in Every Country. Business Insider, 23 February 2020. https://www.businessinsider.com/great-gatsby-curve-relationship-between-Income-Inequality-and-mobility-2020-2.

Hudecz, Gergely, Edumd Moshammer, Alexander Raabe, and Gong Cheng. The Euro in the World. Discussion Paper Series No. 16. Luxembourg: European Stability Mechanism, 2021. https://www.Esm.Europa.Eu/Publications/Euro-World.

Humphrey, Chris; Stephany Griffith-Jones, Jiajun Xu, Richard Carey and Annalisa Prizzon. Multilateral Development Banks in the 21st Century: Three Perspectives on China and the Asian Infrastructure Investment Bank. London: ODI, 2015.

Hydrogen Council. Hydrogen for Net-Zero: A Critical Cost-competitive Energy Vector. Hydrogen Council, 2021. https://hydrogencouncil.com/wp-content/uploads/2021/11/Hydrogen-for-Net-Zero_Full-Report.pdf.

Hydrogen Council. Path to Hydrogen Competitiveness: A Cost Perspective. Hydrogen Council, 2020. https://hydrogencouncil.com/en/path-to-hydrogen-competitiveness-a-cost-perspective/.

IDMC. Africa Report on Internal Displacement. International Displacement Monitoring Centre, 2019. https://www.internal-Displacement.org/Africa-Report.

IEO. IMF Advice on Capital Flows: Evaluation Report 2020. Washington, DC: Independent Evaluation Office of the IMF, 2020.

IFAD. Rural Poverty Report, Fostering Inclusive Rural Transformation. Rome: IFAD, 2016.

IFPRI. Global Food Policy Report. Washington, DC: IFPRI 2017.

IMF and World Bank Staff. Enhancing Access to Opportunities Prepared for the Group of Twenty. Washington, DC: IMF and World Bank, 2020.

Ingraham, Christopher. How Rising Inequality Hurts Everyone, Even the Rich. The Washington Post, 6 February 2018.

Ingram, Elizabeth. World Adds Record New Renewable Energy Capacity in 2020. Renewable Energy World, 6 April 2021. https://www.renewableenergyworld.com/baseload/world-adds-record-new-renewable-energy-capacity-in-2020/#gref.

International Energy Agency. Deep Energy Transformation Needed by 2050 to Limit Rise in Global Temperature. IEA. Last modified March 20, 2017. https://www.iea.org/news/deep-energy-transformation-needed-by-2050-to-limit-rise-in-global-temperature.

International Energy Agency. World Energy Outlook 2021. Paris, France: IEA, 2021.

International Labour Organization (ILO). Global Employment Trends for Youth 2020: Africa. Washington, DC: International Labour Organization, 2020.

International Labour Organization (ILO). ILO Monitor: COVID-19 and the World of Work, Second Edition, Updated Estimates and Analysis. Washington, DC: ILO, 2020.

International Monetary Fund (IMF). Fiscal Monitor, Tackling Inequality. Washington DC: IMF, 2017.

International Monetary Fund (IMF). Corporate Taxation in the Global Economy. Policy Paper. Washington DC: IMF, 2019.

International Monetary Fund (IMF). World Economic Outlook: A Long and Difficult Ascent – October 2020. Washington, DC: IMF, 2020.

International Monetary Fund (IMF). Regional Economic Outlook, Sub-Saharan Africa: One Planet, Two Worlds, Three Stories. Washington DC: IMF, October 2021a.

International Monetary Fund (IMF). World Economic Outlook: Recovery During a Pandemic – October 2021. Washington DC: IMF, 2021b.

IPCC. Climate Change 2007: Synthesis Report. Contribution of Working Groups I, II and III to the Fourth Assessment Report of the Intergovernmental Panel on Climate Change [Core Writing Team, Pachauri, R.K and Reisinger, A. eds.]. IPCC, Geneva, Switzerland, 2007.

IPCC. Climate Change 2014: Synthesis Report. Contribution of Working Groups I, II, and III to the Fifth Assessment of the Intergovernmental Panel on Climate Change. [Core Writing Team, Rajendra K. Pachauri, and Leo Meyer, eds.] Geneva, Switzerland: Intergovernmental Panel on Climate Change (IPCC), 2014. https://www.Ipcc.Ch/Report/Ar5/Syr/.

IPCC. Summary for Policymakers. Climate Change 2021: The Physical Science Basis. Contribution of Working Group I to the Sixth Assessment Report of the Intergovernmental Panel on Climate Change. [Valérie Masson-Delmontte et al., eds.]. Geneva, Switzerland: Intergovernmental Panel on Climate Change (IPCC), 2021.

IPCC. Summary for Policymakers. Global Warming of 1.5°C. An IPCC Special Report on the Impacts of Global Warming of 1.5°C Above Pre-industrial Levels and Related Global Greenhouse Gas Emission Pathways, in the Context of Strengthening the Global Response to the Threat of Climate Change, Sustainable Development, and Efforts to Eradicate Poverty. [Valérie Masson-Delmontte Et Al., eds.]. Geneva, Switzerland: Intergovernmental Panel on Climate Change (IPCC), 2018. https://www.Ipcc.Ch/Sr15/Download/.

IRENA. The Power to Change: Solar and Wind Cost Reduction Potential to 2025. Abu Dhabi: International Renewable Energy Agency (IRENA), 2016.

IRENA. Global Renewables Outlook: Energy Transformation 2050. Abu Dhabi: International Renewable Energy Agency (IRENA), 2020a.

IRENA. Green Hydrgen Cost Reduction. Abu Dhabi: International Renewable Energy Agency (IRENA), 2020b.

IRENA. Renewable Power Generation Costs in 2020. Abu Dhabi: International Renewable Energy Agency (IRENA), 2021.

Jacobs, Jane. Cities and the Wealth of Nations: Principles of Economic Life. New York: Random House, 1984.

Jain-Chandra, Sonali, L. Kochhar, and M. Newiak. Empowering Women, Tackling Income Inequality. IMF Blog, 22 October 2015.

James, Harold. The Bleak Future of the International Monetary Fund. In Bretton Woods: The Next 70 Years, Edited by Marc Uzan, 168–174. ReInventing Bretton Woods Committee, 2016.

Jerving, Sara and Jenny Lei Ravelo. Prospects for Local Manufacturing of COVID-19 Vaccines in Africa. Devex, 6 January 2022. https://www.Devex.com/News/Prospects-For-Local-Manufacturing-of-Covid-19-Vaccines-in-Africa-102300.

Juma, Calestous. Innovation and Its Enemies: Why People Resist New Technologies. New York: Oxford University Press, 2016.

Kanga, Marlene. Global Governance and Partnerships for Engineering Collaboration in the Context of COVID-19 and Beyond. Accessed At https://www.wfeo.org/wp-content/uploads/members/Webinars/CIP_Global_Engg_COVID-19/Dra-Marlene-Kanga.pdf.

Kaplan, George A, Elsie R. Pamuk, John W. Lynch, Richard D. Cohen, Jennifer L. Balfour. Inequality in Income and Mortality in the United States: Analysis of Mortality and Potential Pathways. BMJ 1996;312:999. 1996.

Kar, Dev and Sarah Freitas. Illicit Financial Flows from Developing Countries: 2001–2010. Washington, DC: Global Financial Integrity, 2012.

Karlo Mari Tottoc, Jose. 2 Years Worth of Digital Transformation in 2 Months for Microsoft (MSFT). Yahoo, 8 February 2021. https://www.yahoo.com/now/2-years-worth-digital-transformation-170251059.html.

Kautilya, Ed. L. Rangarajan. The Arthashastra: Part VI, 2.9.32. Loc 5010, Digital Edition. New Delhi: Penguin Random House, 2016.

Keith Fugli, Madhur Gautham, Aparajita Gogul, and William Maloney. Harvesting Prosperity, Technology and Productivity Growth in Agriculture. Washington, DC: World Bank, 2020.

Kling, Arnold and Schulz, Nick. From Poverty to Prosperity: Intangible Assets, Hidden Liabilities and the Lasting Triumph over Scarcity. New York: Encounter Books, 2016.

Kohli, Harinder (ed.). The World in 2050: Striving for a More Just, Prosperous, and Harmonious Global Community. New Dehli: Oxford University Press, 2015.

Kohli, Harinder, Claudio Loser, and Anil Sood (eds.). Latin America in 2040: Breaking Away from Complacency: An Agenda for Resurgence. Washingtington, DC: Emerging Markets Forum, 2010.

Kohli, Harpaul Alberto, Y. Aaron Szyf, and Drew Arnold. Construction and Analysis of a Global GDP Growth Model for 185 Countries through 2050. Global Journal of Emerging Market Economies 4, No. 2 (May 2012): 91–153. 2012. https://Doi.org/10.1177/097491011200040020.

Koyanagi, Ken. India's Unicorn Boom Shows No Signs of Slowdown. Nikkei Asia. Last modified 16 September 2021. https://Asia.Nikkei.com/Spotlight/Comment/india-S-Unicorn-Boom-Shows-No-Signs-of-Slowdown.

Krishnan, Mekala, Hamid Samandari, Jonathan Woetzel, Sven Smit, Daniel Pacthod, Dickon Plnner, Thomas Nauclér, Humayun Tai, Annabel Farr, Weige Wu, and Danielle Imperato. The Net-Zero Transition: What It Would Cost, What It Could Bring. McKinsey Global Institute. 2022. https://www.McKinsey.com/Business-Functions/Sustainability/Our-insights/The-Net-Zero-Transition-What-It-Would-Cost-What-It-Could-Bring#.

Krueger, A. The Rise and Consequences of Inequality. Speech at the Center for Economic Progress. Washington, DC, 2012.

Kumagai, Jean. Power from Commercial Perovskite Solar Cells Is Coming Soon. IEEE Spectrum, 4 January 2019. https://spectrum.ieee.org/power-from-commercial-perovskite-solar-cells-is-coming-soon.

Laberge, Laura, Clayton Otoole, Jeremy Schneider, and Kate Smaje. How COVID-19 Has Pushed Companies over the Technology Tipping Point: And Transformed Business Forever. Edited by Daniella Seiler. McKinsey & Company. 18 February 2021. https://www.McKinsey.com/Business-Functions/Strategy-and-Corporate-Finance/Our-insights/How-Covid-19-Has-Pushed-Companies-Over-The-Technology-Tipping-Point-and-Transformed-Business-Forever.

Lahtinen, Hannu, Hanna Wass, and Heikki Hiilamo. Gradient Constraint in Voting: The Effect of Intra-generational Social Class and Income Mobility on Turnout. 2017. https://Helda.Helsinki.Fi/Bitstream/10138/297763/1/Lahtinenwasshiilamo-ES2017.Pdf.

Lakner, Christoph, Daniel Gerszon Maler, MArio Negre, Espen Beer Prydz. How Much Does Reducing Inequality Matter for Global Poverty. World Bank Policy Research Working Paper No. 8869. Washington, DC: World Bank, 2019.

Lanvin, Bruno, and Felipe Monteiro, eds. Rep. The Global Talent Competitiveness Index: Talent Competitiveness in Times of COVID. Fontainebleau, France: INSEAD, Portulans Institute, and Accenture, 2021.

Lewrick, Ulf and Stijn Claessens. Open-Deed Bond Funds: Systemic Risks and Policy Implications. BIS Quarterly Review, December 2021.

Licholai, Greg. How Is the Pharmaceutical industry Responding to Covid-19? Yale Insights. Yale School of Management. 31 March 2020. https://insights.Som.Yale.edu/insights/How-Is-The-Pharmaceutical-industry-Responding-To-Covid-19.

Loo, Karl. How the Gig Economy Could Drive Growth in Developing Countries. Forbes, 23 March 2017. https://www.Forbes.com/Sites/Groupthink/2017/03/23/How-The-Gig-Economy-Could-Drive-Growth-in-Developing-Countries/?Sh=3286601e4a49.

Lorenzo, George. Collaboration between Community Colleges and Automotive Companies Results in New General Maintenance Mechatronics Curriculum. Training Industry, 15 September 2017. https://Trainingindustry.com/Articles/Workforce-Development/Collaboration-Between-Community-Colleges-and-Automotive-Companies-Results-in-New-General-Maintenance-Mechatronics-Curriculum/.

Loser, Claudio. Commodity Terms of Trade in Emerging Markets: A Fragile Blessing, Global Journal of Emerging Market Economies 5, No. 2 (May 2013): 99–115. 2013. https://Doi.Org/10.1177/0974910113494538.

Loser, Claudio. Where Is Latin America Going: Developments and Medium Term Prospects, Emerging Markets Forum 20-22 October 2019. 2019. http://www.emergingmarketsforum.org/Wp-Content/Uploads/2019/10.

Lowder, Sarah, Marco V. Sanchez, Raffaele Bertini. Farms, Family Farms, Farmland Distribution and Farm Labor: What Do We Know Today? FAO Agricultural Development Economics Working Paper 19. Rome: FAO, 2019.

Lufkin, Bryan. What Were Getting Wrong about the Great Resignation. BBC, 28 October 2021. https://www.Bbc.com/Worklife/Article/20211028-What-Were-Getting-Wrong-About-The-Great-Resignation.

Lustig, Nora, Valentina Martinez Pabon, Federico Sanz and Stephen D. Younger. The Impact of COVID-19 and Expanded Social Assistance on Inequality and Poverty in Argentina, Brazil, Colombia and Mexico. CEQ Working Paper 92. 2020.

Majumdar, Ramita and Kalpana Pathak. Massive Growth in Edtech to Create Fresh Opportunities. Live Mint, 21 August 2020. https://www.livemint.com/companies/news/massive-growth-in-edtech-to-create-fresh-opportunities-11597969127927.html.

Mandavilli, Apoorva. A 'Historic Event': First Malaria Vaccine Approved by W.H.O. New York Times, 6 April 2021. https://www.nytimes.com/2021/10/06/health/malaria-vaccine-who.html.

Manikandan, Ashwin. UPI breaches 2 Billion Transactions Mark in October. The Economic Times, 1 November 2021. https://economictimes.indiatimes.com/tech/technology/upi-breaches-2-billion-transactions-mark-in-october/articleshow/78980584.cms.

Manriquez, Manny, and Jennifer Heckmann. Understanding the Role of Japanese Automakers and Suppliers in the US Automotive industry. In Sasakawa Usas Policy Briefing Series. Sasakawa Peace Foundation, 2021. https://Spfusa.org/Event/Understanding-The-Role-of-Japanese-Automakers-and-Suppliers-in-The-U-S-Automotive-industry/.

Manyika, James, Jaana Remes, Jan Mischke, and Mekala Krishnan. New Insights Into the Slowdown in US Productivity Growth. McKinsey, 31 March 2017. https://www.mckinsey.com/featured-insights/employment-and-growth/new-insights-into-the-slowdown-in-us-productivity-growth.

Marr, Bernard. These 25 Technology Trends Will Define the Next Decade. Forbes, 20 April 2020. https://www.forbes.com/sites/bernardmarr/2020/04/20/these-25-technology-trends-will-define-the-next-decade/?sh=4ef2289629e3.

Mashelkar, R.A. 2018 K.R. Narayanan Oration: Dismantling Inequality through ASSURED Innovation. Accessed on 11 December 2021. http://mashelkar.com/index.php/keynote-addresses/203-dismantling-Inequality-through-assured-Innovation.

Mashelkar, R.A. and Ravi Pandit. Leapfrogging to Pole-vaulting. India Viking: 2018.

Masini, Fabio. Time for a Next Generation Africa. Research Paper. Torino: Centro Studi Sul Federalismo, 2021.

Masterson, Victoria. 5 Milestones in Green Energy. World Economic Forum, 14 April 2021. https://www.weforum.org/agenda/2021/04/renewables-record-capacity-solar-wind-nuclear/.

May, John F. and Jean-Pierre Guengant. Demography and Economic Emergence of Sub-Saharan Africa. Académie Royale De Belgique, 2020.

Mbiti, Isaac M. and Weil, David Nathan, Mobile Banking: The Impact of M-Pesa in Kenya. NBER Working Paper No. w17129. 2011.

434

Mccall, Leslie. Political and Policy Responses to Problems of Inequality and Opportunity: Past, Present and Future. In the Dynamics of Opportunities in America: Evidence and Perspectives, Irwin Kirsch and Henry Braun eds., Springer, Cham. 2016. https://doi.org/10.1007/978-3-319-25991-8_12.

Mccollum, David, Wenji Zhou, Christoph Bertram, Harmen Sytze De Boer, Sebastian Busch, Jacques Després et al. Energy Investment Needs for Fulfilling the Paris Agreement and Achieving the Sustainable Development Goals. Nature Energy 3 (June 2018): 589–99. 2018. https://Doi.org/10.1038/S41560-018-0179-Z.

McKinsey Digital. The Top Trends in Tech. Not dated. https://www.mckinsey.com/business-functions/mckinsey-digital/our-insights/the-top-trends-in-tech.

McKinsey Global Institute. The Bio Revolution: Innovations Transforming Economies, Societies, and Our Lives. McKinsey Global Institute, 13 May 2020. https://www.mckinsey.com/industries/life-sciences/our-insights/the-bio-revolution-Innovations-transforming-economies-societies-and-our-lives.

McKinsey. Net-zero Power: Long-duration Energy Storage for a Renewable Grid. McKinsey, 22 November 2021. https://www.mckinsey.com/business-functions/sustainability/our-insights/net-zero-power-long-duration-energy-storage-for-a-renewable-grid.

Meckler, Laura and Hannah Natanson. Remote Learning Widens Equity Gap. The Washington Post, 6 December 2020.

Mersch, Max and Richard Muirhead. What Is Web 3.0 & Why It Matters. Medium, 31 December 2019. https://medium.com/fabric-ventures/what-is-web-3-0-why-it-matters-934eb07f3d2b.

Michaels, Loretta. Yes, COVID Is the Big Bang of Digital Payments. Center for Financial Inclusion, 8 April 2021. https://www.centerforfinancialInclusion.org/yes-covid-is-the-big-bang-of-digital-payments.

Michailof, Serge. Africanistan: Development or Jihad. Oxford University Press, 2018.

Mikkelson, Gregory M, Andrew Gonzalez, Garry D. Peterson. Economic Inequality Predicts Biodiversity Loss. PLoS ONE 2(5): e444. 2007. https://doi.org/10.1371/journal.pone.0000444.

Milanovic, Branko. More or Less. Finance and Development, Vol 48, No. 3. 2011.

Milanovic, Branko. Introducing Kuznets Waves: How Income Inequality Waxes and Wanes Over the Very Long Run, VOX CEPR Policy Portal, 24 February 2016a.

Milanovic, Branko. Global Inequality: A New Approach for the Age of Globalization. Cambridge, MA: Harvard University Press, 2016b.

Mint. India Sees Carbon Emissions Peaking in 2040-45. Mint, 3 November 2021. https://www.Livemint.com/News/india/india-Sees-Carbon-Emissions-Peaking-in-204045-11635947031283.html.

Mischke, Jan, Jonathan Woetzel, Sven Smit, James Manyika, Michael Birshan, Eckart Windhagen, Jörg Schubert, Solveigh Hieronimus, Guillaume Dagorret, and Marc Canal Noguer. Will Productivity and Growth Return after the COVID-19 Crisis? McKinsey, 30 March 2021. https://www.mckinsey.com/industries/public-and-social-sector/our-insights/will-productivity-and-growth-return-after-the-covid-19-crisis.

Mishke, Jan, Jonathan Woetzel, Sven Smit, James Manyika, Michael Birshan, Eckart Windhagen, Jörg Shubert, Sloveigh Hieronimus, Guillaume Dagorret, and Marc Canal Noguer. Will Productivity and Growth Return after the COVID-19 Crisis?. McKinsey Global Institute, 2021. https://www.McKinsey.com/industries/Public-and-Social-Sector/Our-insights/Will-Productivity-and-Growth-Return-After-The-Covid-19-Crisis.

Mitchell, Timothy. Carbon Democracy: Political Power in the Age of Oil. London: Verso, 2011.

Mokyr, Joel. A Culture of Growth. Princeton, NJ: Princeton University Press, 2017.

Mold, Andrew and Samiha Chowdury. Why the Extent of Intra-African Trade Is Much Higher Than Commonly Believed-and What This Means for the AFCFTA. Africa in Focus, Brookings, 19 May 2021. https://www.drookings.edu/Blog/Africa-in-Focus/2021/05/19/Why-The-Extent-of-intra-African-Trade-Is-Much-Higher-Than-Commonly-Believed-and-What-This-Means-For-The-Afcfta/.

Mongird, Kendall, Vilayanur Viswanathan, Jan Alam, Charlie Vartanian, VIncent Sprenkle, and Richard Baxter. 2020 Grid Energy Storage Technology Cost and Performance Assessment. Publication No. DOE/PA-0204. Pacific Northwest National Laboratory and US Department of Energy, 2020.

Moreland, Will. The Purpose of Multilateralism a Framework for Democracies in a Geopolitically Competitive World. Washington, DC: Brooking, 2019.

Motyka, Marlene, Jim Thomson, Stanley E. Porter, Ben Jones, Tom Keefe, Katie Pavlovsky, Tom Stevens, and Kate Hardin. Renewable Transition- Separating Perception from Reality. Deloitte Insights, 30. No Date. https://www2.Deloitte.com/Xe/En/insights/industry/Power-and-Utilities/Us-Renewable-Energy-Transition.html.

Muller, Christoph, Wolfgang Cramer, William Hure, and Husmann Lotze-Campen. Climate Risks for African Agriculture. Proceedings of the National Academy of Sciences 2011-03-15 108(11): 4313-4315. 2011. https://doi.org/10.1073/pnas.1015078108.

Mullin, Emily. The Price of DNA Sequencing Dropped from $2.7 Billion to $300 in Less Than 20 Years. OneZero, 18 February 2021. https://onezero.medium.com/the-price-of-dna-sequencing-dropped-from-2-7-billion-to-300-in-less-than-20-years-f5e07c2f18b4.

Mungiu-Pippidi, Alina. Corruption: Diagnosis and Treatment. Journal of Democracy, 17(3): 86–99 (2006). 2006.

Narayan, Deepa (Ed.). Voices of the Poor: Can Anyone Hear Us? Oxford: Oxford University Press, 2000.

Nersesian, Ron. Five Key Breakthroughs Needed to Make 6G a Reality. Forbes, 17 August 2021. https://www.forbes.com/sites/forbestechcouncil/2021/08/17/five-key-breakthroughs-needed-to-make-6g-a-reality/.

NOAA. Annual Mean CO2 Concentrations in the Atmosphere. NOAA/ESRL Global Monitoring Division, National Oceanic and Atmospheric Administration (NOAA), 2021.

Nobel Prize. Press Release: The Nobel Prize in Chemistry 2020. 7 October 2020. https://www.nobelprize.org/prizes/chemistry/2020/press-release/.

Nokia. 6G Explained. Nokia, 15 October 2021. https://www.nokia.com/about-us/newsroom/articles/6g-explained/.

Noonan, John T. Jr. Bribes: The Intellectual History of a Moral Idea. New York: Macmillan. 1984.

North, Douglass C. Thomas, Robert P. The Rise of the Western World: A New Economic History. Cambridge: Cambridge University Press, 1973.

North, Douglass C., John Joseph Wallis, Barry R. Weingast. Violence and Social Order, New York, Cambridge University Press, 2009.

North, Douglass C., Barry R. Weingast. Constitutions and Commitment: The Evolutions of Institutions Governing Public Choice in Seventeenth Century England. Journal of Economic History 49(4) 1989, P. 831. 1989.

NTI and the Johns Hopkins Center for Health Security. Global Health Security Index. NTI, the Johns Hopkins Center for Health Security, and Economic Impact, 2021. https://www.Ghsindex.org/.

Ocampo, José Antonio, Building a Better SDR. Project Syndicate, March 5, 2021.

Ocampo, José Antonio. Resetting the International Monetary (Non) System. New York: Oxford University Press, 2017.

Ocampo, José Antonio. The Future of Global Currencies. In Bretton Woods: The Next 70 Years, Edited By Marc Uzan, 271–275. ReInventing Bretton Woods Committee, 2016.

OECD. Inequality Hurts Economic Growth. Paris: OECD Publishing, 2014.

OECD. In It Together: Why Less Inequality Benefits All. Paris: OECD Publishing, 2015.

OECD. Opportunities for All: A Framework on Policy Action for Inclusive Growth. Paris: OECD Publishing, 2018.

OECD. OECD Economic Outlook, Volume 2020 Issue 2. Paris: OECD Publishing, 2020a.

OECD. OECD Employment Outlook 2020: Worker Security and the COVID-19 Crisis. Paris: OECD Publishing, 2020b. https://Doi.org/10.1787/1686c758-En.

OECD. Government Policies Providing More Than USD 500 Billion to Farmers Every Year Distort Markets, Stifle Innovation and Harm the Environment. Paris: OECD Publishing, 2020c. https://www.Oecd.org/Agriculture/News/Government-Policies-Providing-More-Than-Usd-500-Billion-To-Farmers-Every-Year-Distort-Markets-Stifle-Innovation-and-Harm-The-Environment.Htm.

OECD. Climate Finance Provided and Mobilized by Developed Countries: Aggregate Trends Updated with 2019 Data. Climate Finance and the USD Billion Goal, Paris: OECD Publishing, 2021a. https://Doi.org/10.1787/03590fb7-En.

OECD. Forward-looking Scenarios of Climate Finance Provided and Mobilized By Developed Countries in 2021–2025: Technical Note. Climate Finance and the USD 100 Billion Goal, Paris: OECD Publishing, 2021b. https://Doi.org/10.1787/A53aac3b-En.

Olivera, Rodrigo, Jesse Lastunen, Enrico Nichelatti, and Pia Rattenhuber. Imputation Methods for Adjusting SOUTHMOD Input Data to Income Losses Due to the COVID-19 Crisis. Wider Technical Note 19. 2021.

Olson, Mancur. The Logic of Collective Action, Public Policy, and the Theory of Groups. Cambridge, USA; London: Harvard University Press, 1971.

Olson, Mancur. The Rise and Decline of Nations: Economic Growth, Stagflation, and Social Rigidities. Yale University Press, 1982.

Ortiz-Bobea, Ariel, Toby R. Ault, Carlos M. Carillo, Robert G. Chambers, and David B. Lobell. Anthropogenic Climate Change Has Slowed Global Agricultural Productivity

Growth. Nature Climate Change 11, No.4 (April 2021): 306–12. https://Doi.org/10.1038/S41558-021-01000-1.

Ostry, Jonathan D. and Andrew Berg. Treating Inequality with Redistribution: Is the Cure Worse Than the Disease? IMF Blog. Last modified 24 Februar 2014.

Ostry, Jonathan D., Andrew Berg, and Charalambos G. Tsangarides. Redistribution, Inequality, and Growth. IMF Staff Discussion Notes 14/02. 2014.

Ostry, J., Andrew Berg, Charalambos G. Tsangarides, and Yorbol Yakhshilikov. Redistribution, Inequality, and Growth: New Evidence. Journal of Economic Growth 23 (3):259–305. 2018.

Our World in Data. Share of Population Fully Vaccinated Against COVID-19. Our World in Data. Accessed 31 January 2022. https://Ourworldindata.org/Grapher/Share-People-Fully-Vaccinated-Covid.

Ovide, Shira. A Perfect Positive Storm: Bonkers Dollars for Big Tech. The New York Times, 29 April 2021a. https://www.Nytimes.com/2021/04/29/Technology/Big-Tech-Pandemic-Economy.html.

Ovide, Shira. How Big Tech Won the Pandemic. The New York Times, 30 April 2021b. https://www.Nytimes.com/2021/04/30/Technology/Big-Tech-Pandemic.html.

Oxford PV. Oxford PV Hits New World Record for Solar Cell. Oxford PV, 21 December 2020. https://www.oxfordpv.com/news/oxford-pv-hits-new-world-record-solar-cell.

Park, Han Woo, and Loet Leydesdorff. Longitudinal Trends in Networks of University–Industry–Government Relations in South Korea: The Role of Programmatic Incentives. Research Policy 39, No. 5 (June 2010): 640–49. https://Doi.org/10.1016/J.Respol.2010.02.009.

Parry, Ian, Simon Black, and Nate Vernon. Still Not Getting Energy Prices Right: A Global and Country Update of Fossil Fuel Subsidies. Working Paper No. 2021/236, IMF, 2021. https://www.Imf.org/En/Publications/WP/Issues/2021/09/23/Still-Not-Getting-Energy-Prices-Right-A-Global-and-Country-Update-of-Fossil-Fuel-Subsidies-466004.

Parry, Ian. Simon Black, and James Roaf. Proposal for An International Carbon Price Floor Among Large Emitters. Staff Climate Note No. 2021/001, IMF, 2021. https://www.Imf.org/En/Publications/Staff-Climate-Notes/Issues/2021/06/15/Proposal-For-An-International-Carbon-Price-Floor-Among-Large-Emitters-460468.

Pathak, Kalpana. RIL Targets Green Hydrogen Output at a Cost of $1/kg. Livemint, 3 September 2021. https://www.livemint.com/companies/news/ril-targets-green-hydrogen-output-at-a-cost-of-1kg-11630687916328.html.

Perotti, Roberto. Growth, Income Distribution, and Democracy: What the Data Say. Journal of Economic Growth 1 (2): 149-187. 1996.

Perry, M. and Tan Boon Hui. Global Manufacturing and Local Linkages in Singapore. Environment and Planning A: Economy and Space 30, No. 9 (September 1998):1603–24. https://Doi.org/10.1068/A301603. 1998.

Persson, Anna, Bo Rothstein, and Jan Teorell. Why Anticorruption Reforms Fail: Systematic Corruption as a Collective Action Problem. Governance 26(3): 449–471. 2012.

Petrova, Magdalena. Green Hydrogen is Gaining Traction, but Still Has Massive Hurdles to Overcome. CNBC, 4 December 2020. https://www.cnbc.com/2020/12/04/green-hydrogen-is-gaining-traction-but-it-must-overcome-big-hurdles.html.

Plnner, Dickon, Matt Rogers, and Hamid Samandari. Addressing Cimate Change in a Post-pandemic World. McKinsey, 7 April 2020. https://www.mckinsey.com/business-functions/sustainability/our-insights/addressing-climate-change-in-a-post-pandemic-world.

Posner, Eric A. and Weyl, E. Glen. Radical Markets, Uprooting Capitalism and Democracy for a Just Society. PrInceton, NJ: PrInceton University Press, 2018.

Programa De Naciones Unidas Para El Desarrollo (PNUD). Más Allá Del ingreso, Más Allá De Los Promedios, Más Allá Del Presente: Desigualdades Del Desarrollo Humano En El Siglo XXI. Informe Sobre Desarrollo Humano. Nueva York: PNUD. 2019.

Psacharopoulos, George, Harry A. Patrinosvictoria, Collisemiliana Vegas. The COVID-19 Cost of School Closures. World Bank Blogs, 30 April 2020. https://blogs.worldbank.org/education/covid-19-cost-school-closures.

Psious. No date. https://psious.com/.

Putnam, Robert D., Leonardi Robert, Nanetti Raffaella Y. Making Democracy Work: Civic Traditions in Modern Italy. Princeton, NJ: Princeton University Press, 1993.

Putnam, Robert D.. Bowling Alone: The Collapse and Revival of American Community. New York: Simon & Schuster, 2000.

Quibria, M.G. Governance and Developing Asia: Concepts, Measurements, Determinants, and Paradoxes. ADB Economics WP Series No. 388, March 2014., P.2. 2014.

Qureshi, Zia. Technology and the Future of Growth: Challenges of Change. Brookings, 25 February 2020. https://www.brookings.edu/blog/up-front/2020/02/25/technology-and-the-future-of-growth-challenges-of-change/.

Rajan, Raghuram. New Rules for the Monetary Game. Project Syndicate, March 21, 2016.

Ratha, Dilip, Eung Ju Kim, Sonia Plaza, Ganesh Seshan, Elliott J Riordan, and Vandana Chandra. Migration and Development Brief 35: Recovery: COVID-19 Crisis through a Migration Lens. Washington DC: KNOMAD-World Bank, 2021. https://www.Knomad.org/Sites/Default/Files/2021-11/Migration_Brief%2035_1.Pdf.

Raupach, Michael R., Steven J. Davis, Glen P. Peters, Robbie M. Andrew, Josep G. Candall, Philippe Ciais, Pierre Fredlingstein, Frank Jotzo, Detlef P. Van Vuuren, and Corlnne Le Quéré. Sharing a Quota on Cumulative Carbon Emissions. Nature Climate Change 4, No.10 (September 2014): 873-79. https://Doi.org/10.1038/Nclimate2384.

Reuters. Indonesia Signals about-face on COP 26 Zero-deforestation Pledge. Reuters, 4 November 2021. https://www.Reuters.com/Article/Climate-Un-Forests-indonesia-Idafl4n2rv0y0.

Reuters. Thailand's Eastern Economic Corridor: Southeast Asia's New Engine of Growth. Reuters Plus, No. March: 1–5. 2020.

Rickards, James. Currency Wars: The Making of the Next Global Crisis. New York: Portfolio/Penguin, 2011.

Rigaud, Kanta Kumari, Alex De Sherbinin, Bryan Jones, Jonas Bergmann, Viviane Clement, Kayly Ober, Jacob Schewe, Susana Adamo, Brent Mccusker, Silke Heuser, Amelia Midgley. Groundswell: Preparing for Internal Climate Migration. Washington, DC: The World Bank, 2018. https://Openknowledge.Worldbank.org/Handle/10986/29461 License: CC BY 3.0 IGO.

Roberts, J. Timmons, Romain Weikmans, Stacy-Ann Robinson, David Ciplet, Mizan Khan, and Danielle Falzon. Rebooting a Failed Promise of Climate Finance. Nature Climate Change 11, No. 3 (February 2021): 180–2. https://Doi.org/10.1038/S41558-021-00990-2.

Romer, Paul. Cutting the Corruption Tax, Voxeu, 08 October 2018.

Roser, Max, Esteban Ortiz-Ospina, and Hannah Ritchie. Life Expectancy. Our World in Data, 2013. https://Ourworldindata.org/Life-Expectancy.

Rothstein, Bo, and Jan Teorell. Getting to Sweden, Part II: Breaking with Corruption in the Nineteenth Century. Scandinavian Political Studies 38(3): 238–254 (2015). 2015.

Rothstein, Bo. Trust, Social Dilemmas, and Collective Memories. Journal of theoretical Politics 12(4): 477–501, P. 477. 2000.

Rowlatt, Justin. Why Electric Cars Will Take Over Sooner Than You Think. BBC News, 1 June 2021. https://www.Bbc.com/News/Business-57253947.

RTI. Managing Global Liquidity as a Global Public Good: A Report of an RTI Working Party. RTI Paper No. 11. Louvain-La-Neuve and Turin: Robert Triffin International, Centro Studi Sul Federalismo, and Université Catholique De Louvain, 2019.

RTI. Using the SDR as a Lever to Reform the International Monetary System: Report of an SDR Working Party. Louvain-La-Neuve and Turin: Robert Triffin International, Centro Studi Sul Federalismo, and Université Catholique De Louvain, 2014.

Ryan, Vincent. Three Ways Covid-19 Is Accelerating Digital Transformation in Professional Services. CFO, 29 June 2020. https://www.Cfo.com/Corporate-Finance/2020/06/Three-Ways-Covid-19-Is-Accelerating-Digital-Transformation-in-Professional-Services-8840/.

Sachs, Jeffrey D. Time to Overhaul the Global Financial System. Project Syndicate, 3 December 2021. https://www.Project-Syndicate.org/Commentary/Global-Financial-System-Death-Trap-For-Developing-Countries-By-Jeffrey-D-Sachs-2021-12?Barrier=Accesspaylog.

Sachs, Jeffrey. Some Brief Reflections on Digital Technologies and Economic Development. Ethics & International Affairs, Vol. 33, Núm. 2: 159-167. 2019.

Satterthwaite, David, Gordon Mcgranahan, and Cecilia Tacoli. Urbanization and Its Implications for Food and Farming. Philosophical Transactions of the Royal Society B: Biological Sciences 365, No. 1554 (September 27, 2010): 2809–20. 2010. https://Doi.org/10.1098/Rstb.2010.0136.

Schwab, Klaus and Malleret, Thierry. COVID-19: The Great Reset. Cologne, Geneva: World Economic Forum (WEF). 2020.

Science Daily, Whole Genome of Novel Coronavirus, 2019-nCoV, sequenced. Science Daily, 31 January 2020. https://www.sciencedaily.com/releases/2020/01/200131114748.htm.

Seabright, Paul. The Company of Strangers: A Natural History of Economic Life. Princeton, NJ: Princeton University Press, 2010.

Sen, Amartya. Isolation, Assurance, and the Social Rate of Discount. The Quarterly Journal of Economics, Vol. 81, Issue 1, February 1967. 1967.

Sen, Amartya. Development as Freedom. New York: Alfred A. Knopf, 1999.

Sen, Amartya. The Idea of Justice. London: Allen Lane, Penguin Books, 2009.

Sepulveda, Nestor A., Jesse D. Jenkins, Aurora Edington, Dharik S. Mallapragada, and Richard K. Lester. The Design Space for Long-Duration Energy Storage in Decarbonized

Power Systems. Nature Energy 6, No.5 (March 2021):506–16. https://Doi.org/10.1038/S41560-021-00796-8.

Shakespeare, William. The Tragedy of Hamlet, PrInce of Denmark. New Folgers Ed. New York: Washington Square Press/Pocket Books, 1992.

Shell Deutschland Oil GmbH 2017. Shell Hydrogen Study: Energy of the Future. Shell, 2017.

Sheng, Andrew. Re-thinking Emerging Market Debt and Development Finance. Unpublished Paper, April 2021.

Sheth, Hemai. India Is Second-fastest-growing Freelance Market in the World, Says Report. The Hindu Businessline, 11 September 2020. https://www.Thehindubusinessline.com/News/india-Is-Second-Fastest-Growing-Freelance-Market-in-The-World-Says-Report/Article32578886.Ece.

SHL. National Employability Report: Engineers. SHL, 2019. https://www2.Shl.com/En/india/Employability-Reports/.

SHRM. Study Finds Productivity Not Deterred by Shift to Remote Work. SHRM. Society for Human Resource Management, 6 July 2021. https://www.Shrm.org/Hr-Today/News/Hr-News/Pages/Study-Productivity-Shift-Remote-Work-Covid-Coronavirus.Aspx.

Smith, Aaron. Public Attitudes toward Computer Algorithms. Pew Research Center, 2018. https://www.Pewresearch.org/internet/2018/11/16/attitudes-Toward-Algorithmic-Decision-Making/.

Smith, Adam. The Wealth of Nations. Oxford, England: Bibliomania.com Ltd, 2002. https://Lccn.Loc.Gov/2002564559.

Smith, Elliot. Russia Is Building Its Military Influence in Africa, Challenging U.S. and French Dominance. CNBC, 13 September 2021. https://www.Cnbc.com/2021/09/13/Russia-Is-Building-Military-influence-in-Africa-Challenging-Us-France.html.

Sobel, Mark. IMF Shifts Approach to Low Income Countries and Special Drawing Rights. OMFIF, 10 August 2021. https://www.Omfif.org/2021/08/Imf-Shifts-Approach-To-Low-Income-Countries-and-Special-Drawing-Rights/#:~:Text=IMF%20shifts%20approach%20to%20low%20Income%20countries%20and%20special%20drawing%20rights,-By%20Mark%20Sobel&Text=IMF%20concessional%20LIC%20lending%20is,Free%2C%20essentially%20under%20IMF%20programmes.

Sobers, Rob. 134 Cybersecurity Statistics and Trends for 2021. Inside Out Security Blog, Data Security, 115–16. 2021. https://www.Varonis.com/Blog/Cybersecurity-Statistics.

Stiglitz, Joseph. The Price of Inequality: How Todays Divided Society Endangers Our Future. New York: W.W. Norton and Company, 2012.

Stiglitz, Joseph. The Unfinished Task of Bretton Woods: Creating a Global Reserve System. In Bretton Woods: The Next 70 Years, Edited by Marc Uzan, 349. Reinventing Bretton Woods Committee, 2016.

Stiglitz, Joseph. Conquering the Great Divide. Washinton, DC: IMF Finance and Development, 2020.

Stirling, Chris, Anuj Kapadia, Roger Van De Heuvel, and Jia Zhou. Medical Devices in 2030. KPMG International, 2018. https://Assets.Kpmg/Content/Dam/Kpmg/Xx/Pdf/2017/12/Medical-Devices-2030.Pdf.

Stokes, Bruce. Global Publics More Upbeat about the Economy: But Many Are Pessimistic About Children's Future. Pew Research Center, 2017.

Sun, Luna. Is Chinas Version of the Great Resignation Creating an Army of Freelancers? South China Morning Post, 22 October 2021. https://www.Scmp.com/Economy/China-Economy/Article/3152487/Chinas-Great-Resignation-Freelancers-Find-Both-Hope-and?Utm_Content=Article&Utm_Medium=Social&Utm_Source=Twitter#Echobox=1634453078-1.

SWIFT. An Inside Look Into London's Quest for the Renminbi. RMB Tracker, Special Edition, 25 September 2019.

Swiss Re Institute. The Economics of Climate Change; No Action Not an Option. Zurich, Switzerland: Swiss Re Management Ltd, 2021.

Szczerba, Robert J. 15 Worst Tech Predictions of All Time. Forbes, 5 January 2015. https://www.Forbes.com/Sites/Robertszczerba/2015/01/05/15-Worst-Tech-Predictions-of-All-Time/?Sh=28844c4e1299.

Taylor, Paul. The Good News about Labor Shortages. Politico, 7 October 2021. https://www.Politico.Eu/Article/Good-News-Labor-Shortages-Coronavirus-Economic-Recovery/.

Temple, Jonathan. The New Growth Evidence. Journal of Economic Literature 37 (1): 112-56. 1999.

Tett, Gillian. The Dollar Will Dominate for a While Yet. Financial Times, 17 May 2019.

The Economist. The Great Jobs Boom. The Economist, 25 May 2019.

The Economist. Chinas Dual-Circulation Strategy Means Relying Less on Foreigners. The Economist, 7 November 2020.

The Economist. Water in Bangladesh Is Either Unsafe Or Pricey. The Economist, 8 May 2021. https://www.Economist.com/Asia/2021/05/08/Water-in-Bangladesh-Is-Either-Unsafe-Or-Pricey.

The Economist. Why the War Against Jihadists in Mali Is Going Badly. The Economist, 7 November 2021b.

The Global Fund. Results Report 2021: At a Glance. The Global Fund, 2021. https://www.Theglobalfund.org/Media/11309/Corporate_2021resultsreport_Summary_En.Pdf.

Ting, Choo Yun. More ASEAN Start-Ups Became Unicorns Thanks to Robust Funding, Rising Middle Class. Report, Economy News & Top Stories - the Straits Times, No. 202120748: 2021. https://www.Straitstimes.com/Business/Economy/More-Start-Ups-in-Asean-Reach-Unicorn-Status-With-Lift-From-Robust-Private-Equity.

Tongia, Rahul. Flatten the Curve: Why Total Carbon Emissions Matter Much More Than Date to Zero. Working Paper 14, CSEP, 2021. https://Csep.org/Working-Paper/Flatten-The-Curve-Why-Total-Carbon-Emissions-Matter-Much-More-Than.

Tørsløv, Thomas R., Ludvig S. Wier, and Gabriel Zucman. The Missing Profits of Nations. 2018. http://Gabriel-Zucman.Eu/Missingprofits/.

Tran, Hung. New Risks to Global Financial Stability. Issue Brief. Atlantic Council, 2019.

Trebilcock, Michael J. Dealing With Losers: The Political Economy of Policy Transitions. New York: Oxford University Press, 2014. Oxford Scholarship Online, 2014 Doi: 10.1093/Acpr of:Oso/9780199370658.001.0001.

Triffin, Robert. Gold and the Dollar Crisis: The Future of Convertibility. New Haven: Yale University Press, 1960.

Triffin, Robert. The IMS (International Monetary System… Or Scandal?) and the EMS (European Monetary System… Or Success?). Jean Monnet Lecture, European University Institute. Florence: Banca Nazionale Del Lavoro Quarterly Review, No. 179 (December 1991). 1991.

Tuluy, Hasan. Regional Economic Integration in Africa. In Africa Reset: A New Way Forward. Edited by Theodore Ahlers and Harinder S. Kohli, Oxford University Press, 2017.

Turner, Philip. The New Monetary Policy Revolution – Advice and Dissent. NIESR Occasional Paper LX. London: National Institute of Economic and Social Research, 2021.

UN Climate Change Conference UK 2021. COP26: The Negotiations Explained. November 2021. https://Ukcop26.org/Wp-Content/Uploads/2021/11/COP26-Negotiations-Explained.Pdf.

UN Committee for Development Policy. Global Governance and Global Rules for Development in the Post-2015 Era. New York: United Nations, 2014.

UN Department of Economic and Social Affairs. World Population Prospects 2018, Online Edition, Rev. 1. New York: United Nations, Department of Economic and Social Affairs, Population Division, 2019.

UNCTAD. Accounting and Financial Reporting by Small and Medium-Sized Enterprises: Trends and Prospects. New York: United Nations, 2013.

UNCTAD. Economic Development in Africa Report 2020: Tackling Illicit Financial Flows for Sustainable Development in Africa. New York: United Nations, 2020.

UNCTAD. Technology and Innovation Report 2021: Catching Technological Waves—Innovation with Equity. New York: United Nations, 2021a.

UNCTAD. World Investment Report 2021: Investing in Sustainable Recovery. New York: United Nations, 2021b.

UNCTADSTAT. Export Diversification Index. UNCTAD. Accessed 21 December 2021. https://unctadstat.Unctad.org/EN/index.html.

UNDP. State of Biodiversity in Asia and the Pacific. Bangkok: UNDP, 2010.

UNEP. The Emissions Gap Report 2016. Nairobi, Kenya: United National Environment Program (UNEP), 2016a.

UNEP. The Adaptation Finance Gap Report 2016. Nairobi, Kenya: United Nations Environment Program (UNEP), 2016b.

UNEP. Addendum to the Emissions Gap Report 2021. Nairobi, Kenya: United National Environment Program (UNEP), 2021.

UNESCO. Basic Texts: 2020 Edition (revised edition). Paris: UNESCO, 2020.

UNHCR. Data Reveals Impacts of Climate Emergency on Displacement. UNHCR. Last Modified 22 April 2021. https://www.unhcr.org/en-us/news/stories/2021/4/60806d124/data-reveals-impacts-climate-emergency-displacement.html#:~:text=This%20Earth%20Day%2C%20UNHCR%20is,often%20decreasing%20possibilities%20for%20return.

UNICEF. Child Poverty in Perspective: An Overview of Child Well-being in Rich Countries. Innocenti Report Card 7. Florence: Innocenti Research Centre, 2007.

UNICEF. COVID-19: Are Children Able to Continue Learning During School Closures? Accessed 2 January 2020. https://data.unicef.org/resources/remote-learning-reachability-factsheet/.

United Nations. United Nations - Resolution Adopted by the General Assembly on 25 September 2015. New York, NY: United Nations, 2015.

US Department of Agriculture Economic Research Service. Measuring the Number of Adults Economically Active in Agriculture. Washington DC, US Department of Agriculture Economic Research Service, 2018.

US Department of Energy. Hydrogen Shot. Accessed 11 December 2021. https://www.energy.gov/eere/fuelcells/hydrogen-shot.

US Department of Energy. Long Duration Storage Shot. Accessed 11 December 2021. https://www.energy.gov/eere/long-duration-storage-shot.

Uslaner, Eric and Brown, M. Trust, Inequality, and Civic Engagement. American Politics Research, Volume: 33 issue: 6, page(s): 868–894. 2005.

Uzan, Mark, Ed. Bretton Woods: The Next 70 Years. New York, NY: Reinventing Bretton Woods Committee, 2016.

Vogels, Emily A. Millennials Stand Out for their Technology Use, But Older Generations Also Embrace Digital Life. Pew Research Center. Last modified 9 September 2019. https://www.Pewresearch.org/Fact-Tank/2019/09/09/Us-Generations-Technology-Use/.

Vogl, Frank. The Enablers: How the West Supports Kleptocrats and Corruption -Endangering Our Democracy. Lanham, MD: Rowman & Littlefield Publishers, 2021.

Vollset, Stein Emil, Emily Goren, Chun-Wei Yuan, Jackie Cao, Amanda E Smith, Thomas Hsiao, Catherine Bisignano, Gulrez S Azhar, Emma Castro, Julian Chalek, Andrew J Dolgert, Tahvi Frank, Kai Fukutaki, Simon I Hay, Rafael Lozano, Ali H Mokdad, Vishnu Nandakumar, Maxwell Pierce, Martin Pletcher, Toshana Robalik, Krista M Steuben, Han Yong Wunrow, Bianca S Zlavog, Christopher J L Murray. Fertility, Mortality, Migration, and Population Scenarios for 195 Countries and Territories from 2017 to 2100: A Forecasting Analysis for the Global Burden of Disease Study. The Lancet Volume 396. Issue 10258, P1285–1306. 2020.

Walden University. How to Use Technology To Promote Social Change. Walden University. Accessed 25 March 2021. https://www.Waldenu.edu/Online-Masters-Programs/Ms-in-Nonprofit-Management-and-Leadership/Resource/How-To-Use-Technology-To-Promote-Social-Change.

WEF. The Global Information Technology Report 2016: Innovating in the Digital Economy. Cologny/ Geneva: World Economic Forum, 2016.

Wellcome. How have Covid-19 Vaccines Been Made Quickly and Safely? Wellcome, 2021. https://wellcome.org/news/quick-safe-covid-vaccine-development.

Williamson, John. International Monetary Reform: A Specific Set of Proposals. New York, NY: Routledge, 2018.

Witte, Björn, Przemek Obloj, Sedef Koktenturk, Benjamin Morach, Michael Brigl, Jürgen Rogg, Ulrik Schulze, et Al. Food for Thought: The Protein Transformation. BCG and Blue Horizon, 2021.

Wong, Katie. 2021. China Develops $ 26bn Ultra High Voltage Electrical Grids to Stimulate Economic Recovery Announcement of New infrastructure Projects Transmission Utilities to Develop 14 UHV Projects. Power Technology. Last modified on 05 Nov 2021. https://www.Power-Technology.com/Comment/China-26bn-Uhv-Grids/.

World Bank. Governance and Development. Washington, DC: World Bank, 1992.

World Bank. World Development Report, Agriculture for Development. Washington, DC: World Bank, 2008.

World Bank. A Measured Approach to Ending Poverty and Boosting Shared Prosperity : Concepts, Data, and the Twin Goals. Policy Research Report;. Washington, DC: World Bank, 2015.

World Bank. World Development Report: Governance and the Law. Washington, DC: World Bank, 2017.

World Bank. Ending Learning Poverty: What Will It Take?. Washington, DC: World Bank, 2019.

World Bank. Future of Food: Maximizing Finance for Development in Agricultural Value Chains. Washington, DC: World Bank, 2020a.

World Bank. Trading for Development in the Age of Global Value Chains, World Development Report 2020. Washington, DC: World Bank, 2020b.

World Bank. The African Continental Free Trade Area: Economic and Distributional Effects. Washington DC: World Bank, 2020c.

World Bank. Climate Change Could Further Impact Africa's Recovery, Pushing 86 Million Africans to Migrate Within their Own Countries By 2050. Press Release No: 2021/021/AFR. 27 October 2021a. https://www.Worldbank.org/En/News/Press-Release/2021/10/27/Climate-Change-Could-Further-Impact-Africa-S-Recovery-Pushing-86-Million-Africans-To-Migrate-Within-Their-Own-Countries.

World Bank. World Development Indicators. Washington, DC: World Bank, 2021b.

World Bank. Global Economic Prospects. Washington, DC: World Bank, 2022.

World Bank. The Human Capital Project: Frequently Asked Questions. No Date. https://www.Worldbank.org/En/Publication/Human-Capital/Brief/The-Human-Capital-Project-Frequently-Asked-Questions#HCP2.

World Economic Forum. The Global Competitiveness Report 2019. Insight Report. Klaus Schwab (ed.). Cologny/ Geneva. Switzerland: World Economic Forum (WEF), 2019a.

World Economic Forum. Towards a Reskilling Revolution: Industry-led Action for the Future of Work. Cologny/ Geneva. Switzerland: World Economic Forum (WEF), 2019b.

World Economic Forum. The Future of Jobs Report. Cologny/ Geneva: World Economic Forum (WEF), 2020.

World Health Organization and World Bank. Tracking Universal Health Coverage: Global Monitoring Report. Geneva: World Health Organization, 2017.

World Health Organization. Climate Change and Health. World Health Organization. Last modified on 30 October 2021. https://www.Who.int/News-Room/Fact-Sheets/Detail/Climate-Change-and-Health.

WRI Climate Watch. Historical GHG Emissions Data. World Resources Institute (WRI). Accessed on 17 December 2021. https://www.Climatewatchdata.org/Ghg-Emissions.

WTO. Overview of Developments in the International Trading Environment: Annual Report by the Director-General. Geneva: World Trade Organization, November 2021.

Yusuf, Shahid. Productivity Matters: The Big Picture. Unpublished, 2021a.

Yusuf, Shahid. Boosting KSA's Economic Productivity: What NDF Can Do. Unpublished, 2021b.

Yusuf, Shahid. 2021c. Vietnam: The East Asian Model Redux. Center for Global Development, 2021c. Accessed At https://www.cgdev.org/publication/vietnam-east-asian-model-redux.

Zhao, Daniel. Work from Home: Has the Future of Work Arrived? Glassdoor Economic Research, 2020. https://www.Glassdoor.com/ Research/Working-From-Home/.

Zhou, Xiaochuan. Reform the International Monetary System. BIS Review 41/2009. BIS, 2009.

About the Editors and Authors

Editors

Harinder Kohli

Harinder S. Kohli is the Founding Director and Chief Executive of Emerging Markets Forum as well as the Founding Director, President, CEO, and largest shareholder of Centennial Group International both based in Washington, DC. He is the Founding Editor of Global Journal of Emerging Markets Economies. He has written extensively on the emergence of Asia, Latin America, Africa and other emerging market economies; financial development; and infrastructure. He led Centennial Group teams that helped the Asian Development Bank (ADB) and Development Bank of Latin America (CAF) develop their long-term corporate strategies. He is also an author or co-author of some fifteen books published by international publishing houses, the ADB, World Bank (WB) and Japan International Cooperation Agency. Some of the books have been translated into French, Spanish, Chinese, Russian and Japanese. These books include: *The World in 2050: Striving for a Just, Prosperous, and Harmonious Global Community* and *China's Belt and Road Initiative: Potential Transformation of Central Asia and the South Caucasus.* Prior to starting his current ventures, he served over twenty-eight years in various senior managerial positions at the WB and worked in some eighty emerging market economies in Asia, Latin America, Europe, the Middle East and Africa. Earlier, he worked in the private sector in India and France. He has also been independent Director of IT companies based in the US and India. He has lectured at the Emerging Markets Institute as well as many international forums.

Rajat Nag

Rajat M. Nag is concurrently a Distinguished Fellow both at India's National Council of Applied Economic Research, Delhi and at the Emerging Markets Forum, a think tank based in Washington DC. He was a Visiting Professor at the Stephen Zuellig Graduate School of Development Management, Asian Institute of Management in Manila (2014–15) and currently serves as a Distinguished Professor at the Emerging Markets Institute at the Beijing Normal University, China. In addition, he serves as an Advisor and Board Member of several organizations. Mr Nag was the Managing Director General of the Asian Development Bank during 2006–13. His work has given him wide-ranging insight into several issues and challenges relevant to Asia. His particular interest is in working to enhance regional cooperation and integration in Asia and beyond and bridging the gap between the region's thriving economies and the millions of poor people being left behind. He holds engineering degrees (BTech) from the Indian Institute of Technology, Delhi, and an MSc from the University of

449

Saskatchewan, Canada. He also has an MBA from the University of Saskatchewan and an MSc (Econ) from the London School of Economics. Mr Nag was awarded Doctor of Laws (Honoris Causa) by the University of Saskatchewan, Canada in May 2016.

Ieva Vilkelyte

Ieva Vilkelyte is a Senior Research Associate at Centennial Group International and the Emerging Markets Forum. During her time at Centennial Group and EMF, she has collabourated on projects for the African Development Bank, the Japanese International Cooperation Agency, and CAF, among others. She also worked on *The World in 2050: Striving for a Just, Prosperous, and Harmonious Global Community* (2016), *Kazakhstan 2050: Toward a Modern Society for All* (2014) and *Africa 2050: Realizing the Continent's Full Potential* (2014). She graduated from Georgetown University in 2013, where she majored in economics.

Authors

Montek Ahluwalia

Montek Singh Ahluwalia is an economist, civil servant and the former Deputy Chairman of Planning Commission Government of India. He is currently a Distinguished Fellow at the Center for Economic and Social Policy, New Delhi. He has held several positions in the Indian Government and been a key figure in India's economic reforms since the mid-1980s. He began his career at the World Bank and joined the Indian Ministry of Finance in 1979. He subsequently served as Special Secretary to the Prime Minister, Rajiv Gandhi, as Commerce Secretary, Finance Secretary and as a member of the Economic Advisory Council to the Prime Minister. In 2001, he was appointed the first Director of the IMF's Independent Evaluation Office. He is a member of the Governing Board of the Council on Energy, Environment and Water, New Delhi. He has authored several articles and his memoirs *Backstage: The Story of India's High Growth Years* was published by Rupa publications in 2020. Dr Montek Singh Ahluwalia graduated from Delhi University and has an MA and an MPhil in economics from Oxford University.

Manu Bhaskaran

Mr Bhaskaran is a Partner of the Centennial Group, a strategic advisory firm headquartered in Washington, DC. As Founding CEO of its Singapore subsidiary, Centennial Asia Advisors, he coordinates the Asian business of the Group which provides independent economic research on Asian political and macroeconomic trends for investment institutions, government agencies, multilateral institutions and companies with interests in Asia, leveraging off forty years of studying Asia. Mr Bhaskaran is also Adjunct Senior Research Fellow at the Institute of Policy Studies in Singapore where his main interests are in analysing macroeconomic policy frameworks in Singapore. Prior to Centennial, Mr Bhaskaran held senior positions at Societe Generale's Asian investment banking division where he supervised Asian economic and investment strategy analysis and was a member of the Executive Committee, in charge of Asian equity research. In twelve years with the firm, Mr Bhaskaran helped to establish its business presence in Southeast Asia and in South Asia, while also helping to develop the firm's highly-rated equity and economic research. Prior to that, Mr Bhaskaran worked for the Singapore government, supervising a team that prepared strategic political and economic assessments of Asia for senior Singapore government officials. Mr Bhaskaran holds a range of other positions. In terms of public service, he served as Chairman of a high-level government committee reviewing the regulation of moneylenders in Singapore in 2014–15. He is also Member of the Competition Appeals Board, Singapore. In addition, he is a Member of the Regional Advisory Board for Asia of the International Monetary Fund; Council Member, Singapore Institute of International Affairs (SIIA); and Vice-President, Economics Society of Singapore. Mr Bhaskaran also serves on the boards of several companies whose businesses span the ASEAN region including CIMB Investment Bank (a subsidiary of CIMB Bank, Malaysia's second largest bank and which operates across ASEAN), Japfa Ltd (listed in Singapore) and Luminor capital. Mr Bhaskaran was educated at Magdalene College, Cambridge University where he earned an MA (Cantab) and at the John F. Kennedy School of Government at Harvard University where he obtained a Master's in public administration. He is also a Chartered Financial Analyst.

Michel Camdessus

Founding co-Chairman of the Emerging Markets Forum and former Managing Director of the International Monetary Fund, Mr Camdessus is Governor Emeritus of Banque de France. He was a member of the Africa Progress Panel, chaired by late Kofi Annan, and a member of the Commission for Africa, chaired by the then British Prime Minister, Tony Blair. Mr Camdessus was the Chairman of the World Panel on Financing Water Infrastructure. He has been appointed as the Chairman of the French Government's several working groups in charge of preparing the economic, social and structural policies reforms. Mr Camdessus was educated at the University of Paris and earned post graduate degrees in economics at the Institute of Political Studies of Paris (Institut d'Etudes Politiques de Paris) and the National School of Administration (ENA). Following his appointment as Administrateur Civil in the French Civil Service, Mr Camdessus joined the Treasury in the Ministry of Finance in 1960. After serving as Financial Attaché to the French delegation at the European Economic Community in Brussels from 1966 to 1968, he returned to the Treasury and went on to become Director in February 1982. During the period 1978–84, Mr Camdessus also served as Chairman of the Paris Club, and was Chairman of the Monetary Committee of the European Economic Community from December 1982 to December 1984. Mr Camdessus was appointed Governor of the Banque of France in November 1984. He served in this capacity until his election as Managing Director of the IMF in 1987. On 22 May 1996, the Executive Board of the IMF unanimously selected Mr Camdessus to serve a third five-year term as Manageing Director, beginning 16 January 1997. Mr Camdessus retired from the IMF on 14 February 2000. In 2021, President Macron awarded the highest civilian honour in France, the Grand' Croix dans l'ordre national du Mérite, to Mr Camdessus.

Suma Chakrabarti

Sir Suma Chakrabarti is Chair of the Board of Trustees of ODI, a global affairs think tank, and also Adviser to the Presidents of Kazakhstan and Uzbekistan on economic development, governance and international cooperation. Sir Suma also holds positions at the Astana International Financial Centre and with a number of entities tackling climate change. He also served recently as a member of the WHO Pan-European Commission on Health and Sustainable Development and the Commission for Smart Government in the UK Sir Suma was President of the European Bank for Reconstruction and Development from 2012 to 2020, focussed on growing the private sector in emerging markets. Prior to that Sir Suma was Permanent Secretary (most senior civil servant) in the UK Department for International Development and Ministry of Justice. Sir Suma was knighted in 2006 for his work in international development and UK public service reform. He also holds many other prestigious honours from the UK and a range of emerging markets.

Kevin Cleaver

Kevin Cleaver is a consultant specializing in international development, development economics and agriculture. He currently works with the Centennial Group (Washington, DC) preparing a chapter on global agriculture for a forthcoming book on global development. He is the chairperson for the Agriculture and Rural Development Thematic Group of the World Bank's 1818 Society (of alumni and retirees). Dr Cleaver is also co-owner with his wife, Maria Nikolov, of a farm in Peru which produces coffee and cacao. They have created a project to assist Peru's park service to manage the Abiseo Park in Peru (a World Heritage site), including buffer zone activities to protect the park. Prior work with Centennial has included supporting preparation of the African Development Bank's new agriculture strategy; assessing FAO's technical capacity; preparing a chapter on agriculture for a book entitled *Africa Reset* by the Centennial Group; an evaluation of the agriculture situation in China for the Asian Development Bank, and an evaluation of the Asian Development Bank's agricultural strategy and projects. Dr Cleaver was the Associate Vice President (Assistant Secretary General in the common UN system), for Programs of the International Fund for Agriculture Development (IFAD) (a specialized agency of the United Nations) from 2006 to 2014. During 2002–06, he was the Director for Agriculture and Rural Development for the World Bank Group. He also held various positions in the World Bank, including Director for Environment, Rural Development and Social Development in the Europe and Central Asia Region of the World Bank, Technical Director for the Africa Region of the World Bank, and Agriculture division chief in the Africa Region (1976–2002). Prior to joining the World Bank, he was an economist in Zaire's Ministry of Finance while completing research for his PhD. He has a number of publications on agriculture and on the environment. Dr Cleaver earned his PhD in economics from the Fletcher School of Law and Diplomacy, Tufts University (1975). He has a Master's Degree in international law and diplomacy, Tufts University (1973). He received a Bachelor of Arts degree (major in international relations and minor in economics) from the University of Pennsylvania (1970). He also received a World Bank-sponsored executive training program in Harvard Business School in 1995. Dr Cleaver has several awards, including the 2014 IFAD President's Award, and the Chevellier de l'Ordre du Merit Agricole awarded by the French government.

Soumitra Dutta

Soumitra Dutta is Dean Elect, at the Said School of Business, University of Oxford. He is also a Professor of Management and the former founding Dean of the SC Johnson College of Business at Cornell University, New York. He is the co-founder and President of Portulans Institute, a non-profit non-partisan think tank based in Washington DC. Prior to joining Cornell in 2012, he was on the faculty of INSEAD. Soumitra Dutta is an authority on innovation in the knowledge economy, with a refreshing global perspective. He is the author of the Network Readiness Index and the Global Innovation Index—two influential reports in technology and innovation policy. He is/has been on the board of global firms, including Sodexo, Dassault Systemes and

ZS Associates. He is currently the Chair of the Board of the Global Business School Network and is on the advisory boards of several business schools including HEC Montreal and ESADE (Spain). Dean Dutta received a BTech in electrical engineering and computer science from the Indian Institute of Technology, New Delhi, a MS in both business administration and computer science, and a PhD in computer science from the University of California at Berkeley. In 2017, he received the Distinguished Alumnus award from the Indian Institute of Technology, Delhi.

Jose Fajgenbaum

Jose Fajgenbaum is Partner of Centennial Group and Director of Centennial Group Latin America. Prior to joining the Centennial Group, he worked at the International Monetary Fund (IMF) for about thirty years, where he advanced from economist to Deputy Director of various departments. In addition to helping define and supervise these departments work, he led missions to surveillance countries, such as Brazil, Israel, Russia and South Africa, as well as to countries supported by the IMF, such as Brazil in the early 1990s, the Dominican Republic, Kenya, Malawi, Peru and Trinidad and Tobago. His expertise is on a wide range of development and macroeconomic issues. He holds a BA from the National University of Cuyo, an MA in economics from the University of Chicago, and completed his doctoral studies in economics at the University of Chicago.

Katie Ford

Katie Ford is a Research and Project Associate at Centennial. She holds a MA in international development studies specialized in economic development and development in conflict affected countries from The George Washington University's Elliott School of International Affairs. Throughout her graduate studies, she focussed her research on social and economic development issues in the Middle East and Sub-Saharan Africa, and conducted a capstone study on data tool utilization for local governance capacity building in three Myanmar townships. Further, she holds a BA in economics and a minor in French from Georgia State University. Her technical experience in international development research ranges from econometric analysis to evidence-based monitoring and evaluation.

L. Enrique García

Enrique García was President and CEO of CAF—Development Bank of Latin America for twenty-five years between December 1991 and March 2017. He also held professional and managerial positions at the Inter-American Development Bank (IDB) for seventeen years. In his home country Bolivia, he was the Minister of Planning and Coordination and Chief of the Economic and Social Cabinet, and member of the Board of Directors of the Central Bank. He has been a member of the Development Committee of the World Bank and the International Monetary Fund (IMF) representing Bolivia, Chile, Argentina, Peru, Uruguay and Paraguay. He is currently Chairman of the Council of International Relations for Latin America (RIAL), Chairman of the Trust for the Americas (USA), co-President of the Ibero-American Productivity and Competitiveness Council (CIPYC), co-Chairman of the Emerging Markets Forum, co-Vice Chairman of the Inter-American Dialogue (USA) and a member of numerous Boards of public and private institutions. He is a ranking member of the Bolivian Academy of Economic Sciences and a visiting professor at LSE IDEAS at the London School of Economics (LSE), the University of Sao Paulo (USP) and Beijing Normal University. He is the author of many publications on development issues and multilateralism in international journals and books. Mr García holds a Bachelor of Science degree (BS) in economics and political science and a Master of Arts degree (MA) in economics and finance from Saint Louis University in the USA. He has a post graduate in economics from St. Louis University and American University in the USA. Mr García has received Grand Cross grade and other high rank decorations from the governments of Argentina, Bolivia, Brazil, Colombia, Ecuador, Panama, Paraguay, Peru, Spain, Uruguay, Venezuela and the Sovereign Order of Malta, from the General Secretariat of the Andean Community, the Argentine and Bolivian Senates, the Bolivian Legislative Assembly. He is also recipient of awards and distinctions from regional and local governments, public and private institutions and media worldwide.

Werner Hermann

Werner Hermann is a former Director at the Swiss National Bank (SNB). He was responsible for central bank cooperation and represented the SNB at international financial institutions and in international negotiations. He was a member of the foundation council of the Study Center Gerzensee. He started his career in the economics department where he conducted empirical research in macroeconomics and finance, then he headed a group concerned with banking and financial market regulation and supervision, and later was appointed manager of the international department. This allowed him to establish close ties with a group of central banks in transition countries. He was instrumental in establishing the Eurasia Emerging Markets Forum. In the late eighties, Mr Hermann was a visiting scholar at the Federal Reserve Bank of St. Louis. Prior to joining the SNB, he taught at the University of Basel and was a member of the Basel Business Cycle Research Group (now BAK Basel Economics AG), a macroeconomic research and forecasting company. He received a doctorate in economics from the University of Basel. His interests are monetary economics and growth, particularly in transition countries.

Harpaul Alberto Kohli

Harpaul Alberto Kohli is Senior Economist at Centennial Group International and the Emerging Markets Forum, where he is responsible for all econometrics, economic modelling and databases. He previously served as Centennial's Manager of Information Resources and as a consultant for the Asian Development Bank. He earned a degree with honours in mathematics and philosophy from Harvard University, where he served as co-president of both the Society of Physics Students and the Math Club and was elected a Class Marshal for life. He earned his MBA with honours from Georgetown University and his Master of Science in economics from The George Washington University. He is also a Microsoft Certified Technology Specialist, and is owner and CEO of the Abora Music Group. Prior to joining Centennial, he served as a teacher in prisons in Ecuador and Massachusetts, a researcher at UBS and in the US Congress, a field organizer for the 2004 American general election, and a communications staffer for the Wesley Clark presidential primary campaign.

Claudio Loser

Claudio Loser is the Founding Director and Chief Executive Officer of Centennial Latin America, and a Distinguished Fellow of the Emerging Markets Forum. He is a well-known authority on Latin American economies and institutions. During his career at the International Monetary Fund, he held many senior positions, including Director of the Western Hemisphere Department. Recently, he has worked closely with the Latin American Development Bank (CAF), Asian Development Bank (ADB), Japan International Cooperation Agency (JICA), Japan Bank for International Cooperation (JBIC) and with several other financial corporations, mainly dealing with developments in Latin America and the evolving relations between these countries and the International Monetary Fund (IMF). He is a Senior Fellow at the Inter-American Dialogue, a Washington-based forum on Western Hemisphere affairs. He has taught Latin American development issues at the George Washington University. He has published in many journals, mainly on Latin American and Emerging Economies issues. He graduated from the University of Cuyo, Argentina, and obtained a Master of Arts and PhD from the University of Chicago in 1967 and 1971, respectively.

Ramesh A. Mashelkar

Dr R.A. Mashelkar served (1995–2006) as the Director General of Council of Scientific and Industrial Research (CSIR), a chain of thirty-eight national laboratories, also as President of Indian National Science Academy (2004–06), Chairman of National Innovation Foundation (2000–18), President of UK Institution of Chemical Engineers (2007) and also the President of Global Research Alliance (2007–17), a network of RTOs from US, Europe, Asia Pacific and Africa with around 60,000 scientists. Forty-four universities from around the world have honoured him with honourary doctorates. Dr Mashelkar is only the third Indian engineer to have been elected (1998) as a Fellow of the Royal Society (FRS), London, in the twentieth century. He was elected a Foreign Associate to the US National Academy of Science (2005) and also the National Academy of Engineering (2003), and Associate Foreign Member to the American Academy of Arts & Sciences (2011), a Fellow of the Royal Academy of Engineering, UK (1996), a Foreign Fellow of the Australian Technological Science and Engineering Academy (2008), a Corresponding Member of the Australian Academy of Sciences (2017), a Fellow of the World Academy of Arts & Science, USA (2000), a Fellow of the US National Academy of Inventors (2017), the first ever Indian to be elected and TWAS-Lenovo Science Prize (2018), which is the highest science award of the World Academy of Science. Dr Mashelkar has been on the Board of Directors of several reputed companies ranging from Reliance Industries Ltd. and Tata Motors Ltd. to Hindustan Unilever Ltd. He is presently the Chairman of the New Energy Council of Reliance Industries, which is, with multibillion dollar investments, building giga factories in renewable energy, including in green hydrogen. Dr Mashelkar served as a member of Science Advisory Council to the Prime Minister set up by successive Indian governments for over three decades. He has been a member of External Research Advisory Board of Microsoft (USA), Advisory Board of VTT (Finland), Corporate Innovation Board of Michelin (France), Advisory Board of National Research Foundation (Singapore), Corporate Innovation Board (Michelin), among others. On 16 November 2005, he received the Business Week (USA) award 'Stars of Asia' at the hands of George Bush (Sr.), the former President of USA. President of India honoured Dr Mashelkar with the Padmashri (1991), Padmabhushan (2000) and Padma Vibhushan (2014), three of the highest civilian honours.

Celestin Monga

Célestin Monga is Visiting Professor of Public Policy at Harvard's Kennedy School of Government, Faculty Associate at the Center for International Development (CID) at Harvard University, and Fellow at the Harvard University Center for African Studies. He is also part-time Professor of Economics at the University of Paris 1 Panthéon-Sorbonne and Research Professor at Peking University's Institute of New Structural Economics. Monga has held various board and senior executive positions in academia, financial services and international development institutions, serving most recently as Managing Director at the United Nations Industrial Development Organization (UNIDO), Vice-President and Chief Economist of the African Development Bank Group, and Senior Economic Adviser/Director at the World Bank Group. Monga has published extensively on various dimensions of economic and political development. His books have been translated into several languages and are widely used as teaching tools in academic institutions around the world. His most recent works include *The Oxford Handbook of Structural Transformation* (2019), with J.Y. Lin; *Beating the Odds: Jump-Starting Developing Countries* (2017), with J.Y. Lin; the two-volume *Oxford Handbook of Africa and Economics* (2015), with J.Y. Lin; and *Nihilism and Negritude: Ways of Living in Africa* (2016). Dr Monga holds graduate degrees from MIT, Harvard University, and the Universities of Paris and Pau.

Utkarsh Patel

Utkarsh Patel is a part-time Associate Fellow, Sustainability & Climate Change at CSEP. His research focuses on India's climate policy, and the role of deep decarbonization technologies like hydrogen and carbon capture and storage in the country's energy transition. He will soon commence his doctoral research on the Economics and Ethics of Negative Emission Technologies at the Brandenburg Technical University, Germany. He was previously associated with the Indian Council for Research on International Economic Relations (ICRIER), New Delhi, where he worked with Dr Isher Judge Ahluwalia on issues of urbanization and sustainable development in India. He contributed to studies on solid waste management, municipal water supply and electric mobility. He is trained in economics from the Madras School of Economics, Chennai, and has additionally studied energy regulation at the Technical University Berlin.

Jean-Louis Sarbib

Jean-Louis Sarbib is currently Head of the Africa and Middle East Practice at Centennial Group International, a Distinguished fellow of the Emerging Markets Forum, and chair of the ACET Advisory Panel for the G20 Compact with Africa. From March 2009 to January 2019, he was Chief Executive Officer of Development Gateway, an international non-profit social enterprise whose mission is to support the use of data, technology and evidence to create accountable institutions that listen and respond to the needs of their constituents and are efficient in targeting and delivering services that improve lives. From 1980 to 2006, Mr Sarbib was at the World Bank where he occupied a number of senior positions: Vice President for Africa, Vice President for the Middle East and North Africa, and Senior Vice President for human development. Upon leaving the Bank and before leading Development Gateway, Mr Sarbib joined Wolfensohn & Company, a private equity firm, as a Managing Director. He was a non-resident senior fellow at The Brookings Institution and taught at Georgetown University. He serves on a number of non-profit boards (Partnership for Transparency Fund, Feedback Labs and Open Data Watch).

He is a member of the board of governors of the Ben-Gurion University of the Negev, and a non-executive director on the boards of the African University of Science and Technology, the Nelson Mandela Institution and NOI Polls in Nigeria. Prior to joining the World Bank Mr Sarbib taught at the University of Pennsylvania and the University of North Carolina, Chapel Hill and worked for the French Government. In 2006, Mr Sarbib was awarded an honourary doctorate by the University of Ouagadougou in Burkina Faso and received a Lifetime Award for Diversity and Inclusion from the World Bank. He received numerous honours from the countries where he worked. Mr Sarbib is a graduate of the Ecole Nationale Supérieure des Mines de Paris (now Mines Paris Tech) and holds a Master's in city planning from the University of Pennsylvania. He attended the General Manager course at Harvard Business School.

Laura Shelton
Laura Shelton is a Project Associate at Centennial Group International. She holds an MA in international economics and international development with a focus on market-based solutions to development problems from Johns Hopkins University School of Advanced International Studies, and a BA in foreign affairs and in economics from the University of Virginia. In the final year of her graduate program, she consulted on a Supply Chain Analysis focussed on the nexus between nutrition and adolescent girls in Bangladesh. Ms Shelton has also served as an Agricultural Economics Advisor in the US Peace Corps in Madagascar where she worked with farmers, giving trainings on improved agricultural techniques and ag-business skills.

Bernard Snoy
Bernard Snoy et d'Oppuers, Belgian national, is Chairman of Robert Triffin International (RTI) and Honorary Chairman of the European League for Economic Cooperation (ELEC). He is also Professor at the Institute of European Studies at the Catholic University of Louvain (now UCLouvain in Louvain-la-Neuve). Bernard Snoy studied Law, Economics and Philosophy at the Catholic University of Louvain. He holds a PhD in economics from Harvard University. Bernard Snoy started his career at the World Bank in 1974. In the 1980s, he worked for two years at the Economic and Monetary General Directorate of the European Commission in Brussels. Subsequently, he was the Chief of Cabinet of the Belgian Minister of Finance, Executive Director of the World Bank (where, in addition to Belgium, he represented Austria, Belarus, the Czech Republic, Hungary, Kazakhstan, Luxembourg, Slovakia, Slovenia and Turkey), Member of the Board of Directors of the European Bank for Reconstruction and Development (EBRD), Director of the Economic Table of the Stability Pact for South-Eastern Europe, and Coordinator of the Economic and Environmental Activities of the Organisation for Security and Cooperation in Europe (OSCE). Bernard Snoy has been teaching and publishing on a wide variety of subjects, linked to developing countries indebtedness, transition economics, European Union enlargement and financial and monetary reform. In 2019, he chaired an RTI Working Party on 'Managing Global Liquidity as a Global Public Book' (see report on www.triffininternational.eu).

Hasan Tuluy
Hasan Tuluy is an economist with nearly four decades of experience in Africa, the Middle East and North Africa and Latin America, and is currently with the Centennial Group where he advises multilateral and bilateral development institutions and countries on development

strategy and organizational design issues. He has, in addition, periodically consulted for the World Bank on country programs and organizational design. He is on the Board for Partnership for Transparency Fund and formerly served on the Board for IREX, an international NGO. From 1987 to his retirement in 2014, Tuluy held various senior positions at the World Bank. In his most recent assignment prior to his retirement, he served as Vice President for Latin America and the Caribbean region from 2012 to 2014, overseeing the program of engagement with thirty-two member countries. Between 2008–11, he was Vice President for Human Resources for the World Bank guiding the Bank's HR strategy, policy, and implementation. In 2007–08 as the Chief Operating Officer of the Multilateral Investment Guarantee Agency, he initiated a turn-around to bring the agency back to profitability. During the period from 2003 to 2007, Tuluy was Director of Strategy and Operations for the Middle East and North Africa region of the World Bank, responsible for program implementation and portfolio quality. Between 2001–03, he served as Director of Corporate Strategy for the World Bank. Before that, he worked as Country Director in West Africa (1996–2000) and economist in various country and sector programs (1987–95). Prior to joining the World Bank Group, Tuluy worked for around a decade in research and private consulting on trade and price policy issues in Africa and the Maghreb.

Index